Mirage of Destiny

Mirage of Destiny

The Story of the 1990–91 Minnesota North Stars

By Kevin Allenspach

North Star Press
of St. Cloud Inc.

Published by North Star Press of St. Cloud Inc.
Since 1969
www.northstarpress.com

First Edition
ISBN: 978-1-68201-143-0

Printed in the United States of America

Kevin Allenspach is an award-winning writer with more than thirty years experience in journalism, most of them covering sports. He lives with his wife and two children in St. Cloud, Minnesota, about eighty miles from the site of the former Met Center in Bloomington, which is now covered by an IKEA store and the Mall of America. For more information about the author please visit www.kevinallenspach.com

For my family:

My loving wife, Danell; our children, William and Anna,

who will be my most important contributions to this life;

and to loved ones passed and yet to come.

And also to Cinderella, wherever she is...

TABLE OF CONTENTS

A shooting star, sometimes called a falling star, isn't actually a star at all. It is a streak of light in the night sky caused by bits of dust and rock—meteoroids—burning up in the Earth's atmosphere almost as soon as you see them.

The material for the meteors, which can range from the size of a grain of sand up to one meter in diameter, comes from the trail of a comet and travels between 25,000 and 160,000 mph. Green is a common color for a shooting star because many meteors contain nickel and magnesium, which give off a green glow as they burn.

A common superstition is that shooting stars possess magic that grants the observer good luck, positive energy flow, and the opportunity to make a wish.

FOREWORD

By Mike Modano

One of the first times I talked to Kevin Allenspach for this project, my five kids and I were waiting in a drive-through in Phoenix. The conversation Kevin and I had was punctuated by excited requests for ice cream from the back seats, mixing with the memories of cheering fans during an almost fairytale season long ago.

A lot changes in three decades. In 1990, I was twenty years old, in my second full season with the North Stars, and had no idea what lay before me. Looking back now, more than ten years after I retired, hockey seems like it was a fantasy world. As players, we were taken care of, told where to be, what to do, what to wear and sometimes even what to say. When it was all done, it hit me: I'm on my own. I was forced to grow up again.

I didn't start a family until I was done playing. I moved out of Dallas to Arizona—a place where there isn't much hockey at all. The only people who recognize me anymore are snowbirds. In some ways, that's been nice because I needed to separate myself from the game. I was mentally exhausted and, by the time I was 40, the physical toll of training, practicing and playing—everything that goes into being able to compete at a high level—was enormous. Now that's all gone and, if I sit back and think about it, my career was very rewarding. I'm content. I accomplished things I never thought I would, and that's the neat thing about it.

When my career was over, it seemed everyone splintered off in different directions, going back home or settling somewhere with their families. But when I was playing, my teammates were my family—and sometimes I wish I knew what happened to them. Sometimes I see people, like at the inaugural Stars Hall of Fame induction in Dallas, but those situations don't lend themselves to reminiscing much. A lot of the time, we're meeting with fans or season-ticket holders, and then everyone has some family and friends along with them. We're constantly getting tapped on the shoulder or pulled away for a picture. As players and coaches, we never really get the chance to catch up. It would be awesome if we could really reconnect. One thing is sure: we miss those days and the stories that went with them.

Mirage of Destiny serves two purposes. First, it records what happened in 1990–91. What we did was totally unexpected. The Stanley Cup wasn't even on our radar at the beginning of that season. That's why it became so exciting for not only us but the fans, the people of Minnesota, and really anyone who started paying attention. It was such a roller-coaster ride. In comparison, at training camp in '98, we knew the team we had in Dallas by then was Stanley Cup or bust. The expectations in September in Vail, Colorado, were off the charts. If we didn't win it that year, I think we would have felt like it was a failure. At training camp in 1990, we had no idea what we were. We didn't know anything. Come April, we lived one of those lightning-in-a-bottle scenarios like I've never heard of in hockey or any other sport.

Second, this book also gives us that reunion we wish we could have. We wonder what everybody's doing. We bump into each other at odd times and hear what life has handed some of us who were so close so long ago. Others, we haven't talked with for 30 years. Now it's possible to know how life turned out for everyone.

I have a lot of responsibility with my kids now, and that's a whole new game for me. That's where my energy goes and in some ways it's as taxing as any sport can be. My life is so different from what it was. Being Mike Modano these days would maybe be boring to some people. I'm pretty conservative on the business front. I don't dabble with too many investments. I make the odd appearance here or the occasional speaking engagement there, but mainly it's just family stuff—activities and sports for the kids. I play golf as I can but, for Allison and me, our days and nights are pretty full. That's OK, because the kids are young, and I want to be involved in their lives as much as I can. Maybe someday they'll wonder what happened with that team in Minnesota and how it shaped my future. If so, Kevin's book will be a source for them and everyone else—those fortunate enough to remember, and those not lucky enough to have experienced it. Hopefully, other people will feel like I do and be glad this story has finally been told. Being part of it was my pleasure.

Mike Modano
Scottsdale, Arizona
December 2022

INTRODUCTION

Echoes of History, 100 Years Apart

In 1919, four months after the armistice that ended World War I, the National Hockey League finished its second season. With teams in Montreal, Toronto and Ottawa, the champion Canadiens were destined to play the winner of the three-team Pacific Coast Hockey League for the Stanley Cup. Montreal beat Ottawa in a playoff series among the top NHL teams, and the Seattle Metropolitans edged the Vancouver Millionaires in a two-game, total-goals series for the PCHL title. A best-of-five Stanley Cup Finals was scheduled for late March at Seattle Ice Arena.

The Canadiens and Metropolitans each won twice, and one game ended in a double-overtime scoreless tie. That set up a decisive clash for April 1. But in the hours leading to it, several players from both teams became ill as part of a Spanish Flu outbreak then hitting the Pacific Northwest. Half the Montreal roster, including eventual Hall of Famers Newsy Lalonde and Joe Hall, were hospitalized or bedridden. The game was canceled, a decision that became even more solemn when Hall died of pneumonia on April 5.

The Spanish Flu pandemic would go on to claim the lives of at least 17 million people globally (with some estimates as high as 100 million).

We didn't experience another pandemic of similar magnitude for 100 years. But it took one to produce the book you're about to read.

Late in 2019, ominous signs emerged about a virus spreading from China around the globe. Early in 2020, it reached the United States and led to the declaration of a national emergency, travel bans and stay-at-home orders. In less than 24 hours on March 11–12, the National Basketball Association suspended its season and the NHL followed. Sports soon ground to a halt, along with everything else that couldn't be enjoyed in our homes, accomplished outdoors with "social distancing," or conducted via the Internet. For months, we lived in a Twilight Zone devoid of much popular culture for the first time in history.

Few segments of life were unaffected by the Coronavirus, also known as COVID-19. With the advent of testing, Major League Baseball began an abbreviated 60-game season in late July, and the NBA and NHL resumed their seasons with expanded playoff formats a week later. We saw what it was like to play in "pods" and "bubbles," captive environments where participants were quarantined. While NBA teams gathered near Orlando, Florida, the NHL formed two hubs. One was in Toronto, the other in Edmonton—where on September 28 the Tampa Bay Lightning finally won the Stanley Cup, thousands of miles from their adoring fans.

Of course, they might as well have played on the moon. No spectators were allowed in the building.

This was a watershed development. As a child of the North American pro sports explosion of the 1970s, I'd grown up in Minnesota by no means alone in giving disproportionate attention to such games. They set the course for my life as I combined that passion with a talent for writing and became a sportswriter for almost 30 years—most of it with the *St. Cloud Times*.

The Coronavirus taught me something in my 50s that I'd never realized: Without fans, it is impossible for sports to be as meaningful as we've come to know them. You can crown a champion in a vacuum, as the NBA did on October 11, 2020, when the Los Angeles Lakers beat the Miami Heat in an empty, 8,000-seat arena outside of Orlando, Florida. Later that month, after the baseball season and playoffs had mostly been played in empty stadiums, approximately 11,000 people were allowed into 40,000-seat Globe Life Field in Arlington, Texas, for a neutral-site World Series between the victorious Los Angeles Dodgers and the Tampa Bay Rays. With such lack of atmosphere, it was like the games weren't real. How could they be legitimate without a roaring crowd driving the adrenaline of the participants?

I reflected on the countless games I'd attended and perhaps 10-fold as many that I'd watched on television. When each ended, there usually was a line in the box score or summary: "Attendance: XXXX." Now, I've come to believe every person who ever passed through those turnstiles was an *essential* part of the result. Even as one fan, your voice—your *participation*—helped make that game what it turned out to be, regardless of what was on the line, from exhibitions to the postseason.

We learned from the dark days of April, May, and June 2020 that any competition was better than none. Yet even then, the primary interest I had in sports was in how they could beat the virus and help bring our lives back to normal.

My thoughts were anxious, perhaps similar to those of others: Who do I know that will get this disease or die from it? When will there be a vaccine? How long must we wear masks? Why did our response to COVID-19 become so political? How would we get past it, and will our lives return to what they once were?

Pro football provided some intrigue: Which would win out? The irresistible force that has become the NFL in my lifetime? Or the immovable object that seemed to be the Coronavirus?

It was a worthy matchup. The 2020 season kicked off September 10 and, less than three months later, 20 games had been postponed or rescheduled. Local governments determined whether or how many people could attend, and some prohibited play entirely. The San Francisco 49ers had to move games to Glendale, Arizona. Most teams had multiple players test positive, forcing the implementation of new COVID regulations. Yet, amazingly, every game of a full season and the playoffs was played—if in front of no fans or fractional capacities. Maybe there was hope.

Long before the Tampa Bay Buccaneers beat the Kansas City Chiefs in Super Bowl LV before a crowd of 24,835 people—by far the smallest attendance ever at Super Bowl—I had wrestled with the pandemic long enough. I finally realized I'd been given an unbelievable gift: a chance to have something to show for this time in history and my place in it.

I've always wanted to write a book. My shelves are filled with them, thousands of volumes, most about (you guessed it) sports. I wouldn't have become the person I am without the influence of many special authors. As a teen in the early 1980s, I read *The Boys of Summer* by Roger Kahn. It sparked my desire to be a sportswriter. Written in 1972, it's the story of how Kahn came to cover the early 1950s Brooklyn Dodgers for the *New York Herald Tribune*. These were the teams of Jackie Robinson and Pee Wee Reese, Duke Snider and Roy Campanella, Carl Erskine and Preacher Roe—among many others. Immensely talented, they played a major role in America's transition from segregation to the Civil Rights movement but usually came up frustratingly short of a World Series championship. In the early 1970s, Kahn revisited many of those players and contrasted former glory with their lives 20 years later. To label it simply a baseball book is a tremendous injustice.

For even longer, I had an idea percolating within me. At 21, I was a public relations intern with the 1990–91 Minnesota North Stars. In a span of perhaps seven months, I witnessed one of the wildest rides in sports history—with a losing franchise that went from near extinction to the Stanley Cup Finals. I wanted to tell that story and what became of the players, coaches, front-office personnel, and media with whom I came in contact.

I knew if I didn't write it now, I never would.

In no way do I presume what follows is anything close to Kahn's seminal work. But I do hope you find more in it than just hockey. It's meant to be about remembering a historic opportunity, coming to grips with success and failure, and, if we're fortunate to grow old enough to look back, embracing that experience in relation to the rest of our lives.

Mirage of Destiny required months of research and tracking down as many as I could of more than 60 people I wanted to interview. I began in November 2020 and, undoubtedly, wanted my first contact to be with Mike Modano, the only Hall of Fame player from that '91 playoff team. He proved not only gracious during multiple interviews but helped connect me with previously unavailable sources.

After speaking with Mike, the project unfolded as though ordained. I spoke with nearly four dozen people. Bob Gainey, who coached the team after his own Hall of Fame career as a winger with the Montreal Canadiens, reminisced for hours. The entire coaching staff contributed, as did most of the front office, and, from the playoff roster, all but three players gave interviews for this book. Since I'd spoken to the others in the past or could supplement with what has been reported elsewhere, this is the most complete representation conceivable.

By spring 2021, almost exactly thirty years after my last days as a North Stars intern, I'd conducted most of my interviews. COVID-19 not only gave me time for this project, those to whom I reached out faced a similar void of activity that made them inclined to participate. Often, I heard gratitude for dusting off memories and preserving a special legacy.

Much of what follows is assembled chronologically, despite my assumption that readers are likely aware Minnesota lost to the Pittsburgh Penguins in the '91 final, and that the North Stars relocated to Dallas just two years later.

If they'd won the Cup, their story surely would've been told many times over and there would be no need for this volume. But without the immortal bond of a championship, the North Stars have become orphans. Fans of the Dallas Stars have little interest in their team's Minnesota roots. And the Minnesota Wild, born in 2000, has no relation to the North Stars beyond that their departure made the new franchise possible.

Losing the North Stars left a hole in the hearts of some Minnesotans perhaps similar to how the people of Brooklyn lost their identity after the Dodgers moved to Los Angeles in 1958. Minnesota, where hockey is part of the fabric of the state, went seven years without an NHL franchise. During that time, other than my TV set, the closest teams were a six-hour drive to Chicago or seven hours to Winnipeg.

Just as that exile came to a close, the Stars won their only Cup in 1999. Rest assured, had the North Stars won it eight years earlier, it's almost certain the team would still be in Minnesota. As it is, after more than two decades, the Wild have yet to make it to the finals.

Some who you'll read about in these pages, which took a couple years to publish, went on to win it all somewhere else. Like Rob Zettler, a defenseman with the '90–91 North Stars. Thirty years later, he finally achieved his goal as an assistant coach with the Lightning in 2021.

For most, however, there was no Cup. Not in 1991. Not later in the 1990s, or the 2000s or beyond. A generation later, what's the significance of that in the wake of what they've gone on to experience?

In 1991, still nearly a year before I would graduate from the University of Minnesota, I had grand plans. I wanted to be a beat writer covering a major league sports franchise or at least a Division I athletic team. If you'd asked, I would've said covering the Yankees was the top of the mountain. I never got there, but I did spend some time in MLB, NFL and NHL press boxes and even on press row in the NBA. For more than a dozen years, I covered a Division I hockey program. Through it all, I'm proud of my work—voluminous and occasionally flawed, and I still appreciate the games, participants, and fans. Could my career have turned out better? Sure. Could it have been a greater disappointment? Certainly. But whatever it was, I've done my best and it is mine.

With the North Stars, I was a PR intern—about as low as you can go in the organization and still be part of it. But I was there. And if this recollection informs and entertains, 30 years after the team played its last game, hopefully it can be a window into what I've seen and become. To what we've all seen and become.

Star light, star bright,
first star I see tonight.
I wish I may, I wish I might,
have this wish I wish tonight

CHAPTER 1

So Close You Can Almost Touch It

The buzz of conversation, almost a steady drone, reverberated in your ears. The thick concrete walls of the Metropolitan Sports Center muted the noise, but only slightly.

Site of more than 1,000 National Hockey League games prior to Tuesday, May 21, 1991, it should have been quiet. The Bloomington home of the Minnesota North Stars had never seen a game this late in the spring. And since opening in 1967, God knows how many nights the Met sat silent—sometimes with not much of a murmur even when the North Stars *were* playing.

This was different.

The opening faceoff for Game 4 of the 1991 Stanley Cup Finals against the Pittsburgh Penguins was several hours away and the building was abuzz. For the relatively small front-office staff of about three dozen people, it was all-hands-on-deck from early morning. By afternoon, a small army of concessions workers began popping popcorn, heating up hot dog grills, connecting soda canisters, and tapping kegs. Souvenir stands were stocked and programs stacked, ready for sale at stations inside each entrance.

Thirty-five members of a contracted security detail prowled the premises like the US Secret Service preparing for a presidential visit. Each man wore a black clip-on tie, lest the rowdy among a sellout crowd yank a traditional Windsor into a hangman's noose.

In Section 115, just across from the runway that led up to the home dressing room, 105 ushers got their pregame pep talk. They wore black sweaters with "North Stars" woven in white on the front. They sat in vinyl-covered seats, a hodgepodge of greens, whites, blacks and something that perhaps was supposed to be gold but through age was now a faded, mustard yellow.

The fans—most of the capacity 15,378 with tickets, plus additional hangers-on for the tailgating party—jammed the surrounding parking lot as the players began to arrive. Designer-clad but long-unshaven individuals, they waded through hundreds of well-oiled well-wishers at the Met Center's west end cargo ramp.

Mike Modano—at twenty years old unable to produce much more than blond peach fuzz for a playoff beard—pulled up in his white Porsche 911 Carrera Cabriolet. It shone like a beacon with his license plate ("NINE") among other newer cars and trucks in the players' temporary parking area. They hadn't needed this special treatment earlier in the season. Then, they just drove up and stopped in the front row of empty gray pavement crossed with white stripes that stretched about 1,000 feet before ending at the boundary of Cedar Avenue's four lanes.

What would've been vacant this far in advance of a game just two months earlier now looked like a carnival. Barbecue smoke wafted as the thump of bass woofers and rock music vibrated in the air. Old Chevy Silverados and Ford Pacers mixed with modest Oldsmobiles, Pontiacs and Chryslers, and the occasional new Acura or Audi, a Lincoln here and Cadillac there. The crowd trended younger—20- and 30-somethings, college kids, high school students, all eager to turn a gorgeous day (sunny, humid, light breeze, almost 80 degrees) into another pinch-me bash.

The North Stars, having won Game 1 in Pittsburgh 5–4 and Game 3 two nights earlier at home 3–1, were two victories from a championship. In the barnstorming days of the NBA, the Minneapolis Lakers won four titles between 1950 and '54—sometimes before fewer than 4,500 spectators. Only baseball's Twins had previously produced a modern major league title for Minnesota, four years earlier and 10 miles up Interstate-35 at the Metrodome. But this was what would become widely known as the State of Hockey, and you could see the greatest trophy in sports on display just a few minutes away at the Hotel Sofitel.

It was so close you could almost touch it.

That this team and its followers were here seemed impossible. The North Stars had been born not quite 25 years earlier, part of the NHL's original expansion from six to 12 teams—making the league truly national in scope after a quarter-century in only Boston, Chicago, Detroit, Montreal, New York and Toronto. The first 12 years in Minnesota, which yields more pro hockey talent than anywhere in the U.S., produced zero division titles, no trips beyond the second round of the postseason, and indeed six idle springs. From 1974 to 1979, the North Stars played just one home playoff game at the Met—a 7-1 loss to Buffalo in 1977.

As the NHL fought off encroachment from the World Hockey Association, suddenly there were more teams than legitimate markets. That led to a merger of the North Stars with the even more unwanted and unsuccessful Cleveland Barons, owned by George and Gordon Gund. Only temporarily during World War II, when a couple of National Football League teams joined forces for the duration, had any pro sports franchises merged. This one was permanent, and the Gund brothers took over the amalgamation. The consolidation of talent, plus a No. 1 draft pick and clever scouting, produced a long playoff run in 1980 followed by Minnesota's only previous trip to the finals in '81.

Alas, those North Stars were little more than bugs on the windshield of the New York Islanders, who featured Hall of Famers Mike Bossy, Bryan Trottier, Clark Gillies, and Dennis Potvin. Those Islanders were en route to the second of four straight Cups—a run exceeded only once in NHL history. Exactly 10 years earlier, on May 21, 1981, at Nassau Coliseum on Long Island, Isles goalie Billy Smith (who also would find a home in the Hall) stopped 24 of 25 shots to stone the North Stars 5–1 in the decisive fifth game.

Nonetheless, the experience ignited expectations that peaked with a trip to the conference finals in 1984. There, the North Stars were swept away by Wayne Gretzky and the Edmonton Oilers, poised to win the first of four Cups in five years with a nucleus that also included Glenn Anderson, Paul Coffey, Grant Fuhr, Jari Kurri, Kevin Lowe, and Mark Messier.

Diminishing returns brought a second-round loss in 1985, a first-round exit in 1986, and no postseason appearance in 1987 or '88. By 1989, when Minnesota made it back to the playoffs, cracks in the fan base were apparent. Modano, the No. 1 overall selection in the '88 draft, made his first NHL appearances in Games 2 and 3 of the first round series against the St. Louis Blues. It didn't matter. The

North Stars trailed three games to none entering Game 4, which drew 8,013—the smallest Met Center playoff gate since 1968, and they lost the series in five.

Then the milk really began to curdle. In 1990, plagued by mismanagement and poor attendance (the order of which could be argued), the team nearly melted away like so much winter ice in the Land of 10,000 Lakes. Starting in January, the Gunds made public their intent to sell, move to California, or even cease operations with the promise of a future expansion franchise.

The team was "saved" five months later with a much-maligned deal from a couple of investors fronted by Howard Baldwin, a curly-haired entrepreneur and film producer who would go on to earn an Academy Award nomination for a picture about R&B legend Ray Charles.

What subsequently transpired in less than 12 months was too implausible even for Hollywood.

The new owners installed former Philadelphia Flyers legend and two-time Cup champion Bobby Clarke as general manager on June 8. Eleven days later, Bob Gainey—a five-time Cup winner with the Montreal Canadiens—was named the sixteenth head coach (Clarke was the fifth GM) in the 23-year history of the North Stars, for whom stability couldn't be found in a dictionary. Baldwin and his partner, former Budget Rent-A-Car chairman Morris Belzberg, immediately had cash-flow concerns, leading 56-year-old Canadian shopping-mall magnate Norm Green to buy a majority interest even as Gainey and Clarke settled into their new offices.

The season ahead was guaranteed a mammoth distraction engineered by none other than the Gunds, who'd already shredded the Minnesota hockey market through twelve years of ownership. Claiming losses of $16 million in their last three seasons, they weren't going to leave quietly or empty-handed. In agreeing to sell the North Stars for $31 million (which they forwarded along with another $19 million to equal the $50 million NHL expansion fee), they were to get a new team that would play in the San Francisco Bay area in the fall of 1991. They retained former North Stars GM Jack Ferreira, several executives and scouts, and the knowledge they'd accumulated. Plus, unconscionably to fans, many in the media, and most other owners, the Gunds negotiated the right to stock their team with thirty players from the franchise they were *selling*. Except for the most veteran and highly touted North Stars, everyone under contract (including all players in the minors) didn't know if they'd remain with Minnesota beyond the spring of '91.

That haunted like a recurring nightmare, although more pressing was a power struggle atop the team. Baldwin continued as president, despite his minority holdings. But by late July, with Green itching for full control, Baldwin resigned. Green, a minority owner in a group that had brought the Atlanta Flames to Calgary ten years earlier, assumed the title, moved to Minnesota, and immediately infused $2.5 million to spruce up Met Center. New were maroon theater seat coverings in the 10 sections nearest center ice, a club level, four 9-by-12-foot video screens (though they wouldn't all be operational until well after the season started), remodeled dressing and training rooms, and revamped administrative quarters.

The additions were accompanied by even greater subtractions to personnel. By October, Green had fired more than 60 employees and hundreds of contract workers, reducing the nonplayer payroll by more than half, doubtless recouping much of the $2.5 million he'd just spent.

The season opener was a 3–2 home loss to St. Louis on October 4 that drew 5,730—roughly one paying customer for every three seats. Within two weeks, Green was stamping out rumors the team would be sold and moved to Milwaukee or Seattle.

Influenced by the chic NBA atmosphere for the Minnesota Timberwolves, playing their second season overall and first in the new Target Center in downtown Minneapolis, Green tried similar tactics to pump up the volume at the Met. He introduced a dance troupe called the Electric Stars and launched tartakes, a lottery in which ticket holders could win a minimum of $15,000 at each home game.

Nothing seemed to help. Through mid-January, average attendance was 7,319—less than half capacity and assuring the worst season at the turnstile in team history. Green was stunned. Calgary would lead the NHL during the regular season with 19,986 fans per game. None of the other 19 franchises drew fewer than 10,000. Only nine failed to *double* the typical North Stars crowd.

The Flames had won the Cup in 1989, providing a smaller likeness for Green's mantel, and he couldn't understand why the marketing plan in Alberta (unlock the gates) wasn't working in Minnesota.

Part of it was because, on the ice, there wasn't much shine to the North Stars. They won two of their first 14 games and hit rock bottom after 5,375 showed up for a 5–1 loss to Montreal on January 15. That left them 16 games under .500 and just four points ahead of the Quebec Nordiques and Toronto Maple Leafs—locked in a mortal struggle for the worst overall record and the draft rights to Eric Lindros (presumed the "Next One" to Gretzky's "Great One").

Then occurred one of those fickle changes of fate that make spectator sports a passion for those who preach that anything can happen.

On January 17, the North Stars beat Washington 5–2 in their last game before the all-star break. It was obscured, along with almost all sports news, by the onslaught of war in the Middle East. But that victory quietly started a 13-game home unbeaten streak (11–0–2) that matched a franchise record. Two months later, the last of those games clinched the fourth and final playoff spot in the five-team Norris Division. When they next lost in Bloomington, only three games remained in the regular season.

Surely the surge was just a cosmetic conclusion to an otherwise ugly season, right? Minnesota barely made the playoffs with a .425 winning percentage and in the first round drew Chicago (.668), which had just won the President's Trophy with the best record in the league. The North Stars had some biblical battles through the years with the arch-rival Blackhawks, but those were mostly before April. In the postseason, the teams met five times between 1982 and 1990 with Chicago winning four series.

But the North Stars took Game 1 in overtime at cacophonous Chicago Stadium, kept their composure after losing Games 2 and 3, then reeled off three straight victories as the undisciplined Blackhawks blew a gasket. It was the second-greatest NHL playoff upset in forty years. Only in 1982, when Los Angeles (.394) shocked Edmonton (.694), did a more highly favored team fall. And only once since expansion from the Original Six had the team with the league's best record lost in the first round.[1]

Well, anything's possible once. In all likelihood the St. Louis Blues, whose 47-22-11 record fell just one point short of Chicago, would sound the North Stars' swan song. Except Brett Hull, who led the league with 86 goals—a better single-season mark than anyone in NHL history *not* named Gretzky—couldn't shrug off Stew Gavin and Gaetan Duchesne. The scrappy Minnesota forwards hounded him everywhere but the men's room, and Minnesota won Games 1, 3 and 4. Hull didn't score until midway through the last of those, an 8–4 blowout, and he was shut out in Game 5 and the first 57 minutes of the deciding Game 6, by which time the Blues rivaled the Blackhawks in frustration.

It would be too much to ask for a defeat of the dynastic defending Stanley Cup champions, too. Right? The Edmonton Oilers had restored their reputation two years after trading Gretzky to Los Angeles, and, despite a disastrous 5–13–2 start through their first twenty games, they were still steeped in mystique, with Messier as captain and Fuhr back in goal after missing most of the regular season because of a drug suspension. Minnesota entered the Campbell Conference final *winless* at Northlands

1 Boston, which sliced through the NHL with a .776 winning percentage in 1970-71, lost to Montreal in seven games. The Bruins' only solace was that the Canadiens won the Cup.

Coliseum since 1980. But the North Stars again stole Game 1 and blew away the Oilers twice at the Met Center before taking a slim third-period lead in Game 5. Goalie Jon Casey withstood a last-minute flurry, and a mob of green jerseys celebrated before a shocked crowd in Edmonton.

The Minnesota North Stars were going to the Stanley Cup Finals.

To put it in broader perspective, in the history of North American pro sports through 2022, no Major League Baseball or NFL team has ever played for a championship despite a losing regular-season record. Three NBA teams have done so, all lost, and the 1981 Houston Rockets (two games under .500 and including Hall of Famers Moses Malone, Calvin Murphy, and Rudy Tomjanovich) are the only team to do so since the 1950s.

In the NHL, where a majority of teams have made the postseason since 1927, it has happened fourteen times. But only three of those came after expansion in 1967 and none since '91, when the North Stars' 27–39–14 record was worse than all but one. The 1938 Chicago Black Hawks (the name was two words until the 1980s) went 14–25–9 (.385) before incredibly *winning* the Cup—though they had to win only seven games to do so.

Fifty-three years later and through three best-of-seven postseason series, these North Stars had already won 12 times. With each victory, Minnesota went increasingly mad. All Canada was aware of the fairy tale unfolding here and, while much of the U.S. was still indifferent to hockey, *Sports Illustrated* and ESPN had jumped on the bandwagon with cover stories and special programming. And they weren't alone among major media outlets.

So, a decade after the Islanders skated away with the only Cup for which the North Stars had ever contested, 261 credentialed members of the media from all over North America streamed into Met Center. Most were late to catch Neal Broten, the shifty little center by way of tiny Roseau, the University of Minnesota, and the gold-medal-winning 1980 US Olympic team. He arrived just after 4 p.m., 5-foot-9 and 170 pounds, oozing rink rat from every pore—even at 31—as he weaved through onlookers, down the ramp and up the concrete runway to the right and toward the North Stars' dressing room. Bobby Smith, also a center but at 6–4 towering over most everyone, followed with a blank, business-like look on his face—battered by more than 1,000 NHL games over a dozen seasons. The previous year, when he played in Montreal and the Canadiens uncharacteristically failed to make it out of the second round, he'd suffered a broken jaw. Less imposing but perhaps even more competitive came Curt Giles, 5–8 and uncomfortable in a suit that he knew he wouldn't take off tonight—scratched for the fifth consecutive game despite having worn the captain's "C" most of the season.

That trio comprised the last remnants from the team that surprised the league in even getting to the 1981 final.

Broten had never left, becoming the franchise's all-time leading scorer barely a year earlier. With brown hair that always looked a bit disheveled and large eyes that never seemed surprised, he embodied the spirit of hockey in Minnesota. Growing up a few miles from the Canadian border, he watched *Hockey Night in Canada* and wanted to play for the Canadiens. Opportunities to watch the North Stars were rare as he began to make a name for himself, becoming a three-time state tournament participant. In 1979, he was the Western Collegiate Hockey Association rookie of the year and scored the winning goal in the NCAA championship game. The following summer, the North Stars made him a third-round pick and he made it look like a bonanza. Broten took a year away from the Gophers to join the U.S. Olympic team, winning a gold medal at Lake Placid. Returning to college, he won the 1981 Hobey Baker Award, turned pro, and scored in his NHL debut. He played in every game of the '81 playoffs and, within five years, became the first American to post a 100-point season. But on

October 30, 1986, he was checked from behind by Detroit's Lee Norwood and suffered badly torn shoulder ligaments. Surgery would leave Broten a different player, and the seven-inch scar above his left breast is a stark reminder every time he takes off his shirt.

Smith was the North Stars' first No. 1 overall pick, in 1978. His 192-point final season with the Ottawa 67s bested Gretzky head-to-head by ten points and would remain the Ontario Hockey League record more than forty years later. But Smith clashed with former North Stars coach Bill Mahoney and, 15 months after signing a seven-year contract, he forced a 1983 trade to Montreal. Smith won the Cup three years later, but by the summer of '90 it became clear he was dropping down the depth chart and he lobbied to go back where he started.

Giles, a defenseman, perhaps was representative of the Minnesota franchise—an underdog with inexhaustible pride who could be defeated but never broken. He'd migrated here from The Pas, Manitoba, by way of the University of Minnesota-Duluth, where he enrolled as a 16-year-old freshman and was later captain and a two-time All-American before turning pro. Other than 42 games for Oklahoma City of the Central Hockey League in 1979–80 and an abortive year in New York with the Rangers (traded away in November '86 and back in November '87), he'd spent his entire pro career in his adopted home state.

Other than those three players, almost everything else—including parts of the building itself—was new at some point in the previous ten years. Assistant coach Doug Jarvis arrived in 1988 and survived the departure of Pierre Page, Gainey's predecessor as head coach. Of course, as a longtime former teammate and friend with the Canadiens, Gainey perhaps would've brought Jarvis in anyway. As the North Stars filtered in for the biggest game in their history, he camped in the cramped and sterile office he shared with fellow assistant Andy Murray, who like Clarke and several scouts had just come from Philadelphia. They pored over videotape, trying to find the right tweak for a power play that had gone 1-for-18 in the first three games of the series and 0-for-8 since Modano scored Minnesota's only goal of Game 2.

Through an open door that led into the dressing room, they could see Chico Resch exchange a few words with Casey, who'd started every game of the postseason. It was impossible to hear anything from more than a few feet away as a crush of reporters, cameras, and microphones mined any scrap of news. Resch, the twenty-sixth goalie in NHL history to surpass 200 wins, was at ease among the media. He'd won a Cup with the Islanders in 1980, retired in '87 and, after two years as a color analyst on North Stars TV broadcasts, was in his first season as the team's goaltending coach.

Ducking in and out, his young face all business, was Doug Armstrong. A 26-year-old from Sarnia, Ontario, in his first season as director of team services, he was responsible for travel and assisting coaches with stats and video. His father, Neil, worked some of the biggest games in NHL history as a linesman from 1957 to 1978 and had recently been informed he would be inducted into the Hall of Fame. But a game like this was new territory for Doug.

Dave Surprenant, in his third season as head athletic trainer, had almost as many players in the training room for treatment as there were in the dressing room. Dave Smith, a veteran of six seasons in Minnesota, was listed as assistant trainer but spent more time at the skate sharpener than anyone else, mastering a grinder whose whine was juxtaposed with sparks and tiny, flying shards of steel. Mark Baribeau, the 27-year-old equipment manager who joined the North Stars as a part-time gofer before he could even drive a car, shuttled between his office and the stick room, attending to myriad tasks for the players. His assistant, Lance Vogt, was in his first full-time season. A big, quiet kid with a mustache, he arranged jerseys, socks and made sure helmets and assorted armor were ready for battle.

Past the dressing room, in an area between the showers and free weights, Perry Berezan glanced at a TV mounted on a wall and tried to stay out of the way. He'd played in the 1986 finals as a center for Calgary, losing to Montreal (and Gainey and Bobby Smith), but now found himself on the outside looking in. He'd watched the first eighteen playoff games from the press box or, when that didn't appeal, from players' lounges or any perch where he could follow the action. He finally skated four nights earlier in a 4–1 loss at Pittsburgh and wanted to remain as close as possible without infringing on the concentration or superstition of his teammates.

Brian Hayward, about fifteen feet behind Resch, sat between his big white goalie pads, waiting for warmups and wanting his own chance to play—just not at the expense of the team. He had backed up (i.e. watched) Patrick Roy in the finals two years earlier in Montreal. Hayward's desire to be a starter led to a holdout and an eventual trade to Minnesota in November 1990.

Just to Hayward's right, Brian Propp stood in a pair of shorts, a worn blue undershirt, white socks, and tennis shoes. He idly stretched his legs, first the right then the left, against the blond wood of the bench that ran around the room. His face showed grim determination behind a bushy playoff beard. A 32-year-old left wing, he bore the emotional scars of falling short in four previous Cup finals—three in Philadelphia and one just a year earlier in Boston. He desperately wanted this to be The One.

After Broten, Smith, and Giles, the triumvirate of Berezan, Hayward, and Propp were the only other Minnesota players with experience this deep in the postseason.

The remaining seventeen North Stars that Gainey had used in the playoffs included veterans and rookies, snipers and plumbers, bone-crushing body-checkers, menacing enforcers, and assorted journeymen who somehow were playing the best hockey of their careers.

Only one of the six defensemen had more than three full NHL seasons on his resume. That was Jim Johnson, who grew up twenty miles away in New Hope but had spent six years with the Penguins before a midseason trade brought him home along with Fridley native Chris Dahlquist. The most experienced of the rest was Shawn Chambers, a chunky 24-year-old who had been playing on one healthy knee since a preseason exhibition in Russia. Mark Tinordi, a 6–4 brute from western Canada with a take-no-prisoners attitude, was just coming into his own and destined to be a team leader. But up to that point, Tinordi was still unproven. That left 6–4 Brian Glynn, acquired in October from Calgary, just starting to show he could thrive outside of Salt Lake City and the International Hockey League, and Neil Wilkinson, a hard-hitting and hard-living rookie.

Offensively, Brian Bellows—his 26-year-old hairline receding as his self-confidence grew—carried the swagger of nine seasons since he was drafted second overall in 1982. After his rookie year, he never failed to be one of Minnesota's top three goal scorers. But by the spring of '91, he was still reckoning a drop-off of 25 goals and 29 points from 1989–90.

Into that breech stepped Dave Gagner, also twenty-six, an energetic 5–10 center and cast-off first-rounder of the Rangers. Not far removed from the North Stars' IHL affiliate in Kalamazoo, Michigan, Gagner had considered quitting a couple years earlier—only to make his first all-star appearance and finish the '90–91 season as the team's leading scorer with 82 points.

Ulf Dahlen, one of a growing number of Swedes in the league but the only one with Minnesota, was another first-round refugee from the Rangers. A lanky 24-year-old right wing, he could tantalize opponents on the rush by turning his feet so his heels were almost together as he was in full flight—leaving defenders unsure whether he would cut around or behind them. But he'd only scored once in the entire postseason and was scratched through much of the first two rounds.

Mike Craig, a 19-year-old winger who looked and talked like Jeff Spicoli from "Fast Times at Ridgemont High," appeared in ten of the first eleven playoff games but managed just one goal before Gainey replaced him with Dahlen.

Gavin, thirty-one, and Duchesne, twenty-eight, were relative newcomers to the North Stars but veteran NHL wingers nonetheless. Defense was among their best attributes. Gavin, who played every game the previous season, missed much of '90–91 with a knee injury, and Duchesne didn't break double digits in either goals or assists through 68 games—but his plus-4 rating trailed only Gagner, Propp, and Dahlen among the forwards.

Then there was Bump and Thump, otherwise known as Shane Churla and Basil McRae. Churla, a crew-cut and buff 25-year-old right wing who also answered to "Chuck" and "Chainsaw," led the team in penalty minutes (286, or more than seven in each of his forty games). McRae, a grizzled 30-year-old left wing and glue guy in the room after stints with three other franchises, would become the North Stars' all-time leading resident of the penalty box. He'd go on to total 1,567 PIM (more than twenty-six full games) in Minnesota, but "only" 224 of those came in 1990–91 as (like Churla) he missed half the schedule with injuries.

Marc Bureau, a trade deadline pickup from Calgary, provided another French Canadian to go with Duchesne. Bureau, whose twenty-fifth birthday coincided with Minnesota's Game 3 victory two days earlier, joined the North Stars in early March. Less than a month later, he was in the lineup every night—usually as the fourth-line center. That left out Berezan, whose primary press box wingman in the postseason was speedy Doug Smail, acquired from Winnipeg in November. Smail, at thirty-three the North Stars' oldest player, was among the team's top eight scoring forwards. But his only playoff appearance was on a line with Berezan for the Game 2 loss. As the clock high over center ice ticked down the minutes before Game 4, Smail was in the relative eye of the storm. In street clothes, he leaned against the partition behind the North Stars bench, cradling his newly adopted infant son and drinking in the atmosphere of his closest brush with the Cup.

Moving about in the middle of all this noise—this preeminent disruption—was a 21-year-old. About 5–10 with dark hair, he perhaps could've fooled the near-sighted into wondering whether he was a minor-leaguer. However, there were dead giveaways he was no skater; he was clean-shaven and wearing an off-the-rack grey double-breasted blazer over a stiff white shirt and tie. There was a North Stars pin on his left lapel, and credentials and a ball-point pen hung from a chain around his neck.

That was me.

I passed among the players long enough to drop off an armload of game notes. Producing them was among my most important tasks. I was in my fourth year at the University of Minnesota, moonlighting as a public relations intern while I gauged whether my future was inside pro sports or—more likely—outside it as one of the dozens of notebook-wielding reporters I weaved through that day.

At the moment, I was oblivious to the future and barely cognizant of the past. My experience working for a major-league franchise began six months earlier. Walking past a bulletin board in the basement of Murphy Hall—home to the University's journalism school—I'd noticed a post too enticing to pass up: PR Intern with the North Stars. I didn't care that my only compensation would be a $100-a-month stipend, or that it would barely cover my gas to drive to Bloomington most every day. It didn't matter that I was carrying a full class load, less than a year removed from academic probation caused largely by my first serious romance, or that I was working part-time in the sports department at the *St. Paul Pioneer Press* to further my career and pay bills.

I'd grown up in outstate Minnesota, near Mille Lacs Lake and east of Brainerd, where I graduated high school in 1987. Sports were my obsession from my earliest recollection. An annual trip to a

Twins game was a holiday better than Christmas. Fran Tarkenton was my first idol and remains one to this day—perhaps in no small part because I never met him. As a child I played Nerf basketball and drove my mom crazy with jump shots into the lampshades at either end of the living room couch.

Hockey, however, was always a little beyond my understanding—like the metric system or why Canadian quarters wouldn't work in video game slots. My dad grew up along the North Dakota border and even played small-college football and basketball. His interests influenced mine and my only exposure to hockey was the occasional game on television. Pulling the signal more than 100 miles from the Twin Cities sometimes made it hard to follow among waves of interference.

I had a wooden Northland hockey stick and my bedroom overlooked tiny Wilson Lake, which would've been perfect for games—except for the shoveling. I wobbled on tube skates occasionally, at least as long as my ankles could take it. It's hard to pass the puck to yourself and even more discouraging to dig it out of a snowbank.

By high school, it dawned on me that I wasn't going to become a pro athlete, but I'd found other outlets. As a kid I collected baseball cards (and their football, basketball and hockey counterparts). They provided limitless entertainment as I memorized the fronts, devoured information on the backs, and devised games with intricately drawn fields, courts, and rinks on sheets of cardboard or drafting paper. A good early job for me was working at a sports card and memorabilia store (they once had such things, even in Brainerd). Even better, as I matured, I also discovered that if you could write you could get paid to be around sports all the time.

I became a reporter for the *Brainerd Dispatch* while still in high school and, within a few weeks of enrolling at the U, ventured into the mystical offices of the student-run *Minnesota Daily*. It became my home between classes for more than four years. My early exposure to hockey was limited to the occasional sidebar on a Gophers series at antique Mariucci Arena, but much changed in the winter of 1989–90.

My girlfriend at the time overshadowed everything else and, when our relationship disintegrated in November, I needed a diversion. I found one during Thanksgiving break in a new pair of CCM Tacks. I'd become increasingly appreciative of hockey since I lived in Minneapolis and could even afford to attend an occasional North Stars game on student-rush tickets. Now I planned to immerse myself, really learn to skate and play. I quickly added a new pair of gloves and used shin pads, elbow pads—even breezers.

Oof. Some of those early sessions at Van Cleve Park just north of campus were painful. Not so much from falling but because it seemed like everyone else must've been a prep all-star somewhere between Duluth and Austin. Thankfully, a couple of my friends also were on the same learning curve. We gamely stuck with it as others weaved through us like so many short-armed pylons. Eventually, in the heat of a pick-up scrimmage on a Wednesday night or Saturday afternoon, we didn't stand out for being quite so bad anymore.

Thus, in November 1990 I became privileged if not a minor celebrity at our house after I got a call from Joanie Preston, the North Stars' communications manager. The team started the season 1–6–2 before I even applied for the internship and had the third-worst record in the NHL (4–14–5) after a November 21 loss at Detroit. But all I heard was that I was one of two successful candidates.

The subsequent half-year is like alternate reality. Even now, I must remind myself I was there. I suppose that's where this book comes in. Some mornings I would go to class, drive to Met Center for the afternoon, and then go to the *Pioneer Press* to answer the sports department phone and write high school stories in the evening. I'd be up by 7 a.m. and crawl into bed at 1 a.m. Repeat. If I didn't have class, or if it was game day, I was at the rink. It felt ethereal driving my 1981 Buick Regal down I-35 to the Crosstown

Highway, then south on Cedar to the Met. Eventually when I walked in, familiar faces greeted me—just a Minnesota kid from up north, who often called home with an excited update of what I'd seen or done.

From the west end entrance, where the players turn right and head up to the dressing room, I would turn left. It was impossible not to gawk at Norm's black Rolls Royce Silver Spur parked inside the overhead door. A few feet farther there was a glass door on the left. Behind it were the North Stars' administrative offices for marketing, advertising, and public relations. The biggest and most exclusive space—at least as ornate as you can make a room underground with no windows—was to the right, Norm's suite. His two Cavalier King Charles Spaniels (black-haired, 3-year-old Rupert and brown-haired, 4-year-old Charles) barked at visitors—except on Thursday (their shampoo day). To the left was hockey operations, with Bobby Clarke's office opposite Norm's. Straight ahead and around a corner was a room not much bigger than an elevator. This was where we had our desks, mine to the right and, to the left, his chair exposed in a walkway to Joanie's office, sat Dan Stuchal.

A 22-year-old senior at the U, Dan was from Hayward, Wisconsin, and a little closer to the real world. He would graduate with a liberal arts degree that spring. I would need another two quarters. He worked at Coffman Memorial Union and spent the rest of his waking hours at the Met. We were relative minions, answering phones, preparing the press box, fulfilling media requests, helping oversee access to the players, and writing unattributed content that would populate game programs, press releases, and space in smaller newspapers.

And there was copying. Always, copying. The Xerox machine was nearly the size of my car and hid behind dividers just outside our office in the lower concourse. For every home game in the postseason, we printed press packets, standings, statistics, quotes, and other communications totaling more than 17,000 sheets in coordinated colors of white, light green, light yellow, and pink paper. That's 34 *reams* of paper every game day. Earlier in the season, when we weren't exactly drawing a big crowd of media (or fans), the appetite was less. But by conservative estimate we consumed a semi-truck load of copy paper during the season, just for game notes and interoffice use. This was before the Internet. I shudder to think how many trees it took to keep up with our demand.

The copier spat pages all afternoon. Occasionally, Dan or I would take a batch up to the TV booths or to the press dining room, where a wall had been knocked out earlier in the week to make room for more media. During the season, we'd had our choice of dozens of press box chairs from which to watch at least portions of the games. Now there was no place to sit, and we were so busy we couldn't have done so anyway. There was a nervous energy everywhere. Was this team really going to win the Stanley Cup? Were the playoffs ever going to end? Was this all a dream? What would "normal" ever be in the wake of this experience?

We were about to find out. Around 5:30 p.m., the strains of the theme from "The Natural" drifted through the arena. That gave way to the "Top Gun" anthem and then music from "Rocky." A little before six o'clock, fans started streaming in. It was nearly time. Crews from the Canadian Broadcasting Corporation and SportsChannel America began their rink-side live shots. Joanie, Dan, and I gathered outside the North Stars dressing room to herd the media away.

The mood inside was all business. McRae and Churla bumped shoulders and hollered encouragement to no one in particular. Casey was ensconced in his gear, obscured behind his green goalie mask with prominent yellow stars. Broten had a placid expression. The rest looked like they were about to go to war, so nervous they could vomit, or both.

Modano was the only player in uniform younger than me, but he already seemed older with his height (6–3), good looks and two years of NHL experience. But this was new to him, too. He bounced lightly on the toes of his skates, and he looked slightly perplexed—like fellow students I'd seen trying to understand a complex chemistry formula.

We closed the door behind us. The next time it would open to anyone not with the team would be several hours later. At that point, we would either have a stranglehold on the series or it would be tied heading back to Pittsburgh for Game 5.

None of us knew at that moment we were at a fulcrum, the futures of everyone there forever affected by what was about to take place.

Not the players. They just wanted to keep the dream going. Whether a veteran like Smith, who might not get another crack at the Cup, or a kid like Modano, who surely would have other finals in his future, it was all about the next shift.

Not the coaches. Gainey appeared surprisingly years ahead of pace. While winning may not happen all the time, it was certainly an expectation for him and Jarvis.

Not the support staff. Baribeau's first road trip with the North Stars was for the '81 finals, a few weeks before he graduated from Richfield High School. Working at Met Center was all he'd known. He met his girlfriend (and future wife) when she was an usher and never had to contemplate a future anywhere else.

Seventy-five feet down the hall in the visitors' dressing room, the Penguins only knew they were down two games to one. Trottier, in his twilight years as a player, had come to Pittsburgh with his name already on the Cup four times. Coffey, halfway through a twenty-one-year career, had raised it three times. And Joe Mullen won it two years earlier with Calgary. Mario Lemieux, whose absence from Game 3 with a wonky back had seismic consequences, to this point was just a really good player with a fairly bad franchise. In six seasons since he was the first overall draft pick in 1984, Pittsburgh had twice finished last in the Patrick Division and fifth three times. More than half the roster had turned over since a trip to the division finals in 1989. In twenty-three previous seasons, the Penguins finished in the bottom half of the league eighteen times, never made it past the second round, and only got that far thrice.

Bob Johnson, named Pittsburgh's head coach a week before Gainey was announced in Minnesota, held court with a few assistants in a small office off the dressing room. His smile and quick wit couldn't hide an anxiety reminiscent of legendary football coach George Allen. Like Allen, Johnson's hands were always in motion, either to punctuate a point he made verbally, brush his nose, or scribble with a felt-tipped pen in his ever-present spiral notepad. He'd grown up at 43rd Street and Fourth Avenue in South Minneapolis, attended Central High School, played for the Gophers, and later coached at the University of Wisconsin—earning the nickname "Badger Bob" as he won three national titles. He got his only previous NHL shot with Calgary and led the Flames to the '86 final. At 60, with Lemieux and the other building blocks he had with the Penguins, Johnson should have a bright future. But you never know. If this was his best chance at the Cup, he couldn't afford to let it slip.

Upstairs in the TV press box on the south side of the arena, longtime Pittsburgh play-by-play commentator Mike Lange and color analyst Paul Steigerwald prepared to call the Penguins' simulcast on KDKA-TV (Channel 2) and its affiliated radio station. If they were anxious, it was mostly about how the raucous North Stars crowd might treat them. They'd been doused with beer during Game 3, so they had a vanguard of four security guards for Game 4. In a booth to their left, Doug McLeod and Lou Nanne were getting ready for the North Stars' pay-per-view telecast—the feed from Midwest Sports Channel that cost $12.95 for metro onlookers. One of them would be Bob Johnson's 85-year-old mother, Myrna, in her Minneapolis apartment, though her son was footing the extra cost on her cable bill.

McLeod, in just his third season with the team, was thirty-six, dark-haired with a mustache, married and ready to start a family. He was piecing together a full-time existence between high school state tournaments, some Twins telecasts, and even Gophers baseball, of all things. Ratings for North Stars games on KMSP-TV Channel 9 were through the roof, the pay-per-views were hot, and calling a Stanley Cup winner could only solidify his future.

Nanne, twelve days shy of his fiftieth birthday, played during the North Stars' first eleven seasons, then spent the next twelve either coaching or in the front office. The single person who's had the most to do with the franchise, Louie was extremely well-known if not always beloved in the Twin Cities. In 1990–91, he was VP of marketing and public relations (my boss's boss's boss) but had publicly announced his retirement on the eve of the Chicago series to go into financial services with Royal Bank of Canada. His personal interest and a one-year commitment to Green kept Louie involved with the TV broadcasts down the stretch. But the sands were running thin on his tenure—and his chance of being part of a Stanley Cup championship.

Green had Nanne's replacement lined up months earlier. Pat Forciea, a 32-year-old from Coleraine and former goalie at the University of St. Thomas, had made his biggest headlines as a political strategist in November. Just before the North Stars picked up Kevin Allenspach, Forciea helped make possible Paul Wellstone's upset of Minnesota's two-term senator Rudy Boschwitz—the only incumbent to lose in the 1990 mid-terms. Boschwitz outspent Wellstone 7-to-1, so Forciea knew more than a little about succeeding as an underdog. He joined the team in February and later became VP of communications and operations.

Forciea's influence occasionally clashed with Elaine Waddell, in her first year as director of public relations and advertising. She'd promoted Met Center events under the Gunds and was a late addition to Norm's staff before the season began. Somewhat high-strung but with a knack for schmoozing, Waddell was forty-one and between marriages, trying to steady her career in a year of upheaval. Unfortunately, she also was easy to spot during the finals for the eye patch she wore after nearly being blinded by an errant shot from a neighboring fairway while golfing during the St. Louis series.

Joanie was the driving force above Dan and me, though at this stage of the playoffs she was running on adrenalin like the rest of us. Five years earlier, also as a University of Minnesota student, she wrote an unsolicited letter to Dick Dillman, who had been the team's publicity director since 1967. Dillman met with her, offered her a job, and she worked with him until his death in 1988. Joe Janasz, who also worked for Dillman as publications manager, succeeded him and everything went fine until the ownership change in 1990. Janasz left and Joanie was one of the many who got fired that summer. Fortunately, and not without satisfaction, she got a call three days later asking her to return under Waddell.

At this point before Game 4, Joanie was going on nine months of running everything from a PR standpoint. She had her trusty interns, but the stress of nearly six weeks in the postseason without a day off was beginning to show. To top it off, she was planning her wedding for a few months after the finals. Just twenty-seven as she stood, one knee on her press box chair and one hand on the phone extension at her seat, Joanie was about to cram some of the biggest events of her life into a very small window of time.

About thirty feet to her right and under a red-and-blue neon KSTP-AM 1500 sign, Al Shaver and Ralph Strangis wore headsets that made them oblivious to conversation nearby as they painted a verbal picture for those who couldn't or wouldn't pony up for the pay-per-view.

Shaver, sixty-three, was the only radio play-by-play voice the North Stars ever knew, his descriptions rising and retreating with the flow of a game but going down like fine wine and punctuating cold winter nights from International Falls to the Iowa border for decades. He could feel the years, however, and was looking ahead to perhaps calling only home games in future seasons. Would he get another chance to be part of something this special?

If Shaver was like an old dog in the business, Strangis was a rambunctious puppy. Barely thirty, he'd willed himself to become Shaver's partner during a preseason audition with three other candidates. Perhaps equal to if not more important than his vocal ability was his persistence in a nonstop personal marketing campaign targeting KSTP station manager Ginny Morris. Strangis' career was even more patchwork than McLeod's, including all-star wrestling and pro volleyball. And, considering Strangis was less than five years out of treatment for drug and alcohol dependency, his rise might've been as shocking as the team about which he spoke.

The unobtrusive digital clocks at the back of the upper level on each side of the arena clicked past 6:30. The more prominent timer on the scoreboard counted down under thirty-five minutes.

By now, we were all in place or close to it. Norm was in the owner's box, along with a cast of characters that included "Who's the Boss?" actor Tony Danza, Dallas Cowboys owner Jerry Jones, and reigning Tour de France champion Greg Lemond, who three years earlier built a six-bedroom, seven-bath, 11,500-square-foot mansion in Medina that would rival Green's home in nearby Tonka Bay.

Forciea worked the aisle of the press box, shaking hands here and patting backs there—especially lobbying the national writers. Waddell chatted with the well-to-do on the club level at the west end. Preston presided over a brief confab with diminutive Rachel Blount of the *Minneapolis Star Tribune* and bulbous Gary Olson of the *Pioneer Press*. They regularly covered the team year-round. Blount, with short dark hair, had just come to Minneapolis a year earlier, four years out of the University of Missouri School of Journalism and after working at her home-state *Des Moines Register*. Olson, who stood about 6–3 and weighed about 300 pounds, was forty-four and had been working in St. Paul for two decades—assigned to the North Stars since 1985. They weren't Felix and Oscar, but they were an odd couple. Tonight, they were surrounded by dozens of journalists they knew and even more they didn't.

Finally, Casey ambled down the twenty steps from the dressing room to the ice with nineteen teammates behind him. The crowd erupted when he came into view and roared as the players skated out for warm-ups. George Michael's "Freedom! '90" blasted from the sound system.

Dan and I converged on the seated media, handing out rosters—still warm from the copier—denoting who was starting and who would be scratched. Lemieux was back in.

The largest crowd the building could hold was ready. The Twin Cities were electric. Throughout the Midwest, even those who couldn't name a North Star three months ago flocked around TV sets and leaned into their radios. People everywhere, at least the ones who cared about hockey, focused on Met Center.

None of them had ever seen anything like this before.

More than 30 years on, they still wait to see it again.

The words "anything can happen"
have become a cliché.
But they are what sports are all about.
Even more, they're what life is all about.
-Kevin Allenspach

You may glory in a team triumphant,
but you fall in love with a team in defeat.
Losing after great striving
is the story of man.
-Roger Kahn in **The Boys of Summer**

CHAPTER 2

The North Stars' Story

There's a beginning to everything. For the Minnesota North Stars, the path to the 1991 Stanley Cup Finals started 130 years earlier, in 1861, when Minnesota's first governor, Henry Hastings Sibley, chose "*Le Etoile Du Nord*" as the state motto. A French phrase meaning "The Star of the North," it came three years after Minnesota's admission to the union, on the cusp of the Civil War, and 100 years before anyone here ever heard of Andre Boudrias.

Not quite 70 years later, on September 25, 1929, Walter Bush was born in Minneapolis. He played hockey, first at Breck Academy and later at Dartmouth. He went to the University of Minnesota Law School and started his administrative career in the game in 1955 as president of the Central Hockey League. He later owned the Minneapolis Bruins, a farm team for the Boston Bruins, positioning him to be the front man of an investment group if the National Hockey League ever expanded.

By the 1960s, that was a legitimate possibility. The NHL debuted in 1917–18 and its first American team began play in Boston in 1924–25. Nine US franchises followed in the next decade, but most led a nomadic existence. By the 1940s, only the Boston Bruins, Chicago Black Hawks, Detroit Red Wings, and New York Rangers survived.

Just before the St. Louis Eagles began their only season in 1934–35, about 1,000 miles northwest in Winnipeg, Manitoba, a pair of Jewish immigrants from Russia celebrated the birth of a son on June 12, 1934. His name was Norman Green; his father a working-class railroad employee who later moved his family to Vancouver and his mother a store clerk. Norm played basketball and golf (but not hockey) and wore hand-me-down clothes until he attended the University of British Columbia. At twenty-one, he moved to Calgary and began selling houses. Six months later, he started his own real estate company and within three years bought his first commercial building. At twenty-eight, he opened his first shopping center. It was the start to assembling a fortune that would make him an NHL owner, someone who wore $3,000 suits, went yachting on the French Riviera with NHL president John Ziegler, and moved in circles unfathomable to ordinary businessmen.

For anyone coming of age during World War II and the two decades after, the only places you could find major league hockey were in one of the NHL's "Original Six" cities, which also included Montreal and Toronto. It was this combination that forged pro hockey as we know it today, coincident with establishing modern components of the game like the center-ice red line and icing. And the only way Bush or Green could follow the NHL was via the newspapers or, if they could find him on the dial, listening to Foster Hewitt on the radio during Saturday broadcasts of Hockey Night in Canada.

Al Shaver was way ahead of them. Born in 1928 in London, Ontario, Al grew up without his mother, who died in childbirth, leaving him with no siblings and only his father, Walter, who made a living as an auto dealer and farm-implement salesman in nearby Tillonsburg. Al grew up hockey mad, but asthma kept him from playing. One night in 1937, the Shavers drove two hours to a game in Toronto, and they saw Hewitt describe play from the gondola at Maple Leaf Gardens. It was then the self-described "little Shaver" decided to be a broadcaster, and Saturday nights became routine for a bath before pattering downstairs to listen to Hewitt on the big console radio. In 1942, when Toronto beat Detroit in Game 7 and became the only team in NHL history to overcome a three-games-to-none deficit in the finals, Al was fourteen and among the spectators in Canada's first hockey crowd of more than 16,000. At twenty, he graduated from a program at a Canadian broadcasting school owned by actor Lorne Greene. Shaver later hopscotched across the country, working at stations in Guelph (Ontario), Calgary, Medicine Hat and Edmonton (in Alberta), Montreal (Quebec) and Windsor (Ontario) before landing back in Toronto, where he called five Grey Cup football championships.

In the 1950s, soon after Bush took over the Minneapolis Bruins and Green launched Stewart, Green Properties, Ltd., the NHL began to realize it had to look beyond the Original Six to grow revenue. Major League Baseball had two franchises move to the west coast in 1958[2] and, within four years, had expanded by four more teams to a total of twenty. One of those was the "new" Washington Senators, who entered the American League in 1961 to replace a previous incarnation that moved to Minnesota to become the Twins. The National Football League not only expanded (including to Minnesota in 1961), but it faced competition from the new American Football League; there were twenty-two pro franchises between the two by 1961. The National Basketball Association, which had the Minneapolis Lakers move to Los Angeles in 1960, expanded to nine teams a year later and had ten franchises by 1966.

By comparison, the NHL moved slowly, but when change came it was monumental. On March 11, 1965, President Clarence Campbell announced expansion by six teams, doubling the size of the league. That same day, Bush told reporters in the Twin Cities that he and seven other investors would apply for one of the new franchises.

From that moment, the fortunes of Bush and Green, connected in time by Shaver, were on a collision course with a team that could ultimately and simultaneously be called star-crossed and cursed.

On February 9, 1966, Minnesota was awarded an NHL team, joining Pittsburgh, Philadelphia, Los Angeles, St. Louis, and Oakland for the 1967–68 season. Bush hired Wren Blair, previously general manager of the Minneapolis Bruins, to be Minnesota's first GM. Affectionately known as "The Bird," Blair had a reputation as a master at identifying and recruiting prospects, including the game-changing Bobby Orr, whom he'd signed for Boston. The new Minnesota team would be called the "North Stars," and they needed an arena. Minneapolis Arena, which opened in 1924 at Dupont Avenue and Lake Street, was home to pro hockey west of the Mississippi River—but it only held 5,500 fans. To the east, the St. Paul Auditorium opened in 1932 at 175 West Kellogg Boulevard and was the city's first artificial ice rink—but its capacity was 7,000. Neither was big enough for the NHL.

Between the cities, the Minnesota State Fairgrounds also had a rink–the Hippodrome–which was built in 1906 and seated 8,000. Bush considered it for expansion to 13,000, but renovation proved too expensive and the NHL ultimately said it would only accept a new building anyway. The result was the new Metropolitan Sports Center, built just north of Met Stadium, home of the Twins and Vikings. The property under and around the facilities was jointly owned by the cities of Minneapolis, Richfield and Bloomington and governed by the Metropolitan Area Sports Commission. A few weeks after the groundbreaking, team colors of green and white and a logo featuring a stylized capital N were unveiled.

2 Walter O'Malley spirited his Dodgers from Brooklyn to Los Angeles and, as a result, Horace Stoneham took his Giants from New York to San Francisco. It wasn't the first move of a major league franchise. The Boston Braves moved to Milwaukee in 1953. And it wasn't even the first expansion to the west coast. In the NFL, the Rams moved from Cleveland to Los Angeles in 1946. But O'Malley's decision set the stage for pro sports to be truly national in scope at their highest levels.

Home to pro hockey early in the 20th century, Minneapolis Arena opened in 1924 and was home to the Minneapolis Rockets, shown here playing against the St. Paul Saints in 1925. The Rockets soon were renamed the Millers and played in more than a half-dozen different leagues through the early 1960s. The Minneapolis Bruins played here from 1963 to 1965. The building was razed in 1966. (Minnesota Historical Society)

The following spring, Shaver scaled a catwalk at Maple Leaf Gardens and described the action of the 1967 Stanley Cup Finals against Montreal into a tape recorder. That was his audition for the North Stars, launching a career that would last longer than that of any owner. He and his wife, Shirley, moved with their five children to Minnetonka. Traveling in a Volkswagen Beetle, it must've seemed a circus stunt when they piled out.

With the expansion draft, the team finally had some players. Cesare Maniago was the North Stars' first choice among goalies, and Dave Balon became their first skater. Both twenty-eight, Maniago came from the Rangers and Balon from the Canadiens. Another goalie and seventeen skaters followed to give Minnesota its first roster. The following day, amateur drafts and trades resulted in another thirty-nine players. Two weeks later, Blair named himself coach.

On Wednesday, October 11, at St. Louis Arena, Minnesota made its NHL debut against the Blues. The game was supposed to start at 8:30 p.m., but the first puck dropped forty-eight minutes late, thanks to extensive pregame ceremonies that featured Guy Lombardo and Arthur Godfrey before a crowd of more than 11,000. The delay led to some creative pregame commentary and programming for WTCN-TV

A crowd of more than 3,000 fans watches the Minneapolis Millers skate to a 3-0 shutout victory on November 30, 1937, at the St. Paul Auditorium. Saints goalie Sam LoPresti (No. 1) made 26 saves. He played for the Chicago Black Hawks from 1940 to 1942. After his career, LoPresti operated a tavern in Eveleth. His son, Pete, later became a goalie for the Minnesota North Stars from 1974 to '79, making them the first father-son goaltending duo in NHL history. (Note how goal judges of the era stood on the ice behind the net. At the Auditorium, a switch dangled from a cord by which a goal could be signaled.) (Minnesota Historical Society)

Channel 11, which was airing the first of thirty games—mostly on the road. The teams skated to a 2–2 tie, although the North Stars led 2–1 with less than a minute and a half remaining. Bill Masterton, who'd been the first player to sign a North Stars contract, scored the first goal in franchise history, a backhand at 15:20 of the second period that beat St. Louis goalie Seth Martin to make it 1–0. Gary Bauman made 25 saves but couldn't stop Wayne Rivers' 30-foot shot that zipped under the crossbar to clinch a tie for the Blues.

After four games, the North Stars were 0–2–2 and looking up at every team in the division. A welcome luncheon at the Met was intended to be followed by public tours, but the event was canceled a week in advance because halting construction on the arena—even for a day—would mean it wouldn't be ready for the home opener. Crews continued to install seats and the scoreboard and were even painting lines on the ice on October 20.

Less than 24 hours later, a crowd of 12,951 (the largest of the expansion six openers) saw a 3–1 victory over Oakland. Bill Goldsworthy netted the first goal at 8:23 of the second period. Ray Cullen and Balon scored third-period goals to break a tie and Maniago made 21 saves.

Bill Goldsworthy: 1st goal at Met Center. (Vintage Minnesota Hockey)

There were other highlights in the first half of the season: a 3–1 win at Philadelphia, and a home win over the defending Stanley Cup champion Maple Leafs that put the North Stars over .500 for the first time. They won at Chicago in early December and soon after posted the franchise's first three shutouts in a row (all by Maniago). After Christmas, the team went unbeaten in four straight (including another first: Wayne Connelly's hat trick January 10 against Philadelphia) as Oakland came to the Met on Saturday night, January 13, 1968.

That game will forever be remembered for Masterton, a 29-year-old Winnipeg native, former All-American and two-time national champion at Denver University, who became the only player in NHL history to die from a game injury. He was on just his second shift when he carried the puck toward the Seals' goal inside the blue line at the east end of the arena. He angled in from the right and fed a backhand to Connelly. Seals defensemen Larry Cahan and Ron Harris checked Masterton, who fell backward and hit his head on the ice.

It was obvious Masterton was in major distress, already bleeding at the nose and mouth before trainer Stan Waylett—shuffling as fast as possible over the relatively fresh surface—could reach him. Moments later, Masterton was rolled away on a stretcher, the 12,119 onlookers hushed.

An ambulance rushed him to Fairview Southdale Hospital and the game later ended in a 2–2 tie. The North Stars showered, dressed and flew to Chicago. They intended to travel to Boston on Sunday morning, however delays and cancellations made the team late and arriving on multiple planes. By then Masterton was in intensive care, his parents having rushed from Winnipeg to be with their son and daughter-in-law and their two young grandchildren.

Sunday night's opening faceoff at Boston Garden was delayed 45 minutes as Blair informed his players that Masterton wasn't expected to live. Stunned, they went out to face the Bruins, who creamed them 9–2. The North Stars were outshot 55–24 and trailed 8–0 early in the third period before they got goals from Balon and Boudrias (the only Minnesota player to wear a helmet).

In the darkness of early Monday morning, with the NHL's top players soon headed to Toronto for a dinner the night before the all-star game, Blair and assistant coach John Mariucci kept vigil in Blair's room at the Somerset Hotel in Boston. The phone rang just before 4 a.m., informing them that Masterton[3] died. He'd never regained consciousness.

On January 21, more than a week (and four straight losses) since the tragedy, the North Stars beat Pittsburgh 4–3 at Met Center. By February, they'd clawed back over .500 at 22–21–9. It would be the

3 No other North Star ever wore Masterton's No. 19, though it wasn't formally retired until 1987.

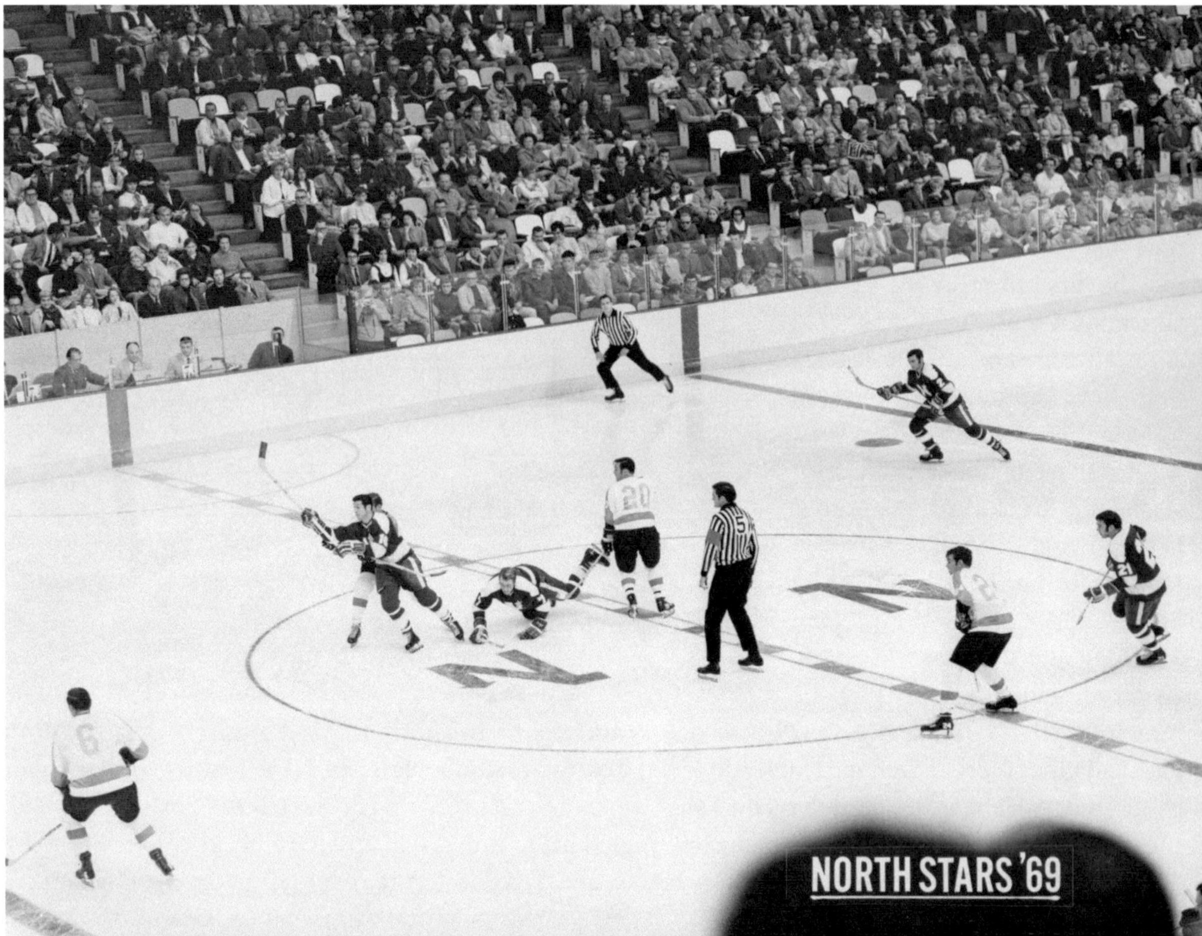

This is what early North Stars action looked like at Met Center. This photo is from January 24, 1970, against Philadelphia. Minnesota captain Claude Larose (16) fights through traffic at center ice as Flyers center Jim Johnson (20) trips Danny O'Shea (7). Also shown are Minnesota defenseman Barry Gibbs (2) and left wing Danny Grant (21), who won the Calder Trophy the previous season. The other Flyers include defensemen Terry Ball (24) and Wayne Hillman (6). Philadelphia cruised to a 6-0 victory with goals from six different skaters, including one from an aspiring rookie – Bobby Clarke. (Minnesota Historical Society)

last time in franchise history the North Stars would have an accumulative winning record. They won one of their next nine games to slide into fourth place.

The newly expanded playoffs pitted the top four expansion teams against each other on one side of the bracket. The North Stars beat the Los Angeles Kings in seven games in the opening round, then played five of seven games on the road in the division final against St. Louis because of a Met Center commitment to the Ice Follies. A national period of mourning in wake of the assassination of Dr. Martin Luther King, which happened the night of Game 1 against the Kings, had pushed the playoff schedule back and the arena was unavailable. Bush appealed to change dates, but the Blues refused. Minnesota played host to only Games 2 and 6, and the series was decided on a crushing double-overtime goal by Ron Schock in Game 7 that gave St. Louis a 2–1 victory.

The inaugural season, greatly because of Masterton's death, cast a pall over the franchise for years. In 1968–69, the North Stars finished sixth and missed the playoffs with the worst record in the league. In 1969–70, they lost to St. Louis in the first round.

Then, early in the morning of November 12, 1970, tragedy struck again when North Stars winger Tommy Williams found his 27-year-old wife, Emily, dead in the garage of their Richfield home. She'd attended the North Stars game against Los Angeles the previous evening and was sitting in their car, which had been run until it was out of gas. She presumably died of carbon monoxide poisoning. Tommy, who'd been slowed by a back injury early in the season, was left with five children—one still in diapers.[4]

One season after losing to Montreal in the Stanley Cup semifinals, season-ticket sales crested at 12,400 in 1971–72, when Met Center played host to its only NHL All-Star Game.[5] A few months later, the North Stars exited in the first round, again against St. Louis, albeit after more than ten minutes of overtime in the seventh game. In '73, they lost to Philadelphia in the first round. They missed the playoffs the following three seasons, and their viability became even more difficult with the advent of the Minnesota Fighting Saints, who began play in the World Hockey Association at the St. Paul Auditorium in 1972 and later moved into the city's brand-new Civic Center.

The North Stars bowed out meekly in a best-of-three preliminary round series against the Buffalo Sabres in 1977, and following another season without a playoff appearance, the team merged with the Cleveland Barons under the ownership of George and Gordon Gund on July 22, 1978.

If Bush was the driving force that gave birth to the North Stars, and Green was their last owner, the Gunds were the link that brought them together. George was born May 7, 1937, in Cleveland, son of the president and chairman of Ohio's largest bank. His brother, Gordon, was born October 15, 1939. While George was a high school dropout who joined the Marines, Gordon graduated from Harvard, where he played hockey—albeit long after Bush and several other original North Stars owners played in the Ivy League. George settled in San Francisco, made a name for himself as a filmmaker, and in 1975 invested in the California Golden (*nee* Oakland) Seals. Gordon made his home in Princeton, New Jersey, and followed his father into corporate finance. By the 1970s, he'd lost his sight to a rare eye

Walter Bush

George Gund

Gordon Gund

4 Williams, a Duluth native, joined the Boston Bruins in 1962 and, for several years, remained the only American playing regularly in the NHL. After his wife's death, his happy-go-lucky attitude darkened to moodiness. He began to drink heavily, fought with North Stars coach Jack Gordon and ultimately was traded to Oakland in February 1971. He later jumped to the WHA and finished his career with the Washington Capitals in 1976. He remarried but his son, Robert (a Bruins prospect), died in 1987 at 23. Tommy Williams died of a heart attack on Feb. 8, 1992.

5 Bobby Orr and the East all-stars beat the West, 3–2, though the magnitude of the game was obscured by a couple other local events. A riot broke out that same night ten miles north at Williams Arena among players and fans at a college basketball game between Ohio State and Minnesota. And, while pro hockey meetings were going on at the Radisson South in Bloomington, Daniel Meyer, the owner of the Western Hockey League's Salt Lake City Eagles, fell to his death from a room on the hotel's nineteenth floor.

condition, retinitis pigmentosa. It kept him off skates, but he excelled at virtually everything else—and his other senses became so sharp that business colleagues weren't always sure he *couldn't* see.

The Seals had floundered in California. They never had a winning record and finished last in their division six times in nine years. By 1976, after several ownership debacles, George Gund, who routinely played pickup hockey and participated in alumni and amateur games into his fifties, helped entice majority owner Mel Swig to move the Seals to Cleveland.

The Barons didn't fly in Ohio. In 1976–77, they drew 10,000 fans for just seven of forty home games. They missed payroll twice in February, and only a late-season loan allowed them to finish the season, last in the Adams Division. George Gund convinced Gordon to invest, and they bought Swig's interest. The Barons won four of their first five in '77–78, were at .500 into November, and attendance seemed to solidify. But they won just six of their final thirty games and, on the eve of the '78 draft, the NHL found itself with two franchises in trouble. The North Stars (18–53–9) were the worst team in the league and in danger of disappearing in an area infatuated with hockey. The solution was to combine them with the Barons in the better of the two markets. The Gunds bought out the original Minnesota investors, took over Met Center, and kept Lou Nanne as general manager.

Nanne drafted well a few days later, selecting Bobby Smith first overall. In his rookie season, Smith led the North Stars in scoring and claimed the Calder Trophy. But, again, they missed the playoffs.

The 1979–80 season, however, proved a turning point. Four teams from the now-defunct WHA joined the NHL, ending that competition, and the North Stars started to shine. They finished third in the Adams Division and their 88-point total was sixth-best in the new 21-team league. They swept Toronto in the preliminary round and stunned four-time defending champion Montreal in seven games to advance to the semifinals for the first time in nine years. Philadelphia put an end to the run, winning the series in five games, but the North Stars were relevant again.

Soon after Philadelphia lost to the Islanders in the 1980 final, Green took the advice of his 13-year-old son, Adam, and became part of the Flames' ownership group. From there, Norm—who served on the NHL's board of governors and was the most visible of the new Calgary owners—had an insider's view to watch what played out through the next decade in Minnesota.

In 1980–81, the North Stars fell one win short of improvement. But on February 26, one of their losses set the stage for a mammoth first-round playoff statement. In a 5–1 loss at Boston, the teams combined for 406 penalty minutes as the North Stars sent a message that they would not be intimidated by the brawling Bruins. Less than six weeks later, Minnesota—which had been 0–28–6 all-time at Boston Garden—won the first two postseason games there.[6] The North Stars went on to sweep the Bruins before vaulting past Buffalo and Calgary en route to the Stanley Cup Finals against the Islanders.

The 1981 finals were anticlimactic, however. The Islanders had far and away the NHL's best record and its top goal scorer in Mike Bossy (68 goals, including 28 on a lethal power play and 10 game-winners). They won the first two games on Long Island by the same score, 6–3. The North Stars tried to answer in Game 3 at Met Center, taking a 3–1 lead into the second period and maintaining a 4–4 tie early in the third. But Bossy added his second of two goals and Butch Goring completed a hat trick to

6 On the advice of a psychic, North Stars coach Glen Sonmor wore a black eye patch for the playoff games against the Bruins. Sonmor, who'd lost his left eye when he was hit by the puck while playing for the Cleveland Barons of the AHL, was a genial showman. When coaching the Minnesota Fighting Saints and later the North Stars he was known for fostering an environment where players could decide games with their fists in addition to their skating and shooting ability. Behind the bench for more than 400 NHL regular-season games, the North Stars of the late 1970s and early 1980s often relate with hilarity what happened when Sonmor would get excited during a game and his glass eye would fall out.

Steve Payne (26) redirects a shot by Brad Maxwell between the legs of Islanders goalie Billy Smith for the winning goal in a 4-2 victory in Game 4 of the Stanley Cup Finals on May 19, 1981, at Met Center. The goal came at 12:26 of the third period and was Payne's 17th (and last) of the '81 playoffs. Also shown for the North Stars are center Kevin Maxwell (9) and, far in the distance, goalie Don Beaupre, who made 33 saves. Islanders in the photo include Dave Langevin (far left), Wayne Merrick (11), John Tonelli (27), Bob Lorimer (4), and Bob Nystrom (23). (Minnesota Historical Society/ St. Paul Pioneer Press/Spencer Hallstadt)

win it 7–5. Finally in Game 4, Minnesota prevailed, 4–2. Steve Payne scored the game-winner late in the third, and 19-year-old rookie Don Beaupre made 33 saves. But it only served to allow the Islanders to win the Cup in New York as Goring scored twice in Game 5 to earn the Conn Smythe Trophy as playoff MVP and the North Stars had only a long flight home to Minnesota.

Still, the North Stars should have been flying high in 1981–82. Instead, they got a reality check. They entered the newly realigned Norris Division and finished in first place, but then lost to fourth-place Chicago in the first round. In '82–83, Chicago won the Norris and ousted Minnesota in five games of the division final. And, less than two months later at the draft in Montreal, the future began to swing south again.

Since their first choice in 1967, the North Stars' draft record was spotty at best. Their first two No. 1 picks never played a game. Their third, defenseman Dick Redmond, played 771—but only 16 with Minnesota. The fourth No. 1 pick (left wing Jerry Byers) came in 1972, and he played 24 of 43 career NHL games with the North Stars. In 1974, defenseman Doug Hicks was the first first-rounder the hometown fans got to see develop. Unfortunately, that coincided with some of the team's worst days. Hicks played all but seven games in four seasons and was minus-102. The next three first-round picks were: Bryan Maxwell (1975), a defenseman who signed with the WHA and later played 43 games for

Minnesota; Glen Sharpley (1976), a center who played four full seasons with the North Stars but was traded midway through 1980–81; and Brad Maxwell (1977), a defenseman who played 471 of 612 career games with Minnesota.

Their fortunes changed as Smith (1978) and defenseman and future captain Craig Hartsburg (1979) helped form the heart of the team that made the '81 finals. Few would argue those picks. But the first round often is where franchises pivot. Great ones are made with shrewd selections. And nothing can hamstring an organization more than poor decisions that lead to a weak pipeline of talent.

In 1980, the North Stars took left wing Brad Palmer[7]. He played 95 games over two seasons in Minnesota, one year in Boston and was out of the NHL. Ron Meighan[8], the first-round pick in '81, played 48 career games—seven with the North Stars.

So, there was some perhaps well-deserved pressure when Brian Bellows was the second overall pick in 1982, and Brian Lawton followed, the first American to go No. 1 overall, in 1983. After an injury to Hartsburg in 1983–84, Bellows became interim captain at 19 years and 4 months of age. That's younger than Connor McDavid, Gabriel Landeskog and Sidney Crosby were when they later became teen captains, although McDavid is recognized as the NHL's youngest at 19 years, 8 months because his "C" was permanent. Nonetheless, Bellows went on to score more goals than any North Star.

But Lawton, compared to the North Stars' only other overall No. 1s (Smith and Mike Modano, the second American to go first), was a major bust. Lawton had a 31-point rookie season and spent half of his second year in the minors. From 1985 through '88, he averaged 19 goals and 40 points per season. That's not terrible, but not worthy of a first overall pick, either—especially when future Hall of Famer Steve Yzerman, who would hoist Stanley three times, went three spots later to Detroit.

Minnesota won the Norris Division in '84 and topped Chicago and St. Louis in consecutive series that each went the distance. But a month after Edmonton swept them in the conference final, the North Stars compounded the Lawton selection by taking defenseman David Quinn in the first round. Diagnosed with a rare blood disease, he never made it to the NHL as a player, though he did become head coach of the Rangers in 2018.

In 1985, the North Stars swept St. Louis in a three-game preliminary series, but the Chicago ended their season, winning Game 6 of the division final in overtime at the Met.

Lacking first- or second-round picks in the subsequent draft, the North Stars changed their look by adding black accents to their uniform and logo—producing the look they would wear through '90–91. They finished second in the Norris but lost to the Blues in the first round in 1986.

Their next two first-round picks were left wing Warren Babe (21 NHL games) in 1986 and center Dave Archibald in 1987. Archibald had two 33-point seasons in Minnesota and was traded to the Rangers in '89. Defenseman Doug Zmolek was the North Stars' prize pick when the draft came to Minnesota that year, but the Rochester native was about to play the first of three seasons for the Gophers and wouldn't be available anytime soon. Defenseman Derian Hatcher was their first-rounder in 1990. Other than Modano, and possibly Bellows, Hatcher had the greatest impact on the franchise of any other top pick. But only 110 of his 1,045 NHL games came with Minnesota.

The '86–87 and '87–88 seasons coincided with back-to-back last-place finishes. In the spring of '87, the Gunds hired as coach Herb Brooks, the St. Paul native who led the Gophers to three NCAA titles in the

7 One pick after Palmer, the Islanders drafted Brent Sutter, who went on to play more than 1,100 NHL games. The player that perhaps most regrettably slipped through the North Stars' fingers, and most other teams, was Jari Kurri, a fourth-round pick by the Edmonton Oilers.

8 Two picks later, Calgary took future Hall of Fame defenseman Al MacInnis. And another, Chris Chelios, was still available in the second round when the North Stars took Dave Preuss, a right wing from St. Thomas Academy. Preuss, who played parts of three seasons for the University of Minnesota, never played pro hockey.

1970s and became a living legend for guiding the 1980 US Olympic team to gold. There was no miracle at the Met, however. The Gunds suffered the embarrassment of the worst record in the league, something that would have a silver lining—but not enough to save Brooks from being fired by the spring of '88.

During this time, the Gunds also failed in a bid to buy the property surrounding Metropolitan Stadium, vacant since the Twins and Vikings moved to the Metrodome in 1982. They were interested in the land with the same intent for its ultimate development—as a shopping mall. When that purchase became seemingly impossible, they focused on upgrading the arena. They wanted to expand concourses, revamp the ticket office, and add a restaurant and forty suites. The price tag was $15 million. They sought help and weren't getting it. They invested $3.5 million of their own money to create twenty suites, but that's as far as the brothers would go without input from what was now called the Metropolitan Sports Facilities Commission.

On January 7, 1989, two weeks after he signed his inaugural pro contract on Christmas Day, Modano made his first appearance in a North Stars uniform. I was in a seat three rows off the ice in the corner opposite the bench for the game, an exhibition against a team from Russia, Dynamo Riga. I was there with a couple young ladies, so I didn't pay quite as much attention to the action on the ice as in the past. One of their roommates soon stole my heart. Likewise, for many North Stars fans, Modano was love at first sight.

Mike Modano, rookie mugshot from 1989.

The third child and only son of Michael Sr. and Karen Modano, Mike was born in Livonia, Michigan. He and his two older sisters, Sandy and Linda, grew up at 1869 Apollo Circle in Highland Township—about 45 miles northwest of Detroit's Joe Louis Arena. His father, who worked in construction and was originally from Boston, got him into hockey at age six to provide an outlet that might dim his mischievous behavior in grade school. When Mike couldn't get to the rink, or when the lake behind his house wasn't frozen, he practiced in the basement. For a while, his mother donned a catcher's mask and clutched a garbage-can lid for a target as he whacked away, sending hundreds of shots in her direction. As was common for many phenoms before and later, he dented duct work and broke several cellar windows. As Mike got bigger, his dad flooded the back yard so his son could skate before and after school. Mike also played baseball, football and tennis. At the age of eight, he made it to the national semifinals of the Punt, Pass, and Kick tournament after winning the event in Michigan—perhaps fittingly at halftime of the Detroit Lions' 45–14 humiliation of the Minnesota Vikings on December 9, 1978.

As a freshman in high school, Mike lettered in tennis. But it was obvious by then where his future would lead. The Modanos moved thirty miles to Westland, Michigan, so Mike could play with the Little Caesar's AAA program. He made the Midget Major team at fourteen, when his teammates were two to three years older. In 1984–85, he scored 50 goals and 100 points en route to helping his team win the USA Hockey National Championship.

The following year, former NHL defenseman Rick Wilson recruited Modano to play with Prince Albert of the WHL. It was a huge change. Prince Albert, Saskatchewan, a town of about 30,000, lies an hour and a half northeast of Saskatoon. That was a six-hour flight from Detroit. The only other way to get there was by car—a 25-hour drive that led right through the heart of Minnesota.

Modano, with braces on his teeth, arrived in Prince Albert in the fall of 1986. He scored a hat trick in his first game and, as a 16-year-old playing against 18- and 19-year-olds, finished fifth on the team in scoring. He lived with surrogate parents Carol and Ralph Ring, a couple who had two sons and had boarded many Raiders players. Carol worked at city hall and sang the anthem before games. Ralph was a team executive. Modano liked going to movies and playing golf, and he also would oblige the neighborhood youth, many at least four years younger, in street hockey.

His first job was working part-time at a lumber mill, and in his second season he went through the WHL like a buzzsaw. In 65 games, he scored 127 points and was an all-star. In nine playoff games, he had 18 points. Most important, thanks to their abysmal finish, the North Stars had the first pick in the 1988 draft. As it approached, they narrowed their focus to two centers, Modano and another WHLer, Medicine Hat's Trevor Linden. They were different players to be sure, Linden a little bigger but not as gifted. He had grit and two Memorial Cups. Prince Albert never finished higher than third with Modano, but no one could go end to end like him, either.

The North Stars brought both players to Traverse City, Michigan, for interviews with the owners. According to Nanne, Lulie Gund, George Gund's wife, was enamored with Linden, who charmed her on their return to Detroit aboard the Gunds' private jet. Modano at that point was listening to music on his headphones. Nanne, however, knew Modano could bring people out of their seats in a way Linden never would. Louie held his ground with the Gunds and picked Modano first, four days after his 18th birthday.

But difficult contract negotiations ensued. And, while Linden went second to the Vancouver Canucks and jumped right into the NHL, Modano returned to Prince Albert. He posted 105 points through 41 games, but also suffered a broken wrist in the WHL all-star game and missed the rest of the season.

For the North Stars, a third-place finish in a weak division and first-round playoff loss in 1989 set the stage for the drama of early 1990.

As a 19-year-old rookie, Modano lived with a host family (Twin Cities artist Bill Mack, his wife, and their children), dated a high school volleyball player, and netted 29 goals and 75 points. He played in all 80 games and, while he was minus-7 in the regular season and had just two points in seven playoff games, it was clear he was The Future. He made the all-rookie team and arguably should have won the Calder Cup, given to the NHL's top rookie. Sergei Makarov, a 31-year-old Russian who scored 24 goals and 86 points for Calgary, hauled off the trophy instead. Modano finished second in the voting and was doubtless more of a true candidate. The ensuing brouhaha forced the NHL to modify its rules, enacting an age barrier of twenty-six to be considered a first-year player.

Any Calder controversy, however, quickly paled in comparison to the ownership soap opera unfolding at Met Center. By 1990, memories of the '81 Stanley Cup playoffs were long gone. The Gunds had presided over a team that from 1986 to 1989 had fewer wins (76) than any other team and had the temerity to do it while living at opposite ends of the continent.

Angst for the owners was mostly on a low simmer, due as much as anything to the team's third-string status on the Minnesota pro sports scene (and later fourth-string following the addition of the NBA's Timberwolves)[9]. On January 21, 1990, George and Gordon Gund were featured on the cover and eight pages inside the *Star Tribune* Sunday magazine. The story detailed their philanthropy, George's soft-spoken nature and interest in the film industry, and Gordon's battle with blindness and reputation as a brilliant entrepreneur. It also pointed out that, with their four siblings, Forbes had estimated the Gunds' net worth at more than $1 billion.

Eight days later, *USA Today* first reported the Gunds were interested in moving the North Stars to Oakland and would soon demand upgrades to Met Center, where the team was playing to about three-quarters capacity. Sure enough, the next day—right next to a front-page wire story about the unification of East and West Germany and its implications for the Soviet Union—the Gunds said as much to Twin Cities readers. They also disputed league attendance figures, saying actual paid ticket sales were about 7,800 per game. To stay, they wanted $15 million in arena improvements and a season-ticket base of 10,000.

By February 2, a *Star Tribune* editorial already said goodbye and good riddance. The next three weeks boiled down to a lot of finger-pointing and behind-the-scenes rumor mongering before the Gunds announced they had lost $16 million in three years and would sell the team—with an April deadline for bids—or move it to California. Longtime Minnesota business executive and author Harvey McKay and future Hartford Whalers/Carolina Hurricanes owner Peter Karmanos quickly emerged as suitors. There was one problem for the Gunds: former Whalers owner Howard Baldwin already had the rights to an NHL expansion franchise in their potential landing spot, the San Francisco Bay area. As a result, the Gunds couldn't move the North Stars to northern California without Baldwin. And, by late March, Baldwin, who made his money in frozen yogurt and would go on to produce such films as "Mystery, Alaska," used that leverage to make an offer on an existing team (the North Stars), giving up the expansion rights in return. He had help from Morris Belzberg, who was the first Budget Rent-A-Car franchisee in Canada in 1965 and moved to the US three years later to take over the entire organization.

Howard Baldwin

The Gunds had to choose between forcing a move of the North Stars (which the NHL didn't want and likely would've required filing an antitrust suit) or selling (which would require watering down the original plan they floated to strip the franchise of its future). They opted for the second choice two weeks after a first-round Game 7 loss at Chicago.

On May 2, the Gunds bit on a Baldwin-Belzberg offer of $31 million plus the North Stars' share of the next three future expansion royalties (value $7 million) and a selection of prospects to stock the Bay Area expansion team the Gunds would purchase. A week later, the NHL approved the deal (deliberating sixteen hours over two days to obtain a three-quarters majority) and gave the Gunds the right to ice a team in the fall of 1991 at the 10,800-seat Cow Palace, a distinctively

9 The Timberwolves debuted Nov. 3, 1989, with a 106-94 loss at Seattle. Five nights later, they played their first home game at the Metrodome, losing to Michael Jordan and the Chicago Bulls, 96-84 (with the author and his girlfriend in attendance among 35,427 fans). The Wolves led the NBA in attendance their first season (1,072,572 for 41 games, an average of more than 26,000 for an all-time league record).

named old rink in Daly City, California, until a new home could be built in San Jose. Fittingly, an organization brought together by a unique sports merger would be divided in two again.

Two days later, Pierre Page resigned as North Stars head coach to become general manager of the Quebec Nordiques. Jack Ferreira, who had been Minnesota's GM since June 14, 1988, three days after the Modano selection, would stick with the Gunds and head to San Jose.

Under Baldwin and with Nanne, who in 1988 had become president, there was preliminary discussion about moving the North Stars to the Target Center. It was opening for the Timberwolves in the fall of 1990 in downtown Minneapolis. However, just when it looked like that was possible, talks fell apart over (of all things) dasher board advertising. The North Stars were aligned with Pepsi and Anheuser-Busch, while the Timberwolves had contracts with Coke and Miller.

Gil Stein, then chief legal counsel for the league and a future NHL president, later said "the obvious one-sidedness of the (San Jose) deal was a testament to the genius of Gordon Gund as a negotiator, the weakness of the Baldwin-Belzberg financial position, or more likely a little of each."

As evidence, just before the financials on the sale were to close, Baldwin and Belzberg recruited Green to avoid "significant financial exposure." They took over a lease that would cost them $250,000 per year. Green owned a dozen shopping malls across North America estimated to be worth $600 million. Tall and thin with silver hair brushed back, hazel eyes, and perfect teeth, Green had introduced Baldwin and Belzberg during their efforts to get an expansion team. Green said he would remain in Calgary and oversee the business from afar as chairman and governor. Baldwin, moving to the Twin Cities, would be president and run the hockey operation.

Two days later, Baldwin announced the hiring of a new GM—never mind that the sale hadn't closed and Baldwin/Belzberg/Green didn't technically own the team yet.

Bobby Clarke didn't worry about such minor obstacles. He'd spent a lifetime going right through them. Born August 13, 1949, in Flin Flon, Manitoba[10], Clarke grew up an eight-hour drive northwest of Winnipeg amid seemingly the last significant population before the Arctic Circle. He started playing organized hockey at eight and, despite battling diabetes, became a star less than a decade later for the local junior team, the Flin Flon Bombers. At nineteen, he was drafted by Philadelphia and made his NHL debut October 11, 1969, at Met Center. He would never play a minor-league game.

Norm Green

After three NHL seasons, Clarke was the last player added to the Team Canada roster for the epic eight-game 1972 Summit Series against the Soviet Union. After going 1–2–1 in four games across Canada and losing Game 5 in Moscow, Clarke showed his character in Game 6. With the reputation of his country on the line, Clarke intentionally and famously slashed Valeri Kharlamov, the Soviets' best player, breaking his ankle. Team Canada won 3–2. Kharlamov didn't play in Game 7, a 4–3 win for the Canadians, and was a non-factor in Game 8—when Paul Henderson scored his historic goal in the final minute for

10 The town of Flin Flon had been formed just twenty-two years earlier, after Hudson Bay Mining and Smelting formed the municipality.

Canada's 6–5 victory, winning the series 4–3–1.

Clarke later captained the Flyers as they won two Stanley Cups. His image, with toothless grin and a wink while holding the Cup after the deciding game in '75, is iconic.[11] Upon retiring in 1984, he stepped right into the role of general manager and Philadelphia lost in the finals in '85 and '87, the second of those defeats soothed by his induction to the Hall of Fame.

Bobby Clarke

In April 1990, the Flyers missed the playoffs for the first time since '72. In an emotional reaction, president Jay Snider (whose father, Ed, owned the team) fired Clarke. Baldwin pounced.

Clarke didn't look much like he did when he was playing. His brown hair now appeared carefully coiffed, graying at the ears, and his false teeth were even more perfect than Green's real ones. Only the scar at the right side of Clarke's chin and the intensity in his brown eyes reaffirmed that this was one of hockey's legends who would always cut down whoever stood between him and victory.

His fierce competitiveness came to the surface quickly with the North Stars. In early June, it was a legitimate question whether the transfer of ownership would be official in time for the June 16 draft in Vancouver. A war of words erupted between Clarke and Ferreira, who would be general manager of whatever franchise the Gunds owned. Ferreira, who was keeping assistant GM Dean Lombardi and pro scouting director Chuck Grillo with him wherever he was the next season, said he was in charge of the North Stars' draft unless a sale closed first. Clarke claimed otherwise, with quite a few off-color phrases sprinkled in. Fortunately, the deal went through on June 15, leaving Clarke a few hours to legally and confidently brush up on his selections. But tension remained and an animosity between the two groups would grow to approximate hatred.

Bob Gainey

Knowing he had to hire a head coach even before the announcement that he was GM, Clarke invited Bob Gainey to his home in New Jersey for a couple of days. They'd had some epic battles on the ice, although surprisingly only met once in the postseason—in the 1976 Stanley Cup Final, when Gainey and the Canadiens swept the series. Four months later, they were teammates en route to winning the Canada Cup. Although they'd also been involved in

11 In 1,144 regular-season games, Clarke netted 358 goals and had 852 assists and 1,453 penalty minutes. In 136 playoff games, he added 42 goals, 77 assists and 152 PIM.

activities together for the NHL Players Association, theirs was a relationship of mutual respect and wary distance. But Clarke soon was convinced Gainey was the man he wanted behind the North Stars' bench.

During the draft weekend, Clarke made the pitch to Green, who approved. Gainey was 2,800 miles away, moving his family back to Montreal before temporarily crashing with Doug and Linda Jarvis in Eden Prairie.

"It was all pretty light," Gainey told me in an interview. "We were optimistic and happy that the North Stars had not folded. The first time I walked into the Met Center that year, there was nobody there. The office had closed. They'd completely turned off the lights. I wanted to get a little swag for my kids but they didn't have any. They'd stopped ordering it. The franchise was basically dormant from when the ('89–90) season ended in April. They had closed up and everybody had been let go. It was a restart.

"I think the Gunds had just decided they wanted to move on," he added. "When the opportunity came up to sell and start with a new franchise in San Jose, that's when the negotiation for the sale came and how the players got split up. I don't know a lot of the details of how that came together, but I know it was messy."

Curiously, three years earlier, Gainey had interviewed with Gordon Gund for the general manager's job that ultimately went to Ferreira. Gainey, then still playing, skated a final season in Montreal before taking an offer in France to coach a second-division semi-pro team. In truth, his job description went far beyond that. He also played, arranged transportation, and even helped carry equipment for the Epinal Ecureuils[12]. He polished his French during seven-hour bus trips and played before crowds of fewer than 1,000 fans.

One season was enough of that, and Gainey began looking for a place to land. He'd interviewed to be the GM in Quebec, but decided he wasn't ready for that responsibility, and the Nordiques tossed Page a lifeline out of Minnesota. Gainey then flew from Paris to Newark and ironed out details and philosophy with an old adversary about to become his new boss.

Born December 13, 1953, Gainey was the fifth of seven children for George and Anne Gainey, who lived in a modest brick house that still stood almost seventy years later in Peterborough, Ontario. A two-hour drive northeast of Maple Leaf Gardens, about 40,000 people lived in the town in the early 1950s. George had served in World War II and for four decades walked daily to his factory job at Quaker Oats, the buildings of which could be seen rising in the distance from his home at the corner of James and Mark Streets. His job as a shipping and receiving clerk wasn't lucrative—his pay ranged from thirty cents an hour when he started to $360 dollars a week when he retired in 1980. By many accounts, George was a humble man and raised his children—most certainly Robert Michael—to be likewise.

Bob had two brothers and four sisters, one of whom became a Sister. The Catholic Gaineys were devoted attendees of The Immaculate Conception Church. Three siblings became teachers, one a dairy farmer and another a nurse. Bob got his initial pair of skates at five and first played hockey as a 6-year-old defenseman in a local church league. He was an altar boy, and his mother later recalled how he overcame a mysterious limp that she believed was cured after nine days of prayer and devotion. She thought perhaps it was a miracle. He watched and rooted for Toronto every Saturday on Hockey Night in Canada.

By seventeen, he'd switched to left wing and was a lanky, strapping young man on his way to a height of 6-foot-2. In the spring of 1971, Bob led his Junior B team to the Ontario championship. The

12 English translation: Squirrels.

following season, he played for his hometown Peterborough Petes and their coach, Roger Neilson. They went to the Memorial Cup final, only to lose to the Cornwall Royals. But by then Gainey had met the most important person in his life: Cathy Collins, two years younger, was an usherette for the Petes. Fortunately, where Bob was reserved, Cathy—the fifteenth of an incredible nineteen siblings—was outgoing. Their courtship lasted more than three years before they married in 1975.

In 1972–73, Gainey parlayed 43 points and 99 penalty minutes in 56 games with the Petes into becoming Montreal's top draft pick (eighth overall). He also was drafted by the Minnesota Fighting Saints, but there was little chance his future would be anywhere but with the Canadiens. He played only six career games in the minors and made his NHL debut October 10, 1973, at Met Center. He scored his first goal two weeks later against Minnesota's Cesare Maniago at the Forum.[13]

By his second season, Gainey was a fixture at left wing on the Canadiens' second line, skating with fellow future Hall of Famers Jacques Lemaire and Yvan Cournoyer. And from 1976 to 1979, Montreal won four straight Stanley Cups.

While Gainey never scored more than 47 points in a season, he became the best defensive forward in the game and a heart-and-soul character for the Canadiens. In 1978, the NHL created the Selke Trophy, honoring the best defensive forward. It was almost as if the league did so for Gainey, who won the award the first four times it was announced. The Russians, acutely aware of North American pro talent even during the Cold War of the '70s and '80s, called him the NHL's most complete player.[14]

Gainey succeeded Serge Savard as Canadiens captain in 1982 and thought it important to be able to communicate in the language of the team's fans. So, Gainey taught himself French, practicing with his francophone teammates and reading grammar books on flights while others played cards or slept. While he never felt his interpretations more than rudimentary, Gainey's example needed no dialogue. He lived close to the Forum so, just as his father before him, he could walk to work. And, just as George Gainey had shoveled his own driveway, Bob did, too, politely declining occasional offers of help from Montreal city crews. After a six-year hiatus from the finals, the Canadiens won the Cup again in '86—Gainey the first to raise it over his head as teammates clutched at his jersey. Montreal, which lost in the conference final in 1984, '87, and '88, played for the Cup again in 1989, when a Game 6 loss at the Forum was his last NHL appearance as a player.[15]

"Bob earned every bit of his reputation," Clarke said. "He was one guy you hated so much, you loved him, eh? I used to hate the guy.

"In Canada, we brag about Wayne Gretzky and Mario Lemieux, but deep down inside, the players we love are the Gaineys and the (Mark) Messiers, the guys who will say, 'If there's someone in my way, I'll go right over them.' There's a toughness to the Canadian people that we take pride in."

Just as Gainey was virtually the same player from the beginning to the end of his career, it seemed all that had changed about him in 15 years was a receding hairline and a few wrinkles. His brown eyes could alternately seem apologetic and then bore right through you. Quicker with a smile than a word, his dimples could make him appear almost shy.

For as much as Gainey seemed uncomfortable in the spotlight, Green relished it. He was omnipresent at the 1990 draft in Vancouver, evidenced by his photo bombing the hockey card of first-round pick Derian Hatcher. By the time it was printed, the North Stars had evolved.

13 The puck from that goal was one of few mementos Gainey kept after selling four of his Stanley Cup rings and many of the keepsakes from his career in 2020.

14 Legendary Soviet coach Anatoly Tarasov, often referred to as "the father of Russian ice hockey," first made this statement in the late 1970s.

15 In 1,160 regular-season games, Gainey scored 239 goals, had 263 assists and was plus-198. He played 182 playoff games, the equivalent of more than two full seasons, adding 25 goals and 48 assists.

This image shows Derian Hatcher's rookie card in the 1990-91 Upper Deck hockey set. The photo was taken at the NHL draft in Vancouver, where new owner Norm Green was eager for any opportunity at publicity. To Hatcher's left is Les Jackson, the North Stars' director of player personnel. (Author's collection)

Les Jackson, the director of amateur scouting, planned to follow the Gunds but reversed course in late June at Clarke's behest and stayed in Minnesota as director of player personnel. Gainey later said the greatest holdover influences for him were Jackson and third-year scout Craig Button, who is from Montreal and the son of Jack Button, a league executive since 1969 and director of the NHL Central Scouting Service in the late '70s. But Craig lived in Ann Arbor, Michigan. Gainey's confidant from within the North Stars' offices became Jackson, whose dark features and mustache couldn't hide a friendly smile. His only concession to age was a tendency to wear glasses to read.

Born December 21, 1952, in Manning, Alberta, Jackson became a Boston Bruins draftee in 1972. A left wing, he played part of the '74–75 season in Kalamazoo but never made it to the NHL as a player. He eventually coached several junior teams, winding up with Brandon of the WHL. His one-time junior teammate, Lorne Henning, became North Stars head coach in 1985 and brought Jackson to Minnesota as an assistant. He became a scout after Brooks succeeded Henning, and was promoted to director of amateur scouting in 1988. Rather than move to San Jose, Jackson decided it was best for him and his wife, Melanie, to keep their home in Bloomington. A modest house with a tuck-under garage on a pie-shaped piece of property on a quiet, curving street, it was perfect for their sons Brock, three, and Drake, just born on June 1.

Unlike others from the organization who followed the Gunds, Nanne still had a year left on his contract and wasn't leaving Minnesota. "Sweet Lou" grew up in Sault Ste. Marie, Ontario, where he played hockey with Phil and Tony Esposito. Recruited by John Mariucci to play at the University of Minnesota, Nanne arrived in Minneapolis in 1960 and never left the Twin Cities. He became an American citizen in 1967, allowing him to play for Team USA in the '68 Olympics at Grenoble, France. After the Games, he signed as a free agent with the North Stars. Other than 13 games in the minors during the '68–69 season, he played his entire career with Minnesota, moving right from the ice into the role of coach and GM in February 1978.[16]

His stint behind the bench was brief as the North Stars went 7–18–4 before Nanne turned the coaching over to Harry Howell to begin the first season after the Cleveland merger. Within weeks, however, Nanne brought in Glen Sonmor to replace Howell. That was the first of six coaches Nanne would hire, sometimes more than once.

Lou and his wife, Francine, were high school sweethearts. They eventually settled in Edina and had four children: sons Michael, Marc, and Marty, and a daughter, Michelle. Michael became a dentist, which was his father's failed pursuit. Michelle married former Minnesota Strikers pro soccer

16 In 635 career regular-season games, mostly as a defenseman but also as a forward, Nanne had 68 goals and 157 assists. In 32 playoff games, he added 4 goals and 10 assists.

Lou Nanne

goalie Tino Lettieri. Marc became a real estate broker. And Marty played at the University of Minnesota, was a Chicago Blackhawks draftee, and had finished the first of two seasons with Indianapolis of the IHL in 1989–90.

Louie was named North Stars executive VP of marketing and public relations in early July 1990—about the same time Clarke added a free agent in former Philadelphia right wing Ilkka Sinisalo. The rest of the month proved tumultuous.

On July 19, Bill Goldsworthy joined the Gunds' new organization as a scout. He had worked in community relations for the North Stars for three years and was arguably their most popular player from the first decade of the franchise.

On July 23, Green said he was moving to the Twin Cities and that the North Stars were "way overstaffed." Some employees would be laid off. Two days later, Baldwin resigned in conflict with Green.

"It's not good for this franchise to go through this B.S.," Baldwin said. "The most important thing is that this crap stop. Two people wanted to run the team, and I decided rather than fight the best thing to do would be to step aside."

Green said he'd been honest in his initial intent to let Baldwin run the organization. But then Green called a friend, John Pickett, who owned the Islanders, to inquire about what it was like to be an absentee owner.

"He said if you have a good president and GM to run the team, you don't have to be there," recalled Green, who at first said he would emulate Pickett and attend about ten games a year. "That was my plan, but he didn't tell me the magnetic power of owning a hockey club. The more I started coming here, the more I got excited about it. I think this was an inevitable conflict. What it boils down to is Howard and I can't both run the hockey club. He felt I was too involved on the operations side, more so than a chairman should be.

"There's no chaos," Green added. "This disturbance is going to be forgotten tomorrow; people don't care about what goes on in the front office."

Perhaps. But by this time Green was having daily 7 a.m. meetings with his executives—Clarke, VP of Administration Dick Arneson, VP of Finance George Wettstaedt, and Nanne, who grew to lament that Green would be "a very hands-on owner."

Clarke also signed left wing Brian Propp, another former Flyer. Propp and Sinisalo, who both played with Clarke, had the distinction of already having played on multiple Stanley Cup losing teams. But they'd come closer (Game 7 against Edmonton in 1987) than anyone else on the current North Stars roster.

Within two days, Green (via Arneson) fired more than forty full-timers—including Joanie Preston—and hundreds of part-time employees whose jobs went to contracted services. The remaining staff, which a *Star Tribune* story pointed out included no minorities, numbered about twenty-five people.

Patty Connolly Reid, a former member of the front office and wife of former North Stars defenseman Tom Reid, was one of them. She was hired to take over community relations and public relations, but lasted less than a week.

Joanie Preston

Elaine Waddell

"It was a chemistry thing," Green told *The National Sports Daily*, a sports-centric newspaper launched six months earlier.

Connolly Reid had a different view.

"It was so bizarre," she said. "He said, 'I don't like you. I look at a person and make a judgment within five minutes and this is never retractable.'"

That provided an opening for Elaine Waddell to return to the North Stars. She'd worked as advertising manager under the Gunds, but also became victim to Green's purge. After his first choice as PR director didn't work out, she got a second chance.

Waddell grew up as Elaine Sullivan on a farm outside Bombay, New York. In the 1950s and '60s, only a few hundred people lived in the crossroads town a few miles south of the Quebec border. Despite her proximity to Canada, she'd never seen a hockey game until she moved to Minnesota. In 1979, she became a waitress at the Carlton Celebrity Room. She worked her way up, helping promote country music stars and guests like Wayne Newton, Bob Hope, George Burns, and Rodney Dangerfield. The Carlton closed in 1987, so she applied for a job with the North Stars—and didn't get it. For nine months, she worked in promotions for a radio station and then tried again successfully after Al Shaver's son, Wally, left his position as the team's director of advertising.

Waddell, who to some seemed to curry favor by playing tennis with Green, wasn't even established in her new role yet when Bobby Smith came home on August 7, traded from Montreal for a fourth-round pick. Two days later, Smith, Propp, and Sinisalo were at Met Center to meet about 100 fans and sign autographs before a news conference.

"There's certainly more pressure on me here than if I'd been traded to Pittsburgh or Washington," said Smith, who never took his Minnesota license plates off his car during the years he lived in Montreal. "I welcome that. They've had trouble here, but I know what kind of hockey town the Twin Cities can be. And I'm at the point in my career where the only thing that's important is winning. With some subtle changes, we can bring this team back quickly."

More changes took place off the ice, too. After two seasons on WAYL-AM, under an agreement that basically had the North Stars buying the airtime, on August 17 it was announced the team (and Al Shaver) would move back to KSTP-AM on a one-year contract. That had been the team's radio home from 1978 to 1988. Ginny Morris, KSTP's vice president and general manager, was in charge of finding a color analyst. Tom Reid had been in the position and wasn't about to continue, considering Green had just fired his wife.

Clarke made two small tweaks to the roster the following week, trading Ken Hodge to Boston for future considerations one day and signing Dan Gratton from the Canadian National Team the next.

Hodge, a center from Boston College, became North Stars property in the original Smith trade to Montreal. Hodge played just five games with Minnesota in 1988–89 and was due to become a free agent with compensation. He'd scored 86 points in '89–90 for the Kalamazoo Wings and didn't want to re-sign. The reacquisition of Smith probably meant there wasn't a spot for Hodge anyway.

Gratton, 23, had played seven games with the Los Angeles Kings in 1987–88. Likely destined for the K-Wings, he had 66 points in 69 games during '89–90 with Team Canada.

On August 24, two weeks before the start of training camp, Baldwin sold his 24.5 percent of the club to Green for about $5 million.

"It's simpler and cleaner this way," said Baldwin, back in Los Angeles after having aborted his move to a Minneapolis condo. "My joy is in running the team, being actively involved. Being a passive investor didn't make sense."

Al Shaver

The North Stars now were three-quarters Green's, with Belzberg retaining 25 percent.

"We were friends before and we're still friends now," Green said of Baldwin. "To have that unsettled between us was unsettling."

Morris Belzberg

The last days of August and the first week of September provided the final calm before the season to come. Players spent time with their families. Homeowners such as Mark Tinordi and Shawn Chambers mowed their lawns. In the afternoon on Saturday, August 25, Modano took time away from boating on Lake Minnetonka to appear at a back-to-school fashion expo (tickets were required) in the eighth-floor atrium at Dayton's in Minneapolis. Some of the *really* cool kids went home and strapped on Rollerblades, invented a few years earlier in Minneapolis, for a little fun before the end of summer.

Bob and Cathy Gainey were just getting familiar with the neighbors around their new home at 4627 Bruce Avenue in Edina—a two-story house with a small yard, a stone entrance and a driveway leading to a garage in back. Their children—Anna (12), Stephen (10), Laura (8) and Colleen (5)—were anxiously waiting to attend a new school in a new country.

And the North Stars were about to get an education under a new owner, a new GM, and a new coach with a preseason trip behind the crumbling Iron Curtain. The world wasn't prepared for what was about to happen.

Weeks turn into years, how quick they pass

And all the stars that never were

Are parking cars and pumping gas

...

Do You Know the Way to San Jose?

-Dionne Warwick, 1968;

lyrics and music by Burt Bacharach

CHAPTER 3

Training Camp, With a Side of Glasnost

Friday, September 7, 1990

A morning thunderstorm hit Bloomington, leaving puddles in the parking lot at Met Center. The new Minnesota North Stars were inside. Fresh gray carpet covered the dressing-room floor, the logo sewn in the floor at each end of the room, walls decorated with pictures of previous teams, and hardwood bench stalls yet to be scarred in celebration or frustration, with overhead shelves and hooks. Twenty-six players drifted in to renew acquaintances or, in a few cases, make them. One by one, they went into the training room and hopped on a padded table for their annual physical, including tetanus and flu shots as well as blood-pressure and vision checks. After everyone had been poked and prodded, they stretched as a team to loosen up for a series of fitness evaluations.

Basil McRae, who'd been captain for a portion of the 1989–90 season—his third in Minnesota—belted out a team-best 79 sit-ups in one minute. He was in the best shape of his life. At 6-foot-2 and 205 pounds, McRae was not exactly a greyhound. He wasn't a greybeard, either, but he did perpetually look like he needed a shave. Nonetheless, it was clear he came to camp ready to set a tone. He'd racked up 351 penalty minutes last season, his lowest total in three years, and would pass Willi Plett as the North Stars' all-time rule breaker with his 40th minute in the box this year. It didn't figure to take long.

Twenty-five-year-old Perry Berezan posted the best results in the sprint bike test. He'd played a career-high 64 games in '89–90 and would've been in more had he not suffered a broken toe, sprained ankle, and broken nose. As a rookie with Calgary in '85–86, Berezan posted 33 points in 55 games. With 20 points in 80 games since being traded to Minnesota in 1989, he felt the pressure mounting to show such ability again.

Brian Propp, who'd played most of his career in the same arena where Dr. J was a "flyer," too,[17] had the best vertical. At 5–9 and 190 pounds, Propp had been Philadelphia's first-round pick, No. 14 overall, eleven years earlier. The five-time all-star put up 97 points in each of the '84–85 and '85–86 seasons. But he was victim of a vicious check by Chris Chelios, then with Montreal, in the Eastern Conference final opener on May 1, 1989. Chelios rammed an elbow into Propp's head in one corner of the Forum. Propp hit the glass and went down, unconscious, his helmet slamming the ice. He suffered a concussion and was carried off on a stretcher. Although he returned before the series ended, Propp had difficulty regaining form. His combined 40 points between Philadelphia and Boston in '89–90 were far below his standard. At thirty-one, he could almost hear the whispers questioning whether he would ever be the same.

17 Julius Erving, known as Dr. J, was the most famous name in the American Basketball Association, helping legitimize its very existence and paving the way for a merger with the NBA in 1976. After ABA stops with the Virginia Squires and New York Nets, he played the rest of his Hall of Fame career from 1976-87 with the Philadelphia 76ers. Playing his home games in the Spectrum, Erving was an 11-time NBA all-star, league MVP in 1981, a championship in 1983 and was one of the game's most legendary authors of the slam dunk.

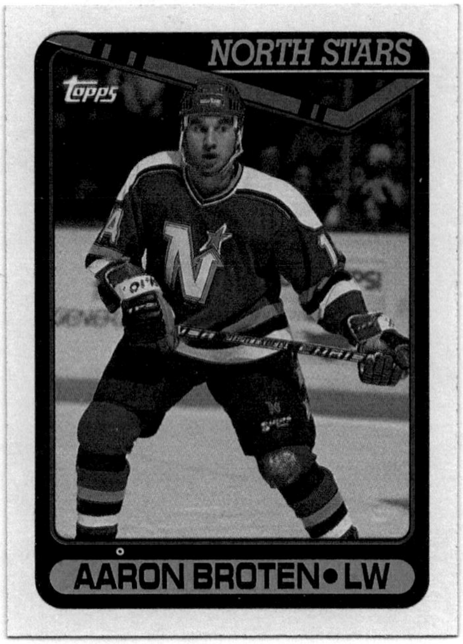

At approximately 12:30 p.m., McRae, Berezan, Propp, and the rest gathered outside, where Doug Jarvis and Andy Murray had stopwatches ready to time a two-mile run.

Over the cracked, drying pavement they went. Aaron Broten, two years younger than his brother Neal, finished first. Aaron, a 29-year-old left wing, had been acquired from New Jersey on January 5, 1990, just in time to witness all the drama in Minnesota. Already with nine full pro seasons behind him, he'd followed Neal from Roseau to the Gophers and the NHL. Their little brother, Paul, was a rookie right wing with the Rangers last season. There could've been an all-Broten line, but the North Stars passed on Paul twice in the 1984 draft. By the time he was taken with the seventy-seventh pick, Minnesota had chosen two players who would never appear in an NHL game.

With conditioning tests over, the players were more enthused for the "optional" afternoon practice. Jon Casey and Kari Takko, Casey's backup last season, got all the action they wanted in goal. Jarmo Myllys, a ninth-rounder who led Finland to a silver medal in the '88 Olympics, would miss the start of camp because of a travel delay. Another goalie, Daniel Berthiaume, who won one game after being acquired from Winnipeg in January '90, was traded to Los Angeles the night before as part of a three-team swap with the Kings and Jets. Winnipeg sent to Minnesota 21-year-old center Brian Hunt, who played at Moncton of the American Hockey League last season and would report directly to the IHL camp on Wednesday at Kalamazoo. By then, the North Stars would be in Moscow and he'd be one of forty players in the organization who wouldn't make the preseason trip to the Soviet Union.[18]

At thirty-two, Bobby Smith grinned like a rookie when he first stepped through the door at the bottom of the steps from the dressing room and onto the ice. Propp and longtime Philadelphia teammate Ilkka Sinisalo were more cautious, skating among former adversaries with whom they would have to forget old scores. Propp, single but engaged to a woman he met in 1987 on a Flyers off-season cruise, was sub-letting former North Star Ron Wilson's house in Eden Prairie while the latter served as a first-year assistant with Vancouver. Sinisalo was married (Carina) and has two children (Tomas, 4; and Niklas, 2). Danny Gratton was the other new face among the players.

They all looked new to 36-year-old Bob Gainey, even though he'd played at least one NHL game against everyone in camp except Gratton, Don Barber, and Mike Modano. In recent years, the North Stars' roster hadn't been too memorable. And, when Gainey arrived in Minnesota, he'd found only a few videotapes left behind by former GM Jack Ferreira and his staff. They'd taken most of their materials to San Jose.

Gainey watched those videotapes but knew he was going to have to discover first-hand what his players could do and how to use them. As they huffed and hooted through a first workout for their new coach, their names already were on a blackboard in his office, the walls covered with new paint, part of Norm Green's remodeling plan.

"There have been a lot of changes made in the past, that's true," Gainey said of the North Stars. "But this is the first time in ten or twelve years that changes have been made from the top right on through the whole organization… There are lots of reasons to think we should be optimistic.

18 Hunt didn't play for the K-Wings and never appeared in another pro game.

"Quite a few of these players have been through this before. I have the feeling, after talking to them, that they have a good feeling about the year ahead."

Stew Gavin did. A member of the 1984–85 Toronto Maple Leafs—owners of the worst record in the NHL—he'd been claimed off waivers from Hartford in 1988. Gavin had seen more than his share of bad hockey and was eager to put the turmoil from the previous season to rest.

"In light of what happened, the outlook is stable, and I think everyone's happy about that," Gavin told the small group of reporters who showed up. "Today we came in here to see changes in the locker room, changes in the building. Mr. Green is gung-ho and he's brought in good hockey people. The guys who felt maybe they didn't get a fair shake with the old management feel like they'll get a new shot. Plus, they brought in some players who will make us a better-balanced team. Everyone knows they have a lot to prove, but everyone seems excited."

No one lingered. By mid-afternoon, the players were gone—beating rush-hour traffic, knowing they would be on the ice for a real first practice early Saturday, followed by an intersquad scrimmage. Only a few people remained in the Met Center offices, where Green had relocated the administration after it had been across the street at the Alpha Business Center for years under the ownership of George and Gordon Gund. The previous owners had moved the staff out because they thought the underground administrative space at the Met too cramped. Green, however, saw an opportunity to save a few bucks by moving them back.

The Gunds also made an announcement Friday afternoon. Their expansion team would be called the "Sharks." Their hockey department was already familiar with the talent taking the ice at Met Center and next week at Wings Stadium in Kalamazoo. The K-Wings' coaches are under contract to the Gunds and scouts will circle all season. So the name seemed appropriate. You could almost hear the theme from "Jaws."

Saturday, September 8, 1990

Just before 8 a.m., Gainey glided onto the ice at Met Center for his first practice. The drills were predictable, but he watched intently as the players wound around the rink, his biggest reaction an occasional pursing of lips.

About three-quarters of the way up Section 102, in one of the maroon theater seats he'd had re-covered, Green sat with crossed legs. His chin resting in the palm of his hand, only his eyes seemed to move behind the large lenses of his glasses. Scattered in seats nearby were Clarke, the media—including Rachel Blount and Gary Olson—and about sixty fans. The North Stars had advertised practices would be open to the public through December 1. On the way in and out, onlookers passed the ticket office on the main concourse where new prices were listed—ranging from $9.50 to $28.50 per seat.

The ice was resurfaced for the scrimmage from 9:30 to 11. The action was spirited but tempered by the fact that everyone would travel to Russia. There was no immediate risk of being cut.

By afternoon, the arena was quiet again. A similar routine would take place earlier on Sunday and Monday to acclimate to the nine-hour time difference with Moscow before leaving Tuesday. The eight-day, four-game, three-city Friendship Tour, during which the North Stars and Canadiens would play Russian teams, was an olive branch between the NHL and the Soviets. It's just the second time such an expedition had been scheduled. Washington and Calgary made the trip last year and reviews were mixed on whether it was beneficial.

The North Stars were scheduled to play Spartak and the Soviet Wings in Moscow before traveling to Voskreshensk to play Khimik, and Kiev to play Sokol Kiev. The team would be paid approximately $200,000 for the trip, a sum that didn't begin to cover expenses.

Dave Smith

Dave Surprenant

Mark Baribeau

Lance Vogt

Sunday, September 9, 1990

It was well before 5 a.m. when Dave Smith, Dave Surprenant, Mark Baribeau and Lance Vogt prepped for practice. Smith, forty-seven, had been born in Toronto and, at an early age, his father chose to move the family to Vancouver. They got as far as Saskatoon, where "Smitty" finished high school and played hockey. He soon realized if his future was going to be at the rink, it wouldn't be as a player. He began working as a trainer for the Saskatoon Blades, a junior team associated with the Los Angeles Blades of the professional Western Hockey League in the 1960s. After three years, he moved back to Toronto and took a similar job with the Marlboros, a junior team associated with the Maple Leafs. NHL expansion opened other jobs in pro hockey, and in 1969 that led Smith to work three seasons for the IHL Saginaw (Michigan) Generals, who actually played forty miles south in Flint. When the WHA expanded opportunities again in 1972, he set aside the primitive training methods he used with his junior teams and in the minors and focused solely on equipment during four seasons with the Cleveland Crusaders followed by eight years with the St. Louis Blues.

Presaging what Smith would experience in Minnesota, the Blues had three ownership groups during his tenure. Insurance tycoon Sid Salomon and his family owned the team from its inception through 1977, when they incurred financial difficulty and sold to St. Louis-based pet food giant Ralston Purina. By 1983, Ralston Purina figured it had lost enough money running the team and agreed to sell to a prospective owner who wanted to move it to Saskatoon. The NHL rejected the sale on the grounds that it wasn't a big enough market to support a major pro franchise, and that led to antitrust suits and countersuits between Ralston Purina and the league. As a result, the Blues didn't participate in the '83 draft, forfeiting their picks. The NHL revoked the franchise and threatened to dissolve it if a new owner couldn't be found. Ten days before the deadline, Harry Ornest led a group of St. Louis businessmen to buy the team.

"That was a schmozzle," Smith remembered. "It was a sideshow once that occurred and I was looking for an opportunity to get out of there."

In 1985, North Stars trainer Doc Rose lost his assistant when Larry Ness left to join the Boston Bruins.

"(Rose) called me and said 'Would you be interested in coming to Minnesota?'" Smith said. "I said 'Sure. Get me out of here. I'm a free agent without compensation. Get me out of this horror movie.' Doc set me up with an interview with Lou Nanne, and they hired me."

By 1988, Rose was suffering from chronic back pain, and the North Stars needed to add someone with formal medical education. That turned out to be Surprenant. Originally from Tracy, Minnesota, he went to Mankato State and, for a couple of summers served as a training camp intern with the NFL's New Orleans Saints. He joined the team full time shortly after graduating in 1983, but a few years later was back in Bloomington, working at a private training facility, when several North Stars came in for rehabilitation. Those contacts led to a spot as the team's head athletic trainer.

"(Surprenant) ran a one-man show," Smith said. "The long-term injury guys left behind were seen by a local rehab clinic to get treatment; otherwise he was with the team all the time. And, by then we needed two (equipment) guys on the road."

There was no question who would be the other. Baribeau started working part-time at Met Center in the late 1970s. He grew up with a transistor radio under his pillow, Al Shaver's voice whispering in his ear from fall to spring. One day, Baribeau and his friends saw an ad in the newspaper. Met Center was looking for ushers. They rode over on their bikes to find all those spots had been filled, but they were hired to work on the arena cleanup crew. Their shifts ended about 1 a.m., after which they got a few hours' sleep and went to school. Partly because he was a clean-cut kid who showed up when he was supposed to, Baribeau eventually was promoted to locker room attendant. By the '81 playoffs, he was helping Rose with laundry and odd jobs in the North Stars' dressing room.

"I was essentially a glorified locker room attendant/stick boy/whatever you want to call it," Baribeau said in an interview.

His parents were divorced. He lived with his mother, "didn't come from money," and wanted to be a sports announcer.

"That went sideways because of the hours we worked," he recalled. "What I earned went into my pocket, and I liked working there. I loved sports. I was there all the time. I would work seventy to eighty hours a week. I'd sleep through school, did what I had to in order to get by. But I wasn't going to get in any trouble. The Met kept me away from all that."

He briefly attended the University of Minnesota, then dropped out after he officially became an equipment assistant in 1982. He was hired full-time in 1985.

"I was content and happy doing what I was doing," Baribeau said. "I should've been more ambitious. If I knew then what I know now, it would be different. But you're just living. I was getting paid a pittance, but I felt like 'Yeah, I'm in.'"

Baribeau specialized in sticks as they became more than rough lumber, with new models featuring aluminum shafts and replaceable blades. For as fussy as players could be about their sticks, they were even more particular about their skates. That was Smith's domain. He spent a couple hours every day at the sharpener, personalizing each hollow to preference.

"If you got a month off in the summer, you were lucky," Smith said. "You're ordering equipment, doing budgets, repairing equipment, moving it from city to city, and I dealt with customs when we went across the border. And all the daily prep for games and practices. There was always plenty to do."

For the first time, the North Stars added a third full-time equipment manager in Vogt, who was single and lived in Minneapolis. He worked part time last season. Among his duties was driving a cargo truck back and forth from the airport, loading or unloading trunks for either the North Stars or visiting teams.

By design, the entire support staff lived nearby. Smith and his wife, Maxine, had a 15-year-old son, Kevin, and lived just across the Minnesota River in Eagan. Surprenant, 32, was single and lived even closer—in Richfield.

But perhaps no one was there more than Baribeau, whose best friends remained on the arena crew. He'll make $35,000 this season, enough to pay for a new navy-blue Jeep and to rent the basement of a friend's house barely a slap shot away—diagonally across the 494-Cedar Avenue cloverleaf. Baribeau's girlfriend of several years, Julie Larson, was a year older at Richfield High, but they met—naturally—

at the Met. A decade earlier, her spot as an usherette was near one end, conveniently where Baribeau often tried to catch a little of each game when he wasn't pushing a broom.

"As rink rats we wore these yellow jump suits," he remembered. "The guys who swept the hallways during the first seven or eight minutes could then go find a spot to stand and watch the rest of the period. I always tried to do that and then stand behind the net. That's where Julie was. She was nice and I had a crush on her, but I was just this kid in a yellow jump suit and braces."

They didn't date until years later, but now she was headed to Russia, too.

It was still dark when the sleep-deprived players grumbled in, rubbing their eyes and downing coffee to either wake up or stave off the effects of the previous evening. New among them was Myllys, arrived from Finland in time for the first of two practices before flying right back around the world again.

About half as many fans as had attended during a more decent hour on Saturday, watched the players tumble onto the ice at 6 a.m. Preteen girls wore Modano jerseys, and several boys hung around to get autographs on pennants. At least *they* looked like they had gotten a good night's sleep.

And, while it made ripples internationally, you probably couldn't have found a North Star who paid attention to a meeting between President George Herbert Walker Bush and Soviet leader Mikhail Gorbachev in Helsinki. They issued a joint statement calling on Iraq to withdraw from Kuwait, which it had seized in August. The action had been condemned by the United Nations, and the allegiance of Bush and Gorbachev was supposed to put increasing pressure on Iraqi dictator Saddam Hussein. However, the Soviet Union, as the North Stars would find firsthand, was in its final death throes and unable to exert much influence. Since the Berlin Wall fell on November 8, 1989, Romania, Lithuania, Latvia, and Armenia had all broken from the Soviet republic, weakening the Russians' grip on Eastern Europe. The world map was changing almost every day.

Monday, September 10, 1990

Like it or not, the players were getting used to Moscow time. Link Gaetz lumbered into Met Center about when he would've been getting home from the bar last season in Kalamazoo—which the players call "The Zoo." Gaetz, 6-foot-3 and 240 pounds, was selected one round behind Modano two years earlier, largely as protection for the latter. Gaetz showed up for the draft with two black eyes from a bar fight the night before and, four months later, was arrested for drunk driving. Increasingly, Lou Nanne began to quip that his third-round pick should've been a lawyer.

Frantisek Musil

The North Stars took the ice at 5 a.m. and had already wrapped up their scrimmage before many people made it to work. The rest of the day was spent preparing for Tuesday's departure.

The support staff was stretched to the limit, arranging for 15,000 pounds of cargo to get across the freeway to MSP for the flight. The travel party of eighty included twenty-seven players. In addition to Gaetz and Modano, they were: Barber, Brian Bellows, Berezan, Neal Broten, Aaron Broten, Casey, Shawn Chambers, Shane Churla, Ulf Dahlen, Gaetan Duchesne, Dave Gagner, Gavin, Curt Giles, Gratton, Dean Kolstad, McRae, Larry Murphy, Frantisek Musil, Myllys, Propp, Sinisalo, Bobby Smith, Takko, Mark Tinordi, and Neil Wilkinson.

Musil, a 25-year-old defenseman, played 152 of 160 games for the North Stars during the lean seasons of '86–87 and '87–88. He grew up in Czechoslovakia and was three when the Soviets occupied his country in 1968. He wasn't so sure his teammates will like what they find.

"It's a completely different lifestyle from anything they've experienced," said Musil, who looked almost cartoonish with a buzz cut, wide-set eyes, large nose, and easy grin. "It isn't someplace I've ever wanted to go just to spend time."

Barber, Gaetz, Kolstad, and Wilkinson all played at least part of last season with the K-Wings. Barber, twenty-five, was the North Stars' sixth-round pick in 1983. He played four years at Bowling Green before turning pro and had 47 points in his first 67 NHL games. A 6-foot left winger who didn't look as solid as his 205 pounds would suggest, Barber's heartthrob looks were marred only by a scar creasing his right eyebrow.

Gaetz, from Vancouver, turns twenty-two on October 2. He had two assists and 86 penalty minutes in 17 NHL games during his first two pro seasons.

Kolstad was a 6–6, 230-pound defenseman from Edmonton. The 22-year-old was a second-rounder in 1986, Modano's teammate at Prince Albert, and became an IHL all-star in 1990. But Kolstad, who played 25 games with Minnesota, doesn't know if the trip to Russia signals a move to Bloomington or a return trip to Kalamazoo with his new wife, Amelia. They'd just gotten married, but not in time for her to get travel documents to come on the trip.

Wilkinson, twenty-three, was 6–3 but raw-boned and tough, with long hockey hair and a smile that curled his mouth into something of a smirk. He teased star potential in his first 36 NHL games last season.

The traveling party also featured Bobby Clarke, the coaching staff—including Chico Resch, trainers and equipment men, three team doctors (Latvian native George Nagobods, orthopedic surgeon William Simonet, and Fairview Southdale ER physician John Schaefer), a U of M dietitian, an interpreter, and their approximate equal number of guests. They even had their own chef, Jim Hawley, a college football teammate and friend of Andy Murray. There was a strong media contingent, including reporters from both metro newspapers, columnist Tom Powers from the *Pioneer Press*, and several television crews—including reporter Robb Leer and a photographer from the Twin Cities ABC affiliate, KSTP-TV. Elaine Waddell represented the front-office as Green and everyone else remained behind to prepare for the start of the season.

Every person on the trip was issued a two-liter bottle of spring water. They would be refilled daily at the US Embassy. And the players were given instructions on dos and don'ts for avoiding the Russian mafia. With nervous excitement, all that remained was to embark.

"We're going to get to see a country most people would never get a chance to see," said Gavin, whose wife, Phyllis, joined him on the trip while their 2-year-old son, Max, stayed behind at their Edina home with grandparents. "Because of the NHL, a few more doors will probably be opened to us than regular tourists. It's not really the most ideal conditions for training camp, but for twenty-seven guys to go over there with their wives and significant others, we'll get to know each other in a different light. I'm looking forward to it."

Some of the players' wives remained in Minnesota. Cathy Gainey and Beth Smith each had children starting school and thought it better to stay home. Kirsi Takko, who knew what conditions will be like, didn't *want* to go.

Tuesday-Wednesday, September 11–12, 1990

The Longest Day of the 1990–91 season began with a 9 a.m. charter to New York. The North Stars and their companions waited out a two and a half-hour mechanical delay at LaGuardia before finally boarding Pan Am Flight 30 for Moscow at 5:25 p.m. The flight took nine and a half hours and covered eight time zones, arriving in the Russian capital at 1:30 p.m. Wednesday. Two buses ferried the group to the Belgrade Hotel, which an American tourism guide listed as in a "grim zone." Some rooms didn't have toilet paper. All had single beds that could comfortably accommodate anyone under 5-foot-6—a description that fits none of the players.

Perry Berezan documented the trip with an ever-present video camera. On settling in, he filmed Basil McRae pointing out to his wife, Jill, that a child could probably pick the locks to the rooms. Their children (Alexandra, not quite 2; and Phillip, born March 15 in Minneapolis) remained in Minnesota, as did Jeremy Duchesne, 4-year-old son of Gaetan and Gina Duchesne. Gaetan, his black tie still cinched tight after the marathon journey, looked over the accommodations.

"Gator, what do you think?" Berezan called from behind the lens.

"I think it is a small room," Duchesne said with a wry smile. "But in Quebec we're used to small rooms, you know?"

Duchesne grew up in Quebec City with ten siblings—enough to make any house feel claustrophobic.

After practice, the team donned matching black running suits with the team logo on the jackets and pants with green-and-gold piping down each leg. They visited Red Square and gawked at the golden domes of the Kremlin. Musil served as guide for several players as they watched the changing of the guard at Lenin's tomb. At the rink, Musil had dressed in the same locker room he visited nearly four years earlier with the Czech national team. That was before he defected, making part of the journey in the trunk of a car to escape the communist empire.

The North Stars, who drafted Musil in 1983, worked three years arranging for his legal entry into the United States. By the summer of '86, he'd completed the last of his military obligations and obtained a holiday pass to travel to Yugoslavia with his girlfriend. Leaving her at a resort, Musil met Nanne and player agent Ritch Winter, who had quietly arranged an American visa for the defenseman. It took several days to find an exit point, but on July 17, 1986, Winter and Nanne fooled border guards, unaware a hockey star was defecting before their eyes. Musil had secretly studied English to prepare for his attempt and even refused a five-year contract with the Czechoslovakian national team. Signing would have required he promise not to defect. He was never considered a defector by the US government because he had come to America on a work permit rather than as an individual seeking political asylum. And, since he had fulfilled his army obligation, he could never be considered a deserter. Nevertheless, the Czechs viewed him as a fugitive until he gained US citizenship.

Just because he made it to Minnesota didn't mean he'd found a pot of gold, however. Musil supplemented his income during off-seasons by selling cars. Eventually, he married Andrea Holikova, a pro tennis player and sister of NHLer Bobby Holik, and no longer needed a part-time job. Musil made $155,000 in 1989–90.

The Russians' reluctance to adopt international contract standards left them vulnerable to more defections. Sergei Fedorov, a 20-year-old Detroit Red Wings prospect, snuck away from the Goodwill Games less than two months earlier in Seattle. That had the Soviet hockey federation extremely agitated. In fact, there was such ill will that the Friendship Tour was in doubt until shortly before the North Stars left, and there was speculation that perhaps the Russians weren't trying to make their stay very pleasant as retribution.

Thursday, September 13, 1990

Wearing their green road jerseys, the North Stars stood at one blue line of the Luzhniki Ice Palace—the same arena where the '72 Summit Series was played—and listened to the strains of the US and Soviet anthems. Then several tiny skaters—young girls perhaps five years old—delivered flowers to the participants. Moscow Spartak showed no deference, however, winning 8–5 before about 6,000 fans who cheered and clapped in unison, many wearing striped shirts that made them look like escaped prisoners.

The North Stars got two goals from Modano in the first six minutes, and Sinisalo, Duchesne (short-handed) and Barber scored on the Olympic-sized surface to take a 5–4 lead in the third period. But, as NHL president John Ziegler looked on, the Russians stormed back and added two empty-net goals as a measure of revenge for a 5–3 loss to Montreal the night before in Leningrad.

Doug Armstrong

Friday, September 14, 1990

After practice, the North Stars attended the Moscow Circus. Kari Takko bought cases of Coke from a Finnish grocer and the team ordered crates of hamburgers from a recently opened McDonald's delivered to the Belgrade. Dahlen and his fiancée, Maria Forslund, resisted in favor of Russian soup.

Arranging dinner turned out to be an adventure for Doug Armstrong, the director of team services. He tried to do so and still catch the team bus back to the hotel. But there's time, and then there's Gainey Time—at least according to Murray. That means if the bus is scheduled to depart at five o'clock, Gainey boards and tells the driver to leave at four or three minutes to five.

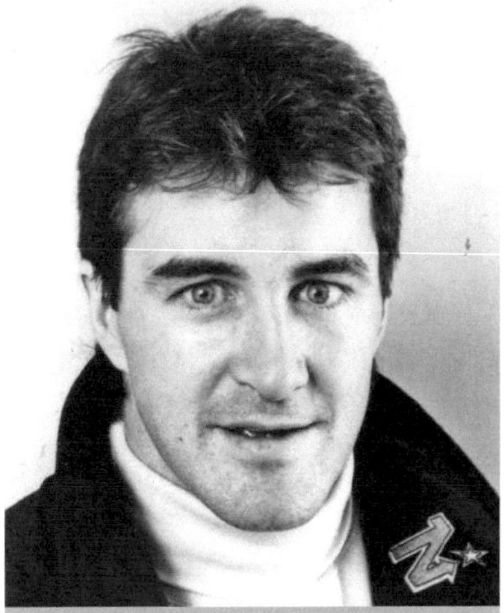
Stew Gavin

Never mind that Armstrong wasn't aboard.

"I was on there with my wife and Doug Armstrong's wife (Kelly) and I think Doug and Linda Jarvis were there," Murray recalled in an interview for this book. "I don't know if Doug Armstrong knew where he was or how to get back, but Bob said, 'We're going,' and we left. Doug's wife is sitting in the seat right behind Bob. They hadn't been married that long and she started to cry. But, I mean, we were *leaving*."

It was a long way from the Armstrongs' home in Bloomington. Somehow, Doug found his way back.

Basil McRae

Saturday, September 15, 1990

Surprenant treated the first real injury of the season. Chambers was behind the net with a Russian player when they grappled. As they fell, Chambers suffered a dislocated kneecap. He said it felt like someone chopped off his leg.

Eventually, the Soviet Wings beat the North Stars 3–2 in overtime before about 2,000 people. Gavin and McRae each scored but Minnesota couldn't hold a 2–1 lead.

Gavin once scored 26 goals after joining the Whalers on the eve of the 1985–86 season. And don't let the penalty minutes fool you—McRae could surprise with an occasional slick move, too. But the North Stars' outlook wasn't bright if those two had to provide all the offense.

Gavin was a reasonable offensive prospect with the major junior Toronto Marlboros from 1977 to 1980, averaging 22 goals and 48 points per season. But he never approached those numbers with the Maple Leafs, who made him a fourth-round draftee. He scored 34 goals in 272 games before Toronto traded him to Hartford. While that at least temporarily provided a spark, his production declined until the Whalers let him go at the end of training camp in 1988. Despite a career minus-36 rating before coming to Minnesota, Gavin settled into the role of checking winger. He was plus-12 in 153 games his first two seasons with the North Stars, also chipping in 20 goals and 31 assists.

McRae was a major junior prospect with the London Knights more than a decade ago. In 198 Ontario Hockey League games, he scored 65 goals—his total increasing in each of his last two seasons. He also had 461 PIM. The Nordiques liked what they saw, made him a fifth-round pick in 1980, and he played 20 games for them in '81–82. Subsequently, a season never passed when he didn't play at least one NHL game. But mostly he became an AHL fixture and fighter who cycled through three organizations before signing with the North Stars in '87. Nanne had seen many players "come in as crushers, try to be rushers and end up as ushers." But he thought McRae would thrive if he didn't let a little skill go to his head. He played 158 of 160 games in his first two seasons in Minnesota, 39 more than the rest of his career combined to that point. In three years, he'd averaged nine goals, 16 assists, and 365 PIM, an enforcer who could contribute a few points.

"As a kid, Basil was a goal-scoring machine," said Gagner, who played three OHL seasons with Brantford—an hour east of London—immediately on the heels of McRae. "But when you've got to think about dropping the gloves at any minute, it's not so easy to be skillful. We used to laugh at him in the summers because he'd come down to Minnesota and do toe-drags on guys and waltz around them. He'd say, 'I *told* you I can do it.'"

Sunday, September 16, 1990

Fortunately, Chambers' kneecap popped back in place. Otherwise, he would've been flown to Helsinki for surgery. He'd heard horror stories about the medical care available in the USSR and couldn't have been dragged before a Russian doctor. Nonetheless, he hobbled around on crutches while his fiancée, Lisa Miller, grudgingly killed more time than anyone else the rest of the trip.

After morning practice, the North Stars went to the newly opened Moscow Pizza Hut and then watched the Canadiens lose to Moscow Dynamo, 4–1. Some of the players wanted to go to the opera with their wives and girlfriends instead, but Gainey made the game mandatory. He said these games are different from the routine NHL exhibitions about to start up in the states. There, many younger players getting exposure wouldn't be on regular-season rosters and teams weren't already in midseason flow.

"When these teams play North American teams in their hometown, they have so much pride in their hockey they want to make sure they play well enough to win," Gainey said. "I don't think they could play at this level every night."

Bobby Smith said with even just another week of practice the North Stars likely would've won both exhibitions.

"The competitive side of the game doesn't come back to you in two games," Smith said. "We've been sitting around lifting weights and barbecuing for the last 11 weeks, remember."

Monday, September 17, 1990

The North Stars traveled to Voskresensk, a southeastern suburb of Moscow, where Bellows, Modano, and Aaron Broten scored in a 3–2 win over Soviet Khimik. But the game turned sour after Gaetz flexed his muscles in front of the Khimik bench, leading to the first of two brawls. Gaetz was ejected and unable to later protect Gagner, who was high-sticked in the face and cut for twenty-five stitches—most of them to the right side of his upper lip.

"I remember thinking I was just going to poke the puck by a guy, and… all of a sudden, he just pitch-forked me in the face," Gagner recalled in an interview for this book. "We had come out in the first period and played them a little bit probably too aggressively over the edge of, uh, outside the rules, I guess you'd call it. You know, everybody from North America gets a little tougher when they go to Europe. I think they came out in the second period thinking, 'To hell with you guys, we're going to even the score.'… It was a good thing we had Dr. (John) Schaefer there. He stitched me up and took a lot of time, to the point where you could really hardly see it. I don't know if I'd have felt the same if I saw a Soviet doctor. I might not be as pretty today."

Tinordi, Kolstad, and McRae each took runs at Gagner's attacker as fans threw bottles, coins and apples on the ice, along with pieces of wooden seats they ripped apart. The Minnesota traveling party moved from the stands to the dressing room for safety during the third period. Surprenant wrapped Gagner's head in gauze, as much for theatric sympathy as anything, and everyone rushed a short gauntlet of onlookers to the buses. Rocks hit the exterior, cracking some of the windows, making a staccato sound until they rolled away.

Outside Voskresensk, police stopped the buses and police took the drivers off for questioning. After some anxious moments for those on board, they returned and drove back to the Belgrade.

"The Russia training camp could've been a movie on its own," Churla told me more than thirty years later. "Tanks were going by us and all kinds of stuff you never expect to see on a freeway… and they didn't put us in the best of hotels. When you walk in the lobby and the guy is mopping the floor with a burlap sack attached to a hockey stick shaft, you know weren't in a five-star establishment."

Stephanie Churla wouldn't let her husband turn off the light in their room for fear of cockroaches.

And when Bellows asked one of the cleaning ladies for a towel, she walked ten paces down the hall, grabbed one from a dirty pile, folded it up and handed it back to him.

Tuesday, September 18, 1990

The North Stars herded to Moscow's Shrementyevo airport and an Aeroflot transport to Kiev, a city of 2.5 million people about sixty miles from where the world's worst nuclear accident occurred four years earlier at Chernobyl. Departure was delayed by an electrical malfunction, leading to several hours waiting in a cramped terminal. On arrival, however, the players and their companions found Kiev much better than Moscow—especially the Salyut Hotel, where accommodations were nicer and the TVs showed CNN.

After practice, dinner included squid, beef stroganoff, ice cream, and a traditional Soviet dish of mushrooms, sour cream and cheese. A pianist and strolling violinists serenaded the group, and Gainey served wine. Dairy foods were considered dangerous because of radiation and Gagner's wife, Jo-Anne, who just learned she was pregnant with their second child, was among the Minnesotans who avoided anything locally sourced.

Back in Minnesota, Green already sounded like he had indigestion from the way his team was playing.

"Of course I'm disappointed, but the only thing that's really going to count is the regular season," he told *Pioneer Press* columnist Charley Walters. "The reason they lost, more than anything else, probably is conditioning."

Wednesday, September 19, 1990

The North Stars lost to Sokol Kiev, 5–0 at the Kiev Palace of Sport before about 4,000 fans. At least seven of them, foreign-exchange students from the US, cheered for Minnesota. And, ironically, one of the Sokol players was Tod Hartje, an Anoka High School and Harvard graduate who was property of the Winnipeg Jets. While the Russians were worried about defectors, he'd become the first North American to play in the Soviet Union.[19]

Thursday-Friday, September 20–21, 1990

The North Stars landed in Minnesota after a travel odyssey that seemed even longer on the way home.

"It was a great experience and, like a lot of great experiences, they're not easy when you're going through them, but they leave a mark," Gainey recalled for this book about the Friendship Tour. "I think that was the most important thing about the trip to the Soviet Union. It was just months after the (Berlin) Wall had come down, and we still had opportunity to look in on society as it had been there with the occasional glimmer of transition. But there was still a lot of communist anxiety around, like we were being watched and followed. That doesn't just go away six months after the transition begins. It wasn't an easy trip. I can't say it was a positive thing for us or that it had any real benefit in us coming together as a team. There was a lot of anxiety and drama and I think everybody was ready to get back home."

The players, other than Chambers—who underwent arthroscopic knee surgery at Fairview Ridges Hospital—returned for practice Friday at Met Center.

Gainey gave a scouting report on who had played well to *Star Tribune* reporter John Gilbert, giving Rachel Blount a needed break. Gainey cited Myllys, Kolstad, Dahlen, Gratton and Barber.

Dahlen was under special scrutiny as Clarke had secretly negotiated a handshake deal that would allow the North Stars to keep the Swedish winger or let him go to San Jose for Clarke's choice among the others exposed to the Sharks. Dahlen grew up in Ostersund, Sweden, an eight-hour train ride north of Stockholm. His Swedish friends would say he was "from the sticks." At eighteen, he'd been discovered by the Rangers, who made him the seventh pick in the 1985 draft. He moved four and a half hours east to play for Bjorkloven IF in the Swedish Elite League and, by the fall of '87, the Rangers wanted him in New York. He scored 52 points in a 70-game rookie season, but declining totals the next two years left him available at the trading deadline. By then, Ferreira had left as director of player development with the Rangers to become GM of the North Stars, and he thought Dahlen too valuable to leave behind. On March 6, 1990, Ferreira acquired Dahlen and a fourth-round pick in the coming draft (Cal

Ulf Dahlen

19 Hartje scored two goals and had four assists in 32 games in 1990–91 with Sokol Kiev. During a return to the US for the holidays, he appeared on *Late Night with David Letterman*. Beginning in '91–92, Hartje played 297 career games in the AHL and IHL during the next five years—including a six-game stint with the Minnesota Moose in 1994–95. He never made it to the NHL.

McGowan) for Mike Gartner and future considerations. Minnesota fans have boisterously questioned the move, but Dahlen became popular with his new teammates. They teased him about his accent, which made him sound like a character from the Hans and Franz sketches on "Saturday Night Live." Dahlen twisted the needle right back about whatever he saw as foolish in North America.

Drafted three spots behind Dahlen by the Kings, Gratton stood out with the Canadian National Team in 1989–90. But he was still trying to prove he could score more than 10 goals in a pro season—something he'd done once in three attempts.

The North Stars recalled Derian Hatcher, Dan Keczmer, Warren Babe, and Mike Craig from Kalamazoo ahead of a stretch of three exhibition games in as many days starting on Monday.

Keczmer, a 10th-round draft pick in 1986 out of Mount Clemens, Michigan, played the past four seasons at Lake Superior State, winning an NCAA championship as a sophomore in '88.

Craig was the North Stars' second-round pick in 1989. He grew up in Thorndale, Ontario, a farming community of about 800 people just north of London. At fifteen, he moved two hours east, on the other side of Toronto, to play junior hockey in Oshawa. Despite being underage, he doesn't have a fake ID. Perhaps he figured his prominence as a player would be good enough to pass the most unforgiving bouncer. Only he doesn't have a biography in the media guide, either. Traditionally, that would mean his chances of playing in the NHL already were about zero.

Saturday, September 22, 1990

Gainey split the players into two groups for morning practice and then brought them together for a 3 p.m. intrasquad game. A small group of fans entered through the north gate and watched quietly.

Larry DePalma, a bruising, 24-year-old left winger whose nickname was "Repo," hadn't signed his contract. He had an injured hand and was cleared to practice beginning Thursday in Kalamazoo but was told not to report until after meeting with Clarke.

Larry DePalma

Five years earlier, DePalma had 232 penalty minutes and 61 goals in 65 games in the WHL—and another 58 PIM and seven goals in 13 playoff games. That made him enticing to the North Stars, who signed him as a free agent and put him right into their lineup.

Scoring in Minnesota proved a lot tougher, however. He had nine goals and 15 points in 56 games as a rookie and stuck around, largely, because he could always fight. He did so 13 times and racked up 219 PIM. But by 1989, Pierre Page told DePalma he wasn't good enough and banished him to The 'Zoo.

It'd been more than a year and a half since his last NHL game. DePalma, who sported a Fu Manchu mustache and shaved head, was married (Jacquie), had a son (Larry), and was scheduled make $160,000 under a termination contract.[20] Then he'd again be a free agent—unless Clarke decided to make a different offer.

20 Termination contracts were a popular process in the 1980s whereby an NHL team would sign a player it didn't believe had a very promising future—with the prospect for the player that he would become an unrestricted free agent when the term ended. Under the Collective Bargaining Agreement at the time, teams were required to compensate any team from which they signed a free agent. The practice served to chill the market for the best players because a team might sign an expensive free agent only to find the league would require a comparable player be given to the team from which he was signed.

Sunday, September 23, 1990

MC Hammer (who had one of the summer's hottest singles, "U Can't Touch This") played Met Center before a crowd of 12,390. It was the first concert at the Met since training camp began. As a result, the North Stars played another intersquad scrimmage in Eden Prairie. Craig, among players uncertain to make the team who were living at the Registry Hotel during camp, raised a few eyebrows with a hat trick.

Monday, September 24, 1990

Hatcher was returned to his junior team, the North Bay Centennials. Later, while James Taylor played to a crowd of 8,303 at Met Center, the North Stars lost to Winnipeg 5–1 before 3,123 fans at the National Hockey Center in St. Cloud.

Most of the action for Minnesota came during the third period, and that suited Ralph Strangis fine. He was the fourth of as many analysts auditioning next to Al Shaver, following former North Stars Bob Paradise and Dan Mandich and UPI sportswriter Dan Stoneking. Strangis, an underdog at best, was on the air for the final ten minutes when Churla fought Winnipeg's Steve Martinson for a second time. Gaetz then battled Daryl Stanley, giving Strangis plenty to talk about, including perhaps the scariest moment—when Bellows went down clutching at his knee after a hit by Bryan Marchment. Finally, Sinisalo snapped Stephane Beauregaurd's shutout bid at 18:22 of the third period, a play set up by Smith and Barber. But it was far too little too late to help Takko, who stopped 19 shots.

Takko had come to North America in 1985. Although he learned English in his native Finland, he hadn't used it much and found it a barrier. Sent to Springfield of the AHL, he didn't know how to ask at the grocery store for the ingredients to Swedish meatballs.

Takko made his NHL debut on March 8, 1986, allowing three goals in a 4–2 loss to the Jets. Unfortunately, it became a familiar occurrence. He entered the season 33–65–14 (.357). At twenty-eight, he's making $215,000 in the last year of his contract. His family (including son, Karri, nine, and daughters Kira, seven, and Karla, three) enjoys skating and sledding in the winter near the house they rent in Eden Prairie, and days off mean trips to the movies or even occasionally Duluth so the kids can ski.

Kari Takko

"At first you're just excited to be in the NHL, but then the feeling during those years was that they started making a lot of trades and they didn't always click," Takko recalled more than three decades later. "The team started to go into a downfall, and the financial troubles started. I thought we were going to be in trouble. When Lorne Henning was fired, we still had a chance to make the playoffs (in '87), and Glen Sonmor took over with two games to go. We got into an argument in the room. Keith Acton and Dirk Graham were upset with Lou Nanne, and they got traded the next year. They were a big part of keeping the group together, and we didn't make the playoffs. And then having so many coaches got confusing for everyone. We lost our direction.

"When Bobby Clarke and Bob Gainey came in, you could see it was business again."

Tuesday, September 25, 1990

McRae scored the deciding goal in the third period, deflecting Berezan's shot past goalie Tom Draper, as the North Stars downed the Jets 4–1 at Winnipeg Arena. Propp scored first and newly acquired Winnipeg defenseman Phil Housley, a South St. Paul legend, beat Myllys late in the second to tie it. But Gagner made it 3–1 in the third, and Modano added an empty-net goal with 28 seconds left as Myllys finished with 31 saves.

Earlier in the day, at an NHL board of governors meeting in Toronto, Green said he wanted to renegotiate the arrangement to stock the San Jose Sharks.

"I think it is a shame this deal happened," Green said.

Meanwhile, Mario Lemieux left the Pittsburgh Penguins to get treatment for a sore back. He had surgery July 11 to remove a herniated disk. The latest pain apparently was not related; however, Lemieux couldn't tie his own skates. He entered a Pittsburgh hospital for tests and wouldn't be ready to start the regular season.

Wednesday, September 26, 1990

President Bush arrived in the Twin Cities for a couple of fundraisers, including one where he spoke in support of Jon Grunseth, a Republican candidate for state Governor. The appearances were Bush's first in Minnesota since taking office in 1988.

As Bush and Grunseth smiled, waved, and shook hands, the North Stars beat the Chicago Blackhawks 5–2. A crowd of 7,457—many of whom paid just five dollars to get in—saw the only preseason action at Met Center. It wasn't televised, and Strangis got a full-game audition on the radio. KSTP had been impressed with his broadcasting knowledge, the homework he'd done, and his bravado.

Murphy scored in the first period on the power play. Gavin (short-handed), Aaron Broten, and Gaetz scored in the second, and Neal Broten made it 5–1 on the man advantage midway through the third.

Bellows (bruised knee) did not dress.

The game was marred by 46 penalties (25 in the third period) for 189 minutes. Tinordi, who left the penalty box momentarily in a fit of rage after fighting Chelios, was one of five players given game misconducts.

Green, who earlier fired longtime public address announcer Dick Stanford, brought in Twins PA man Bob Casey to work the game. Afterward, Green decided to rehire Stanford.

Green also revealed the NHL would abandon the Friendship Tour. The Canadiens had suffered thefts from their hotel as well as hostile crowds and other travel nightmares similar to the North Stars, and there was little appetite for a third attempt.

Thursday, September 27, 1990

The NHL suspended Tinordi ten games and fined him $10,000 for his role in the melee. He'll lose $25,000 of his $200,000 salary, hefty for a guy who just bought his first house (in Eagan).

Tinordi was suspended the first four games of the '89–90 season following an altercation with Chicago's Al Secord, and the teams had a bench-clearing brawl before a game last December that led to future restrictions on how many players could dress for warm-ups.

"I guess when we play them it does get kind of busy out there," McRae said of the Blackhawks. "I don't think that will change.... You learn after awhile, against a team like that, it's either hit or be hit."

Tinordi usually does the hitting. He grew up in Red Deer, Alberta, which had a population of roughly 30,000 in the 1970s.

Mark Tinordi

"Either you were a farmer, or you worked in the oil business, but hockey ran that town at the time," said Tinordi, who didn't start playing on an organized team until he was thirteen.

At sixteen, he moved three and a half hours south to live with his aunt and uncle and play for the WHL team in Lethbridge. Despite his size, he went undrafted after five junior seasons, the last of which was with the Calgary Wranglers. But Ferreira signed Tinordi as a free agent, and he played 24 NHL games in 1987–88 with the Rangers. His defensive partner in his debut was Giles. The next day, Tinordi was sent to Denver, and Giles was traded to the North Stars. The following October, Tinordi joined him in Minnesota.

"That tickled me to no end," said Tinordi, who was demoted on the day his car and furniture arrived in Manhattan from Colorado. "I didn't like New York too much for a whole bunch of reasons, starting with the fact that I'm a defenseman—played my whole life as a defenseman—but the Rangers played me at left wing. Not only that, but (then head coach) Michel Bergeron put me in the role of fighter.... I didn't want to get tagged in that role because I felt I was capable of being a regular defenseman, not a left wing who would go out fighting."

For at least the next couple weeks, Tinordi—who drives a 1979 Ford F-150—will have a little less money in his pocket and more time to spend with his wife, Lorene, and their 1-year-old son, Matthew.

Tinordi's wasn't the only suspension of the day. The NHL also banned Edmonton goalie Grant Fuhr for one year because of cocaine use, although meeting conduct requirements could allow him to return in February.

The North Stars sent Babe and Keczmer to Kalamazoo, along with DePalma. Bellows returned to practice but wouldn't make the trip to Oakland for Friday's exhibition against Pittsburgh.

The team also announced that Strangis won the seat next to Shaver. The 29-year-old son of the chairman of the racing commission governing Canterbury Downs, Strangis was single and living in a $52,000 condo at 694 and Silver Lake Road in New Brighton. He grew up in Northeast Minneapolis, his father a well-connected attorney who helped pave the North Stars' merger with Cleveland. For his twelfth birthday, Ralph Jr. got to visit the press box at Met Center and glimpsed Shaver at work.

"I went, 'THAT! I want to do that!'" said Strangis, who began calling play-by-play of basketball games into a tape recorder as a sixth-grader in the balcony at St. Charles Catholic School in Northeast Minneapolis.

He attended Totino Grace High School and, soon after, had his first radio broadcast roles at KTWN in Anoka and WMMR at the University of Minnesota from 1977 to 1980. He called play-by-play of football and hockey at WJON in St. Cloud before gravitating to various roles in the greater Twin Cities, calling pro volleyball, pro wrestling, and high school and small-college hockey. Hired in 1983 as production coordinator for a company in Hollywood, he supervised projects for TV, film, local news, and sports packages. He received his first national producing award in 1986 as co-producer and host for "The Minnesota Hockey Report."

Ralph Strangis

But struggles with drugs and alcohol led him to seek treatment that same year. After his release from Hazelden, he had to restart his career and overcome depression, fear, and anxiety—conditions he would battle much of his life. This was the chance of that lifetime.

After he learned Tom Reid had left the radio and TV broadcasts, replaced on the latter by Nanne, Strangis launched an all-out blitz on KSTP and the North Stars. He had his sister pretend to be his personal assistant, calling station manager Ginny Morris to try and arrange an interview. He pleaded with his father to get Walter Bush to appeal to Morris for an audition. Ralph Jr. even wrote letters to Green.

"At some point, it became 'Fuck you. I'm getting an audition,'" Strangis told me. "I'm just annoying the shit out of these people, although I'm charming about it."

He signed a one-year contract paying $200 per game at home and $250 on the road—the first time that has happened with a color commentator in franchise history. Morris said that decision, along with the choice of analyst, was "Norm Green's idea."

Once addicted to Scotch and cocaine, Strangis now goes through as much as a 12-pack of Diet Coke every day.

Friday, September 28, 1990

As Robert Plant played before 6,170 at Met Center, the North Stars lost to the Penguins 3–1 at the Oakland Alameda County Coliseum. Pittsburgh scored three times on the man advantage and Gavin netted Minnesota's only goal with a 20-foot shot in flight from the right wing.

In the crowd of 9,497 were fifty San Jose Sharks employees (including Ferreira, scouting director Chuck Grillo, and PR director Tim Bryant) and many future season-ticket holders.

Saturday, September 29, 1990

The North Stars flew to Chicago and practiced ahead of Sunday's exhibition against the Blackhawks. Back in the Twin Cities, Green defended his decision to fire more than half of the team's staff during the off-season.

"Because there was no local ownership, what developed in Minnesota is a bureaucracy of inefficiency," he said. "The North Stars were a very loosely run organization with far too much staff and a poor business philosophy. I reduced the staff, eliminated the free tickets and the barter program and moved the offices back to the original building. There's an enthusiasm among our staff that wasn't there before. The people we have feel like they were hand-picked."

Or something like that.

Green, who wears a Flames Stanley Cup ring, vows the North Stars are not a rich man's plaything.

"I wouldn't work this hard for a toy," he said. "This is a career, something I've always wanted to do. I can feel the adrenaline flowing again. It's a chance to be involved in an area I love."

Fans won't like his increased ticket costs, including a new benchmark of $50 to sit in the lower level between the blue lines. As a way of protecting that perceived value, he's instructed ushers to prevent fans in cheaper seats from moving down.

"I'm afraid we're going to offend some high school kids and some of the people who can't afford the higher prices," Green said. "But the reality is we need people in our seats who can afford to buy them. If we didn't make any changes, if this team continued to lose money, it would wind up in someplace like San Jose."

Sunday, September 30, 1990

Before the preseason finale, the team recalled Rob Zettler from Kalamazoo and acquired Winnipeg defenseman Peter Taglianetti for future considerations. The moves were necessary after Chambers underwent surgery and Tinordi was suspended.

By trading unnamed "future considerations," Clarke circumvented the San Jose agreement. Taglianetti, twenty-seven, was the Jets' third-round pick out of Providence College in 1983 and led the Jets last season in plus-minus (plus-20), although he was minus-36 from '87–89. Other than portions of the '85–86 and '86–87 seasons, he stuck with Winnipeg, totaling 10 goals and 37 assists in 207 career regular-season games. But he also was an active unionist and always one to speak his mind. That ran afoul of Jets GM Mike Smith, making Taglianetti expendable. He'd join the North Stars on Tuesday. His wife, Allison, and their three sons (Patrick, 4; and twins Andrew and Jonathan, 2) would follow soon.

In a letter to the editor in Sunday's *Star Tribune*, former North Star Steve Payne reacted to the ambivalence toward the team from Minnesota fans, calling them "fair-weather" and "bandwagon" jumpers. Gainey wasn't sure how to describe the aura around the North Stars, only that it was unique.

"The team had performed pretty well the previous season and lost in a seventh game at Chicago, so they had a base there," Gainey recalled for this book. "They had a culture but then Bob Clarke comes in with a certain culture and I come in with a certain culture and it took some time to bring all of those together. I wouldn't say the North Stars had a poor culture. I'd say they had their own culture. And as much as Bob or I brought in a different culture, we had to adapt to some of that culture, too. We had to find this new spot for all of us. It wasn't the Flyers, where Clarke had spent twenty years. It wasn't Montreal, where I had spent fifteen years. And it wasn't the old North Stars. It was a combination that needed time to settle in before we said, 'This is who we are and this is what we need to do.'"

In one last tune-up, Craig and Modano scored power-play goals before the Blackhawks tied it. Smith scored late in the second, and Wilkinson restored a two-goal margin early in the third, only to have Chicago tie it again. But Propp converted a power play at 18:49 to earn a 5–4 victory.

Dead ahead was the six-month regular season, during which the North Stars would take a lot of lumps—at the Stadium and most other arenas around the NHL. No one could've known that last goal would echo a distant future.

CHAPTER 4

October: Dismal in the Standings and at the Turnstile

Monday, October 1, 1990

After the North Stars returned on their commercial flight to MSP, Rob Zettler grabbed his bags and checked into the Marriott, across the street from Met Center. He didn't know it, but he would be there nearly a month.

Bobby Clarke monitored the waiver draft[21] from his office. Quebec selected Aaron Broten—whose family had just moved into a new home in September. Clarke accepted $10,000 in compensation instead of Tony McKegney, a former North Star who could have reverted to Minnesota. Teams could protect eighteen skaters with more than two years' NHL experience and two goalies with more than three. But with Shawn Chambers injured and Mark Tinordi suspended, the acquisition of Peter Taglianetti left Broten the odd man exposed.

As evidence of how the league sometimes ruled at random, Edmonton was allowed to protect three goalies because Grant Fuhr was under suspension. If Clarke could've made the same claim for Tinordi, Broten might have remained a North Star.

Kari Takko also cleared waivers, paving the way for him to be sent to Kalamazoo if necessary.

Danny Gratton

Tuesday, October 2, 1990

Clarke sent Link Gaetz and Dean Kolstad to Kalamazoo and dispatched Danny Gratton[22] to the Canadian National Team. That left Mike Craig as the sole rookie on a roster of twenty-six for the season opener in two days against St. Louis.

The average NHL salary for 1990–91 was $210,000, with Blues winger Brett Hull the poster boy for expanding payrolls. He made $125,000 in '89–90, but that jumped to about $1.5 million.

21 The NHL waiver draft was in place from 1977-2003 except for the 1979-80 and 1991-92 seasons because of the merger with the WHA and the expansion to San Jose, respectively. The draft was in the week before the start of the regular season, at which time each team could designate a number of protected players. Anyone unprotected was exposed to selection by the other teams in the league, with the draft order the reverse of the previous season's standings. Seldom did a great number of players change organizations. The largest number of picks was 18 in 1988 (when the North Stars made Stew Gavin the No. 1 pick from the Hartford Whalers) and 2003. Compensation was either cash or the player the claiming team dropped to make room for the one they picked.

22 Gratton would go on to play eight games with Team Canada before spending most of the season at Kalamazoo, where he would score 20 points in 44 games. By '91–92, he began playing intermittently in Europe and just two of the remaining 108 minor-league games in his career would come as high as the AHL. He never played for the North Stars and retired in 1998.

Wednesday, October 3, 1990

Tinordi practiced with the team at Met Center. Chambers watched. Neither would be available for Thursday's opener, which would be televised at 7:35 p.m. on KMSP-Channel 9.

At the east end of the arena in section 234, one new video screen was in a temporary location. That screen, along with three more made by Electrosonic of Eden Prairie, was expected to be installed on the center ice scoreboard by January—if not sooner.

At the Metrodome, in an afternoon game that drew 9,826, the Twins beat the Seattle Mariners 7–4. They finished in last place in the American League West with a record of 74–88 (.457). The only team worse in the AL was the Yankees (67–95). In the National League, only the Atlanta Braves (65–97) and St. Louis Cardinals (70–92) lost more.

Thursday, October 4, 1990: Blues 3, North Stars 2, at Met Center

In the early morning darkness, Norm Green left his expansive home at 80 Gideon's Point Road in Tonka Bay. A wide stone parkway circled around an island of greenery up to three large garage doors. To the left, three wings formed the residence. One faced the front, sheltered by a grove of tall maple, oak and ash trees. Another pointed toward a long dock and a 28-foot Skiff Craft inside a boathouse extending into Lake Minnetonka. A third sloped down to an immense patio with a swimming pool.

Green and his wife, Kelly, have three children—Cheryl (32), Howard (30) and Adam, who turned 23 on August 7. Kelly will join him later, as will Adam, an assistant to the North Stars' director of operations, Eric Kruse.

But none rose as early as Norm, whose chauffeur-driven Rolls made the half-hour trip on Highway 7 and I-494 to Met Center. He passed steel girders rising on what would become Mall of America, slated to open in approximately two years, and arrived at the arena, eager for his first season opener as majority owner of an NHL franchise, just after 5 a.m.

More than twelve hours later, few fans followed. Perhaps attendance was dampened by road construction, or maybe people were taking a wait-and-see approach. Only 5,730 turned out, nearly 2,000 fewer than the attendance at the home exhibition. One person counted at the turnstile was Bill Goldsworthy. The North Stars wouldn't offer credentials to the Sharks, as they did to the other twenty NHL teams, because of the ongoing player dispersal dispute. So, Goldsworthy had to buy a ticket.

Because of the numerous firings made by Green since he took over the team, *Star Tribune* columnist Dan Barreiro has dubbed him "The Smiling Assassin." Green had a penchant for straightening crooked lapel pins on his employees and lecturing those without one. Doug McLeod and Ralph Strangis were transgressors at this week's welcome luncheon.

Green told *The National Sports Daily* that his team would be run different from the one under George and Gordon Gund.

"We cleaned up the building and got rid of the drunks[23]," said Green, who also prohibited smoking in the concourse. "I moved here. I'm here twelve hours a day. Yes, we had to let some people go. The result is a far more efficient organization."

As expected, lining up for the National Anthem, Curt Giles wore the captain's "C" on his jersey. The alternates were Basil McRae and Stew Gavin.

Dave Gagner scored a power-play goal late in the first period to give the North Stars a 1–0 lead. But Hull put the Blues in front late in the second, scoring immediately after a face-off. He added an

23 One of the excuses for the lack of attendance in the late 1980s was an atmosphere fueled by alcohol. Some season-ticket holders cited the rowdiness of some fans as a reason they did not renew.

unassisted goal at 11:40 of the third for what stood up as the game-winner, beating Jon Casey after picking off a pass Gagner intended for Zettler.

Despite what took place on the ice, the story was the attendance. It was the smallest crowd for a home opener[24] in North Stars history. It wouldn't be easy going head-to-head with the Timberwolves, who averaged 26,160 per game in their first season at the Metrodome. They finished just 22–60 (.268) but have moved into the brand-new Target Center, where they'll tip off their first exhibition on October 16.

The North Stars went 26–12–2 at the Met in '89–90, including thirteen wins in their first fourteen home games. That made Gagner wonder where the fans went.

"We were really bad on the road, but they didn't have to watch us on the road," he said, glumly.

Friday, October 5, 1990

The broadcast of Thursday's opener drew a 7.5 rating and a 12 share, meaning about 200,000 people in Minnesota watched on television—more than tuned in to "The Simpsons." Ironically, it was the best TV audience in years for a North Stars game.

Green said he was "disappointed but not surprised" by the attendance. He hoped by mid-season there would be sellouts.

Saturday, October 6, 1990: North Stars 4, Islanders 2, at Met Center

Craig, who wore No. 50 in the preseason and in Thursday's opener, switched to No. 20—last routinely worn by fan favorite Dino Ciccarelli.

Making sure Craig had the right number was one of myriad tasks before the game for the equipment staff. They also had to make sure sticks, skates, helmets, and other gear did not display logos from companies that hadn't abided by new NHL rules requiring endorsement. Manufacturers, such as the maker of Gagner's helmet, had to pay a $12,500 fee plus 8.5 percent of all sales of such equipment to the NHL. When they didn't, as in Gagner's case, his Cooper insignia was covered in white paint (green on the road) and the only decorations were two reflective star stickers—new to the uniform that season. Sticks often were hastily spray-painted to obscure noncompliant brand names. By its own estimate, the league figures fifty-five percent of sticks and eighty percent of skates must be made generic.

Brian Propp

Attendance blossomed (?) to 5,970, more than a few cheered, and Bob Gainey smiled (!) as the North Stars outshot the Islanders, took a 3–0 lead early in the second period, and held on. Gagner and Brian Propp each had a goal and an assist.

"I think it's always special to accomplish something for the first time," Gainey said. "It will be another of those posts along the road someday."

After Propp poked in a loose puck in the third period, he unleashed his signature celebratory move: The Guffaw. In 1986, Propp was at a stand-up comedy show featuring Howie Mandel, who made a movement he called a "Guffaw"—with his right arm a short left-to-right wave followed by extending his hand up toward the ceiling. Mandel intended for the crowd to repeat the motion and tease the subsequent comic, substituting the Guffaw for regular applause. Propp

24 It also was the earliest home opener the North Stars ever played.

liked it so much he appropriated it to demonstrate his charisma after he scored a goal. He'd used it after most of his 140 regular-season and playoff goals of the past four seasons—but this was his first chance to unveil it in Minnesota.

As a 16-year-old in 1974–75, Propp was MVP of the Saskatchewan Junior Hockey League with Melville, a town of a few thousand people not quite two hours east of Regina. He posted 168 points in 57 games, then moved on to the Brandon Wheat Kings of the WHL. There he totaled 511 points in 213 regular-season games over three seasons. In 1979, Brandon lost to Peterborough, 2–1 in overtime, in the Memorial Cup final. For Propp, it was the beginning of some seriously bad fortune with a championship on the line.

Propp scored the winning goal in his first NHL game, October 11, 1979, against the Islanders, and became a regular for one of the league's most dominant franchises for the next decade. The Flyers finished first in their division five times in eight seasons and had the best record in the league in 1980 and '85.

But they lost to the Islanders in a six-game Stanley Cup Final in 1980, and fell to Edmonton in five games five years later. In a 1987 rematch, Propp was second to Wayne Gretzky in playoff scoring and Philadelphia forced the Oilers to a seventh game. The Flyers took an early lead—only to have Mark Messier, Jari Kurri, and Glenn Anderson score to win 3–1. At the trade deadline in '90, with Philadelphia out of the playoffs, Clarke sent Propp to Boston. He latched onto a team that won the President's Trophy and, after a harrowing Game 7 win over Hartford in the first round, won eight of nine games to get to the final again. But then Edmonton proved it could win without Gretzky.

Two games into his North Stars tenure, Propp could only wonder whether he'd get another chance at the Cup.

<u>Sunday, October 7, 1990</u>

Jarmo Myllys, Kalamazoo's No. 1 goalie last season, at least temporarily became Casey's backup and flew with the team to New York for Monday's game against the Rangers. Had they been interested, none of the players could have watched the Vikings fall to 1–4 with a loss to the Detroit Lions before 57,586 at the Metrodome.

<u>Monday, October 8, 1990: Rangers 6, North Stars 3, at Madison Square Garden, New York</u>

With no Twin Cities TV option, Minnesota fans were deprived of—or perhaps saved from—watching former North Star Mike Gartner score twice in New York's home opener as the Rangers bombarded Myllys with 39 shots. With San Jose GM Jack Ferreira and Sharks owner George Gund on hand and a crowd of 15,286 watching, it was 4–0 early in the second period.

With the loss, the North Stars sank to what would become a familiar fourth place in the five-team Norris Division.

Meanwhile in Montreal, goalie Brian Hayward was suspended by the Canadiens after he walked out of their morning skate as part of a demand for more playing time or a trade. His contract called for a salary of $300,000 this season.

<u>Tuesday, October 9, 1990: Devils 5, North Stars 2, at Meadowlands Arena, East Rutherford, NJ</u>

Ordinarily road roommates, Chambers (knee) and Tinordi (suspension) were back in Eagan, their houses across the road from each other. They tuned in KMSP-TV to watch the game at New Jersey and didn't like what they saw.

The Devils scored three power-play goals—already enough to win early in the second period—as the North Stars went short-handed seven times for the second consecutive game.

"We're just not very good right now," Gagner said. "We're playing sloppy and taking too many chances."

The attendance was 8,448—large by North Stars standards, but the team's smallest road crowd of the season and the only one under 10,000. The IHL's Milwaukee Admirals drew more than that. And while their owner, Lloyd Pettit, formally dropped his bid for an NHL expansion franchise, that didn't stop speculation the North Stars could move to Milwaukee.

"It is a terrible shame the Minnesota North Stars can't outdraw the Milwaukee Admirals," Pettit said, not exactly discouraging the rumors. "We are constantly keeping aware of what is available and what might be available."

Wednesday, October 10, 1990

The North Stars returned to MSP on a morning commercial flight (the younger players and unfortunates like McLeod crammed into the middle-row B and E seats).

The team practiced in the afternoon at Met Center. Gainey said he would keep Craig at least through October. He could play ten NHL games and still retain his eligibility with the OHL's Oshawa Generals, where one of his linemates last season was Eric Lindros.

Gagner learned of the death of his father, Armand, who was 68, and returned to Chatham, Ontario. He would miss the next two games while spending time with his family.

Dave Gagner in 1990.

"My dad was forty-two when I was born and I was the youngest of seven kids," Gagner told me in a 2021 interview. "I left home at fifteen to pursue a hockey career. So, I don't think we had as close of a relationship as some people. We always got along really well, and he was very supportive. He didn't push me hard in hockey. That was my mother's job, I guess, and my brothers."

One of them maintained a satellite dish so their parents could watch North Stars games.

"I think it was great that he got to see me make the NHL," Gagner said. "That was important for me, and he saw a lot of my games. I'd done well the season before and we all want to make our dads proud, right? I was at peace with that.... I didn't find it as emotionally hard as I probably would have a few years earlier."[25]

Thursday, October 11, 1990: North Stars 3, Bruins 3, at Met Center

A "crowd" of 5,280 booed after the North Stars fell behind 3–0. The biggest home highlight to that point was first-period fisticuffs between McRae and Stephane Quintal.

But Mike Modano assisted on Ulf Dahlen's first goal and set up Propp in the second. Then, midway through the third, Modano scored a coast-to-coast power-play goal, and Minnesota held on without two key players: Gagner and Giles (flu).

"Under the circumstances, being down 3–0, we're happy with the point," Gainey said. "This is a great building block for the club, to say this is the way we have to play to win games."

Brian Bellows agreed to a three-year, $2.1 million contract extension. Bellows made $300,000 in 1989–90.

25 Gagner's mother, Helen, died in 2021 about a week before we talked for this book. She was 97.

Brian Bellows

"The price of hockey is going up," said Clarke, who also signed Frantisek Musil to a multiyear extension starting at $210,000—a $55,000 raise.

Friday, October 12, 1990

The North Stars announced several marketing initiatives to improve attendance, including one that would provide $3 admission to youth hockey players wearing their team jerseys. An advertising campaign and promotional giveaways also were designed to spur interest. Later, about an hour up I-94, a standing-room sellout of 7,051 jammed the National Hockey Center to see the University of Minnesota tie St. Cloud State 3–3 in the latter's first game in the Western Collegiate Hockey Association.

Saturday, October 13, 1990: Blackhawks 4, North Stars 1, at Met Center

Hours before his team would take the ice against Chicago, Green was guest speaker for the Gophers hockey team's Blue Line brunch at Jax Café in northeast Minneapolis. He said the North Stars had no marketing plan entering the season and, when asked if attendance could turn around in one year, said, "It would be a miracle."

The team launched a Family Section against Boston where anyone who bought a $19.50 ticket could add admission for two kids fourteen and younger for $2 each. Such accommodations were possible with so many seats available.

A Saturday night game against the rival Blackhawks with no local TV and a Fina Flag Night[26] promotion brought 9,129 fans to the Met. (There would have been more, but the $9.50 seats sold out and more than 400 people who wanted them were turned away when they decided not to pay as much as twice that to get in.) Unfortunately, Modano's second-period power-play goal, which briefly made it 2–1, was about all they had to cheer. Kolstad fought Mike Peluso, only a couple of months after they'd lived in the same cabin and trained together at Minnesota Hockey Camps in Brainerd. And McRae squared off with Stu Grimson twice in the second period.

"Too many guys are standing around," McRae said in his postgame analysis. "Even the bench is dead. In the NHL, you've got to get excited."

The North Stars had three shots in the first period, and just nineteen in the game—not nearly enough to overcome Steve Larmer's hat trick.

"I think we have to play at a higher level or find other players who can," Gainey said.

At Kalamazoo, where players were known to whistle on the bench to the tune of the Dionne Warwick song "Do You Know the Way to San Jose?", Takko won his second game in as many nights as the K-Wings started the season 5–0.

Sunday, October 14, 1990

With the Vikings idle heading into a Monday night game at Philadelphia, the North Stars about to hit the road for L.A., and the Timberwolves yet to start their season, Minnesotans' attention was diverted to a political scandal. Republican gubernatorial candidate Jon Grunseth was accused of

26 This was the first of the promotional giveaway nights designed to stimulate attendance. The item was a North Stars flag—ironically white in color—with the Fina logo that could be extended from within a carrying case.

swimming nude with four young teenage girls at a party in 1981 at his home in Hastings. The resulting outcry dealt a heavy blow to Grunseth, whose campaign benefitted from President Bush's recent visit.

Monday, October 15, 1990

Green denied rumors the North Stars would be sold or move to Seattle or Milwaukee. The *Seattle Times* reported that he was in talks with groups bidding for expansion teams in Florida.

"The last thing I would do is move or sell this team," he said. "Why would I move the team when we've only been here a few months? We're in this thing for the long haul. We're not giving up."

Tuesday, October 16, 1990

Gagner returned to the Twin Cities and practiced before the team left for Los Angeles. Later, the Timberwolves played their first preseason game at Target Center before a crowd of 18,296. As a stunt for NBC Sports, former Vikings receiver Ahmad Rashad played three minutes of the third quarter with the Philadelphia 76ers, who went on to win 102–96.

Wednesday, October 17, 1990: Kings 5, North Stars 2, at Great Western Forum, Los Angeles

It was a high school football Wednesday in Minnesota, the day before a four-day Minnesota Education Association break, but Chambers, Green, and plenty of other viewers caught some late-night hockey on Channel 9.

Just before Los Angeles took a 2–0 first-period lead, play was paused while an electrician fixed the goal light behind the Minnesota net. It was malfunctioning, flashing repeatedly—a harbinger of sorts.

Gretzky and Luc Robitaille each had a goal and two assists, and Kings goalie Daniel Berthiaume, who'd gone 1–3 with the North Stars before his trade on the eve of training camp, frustrated his former team with 41 saves.

In five consecutive games, Minnesota had fallen behind by at least two goals before attempting a rally. They had only the October 11 tie against Boston to show for it.

"The disappointing thing is that nobody is really disappointing," Gainey said. "I don't think I can say I'm happy with the effort of all the players, but I don't think it's a lack of effort that's putting us in this position."

Thursday, October 18, 1990

The North Stars practiced in LA before flying to St. Louis. Neil Wilkinson met his future wife, the former Kristin Pendleton, on the flight. The North Stars were playing "Snarples," a card game, and his partner took a break to go to the bathroom.

"She walked down the aisle, and I said 'Hey, I need a partner,' and handed her the cards," Wilkinson recalled more than 30 years later.

Whether she felt sympathy for his lingering bruises from taking a puck in the face at New Jersey or the black eye he got in a fight Wednesday, Kristin stopped and sat down. Originally from Portland, Oregon, she was an off-duty flight attendant on her way home.

They talked the rest of the way to St. Louis, exchanged numbers, and met later for dinner.[27]

Neil Wilkinson

27 That date for Neil and Kristin began a nine-year courtship that resulted in their elopement to Jackson Hole, Wyoming, during the 1998 Olympic break.

Friday, October 19, 1990

The North Stars held a team meeting for more than an hour and then practiced at St. Louis Arena, where they experimented with new line combinations—including one with Modano centering McRae and Shane Churla.

Last season, McRae and Churla combined for 12 goals. Modano had 29 by himself.

Saturday, October 20, 1990: North Stars 2, Blues 2, at St. Louis Arena

While much of America watched the Cincinnati Reds complete a sweep of the Oakland A's in the World Series, the North Stars earned a point before more than 17,000 fans in St. Louis. Gagner tied it midway through the third period, pleasing Green—who flew with his personal pilot to St. Louis aboard Green's six-seat jet.

Midwest Sports Channel carried the action back to Minnesota with its first telecast of the season, but even if every subscriber were tuned in around the Twin Cities, that would've only amounted to an audience of 11,000 homes.

McRae became the North Stars' all-time penalty minute leader with a second-period fight against Dave Lowry.

"Fifty percent of the game is mental, and the other fifty percent is *being* mental," McRae said of his abilities. "I've got that part down, no problem."

Early in the third period, Modano roughed Rod Brind'Amour, and the two recent candidates for the Calder Trophy got into a fight. It was the first of Modano's career. He was cut and needed several stitches but returned later in the third.

Sunday, October 21, 1990: Blackhawks 7, North Stars 1, at Chicago Stadium

The KMSP-TV audience tuned in around 7:30 p.m. and saw a shellacking that delighted most of the 17,782 who attended in person. It was 7–0 before Modano scored with 2:47 remaining. It was the North Stars' most lopsided defeat since a 9–0 loss January 9 at Detroit.

Giles, often the team spokesman when others ducked the media, sat in a tense dressing room and couldn't even speak. As head coach, Gainey generally had little choice but to address reporters.

"Is it as disappointed as I've been this season?" Gainey said, echoing a question as his gaze rose to the ceiling. "It feels like it."

While Giles and many others had nothing to say afterward, Bobby Smith—playing in his 900th NHL game—at least responded.

"We're lacking something," he said. "I don't know what the solution is."

Monday, October 22, 1990

As a Republican named Arne Carlson called a noon press conference at the state capitol in St. Paul to enter the race for Governor, Green made an announcement of his own: He had bought the remaining 24.5 percent of the team from Morris Belzberg. Green purchased Howard Baldwin's 24.5 percent for $5 million and, while terms were not disclosed, it was expected Belzberg would realize approximately the same amount.

Green said owning 100 percent of the team is a dream come true and shows his commitment to keeping the North Stars in Minnesota and "building a franchise everyone can be proud of."

Jarmo Myllys

"Mark it on your calendar," Green told *USA Today*. "One year from today, the North Stars' turnaround will be the biggest story in sports.... We have a scorched-earth fan base. Our fans have been injured. Someone told them they weren't good fans, so the team was going to be moved. There is no price or circumstance in which I would be interested in selling or moving. It's not negotiable or open for discussion."

Smith appeared in a print ad with Beth and their children: Ryan (5), Meg (3) and Daniel (2). It promoted the family section for this week's games against Hartford and Detroit.

The North Stars also ended the Jarmo Myllys Experiment, giving the goalie a one-way ticket to the 'Zoo. He was 0-2-0 with a 6.15 goals-against average and an .867 save percentage in two appearances. Combined with brief stints in 1988–89 and '89–90, his North Stars career numbers would forever remain: 1–9–0, 5.84 and .835.

"It was crazy; Jarmo was the perfect example of the best minor-league goalie you'd ever see," Kolstad remembered for this book. "Better than Ed Belfour. Better than Jimmy Waite, Ray LeBlanc.[28] (Myllys) would play four games in Kalamazoo and allow two goals total. They'd call him up to Minnesota, and he'd let in eight. He'd go back to Kalamazoo and have three shutouts in a row, and they'd call him back up, and he'd lose again. I think he was comfortable with the non-pressure in Kalamazoo."

Tuesday, October 23, 1990

Clarke, one of the most competitive individuals to ever play the game, expressed his displeasure at a 1–6–2 start.

"I just don't think we're giving the effort necessary to win," he said. "Obviously, we're not an elite team so everyone has to give all they've got every night.... There are some concerns, but we're not anywhere near the stage where we think we can't recover."

He added, "If you have players that don't want to push hard, it's the responsibility of management to do something about it."

The players had the latest of multiple meetings in an effort to stop the slide.

"It's not from a lack of hard work," Giles said. "The problem during a time like this is that the guys start trying to do too much. Pretty soon, if everyone starts doing that, it becomes a big circle. No one does what they're supposed to do, and everyone's trying to do everything. If every player realizes he has a certain job and he does it as well as he can, we can be a successful team."

While it remained to be seen what kind of team Craig would be part of, it became clear it would be in Minnesota. His next game would be his tenth, negating any chance to send him back to the OHL. The North Stars made arrangements for him to live with a billet family[29]—that of Jim and Donna Hawley, the chef from the Russia trip and his wife.

28 Waite was one of the top goalies in the IHL during Kolstad's career, posting a 60-32-8 record with the Indianapolis Ice in 1989-90 and 1990-91. However, he could never displace Belfour in goal for Chicago. LeBlanc had a legendary IHL career from 1986-98, winning more than 220 games, but only played 1 in the NHL—beating San Jose 5-1 on March 10, 1992, at Chicago Stadium. His appearance came a few weeks after he was the goalie for Team USA in the 1992 Olympics in Albertville, France, and came about because it allowed the Blackhawks to leave him exposed and protect Belfour, Waite and Dominik Hasek in the 1992 expansion draft. In three seasons at Kalamazoo, Myllys was 68-30-8.

29 A billet family opens its home to players—often in junior hockey—because they are teenagers and not mature enough to live on their own. Often they are compensated for food and other expenses that it takes to provide room and board for the players, usually no more than two per household. Sometimes the players and their billets develop lasting relationships that extend throughout their playing careers and beyond.

Mike Craig

"I was so young and immature," Craig recalled more than thirty years later. "I was nineteen and green. I don't even know if I should've been there. I maybe should've been in junior the whole year to physically develop and mature."

He didn't own a vehicle or have a financial advisor—didn't even have a checking account. Jane Marostica, Clarke's administrative assistant, banked all of Craig's pay and provided him an allowance. Basil and Jill McRae also engaged him as a babysitter.

"There weren't many young guys on the team," Craig told me. "Me and Mike (Modano) were the youngest and pretty much everyone else was married. But we had a lot of characters, awesome personalities in the dressing room from all over the world. Everyone brought some kind of charisma."

Bellows, whose stall was just to the right of Craig in a distant corner of the dressing room, became a mentor of sorts.

"The year before, he sniped 55 (goals)," Craig said of Bellows. "So, I was trying to take up as little space as I could with my stall in the corner. He's got his six Sherwoods there, and I'm trying not to touch them or spill his coffee that's sitting there. The first day, he had me look up in the corner and said 'These are all the tape rolls. If somebody asks, it's your job to grab it and throw it to the guys.'"

Craig couldn't have cared less about any indignation. He was just happy to be there.

Wednesday, October 24, 1990: North Stars 3, Whalers 0, at Met Center

With no local TV for the game against Hartford, the only way to see the North Stars snap their seven-game winless streak was to attend in person. The anticipation was so great that 4,646 fans showed up to see a 33-save shutout by Casey, supported with two goals from Gagner.

Trumpeter Phil Holm and organist Sue Nelson tried in vain to generate noise from a crowd presumed smallest in franchise history. Individual game attendance was first officially recorded by the team in 1984–85, but it's likely there was never a turnout as sparse, even in the lean years of the mid-70s.

"I think we started to rebuild our confidence last week, then it was shattered with the trip into Chicago," Gainey said. "What we should read into that is we shouldn't read too much into any one game. We shouldn't read too much into this one."

Casey's shutout was the fifth of his career but first in more than eleven months. Thus far, he'd proved to be something of an enigma. A native of the Iron Range, he moved from Coleraine to Grand Rapids as a junior in high school when his dad took a job there in the Blandin paper mill. That led to some hard feelings seven miles east in his former hometown as Casey led Grand Rapids to a state title as a senior in 1980. He then helped win an NCAA title two years later at North Dakota.

"He had a temper," recalled Perry Berezan, whose first college season with the Fighting Sioux overlapped Casey's last. "He'd hold things together, but my freshman year at North Dakota we went to the NCAA final four. Eddie Christian, Dave Christian's younger brother, was on that team and was the guy who would poke you. He'd wink and say, 'Watch this one with Casey.' He'd let go a slap shot high over his head off the glass and watch Casey lose his shit. In the warm-up for the semifinal, you know how they do the half-moon (shooting exercise) in front of the goalie? Eddie decides he wants to wake up Jon, so he takes a high slap shot. Casey charged out and tomahawked his goal stick at him. How many goalies, before the biggest game of their life, would do that? Jon was capable of snapping. Sometimes he could pull it back together, and sometimes he couldn't."

Jon Casey

Casey joined the North Stars as a free agent in the spring of '84. He appeared in two games and won his only decision, then played the entire '84–85 season with Baltimore of the AHL. He got a 26-game trial with Minnesota in '85–86 and went 11–11–1 before landing back in the minors most of the next two years. In '87–88, Casey went 1–7–4 with the North Stars and appeared sent to the minors for good by the '88 IHL playoffs.

But Ferreira happened to be in the stands because Kalamazoo's opponent was the Rangers' top farm team. He saw something he liked in Casey, who won three times before the K-Wings lost the first-round series in seven games. Two months later, Ferreira became the North Stars' GM. He hired Dean Lombardi, Casey's agent, to be assistant GM. Casey had to find a new agent, but he then negotiated a new deal with Ferreira and stuck with the North Stars the next two seasons, going 49–39–16 with a 3.15 GAA and an .898 save percentage. In 1989–90, Casey tied for the NHL lead in victories (31).

But in his first eight decisions of '90-91, he was 2–4–2.

Thursday, October 25, 1990

As the North Stars flew to Detroit, the Penguins announced that Mario Lemieux was being treated for a rare bone infection that often leads to debilitating pain and cripples many people who have it. Lemieux's bone disease, a form of vertebral osteomyelitis, was attacking the fourth lumbar vertebra in his back. It was the same spot where he'd had surgery this past summer.

Kolstad was flying to Michigan, but not Detroit. He was headed to Kalamazoo with the impending return of Tinordi and Chambers. And three forwards stayed behind in the Twin Cities. Dahlen had a wisdom tooth removed, while Gaetan Duchesne and Don Barber were left to skate on their own Friday at Met Center.

Friday, October 26, 1990: Red Wings 8, North Stars 6, at Joe Louis Arena, Detroit

A standing-room sellout crowd of 19,875—largest to see the North Stars during the 1990–91 regular season and playoffs, and perhaps twice as many as tuned in to be disappointed on MSC—had eight opportunities to erupt, each following a different Red Wings goal scorer.

Four players (Shawn Burr, Jimmy Carson, Johan Garpenlov, and Bob Probert) had three points. Sergei Fedorov, Steve Yzerman, and Rick Zombo each added a goal and an assist. Only five skaters *failed* to make the scoresheet for Detroit.

Probert was only playing because a federal judge declared it unconstitutional that he had been ordered to remain jailed while appealing a deportation order related to a conviction on drug charges. He was arrested March 3, 1989, trying to cross the US-Canada border with 14.3 grams of cocaine concealed in his underwear. According to *Sports Illustrated*, US Customs agents stopped Probert, who was driving a borrowed car littered with empty beer cans and an empty liquor bottle. The agents became even more suspicious after they found a cocaine mill in his coat. That led to a strip search, and Probert wound up serving three months in a Rochester, Minnesota, prison. For 1990-91, he could only play in US games while undergoing a urine test twice every week.

The North Stars actually led 4–3 early in the third period, but Detroit strafed the net behind Takko four times in a span of fourteen minutes.

Gainey trimmed the bench almost by half as the game wore on and said he had no choice.

"There was a group of players who were up to their ears, and others weren't involved at all," he said. "I'd rather lose with players who are trying than those who aren't trying."

Tinordi played for the first time since his suspension. That allowed Clarke to make a pregame trade of defensemen that was at least somewhat about offense. Clarke sent Musil to Calgary[30] for 22-year-old Brian Glynn, who had 20 points in 77 NHL games and 78 points in 119 IHL games.

Glynn, who scored in his NHL debut three years earlier, played 67 games with the Flames in 1987–88. He got that opportunity because Jamie Macoun had been injured in a car accident. In '88–89, Macoun returned, and Glynn couldn't crack a lineup that also included Gary Suter and Al MacInnis, two of the better offensive defensemen in the league. Playing a ton of minutes in the minors as a 21- and 22-year-old was ideal for Glynn's development, however. He had 17 goals and 44 assists in 80 games last season.

Less than a month from his 23rd birthday, Glynn kissed his wife, Cindy, in Salt Lake City and flew to Detroit. When he arrived, he went to his hotel room. A few hours later, he heard a key in the lock and in walked his new roommate, Bobby Smith. As they got acquainted, Toronto fired coach Doug Carpenter. The Maple Leafs (1–9–1) were the only team in the Campbell Conference with a worse record than Minnesota.

Saturday, October 27, 1990: North Stars 2, Red Wings 2, at Met Center

The sole TV signal emanating from Met Center tonight was from PASS, a regional cable outfit for the Detroit area. Significantly, and perhaps not coincidentally, Modano—who had family and friends tuning in—was a healthy scratch for the first time in his career.

"It was time for him to watch and see the game from a different place," Gainey said. "We talked quite a few times, and I thought we were communicating two ways. I thought he was hearing and understanding. But I didn't see that in games."

In 11 games, Modano had three goals and five assists but also was minus-1.

"I was just like really snaked and couldn't get out of the gate at all," Modano recalled thirty years later. "That first month or two was painful, and that's when Bob kind of tried to get through to me. He and I really struggled at first. I had a hard time getting on Bob's wavelength, and he didn't really know how to handle me. I was just kind of in a fog at that point.

"It was probably self-induced pressure on my part to come out and pick up where I left off (as a rookie). When you try to do that, it can snowball out of control, and you just dig yourself a ditch. The games go flying by, and you're like fifteen games into it and haven't done much. Then, you try to make up for fifteen games in two games and that just doesn't happen. So, it was really hard to let go of what happened in October and start from scratch. We were all struggling. Bobby Clarke, you know, he's always been very, uh, *opinionated* about everything. At that point, there was talk about 'Did they make the wrong choice with the draft with (Trevor) Linden?' Because he was having a good year. Do we move Mike? But Bob (Gainey) was always in my corner. He's like, 'No, we're going to hang with this. There's something there. We'll work with him and see where this goes. But we're not going to sell the farm.'"

30 Musil totaled 60 points in 271 games with Minnesota. Despite playing on some of the North Stars' worst teams, he was a career minus-6 with 547 penalty minutes.

Rob Zettler

In addition to Modano, Wilkinson and Zettler were scratched after playing in Friday's loss. Zettler was pleased, however, that he'd been told to move out of the Marriott and get a permanent place to live. He found one, thanks to Friday's trade. He moved into Musil's furnished condo near 494 and France Avenue and became a regular at nearby Joe Senser's and Fuddruckers.

The North Stars further revealed McRae had an abdominal strain. Ilkka Sinisalo had a strained groin—though that was not yet public.

Larry DePalma was from Trenton, Michigan, about the same distance southwest of Joe Louis Arena as Modano's native Livonia. DePalma was recalled from Kalamazoo and celebrated his 25th birthday by taking Modano's spot in the lineup.

The game drew 6,164 fans, who watched the home team blow a 2–0 lead in the third period. That was slightly fewer than the 6,241 who braved a windy fall night *outdoors* at the National Sports Center in Blaine to see the US men's national soccer team beat Moscow Spartak 1–0 in an *exhibition* as part of an effort to bring the World Cup to Minnesota.

Oh, and the Gophers hockey team drew 6,470 to Mariucci Arena for an exhibition against Team Canada.

Sunday, October 28, 1990

Just after the Vikings fell to 1–6 with a 24–10 loss to the Green Bay Packers in Milwaukee, Grunseth announced from his Afton home that he would quit his campaign for Governor. That left the race to incumbent Rudy Perpich and write-in candidate Carlson.

Buried in the agate type of the transactions in Sunday's newspapers, Pittsburgh acquired former North Stars defenseman Gordie Roberts from St. Louis for future considerations. Roberts had spent most of the first month of the season in the IHL with the Peoria Rivermen.

Monday, October 29, 1990

Before leaving for Toronto, the North Stars practiced at Met Center. Giles acknowledged that the attendance at the home opener (if not other games since) really bothered him.

"We were really geared up to start a new season, and we were looking for a big crowd," Giles said. "So, it was disappointing when it didn't happen."

Gagner said there were bright spots in the sparse home attendance, such as against Hartford.

"At least it was a good, loud 4,600," Gagner quipped. "What's tough to swallow is that the guys are working hard. We know (the fans) are dissatisfied. But everyone wants to win really bad. Everyone wants people to come and see us."

Tuesday, October 30, 1990: Maple Leafs 5, North Stars 4, at Maple Leaf Gardens, Toronto

Game days were developing into a new and wonderful routine for Strangis.

"I'd go to morning skate, because Al was getting to the age where he had no interest in it," he recalled for this book. "He'd be in a sweater or a hotel bathrobe or something outside his room and say, 'I'm going to work on my notes, but we're going to have lunch, aren't we?'"

Gary Olson was Shaver's fellow dining connoisseur. Inevitably Strangis, Rachel Blount, and sometimes McLeod joined them.

"We'd have this huge lunch someplace," Strangis said. "Then I'd come back and work on my notes for a bit and take a nap or something, and then we'd get on the bus and go to the game. We'd eat the press meal at the game, and then Al and Gary would have a reservation after the game if we were in a town with a good steakhouse. At 10 o'clock, we'd go and have a full-on dinner at Hye's."

Hye's Steakhouse, which has locations in Toronto, Winnipeg, and Vancouver, featured Shaver's favorite: a steak called "The Only." He ordered it charred but pink on the inside with a tomato-and-onion salad and twice-baked potato. The meal was bookended by a cheese bread appetizer and dessert.

"Gary and Al were big men," Strangis said. "I thought, 'If I eat like this for twenty years, I'm going to look like they do.' There was no way I could keep up this pace. But I remember Al at the beginning of the season said, 'Ralphie, we may not have a very good hockey team this year, but we're sure going to eat good.'"

For a while tonight, it looked as though the North Stars might devour a team they should beat. Midway through, they led 4–1, and a crowd of more than 15,000 began to boo the Leafs loudly. Then Toronto torched Takko for four consecutive goals. Casey was in uniform but suffering from the flu.

"I can't really explain it," said Bellows, his ample forehead creasing in conversation with Blount and Olson. "It was just another frustrating night. We did some things right and a lot of things wrong."

Wednesday, October 31, 1990

As Clarke walked off the jetway into Philadelphia International Airport, two TV crews stopped him to ask about his return to where he was fired after six seasons as GM of the Flyers. Now holding the same job with a team that was 2–8–3, Clarke gritted his teeth and managed not to smash either camera.

CHAPTER 5

November: Electric Stars and tartakes Distract from Reality

Thursday, November 1, 1990: Flyers 6, North Stars 3, at Spectrum, Philadelphia

Same old story: The North Stars trailed 3–0 and clawed back to trail 4–3 with more than 12 minutes remaining. But Philadelphia's Derrick Smith scored midway through the third and Dave Gagner drew an unsportsmanlike penalty for shooting the puck down the ice after the goal. The Flyers scored on the ensuing man advantage, and Minnesota was left coughing in their vapor trail.

Gagner said he got the penalty immediately after he hollered at referee Rob Schick to pay attention.

"A guy cuts my feet out from under me and they score right after," said Gagner, who pointed out that Shane Churla was cross-checked in the face and given a 10-minute misconduct when he complained. "I know you're not supposed to be yelling at the (referee) and calling him every name in the book. I just tried to tell him to look."

Brian Propp, who scored on the power play and drew cheers in his return to Philadelphia, said, "Everyone's lacking in confidence right now. We need a win to spark us."

The postgame meal was pizza, delivered to the airport hotel.

Back in Minneapolis, the Timberwolves opened the season with a 98–85 win over Dallas before 19,006 at the Target Center.

Friday, November 2, 1990

The North Stars had lunch at a fast-food restaurant but made up for it with an expensive team dinner in Quebec City.

Back in the Twin Cities, Norm Green said he was seeking $13.5 million for his 18 percent share of the Calgary Flames that has been put in trust since he became owner in Minnesota.

"The one thing I didn't expect was for our team to have this type of a poor start," he said. "It might be the impact of all the offseason nonsense, a new coach, and a new general manager. I'm not discouraged because I've given myself a couple of years to get things done. If I don't get it done, I will consider myself stupid."

He didn't specify just *what* he meant to get done.

Saturday, November 3, 1990: North Stars 2, Nordiques 0, at Le Colisée, Quebec City

Larry DePalma showed a flash of the talent that was always within him. Late in the second period, he caused a turnover at the Quebec blue line and used a defenseman to screen his shot through rookie goalie Scott Gordon.

Shane Churla

Propp added an empty-net goal, and Jon Casey earned a 24-save shutout as the North Stars won on the road for the first time since March.

Bob Gainey admitted the low-scoring game may not have been exciting, but his team allowed half as many shots as in the 8–6 loss at Detroit, and he didn't find that particularly exhilarating, either.

Not about to mess with a strategy that worked, the players celebrated with postgame pizza before busing two and a half hours to Montreal.

Sunday, November 4, 1990: North Stars 2, Canadiens 2, at Montreal Forum

The North Stars rewarded Gainey with a point in his return to Montreal, where he is a veritable saint in the religion of the *bleu-blanc-et rouge*. He was met with an ovation from the Forum faithful as he walked to the bench before the game and given another afterward.

In between, Larry Murphy scored an unassisted goal when his pass deflected past goalie Patrick Roy, and Gagner made it 2–1 8:25 into the third with a shot from the slot. But Brian Glynn coughed the puck up to Andrew Cassels, who beat Casey for the tying goal with more the seven minutes to go.

Churla fought Todd Ewen late in the second period, although Churla got a minor charging call instead of a fighting major. He wasn't nearly as upset about the penalty or the result of the game compared with the lack of support in Minnesota.

"It's like we're playing 80 games on the road," Churla moaned to a *Montreal Gazette* columnist.

Churla was a sixth-round pick of Hartford in 1985, after he totaled 34 points and 370 penalty minutes in 70 games with Medicine Hat of the WHL. He spent most of the next three seasons at Binghamton of the AHL. In 22 games with the Whalers, he had one assist and 92 PIM. Traded to Calgary, he managed one goal, six points, and 157 PIM in 34 games with the Flames.

Dealt to Minnesota at the deadline in '89, Churla missed a shot at winning the Stanley Cup in Calgary but established himself as a true NHL heavyweight. In 1989–90 he had 292 PIM. He wouldn't return to the minors, and there's something to be said for that since he and Stephanie had a newborn daughter, Morgan.

Gaetan Duchesne was scratched as precaution after he was knocked out by an elbow from Craig Wolanin at Quebec. MSC again televised the game back to Minnesota; however, most people tuned to see the Vikings play the Denver Broncos in a night game at the Metrodome. Despite having lost six of their first seven, the Vikings overcame a 16-point deficit to win 27–22 and thrilled a crowd of 57,311.

Monday, November 5, 1990

As the North Stars flew to MSP, the DFL candidate for US Senate, Paul Wellstone—with senior campaign adviser Pat Forciea in tow—spent his last day campaigning in Virginia, Duluth, and at the University of Minnesota. Wellstone, a 46-year-old political science professor from Carleton College, made issue of incumbent Rudy Boschwitz's negative campaign tactics and a claim that he was the better Jew. (Both candidates are Jewish.) Wellstone's wife was a Christian, and Boschwitz suggested in a Saturday campaign speech that Wellstone was raising his children as "non-Jews." Boschwitz also sent a letter to people in the Minnesota Jewish community stating Wellstone has no connection to it. A *Star Tribune* editorial called Boschwitz's actions "the lowest political blow of them all."

Tuesday, November 6, 1990

Wellstone, who campaigned in an old school bus painted green, won nearly 52 percent of the vote to earn a seat in the US Senate. Arne Carlson squeaked out victory in the Minnesota Governor's race over DFL incumbent Rudy Perpich by a similar margin, about 36,000 votes out of more than 1.6 million cast. And nationally, the Democrats solidified control of the House of Representatives and the Senate.

Meanwhile, the North Stars lost Stew Gavin, who'd suffered a knee injury late in the game at Montreal. He was diagnosed with a torn left MCL.

Wednesday, November 7, 1990

Bobby Clarke pulled the trigger on two more trades. He sent Don Barber[31]—scratched in nine of 16 games—to Winnipeg for Doug Smail in a swap of left wingers. Clarke then thumbed his nose at the proposed San Jose deal by shipping minor-league defenseman Jayson More to Montreal for holdout goalie Brian Hayward.

Smail was in his eleventh NHL season, all with the Jets after a three-year standout career at North Dakota. He had 189 goals and 208 assists in 691 games with Winnipeg and once tied an NHL record for fastest goal after the opening faceoff, scoring just five seconds after the puck dropped. While the Jets were perennial also-rans through the 1980s, he had the second-best year of his career in '89–90, totaling 49 points. But he had just three through the first 15 games this season, for which he'll make $205,000 and become a free agent when it's over. His temporary status means his wife, Lisa, will stay in Winnipeg for a while with their newly adopted son, Cody, who was born July 11.

Because More had played in fewer than fifty career NHL games (just six, including five with the North Stars), he was ineligible for protection in the postseason dispersal draft that Green was trying to revise. The agreement, as negotiated by Howard Baldwin and Morris Belzberg, was for the North Stars to protect fourteen skaters and two goalies with more than fifty games' experience. San Jose would then choose fourteen skaters and two goalies from the organization, and subsequently alternate picks with the North Stars from what's left until the Sharks had fourteen more skaters. Under the agreement, trading More should have triggered a penalty that would limit the North Stars to protecting nine skaters instead of fourteen.

Don Barber

Sharks president Art Savage told the *San Jose Mercury News* that, in addition to dealing More, the North Stars also should be penalized for the preseason trade of Ken Hodge to Boston. That would mean the North Stars could protect only eight skaters. Savage said Green should have to live with the deal because he was at the meeting where the governors approved the agreement and joined the North Stars before the sale was finalized on June 14.

"He didn't have to close," Savage said. "Nobody held a gun to his head."

Of course, the one-page agreement between the North Stars and Sharks also doesn't specify how many players the former must

31 Barber had 23 goals and 24 assists for 47 points in 74 career games with the North Stars.

Gaetan Duchesne

make available to the latter. If the North Stars released all their players except the 14 skaters and two goalies they can protect, the Sharks would have an empty pool in which to swim.

Hayward, who was thirty, had practiced with the McGill University hockey team since he left the Canadiens on October 8. After playing three seasons at Cornell, he originally signed with the Jets as a free agent in 1982 and was traded to Montreal in '86. That was just in time to watch Roy—then just twenty—become the youngest Conn Smythe winner in league history. In time, it became obvious who was going to get most of the minutes in goal. Sometimes you just need a change of scenery. Or at least a coach who believes in you.

You couldn't blame Duchesne if he was getting near his breaking point, too. Despite a contract that called for him to make $190,000, he'd been healthy scratch in nine of sixteen games, had just one assist, and was minus-1. But his sunny disposition belied dogged determination. Chosen in the twelfth round of the 1979 Quebec Major Junior Hockey League draft, he totaled nine goals in 46 games as a rookie with the Quebec Remparts and was passed over entirely for the 1980 NHL draft. But he scored at a point-per-game pace in '80–81, good enough to warrant Washington's eighth-round selection that summer. Duchesne arrived at the Capitals' training camp as a 19-year-old who spoke virtually no English. He wasn't part of Washington's travel squad that played a series of exhibitions in Sweden, and it looked like he had little chance of making the team. But he did.

Duchesne immersed himself in English lessons and conducted his first media interview already in November of his rookie season, alternating between broken syntax and help from interpreter/teammate Jean Pronovost.

"I made the team because I worked hard," Duchesne said at the time. "There's really no big difference between me and another eighth-round draft choice but, when I was drafted, I decided I would work very hard to make the team. In the draft, number is not important."

He was remarkably consistent with 37, 36, 38, and 39 points in four seasons before posting a career-best 52 in 1986–87. But Washington GM David Poile swapped Duchesne, Alan Haworth, and a first-round pick in the '87 draft to Quebec for Dale Hunter and Clint Malarchuk. Duchesne was happy to be home, but two seasons with the woeful Nordiques almost killed his career. He totaled 29 points in 1988–89, after which he was traded to Minnesota for Kevin Kaminski, who'd played one game for the North Stars.

Duchesne had just 20 points in his first season in Minnesota, the worst output of his career to date. While he hadn't had a minus rating since his rookie year, it was obvious Gainey wasn't quite sure what to do with him.

Thursday, November 8, 1990: North Stars 3, Nordiques 2, at Met Center

As President Bush doubled to nearly 500,000 the number of troops deployed to the Persian Gulf in response to Iraq's invasion and occupation of Kuwait, Green also unveiled a new plan of attack on the empty seats at Met Center. Before the start of a season-long five-game homestand, he announced "tartakes," a cash drawing at every home game, including a $5,000 grand prize that would appreciate with unclaimed winnings, through December. Green said the odds of winning were 1 in 423.

"I think I might have been naïve coming in," Green said. "In Calgary, our marketing program was to open the doors. The fans here have told us that we need a very strong marketing plan. It's an expensive giveaway for us, but, if it draws enough people into the seats, it's a wise investment."

Green also made 60 percent more seats available for the lowest ticket price of $9.50, created a $14.50 ticket, eliminated the $50 ticket, and brought back a student-rush program.

While the season was more than a month old, this was a night of firsts. It was the first game to feature video screens on the scoreboard. The first chance at a $100,000 fan shootout came during the first intermission. It was the debut of the Electric Stars dance troupe. And, for the first time, the North Stars maintained an unbeaten streak longer than back-to-back games—though it helped that they were playing Quebec for the second time in less than a week. All of that combined to keep a crowd of 5,286 fairly engaged.

The Electric Stars included eight women and five men from United Performing Association, Inc., each earning $75 per game, which reportedly matched what the Los Angeles Laker Girls got. According to Lisa Kubinski, the president and director of UPA, they were the first dance team to work NHL games. Kubinski was Miss Teen Minnesota as an 18-year-old Osseo High School graduate in 1984. She became a Vikings cheerleader from '84–88 before recruiting her own dancers.

The Nordiques took a 1–0 lead, but newcomer Smail created a turnover and set up Duchesne's first goal of the season to tie it early in the second. Churla scored on a rebound and Gagner added the eventual winner on a breakaway midway through the third. Still, Gainey wasn't happy.

"I don't think we played as hard," he said. "I can't say that for all the players, but it wasn't a complete team effort."

Hayward arrived, skated, and took sweater No. 33. But Kari Takko dressed as the backup to Casey, who made 24 saves.

"It was bizarre coming into that situation," Hayward remembered for this book. "I landed in Minnesota, and someone picked me up and they said, 'Bobby Clarke wants to get you on the ice.' So, I went on the ice with Bobby Clarke and Ilkka Sinisalo. They fired pucks at me for forty-five minutes, and I was so tired I could hardly stand up. Bobby said, 'Are you in shape? Do you need games?' I hadn't played since September, so I said, 'Give me a couple games with your minor-league club, and I'll be good to go.'"

Perry Berezan was getting concerned after playing in just 8 of 17 games. Twenty-six, married (Marie), and making about $170,000, he'd already sunk $160,000 into his first home. A two-story house at 1982 Safari Trail in Eagan, it was typical for any of the North Stars except established superstars, of which there are few. Behind a double garage on a lot with some woods was a pond. Berezan took out his frustration by smacking golf balls into the water.

Brian Hayward

Perry Berezan

"I felt like I was clinging to a career at that point," Berezan told me in 2021. "It was rough, and mentally I was ready to pack it in. It's one thing to be there, but there has to be some sustained positive growth, and you have to get that feedback from teammates and coaches. I wasn't getting either because I was struggling so bad. And that self-perpetuates.

"When Bob came in, he made it quite clear, 'I don't know who any of you are.' I'd played against Bob, but he didn't remember me. He wasn't a scout. He was like, 'You each need to prove to me that you'll fit a slot in this lineup and do what I need you to do.' I don't think they knew what the hell I was or how I could fit in. All year, I felt like that was a make or break for the rest of my career."

Friday, November 9, 1990

Hayward and Neil Wilkinson went to the 'Zoo. For Hayward, it was a brief conditioning stint. For Wilkinson, who had played once in the past six games, it threatened to be a longer sentence.

To create a spot for Wilkinson, Link Gaetz, with the K-Wings since the preseason trip to Russia, was loaned to Kansas City of the IHL. He refused to report.

Saturday, November 10, 1990: Whalers 3, North Stars 2, OT at Met Center

Rookie referee Lance Roberts whistled 38 penalties, including 12 after a second-period brawl in front of the Hartford bench that made him call for an early intermission to sort it out. With the score 1–1, 2:11 of the second period carried over to the start of the third.

Twenty-nine seconds after the third period started for real, Glynn scored his first goal as a North Star. But, moments later, Neal Broten—wearing Gavin's alternate "A"—went off for tripping, and Pat Verbeek tied it again.

Just 49 seconds into overtime, the deciding goal came following a play the North Stars were sure should have been a penalty. Verbeek appeared to trip Shawn Chambers but Roberts never raised his right arm, and the resulting 2-on-1 led to a rebound goal for Randy Cunneyworth.

The crowd of 8,624, boosted by a Year of the Uniform promotion that provided replica jerseys to the first 3,000 kids sixteen and under, voiced its displeasure. Its echoes soon were heard in a Minnesota dressing room steamy from more than the nearby showers.

Link Gaetz

"I couldn't figure out the referee tonight," Gainey said. "I don't think he had a rhyme or reason."

"I thought it was a penalty, and there are twenty guys in here who will tell you the same thing," Chambers said. "(Verbeek) stuck his stick up between my legs and tripped me. If that's not a penalty, then half the other things shouldn't have been, either."

Unknown to most at the time, Gaetz was watching the game—in person. He was supposed to be in Kansas City and undergoing treatment for alcohol abuse. But Gaetz told his minor-league teammates he was going hunting instead, and then showed up in the second-level seats to the right of the Met Center press box.

"We didn't know where he was," said Clarke, sounding exasperated. "He didn't show up for practice and didn't go to Milwaukee for a game. And then he shows up here, in the stands. Our coaches can't be wasting time on guys like that."

Sunday, November 11, 1990

Gagner, leading the North Stars with nine goals, underwent arthroscopic surgery. He aggravated a knee injury when he was checked during the first period against the Whalers. He was originally hurt on the Russia trip but played through it. He finished Saturday's game, but Dave Surprenant said Gagner wouldn't have been able to skate Sunday if he had to and was likely to miss two to three weeks.

It was a major blow. Gagner collected more points (156) than any other North Star the past two seasons. Not bad for a player the Rangers gave up on after 80 games. He grew up on a farm east of Detroit, just over the Canadian border. Chatham, Ontario, is perhaps best known as the home of Hall of Fame pitcher Fergie Jenkins. But for Gagner, hockey was always No. 1. He had three sisters, and three older brothers who played, so he learned quickly about overcoming a size disadvantage. Topping out at 5-foot-10 and 188 pounds, he made up for any lack of brawn by skating like a dynamo and with an exuberant, desperate style.

"It was never hard for me to get up for games," said Gagner, who by his own estimation was obsessed with hockey from age twelve. "I was always able to get my emotions going, though coaches always said that my strengths could be my weaknesses if I let my emotions get the best of me. I used to try to manufacture some anger before a game—think about something to get me going. On the flipside of that, I wasn't always the easiest guy to play with."

In the second of three major junior seasons, Gagner scored 121 points in 70 games in 1982–83. Within the span of a few months, the Rangers drafted him twelfth overall and he played for Team Canada at the World Junior Championships and in the Olympics.

Once he signed professionally, however, it seemed like the Rangers suddenly doubted his ability. Gagner split the 1984–85 season between New York and New Haven of the AHL. That pattern would be repeated in '85–86 and '86–87. With the Rangers, he managed 11 goals, 16 assists, and was minus-16.

"If I wasn't a really motivated kid, I probably wouldn't have been playing after my third or fourth year," Gagner said. "As a kid, you don't realize that you have to earn your job every day. In the pros, you have to succeed before you get the ice time. That means playing well with less minutes. It's not all about talent—it's about dealing with adversity. I didn't have the understanding of that when I was with the Rangers. I can cry about it and say they didn't give me a chance but, honestly, I probably didn't deserve a chance."

On October 8, 1987, Lou Nanne made what he later said was his best trade, acquiring Gagner and Jay Caufield for Paul Boutilier and Jari Gronstrand.[32] Caufield played one game for the North Stars and was waived to Pittsburgh in 1988. He'd be in the lineup for the Penguins on Thursday, but—with three goals in his last 100 games—what good is a right winger who can't score?

At first in Minnesota, it didn't look like Gagner would do much better. Playing for Herb Brooks, who had coached and liked him in New York, Gagner had 19 points in 51 games. Then Brooks got fired and, at the beginning of the '88–89 season, new GM Jack Ferreira told Gagner he was going to Kalamazoo, where he'd played part of '87–88. Gagner burst into tears.

"I had a really strong camp, but they sent me down again," Gagner said. "I was labeled a minor-league guy and an underachiever. That's when I thought about quitting. There are only so many rejections you can take. I was going to go back to school, maybe play in Europe the next year. But my wife was very influential in my decision to stay. She said 'This has been your dream your whole life. You're hurt right now. Don't let your feelings get the best of you.'"

32 Boutilier played four games for the Rangers, nine others in the NHL, and played his last pro season in Switzerland in 1990–91. Gronstrand had 14 points in 62 games with New York and foundered with Quebec and the Islanders, appearing in his final three NHL games in 1990–91.

Bless Jo-Anne. Her husband was recalled after one game with the K-Wings, the last he would ever play in the minors, and broke out with a team-best 35 goals and 43 assists under Pierre Page. Last season, their Apple Valley home brightened by the arrival of a son (Sam), Dave had scored 40 goals (trailing only Brian Bellows) and added 38 assists. Gagner—who drove a used Toyota—became a bargain at $215,000 for 1990-91.

Monday, November 12, 1990

Gainey wanted to evaluate Kevin Evans, who came to Met Center and practiced with the North Stars even though he technically was not recalled from Kalamazoo. Hayward *was* recalled after 3–2 and 4–3 victories in two conditioning starts for the IHL East Division-leading K-Wings.

More than $26,000 remained available in Tuesday's tartakes drawing. Before a winning seat was announced, the "Lucky Stars" (University of Minnesota students Blake Martin and Dave Bernhofer, wearing jerseys and white goalie masks right out of "Friday the 13th") would follow a spotlight around until it settled on the occupied (or not) seat. If someone was there, they'd be handed a winning envelope.

Tuesday, November 13, 1990: Penguins 4, North Stars 1, at Met Center

Former Gophers goalie Frank Pietrangelo stopped 42 shots and permitted little excitement among 5,429 fans in the Met's multi-colored seats. Penguins center Barry Pederson didn't figure in any of the goals but nonetheless scored the line of the night. Waiting to take a faceoff with Bobby Smith while spotlights swirled, music blared and two college kids ran around looking like Jason Voorhees, Pederson deadpanned, "Just like the Forum, right Bobby?"

In an interview for this book, the best Nanne could say about Green's ideas is that they were "different."

"Even if I didn't agree with them, it was worthwhile to try anything you can to get things going," Nanne said. "I guess there were some other things that I didn't like, and I told him. He came down and gave me a new idea during the game all the time, and I'd say 'You gotta quit walking the corridors 'cause the last guy you talked to has an idea, you come down here, and wanna bring it to me.' That's the way it was. He'd walk, and anybody who talked to him and gave him an idea he thought was good, he'd come down and say, 'Let's do that.' And I'd say, 'No, we're not doing that.' He wanted to try everything, but you can't try *everything*. You've got to target what you want to do and complete it and give it an opportunity to succeed."

Nanne spent much of his time trying to convince corporations to buy more tickets or arrange advertising deals.

"I was doing the same thing when I was president," he said. "There wasn't much that I wasn't involved in. When I was president, I'd have final say in the budget, whereas at this time Norm would have final say. But other than that, I was doing all of the same things. Norm was more interested in being around the hockey team than he was the operation. I was taking him all around town to try and meet the CEOs of businesses to try and get them to know who he was and get them interested in us. I'd take him to St. Paul Fire and Marine, the Minneapolis *Star Tribune* and Pillsbury. I'd take him to meet people that he didn't know. He was new in town, so, I was just trying to get him involved in the community."

It wasn't an easy introduction.

<u>**Wednesday, November 14, 1990**</u>

Chico Resch

Gainey met with Casey, Hayward, and Takko to discuss the North Stars' goaltending plan. With Casey the obvious No. 1, and Hayward recently brought in via trade, it looked like Takko—who had allowed 12 goals in two losses—would be the odd man out.

Hayward was in the process of transplanting his wife, Angela, and their daughter, Courtney-Marie, to the Twin Cities.

"I looked at the personnel on that roster and thought 'This team should be a lot better,'" Hayward said in an interview for this book. "But what was going on around it was just bizarre. You think you're in a hockey hotbed in Minnesota, but it felt like there was a real animosity toward the team. And I didn't know any of the back story or what had happened. There was a guy giving away cash in the stands and people dancing and all this weird stuff, but I'm a new player trying to make a good impression. I was trying to help the team win, and I was appreciative that Bob Gainey had vouched for me. But there was so much going on behind the scenes; it was a very strange year."

Chico Resch, speaking to reporters, said Hayward was sound technically and solid under pressure.

"He's coming here with a winning feeling," Resch said. "He's a confident, well-balanced guy with a desire to do well and establish himself."

At forty-two, Resch still looks like he could be a competent NHL backup—if not a starter. Originally from Moose Jaw, Saskatchewan, he played at Minnesota-Duluth before joining the Islanders during their second season, in 1973–74. He played a pivotal role in bringing them to prominence. He never had a losing season in New York, and his eight-year record with the Islanders was 157–69–47 (.661).

Resch said the biggest change in his life occurred in 1980, but it wasn't winning the Stanley Cup. It was when he became a Christian. Traded to Colorado at the deadline in '81, prosperity took a nose-dive. He went 18–35–13 for the Rockies, who moved to New Jersey in '82. With the Devils, he was 49–113–20. After another deadline deal in '86, he concluded his career in a reserve role for Philadelphia—going 7-7–2 before he retired in 1987.

Most recently, Resch was the color analyst for North Stars action on KXLI-TV (Channel 41). The station, whose format included reruns of classic TV shows such as "McHale's Navy" and "Gunsmoke," emanated from St. Cloud and was included in a patchwork of cable-access packages. In the North Stars' early years, their games had been on WTCN-Channel 11. From 1980–85, they moved to KMSP-Channel 9. After three years with KITN-Channel 29, the team took an attractive three-year offer to move to KXLI—largely because it was willing to pay $675,000 per year for the rights. After one season, however, ratings sagged to less than 1.0 (percentage of TV households tuned to a program) with a typical share less than 2.0 (percentage of sets in use tuned to a program).

"It was called TV Heaven," Resch recalled of the channel's format. "After two years, it got shot up into TV Heaven because the station folded."

After KXLI went dark in December of 1989, Resch and Doug McLeod finishing calling the rest of the season under a new contract with KMSP. Clarke, who as Flyers GM had recruited Resch to be a

Kevin Evans

part-time goalie coach, negotiated a similar arrangement with him in Minnesota. Resch, who lived in Brainerd with his wife, Diane, and their 17-year-old daughter, Holly, drove down about once a week to mentor the goalies and wouldn't travel on the road during the regular season. For this, he made $12,500.

Gainey also decided to recall Evans after all. He had 10 goals and 12 assists at Kalamazoo but, make no mistake, his reputation was as a fighter. Although he stood just 5–10 and 182 pounds, Evans set a minor-league record with 648 penalty minutes in his first season with the K-Wings in 1986–87.

Thursday, November 15, 1990: Rangers 4, North Stars 2, at Met Center

The good news (sort of): Attendance was 6,677, largest for a weeknight game so far. Perhaps the tartakes grand prize ($28,600, which went unclaimed) was beginning to have an effect.

The bad news: Those fans booed loudly after two periods and started for the exits with four minutes remaining. New York scored twice early in the second and, 27 seconds after Smail made it 2–1 midway through the third, Ray Sheppard scored his second goal and what proved to be the game-winner.

Evans made his NHL debut, wore No. 44, and, of course, registered his first fight. He battled Kris King shortly after the Rangers made it 4–1. Gainey said the North Stars were playing scared and suggested Hayward gave up a crucial soft goal.

Bernie Nicholls, who didn't figure in the scoring but was plus-3 for New York, bought several tickets to try and make a run at tartakes. He wouldn't be the last opponent to do so.

Friday, November 16, 1990

Bob Sansevere led his *Pioneer Press* column with Rupert and Charles. They followed Green everywhere, which was quaint considering dogs weren't allowed in the condominium where he lived in Calgary. Buying the two spaniels, descended from a breed favored as lapdogs by King Charles I of England in the 1600s, was one of the first things Green did when he moved to Minnesota.

Having just recently heard from Joanie Preston about my internship with the North Stars, I made my first visit to the Target Center, attending a Billy Joel concert with a woman from one of my journalism classes. As I listened to Joel perform his hits and songs from his latest album, "Storm Front," Berezan was sent to Kalamazoo. He'd played in four of 14 games since mid-October.

Saturday, November 17, 1990: Blues 3, North Stars 2, at Met Center

Paul Cavallini and Bob Bassen scored a minute and a half apart midway through the first period and St. Louis never trailed. Casey was pulled for the first time this season, allowing three goals on 20 shots. And Churla suffered bruised ribs late in the game.

The big winner was Lenore Mamer, a Burnsville resident and 26-year-old musician and student at the College of St. Thomas. She was among the 7,926 fans and won the $39,900 grand prize out of $49,900 total available in tartakes.

Sunday, November 18, 1990

The North Stars flew to New York for Monday's game against the Rangers. Minnesota, with 12 points, was ahead of only Toronto and Quebec, which both had nine.

Monday, November 19, 1990: North Stars 2, Rangers 2, at Madison Square Garden, New York

Hayward stopped 35 shots, including 21 in the third period, and Propp scored one goal and set up another. Since the game wasn't televised in the Twin Cities, Green naturally watched in person.

Ulf Dahlen's agent has asked that his client be traded somewhere he could play. Dahlen told the *Pioneer Press* he was surprised because he didn't know anything about it. Clarke said he had no intention of trading Dahlen, who has dressed for 11 of 22 games despite a $200,000 salary.

Berezan was recalled from Kalamazoo but only took a holding penalty in the third period. After the game, the stereo in the Minnesota dressing room blared Madonna's "Lucky Star."

Tuesday, November 20, 1990

The North Stars flew to Detroit and practiced in the afternoon at Joe Louis Arena. There they saw the welcome face of Gagner, who flew in from Minnesota and said he might be able to play already—ten days after arthroscopic knee surgery.

"The whole year has been kind of frustrating," Gagner said. "It hasn't been a lot of fun. You don't feel very proud to walk around and be a North Star in Minnesota right now.... I don't think the fans have to sympathize with us. But until we start winning, we're not going to have a lot of pride."

Wednesday, November 21, 1990: Red Wings 4, North Stars 3, at Joe Louis Arena, Detroit

On the night before Thanksgiving, the Red Wings made turkeys of the North Stars, who had three different one-goal leads, only to lose on a third-period goal by Johan Garpenlov and a failed power play of more than three minutes late in the game.

"There are no excuses anymore," fumed Propp, who had two assists. "We just got outworked. We didn't forecheck or take the body... and they just took the puck away from us. We can't allow that to happen. We just can't stand for it. Every player has to get himself prepared. And every player has to understand that he's playing for the guy next to him and for himself. We're not getting a total team effort, and that's what we have to have to win."

Larry Murphy

Garpenlov cut between Murphy and Glynn and scored on a falling shot. Murphy and Glynn each were a minus-3.

"We don't expect our players to get beat two-on-one," Gainey said. "We were moving onto the wrong people and hesitating in our checking."

Murphy was not yet thirty but looks much older, largely because his hair was fading from brown to silver. He grew up in Scarborough, Ontario, where his father worked for Bell Canada. Larry lived and died with the Toronto Maple Leafs, a love for players like Dave Keon and Eddie Shack forever cemented when they won the Cup in 1967. Murphy was six and had just started playing. His father flooded a backyard rink, and ten years later,

Larry jumped to a junior career with the Peterborough Petes. He won a Memorial Cup, and Los Angeles made him the fourth overall pick in 1980. He never played in the minors. In his first 11 seasons, he amassed 629 points. From '80–83, he played all but four games with the Kings before a trade to Washington. The North Stars got him from the Capitals on March 7, 1989, along with Mike Gartner, in exchange for Dino Ciccarelli and Bob Rouse. Murphy was a career plus-50 entering the season. That may not sound bad but, with his prodigious offensive totals, it meant he'd been on the ice for an awful lot of goals against.

About 140 miles west of Detroit, Gaetz grudgingly arrived back in Kalamazoo after he went pheasant hunting in South Dakota. He'd stayed with DePalma for a few days until the North Stars hit the road. And Wilkinson was given an alternate captain's "A" with the K-Wings. That's not a good sign for a quick recall.

Thursday, November 22, 1990

As President Bush spent Thanksgiving with US troops in the Persian Gulf, the North Stars returned to Minneapolis and practiced.

During the workout, Takko was called off the ice. Clarke wanted to see him. Takko showered, dressed and went to Clarke's office to learn he was being sent to Edmonton for defenseman Bruce Bell[33], who had appeared once for the Oilers. Bell would report directly to Kalamazoo and the media playfully referred to it as the Takko-Bell trade, but one of those involved wasn't laughing or in the mood for a run to the border.

"I cried," Takko told me for this book. "It was tough to handle my first trade. Coming from Europe, you are not used to that. Minny felt like home, and I had to leave my family.

"Bob got Glen Sather on the phone, and I flew that night to Edmonton. But when I got there, Esa Tikkanen took me under his wing and, after the first practice, I felt good again. They wanted me. Grant Fuhr was out. I was surprised to see all those superstars were such good human beings, and that's why I figured they had won a championship."

Friday, November 23, 1990: North Stars 6, Canucks 4, at Met Center

Bellows scored a hat trick, and Gagner assisted on four goals, pleasing a crowd of 7,889. Some fans celebrated with a postgame skating party. The win made it worthy of an appearance by Green, who joined his customers on the ice for the first of several chances to do so following Friday or Saturday games during the next four weeks. Fans could bring their skates and circle to music until 11:30 p.m.

By that time, Bellows was long gone, having found better ways to celebrate a three-goal game.

Saturday, November 24, 1990: Devils 5, North Stars 3, at Met Center

Duchesne scored his second goal, Smail got one short-handed, and Gagner netted his tenth on the power play—all in the first period. But the North Stars squandered a 3–1 lead when New Jersey scored four times in the third.

At the last of those, most remaining in the crowd of 8,138, not counting a blonde mannequin wearing a North Stars sweater next to a guy behind the west net, headed for the exits. It was yet another disappointing loss for a team trying to build momentum.

"There was a lot of disruption around the team… players who were on the team but weren't going

33 Bell was one of the Wings' best defensemen the rest of the 1990–91 season. Although he played professionally until '98, he never returned to the NHL.

to remain on the team," Gainey told me for this book. "There were injuries. There were players who had been in Pierre Page's plans and Jack Ferreira's plans that didn't seem to be in our plans. We had a rookie head coach. Some of the warts of the past years of the North Stars surfaced and, like the support we saw opening night, it became apparent we weren't too important. There were a lot of things going on and it didn't click where we looked and acted like a group, a team with a common goal, until December."

But it was going to get a lot worse before it got better.

Sunday, November 25, 1990

Once given up for dead, the Vikings throttled the first-place Chicago Bears 41–13 before 58,866 at the Metrodome to improve to 5–6.

Evans, minus-2 against New Jersey, was returned to Kalamazoo.

Monday, November 26, 1990

The North Stars flew to Vancouver. Basil McRae made the trip to be examined by a west coast doctor who specialized in abdominal injuries.

Tuesday, November 27, 1990: North Stars 1, Canucks 1, at Pacific Coliseum, Vancouver

Mike Modano scored on a power play early in the second, but Gino Odjick tied it with his first NHL goal late in the period and the North Stars couldn't score the rest of the way, despite a five-minute penalty on Trevor Linden for slashing.

Casey stopped 32 shots and left Vancouver coach Bob McCammon lamenting, calling the North Stars "one of those teams that you know you should beat."

The game ended around midnight in the Twin Cities and was the ninth consecutive loss on Channel 9, dating to last season—when they started 0–21–2 on KMSP-TV before a March 12 win at Toronto.

Wednesday, November 28, 1990

McRae returned to Minnesota and was scheduled to undergo surgery on Friday at Fairview Southdale. He would be out indefinitely, leaving him mostly confined to his home in Apple Valley. The rest of the North Stars moved on to Winnipeg, where they were unable to get ice time for practice. They spent the day watching television and playing cards at their hotel. Those who tuned in CBC or CNN heard that the United Nations had authorized the use of force against Iraq if it did not pull out of Kuwait by January 15.

Thursday, November 29, 1990

The North Stars skated at Winnipeg Arena, then went back to their cards and TVs.

Friday, November 30, 1990: North Stars 4, Jets 2, at Winnipeg Arena

Gainey walked into his hotel room at about 3 p.m. and got a message to call home. His youngest daughter, Colleen, who had just turned six, answered. She was crying and related that her mother was "asleep" on the bathroom floor. Bob immediately called a neighbor, who went over to investigate.

Before the bus left for the arena at 5 p.m., Cathy Gainey had regained consciousness, said she felt better, and they thought perhaps she fainted from the flu. Cathy said she was going to see a doctor and Bob left for the game.

Smail opened the scoring early in the second period with a goal in his return to Winnipeg. Chambers and Sinisalo added their first goals, and Gagner made it 4–1 late in the third to crack the KMSP curse.

Casey, who had planned to play out his option at $145,000 this season, agreed in principle before the game to a new deal. It would pay him $325,000 for the rest of this year and called for $350,000 in 1991–92 and an option for 1992–93 at the same salary. He then went out and stopped 32 shots.

Minnesota's other ex-Jet, Peter Taglianetti, was conspicuously scratched. In a role reversal, his wife had just got settled in a new rental home in Edina and he was back in Winnipeg, where they were still trying to sell their house.

Afterward, the North Stars were able to get a late flight back to Minnesota. Clarke met the arrivals and Gainey got a sense something was wrong—especially when he saw the team doctors there, too.

Clarke told him, "Cathy is sick, and it's serious."

Gainey knew almost before he heard anything what that meant. Cathy's father and an older brother had died of brain tumors. After getting the essentials from Clarke and the physicians, he rushed home.

CHAPTER 6

December: Bob Gainey's Burden

Saturday, December 1, 1990: North Stars 6, Penguins 3, at Met Center

Bob and Cathy Gainey explained to their kids what happened with their mother and started to make plans for Cathy to undergo surgery next week. Amazingly, Bob was behind the bench against Pittsburgh—with most people around the team none the wiser.

I certainly wasn't among the informed. This was the first game I attended as an intern. My head was spinning with everything that went on behind the scenes to put on a pro hockey game. But a win was a good start.

Larry Murphy scored on a shot from the right point, and Perry Berezan (!) added his first two goals of the season on back-to-back shifts early in the third period.

"Everything seems to be breaking for us right now," said Jon Casey, who made 19 saves. "I'm confident we will be in the playoffs."

Of course, there were still fifty-two regular-season games to play—two-thirds of the schedule.

The performance was especially important for Berezan, who had just three goals last season and one in sixteen games after a deadline deal brought him to Minnesota in March 1989. He usually centered a checking line but got to play with Neal Broten and Doug Smail against the Penguins. Both linemates figured in Berezan's scoring. His first goal came from the slot, and the second when he and former Gophers goalie Frank Pietrangelo dived for a loose puck. Berezan got there first and shoved it over the goal line.

"Those kind of chances are going in for us now—those garbage goals," Berezan told reporters afterward. "Those are the ones that win hockey games."

In his own mind, however, Berezan was still wracked with self-doubt, demonstrating a mindset often found among role players and those at risk of being waived.

"I *still* didn't feel good," Berezan told me in a 2021 interview. "It was one of those moments where I thought 'If this doesn't feel good, what's wrong with me? Why is this so difficult?' It was because I knew I couldn't find a role. Sure, I'd scored two goals, but they don't need me to score goals. They need me for something else.

"When you're in and out of the lineup, it's exhausting. You're holding on for the next day to be better. When it's good, you're just hoping that something doesn't break it. The longer it's good, you start getting into a groove. You need a coach to give you the benefit of the doubt when you have a hiccup. When you're trying not to make a mistake, that's when you end up doing nothing."

Doug Jarvis

Sunday, December 2, 1990

Gainey again spent the day with his wife and children, and they had visitors. Doug Jarvis' wife, Linda, checked in and would increasingly do so in the coming months. She and Cathy Gainey had become close friends, as were their husbands, during a long tenure in Montreal.

The Jarvises lived in Eden Prairie. Their oldest daughter, Laura, was the same age as the Gaineys' youngest, Colleen, and they also had a 3-year-old son, Landry.[34] It was only a fifteen-minute drive to the Gaineys' home, and the two families saw each other frequently.

That's what happens when you're almost as close as brothers. Doug, whose youth hockey coach was Walter Gretzky (Wayne's father), played with Bob for one season at Peterborough. Then, in 1975–76, they became linemates in Montreal for the first of seven straight seasons. Doug became best known for playing in 964 consecutive games—an NHL record that stood for more than thirty years. He retired with 139 goals and 264 assists. He never had more than 48 points in a season but was imminently responsible defensively, going plus-121 in his career.

For all the people Gainey knew, perhaps none had his back more than Doug Jarvis.

While much of Minnesota was glued to the evening's telecast of the Vikings beating the Packers 23–7, all games—football, hockey, anything—suddenly might've seemed irrelevant to viewers or the 62,058 people at the Metrodome if they'd known about Cathy Gainey.

Monday, December 3, 1990

Bobby Clarke left early in the morning from his home at 6020 Pine Grove Road in Edina. Constructed to look like a Swiss chalet, it's large but unpretentious and guarded by trees about four lots west of Mirror Lake.

The Gaineys' house was just three miles away. Clarke's wife, Sandy, would pitch in with what support she can provide, and her husband was reflective as he drove to Met Center. What could he say? What tone could he set? Their children included Wade (19), Jody (16), Jakki (13), and Lucas (10). Jakki and Lucas were virtually the same age as the Gaineys' oldest children, Anna and Steve.

Andy Murray

Clarke addressed the team before practice, informing the players and staff about Cathy's condition and how it might impact their head coach. Jarvis and Andy Murray ran the workout. In their late 30s, each about 5-foot-9 with rusty hair and freckles, they *looked* like brothers—especially since both had a serious demeanor by default.

The players met afterward, and Clarke informed the media as discreetly as possible, relating that Cathy had suffered a seizure on Friday and underwent tests during the weekend. She was expected to have surgery Wednesday.

34 Jarvis named his son in honor of Dallas Cowboys coach Tom Landry, who had winning records every year from 1966-85, won two Super Bowls and made 10 NFC Championship appearances in a 13-year span from 1970-83. From 1986-88, however, he went 17-30 and was fired by Jerry Jones the day he bought the team in 1990. Later that year, Landry was inducted into the Pro Football Hall of Fame.

"We're shocked," Bobby Smith said.

He'd sat beside Gainey for six years in the Montreal dressing room. Their wives had become friends and, in April 1985, they'd even been pregnant at the same time—Beth with her first child and Cathy with her fourth.

Bobby Smith

"Everyone is very concerned, and we're hoping for good news over the next few days," Smith added.

He knew it didn't always work that way. Smith's mother, Jeanne, died on April 22, 1981, after a long battle with cancer. The North Stars were in the playoffs then—still sky high after their first-round win over Boston and winning the first three games against Buffalo in the quarterfinals. But they were sobered by an overtime loss in Game 4 at the Met. The Sabres had life going home for Game 5 and Smith's father, Gerald, planned to wait until after the game to tell Bobby of his mother's death. But one of Bobby's uncles unwittingly called the hotel and revealed the news. Bobby instinctively headed for the airport, en route to his family in Ottawa, but his father called Lou Nanne, who reached Bobby as he was changing planes in Toronto. Nanne passed on the message from Gerald, that Jeanne had wanted her son to play in the game. So, Bobby flew back to Buffalo, skated in a series-clinching 4–3 victory and went plus-1 with a team-best four shots. Afterward, he took Gordon Gund's offer to use his private plane to get to the funeral. Bobby was back in the lineup when the North Stars opened the semifinals six days later in Calgary.

He hoped the Gainey children would never experience the pain he felt that week.

Andy Murray and Doug Jarvis were featured on the cover of a North Stars program on March 24, 1992.

Tuesday, December 4, 1990

The North Stars traveled to Toronto. Gainey did not go. Team Services Director Doug Armstrong would be in the press box and connected via radio to Jarvis and Murray, who would run the bench. It was a great opportunity for Armstrong, who'd just joined the North Stars after working in his first hockey job last season on the Washington Capitals' marketing staff. Marketing was his major at Florida State University, where he graduated after an abortive two years at Western Michigan.

Jarvis or Murray usually watched at least part of each game from upstairs to provide a different perspective. The best way the players could change their own view was to win.

"As an athlete, the best thing you can do is to try and keep things on an even keel," Curt Giles said. "You don't want the highs to

Curt Giles

be too high or the lows to be too low. It's awful hard to do that with the situation we're in now. All we can do is hope for the best and let the family know our thoughts are with them. And for Bob, the best thing we can do is keep playing well and winning games."

Giles knew the benefit of victories, even when they didn't arrive on your schedule. In the late summer of 1975, his father, Jack, made the 13-hour drive from The Pas with Curt to drop him off at the Minnesota-Duluth campus. They never saw each other again. Jack, who drove a truck, was killed in an accident that November, just before Curt turned seventeen. To persevere, Curt found the purpose and support he needed with the Bulldogs, who had some older players already married and with children. After posting a 40–63–4 record during his first three seasons, as a senior he led UMD to its first No. 1 ranking and a third-place finish in the WCHA—best to that point in school history. He could only hope now that it wouldn't take as long for the North Stars to provide Gainey some pleasant distraction.

"You can eliminate a certain percentage of what's going on outside the rink, but anyone who tells you they can block it all out—don't believe it," said Giles, who had two children (Michael, 8; and Ashley, 6) with his wife, Mary-Pat. "We're one big family. We have jobs to go to that can help take our minds off of things, but we have the same feelings or reactions as any other person. This is a very tough situation for all of us."

It wouldn't be any easier if Toronto, which had the worst record in the NHL, continued to improve. The Maple Leafs—who started 0–10 on the road—were coming off victories at St. Louis and Los Angeles.

"The bottom line is we have a lot of things on our minds now, but we'll have a hell of a lot of things on our minds if we lose," said Dave Gagner, barely a month removed from the death of his dad. "It's something we can do something about. If we can win some games, we can make Bob's life a little happier for a while."

Wednesday, December 5, 1990: North Stars 3, Maple Leafs 2, at Maple Leaf Gardens, Toronto

Elaine Waddell informed reporters that Cathy Gainey had morning surgery at Abbott-Northwestern Hospital. By afternoon, she was speaking, moving, and recognizing visitors. Waddell said doctors removed as much of the tumor as they could, and a biopsy would inform treatment. Bob Gainey was with his wife and would catch the game on KMSP-TV.

Shawn Chambers

Toronto took a 1–0 lead and later tied it 2–2, both on power-play goals. Now wearing the alternate captain's "A" because Basil McRae was out, Mark Tinordi scored his first goal of the season on a shot from the left point late in the third period, keeping the North Stars' unbeaten streak alive at four games.

But it wasn't all good. Shawn Chambers suffered a temporary dislocation of his left knee—the same one on which he had arthroscopic surgery September 21.

Chambers grew up with three sisters and was a close friend of Washington Capitals defenseman Kevin Hatcher, older brother of

Derian Hatcher—the North Stars' top pick in the latest draft. They lived five houses apart in Sterling Heights, Michigan, and were all Red Wings fans. Chambers was recruited sight-unseen at Alaska-Fairbanks and eventually migrated to Seattle of the WHL before signing with Fort Wayne of the IHL. Selected by the North Stars in the 1987 supplemental draft, early in his career he struggled to keep his weight under control. Some teammates even called him "Baby Huey,"[35] though that nickname eventually gave way to "Bundy," after Al Bundy from the TV show "Married... With Children."

Chambers drove a blue IROC-Z Camaro that he bought with his first bonus, and owned a house in Eagan, near Highway 77 and Johnny Cake Ridge Road. He played softball during the summer with Mark Baribeau. But after playing 78 games for the North Stars last season, Chambers had to wonder if that would ever be possible again.

Thursday, December 6, 1990: Maple Leafs 2, North Stars 1, OT, at Met Center

Charley Walters' column in the *Pioneer Press* reported, without naming names, that Chuck Grillo was at the heart of accusations by the North Stars that the Sharks had tampered with players under contract to Minnesota. Grillo, a 51–year-old Hibbing native who served in the Marines, was a former North Stars scout who followed Jack Ferreira to San Jose. Grillo, who was the Minnesota State High School League hockey coach of the year in 1973, also ran Minnesota Hockey Camps in Brainerd.

Let's Play Hockey later named Grillo and reported the North Stars' Rob Zettler, Neil Wilkinson, Pat MacLeod, Mario Thyer, Clark Donatelli, J.F. Quintin, and Pete Lappin all skated during the summer at MHC. MacLeod, Thyer, Donatelli, Quintin, and Lappin had all played at Kalamazoo, and all but Quintin had appeared in at least one game for the North Stars in previous seasons. *Star Tribune* columnist Sid Hartman wrote that Norm Green confirmed the allegations, added Ferreira and Dean Lombardi to the list of those implied to have tampered with the prospects, and said that George Gund admitted he may have to make concessions on the player disbursement deal to avoid a court challenge.

Gainey missed the game to remain with his wife as she recuperated. There was no local TV, but perhaps it was just as well, as Rob Ramage snapped the North Stars' modest unbeaten streak 2:57 into overtime.

Peter Taglianetti, who had played 15 games and remained the only player on the roster without a point, skated for the first time after being a healthy scratch in eleven straight. It probably hadn't helped that he recently clashed with Clarke about moving expenses. NHL teams are only bound to pay them if a trade occurs during the season. Taglianetti arrived two days before the season opener, so Clarke refused.

Peter Taglianetti

"You remember talking to him? How he always used to click his teeth (with his tongue)?" Taglianetti asked me in a 2021 interview before doing an imitation. "He just kept making that sound across his desk and said, 'No, we're not paying for it.' It was a dink move, but I said, 'Aw, fuck it.'"

In downtown Minneapolis, on the first night the North Stars and Timberwolves played head-to-head home games, the Timberwolves

35 The nickname was a not-very-nice dig at Chambers' weight. Baby Huey was a Paramount cartoon introduced in 1950, depicting a gigantic and naïve duckling. Baby Huey also was the stage name of a 1960s Chicago soul singer, James Ramey, who weighed about 350 pounds because of a glandular disorder. Chambers was 6-foot-2 and weighed 200 pounds in 1990, though that weight ebbed and flowed depending on how much he played and whether he was committed to staying in his best shape. The "Bundy" reference treaded on a likeness in character to that which actor Ed O'Neill portrayed on the popular sitcom from 1987-97.

Warren Babe

drew the typical Target Center sellout (19,006) to see an 83–73 loss to the Los Angeles Lakers.

There were 6,345 at Met Center.

Friday, December 7, 1990

Warren Babe and Wilkinson were recalled from Kalamazoo to fill spots vacated by McRae and Chambers. Babe, twenty-two, said it was a big surprise. He had appeared in 20 NHL games but none since April 2, 1989. Chronic concussions (ten in two seasons) forced him to miss all of '89–90.

"It was pretty discouraging last year," said Babe, who took college classes in Alberta, lifted weights, and played basketball. "What I really missed was the competition. It got to the point where playing cards with my wife (Paige) was a big deal."

Saturday, December 8, 1990: North Stars 7, Flyers 0, at Met Center

A tartakes grand prize of more than $30,000 in cash perhaps partially precipitated a crowd of 6,711 just a few hours after a Gophers matinee against Wisconsin drew 7,514 at ancient and quirky Mariucci Arena. About thirty Philadelphia players and coaches, including former North Stars Paul Holmgren and Craig Hartsburg, bought tickets at the Met in an effort to cash in.

Mike Modano struck it big, on the ice that is. He assisted on the first goal by Tinordi and later set up Brian Glynn before adding a power-play goal in the third period of a rare blowout for the NHL's second-lowest scoring team.

Brian Hayward, whose wife and daughter just moved to a house he rented in Apple Valley, earned a 22-save shutout.

The North Stars were 4-1–1 in six games and haven't lost in regulation since November 24 against New Jersey.

"Other teams start with the same coach and lines in September as they had the previous April and May," said Smith, who scored the seventh goal with 1:03 remaining. "We started with a lot of uncertainty—new coaches and new faces from the general manager all through. I think we are a lot more used to each other now, a lot more comfortable and are playing a lot better hockey.... There are still 50 games to go, and anything can happen."

As for tartakes, no one claimed the grand prize. It would roll over to Tuesday's game against Calgary with $42,300 on the line.

Gainey returned to the bench after missing two games, and there was no putting a value on that—or how friends had provided meals since Cathy underwent surgery.

"We had the occasional message that things were getting better," Gainey told me for this book. "I remember the game against the Flyers... we beat them soundly. Other games, we would stumble. But we showed the occasional flash of acting and performing as a group. And some of our moves had really good impact. For instance, it seemed like a minor thing, but we sent Don Barber to Winnipeg for Dougie Smail. Don Barber looked like a player. He was big. He was strong. We gave him time. The people before us had given him time. But there wasn't production. Dougie Smail bounces in, and he's got incredible energy and experience, and he's productive.

"We'd got Shawn Chambers back. That was a huge difference because Shawn is a very subtle and underrated workhorse. He could take thirty minutes of shitty defensive ice and turn it into productive ice. We traded for Brian Hayward, who gave us a goalie. Kari Takko had been there, and he hadn't won a game. I don't think anybody thought there was a possibility with him in the game that we would win. These are real tangible changes that don't show up on the radar, but they start to shape your team so it can function. You take out dysfunction and put in function, and then the guys who function are able to do it better."

Sunday, December 9, 1990

A US-chartered Iraqi Airways jet landed in Frankfurt, Germany, with 175 Americans who had either been prisoners or hiding in Iraq. It remained to be seen whether the gesture of letting US citizens leave the country would be a step in avoiding war over the insurgence in Kuwait.

Monday, December 10, 1990

Chambers underwent reconstructive knee surgery at Fairview Ridges. He won't return until March.

Tuesday, December 11, 1990: Flames 5, North Stars 4, at Met Center

The North Stars arrived at the rink to find two new teammates, defensemen Chris Dahlquist and Jim Johnson, just arrived from Pittsburgh in a trade for Murphy and Taglianetti. Johnson was twenty-eight and Dahlquist would turn twenty-eight in three days. Both were 6-foot-1 and originally signed as free agents in 1985 following their college careers.

Clarke said the team needed to be more physical at the blue line, and Murphy's offensive skills weren't as valuable to the North Stars as the defensive abilities of Dahlquist and Johnson.

Murphy[36] hugged his wife, Nancy, and their 2-year-old daughter, Madison, and caught a flight to Chicago where the Penguins were playing the Blackhawks. So did Taglianetti, who had one assist in 16 games and had played in just three of the last 17.

Johnson, who played at Robbinsdale Cooper High School and was a college teammate of Brett Hull at Minnesota-Duluth, was one of two college players (Gary Suter being the other) on the US roster for the 1985 World Championships in Czechoslovakia. The experience translated to thirteen NHL offers. Johnson chose Pittsburgh and played all 80 games in each of his first two seasons. He bought a home and even worked in sales and marketing for Orbital Engineering during the offseason because he wasn't too sure how "this hockey thing" was going to pan out. Through 390 career regular-season games, he has 14 goals, 95 assists and 658 penalty minutes. That's why his contract calls for $225,000 and he's not too worried about a life after hockey just yet.

Chris Dahlquist

Jim Johnson

Dahlquist, whose family moved from Fridley to California when he was five and later relocated to Pennsylvania, played at Lake Superior State. He made his NHL debut on December 31, 1985, setting up the first of Mario Lemieux's four goals in

36 Murphy, who made $270,000 for the 1990-91 season, totaled 18 goals and 75 assists for 93 points in 121 career games with Minnesota.

an 8–4 win over St. Louis. Lemieux also had three assists in that game, and it would take Dahlquist 53 more appearances over three seasons to amass as many points as Lemieux did in one night.

Only in '87–88 had Dahlquist avoided spending at least part of a season in the minors. He has 10 goals and 26 assists in 197 career regular-season and playoff games.

He and his wife, Jeanie, were renting a house in the Mount Washington section of Pittsburgh, right across the Monangahela River from Civic Arena, otherwise known as The Igloo. As fate would have it, on Monday night he'd made a down payment on property where they planned to build a home in the North Hills area. Hours later, he learned of his trade via a call from Penguins coach Bob Johnson.

Clarke called his new players and said he'd reserved a spot on a 2 p.m. flight so they could play tonight.

"I'm like, 'What? You've got to be kidding,'" Jim Johnson recalled for this book. "I hung up the phone, and I was scrambling—like, how long am I packing for? What am I packing? What about my sticks? My skates? My equipment? How's this all going to happen? I've got about an hour and a half to get to the airport."

Clarke's calls to Murphy and Taglianetti were comparatively much shorter.

"It was about 12:30, and I was eating my pregame meal," Taglianetti recounted. "The phone rings, and it's Bobby Clarke. His exact words: 'Peter, we traded you to Pittsburgh. (Penguins GM) Craig (Patrick) is going to call you.' *Click*.

"I'm trying to call my agent, going, 'What the fuck?' Then the phone rings, and it's Craig Patrick and he's like, 'Hey, Pete, can't wait for you to get here. The problem is, you've got two hours to get on a plane, and you play tonight. Minnesota's going to meet you and Larry with your equipment.' I threw everything I could in two duffel bags and took off."

Johnson and Dahlquist got their bags and sticks at the curb near the terminal at Pittsburgh International Airport, then lugged them at a trot out of MSP when their plane landed. Armstrong picked up the players and delivered them to Met Center just before 6 p.m. The equipment staff fitted them for new gloves, breezers, and helmets, and, by the time they were dressed, only about ten minutes remained in warmups. By then, Murphy and Taglianetti both were skating in the Penguins' 4–1 loss to Chicago at Civic Arena.

Dahlquist and Johnson, introduced to the other North Stars' defensemen twenty minutes before the opening faceoff, were in the lineup before 6,581 fans (not counting the mannequin again). They made an inordinate amount of noise thanks to a three-goal third-period comeback that came up just short.

Calgary led 5–1 before a minute was gone in the third, but Modano, Broten, and Gagner scored in a seven-minute span to make it a one-goal game with more than five minutes to go.

Pat MacLeod

"The team and the crowd feed off each other," said Smith, who'd played before crowds that averaged 107 percent capacity in Montreal. "We really started taking advantage of the scoring chances and the crowd responded."

Wednesday, December 12, 1990

As Mike Craig joined the Canadian national junior team, Babe and Larry DePalma were sent to Kalamazoo—the former never to return. In exchange, the North Stars arranged for rookie defenseman Pat MacLeod to meet them Thursday in St. Louis.

Thursday, December 13, 1990: Blues 4, North Stars 2, at St. Louis Arena

MacLeod was born in Melfort, Saskatchewan, about twenty miles up the Can-Am Highway from his hometown of Kinistino (population 700). When he was five, his parents moved to Fort Saskatchewan, Alberta, near Edmonton. There he developed as an offensive defenseman. After two seasons with Kelowna of the WHL, the North Stars made him a fifth-round pick in 1989. He responded with 47 points in 82 games in the 'Zoo, routinely playing with Dean Kolstad or Link Gaetz. That gave him space but also a chip on his shoulder after they were taken to Russia and he was not.

"For me, not getting to go to Russia was kind of a slap in the face," MacLeod told me. "I'd had a great first year pro, and I thought maybe I'd get an opportunity. So I thought, 'I'll go to Kalamazoo and make the most of it and bust my butt and try to show them they made a mistake.'"

So, he felt a small sense of satisfaction as he arrived at St. Louis Arena, shouldering his equipment and what clothes he'd packed, about two hours before game time. Before he could even drop his gear, Murray grabbed MacLeod by the elbow and walked him over to a whiteboard. Murray sketched a diagram and told him "You're running the power play. You'll be here. You'll be the quarterback… this is the breakout we're doing, and it's all going to run through you."

With a man advantage on his first NHL shift, MacLeod was at the right point. He faked a shot and fed Ilkka Sinisalo, who'd curled in the left circle to come down the slot. Sinisalo scored, and MacLeod had his first NHL point just 3:16 into the game.

He played almost exclusively on the power play. Afterward, Murray told MacLeod he'd be going back to Kalamazoo.

Friday, December 14, 1990

An ad on page 5C of the *Star Tribune* sports section touted Saturday's 1:35 p.m. matinee against Chicago at Met Center, featuring the words "Open season on Hawks" with the Blackhawks' Indian head logo in the crosshairs of a scope. It didn't take long for our phones to start ringing with indignant callers. They sounded a lot like Lisa Bellanger, an administrator at Heart of the Earth School in Minneapolis.

"It's just terrible," she said. "It's just another sign of how uneducated people are about stereotyping and what it does. Open season on an Indian? The fun is at our expense."

Waddell took the heat, perhaps rightfully since she had to approve the ad.

"It wasn't meant to offend anyone," she said. "It was done in the spirit of the rivalry. It was the Blackhawks' logo. Of course we didn't mean it to reflect Native Americans… you will never see that again."

Saturday, December 15, 1990: North Stars 5, Blackhawks 1, at Met Center

It's hard to imagine how the 9,438 fans at the Met Center (the first matinee and largest home attendance so far) could feel like they got more for their money. Especially Scott Peterson, a 23-year-old machinist from Continental Machine in Savage, who sat in the upper level, saw the North Stars stomp Chicago, and also won the largest tartakes prize to date: $53,700. It was his first North Stars game.

Dan Stuchal had been to dozens. But this was his first as my fellow PR intern, and he got the honor of writing the postgame tartakes press release.

The Blackhawks didn't get a shot until thirteen minutes were gone. By then, Glynn had given Minnesota a 1–0 lead, and soon after, Smith scored what proved to be the game-winner on the power play.

Johnson endeared himself to fans and teammates when he blasted Jeremy Roenick, who was cutting through the neutral zone with his head down just before the first intermission. Roenick went head over heels and crashed to the ice. He was helped to the bench, collapsed momentarily, and had to be led up the steps to the dressing room. Trainers asked him if he knew he was in a hockey game. He couldn't answer at first and didn't return until the third period. Johnson was called for charging, though he maintained afterward that it was a clean hit. Gainey called it a "great bodycheck."

Sunday, December 16, 1990: Blackhawks 5, North Stars 2, at Chicago Stadium

Despite having suffered a concussion the day before, and playing against the advice of team doctors, Roenick scored his third career hat trick to get revenge on Johnson and the North Stars.

Johnson was booed every time he touched the puck by a sellout crowd of 18,059. A banner strung across the facing of the second deck had Johnson's number next to the words "You're cheap."

Giles was clipped by Greg Gilbert's skate and cut for seven stitches in the second period but returned in the third. No one questions Giles' toughness. He once had a tumor in his left ring finger and had a portion of it amputated on March 24, 1987, so he would be available for the playoffs. He appeared in five of six games in the Rangers' first-round loss to Philadelphia and was the only New York defenseman with a positive plus-minus rating.

Monday, December 17, 1990

The North Stars recalled Steve Gotaas, Kolstad, MacLeod, Mike McHugh, and Mitch Messier for Tuesday's exhibition against Soviet Khimik. Minnesota was 1–8 all-time against Russian teams, the only win coming September 17 against Khimik—the night Gagner was slashed in the face.

Gotaas, twenty-three, had close-set eyes, resulting in the nickname "Mouse." He won the Memorial Cup with Prince Albert in 1985 and was nineteen in '86–87 when one of his teammates was 16-year-old Mike Modano. That season, Gotaas was second in team scoring with 108 points. Modano had 62. Gotaas' last appearance with the North Stars was in the '89 playoffs, when he had one assist in three games. He and MacLeod shared an apartment convenient to the campus at Western Michigan, where the K-Wings occasionally practiced.

Kolstad was coming off surgery at the end of October to repair a torn stomach muscle originally injured in Russia.

Messier, twenty-five and a second cousin to Edmonton captain Mark Messier, led Kalamazoo in scoring with 16 goals and 34 points.

Steve Gotaas

Dean Kolstad

Mitch Messier

Mike McHugh

McHugh, also twenty-five, was known as "Huggy," like the character from "Starsky and Hutch." Selected by the North Stars first overall in the 1988 supplemental draft after a standout college career at Maine, he played three games for Minnesota without a point in each of the '88–89 and '89–90 seasons. His wife, Cindy, helped him maintain a four-unit rental property in Portage, Michigan, just south of Kalamazoo. They lived in one apartment and rented the other three, including one to the Kolstads.

Playing for a centrally located team in the "I," as the players call it, many of the trips were by bus. Pregame meals were at places like Sizzler or somewhere they could grab a bag of hamburgers. The NHL, with its accommodations for nutrition and fitness, felt like a different world. The Marriott, where the players were staying and McHugh found to his delight, has *tablecloths*. You don't get that kind of treatment at minor-league buffets.

Tuesday, December 18, 1990: North Stars 6, Soviet Khimik 4, at Met Center

A crowd of 4,250 showed up and heard Jim Bowers sing the US *and* Soviet anthems (the latter in Russian). The fans then saw why the North Stars drafted Messier in the third round seven years earlier. He netted two goals and scored in an exhibition shootout.

Wednesday, December 19, 1990

While Dahlquist and Johnson caught a flight to Pittsburgh immediately after Tuesday's exhibition, the rest of the North Stars had a light skate and followed in advance of Thursday's game at Civic Arena. There, Lemieux was cleared to begin stretching exercises but remained at least a month away from being able to play. Pittsburgh was in fifth place in the Patrick Division, which wouldn't mean the playoffs if the season ended today. However, even without Lemieux, the Penguins had the best offense in the NHL with 146 goals through 35 games. Without Lemieux in 1989–90, Pittsburgh was 5–13–4. So far this season, the Penguins were 16–16–3.

Thursday, December 20, 1990: Penguins 4, North Stars 3, at Civic Arena, Pittsburgh

The first blast of winter hit the Twin Cities, leaving residents seeking shelter from temperatures hovering in the single digits and wind chills below zero. Some tuned in KMSP-TV to see the North Stars jump to a 2–0 lead, trail 3–2, tie it, and then fall on a goal by Mark Recchi in the game's final minute.

Dahlen and Broten each had a goal and an assist.

Friday, December 21, 1990

The North Stars moved on to Boston and checked into the Cambridge Hyatt. Had Green or Clarke known the hotel was owned by the Gund brothers, they might've stayed anywhere else—even the Red Roof Inn or Motel 6.

Al Shaver, Gary Olson, and their entourage dined at Anthony's Pier 4. It was an old haunt of the Kennedy family and home to the best seafood Shaver ever ate.

In the Twin Cities, slippery roads and wind-whipped snow on the year's shortest day complicated the final rush hour before Christmas. It was rougher for Cathy Gainey, who underwent her fifth day of radiation therapy. Her treatments would continue until February.

Saturday, December 22, 1990: Bruins 6, North Stars 2, at Boston Garden

Soon after many Minnesotans watched the Vikings' playoff hopes die in a 28–24 loss to the Raiders in front of 53,899 at the Metrodome, some at home flipped the dial to Channel 9 in time to further their misery.

The Bruins raced to a 5–0 lead before the game was half over.

"This was the first one in a long time where we didn't have the effort," Gainey said.

The North Stars had no punch until Modano and Brian Bellows scored in the final five minutes—after it was 6–0.

While Hayward lost his third straight game and Casey's save percentage in his last five appearances had dipped to .858, Takko was 4–0 with a 2.48 goals-against average for Edmonton.

Sunday, December 23, 1990: North Stars 5, Whalers 2, at Civic Arena, Hartford

The North Stars scored three goals in the final six minutes to ensure a little cheer for the Christmas break. Modano netted the game-winner on a power play at 14:04 of the third period, and Gagner completed his third career hat trick three and a half minutes later.

"It was going to be a long flight home if we didn't get some points," Gagner said.

Smith suffered a broken foot when he was hit with a shot and was expected to miss 3-4 weeks.

Monday, December 24, 1990

Johnson flew to Pittsburgh, where he'd spend the night with his wife, Jody, and their infant son, Derik.

"I didn't ask for a trade, but down the road, I know I'll look at this as the best thing that ever happened in my career," Johnson said.

The rest of the North Stars flew back to MSP. During the flight, the players exchanged gag Christmas gifts and arrived just in time for Chris and Jeanie Dahlquist to spend the holiday in Fridley for the first time in seven years. It was an occasion all the happier because they got back the down payment they'd put on the property in Pittsburgh.

To help spread the spirit of the season, Dahlen got dressed up as Santa Claus. He left his West Bloomington townhome, climbed into his Volvo, and drove to Sinisalo's house.

Four-year-old Tomas Sinisalo answered the doorbell. His parents excitedly questioned him as to who was standing in the hallway in a red suit and hat with a flowing white beard.

The boy turned, unimpressed, and left the door open saying, "Oh, it's only Ulf."

Ilkka Sinisalo

Tuesday, December 25, 1990

Messier, recalled to take Smith's spot, got the pleasure of traveling and staying at the Bloomington Marriott on Christmas. The *Pioneer Press*, available in the hotel lobby, contained Gary Olson's story detailing for the first time Wilkinson's struggles with alcoholism.

In some ways, it was a victory Wilkinson was still alive. He had a strained relationship with his father, and Neil's mother, Muriel, died of cancer in 1984. He gave her morphine injections during her final months, and, at sixteen, began drinking hard. That didn't stop him from excelling on the ice with his hometown Manitoba Junior Hockey League team, the Selkirk Steelers, and he was the North Stars' second-round pick in '86.

Wilkinson went to Michigan State but didn't care for college, or Spartans coach Ron Mason. Next stop was Medicine Hat of the WHL, where Wilkinson was tutored briefly by Barry Melrose before coming to Kalamazoo in the fall of '88. That was when alcoholism nearly ended Wilkinson's career. After practice, he'd join his teammates for lunch at a bowling alley across the parking lot from Wings Stadium. They'd bowl a little and drink some beer. Then he'd go home, nap and get up feeling lousy. He'd have a couple more beers to feel better. If there was no game that night, he'd switch to vodka Coke with a squeeze of lime.

"I was a quiet drunk," Wilkinson later told the *Chicago Tribune*. "I never dropped anybody with a punch. No one knew. I didn't hide, but I wasn't seen, either… It shouldn't have been hard to figure out that if I stopped drinking all night, I would feel healthier and prepared to play the game. It was stupidity on my part."

The North Stars assigned him a mentor in Bill Goldsworthy, who once had his own legendary battles with the bottle. To Wilkinson, the Minnesota hockey legend became like an uncle and best friend.

"Goldy didn't ask me if I wanted to play hockey," Wilkinson said. "He asked me if I wanted to live or if I wanted to die. That scared me. I was too young to die."

He said his November demotion may have been as much about testing his sobriety as improving his game. As a coveted prospect in the Minnesota/San Jose tug-of-war, Wilkinson's future was further complicated by Goldsworthy's status as a Sharks scout, especially since he lived in the basement of Goldsworthy's home, just off Highway 7 in Minnetonka.

Wednesday, December 26, 1990: Jets 6, North Stars 4, at Met Center

Bobby and Beth Smith drove an hour from their Eden Prairie home to Red Wing, where the local footwear specialists fitted him with a special skate boot that might allow his return sooner rather than later.

For the ninth consecutive year, Winnipeg played Minnesota on the day after Christmas (Boxing Day in Canada). Paul MacDermid scored with a shot off the post behind Casey 1:15 into the game. The North Stars took a 2–1 lead late in the first period after Broten beat Jets goalie Bob Essensa. But Winnipeg potted the next four goals.

Thursday, December 27, 1990

Craig scored the tying goal as Team Canada rallied to a 4–4 tie against the United States at Saskatoon, where Clarke was scouting the World Junior Championship. It was the second game for the Canadians, who got a goal and four assists from Eric Lindros in a 6–0 win over Switzerland on Wednesday.

Friday, December 28, 1990

While Green was the guest of Timberwolves president Bob Stein for a game against the Detroit Pistons at the Target Center, the North Stars needed a day off. They had twenty healthy players.

That meant Berezan would play Saturday against Boston. After sitting out 15 of the first 25 games, he has four goals in December. The last time he scored more in a *season* was 1987–88 with Calgary, when he had a career-best seven.

Berezan was credited with one of the most famous goals in the Battle of Alberta, Calgary's rivalry with Edmonton. During Game 7 of the '86 Campbell Conference Finals, he dumped the puck into the Oilers' zone and was sitting on the bench moments later when Edmonton defenseman Steve Smith banked a pass off Grant Fuhr and into his own net. Berezan, the last of the Flames to touch the puck, was credited with the goal that eliminated the two-time defending champions before a bewildered crowd at Northlands Coliseum.

Then his luck began to change. Berezan played in less than half of the games the next two seasons and came to the North Stars with Shane Churla as part of a deal for Brian MacLellan in '89.

"When I got with the North Stars, I realized not everyone was like the Flames," Berezan said. "That team (in Minnesota) was a bunch of misfits, selfish players."

Less than three months following his trade to Minnesota, Calgary won the Stanley Cup.

Heading into the game against the Bruins, the only team between Berezan, the North Stars and the basement of the Campbell Conference was Toronto, four points back.

Saturday, December 29, 1990: Bruins 4, North Stars 4, at Met Center

With less than three weeks before a UN sanction was to expire and give the US the right to attack Iraq if it doesn't withdraw from Kuwait, the North Stars debuted American flag stickers on their helmets. They joined the Los Angeles Kings as the first teams to do so. With a promotion providing free life-sized posters of Modano to everyone under eighteen, the game drew a crowd of 11,639. It was the first time the North Stars had drawn more than 10,000 at home since Game 6 of the 1990 playoffs.

As an intern, one of my jobs—thrilling and nerve-wracking at the same time—was to grab the three stars after they exited the ice following a game. For more than 50 years, the NHL had honored the three best players as chosen by an impartial observer, usually a member of the local media. After a game ends, the three stars return to the ice for an announcement of their performance.

If a game was lopsided, most of those honored would be from the winning team and usually wouldn't be opposed to taking a postgame pivot. If the score was close, it was often a two-person job. One intern would wait just off the bench for the home team and the other would wait in the visitors' runway. Picture twenty large hockey players clomping past you after a game. You literally had to grab them by the sleeve and inform them they were one of the three stars. If their team won, especially the North Stars, it was no problem to get them to wave to the fans. Otherwise, it depended on whether a player had a good enough game and felt agreeable to get both sides to participate.

There was just one problem. The three stars were picked late in the third period. The interns had to be dispatched from the press box to run downstairs and get in position before the final horn. If the game turned in the closing minutes or was decided in overtime, we often had to discern hand signals from high across the arena or go with our best guess to change selections—even if sometimes we hadn't seen the key action.

Imagine my plight then when it looked like the Bruins were going to cruise to victory. With five minutes to go, Cam Neely had just scored twice, Ray Bourque had three assists, and Andy Moog had allowed two goals on 30 shots. Easy. Those are your three stars, in order.

Only, while I jogged down in my suit, credentials waving, Dahlen and Gagner scored twenty seconds apart, and Casey held on for the tie.

Uh oh. Dahlen, with two goals and an assist, clearly had to be one of the stars, and Neely was another. I don't recall the third. We got word to Dahlen, and I had to try to grab Neely, who was not happy, to put it mildly. Since the North Stars lost in Boston a week earlier, the Bruins had blown a three-goal lead in the final nine minutes of a 5–5 tie with the Rangers, botched a one-goal lead with 1:20 left at Buffalo, and were thumped 6–0 at Winnipeg the night before.

I can still see the whites of Glen Wesley's eyes, blood-burst from a recent fight, as he exited the bench. The rest of the Bruins looked equally irate. Even backup goalie Reggie Lemelin looked like he wanted to steer clear of his teammates. As they marched past me on the steps, about two-thirds of the way through the line steamed Neely, who was 6-foot-1 and 218 pounds *before* he put on his skates and equipment. His mood was black as his jersey and, after I stammered something about him being one of the three stars, he broke his stick against the concrete, dropped what was left and stomped up to the dressing room.

Halfway through the season, the North Stars were 11–22–7.

"By December we had started to create this new platform we were going to work from," Gainey told me for this book. "There were a number of player movements that happened in those first three months. We were in transition. I was trying to understand the players. The players were trying to understand the coaches. And with all the movement, it just wasn't happening. On my personal side, once Cathy was diagnosed, my dynamics really changed and our neighbors, who we barely knew, were all very helpful. We found a way to deal with it, and, probably by January, the worst of it was over. We'd settled into a new family routine. The kids were in school, and we had help at home, and it became a little more normal. We had a lot of support, and we wouldn't have survived without it."

Sunday, December 30, 1990

Wayne Gretzky and the visiting Los Angeles Kings practiced at Met Center, about the same time Craig had two goals and two assists to lead Canada past Sweden 7–4 at the World Junior Championship.

Few Minnesotans knew or cared as they watched the Vikings' season end with a whimper, 20–17 to San Francisco before 51,590 at the Metrodome. They finished 6–10 and last in the NFC Central.

Monday, December 31, 1990: Kings 4, North Stars 2, at Met Center

Hours after Lemieux leisurely skated alone in Pittsburgh for the first time since the season began, 12,015 fans—the largest crowd yet this season—turned out in Minnesota. They got free New Year's Eve party horns beforehand and a skating party afterward.

Before the opening faceoff, Green issued a "State of the Stars" statement, listing the lack of corporate support and the ineffectiveness of tartakes among his biggest disappointments.

The game was televised on MSC, for those who could get it. The star of the show, hyped in advertisements all week, was Gretzky, who assisted on two goals—including the game-winner. Gagner scored his 22nd of the season to give the North Stars a lead, and Dahlen's goal with 52 seconds left made the final appear closer than it was. Casey made 19 saves while Hayward, 2–6–1 since his trade in early November, switched his uniform number from 33 to 1 and watched from the end of the bench. Churla drew his third non-stick-foul game misconduct of the season with a boarding major in the third period, earning a one-game suspension.

tartakes finally ended when the clock hit 0:00. The team gave away $224,300 of the planned $225,000 (the $700 carryover would be donated to charity) during 15 games. Average attendance rose from 5,601 on November 10 to 7,371. Not counting the usual increase as winter arrives, or that the North Stars won more than twice as often after the promotion was announced, tartakes cost approximately $8.50 for every extra fan in the building. It probably wasn't a good return.

Before anyone sang "Auld Lang Syne," the second of five kids born to Margret and Reinhold Propp, the latter a Lutheran preacher in the 300-strong farming community of Neudorf, Saskatchewan, sounded like he was giving his best toast to 1991:

"We've got a lot of very proud guys on this team," Brian Propp said. "We're very disappointed, but we can't look at the past. We've got to look to the future. And the only way out of this is to work harder and smarter."

CHAPTER 7

January: War and Nowhere to Go but Up

Tuesday, January 1, 1991

While the rest of the country slept in and watched college bowl games, the North Stars flew to Detroit. It was no holiday for Mike Craig, but he still had something to celebrate. Craig scored a goal for Team Canada in a 5–1 win over Finland at the World Junior Championship.

Wednesday, January 2, 1991: Red Wings 6, North Stars 2, at Joe Louis Arena, Detroit

It took 44 seconds for Yves Racine to beat Brian Hayward. Soon it was 4–1 and Bob Gainey pulled Hayward for Jon Casey, only to put Hayward back in after the first intermission.

"It wasn't Brian's fault," Gainey said. "We left him stranded out there. ...right now we have the worst penalty killing in the league."

With the worst divisional record in the NHL (2–11–2 vs. the Norris), the North Stars' 29 points were more than only Toronto (26) and Quebec (25).

"There is a lot of tension in the air, a lot of frustration for guys who are fighting for their jobs," Mike Modano said. "There's a lot of pressure."

Thursday, January 3, 1991: North Stars 3, Maple Leafs 3, at Met Center

Norm Green unveiled next season's uniforms before the game. The jerseys will be predominantly black and white with green trim and the word "Stars" in gold on the crest. The N-star logo, in use since 1967, was nowhere to be found. The "Stars" secondary logo, which henceforth would appear in the neutral zone ice for the remainder of the season, also would be prominent in marketing materials—on everything from buttons to stickers.

Green later said, "The only person who questioned it was my mother. She thought the reason I bought the team was because the logo was an 'N,' and the team color was green."

Bobby Smith, returning just ten days after he suffered a hairline fracture on the instep of his left foot, scored on a wraparound to give the North Stars a 2–1 lead midway through the game. And Dave Gagner made it 3–2 early in the third. But Doug Sheddon tied it with 4:20 to go.

"What do you want me to say?" Gagner angrily responded to reporters after the game. "I don't know. We haven't improved from last year, but we have a totally different makeup. There were so many changes from the old management. It takes a lot of time for people to jell together, for the pieces of the puzzle to fit. Every guy is coming out and working as hard as he can every night."

Friday, January 4, 1991

Craig was happy. He and Team Canada won the gold medal at the World Junior Championships with a 3–2 win over the Soviet Union.

Just about everyone else connected with the North Stars was growing increasingly disillusioned. Minnesota was averaging 2.93 goals per game. No team has averaged fewer than three goals per game during a full season since the 1983–84 New Jersey Devils (2.89 per game), who finished 17–56–7. And while Gainey already proclaimed it, statistics through 43 games showed that the North Stars' penalty kill (48 goals allowed) was indeed now the worst in the NHL.

Only Gagner and Neal Broten were on pace to equal their scoring totals from last season. Brian Bellows led the team in '89–90 with 55 goals and 99 points. But his new contract has become a millstone. In the past 19 games, he's scored twice and has 12 goals and 35 points to date.

Modano also is off his 1989–90 pace of 29 goals and 75 points, but he's often been placed on a checking line with players of questionable offensive talent. So, at least he has an excuse.

"I'm not saying they're not trying, but your scorers have to score," Bobby Clarke said. "That's what they're there for."

Modano's agent, Howard Gourwitz, watched Thursday's game, met with Green, and would be back Saturday to conclude a visit with his star client. That led to speculation a trade could be in the works, but Clarke said several players are untouchable. He didn't specify which, but there was enough underperformance to go around he knew he might have a hard time making a deal of consequence.

"I'm not very happy about it, but you're not going to see me jump off a bridge," Clarke said. "Winning some games can solve a lot of problems."

Steve Gotaas and Mitch Messier are touchable. They were sent back to Kalamazoo.[37]

Saturday, January 5, 1991: Canucks 6, North Stars 5, at Met Center

The North Stars' penalty kill got *worse* en route to a loss against a team they traditionally dominated. A crowd of 9,445, fueled in part by the second Year of the Uniform Night[38], booed loudly in the third period as the outcome became clear.

Vancouver, 9–28–7 all-time at Met Center, scored three power-play goals. In the third period with the score 3–3, Modano lost his man defensively, and Igor Larionov scored unassisted. Although Modano got that back with his second goal of the game and 14th of the season, Dan Quinn picked off Casey's clearing attempt from the left-wing boards and fired a shot past Rob Zettler, alone in front of the net, giving the Canucks the lead for good.

"It's frustrating, I'm sure, for everyone here," Modano said. "It was good for me to get a couple of goals, especially when I gave one away, and it'll help me feel better about the way I'm playing. But winning is the bottom line."

"We're making mistakes we shouldn't be making," Gainey added. "We're losing pucks and giving up pucks we're not being forced into giving up. Emotionally, we're wound up too tight. I suppose all of those things are a symptom of a team with a record like ours."

As usual, however, Toronto and Quebec were just a little worse. The Maple Leafs lost at home to Los Angeles 4–2, leaving them three points back of the last playoff spot in the Norris. The Nordiques (9–27–7) were shut out at Montreal and had a two-point margin in the Eric Lindros Sweepstakes. If the Leafs were to fall behind them, Lindros's draft rights would go to New Jersey, because the Devils had acquired Toronto's No. 1 choice in a previous trade.

37 Neither Gotaas nor Messier ever played another NHL game.

38 The first 3,000 youth received a full-size wooden hockey stick.

Lindros and Craig were the only members of Team Canada to make the all-tournament team at the World Junior Championship. Craig, who flew from Saskatoon back to MSP, had six goals and 11 points in seven tourney games.

Sunday, January 6, 1991

Arne Carlson, due to be sworn in as Governor on Monday, attended services at Central Lutheran Church in Minneapolis. It was the beginning of a week-long schedule of inauguration activities.

Monday, January 7, 1991

The North Stars practiced ahead of a flight to New York. The big news of the day was that Gagner had been named to the Campbell Conference all-star team.

Stew Gavin shook Gagner's hand and talked wistfully about the chance to play with Wayne Gretzky. Ulf Dahlen clapped Gagner on the back and boasted of how he'll get to play with another Swede, Gretzky's teammate, Tomas Sandstrom.

Gagner said his first-time honor was nice, but he'd enjoy it a lot more if the North Stars were higher in the standings.

"When you don't win, a lot of guys are in bad moods," he said. "We've been finding ways to lose and we've got to change that. It's not fun to come to the rink. And the fans who come to watch us deserve better."

Tuesday, January 8, 1991: North Stars 3, Islanders 0, at Nassau Coliseum, Long Island, New York

Gagner and Perry Berezan (short-handed) scored first-period goals, Doug Smail added another in the third, and Hayward had to make just 15 saves to earn his second shutout and the North Stars' fourth of the season. The last time the North Stars had four shutouts in one season was 1973–74.

Wednesday, January 9, 1991

As the North Stars flew to Minnesota, Mario Lemieux returned to practice with the Pittsburgh Penguins.

Thursday, January 10, 1991

According to *Star Tribune* columnist Sid Hartman, Clarke has been shopping Bellows on the trade market, and Green says he expected to lose at least $2 million this season.

Later, Toronto lost 7–2 at Chicago. Nonplussed, Maple Leafs coach Tom Watt afterward predicted his team would overtake Minnesota and beat Chicago in the first round of the playoffs.

Friday, January 11, 1991

Modano made a promotional appearance at Northtown Nissan in Fridley, signing autographs and meeting fans from 6 to 9 p.m. Even as he did, Rachel Blount was putting the finishing touches on a feature for Saturday's *Star Tribune* about the debate surrounding the way the No. 1 overall pick from less than three years ago was being used—or not.

Modano's ice time has diminished from last season, and he has sometimes been paired with wingers who are not exactly offensive wizards. Other than his two-goal, three-point outburst in Saturday's loss to Vancouver, he had three goals and two assists and was minus-3 in twelve other games since December 11. He has been the subject of calls to sports talk shows and letters to the editor. One radio station even reported he wants to be traded.

"It's been kind of frustrating," Modano told Blount. "In my first year, things went well for me quickly and it made the rest of the season relaxing. This has been totally opposite… but I'm not upset with anyone. I'm not mad at anyone but myself."

Modano, who is making $150,000 this season, is living on his own for the first time, in a warehouse converted to large, open loft-style apartments in St. Paul's Lowertown, across from the Farmer's Market. The main living area is cavernous, with tall windows and doors to a couple of bedrooms and a bathroom. Although he likes to haunt places along Grand Avenue, especially for dinner, it's a quiet existence compared to living with a billet—let alone the temptations he'd find in downtown Minneapolis. It's less than a 20-minute drive to the rink in his Jeep Laredo, bought with part of his rookie signing bonus and a much better winter vehicle than his Porsche.

Getting traction with Modano has been difficult for Gainey. How to implement his young star has been a delicate challenge because he wants Modano's offensive talent on the ice but also a better work ethic to go with it.

"Earlier in the season, we were trying different methods of jump-starting Mike's production," Gainey said. "We played him from 23 to 25 minutes in a number of games. That didn't necessarily make his play better; it just made it more often."

But Modano is the promise of the future. He needs to play in order to deliver, and the reality is he's going to be given every opportunity.

"He sells tickets," Lou Nanne said. "There are very few players who can bring you out of your seat. Mike is one of them. He is so explosive on the ice and, besides, he's a matinee idol. Just look at the jerseys in the stands. You used to see guys with them; now it's girls, and they all have his name on the back.… You can't help but promote a kid like that."

Saturday, January 12, 1991: Sabres 5, North Stars 3, at Met Center

Hours after Congress gave President Bush authority to use force against Iraq (although Paul Wellstone was one of forty-seven senators to vote against it), the North Stars held three one-goal leads, the final one at the midpoint of the third period. But they wound up buffaloed by three late goals.

"This was a really poor game for our team," Gainey said. "When you take it in the time frame, when we're trying to get things regrouped, it's not acceptable to have a game like this on your home ice against a team you should beat. We worked the game to where we had the advantage on the scoreboard and seemed to be carrying the play, and the players didn't carry the day when they had the opportunity."

Attendance was 7,045, not including Ilkka Sinisalo, who watched from the press box after trying to play through a thumb injury, only to find it was broken.

Elsewhere, Toronto tied Hartford and Quebec tied St. Louis. The North Stars held a four-point lead on the two worst teams in the NHL.

Sunday, January 13, 1991: Blackhawks 5, North Stars 3, at Chicago Stadium

Curt Giles and Jim Johnson took holding and cross-checking penalties twenty-eight seconds apart midway through the game with the score 2–2.

Chicago scored two goals twenty-six seconds apart on the ensuing power play.

"Some nights you survive bad penalties, but they always cost you in the end," Gainey said. "That was the turning point of this game."

Earlier in the day, more than 10,000 people at the University of Minnesota rallied against the potential war in the Middle East. The crowd filled Northrop Auditorium and spilled outside the building, where speeches could be heard on loudspeakers. It was the biggest antiwar rally at the U since Vietnam.

Monday, January 14, 1991

The day's marketing effort: A newspaper print ad reading, "Denis Savard will be seeing Stars on Tuesday." The new logo also appeared in the ad next to the words, "Something to shout about!"

Fans were further encouraged to "avoid ticket lines on game days by purchasing tickets in advance."

Tuesday, January 15, 1991: Canadiens 5, North Stars 1, at Met Center

Smith and Guy LaFleur were added to their respective all-star teams in a new senior category for Saturday's game at Chicago. Smith had earned three previous all-star appearances. This trip would honor his career, the height of which came when he scored the Cup-clinching goal for Montreal in a Game 5 win in 1986 at Calgary. He didn't want to go to the all-star game this time, but Clarke talked him into it.

Coming into the game against the Canadiens, Bellows had taken more shots (175) than all but two players in the NHL. He was scoring at about 8 percent and was 17 goals off his pace from last season.

"I'm really concerned about it," he said. "If you don't perform, you start putting a lot of pressure on yourself, and you should."

Bellows and Craig also entered the game with team-worst minus-12 ratings. Bellows, Broten, and Brian Propp were the only players who had appeared in every game. Broten led the team with 36 assists and 47 points. Gagner had 26 goals.

None of them added to their totals against Montreal, and Gagner later wondered if any of the 5,375 fans would come back.

The North Stars had just three shots on goal in the first period, and their only offense was a goal by Sinisalo in the second. However, they trailed just 2–1 until more than 7 1/2 minutes were gone in the third. But that was also the midpoint of a fifteen-minute stretch where they had just two shots. That's why they fell to 0–19–3 when trailing after two periods.

"After one period, we had no life," Giles said. "The second period had to be an improvement. Any kind of life would have been more than we showed."

At the first intermission, Gainey swapped Hayward for starter Casey, who saved 11 of 13 shots. Hayward stopped 11 of 14 the rest of the way.

"We have to be disappointed," Gainey said.

Johnson, who recently moved his family into a rented condo near France Avenue and I-494, was scratched with a sore neck. Dan Keczmer was recalled early in the day, but his initial flight from Kalamazoo was canceled. He was rerouted through Chicago but didn't arrive until game time.

Dan Keczmer

Attendance wasn't helped by a Timberwolves game downtown. The Wolves lost to the Portland Trail Blazers 132–117, but the customary crowd of 19,006 continued to ogle the new Target Center even with Minnesota's record (11–23) better than only six of the other 26 NBA teams. The disparity in support (13,631 fans) finally eroded Green's enthusiasm.

"I had managed to stay positive through the small crowds earlier in our season," Green later told *Star Tribune* columnist Patrick

Reusse. "Our crowds did get better—11,000 for Boston and 12,000 for the Kings. Then the Montreal Canadiens, the greatest name in hockey, came and we had a crowd of 5,300. I was shocked. Then I was in a serious state of depression. I went home and told Kelly that maybe I had been wrong—maybe this wasn't going to work."

The theme for Green's real estate firm was: "We build, and we keep. We do not build and sell." With experience running the Calgary Flames for much of the 1980s despite his minority interest, he said he never considered pulling out of his investment in Minnesota.

"To have somebody come and save the team, somebody who had a great deal to do with building the Flames from eleventh in the NHL to Stanley Cup champions, to spend two and a half million fixing up Met Center… to do that is quite a commitment," Green said. "The idea was if you get people to come to a game once, they will see something they like and come back. We had Montreal here and those people who took a look in December because of the (tartakes) lottery did not come back. The report card on tartakes was in, and we received an F.

"I've been studying the situation. You go back to the 1982–83 season, and the attendance has declined every year. The North Stars have been going down, and teams with worse records have been going up in attendance. Why? This organization has been out of focus when it comes to selling tickets…. Our focus has to be 100 percent on season tickets. We're selling 3,500 (actually 3,331 for the regular season). No other NHL team sells less than 8,000."

This became prelude to a late-January press release devised as a "Thank you for saving the North Stars" ticket campaign. While not explicitly stated, the thank you actually was supposed to be *from* the fans *to* Green, who approved an offer where those buying two season tickets for '91–92 would get another season-ticket free (though not in the red seats) if they paid half the bill by March 31. Pay immediately and you also could get tickets for the remaining 12 home games. Brochures with a letter from Broten were sent to more than 60,000 recipients.

"We're averaging 7,000, which means 3,500 people are making a decision every night to go to a hockey game," Green said. "If you have 8,000 season tickets and another 3,500 decide to go to a game, you're OK. If you have 3,500 season tickets and another 3,500 people decide to go to a game, you have a disaster. The backup for all this is the opening of the Mall of America. If we can start the building process, get to 8,000 season tickets, and then the mall opens, that will put us over the top."

Green later told *USA Today* that the game against Montreal was the point at which he started to think there was too much competition in Minnesota and he had to look at other places to go.

"If our team continues to lose, if this season-ticket program doesn't make a difference, if the Mall of America opens and things still don't change—of course, you can't make it work with 5,000 people in the stands," Green said. "If someone else had owned this team, you might already have seen it sold to Milwaukee for $60 million. I'm still here. I made the ultimate commitment. I moved here. This is our home."

The North Stars had hit rock bottom for 1990–91. After the game, a group of players gathered around a TV to get the latest update on the Middle East. The deadline after which the US could begin hostilities in the Persian Gulf expired at midnight.

Wednesday, January 16, 1991

Beginning this morning at MSP, the only people allowed past the metal detectors were ticketed passengers. One of them was Keczmer, traveling back to Kalamazoo after a whirlwind trip the day before and an overnight hotel stay—all for a seat in the press box. Large concrete barriers protected sliding glass doors on the terminal's main level from a potential terrorist attack.

Halfway around the world, under cover of darkness, Operation Desert Storm began. US and allied air forces destroyed Iraqi airfields and struck missile bases in western Iraq. Hostilities started at 2:30 a.m., which was 6:30 p.m. in Minnesota.

Thursday, January 17, 1991: North Stars 5, Capitals 2, at Met Center

Several Iraqi missiles struck Israel and two US warplanes were shot down. The pilot of the first, 33-year-old Lt. Commander Michael Speicher of Mayport, Florida, became the first American war casualty. He was married, with a 3-year-old daughter and 1-year-old son.

A 4 p.m. anti-war rally drew several thousand people to Peavey Plaza in downtown Minneapolis.

The NHL announced this weekend's all-star festivities would carry on in Chicago, though Gretzky—whose cousin is a pilot deployed to the Gulf—said they should be canceled. The NFL would move forward with Sunday's conference championships and Super Bowl XXV on January 27 in Tampa.

A crowd of 6,301 showed up for Cap Night. Hayward made 34 saves and helped the North Stars win after a 1–7–2 stretch in their previous 10 games—the worst slump of the season.

"This is a big lift to us," said Hayward, spotted a two-goal lead by Bellows and Dahlen.

Washington tied it seven and a half minutes into the second period on a goal that appeared to be kicked in by Kelly Miller, but Craig beat former North Star Don Beaupre a minute later. Late in the second, Johnson fought Alan May, who took an instigating minor and was ejected for attempt to injure.

In the final five minutes, Gagner provided some breathing room and Smail scored short-handed. After Smail's goal, Neil Wilkinson fought Calle Johansson, and Zettler instigated a fight with Al Iafrate, who'd drawn a double-major for spearing.

It seemed like everyone was on edge. Former North Star and current Capitals winger Dino Ciccarelli squirted an obnoxious fan with a water bottle. The fan filed a complaint with Bloomington police. It'd been a rough go for Ciccarelli in recent years. On January 20, 1988, he was arrested for indecent exposure after being seen wearing only a sweatshirt (and nothing else from the waist down) outside his Eden Prairie home. He pleaded guilty to indecent exposure. Traded to Washington, he was among four players named in a sexual assault investigation during the offseason—however, the case fell apart before it could get traction in court.

Shane Churla suffered a separated shoulder in the first period and was taken to Fairview Southdale. It was only the latest among many times it had happened. His shoulder was getting so loose that he'd separate it lying in bed if he lifted his arm over his head. He'd been setting it himself, which wasn't a long-term solution. This time, Churla was expected to miss six to eight weeks.

Friday, January 18, 1991

As more Iraqi Scud missiles hit Israel, Gagner, Smith, and Clarke all caught a flight to Chicago for Saturday's all-star game at the Stadium.

Green and Jim Erickson, the North Stars' lead counsel, were already there. They met with representatives for George and Gordon Gund regarding the San Jose agreement. The league requested both teams refrain from public comment.

In a skills competition that drew less than capacity, Gagner helped the Campbell Conference win the puck control relay. Earlier, Clarke centered a line with Bill Goldsworthy, and Chico Resch played in goal for the NHL Heroes of Hockey in a 3–1 loss to Blackhawks' old-timers. Goldsworthy wore a North Stars jersey even though he now had to pay his way into Met Center.

While an official announcement would not come until Sunday, the first Minnesotan went missing in action in the war after his US Navy jet was shot down over Kuwait. Twenty-nine-year-old Charley Turner, who graduated from Richfield High School and the University of Minnesota, was a bombardier/navigator. His body would be recovered in March.

Saturday, January 19, 1991

US forces claimed air superiority over Iraq at the same time they deployed Patriot missiles to Israel to defend against Scud attacks.

That set the stage in Chicago for one of the most star-spangled events in NHL history. A crowd of 18,472 jammed the Stadium, and NBC televised the action to a world-wide audience that was the largest ever to see an all-star game. It was the only time all season the NHL would be on network TV in the US, and it made for compelling viewing as the crowd went berserk during the American anthem, waving flags and holding sparklers.

Gagner scored the first goal of the game at 6:17 on assists from Blackhawks Jeremy Roenick and Steve Larmer. Gagner flubbed several other scoring chances and said he likely cost Roenick the new Chrysler as prize for MVP honors. Toronto's Vincent Damphousse took it home instead, scoring four goals as the Campbell Conference beat the Wales Conference 11–5.

During the all-star break, the NHL Players Association released its top 100 salaries. Wayne Gretzky was the NHL's highest-paid player at $3 million, followed by Mario Lemieux ($2,330,000), Brett Hull ($1,366,000), Steve Yzerman ($1,300,000) and Savard ($1,250,000). Bellows ranked nineteenth at $675,000. Other North Stars in the top 100 included: Smith ($400,000), Broten ($348,000), Casey and Propp ($325,000 each), and Basil McRae ($230,000).

The entire Minnesota salary pool was approximately $6 million.

The average per capita Minnesota income in 1990 was $17,657.[39]

Sunday, January 20, 1991

At 4:40 a.m. in Peoria, Illinois, Link Gaetz was arrested and charged with felony criminal damage to property worth more than $300 when he threw a TV out a fifth-floor window at the Continental Regency Hotel. Gaetz, who had bounced between Kalamazoo and Kansas City all season—when he wasn't AWOL—had been in the lineup Saturday night when the Blades played the Rivermen. He was released on $100 bond and scheduled to be arraigned February 25. The incident didn't come to light in the Twin Cities until midway through next week, when Gary Olson reported it in the *Pioneer Press*. Gaetz later told the *Star Tribune* he expected to pay $1,200 in damages in order for the charges to be dropped.

"In order to play, I had to follow certain rules," Gaetz said. "It had worked out all right until now. Anytime you throw a TV out the window, it's not too good."

Last season, Gaetz punched the wife of a Kalamazoo teammate.

"Link's not just ruining his career, he's ruining his life," Clarke said. "He has no one to blame for his problems except himself. We want to get him help, but you can't help a guy unless he's willing to help himself.... He's worn out his welcome in this organization."

As the North Stars flew to Winnipeg, three American pilots were shown on Iraqi TV as reported prisoners of war.

---

39 Between 1990 and 2021, the cumulative rate of inflation was 104.3 percent. In today's dollars, a typical 1990 Minnesota worker made $36,078. Gretzky's 1990-91 salary would've been worth $6,130,000 and Bellows' would equate to $1,379,000 in 2021. According to the US Census Bureau, the per capita income in Minnesota during 2020 was $37,625—a thirty-year increase of just $1,547. Meanwhile, the top NHL salary for 2020–21 was $14,500,000 (Erik Karlsson of the San Jose Sharks) and eighty-eight other players made more than $6,130,000.

Churla underwent shoulder surgery. The operation took three inches off his collarbone, ensuring he wouldn't be able to separate his shoulder anymore.

Monday, January 21, 1991: Jets 2, North Stars 0, at Winnipeg Arena

American prisoners were moved into positions as human shields at military targets in Iraq, though the US said that would not change the course of the Gulf War campaign.

While most of America's cable audience tuned in to CNN, the North Stars were on MSC. Hayward was excellent, stopping 26 of 27 shots. But Bob Essensa was perfect on 28 for Winnipeg. He stoned Craig early in the third period on the North Stars' only penalty shot of the season. Then former North Star Moe Mantha celebrated his thirtieth birthday with a shot from the point that went through a screen at 10:35, and Danton Cole added an empty-netter in the final minute.

Zettler suffered a hip injury. Defending against a rush, he lost his balance and did the splits on his knees.

"The whole club has (bad luck)," Hayward said. "We've been close all year. I don't think our record is an indication of how well this team has played at times. We're not one of the best teams in the league, but we're close every night. It just seems we're not quite good enough."

Tuesday, January 22, 1991: North Stars 7, Blues 3, at Met Center

Iraqi forces sabotaged oil installations in Kuwait, setting fire to two large refineries. In the first week of the conflict, the US and its allies flew more than 10,000 sorties and lost eighteen planes to Iraq's seventeen—but took twenty-three Iraqi prisoners of war.

The North Stars launched an all-out blitz against St. Louis goalie Curtis Joseph, who faced 40 shots. Modano was the only forward and Chris Dahlquist and Wilkinson the only defensemen without a point. Propp had a goal and two assists, Bellows scored twice, and Hayward made 22 saves. Keczmer, whose teammates in Kalamazoo call him "Crazylegs" because of his skating prowess, was recalled for the game—and promptly scratched. Casey, his curly blond hair dripping with sweat, pedaled furiously on a stationary bike long after most others had dressed and left.

Wednesday, January 23, 1991

US ground troops met Iraqi forces for the first time as fleets of tanks clashed near the border of Kuwait, Iraq, and Saudi Arabia. Defense Secretary Dick Cheney told a media briefing that Saddam Hussein "will be defeated." And General Colin Powell described the coming ground campaign.

"Dealing with this army is very simple," Powell said. "First we're going to cut it off. Then we're going to kill it."

The US briefing detailed the loss of twenty allied planes, compared to forty-one by Iraq. The Iraqis countered with a claim that they had downed more than 180 planes and taken more than twenty prisoners.

It was hard to confirm, but the best guess was Hussein is hiding in a nuclear-proof bunker in Baghdad.

Thursday, January 24, 1991

The US Navy took fifty-one prisoners on a small Iraqi-held island in the Persian Gulf and also sunk a minesweeper. With more than 600,000 troops deployed to the region, there were thirteen US soldiers missing in action, as well as the same number from allied forces.

The North Stars—including McRae, who made the trip and has resumed skating—worked out at the Capital Centre ahead of Friday's game at Washington, where the Caps have closed practices since the start of the war to thwart any potential terrorist activity. The equipment staff was under orders to leave McRae's jersey behind, so he covertly packed it himself in order to skate during pregame warmups.

Friday, January 25, 1991: North Stars 2, Capitals 2, at Capital Center, Landover, Md.

Iraqi forces sabotaged Kuwait's main supertanker loading pier, dumping millions of gallons of oil into the Persian Gulf in what Pentagon officials called "environmental terrorism." And a Scud attack killed one person in Israel.

In Washington, where most attention was on the Gulf War, a crowd of 16,859 still found time for a hockey game. Iafrate beat Hayward early in the second period, but Dahlen and Propp (on a power play) gave the North Stars a one-goal lead in the third. Then, as Minnesotans who tuned in to KMSP-TV could testify, Ciccarelli scored a controversial goal with just more than nine minutes left in regulation.

"He kicked it in," complained Johnson, defending on the tying goal. "I had his stick tied up. His skate was all he had left. It was a bad goal and it lost us a point."

Beaupre made 21 saves. Hayward had 18.

Giles suffered a sprained left knee and might miss the next two weeks.

Saturday, January 26, 1991: North Stars 3, Devils 1, at Meadowlands Arena, East Rutherford, N.J.

Smith scored on the power play and Propp got credit for a goal Viacheslav Fetisov knocked into his own net.

Casey, making his first start in a week and a half, finished with 32 saves.

"In the last 10 days, I had time to personally reflect on what was happening and what was going wrong," Casey said. "I tried to get back to basics, work hard on my game, and get in better shape. Also, my outlook got better."

Since Hayward arrived, Casey had started 16 of 32 games and been on the bench for six of the last eight.

"Jon didn't look sharp (against Montreal)," Gainey said. "It got to the point where I felt the goalies had to know they would stay in if they were playing well. I didn't want to just automatically transfer them in and out because of the schedule."

At Quebec, Lemieux played his first game of the season, collecting three assists in Pittsburgh's 6–5 win.

Sunday, January 27, 1991

As the North Stars traveled to Toronto, General H. Norman Schwarzkopf appeared at a briefing and explained how the US had used "smart bombs" to destroy valves contributing to the oil spill in the Persian Gulf. On more than 22,000 missions, the US and its allies had lost twenty-three planes to Iraq's forty-nine. A total of twenty-seven US and allied soldiers were missing in action.

Most of America tuned in Sunday night to watch the New York Giants beat the Buffalo Bills 20–19 in Super Bowl XXV. Whitney Houston created a sensation with her version of "The Star-Spangled Banner," and Scott Norwood's potential game-winning 47-yard field-goal attempt sailed wide right with four seconds left.

Monday, January 28, 1991: Maple Leafs 4, North Stars 0, at Maple Leaf Gardens, Toronto

Wendel Clark started a fight with Wilkinson in the first period and, by the time Clark exited the penalty box, Toronto had two goals—more than enough to beat the North Stars.

Hayward stopped 23 shots, but one hit him and barely dribbled over the goal line, and another deflected in less than three minutes later. It didn't matter because the North Stars had just six shots in the first period, were punchless on a four-minute power play in the second, and did nothing with a 5-on-3 advantage for 1:26 in the third. Toronto's last shutout of anybody came more than two years earlier.

"There was no intensity," Smith said.

"I don't think I have anything to offer to say why this happened," Smail said. "I guess the outcome speaks for itself."

Johnson played despite suffering a knee injury at New Jersey, rendering meaningless the call-up of Pat MacLeod, who raced from Kalamazoo to Toronto only to be scratched. Turns out he had a torn tricep muscle in his left arm and the coaches didn't know that until he got to Toronto. If he'd played and then revealed the injury, the North Stars could've been stuck with him and forced to pay his NHL salary rather than the IHL rate until he was healthy again.

"This is my one Bob Gainey personality story," MacLeod said with a chuckle thirty years later. "We had not played very well and the room was real subdued. I hadn't played and he looked right at me and said 'So, ah, you'll be coming back with us to Minnesota?' He said it like it was a question. That was the inflection in his voice. I said (with an unsure tone) 'Sure?' I didn't know if it was my choice or what. If it was, 'Yes, I'm coming back to Minnesota and I think I should get a contract extension.' It was weird."

Tuesday, January 29, 1991

Allied warplanes destroyed twenty-four enemy tanks, and US officials said ninety Iraqi aircraft had fled to Iran to escape destruction.

Green was so angered by the effort at Toronto that he told Clarke to do whatever was necessary to ensure maximum effort each night. It was Green's first public criticism of the team.

"Watching that game made me very upset," he said. "As of today, there are no sacred cows. Whatever he has to do to make sure there is a total commitment to the team, Bob is free to do."

Clarke said he was pleased with the effort of Giles, Gagner, Mark Tinordi, Propp, Zettler, and Johnson. Giles and Zettler were injured. That means Clarke complimented just four of twenty players in the lineup, although he added that he could count on one hand the players he was disappointed in.

"I don't want it to be thought that the players aren't working," Clarke said. "But when you're near the bottom, you expect and need everyone to give their full effort every night. Any lack of effort just makes the situation worse.... Norm is feeling some frustration."

Green wouldn't name the players he thought weren't giving their best. He said he backed Clarke and Gainey "one million percent" and that the Stars should be tenth or eleventh overall in the NHL standings instead of nineteenth. Green said injuries, a period of adjustment for new players and coaches, uncertainty about the future with San Jose, and low home attendance were excuses.

"We can't promise our fans a championship team the first year, but we can promise the team will work to its full potential," Green said. "We can't accept underachievers. Some of the kids are working their hearts out. For the ones who aren't, it's not fair to their teammates or to the fans."

Green and Clarke made their comments before the North Stars returned from Toronto, converged on Met Center for a late-afternoon practice, and learned about the squall from the media.

Wednesday, January 30, 1991: North Stars 5, Red Wings 2, at Met Center

Green was back in Chicago with Clarke and Erickson, negotiating with George Gund, Sharks president Art Savage, and GM Jack Ferreira. So Green was unable to see firsthand the North Stars' response to his message from a day before, but clearly it was received.

Pat Forciea

Bellows scored twice as part of a four-goal second period and Casey finished with 32 saves to pull within eight points of Detroit for third place in the Norris.

"I think (Green's comments) had an effect on all of us," Gainey said. "No one likes to feel like they aren't pulling their own weight. When it comes from the top, it goes all the way to the bottom."

Keczmer collected his first NHL point with an assist on Broten's goal 2:17 into the second. Sinisalo made it 4–2 four seconds before intermission, and Gaetan Duchesne scored in the third period.

McRae played his first game after missing thirty-six. He fought Randy McKay early in the third.

"Something positive did come out of all this," McRae said of his three-month absence. "It made me think about how important it is to prepare for life after hockey and how much I enjoy playing the game."

Later in the third period, Bob Probert took a holding penalty and, after he got to the penalty box, fans tossed beer at him. As he left the ice in the final minute following a scuffle with McRae, a fan leaned over the glass near the Red Wings bench, called Probert a "fucking cokehead," and spat at him. At 6-foot-3 and 225 pounds, Probert was as menacing as any player in the league. He responded by firing his helmet into the crowd. One fan was ejected and another arrested following the incidents.

"I get beer dumped on me and a guy spits in my face," said Probert, who earned an automatic $100 fine for the confrontation. "Nice fans they have here. No wonder no one comes to the games."

Well, 5,965 people did. And they heard Jim Bowers sing the rarely played *second* verse of the Star-Spangled Banner, with virtually no accompaniment from onlookers.

Meanwhile, twelve US Marines were killed in the first major clash of ground forces in the Gulf War near a small Saudi Arabian border town. Twenty-three-year-old Corporal Stephen Bentzlin of Wood Lake, Minnesota, was one of them. Bentzlin's family would learn in February that his death was caused by friendly fire.

Thursday, January 31, 1991

A US plane with a crew of fourteen was shot down behind Iraqi lines and all were missing. US officials said they had lost fifteen aircraft so far.

As MacLeod flew back to Kalamazoo for the rest of the season, Pat Forciea accepted Green's offer of a new role in the organization.

Forciea, who graduated from St. Thomas in 1980 with a degree in journalism and finance, lived near 29th Street and Freemont Avenue in the Uptown area of Minneapolis with his wife, the former Cathy Lawrence. Pat had worked full-time in politics since '87, when he directed the Michael Dukakis campaign in Minnesota, Wisconsin, and California in the run-up to the '88 election against George Bush. That was a landslide for Bush, although Minnesota and Wisconsin were among the ten states Dukakis carried. Two years later, after a much different result for Paul Wellstone, the Forcieas declined an offer in late November for Pat to become Wellstone's chief of staff. They didn't want to move to DC, so Pat was a free agent when he got a call from Erickson on Green's behalf just before the holidays.

"Jim said, 'Pat, I know you're a big hockey fan, a North Star fan and an old hockey player; would you have an interest in sitting down with Norm Green?'" Forciea recalled in an interview for this book. "I had never met Norm. I only knew him based on what I'd seen that summer (of 1990) and as the season began. I said, 'Sure.' We went out to meet with Norm and talked about having me get involved in the public relations/marketing side of life. As someone who grew up on the Iron Range and loved hockey, it seemed like it was a pretty straight-forward opportunity. So, I said yes."

Forciea said Green was frustrated at his inability to draw crowds at Met Center, although he wasn't ready to blame anyone but himself.

"He said, 'Pat, I need a new set of eyes,'" Forciea told me. "'Since you haven't been involved in sports, I view you as a plus right now rather than a negative.' I think I was aware of how dire the situation was, in terms of the North Stars' relationship with the hockey community. I was eternally confident that relationships could be rebuilt and built anew, but I certainly didn't think it could happen quickly."

CHAPTER 8

February: Winning in the Gulf. And at Met Center?

Friday, February 1, 1991

Twenty-year-old Army Specialist Melissa Rathbun-Nealy became the first US female soldier missing in the Gulf War. Her parents lived in Newaygo, Michigan, about an hour and a half north of Kalamazoo. American casualties were confirmed to include eleven dead, nine wounded, twenty-three missing, and eight taken prisoner.

TCI (Telecommunications Inc.) began a new contract with MSC. That meant about 150,000 more cable subscribers in outstate Minnesota would receive its programming, including North Stars games. The five major cable operators in the Twin Cities, however, remained blacked out.

Saturday, February 2, 1991: North Stars 6, Nordiques 4 at Le Colisee, Quebec City

In the Gulf, two US planes were shot down by Iraqi fire and an American Marine was killed by an allied bomb dropped off-target.

That all seemed far from Quebec, where Jon Casey gave up three goals on the first five shots he saw. But Dave Gagner responded with a goal and four assists and Brian Propp scored twice and set up two others in a comeback not televised in Minnesota.

"We got pulled into a wide-open style, which is a sloppy way for us to play," Gagner said. "If it means we get two points, we'll take them any way we can get them."

In Pittsburgh, Mario Lemieux left a 6–2 win over Boston early in the second period with a pulled groin.

Back in the Twin Cities, TwinsFest debuted at the Metrodome. The Twins, who finished last in the American League West in 1990, had 8,300 season-ticket holders and expected a crowd of more than 25,000 for the weekend event.

Sunday, February 3, 1991

Former North Stars hockey department secretary Brenda Knight was accused in the *Boston Herald* of pirating scouting information from her computer before moving to San Jose. She denied it. Sharks assistant GM Dean Lombardi was accused of the same thing. They also supposedly took trophies and photos out of the Met Center offices. Lombardi rejected the accusations, recycled from *Let's Play Hockey*—among other sources—in a seven-page letter to the *Herald*. He called comments by Norm Green and Bobby Clarke toward the San Jose franchise akin to "Scud missiles from Saddam Hussein." Lombardi also labeled his letter a "Patriot Missile."

In the real Gulf War, an Air Force B-52 bomber and a Marine Cobra helicopter crashed in separate incidents—leaving at least two airmen dead and three missing.

Monday, February 4, 1991: Canadiens 5, North Stars 3, at Montreal Forum

Gagner and Perry Berezan scored 1:04 apart in the first period, and the North Stars held a 2–0 lead early in the second. But Montreal scored four consecutive goals to take control. Bobby Smith scored with a minute to go, but Mike McPhee completed a hat trick with an empty-netter at 19:25 of the third. McPhee's linemates, Guy Carbonneau and Russ Courtnall, each had three points to the delight of 19,875 fans—matching the October 26 crowd at Detroit for the largest to see the North Stars all season.

Curt Giles, Brian Glynn and Mike Modano each were minus-3. Neal Broten, Doug Smail, and Berezan were the only forwards who managed to finish even.

"We spent a lot of time in our own end in the second period," Bob Gainey said. "Because the Carbonneau line was playing so well, we were forced to take the Modano line (with Brian Bellows and Ulf Dahlen) off the ice. In all honesty, I didn't feel secure putting them on the ice, and they should create scoring chances for us."

Brian Hayward took the loss in his return to the Forum. And Mike Craig suffered a broken bone at the base of his right thumb. It allowed Gainey to move Modano into Craig's spot as right wing on a line with Gagner and Propp.

"I think Bob's concern as the season went on was my play without the puck," Modano told me in one of several interviews for this book. "Being a centerman, there's a lot of responsibility all over the ice, and strictly in your own zone where you have to be a little bit supportive of everybody. You can't be on the fly, and I was always trying to time it where you can fly the zone and we weren't coming out at the same time. Back then the structure coverage in your own zone was like: OK, the D were IN-active. They didn't move off the blue line in the offensive zone. They weren't going anywhere. No one activated down low. No one walked the blue line—they just stood there. So as a winger, I mean, you just stand there and don't move at all. Your only job was to be someone close to that D. Then you're conserving energy. You're not really gassed if you're working down low as a centerman, going corner to corner. So it alleviated responsibility, and I think Bob just thought 'Hey, let's move him over there. You know, Dave can do the work down low.' It freed me up."

Modano said he didn't resist, then revised that statement.

"Well, I guess maybe a little bit, because you feel like you are getting moved out of the position you're supposed to be playing," he said. "You're like, 'Ok. I'm doing something wrong. I'm not pulling my weight as centerman.' But I knew going in to play with Dave and Brian, there's some creativity. These are guys who think offense, who can play the game. So, I started thinking 'This could turn out to be a good thing.'"

Perhaps after thirty years, Modano and Gainey truly understand each other—or at least got their story straight.

"One of the things that came to us over time is that we had a strength that most teams crave, and that was that we had strength at center ice," Gainey told me. "We had four above-average centers (Gagner, Broten, Smith and Modano). In 1990, Neal might have been as talented as Mike, but he would've been the only one with that kind of skill set. But Mike, on a full-blown description of what a center was, wasn't as capable as any one of those guys. Until we got that ironed out, and I sat out Bobby Smith (later) that year also, our centers were going to be Smith, Gagner and Broten, with Mike used in an alternative role as a winger and a secondary defenseman on the power play and wherever else we could spot him. Then we found we had a strength that was buried and hadn't been accessed. It gave me more flexibility as a coach, but he didn't want to move out of position because he's a centerman, and 'This is what I am, and I'm a first pick, and this is where I should be.' That's a battle and you don't come to the end of that kind of negotiation in a week or even a month. At some point, somebody's got to give in and say, 'OK, let's give this a shot and I'll try my best at it.'"

Earlier in the day, the NHL reinstated Edmonton goalie Grant Fuhr from his one-year drug suspension. He was allowed to return to action for the Oilers beginning February 18.

But the big news in the Twin Cities was the hot-stove agreement of St. Paul native Jack Morris, who won more games in the 1980s than any pitcher in baseball, to a free-agent contract with the Twins. A four-time all-star and two-time 20-game winner, Morris was seen as the veteran starter to put the team in contention again.

Tuesday, February 5, 1991

As the North Stars returned home, temperatures in Minnesota reached nearly fifty degrees. Perhaps because of Green's recent outburst, it seemed a little chillier at Met Center. There was an atmosphere of tension around the office that was even more heightened than usual. It came to a head of sorts for me. Unthinking, I had gone through the mail, and, out of one of the magazines we got, there was a poster of Winnipeg Jets captain Thomas Steen. Since our little intern cubicles were somewhat like a dungeon and we didn't have much decoration, I stuck it on the wall.

That was a mistake. Joanie Preston told me so, in not so many words, and I quickly yanked down the offending picture of an enemy player. My day went worse when Green, who had scribbled a compliment on a how-to-play-defense instructional story I wrote with Glynn a few weeks earlier, saw me in the office dressed business casual. I mean, I didn't have holes in my pants. I looked decent, wearing Dockers, a sweater and dress shoes—and it wasn't game day. Uh-uh. Green told Joanie I needed a tie. So, I drove home, put one on and drove back, muttering along the way.

"He was a complex guy," Pat Forciea said of Green in an interview for this book. "Like some successful entrepreneurs I've met in my life, part of him was an incredible, decent guy and part of him was very cold, kind of steely almost. I remember, after I had been there about a week, I sat him down. I said, 'Norm, you must be aware of how nervous people are here.' He acted a little bit incredulous. I circled back and said, 'Norm, whether you realize this or not, people are scared to death of you.'"

The feeling filtered to a team meeting. With Gainey standing by like a disapproving parent and Clarke's voice turning the air blue, each player had to stand and give their assessment of what was going on and how to fix it. Some were pointed in their criticism. Broten, Bellows, and Smith had earned the right to speak their mind. Others made generic allusions, reluctant to call anyone out or tempt the ire of Clarke or Gainey.

Brian Glynn

"You sort of cringed," Glynn told me thirty years later. "Fortunately, as a young guy, not a whole lot of people were looking to me to say what's wrong with our team. But Bob Clarke played the game the way he did, and his approach is no secret to anybody. He's going around the room and typically either telling the reasons why you got traded or you're this or you're that. Everyone was walking on eggshells."

Wednesday, February 6, 1991

Broten continued to lead the team in scoring. But that didn't mean everything was great for Minnesota's favored son. Playing in

Neal Broten

the final year of his contract, Broten was miffed the team hadn't made a stronger push to sign him, and there had been suggestion that perhaps the Sharks may try to steal him away.

Broten has 52 points but only 12 goals. He had 23 last season and has finished with fewer than 18 in a full season only once in nine years.

"I wish it was going better," Broten said. "It's been a different year for me because I've been used on a checking line for awhile, and before I've usually been on an offensive line. I'll do what they want me to do because I like to prevent goals as well as score them."

Gainey said Broten had experienced peaks and valleys but, "his value is different this year because that's what the team needs of him."

Green, meanwhile, was in Montreal, selling his new uniform design to the NHL board of governors.

"The North Stars have a great sense of history, but last year I think they turned some people off," Green later told *Pioneer Press* columnist Bob Sansevere. "We have a new team now. A new dimension. I walk the concourse and talk to fans. Not a single fan said to keep the green. They all love the idea of black uniforms. I'd say 100 percent of them like calling the team the 'Stars.' A guy who pays to come in, his advice I really listen to."

Thursday, February 7, 1991: North Stars 4, Maple Leafs 2 at Met Center

A crowd of 7,084 saw Bellows score twice on plays started by Broten, and Casey stopped 16 shots (only three in the third period). They also held their collective breath late in the game after Modano crashed into the boards following a hit by Lucien Deblois. Modano had to be helped from the ice. He suffered a bruised knee and would be re-evaluated Friday.

If Modano can't go Saturday, perhaps Bellows will continue to take up the slack. After scoring two goals in a 22-game stretch, he has 10 in his last 12—including four two-goal games.

"People start to think that when you're not scoring goals you have to shoot quicker," Bellows said. "Actually, it's just the opposite. What you really have to do is take more time. Wait to see what the goalie is going to do first."

Perhaps equally important, the penalty killers (Broten, Mark Tinordi, Curt Giles, and Smail were the No. 1 unit) have grown more aggressive and successful. They've killed 28 of their last 30 chances—a big reason why the North Stars have improved.

More than a quarter of the schedule remained, but it increasingly looked like Minnesota would make the postseason.

"If you've got a ticket, you've got a chance to win the lotto," Gainey said.

"If we can get everybody healthy and score some goals on the power play, we could cause some problems in the playoffs," Clarke added.

Green was contemplating a change of the arena name to Megamall Center. Such a sponsorship would include the purchase of season tickets by the Mall of America. The North Stars' week-old campaign had yielded about 100 buyers.

Season-ticket holders comprised roughly half of the crowd against the Maple Leafs. In 1980–81, when the team went to the finals, the team sold 9,839 season tickets.

"Think how great it would be if we can turn it around here," Green told *Star Tribune* columnist Dan Barreiro. "I'll tell you something I don't think I've ever said before. If it works out here, great. But if it doesn't, then I'll get out of hockey. I'll never go through this again."

Allied pilots shot down two Iraqi jets, but a Navy F-18 went down in the Persian Gulf (its pilot missing), and an Army helicopter crashed in Saudi Arabia, killing one and injuring four.

Friday, February 8, 1991

Modano skated in practice and expected to play despite his bruised knee.

Saturday, February 9, 1991: North Stars 6, Red Wings 5 at Met Center

The Year of the Uniform continued with Gear Bag Night for the first 3,000 kids. It helped spur the second-best crowd of the season so far—11,838 people.

They were treated to plenty of action. Gagner had a goal and two assists, and Modano and Propp each had a goal and an assist. Berezan's backhander made it 6–2 early in the third, but it proved to be crucial as the Red Wings scored three goals in an eight-minute span and trailed by one for the final 1:28.

Gainey said it was perhaps the best game he's seen Modano play.

Sunday, February 10, 1991

A Marine Corp Harrier jet was downed over Kuwait, and the pilot was missing. But after three weeks of heavy bombing, US Defense Secretary Dick Cheney said of Saddam Hussein's forces, "I don't think it's the world's fourth-largest army anymore."

Monday, February 11, 1991

The North Stars flew to New York ahead of Tuesday's game against the Islanders, who have joined Quebec and Toronto among teams trailing Minnesota.

Later in Edmonton, Peter Taglianetti suffered a collapsed lung during Pittsburgh's 7–5 loss. He was taken to University of Alberta Hospital, had a sixteen-inch tube placed in his chest, and would be out indefinitely. Taglianetti was plus-7 in his first 26 games with the Penguins while being paired with Paul Coffey.

Tuesday, February 12, 1991: Islanders 5, North Stars 4 at Nassau Coliseum, Long Island, N.Y.

The teams traded goals three times until New York finally got two back-to-back in the third period.

"In the last five games, we've had over four goals scored against us," Gainey said. "That doesn't work in my math."

Neither did an uncharacteristic minus-3 rating for Broten. Hayward made 21 saves but was victimized by two breakaways.

"We can win a hockey game against anyone, but not if we have to score six goals to do it," Smith said.

Wednesday, Fed. 13, 1991: North Stars 6, Sabres 6 at the Auditorium, Buffalo

Smith was right, but at least this time the North Stars were able to score six goals and earn a point. The egregious part was they let a 4–1 lead get away and couldn't hold a one-goal margin more than eight minutes into the third period.

Steve Bellows (and several relatives) made the 45-minute drive from St. Catharines, Ontario, to Buffalo and was rewarded as his son, Brian, scored two goals (including the 300th of his career) and assisted on another.

The North Stars deserved better after they scored three power-play goals on six chances, killed all nine penalty situations they faced, and outshot the Sabres 9–0 in overtime. But 22-year-old rookie Darcy Wakaluk relieved Darren Puppa and stopped 31 of 33 shots in more than 56 minutes to force the tie.

Mike McHugh, played six games with the North Stars in 1991. He totaled four shots and was destined to be one of the players Minnesota would lose in the dispersal draft with the San Jose Sharks. (Photo courtesy of Mike McHugh)

After the game ended and the teams were leaving the ice, Lou Franceschetti hit Bellows from behind and coaches, security, and police were needed to quell an uprising. Earlier, Franceschetti ran Jim Johnson into the end boards and put him out of the game with a sprained neck.

"We were yapping at each other, but I'd turned my head when he hit me," Bellows said of Franceschetti. "Some guys are pretty tough when you're not looking. He had 65 minutes to do something if he's so tough."

There was no Minnesota TV for the game, but there was news on that front. King Videocable reached an agreement to begin carrying MSC on April 1. That's when 70,000 subscribers spread over more than twenty suburbs would begin to get the programming—just after the end of the regular season.

Until then, just 47,000 of the 400,000 cable subscribers in the metro area would have access to MSC.

Thursday, February 14, 1991

As the North Stars moved on to Detroit, two US Air Force crewmen were killed when their plane went down in combat over northern Saudi Arabia. In the first month of conflict, American forces lost fourteen people killed and twenty-eight more missing in action.

Smail, who was injured against Detroit and scratched against the Islanders, returned to the Twin Cities, underwent arthroscopic surgery on his left knee, and was expected to miss two to three weeks.

Friday, February 15, 1991

Johnson, with soreness lingering after he aggravated a neck injury at Buffalo, flew to MSP to get some rest.

The Iraqis offered a conditional withdrawal from Kuwait. They held to 10 conditions, including that Israel withdraw from Lebanon, that foreign forces with leave the region within a month of a cease-fire, that economic sanctions against Iraq end and that the US and its allies pay reparations to repair war damage. President Bush told them where they could stick it.

Saturday, February 16, 1991: North Stars 3, Red Wings 0, at Joe Louis Arena, Detroit

The North Stars moved within seven points of third-place Detroit as they beat the Red Wings for the third consecutive time.

Casey stopped 18 shots in a game that started at 12:05 p.m. Central time and was not televised. It was his NHL-best third shutout of the season, tying him with John Vanbiesbrouck of the New York Rangers and Winnipeg's Bob Essensa.

"I've been a little disappointed with the high scores lately," Casey said. "Even though we were still getting some points, I knew we couldn't play that way and expect to win."

The game drew a standing-room sellout of 19,875. If Green needed inspiration, he could look to Detroit. Eight years earlier, the Red Wings had sold just 2,200 season tickets. Then Mike Ilitch bought the team, drafted Steve Yzerman, and gave away a car at every home game to ignite interest. The fans responded with eight consecutive seasons averaging more than 15,000 per night. Demand was so strong this year they had to cut off season-ticket sales at 16,000.

Sunday, February 17, 1991

Two US soldiers were killed by friendly fire in the Gulf when a helicopter destroyed two ground vehicles by mistake.

Monday, February 18, 1991

As parts of the metro area got more than six inches of snow, the North Stars plowed ahead with a new ad campaign pushing season tickets. Forciea took charge of the drive during the weekend.

"The Gunds did quite a job of scorching the earth here," Forciea said. "It was unlike anything I've seen. The anger toward the Gunds was as hot as it could get. That's why I hope I have some sense for how people feel. We have to show them that the confusion and chaos has ended and that we plan to do everything we can to win them back."

That's why Forciea has critiqued the way staff answer the phones and even the manner in which ushers helped the customers.

"Over the past few years, a lot of fans have been frustrated with their experience at the game, not just with the team," Forciea said. "It's a cop-out to say we can't sell tickets if the team is losing. Many of the former season-ticket holders have told me stories of the organization doing nothing to find out what went wrong or how to win them back. One reason sports franchises get in trouble is because they act as if they're doing the fans a favor by opening the doors. I understand very clearly that we're in the entertainment business, and people deserve that kind of personal attention."

Forciea said he planned to stay on the political sidelines as long as he worked for the North Stars. He also noted that changing fortunes—for a politician or a hockey team—wouldn't be instantaneous.

"It took eighteen months for Paul Wellstone to win," Forciea said. "Things don't happen overnight. I wish we could turn it around by the end of March, but that's not doable; we're not going to gimmick our way to respectability, because it doesn't do much good to win people back for one night. But we don't have an infinite amount of time to correct the situation either. I just hope people are impressed with our commitment to stay and make this organization healthy again."

Tuesday, February 19, 1991

As a US A-10 Thunderbolt attack aircraft was lost in Gulf War combat, a survey of Twin Cities gas prices revealed they had returned to levels prior to Iraq's invasion of Kuwait. A gallon of unleaded (self-service) cost $1.12.9.

Smail skated in practice already after undergoing knee surgery last Thursday.

Edmonton arrived and practiced later. Among the Oilers, on his first trip back to Minnesota, was Kari Takko. But there was little chance he'd supplant Grant Fuhr or Bill Ranford.

"What are you going to do?" Takko said. "This team has two of the best goalies in hockey and it looks like that's going to put me in the press box again. I understand; I'll wait and see how it all works out. It's nothing I can control."

Takko won his first four games as an Oiler but saw his playing time gradually diminish. His record stood at 4–4–0 with 4.20 GAA.

"I knew Grant would be back when I went to Edmonton," Takko said. "I knew I might have to move again. That's why my family stayed in Minnesota. Four months in Finland, two months in Minnesota, a few months in Edmonton is not good for the kids."

He said he'd either play in Europe next season or return to the NHL as a free agent.

"Maybe I'll be available if Minnesota is looking for a goalie after their deal with San Jose is finished," Takko said. "The guys who are here should realize what a great place the Twin Cities is, a great place to live and play hockey.

"The biggest difference I've noticed in Edmonton? They're a team. The big stars aren't stars in the locker room. Inside that room, everybody's equal. Even goalies who don't play much."

The North Stars announced a multi-year renewal of an agreement with Kalamazoo to be their top minor-league affiliate. One player who may never return is Link Gaetz, who entered an inpatient treatment program at Hazelden after being suspended indefinitely by Kansas City coach Doug Soetaert. Gaetz's latest misstep was ramming a pool cue through the glass of a pinball machine.

Later, Lemieux had four assists in a 6–3 win over Buffalo to extend Pittsburgh's home winning streak to eight games—one short of a franchise record. And St. Louis and Boston became the first teams to clinch playoff berths.

Wednesday, February 20, 1991: North Stars 5, Oilers 1, at Met Center

Casey had a game-day breakfast of Cheerios and peanut butter-and-honey sandwiches at the home he shared with his wife and three kids in Apple Valley. After he returned from the morning skate, Brenda Casey, who met Jon in college and is from Cavalier, North Dakota, tried to keep 5-year-old Jonathan and 3-year-old Joshua occupied during their father's afternoon nap, which usually ends about the time 7-year-old Crystal gets home from school. Then he ate a pregame meal of barbecued beef with corn and baked potatoes. Such was his routine on game days, a structured study in contrast to the summer, when the family vacationed in a travel trailer on a leased lot at a resort near Cass Lake. He loved to go boating and fishing and play cards with the retired guests.

"Jon would spend all summer fishing for muskies," Chico Resch said in an interview for this book. "He might only catch ten of them a year—and we would laugh about that—but they were big and it was quality over quantity for Jon."

There were different ways Resch tried to help Casey reach his potential.

"Through fishing as well, we built a relationship," Resch told me. "My job was to accentuate his strengths and tell him why they can work, how he can round off some edges and mostly keep feeling good about himself. But Jon liked the big splash. He didn't want to be a cookie-cutter goalie. Jon was a free spirit. He was doing things that other goalies weren't doing. He was aggressive. He relied on a very effective poke check. He would surprise shooters. He would challenge, but then sometimes over-challenge. It was like, 'Jon, when do you really want to use this?'"

Casey's aggressiveness became a key component in the North Stars' resurgence.

"Jon was so good at getting out of the net and his puck-handling was a catalyst for us," Hayward recalled thirty years later. "He did that weird thing where he switched his hands around on his stick for how you thought he should play it, but he could pass very well. Our philosophy became: stand everyone up at the blue line and let Jon or me—and he was better at it, frankly—handle the puck. Our D were able to peel off instead of going behind the net. I don't know of any team that was doing it that way at that time."

Hayward also remembered his relationship with Casey as different from other goalies.

"I was used to talking all the time with my goaltending partner in Montreal and Winnipeg," Hayward said. "There was a lot of turmoil around that time. Jon was one of the guys you couldn't talk to on game day. He didn't want to talk. So, I respected that and just stayed away from him. He was just a quiet, go-about-your-business kind of guy."

Resch said that may have been a misinterpretation or exaggeration of how Casey's reticent Iron Range roots manifested in the locker room.

"I don't think he was necessarily shy," Resch told me. "He was like a lot of Minnesota guys. They weren't arrogant. He grew up in a little town. He was a little like Billy Smith, the Hall of Famer who I played with, too. (Casey) loved the game, but he didn't like all the stuff surrounding it—like the interviews. It was like, 'Let's be doing something, otherwise I'm going to go and do what interests me.' With the media, he would tell the basics, but it wasn't like, 'I've got to be noticed.' That wasn't him."

Prior to the game, newspaper clippings highlighting team history were posted under glass in the concourse. The displays would rotate every month. If you examined them while sipping a beer between periods, you'd have had a hard time finding the last time the North Stars defeated Edmonton. To that point, it had been a stretch of thirteen games over five years. But a crowd of 6,195 and a KMSP-TV audience for a rare home game saw Modano score twice and set up two other goals as they knocked off the defending Stanley Cup champions.

The North Stars set their only team record of the regular season by allowing zero shots in the second period. By then, Propp had taken a high-sticking major for clipping Ken Linseman in the face. Propp was ejected and earned a one-game suspension for his second major stick foul of the season.

Casey daydreamed his way to 16 saves and, in the process, improved to 7–0–1 in his last eight games—the longest unbeaten streak of his career. From the beginning of the season through early December, he'd gone 2–8–2.

"In my mind, I was in danger of losing my job," Casey told the media after the game. "They traded Kari Takko, and I was used to talking through the tough times with him. As a team, we started to feel comfortable playing at home, and I worked through my own problems."

Ilkka Sinisalo changed his number from 25 to 32 but joined Mike McHugh as the only North Stars who registered no points, no penalty minutes and no shots.

Regarding Modano's move to right wing, Clarke said: "It's just a place to line up on a faceoff. It's a big rink, and he's a player who uses the whole ice surface."

Maybe. But Gainey always put a lot of thought into why he put Modano anywhere on the ice.

"I think you have to take into consideration that Mike was over-the-top talented in terms of physical skills," Gainey told me for this book. "He was a great athlete. Very committed. But there's a textbook that you have to learn when you go from playing with young men and boys to playing with adults. It takes time. Sometimes a player easily walks through those learning doors, and other times they've got to be kicked and pushed and shoved through because they're not all easy learns. If you don't learn, then you become a player with a lot of flaws in your game.

"To Mike's credit, over time he got past the learning curve and learned to play different ways in different situations, and that's one of the reasons he became such a well-rounded, skilled, beautiful player."

Thursday, February 21, 1991

Chicago, which comes to Met Center on Saturday night, and Montreal became the third and fourth teams to clinch playoff berths.

Since their 4–0 loss January 28 at Toronto, after which Green blasted his team, the North Stars have scored 42 goals in nine games (6–2–1)—an average of 4.67 goals per game. They have not been held to fewer than three during the stretch.

They're also 9–4–2 in 15 games since their mid-January loss to Montreal.

"With new guys there's so much guesswork," Gagner said. "I know we've talked about this until it's a dead issue, but there were just too many new faces. It took us some time to jell."

Perhaps as important, in the past 12 games since Doug Jarvis implored them to be more aggressive, the penalty killers have improved from worst in the league to allowing five goals on 58 chances (killing 91.4 percent of opportunities). Meanwhile, the power play—which was more or less Andy Murray's department—clicked 14 times in 38 attempts (36.8 percent).

"Special teams are funny," Jarvis said. "You have to be confident to be successful, but you need the success to gain confidence. The guys are at the point now where they are excited about getting out there."

Lest anyone get too cocky, Gainey said "I don't think you can call 15 games a roll."

Friday, February 22, 1991

President Bush issued an ultimatum to Saddam Hussein: Withdraw from Kuwait within twenty-four hours or face an imminent ground war. In absence of a response, one US Marine was killed in an artillery attack.

Rob Zettler, sent to Kalamazoo on a rehabilitation assignment, appeared in one game and reinjured his hip. He would return to MSP on Saturday for re-evaluation and was likely to be out indefinitely. His two-way contract paid him just $30,000 in the minors, but since his original injury came in the NHL, he'll make about $130,000 this season. A big Michael Jackson fan, it looks like Zettler is going to have plenty of time to study the man in the mirror.

Saturday, February 23, 1991: North Stars 3, Blackhawks 3, at Met Center

Saddam Hussein ignored President Bush's noon deadline for a withdrawal from Kuwait, and more than 530,000 US soldiers began a ground offensive at approximately the same time the North Stars faced off against Chicago. Iraq outnumbered the US in troops, tanks, and artillery pieces. The only American advantage remains a 2:1 margin in combat planes.

The biggest home crowd yet this season (14,832 fans, 261 short of a sellout) saw Casey stop 36 shots. Minnesota native and pro tennis star David Wheaton offered to buy the remaining tickets, but Green demurred. He did, however, direct free hot coffee be given to fans waiting in the snow to pay their way in.

A Bloomington company distributed 4,000 US flags, waved enthusiastically as the North Stars took a lead on three different occasions. Glynn scored 2:26 into the game, Bellows added a power-play goal at the nine-minute mark, and Gagner deflected home Modano's shot with a two-man advantage early in the third period. But Michel Goulet countered each time for his 14th career hat trick—completing it with his 1,000th NHL point.

Blackhawks goalie Greg Millen, who had played just 49 minutes all season, started for the first time since last year's division finals. But he lasted just nine minutes before Chicago coach Mike Keenan hooked him for Eddie Belfour.

Bellows taught me a quick lesson in PR after the game. I cornered him for an interview to put on the North Stars Hockey Hotline, another of my responsibilities. My first questions, as I saw it from a reporter's viewpoint, were about how the team had to be disappointed to let three separate leads get away. After about thirty seconds of that, he asked me to stop my tape recorder and start over.

"Positive, positive," he said, coaching me as he might a peewee at a hockey camp. "Everything we put out should be positive for the team."

Take 2 seemed to suffice and I loaded the cassette of his conversation into a machine that fed into a fan line. Then I ran summaries and stats to the dressing rooms and helped any straggling media corral the players they wanted. By the time we were done, it was perhaps an hour after the game ended. To drink in the atmosphere, I made a trip around the walkway between the upper and lower decks on my way back to the northwest corner of the building and the administrative offices. The arena was empty except for a few sportswriters in the press box and the cleanup crew. As music from KQRS-FM came through the arena speakers, perhaps two dozen men and women of all ages used brooms to push popcorn boxes, hot dog wrappers, napkins, and peanut shells into the aisles. There, the refuse was either scooped up or shoveled down to where it was collected in large garbage bags. The smell of stale beer was almost overpowering. After a large crowd like that, sometimes my dress shoes would stick to the floor. It felt like Met Center had been the scene of a colossal and successful house party. The fans left a mess that had to be cleaned up, but you knew they had a good time and would be back. By the time they did, everything would be clean and fresh again.

Sunday, February 24, 1991

Striking along a 300-mile front, US forces were on the outskirts of Kuwait City after one day of fighting. Marines, Army paratroopers, and Special Forces led the attack.

A *Star Tribune* reporter came to the U seeking reaction about the war and interviewed, among others, Dan Stuchal as he worked his "other" job, at the recreation desk in Coffman Union.

"It distracted me and worried me a lot more at the beginning," said Stuchal, who had a friend from Hayward High School flying F-16s in the Gulf. "It's terrible to say, but I sort of got used to it (the war). But now that there's a ground war and there's going to be a lot heavier casualties, it's going to be a lot more on my mind again."

Maybe. But he was working so many hours between Coffman and Met Center that the crash of bowling pins, the click of billiard balls, and the clack of ping-pong volleys barely kept him awake.

Monday, February 25, 1991

An Iraqi Scud missile killed twenty-seven soldiers and injured ninety-eight when it hit a barracks in Saudi Arabia. It's the worst US loss from a single battle scenario so far in the war. Since the ground campaign began on Saturday, American forces had taken more than 20,000 Iraqi prisoners at a cost of four US soldiers killed and twenty-one injured. Four more US aircraft were lost, and two pilots remained missing.

At Met Center, Broten told reporters he would play out his contract and become an unrestricted free agent. He didn't put much faith in the idea that the North Stars' recent advertising push over his name would signal a new deal.

"I hope they'd like to have me for playing hockey," Broten said. "I mean, I averaged a point a game for ten years. My family and I would like to stay. But if it's not going to happen, we'll make a change."

Les Jackson

Tuesday, February 26, 1991: North Stars 2, Flyers 2, at Met Center

The North Stars outshot Philadelphia 44–21 but trailed 2–0 until early in the third period when Modano scored his 20th goal of the season. Broten then tied it with 1:09 left in regulation before a crowd of 8,866.

In the first nine days of the coordinated drive under Forciea, the team had sold 537 season tickets.

"The timing of the season tickets offer, the timing of the players playing good ... it's some kind of miracle—like the parting of the Red Sea," Green gushed to Sansevere before the game.

By comparison, from October 1989 through mid-February 1990, the North Stars sold fifty-three season tickets.

"Pat is blessed with terrific instincts, a mind full of ideas, a sense of humor, an ability to see the big picture and, most of all, great timing," Senator Wellstone said later, comparing Forceia's political promotional flair with what he did with the hockey team. "He also has a commitment to underdogs and long shots. He's practically made a cottage industry out of them. Maybe he likes to gamble or maybe he knows something the others don't, or maybe he just has the confidence to make things happen."

Forciea may have looked calm on the outside, but inside he was a bundle of nerves—especially during games. A self-professed "worry wart," he watched the first period from his season-ticket seats in one corner of the North Stars' end. He usually reserved the second period to make corporate contacts. During the third period, he'd bite his fingernails while watching from the glass of the Zamboni doors. Since the team had yet to lose a home game under his watch, his routine wasn't about to change.

Neither was Les Jackson's. He'd get to the rink around 4 p.m. and wouldn't leave until after midnight, following postgame chats with a few players and a briefing with the coaching staff. Jackson had traveled all over Europe and North America looking for Minnesota's No. 1 pick in the coming draft, and he was beginning to conclude it wouldn't be Eric Lindros.

Just before Jackson headed out the door, Los Angeles became the first team in the Smythe Division to clinch a playoff spot.

In the Middle East, Iraqi forces began leaving Kuwait as US and allied troops secured the country.

Wednesday, February 27, 1991

Four days after the ground assault began in Kuwait, President Bush proclaimed the country liberated and ordered the suspension of offensive combat tactics.

Thursday, February 28, 1991

The Gulf War was over. Iraq accepted a cease-fire, ending a conflict that included more than three dozen nations, the largest military alliance since World War II. It lasted one month, one week and four days. The cease-fire allowed Saddam Hussein to remain in power, despite 146 US casualties and a total cost that would eventually exceed $60 billion, of which Kuwait and Saudi Arabia would reimburse $32 billion. The US lost more troops to enemy fire than the rest of the coalition combined, and 458 were wounded. But more than 20,000 Iraqi soldiers were dead, as well as more than 140,000 civilians from military strikes or factors tied to the destruction of the country.

Far from the conflict, in Edmonton, the North Stars practiced ahead of Friday's game against the Oilers. Conceding that Fuhr and Ranford would carry Edmonton in the playoffs, Takko announced his retirement. He could've accepted an assignment to Boston's AHL team, but instead would return to Finland.

"I regret it," Takko told me in 2021. "I should have taken a chance because Reggie Lemelin was going to retire, and it was a chance to take a spot. But I didn't challenge for it. Moving back, I kind of knew I was done with the NHL. Team Finland asked if I wanted to play at the World Championships, and I did because they were in Finland. You might have that chance once in your lifetime."[40]

40 Takko backed up Markus Ketterer, the top goalie in the tournament, as the Finns went 3–3–1, took fifth and won the consolation round.

Gary Olson (left) and Rachel Blount were featured on a North Stars game program in the fall of 1991. Note the cutting-edge laptop computers of the day

CHAPTER 9

March: Somebody Has to Make the Playoffs

Friday, March 1, 1991: North Stars 1, Oilers 1, at Northlands Coliseum, Edmonton

Brian Hayward, making his first appearance since February 12, stopped 30 shots and Dave Gagner scored a second-period power-play goal. Martin Gelinas tied it early in the third, but the North Stars stifled the Oilers much of the night. It got so quiet that people in the upper reaches of the arena could hear the players shouting to each other.

Gagner also took a high-sticking major in the third period. He raked Craig MacTavish across the face and earned a one-game suspension.

Al Shaver, Gary Olson, and Doug McLeod went out to dinner after it was over. Rachel Blount joined them at the last minute.

"She had a salad, and the rest of us had steaks," Shaver recalled with a hearty chuckle in an interview for this book. "We split the bill four ways. Rachel's share was $52. She was about to protest when Gary said, 'Rachel, you pay for the company.' Gary always had some smart remark like that. He had a good sense of humor, God bless him. He was a wonderful guy and a great writer."

Saturday, March 2, 1991: Flames 5, North Stars 1, at Saddledome, Calgary

With their top scorer watching in a suit and tie, the North Stars had little clout against Calgary. They've won once here since 1980, same as in Edmonton.

Frantisek Musil high-sticked Ilkka Sinisalo 33 seconds after the opening faceoff and Ulf Dahlen scored on the ensuing power play. But the Flames roared back with five consecutive goals—including two by Theo Fleury.

While the game was televised on MSC, there was no way Norm Green wasn't returning to Calgary at his first opportunity since taking over the North Stars. He left disappointed, as Jon Casey lost for the first time since January 15.

"That was the worst game we've played in ages," Mark Tinordi said.

Back at Met Center, Bloomington Kennedy and Richfield punched tickets to the state high school tournament with wins in a pair of section finals—the second of which was the last game in the career of legendary Edina coach Willard Ikola. The doubleheader drew 14,933 fans—more than any North Stars game to date.

Sunday, March 3, 1991

Shawn Chambers scored a goal and assisted on another in the last of a three-game rehabilitation assignment to Kalamazoo. He was expected to be in the lineup on Wednesday against Edmonton. With Chambers' expected return, Dan Keczmer and Mike McHugh were returned to the K-Wings for

Marc Bureau

the rest of the season. During the 18 games he was with the North Stars, Keczmer dressed nine times and had one assist. McHugh was pointless in six consecutive games and minus-3.

Monday, March 4, 1991

Bobby Clarke said he didn't intend to make any deals ahead of Tuesday's 3 p.m. trading deadline.

Pittsburgh wasn't waiting. The Penguins added Ron Francis, Ulf Samuelsson, and Grant Jennings from Hartford in exchange for John Cullen, Jeff Parker, and Zarley Zalapski.

Tuesday, March 5, 1991

Clarke lied.

The North Stars acquired center Marc Bureau from Calgary and dealt Sinisalo to Los Angeles. They gave up a third-round pick for Bureau, who had 40 goals and 88 points in 54 games at Salt Lake of the IHL, and received an eighth-rounder for Sinisalo, who had five goals and 17 points in 46 games.

Bureau played four seasons in the QMJHL, totaling 399 points in 282 games, before signing with the Flames as an undrafted free agent. He won a Turner Cup in 1988 with the Golden Eagles.

After playing right wing for his entire career, Calgary recently converted Bureau to center. His two-way contract would pay him approximately $45,000 if he spent the rest of the season with Minnesota. He packed a few suits, and his wife, Louise, dropped him off at the airport for the flight to Minnesota. Doug Armstrong picked up Bureau at MSP and got him settled at the Registry Hotel.

"I never heard anything about Minnesota North Stars, so I read about the team a little after I got there," Bureau remembered thirty years later. "Mike Modano was in my spot the year before on a line with Basil McRae. It felt flattering to be asked to do the same thing. Being at Salt Lake City, I was averaging two to three points a game. You move to the NHL and that's not the way it is, but if you get the ice time, anything's possible."

In Pittsburgh, Peter Taglianetti returned after missing nine games because of a collapsed lung and the Penguins beat Vancouver 4–1. It would start a 9–3–2 streak to finish the regular season.

It was hard to believe the Gulf War is over less than two months after it began. The last allied prisoners were returned from Iraq and US troops would begin heading home by the end of the week.

Wednesday, March 6, 1991: North Stars 5, Oilers 1, at Met Center

The North Stars finished the regular-season series unbeaten (2–0–1) against Edmonton for the first time in franchise history. A crowd of 6,882 saw Brian Bellows and Brian Propp each collect a goal and an assist and Gagner set up three goals. Casey stopped 23 shots.

"We have to save face here and turn attitudes around about our organization," Gagner said. "Making the playoffs isn't enough. It's time everybody puts a little extra pressure on themselves and starts believing we have to win. Maybe to save face, to turn people's thoughts about this organization around, we need to do more than make the playoffs. Maybe we need to win a couple of rounds."

Neil Wilkinson suffered a bruised thumb in a fight with Steve Smith.

The season-ticket campaign reached 860 sold.

Marc Bureau, recently arrived via trade, skates during practice on March 8, 1991, at the Met Center. (St. Paul Pioneer Press/Joe Oden)

Thursday, March 7, 1991

The last one-class Minnesota State High School boys hockey tournament began at the St. Paul Civic Center, which was an anomaly in that it featured clear Plexiglas dashers. It was one of the only rinks in the world where you could see what happens below waist level if you were sitting in the stands and play came to the near boards.

The afternoon session, featuring victories by Grand Rapids and Hill-Murray, drew 17,931 fans. In the evening, 17,448 gathered to see Burnsville and Duluth East win.

Friday, March 8, 1991

Hill-Murray and Duluth East each won semifinals in the boys hockey tournament before crowds of 15,969 and 16,772 in St. Paul.

In Fort Myers, Florida, the Twins played their spring training opener—a 5–3 win over Pittsburgh—before 6,962 fans. It was their first game in a new $11.5 million spring training facility after almost thirty years at aging Tinker Field in Orlando.

Rob Zettler celebrated his 23rd birthday by testing his injured hip in practice at Met Center. He hadn't given up on getting back in the lineup, but time was running out.

Later, a large group of players and their wives met for dinner at Manny's Steakhouse in Minneapolis. It had become an occasional event and was one reason the team had begun to gel.

Saturday, March 9, 1991: North Stars 6, Red Wings 2, at Met Center

Dahlen posted a career-best five points, including a hat trick, to demolish Detroit in a matinee that started at 1:35 p.m. to avoid a conflict with the state high school championship.

"I'm not a great skater," said Dahlen, who nonetheless could maintain full speed even when his feet were in the same position as the hands on a clock at a quarter to three. "So, I always want to be good along the boards, even back home. The game is played there a lot, and that's where I know I can contribute."

This was Clarke's best example yet of Dahlen being a first-round talent.

"There's a lot more to the game than flash, eh?" Clarke said. "A lot of players skate like hell and nothing ever happens. Ulfie brings substance to the game. He plays well in traffic, and he comes up with the puck when two or three guys are around it. He's not a bad skater. He has kind of a different stride, but he's agile on his feet, and he gets there fast enough. And when he gets there, he does something. He makes something happen."

Lately, anyway. Dahlen had 12 points in 26 games before Christmas. Now he has 22 points in his last 29 games.

"It's funny—I had a slow first half and things didn't go my way," he said. "That's the way it is sometimes. You do everything the way you want to, and it still doesn't work out. Today my first two shots weren't perfect, but the puck went in. It seems like that's what's happening with the team. We just kept trying… and the puck finally started going in for us."

Casey allowed only a short-handed goal to Dave Barr and a power-play goal by Bob Probert on 28 shots.

"I can't think of a game this year where we could say he was the reason we didn't win," Gainey said of Casey. "But I can think of a lot of games where we could say he's the reason we came away with points."

A crowd of 11,607—goosed by a Year of the Uniform promotion ("Moon wear" pants to the first 3,000 kids)—roared when an announcement was made that playoff tickets would go on sale. They'd cost $31 and $28.50 in the lower bowl. The upper bowl ranged down to $11.

And season-ticket sales passed 1,000 since February, prompting Green to celebrate by pouring champagne in the press box.

Casey took advantage of a rare Saturday night off at home to tune in WCCO-TV Channel 4 and watch Hill-Murray defeat Duluth East 5–3 to win the final single-class state title.[41] Attendance was 16,935, totaling 99,507 for the tournament. Eleven years earlier, Casey was in goal when Grand Rapids won the championship. Nine years ago, he helped win an NCAA title at the University of North Dakota. He continued to search for such satisfaction as a pro.

Sunday, March 10, 1991: North Stars 7, Flames 3, at Met Center

Eight days after losing by four goals in Calgary, the North Stars exacted their revenge before 7,082 fans and an MSC-TV audience.

Curt Giles and Bellows scored in the first period as the teams twice traded goals. But the North Stars blew it open with four unanswered in the second. Modano and Brian Glynn scored on the power play, Gaetan Duchesne added the game-winner at even strength, and Perry Berezan converted a short-handed breakaway. Hayward made 26 saves.

41 In 1992, the MSHSL would go to a much-maligned two-tier system.

It was almost enough to put a smile on the head coach's face.

"When will I get excited? When we're still playing in May," said the always-unruffled Gainey, whose wife, Cathy, was nonetheless energized in her recovery from surgery by the prospect of the playoffs. "There are people who like to call our team hot. I don't know if they're hot or that's just our team. We are much better than we were."

Bureau played his first game against his former organization and collected his first NHL points with assists on the goals by Duchesne and Glynn.

"In Salt Lake, sometimes we had 10,000 people," Bureau recalled in an interview for this book. "There were pretty good crowds there, especially when you had special events—like Bikini Night or something like that. In Minnesota, for me just to be in the NHL I didn't look too much at the 7,000 fans, and they had the seats with yellow and green and black that looked like people in the stands. I was in The Show. I was getting dressed and jumping on the ice. It felt packed for me."

While he may have been in "The Show," the rental car the North Stars provided was a Subaru Justy, a three-cylinder subcompact with a manual transmission. And Louise Bureau, who had joined Marc at the Registry, felt marooned because she knew no one in the Twin Cities yet.

Bobby Smith was scratched. He was goalless with three assists, five shots and minus-1 in his last seven games. His status as Gainey's former teammate earned him no favors as the team battled for playoff position.

"There was a line there between coach and player," Smith told me thirty years later. "But it was kind of funny or strange, when you look back at the fact that my wife might spend the entire day with Cathy Gainey, and yet Bob treated me like one of his twenty-three players, and I treated him like a coach, and that was it."

Earlier in St. Paul, 13,476 fans watched in person and more tuned in KITN-TV Channel 29 as the Gophers beat Wisconsin 3–2 in the WCHA semifinals.

Monday, March 11, 1991

The North Stars gathered for an informal team photograph at Peavey Plaza. It would be used as part of a promotion Lou Nanne organized with Pillsbury. It also was the beginning of the end for Nanne's tenure with the team.

Seeing the players depart from Met Center, Green wondered what it was all about. Nanne explained that Pillsbury would pay $25,000 for the sponsorship and buy season tickets on top of that. Green wanted more. He said he hadn't signed off on the deal and Nanne should go back to Pillsbury and say so. But Nanne wouldn't budge, saying he'd given his word on the arrangement. Green told him they wouldn't be able to continue working that way, and that's when Nanne decided there was no chance he would remain with the team beyond the end of the regular season. Green did, however, persuade Nanne to be the TV color commentator for the playoffs—which look increasingly likely.

On Monday night, Northern Michigan knocked off the Gophers 4–2 to win the WCHA playoff title on Channel 29 and before 11,028 fans at the St. Paul Civic Center.

Tuesday, March 12, 1991: North Stars 5, Sabres 2, at Met Center

The Met Center media lounge featured an elevator that also served suite holders on the east end of the building. A guest book and game notes stood nearby and there were free mineral waters and sodas. A steam table warmed food for those fortunate enough to gain admittance. The press box was out a door and up a few steps to the west. Earlier in the season, pregame meals were served in the lower concourse to the left as you went out of the North Stars' offices. That amenity has been moved here and, for the first time this season, representatives of the San Jose Sharks could attend just like those from the other 19 NHL teams. After charging admission to Bill Goldsworthy and other Sharks scouts earlier in the season, an agreement in principle on a deal to divide the North Stars' players at season's end led to a relaxation of hostilities.

"Representatives of the San Jose team are welcome in our press box, in the president's suite—well maybe not that welcome—and in the press lounge," Green said. "Right now, we're trying to decide if we'll refund the money they spent on tickets to see our games. We may need receipts."

Casey was the star of tonight's show, stopping 30 shots and improving to 10–1–3 in his past 14 decisions. The North Stars—for the first time since the second game of the season—raised their point total ahead of five teams (Toronto, Winnipeg, Vancouver, Quebec, and the New York Islanders).

"I've got to keep working to keep my job," Casey said afterward with a poker face as he huffed and puffed on an exercise bike.

Wednesday, March 13, 1991

The North Stars flew to St. Louis ahead of Thursday's game against the Blues. Detroit beat the Rangers 4–1 to clinch the third playoff spot in the Norris Division. That left the North Stars, with 63 points, and Toronto, with 49, battling for the remaining berth.

In all reality, it was likely over as Minnesota had nine games left and could clinch with any combination of five more points or five points dropped by the Maple Leafs.

Thursday, March 14, 1991: North Stars 2, Blues 2, at St. Louis Arena

As the state girls high school basketball tournament tipped off on a court laid down over the ice at Met Center, there was no room on the TV dial for the North Stars' game at St. Louis.

Too bad. No one got to see Modano tie it with 11 seconds left in regulation, slamming a slap shot past Blues rookie backup goalie Pat Jablonski.

Green flew to St. Louis to attend in person and saw Neal Broten lay a perfect pass for Modano with an extra attacker on for Casey, who finished with 26 saves.

At the Metrodome, the NCAA men's basketball Midwest Regional drew crowds of 25,348 and 25,759 for the afternoon and evening sessions. Only the evening session, when much-hyped LSU sophomore center Shaquille O'Neal scored 27 points in a loss to Connecticut, was televised locally.

Friday, March 15, 1991

As the North Stars moved on to Toronto, the Gophers dropped their first game in a best-of-three NCAA Tournament series against Providence. The game drew 4,315 fans, easily the smallest crowd of the season at Mariucci Arena—largely because it was spring break for the students.

Saturday, March 16, 1991: Maple Leafs 4, North Stars 3, OT, at Maple Leaf Gardens, Toronto

Michel Petit scored 2:44 into overtime to save face for Toronto and delay the North Stars' inevitable clinching of the final Norris Division playoff spot.

Modano's 25th goal had given Minnesota a 3–1 lead early in the second period. But Mike Foligno answered 23 seconds later with a bad-angle shot that beat Hayward, and Vincent Damphousse tied it in the third with McRae off for holding.

"We're not a powerhouse that can have a sixty percent effort or an eighty percent effort," Bob Gainey said. "A lot of players had off games. We didn't have a good effort right through our team."

In Minneapolis, Duke and UConn advanced in the Midwest Regional before 28,114 fans at the Metrodome, which would host the 1992 Final Four, while the Gophers forced a third game of their NCAA series with Providence, winning 8–4 before 5,197 at Mariucci Arena.

Sunday, March 17, 1991: North Stars 4, Maple Leafs 3, at Met Center

Wearing green jerseys on St. Patrick's Day, the North Stars finally clinched the last playoff position in the Norris Division and tied a franchise record for remaining unbeaten at home through 13 straight (11–0–2), this time before 7,234 fans.

"We knew it was a matter of when we would do it," said Modano, whose slap shot 5:22 into the third period broke a 3–3 tie.

Since the January 15 home loss to Montreal, Minnesota was 14–6–6.

"We had started to buy in during January, February, and March," Gainey told me for this book. "There was an improvement there that was very tangible. Players are placed in roles they're OK with, and they're having success. We're beating good teams. We're very strong on defense. Our goaltending is above average, and our special teams are good. We looked like a different team from earlier in the year."

Giles suffered a bruised knee in the first period and was taken to Fairview Southdale for x-rays. Wilkinson returned after missing five games with a bruised thumb.

"No one wanted to go out of the lineup because you didn't know if you were going to get back in," Wilkinson recalled in a 2021 interview.

Scratches were Berezan (for the first time in 18 games), Chambers (first in seven), and Stew Gavin (healthy, in back-to-back games for the first time this season). It was a continuation of a frustrating time for Berezan.

"I was never able to find a role where (Gainey) was happy with what I could bring to the table," Berezan said thirty years later. "He looked at me and said, 'I need to find somebody else.'"

That turned out to be Bureau. They were close to the same size and the only right-handed centers the North Stars had. Gainey just thought Bureau was more "rugged."

"I have the utmost respect for what (Gainey) did with the organization that year—even though it was basically the writing on the wall for me because I was never going to be loved by him," Berezan said. "He wanted me to be someone I couldn't be, which was that real tough player. I just couldn't be that gritty. He was hard on others, and it helped me that I had some good friends there who could help me put it in perspective. I'm talking about a guy like Andy Murray. They were pretty much asking me, 'Perry, what are you?' At that point in my career, I had no idea. When I first got into the league, Badger Bob (Johnson) was my coach and he loved and praised everything I did. Everybody needs to be pushed differently. Then you either crack or you don't. Badger Bob praised outwardly the things that he needed me to do the most. Instead of slamming me, 'You're horrible at this, you're horrible at that,' I was getting praise. 'Keep doing this. Keep doing that.' When Terry Crisp came to Calgary, he basically was slamming me for everything Badger loved.

"When I arrived in Minnesota, Pierre Page was there, and he'd been an assistant coach with Badger. So, he was pushing those same buttons, and it was working out good, and, boom, Pierre's gone. Having someone like Bob come in, we knew what he wanted from that slot position on the third and fourth lines, and I wasn't ever going to be that guy. Every practice, you were just wondering, 'Is this drill going to be good enough for him?' It was a grind. That's why, when you reached out to me for this book, I was like, 'You don't want to talk to me.' My years living in Minnesota were enjoyable but, personally, that last year was tough."

Armstrong, a favorite of many of the players, was Berezan's conduit to Gainey.

"I'd go talk to him and say, 'What's going on?'" Berezan said. "He kept saying, 'You need to find a way to get into Bob's books.' Whether I didn't have it in me anymore or I just couldn't find it, I don't know. Trying to reinvent yourself is hard. At the end of the day, you are who you are. When I was getting scratched regularly, you can only keep up your positivity for so long before they break you. When they told me they were going to send me down, I was like, 'All right. Do what you've gotta do. Whatever.' Then Doug told me, 'Bob was upset that you didn't come in screaming and yelling at him.' He was looking for someone who would fight to the death. When I did try that one time with Bob, it didn't go over very well. He said something about me in front of the whole team. I thought, 'OK, if he wants me to I will.' He basically told me to get the hell out, and I don't think I played much after that."

Elsewhere, Buffalo clinched the final playoff spot in the Adams Division. One spot remained in the Smythe Division for either Vancouver or Winnipeg. Amazingly, no playoff spots had yet been clinched in the Patrick Division, where first-place Pittsburgh held a one-point lead over the Rangers.

Ralph Strangis later said the lack of drama in the Norris Division helped the North Stars.

"Somebody had to finish fourth," Strangis told me in an interview for this book. "It's the old story where the guy and his buddy are walking through the woods and a bear comes up. The guy sits down and puts his track shoes on. The other guy says, 'What are you doing? You can't outrun the bear!' He's like, 'I don't have to outrun the bear. I just have to outrun you.' That's what this was. All they had to do was be better than Toronto. That wasn't a high bar. So, they were going to be in the playoffs, and I think once they realized that they thought, 'Wow. We know who we're going to play.' That was a huge advantage. Nobody knows who they're going to play now; you're scouting six teams until the last night of the season. They were going to play (Chicago or St. Louis) two more times before the season ended.... I don't think they had big aspirations but, OK, there's the target."

Going head-to-head with a 7:05 p.m. faceoff at Mariucci Arena, the Gophers drew 7,626 and advanced to the NCAA quarterfinals with an 8–3 win over Providence.[42]

And in Kalamazoo, the K-Wings clinched a Turner Cup playoff spot. They led the IHL's East Division but had trailed Peoria all season for best record in the league.

Monday, March 18, 1991

Tinordi suffered several cuts, including one to his face, after Broten fell forward in front of him at practice. Tinordi was taken to the hospital for more than thirty stitches.

After more than three months of working seven-day weeks between Met Center and the *Pioneer Press*, I needed some rest or I was going to be right there with Tinordi. So, I flew to Fort Myers, Florida. Jim Caple, who covered the Twins for the St. Paul paper, offered to let me crash at his condo as respite during a week when the North Stars were idle except for a Friday game at Washington.

Tuesday, March 19, 1991

INXS (whose recent hits included "Suicide Blonde" and "Disappear") played to 8,528 fans at Met Center.

42 They would be swept out of the tournament the following weekend at Maine.

Wednesday, March 20, 1991

After a few days of wondering whether I had mononucleosis, I finally climbed out of bed to see the Twins beat Texas 3–0 in Fort Myers. I watched from the press box, but more than 7,000 fans paid their way in to see the Twins improve their spring record to 11–3, best in the American League.

The weather was sunny with temperatures in the low eighties. That was 35 degrees better than cloudy, windy, and wet Minnesota.

Thursday, March 21, 1991

The North Stars flew to Washington ahead of Friday's game against the Capitals.

Pittsburgh beat the Rangers 5–4 on Kevin Stevens' goal just 13 seconds into overtime. As a result, the Penguins became the first team in the Patrick Division to clinch a playoff spot. Twelve of their nineteen players, including goalie Tom Barrasso, registered at least one point. Mario Lemieux was not one of them.

Friday, March 22, 1991: Capitals 3, North Stars 1, at Capital Centre, Landover, Md.

Doug Smail

Casey (23 saves) lost a duel with Don Beaupre (33 saves) and Calle Johansson scored in the first period on a shot from the neutral zone that slipped past Casey. Propp averted the shutout with a power-play goal 1:15 into the third.

Giles (knee), Zettler (hip), Shane Churla, Doug Smail, and Smith all were scratched as the North Stars had the maximum twenty-five players available.

Not playing was a wakeup call for Smith, straining his relationship with Gainey. It hasn't been easy for Smail, either.

"I started out playing well, but the pounding on that (left) knee wasn't going to allow me to be what I could have been," Smail recalled in an interview for this book. "I'd had seven surgeries on that knee. It took awhile to come back after that arthroscopic thing—it just didn't feel right… it wasn't carrying me like it should have been and I was in and out of the lineup. Bob Clarke and Bob Gainey both gave me opportunity, but I didn't have discussions with them about my knee. At that time, it was something you just sort of hid."

Saturday, March 23, 1991

The North Stars flew to Chicago ahead of Sunday's matinee to wait for the Blackhawks, who were playing in Pittsburgh.

Beginning January 5, the Penguins won a franchise-record 11 in a row at the Igloo. They tied Montreal on March 12 and then won two more to go 13–0–1. Chicago snapped that streak with a 7–5 win.

Sunday, March 24, 1991: Blackhawks 5, North Stars 4, at Chicago Stadium

I returned from Florida in time to join a KMSP-TV audience that watched Hayward allow five goals in a span of nine minutes in the second period, turning the North Stars' 1–0 lead into a 5–1 deficit. Bellows scored twice, the second making it a one-goal game with 2:17 left, but Belfour made 30 saves and hung on.

"We need to grit our teeth a little more, clench our fists a little tighter," Gainey said.

Churla and McRae clenched their fists plenty. Churla fought Stu Grimson when it was 1–1 but drew an instigating minor that led to a power-play goal. McRae fought Bob McGill when it was 4–1, and Troy Murray scored the game-winner before they returned to the ice.

Hayward made 21 saves, and Bureau was the only Minnesota player who was minus-3.

Monday, March 25, 1991: Blues 5, North Stars 4, at Met Center

The North Stars lost their third straight since clinching a playoff spot. Bellows' power-play goal 20 seconds into the third period gave them a 4–3 lead, somewhat magical considering they'd trailed 3–1 midway through the second. But Brett Hull tied it with his 83rd goal of the season, and Rod Brind'Amour won it as Mike Craig sweated out a hooking penalty. The crowd of 10,070 was disappointed in a home effort for the first time since January 15 against Montreal—also the last time Casey lost at the Met.

Off the ice, there were losses, too. George Wettstaedt, VP for finance, and Dick Arneson, VP of administration, were told their contracts would not be renewed. Arneson, who had been given the task by Green of firing more than half of the team's personnel the previous summer, was the last of the original North Stars employees.

Tuesday, March 26, 1991

Lemieux scored a hat trick in Pittsburgh's 3–1 win at Philadelphia. The first two goals came on breakaways. Later, a puck struck him in the face and he needed fourteen stitches near his left eye, leaving him out for the Penguins' next game Wednesday at Detroit.

Wednesday, March 27, 1991

Most of the North Stars flew to Los Angeles—all but Broten, Duchesne, Chris Dahlquist, and Giles. Dahlquist bruised his knee against St. Louis, similar to the injury that kept Giles out of action on the previous road trip. The others were resting because, with three games left, the team couldn't escape fourth place anyhow. The only question was whether Chicago or St. Louis would be the opponent in the first round of the playoffs, starting on April 4.

"We've got to be concerned, and our goal is to win games," Gainey said. "But we still have a lot of parts of the engine in good working order. We just have to clean up the small parts that are not. What we need to understand is that everyone needs to be at his very best to beat the kind of competition we will face in the playoffs. We have to be better than good."

Pittsburgh clinched the Patrick Division title with a 7–4 win over the Red Wings.

The NHL Hall of Fame added two members: Scotty Bowman, the winningest coach in history and current director of player development for the Penguins, and Doug Armstrong's father, Neil, a linesman for 21 seasons.

Thursday, March 28, 1991: Kings 6, North Stars 5, at Great Western Forum, Los Angeles

Trailing 5–2 with barely five minutes to go, Modano sandwiched goals around one by Glynn, and twice cut the deficit to one. But there they stalled as Casey stopped 19 shots and the North Stars lost their fourth straight game.

Los Angeles got goals from six different players, including Wayne Gretzky—who netted his 41st—and clinched the Smythe Division title.

Elsewhere, Washington and New Jersey clinched the last two playoff spots in the Patrick Division, and Vancouver defeated Winnipeg to claim the last berth in the Smythe.[43]

43 Of sixteen playoff teams, only the Canucks would have fewer points (65) than Minnesota. The Philadelphia Flyers posted 76 points in the Prince of Wales Conference Patrick Division but missed the postseason.

Friday, March 29, 1991

The North Stars flew back to prepare for Saturday's regular-season home finale against Chicago.

After four consecutive losses, the players expected the worst from Gainey at practice. Shortly before they were to take the ice, Murray burst into the dressing room and screamed something about a video meeting, "Now!"

"We looked at each other like, 'Wow. Even Andy's pissed off,'" Berezan remembered in 2021. "After a few losses in a row, Bob was not a good person to be around. But Andy was Mr. Positive. He gets us together, and he's got whatever he has queued up. Bob's pissed off, and Andy was like, 'This is going to be the difference in how we play.' It was an interview with Esa Tikkanen on Hockey Night in Canada. You couldn't understand a word he was saying. They called it 'Tikkanese.' Eventually, everyone in the room is laughing their butts off about the worst interview you could possibly have. Andy turned it off and said, 'OK. Go get ready for practice.' It was a little sense of humor and even Bob smiled."

The Blackhawks practiced at Met Center during the afternoon. I sneaked up from my cubicle to watch a few minutes. Shortly after warming up, the two dozen players in uniform began skating in a circle in the zone at the west end of the arena. They moved so fast, and the players were so big, you could hear the howl of the wind as they went around and around.

We also announced our home playoff games would be televised on MSC and offered via pay-per-view through any cable provider that didn't have an agreement for the coverage. Cost would be $9.95 per game. While 425,000 households in a five-state area had access to MSC, about 350,000 households in the Twin Cities would have to go the pay-per-view route in order to watch.

Saturday, March 30, 1991: North Stars 2, Blackhawks 1, at Met Center

Casey stopped 27 shots and didn't allow a goal until the final 16 seconds, and Propp and Bellows provided enough offense to satisfy the only sellout crowd of the regular season: 15,213—with 120 of those in standing room. It was the North Stars' biggest non-playoff home crowd in more than four years.

"After the run we've had, it was important just to get a win and create some momentum going into the playoffs," Casey said.

There were no fights, but there were twelve minors for unsportsmanlike conduct and three 10-minute misconduct penalties (to McRae, Churla, and Chicago captain Dirk Graham). Still, Gainey was puzzled by the way the on-ice officials called the game.

"I haven't quite figured out how we could be at home, against the most penalized team in the league, and be out-penalized 6–3 with one more misconduct," Gainey said. "Our penalty killing was good, and our goaltending was much stronger. But it scares me about going out on the road and playing with a referee like Ron Hoggarth."

The Blackhawks lost for the first time in eleven games and would need to beat Detroit on Sunday night in Chicago to assure themselves of the President's Trophy and the Norris Division title. The North Stars headed to St. Louis knowing that, if they lost to the Blues and Chicago couldn't beat the Red Wings, it will be St. Louis against Minnesota in the first round instead of the expected Blackhawks-North Stars matchup.

"Do I have a preference between Chicago and St. Louis?" Gainey said, repeating a question. "We'd like to play them both… We're going to St. Louis to win."

In some ways, he already had. Cathy Gainey attended the game. She had a large scar on the right side of her head, and her hair has receded around her ears but remained jet black. She had lost some memory and organizational skills, but only grudgingly allowed hired help into their home for cleaning and cooking.

Anybody who wanted one walked out of the arena with the team poster sponsored by Pillsbury. One of those fans was Senator Paul Wellstone. Another was Link Gaetz, who had just completed rehab at Hazelden and moved into a halfway house. Saturday's attendance stood in stark contrast to the season average: 7,838.

The North Stars had sold 1,703 new season tickets, more than doubling their total from prior to the campaign that began in February. Twelve players' wives called buyers this week to thank them.

The game was televised on MSC and, nonetheless, *outdrew* the NCAA championship hockey game being played in St. Paul—shown nationally on ESPN but blacked out in the Twin Cities. Northern Michigan beat Boston University 8–7 in triple overtime before 12,564.

Sunday, March 31, 1991: Blues 2, North Stars 1, at St. Louis Arena

Hull scored his league-leading 86th goal midway through the second period and set up Dan Quinn on the power play 1:46 into the third to break a 1–1 tie.

Bellows scored his 35th goal 5:15 into the game, which started at 6:05 p.m. on Easter, but that was most of the excitement for a KMSP-TV audience. In the twenty-six regular-season games on Channel 9, the North Stars went 4–19–3.

Hayward, 1–6–2 with an .882 save percentage since January 25, finished with 29 saves.

McRae didn't make the trip after he was hit in the face by Belfour's blocker on Saturday.

With Hoggarth the referee for the North Stars' third straight game and fourth of five, Churla and Gagner each got 10-minute misconduct penalties. The Blues had none. And Minnesota had four power-play chances to St. Louis' eight.

"He was skating around with a smile on his face," Gagner said of Hoggarth. "I think it's obvious he has a grudge against us. He's not being objective."

After the game, Gainey tried to accost Hoggarth, but he skated away with police flanking him on either side.

"After having him work four of our last five games, we deserve a medal," Gainey said of Hoggarth. "Or maybe he does.… Maybe we've seen him too much, or maybe he's tired of seeing us."

Even after the game concluded, the playoff matchups weren't certain until Chicago finished a 5–1 win over Detroit. The Blackhawks won the President's Trophy with 106 points and would play host to Minnesota, which finished with 68.[44] The Blues, who finished with 105 points, would play host to the Red Wings, who totaled 76. Both series were set to begin Thursday.

"We knew a long time ago that we would have a great challenge ahead of us in the playoffs," Gainey said. "We will have to be great."

If there was an omen going into the postseason, it had to be Saturday's victory.

"We didn't need to win that game," Gainey told me for this book. "Our playoff spot was secured, and we were going to be (fourth) in the division. But we needed to do some things in that game that were going to justify what we were going to do next week. And Chicago had to go home for their final game on Sunday, and because we beat them, they had not secured first place. So, they had to play for that. They had to play their final game with intensity, and in that game, Michel Goulet got hurt. If we had not played the game we did on Saturday, would Michel Goulet have been in the game on Sunday, and would he have been hurt, and would it have mattered? Taking Michel out, that was a big piece out of their lineup."

44 Since 1991, only the 1991–92 Hartford Whalers, with 65 points, ever made the playoffs with fewer than 68 points during a full season, and they went one-and-out, losing a seven-game series to Montreal.

The North Stars finished with 256 goals scored (3.2 per game) and 266 goals allowed. The league average was 276. They scored 76 power-play goals and allowed 75, (league average 71). They scored nine short-handed goals and allowed seven, (league average 11).

Gagner led in goals (40; a team-best half of them on the power play and five for game-winners) and points (82). Broten led in assists (56). Bellows, who totaled 75 points but was a team-worst minus-13, was the only player to appear in all 80 games. He also totaled 296 shots—64 more than Modano, who was second. Gagner and Jim Johnson each were a team-best plus-9. Churla led with 286 penalty minutes, Berezan had three short-handed goals, and Casey finished 21–20–11 with an .891 save percentage and a 2.98 goals-against average.

The North Stars started 4–14–5 but then went 23–20–9 to finish 27–39–14. They spent the entire season in fourth place and finished the regular season with five losses in their last six games.

Before the team boarded a late Sunday flight for home, Gagner put the season in perspective and previewed the playoffs: "There has been a lot of turmoil with this club, but I think we've put all the changes in the past. This is our chance to turn people's heads and make something meaningful out of this season."

Cinderella is the central character in a folk tale about unjust oppression and triumphant reward. The protagonist is a young woman whose circumstances are suddenly changed by remarkable fortune. Its roots date back more than 2,000 years—the first European literary version was published in 1634. Perhaps the most famous interpretation was printed in Grimm's Fairy Tales in 1812. In 1950, Disney created an adaptation that adds a twist where Cinderella's glass slipper is shattered just before she can try it on and prove her identity. Also unique to that film was how Cinderella's Fairy Godmother transformed a pumpkin into a carriage, mice into horses, and Cinderella's horse "Major" into a coachman and dog "Bruno" into a footman before giving her a shimmering gown and glass slippers. In the story, the Fairy Godmother also issues the warning that the spell making those things possible will expire on the last stroke of midnight.

Ironically, Disney itself became somewhat of a Cinderella story with the success of the tale. Walt Disney Productions was in dire financial straits in the 1940s after losing access to European film markets in World War II. Pinocchio (1940), Fantasia (1940,) and Bambi (1942) all bombed initially at the box office. As a result, the studio was more than $4 million in debt and on the verge of bankruptcy until Cinderella became its biggest critical and commercial success since Snow White and the Seven Dwarfs (1937). Cinderella earned three Academy Award nominations, and a children's album coordinated with the release sold 750,000 copies and hit No. 1 on the billboard pop charts. The film was re-released in 1957, 1965, 1973, 1981, and 1987. In 2018, it was selected for preservation in the United States National Film Registry by the Library of Congress because it is "culturally, historically, or aesthetically significant."

Cinderella, one could argue, made the long-term success of Disney possible, leading to an empire that would include television, movies, and theme parks. In the 1990s, the conglomerate also would invest in a National Hockey League team, the Mighty Ducks of Anaheim.

CHAPTER 10

Norris Division Semifinals: Cinderella Steps Out

Monday, April 1, 1991

It was 53 degrees and sunny as Andy Murray left the rented house he shared with his wife, Ruth, and their three kids (Brady, 6; Sarah, 2; and Jordy, 1) in Eagan and drove up I-35E and Cedar Avenue to Met Center. If you didn't know better, recognizing him as an NHL assistant might've seemed an April Fool's joke.

Murray grew up in Gladstone, Manitoba, where his family operated a second-generation auto dealership. While he played hockey, as virtually every Canadian kid did, he recognized excelling in the game might require him to move behind the bench. He became a Junior A coach at twenty-five, and three years later he vaulted to head coach at Brandon (Manitoba) University. After his father died at fifty-nine in 1981, rather than continue in car sales, Andy took a job coaching in Switzerland. He returned to the US in 1988 to become an assistant with Hershey of the AHL, the Philadelphia Flyers' top affiliate. The Bears conveniently won the Calder Cup, and Murray found himself in the right spot at the right time. St. Paul native and former Flyer Paul Holmgren invited him to join the Philadelphia staff, and that was how Murray made the unlikely jump to coaching in the NHL without much of a pedigree as a player.

"If you haven't been a player in the league, you have to earn your credibility in other ways," Murray told me in 2021. "I think I was kind of there as an idea person."

He was ahead of the curve as a tactician and someone who looked for innovative ways to coach and influence the game. Now he was going to try to convince the players, and especially Bob Gainey, that he had a philosophy that could help them win.

The North Stars met in the dressing room for an hour to review, discuss, and prepare for the first round of the playoffs against Chicago. The coaches split the players into position groups and gave them an assignment: What could they come up with that would be part of the game plan to beat the Blackhawks?

They had some ideas, and Murray certainly did too. That didn't mean they were brimming with confidence or feeling like it wouldn't be an uphill battle. Chicago finished the regular season 49–23–8 (.663). Since 1985–86, only two teams had posted more points. That was in '88–89 when Calgary and Montreal steamrolled to 117 and 115, respectively, and met in the finals.

"I think if you walked down the street and asked 100 people, all 100 would tell you Chicago's going to win," Doug Smail said.

Steve Larmer totaled 44 goals and 101 points. Could Dave Gagner raise his game to nullify that?

Jeremy Roenick scored 41 goals—including 29 at even strength and 10 game-winners. Was Brian Bellows prepared to be his equal or better?

Michel Goulet's loss for the Blackhawks was statistically comparable to the North Stars losing Brian Propp, Neal Broten, or Mike Modano. But Chicago also had Chris Chelios, a defenseman who totaled 64 points, was plus-23, and had 192 penalty minutes. Was Mark Tinordi ready to answer?

And even if they negate everyone else, there was Ed Belfour. The last goalie to win more games in a season than Belfour's 43 was Bernie Parent (47 in 1973–74). The only rookie ever to win more was Terry Sawchuk (44 in '50–51). Could Jon Casey shave a goal off every game to keep pace with Belfour?

Chico Resch, in a suit and slipping side to side in wingtips on the carpet in front of them, demonstrated Belfour's tendency to butterfly and cover the bottom part of the net.

"A lot of people would say, 'Yeah, Eddie Belfour, you can beat him over the glove,'" Resch remembered for this book. "But it's much more complicated than that."

He told the players how to come out of the corner against Belfour and what he would do. Resch went over at least a half-dozen keys, breaking it down to specifics: What's Belfour going to do following a point shot? On a wraparound, what's he going to do?

The basic message is to shoot high. During practice, each skater had to shoot twenty pucks at the crossbar. Since Bellows was the only one who could get away with that on Casey, Gainey brought in a college goalie and dressed him in a Blackhawks jersey for a target.

"The regular season is to prepare for the playoffs," Gainey said. "The teams you respect are the ones that are still playing in late May."

Only in the 1981 finals had the North Stars ever played after May 9. Those days and expectations were long gone.

"There are still a lot (of people) out there who don't know who we are," Gagner said. "The hardcore hockey fans know us, but we can gain the attention of a lot of other people with a good showing in the playoffs. We're still trying to change attitudes about this team, and that's the way we'll have to do it. They don't care if we're underdogs. They just want to see us win."

Game 1 was set for 7:35 p.m. Thursday in Chicago, followed by Game 2 on Saturday. While most regular-season home games started at 7:35 p.m., the North Stars' home playoff games, starting with Game 3 on April 8, would begin at 7:05 p.m.

Game 4 was scheduled for April 10 at the Met Center. Games 5 and 7, if necessary, would be April 12 and 16 at Chicago. Game 6 would be April 14 at the Met.

Tuesday, April 2, 1991

Lou Nanne finalized his decision to resign and become VP of Piper Capital Management Company, a division of Piper Jaffray. He'd remain on TV broadcasts as color commentator in the playoffs.

Nanne, forty-nine, was easily the most recognizable face of the franchise throughout its history. He played eleven seasons, was general manager for ten, and president for two before taking the VP of marketing and public relations post under Norm Green.

A good portion of this day was spent making preparations for a news conference announcing Nanne's decision to be held Wednesday morning in the media lounge off the press box. On the ice below, the team practiced before leaving for Chicago.

"If you can't get up for a game at Chicago Stadium, you can't get up for a game anywhere," Casey said. "Everything seems like it's right on top of you. They can score from anywhere, and they always have the pressure on. But I don't think they have the most talent in the league; they just outwork everyone else. We have enough talent to win."

Tinordi sounded psyched. And Chicago was just the team he wanted to play.

"Obviously, there is something about the Blackhawks that gets me excited," Tinordi said. "There is a group of people that sits upstairs at Chicago Stadium. When we go in there Thursday night, the first guy they will get on is Basil (McRae), then Shane Churla, then me."

Before they checked into the Drake Hotel, Murray handed everyone a three-ring binder. On its cover was the Blackhawks logo covered by a red circle with a slash. Fortunately, it wasn't for public consumption. Otherwise, Elaine Waddell might've had to take the fall again.

Wednesday, April 3, 1991

Nanne's news conference seemed more like a roast. With the team away and an empty arena providing the backdrop, a couple dozen people gathered in the media lounge—basically to listen to people fete Nanne and hear him tell stories.

"He was the single most important conduit between the Gunds, Howard Baldwin, and myself," Green said. "He is the reason the North Stars are still in Minnesota."

Nanne said failing to win the Stanley Cup was his biggest disappointment. Both men said the parting was amicable and unforced.

"I wouldn't be here if it wasn't for him," Green said. "He knows this community better than anybody else. He could have worked for me as long as he wanted to.... He has a chance to make some big money. He can't make that money with us."

In Chicago, the players continued to go over the game plan, which was to make the most of the fact that the Blackhawks were the most penalized team in the league during the regular season. To take advantage of that, the North Stars had to make sure they weren't goaded into the wrong situations. In eight meetings this season, the teams totaled 690 penalty minutes—an average of 86 per game. Chicago withstood its aggressive play, however, with the league's No. 2 penalty kill.

"We're not going to beat the Blackhawks by out-fighting them," Gainey said. "We know that, without being a robust, physical team, our chances of beating them diminish. We're depending on all our players to be that way, but we also expect them to be smart."

The North Stars hoped to go further than their last playoff appearance a year earlier, when they forced a seventh game but lost at Chicago, 5–2. Casey had a lot to do with getting that far. He allowed a total of three goals in Games 1, 4, and 6. As a result, Blackhawks captain Dirk Graham—formerly Casey's teammate—tried a little gamesmanship via a pre-series media interview.

"Jon (Casey) is a good goaltender, and he got hot," Graham said. "I don't want to take anything away from him, but I think it got out of proportion about how good he was. We were throwing a lot of rubber at him, but a lot of the shots were right in the stomach."

The Blackhawks also ended Minnesota's playoff aspirations in 1985, '83, and '82, though many of these North Stars weren't around for those series.

"The mood of the team is 'enough's enough,'" McRae said. "It's time for us to do something about Chicago. We all but eliminated them last year, and when we lost, we had a long time in the summer to think about it. We'd like to play a little longer this year."

Cathy Gainey would watch Thursday's game on TV but expected to be in the crowd when the series shifted to Minnesota. Since undergoing surgery in December, and following subsequent radiation and chemotherapy treatments, she remained unable to drive and hadn't yet resumed her aerobics classes. But she was sunbathing already this week when the temperatures hit the 60s.

"The sun is out; the birds are chirping," she told Rachel Blount. "I've got no complaints."

Except maybe about the strain on her husband, who soon would coach in the Stanley Cup playoffs for the first time. She was amazed at how he handled the stress and suppressed it at home. That's not to say the roller-coaster season, and especially Cathy's illness and surgery, didn't take their toll.

"He is on the verge of tears a lot," she said. "You're seeing what he's feeling."

Bob Gainey rarely showed such emotion publicly, though, and you got no inclination from talking to him at the rink—even about his wife.

"I think she's doing fine, and I believe she's going to do well," he said. "I don't sit and mope about it. I don't think it's going to make her feel any better, and I honestly don't feel like sitting and moping."

The playoffs opened with two upsets Wednesday night in the east. John Cullen scored a goal and assisted on two others to help Hartford win at Boston, 5–2. And, while Mario Lemieux scored, New Jersey shut down everyone else and got two goals from Peter Stastny in a 3–1 victory at Pittsburgh. It was especially shocking for the Penguins, who were 13–1–2 in their final 16 home games and 9–3–2 overall after the deadline deal that brought Ron Francis and Ulf Samuelsson from the Whalers for Cullen.

Elsewhere, Montreal mauled Buffalo 7–5, and the New York Rangers nipped Washington, 2–1.

Back at the Met Center, the Scorpions (of "Wind of Change" fame) played to a crowd of 7,062 people.

In Las Vegas, the odds on the North Stars winning the Stanley Cup were 10,000 to 1. On the Pittsburgh Penguins, they were 8 to 1.

Thursday, April 4, 1991: North Stars 4, Blackhawks 3, OT, at Chicago Stadium

In perhaps the most important game of the postseason, Propp scored at 4:14 of overtime, tucking the rebound of Tinordi's shot from the high slot underneath Belfour's left arm. The play came shortly after Keith Brown took a double-minor for high-sticking Gagner.

"I just got in front of the net and stayed in front of it," Propp told me in an interview for this book. "Sometimes it might go in off your ass, but that counts.... I was ready. I knew that you had to play much better in the playoffs. To win the first game, especially in overtime, made a huge difference because now we have a little confidence against Chicago. They were so good, but that made us think we could win."

It was the North Stars' first overtime victory in the playoffs since April 28, 1985, also at Chicago Stadium. The arena opened in 1929 and, for more than 60 years, it dominated the block at 1800 West Madison Street as one of the most nostalgic settings in NHL history. That title, of course, comes with a few inconveniences.

The near-west side neighborhood was rough. The acoustics were deafening to visitors. The fans were so loud their ovation drowns out the national anthem, played on a 3,363-pipe Barton organ built into the rafters. At full volume, it was louder than 25 brass bands and could shatter every piece of glass in the building.

The Stadium was a bandbox. None of the outer walls were more than 100 feet from the ice, which was shorter than standard length (185 feet long instead of 200).[45] Spectators were stacked on top of each other with two balconies above the main seating area, and the press box hung over one end of the rink, within easy reach of deflected pucks.

By late afternoon, the players honed their stick blades with files, heat guns, and blow torches beneath the lower stands before clomping up twenty-two wooden steps to enter the rink behind one net for warmups. By then, Mark Baribeau had carried the sticks up a ramp from the lower level, into the concourse, down a tunnel and through a couple of seats to get behind the bench. As with some other antique buildings (notably the Montreal Forum and St. Louis Arena), the quickest way from the dressing room to the bench was across the ice. That becomes an adventure for coaches, who tread

45 The regulation NHL rink was deemed in 1929 to be 200-by-85 feet. Older arenas, however, were grandfathered as official even if they didn't meet those dimensions. Boston Garden, for example, was nine feet shorter and two feet narrower than the rules required. The Montreal Forum was 200-by-80, and the Memorial Auditorium in Buffalo was 196-by-85. The Cow Palace, where the San Jose Sharks played their first two seasons, was 185-by-85—the smallest surface in NHL history. It wasn't until 1996, when the Sabres moved to a new arena, that all league rinks were 200-by-85.

lightly before each new period. As a result, Dave Smith keeps a sharpening stone in his pocket in case any of the players lose an edge. Otherwise, they're all on an island until intermission.

There were more fireworks than anyone could've expected in the first few minutes after the opening faceoff. Roenick shoved a rebound under Casey 13 seconds into the game. But Graham ran Casey 34 seconds later and drew a five-minute major for charging.

Tinordi scored a power-play goal at 1:24. Belfour was incensed at what he thought was interference and got an unsportsmanlike conduct penalty from referee Terry Gregson. Broten then beat Belfour with a slap shot during a two-man advantage at 2:08.

Doug Wilson tied it at 4:06 with Mike Craig and Neil Wilkinson off for roughing. Gregson then waved off a potential North Stars goal late in the first because he saw Propp poke Belfour's foot just before Tinordi's shot went in.

Graham put the Blackhawks in front in the second period when he converted a pass from Chelios. But Broten tied it again early in the third, capitalizing on a 3-on-2 breakaway. His two goals matched his output from December 26 to the end of the regular season.

"We have more confidence against Chicago than we did earlier," said Broten, whose wife, Sally, cheered and jeered with other wives while watching the KMSP-TV broadcast. "We've started on a good note, but we realize it's an uphill climb. We recognize who we're playing, and it's not the Roseau peewees."

Minnesota, which also won Game 1 in the 1990 first-round series at Chicago, had three power-play goals on eleven chances, and the penalty killers killed off five of Chicago's six. The North Stars, who once had the worst PK in the league, improved so much in the second half that they wound up 12th of 21 teams.

"No one expected us to win, and we weren't scared of losing," Tinordi said.

Tinordi had 11 power-play assists during the season. While his penalty minutes would always far exceed his point totals, he was growing more confident in his offensive ability.

"When I came back (from suspension), Bob Gainey started putting me on the power play," Tinordi said. "I was scared out of my pants. I made some mistakes on the point, but Bob stayed with me."

Green, accompanied regularly now by Pat Forciea, watched from the press box. And Gophers coach Doug Woog flew to Chicago to scout the series as a favor to Gainey.

Upsets were the rule in the other Campbell Conference playoff openers, too: Steve Yzerman scored a hat trick to lead Detroit to a 6–3 win at St. Louis; Geoff Courtnall's hat trick powered Vancouver's 6–5 stunner at Los Angeles; and Mark Messier set up two goals to lead Edmonton to a 3–1 victory at Calgary. The Red Wings finished 29 points behind the Blues, the Canucks were 37 points back of the Kings, and the Oilers are trying to overcome their worst regular season in 10 years.

Friday, April 5, 1991

The North Stars were forced to practice at a suburban Chicago rink because ice time at the Stadium was unavailable.

Green delivered about a dozen copies of the morning newspapers to the dressing room, underscoring the accomplishment of Game 1. As soon as he left, Gainey went around, gathered them up and threw them in a garbage can.

"If we had lost, we wouldn't be ready to cash in our chips," Gainey said. "Just because we won, we can't react the opposite way."

Later, after several Chicago reporters pressed him, trying to elicit some emotion after the upset, Gainey asked, "What do you want me to do? A back flip?"

"He has always stayed calm," Gagner said of his head coach. "He has never exploded. And I don't want to be around when he does."

Doug McLeod returned to MSP to emcee the Hobey Baker Award dinner and would be back Saturday to call a Gophers baseball doubleheader at Northwestern, followed by Game 2 at Chicago Stadium. On Sunday, he'll call another Gophers game before flying to the Twin Cities to prepare for Game 3 on Monday. McLeod grew up in Centerville, Iowa, which isn't exactly a hockey hotbed, and studied radio and TV journalism at Drake University. It took him twelve years after graduation to get a shot with the North Stars and, once he got his toes in the door of major league sports, he wasn't about to back down because of a little red-eye travel.

The NHL fined Montreal's Denis Savard $400 for spitting at an opponent in Game 1 against Buffalo. On Friday night, the Canadiens took a 2–0 series lead on the Sabres with a 5–4 win—Guy Carbonneau scoring the deciding goal with 1:21 remaining. Pittsburgh squared its series with New Jersey when Jaromir Jagr wriggled through two checks and beat goalie Chris Terreri 8:52 into overtime. Cam Neely completed a hat trick with a 15-foot shot from the right of the net as Boston pulled even with Hartford, 4–3. And Don Beaupre had 35 saves as Washington beat the Rangers 3–0 to even their series.

Even before the last of those games was complete, Bobby Smith had retired to his room at the Drake. His latest roommate, 24-year-old Marc Bureau, had little choice but to do the same.

"Bobby wanted to go to bed about nine o'clock," Bureau remembered for this book. "It's not like you were going to spend a lot of time in the clubs, but I'm lying there looking at the ceiling and thinking about what I could have been doing. That was pretty hard."

Saturday, April 6, 1991: Blackhawks 5, North Stars 2, at Chicago Stadium

Five weeks after most hostilities had stopped in the Gulf War, Iraq formally agreed to a permanent cease-fire.

There was no chance of any such de-escalation in Chicago, where the North Stars set a franchise record for penalty minutes in a playoff game with 146.

Jim Johnson and Wayne Presley got their sticks up, fought and received 10-minute misconduct penalties 3:16 into the game. Larmer beat Casey from the right circle at 12:58, and then the North Stars got in trouble. Roenick scored on a rebound three and a half minutes into the second period. Then a hooking call on Chris Dahlquist and tripping penalty against Casey led to a pair of power-play goals for the Blackhawks. Warren Rychel—who also had two assists in just his third NHL game—fired past Casey's glove at 14:40. After Steve Konroyd scored at 16:39, Gainey sent in Brian Hayward and it stayed 4–0 until almost four minutes remained in the game. McRae scored an unlikely goal on a penalty shot, and Bellows cut the margin to two on the man advantage less than two minutes later, causing McLeod and Nanne to come alive on Channel 9. But Larmer doused any comeback hopes when he scored his second goal of the game into an empty net.

In addition to the Johnson-Presley bout, McRae fought Stu Grimson midway through the game and, six minutes later, it was Churla's turn to go with Grimson. Both got 10-minute misconducts, as did Bureau and Tinordi later in the third.

"That was some ugly hockey," Dahlquist told me thirty years later. "Pucks were optional. At every whistle, someone was getting cross-checked in the back of the head and there was a scrum. Everybody and anybody played physical, and you just expected something was going to happen after every whistle. It's just a draining game. If anybody had the puck for more than a nanosecond, they were really controlling it. It was basically, move it and get your stick up because somebody was going to hit you. I don't think you could even fathom that game these days.… Guys were absolutely getting bear-hugged in the corner. Guys are skiing on the backcheck, hooking another player for a ride. It was crazy the different level of things you could do to compete and what was allowed."

The North Stars were outshot 26–13 through two periods, and Propp was one of five forwards without a shot in the game. Belfour finished with 28 saves. Casey had 21, and Hayward stopped all 10 shots he faced.

Retribution was the theme in every Campbell Conference series as the home teams all won Game 2. St. Louis scored four goals in the third period to roar back on Detroit, 4–2. Paul Ranheim, back from a broken ankle he suffered December 11 at the Met Center, had a goal and an assist in Calgary's 3–1 win over Edmonton. And Wayne Gretzky scored in overtime for Los Angeles to beat Vancouver.

That last game was still under way as the North Stars chartered back from Chicago. They arrived just as Daylight Savings time kicked in and stole an hour of their rest before Game 3.

Sunday, April 7, 1991

The North Stars practiced at Met Center in the afternoon. More than 3,000 tickets remained for Monday's Game 3 and more than 5,000 were left for Wednesday's Game 4. The parking lot wouldn't open until 5:30 p.m. That would be standard throughout the playoffs in an effort to prevent drunkenness and rowdiness. It took a sixty-member arena crew to clean up about fifteen cubic yards of trash after every playoff game, when tailgating was allowed. (It is forbidden—if mildly enforced—at all other events.)

The Blackhawks practiced, too, although roommate goalies Belfour and Dominik Hasek overslept, supposedly because they didn't set their alarm clock ahead. Greg Millen and a canvas bag provided the Hawks something at which to shoot.

That night, Mark Recchi scored unassisted off a turnover as Pittsburgh won at New Jersey, 4–3, and went up 2–1 to yank back home ice in their Patrick Division series. The Rangers (6–0 at Washington) did the same, as did Boston (6–3 at Hartford) in the Adams Division. Buffalo showed some life with a 5–4 home win over Montreal, with Minneapolis native Mike Ramsey scoring the game-winner.

Monday, April 8, 1991: Blackhawks 6, North Stars 5, at Met Center

Roenick scored a controversial goal 6:15 into the third period, completing the North Stars' collapse despite leading by three goals heading into the second. On the winning goal, Mike Hudson, Wilkinson, and Hayward were in a scrum in the Minnesota crease. The net was knocked loose, but referee Denis Morel ruled the puck had gone over the goal line first. Video replays appeared to show that Hudson shoved Wilkinson into Hayward. During this, Roenick converted a 25-foot shot into the upper left corner.

It rendered meaningless the best first period in postseason history for the North Stars, who led 5–2. But the Blackhawks countered with two power-play goals in the second, and Steve Thomas tied it early in the third before Morel found himself in the middle of a firestorm.

Another of my duties as a public relations intern was to supervise a visit by pool reporters, in this case Gary Olson and the Star Tribune's John Gilbert, to interview Morel in the officials' dressing room at the east end of the arena. Reporters almost never talk to referees. When they do, those in the press box elect proxies to handle the chore so a horde of sportswriters don't act like a lynch mob. The interview was like pulling teeth, and neither Morel nor linesmen Bob Hodges or Mark Vines spoke more than a few words, none contradictory to the result.

Dave Gagner (15) slips a shot under Blackhawks goalie Ed Belfour (30) during the first period of Game 3 on April 8, 1991, at Met Center. Gagner scored two goals as part of a franchise-record five-goal outburst for the North Stars in the first 20 minutes, but Chicago scored the last four goals of the game – including a controversial game-winner in the third period. (St. Paul Pioneer Press/Buzz Magnuson)

By the time I got back to the North Stars' dressing room, nobody had cooled down.

"Denis Morel blew the call," Hayward howled. "(Hudson) backed in and had both feet inside the rectangular part of the crease. The referee is supposed to keep that from happening. Otherwise all you need to do is throw the puck at the goal and knock over the goalie. It's awful for a game to be decided that way."

Gainey barked at the officials several times during the game and disputed multiple scoring plays.

"The winning goal was a goal that should not have been allowed," he said.

Wilkinson said Hudson effectively set a pick.

"All he did was cross-check me and drive me into the goal," Wilkinson said. "I ended up under the crossbar, and Brian ended up in the net. I tried to get out, but (Hudson) had me pinned. I saw the shot coming and tried to get my hand up, but it had already gone by."

So had their chance to go up 2–1 in the series. Smith, Bellows, and Gagner all scored power-play goals, and Gagner and Modano scored at even-strength in the first period—when Gagner tied an NHL record for points in a period with four. Modano missed on a breakaway for a potential sixth goal that might've changed the tenor.

But Wilkinson's high-sticking penalty at the end of the first led to one Chicago goal. Then Brian Glynn went off for tripping 3:56 into the second, Johnson took a major and game misconduct for high-sticking Larmer shortly after, and Wilson blasted a slap shot past Casey during a 5-on-3.

That made it 5–4 and brought Hayward off the bench. Casey made 14 saves, and Hayward had 11 the rest of the way, but he couldn't stop Thomas' rebound chance or the mass of humanity that came at the crease soon after. Gainey said he thought Casey should've stopped the first two goals—by Larmer and Chelios—in the opening ten minutes. Casey, as could be expected, wasn't happy about being pulled in Games 2 and 3.

"When you do that, I think you take a little something away from your goalie and give a little confidence to the other team," Casey said.

Blackhawks coach Mike Keenan yanked Belfour after the North Stars' fourth goal but put him *back* in when they got a penalty 8:40 into the second, trailing 5–4. Belfour made 37 saves. Hasek had five in 10:45.

"We're not going to talk about this loss," said Tinordi before he walked outside into a cold drizzle. "We just have to put it out of our minds.... There's not much we can do except play our hardest and not overthink what happened."

Earlier in the day, the North Stars had adjourned to the Decathlon Club after meeting at the rink. There they were able to nap in hotel-like rooms and eat a pregame meal in peace. It was a practice they would continue despite the loss.

Hundreds of people missed the start of the game because of a bottleneck at the will-call windows. About 4,500 were estimated to have waited in line as the opening faceoff approached. Attendance was 12,753—good by regular-season standards but smaller than any 1990 playoff crowd.

The first foray into pay-per-view of the MSC telecast didn't go very well, either. Cable subscribers in five suburbs didn't receive the whole game. Depending on location, it cut out in either the first or third periods.

More than 100 customers called to complain, and the team issued refunds for those who missed some or all of the game in person or on TV.

It wouldn't be public knowledge yet for days, and was never fully reported, but Johnson suffered a hip injury that would get worse as the series went on. Stew Gavin returned after sitting out both games at Chicago, while Craig and Curt Giles stayed in street clothes.

"We were watching the game in the video room," Perry Berezan recalled for this book. "Craiger says, 'Hey, any of you guys getting a little growly? I'm getting a little growly.' We're like, 'Go get some food.' He's like, 'But I want pizza.' And Met Center didn't have pizza then. He's like, 'I'm going to call Domino's.' We're like, 'You can't fucking call Domino's, Craiger.' Probably halfway through the first period, he calls Domino's from the phone in the video room. You knew Craiger. He was off the walls.

"This was the conversation: 'Yeah, I'd like to order a pizza. Delivered. Cheese, pepperoni, whatever, whatever. Address? Uh, yeah. Met Center.' The guy goes, 'We don't deliver to Met Center.' Craiger said, 'Yeah, this is Mike Craig from the Minnesota North Stars. Me and a couple of the boys in the dressing room, we're getting a little growly. Just tell your delivery guy to go to the back entrance and ask for Steve.'"

That would be Steve Ruane, Met Center's primary security guard.

"Remember Steve the security guy? He always had a gun with him," Berezan said. "That makes the story even better. Craiger has to explain the story again to the Domino's manager, and they were going to do it. We were like, 'Oh, my God. What if Bob Gainey finds out?' Then we hear—and I swear to God this isn't made up—Craiger, 'Uh, I don't have any money with me. Can I trade you a stick?' The Domino's guy is like, 'OK, we'll be there in thirty minutes.' He hangs up and the rest of us all had our hands on our heads, and Craiger is like, 'Don't worry about it. I've got it under control.' He went out and told Steve the whole story, came back and said, 'It's all set up.' I'm like, 'I don't even want to fucking be here. I wish I had somewhere else to go.' The period ends. The guys are in the locker room. There's a knock on the back door. I stick my head out, and Craiger shoves me aside. There's Steve with his hand on his gun, and he looks both ways like he's seeing if the coast is clear. Here's this Domino's guy behind him and his eyes are as big as fucking pizzas. They escort him right into our video room between periods. Bob Gainey could run in wanting to see something any minute, and we've got a Domino's pizza guy hostage. Craiger's smelling the pizza and wants to dig in, and then he says, 'Oh, shit. I forgot about the stick.' He runs right through the dressing room, down to the bench and grabs Brian Bellows' extra game stick and hoofs it back through. He grabs a Sharpie and asks a few of us to sign it for this guy, and then he gives it to him. Craiger said, 'I hope this is OK.' The guy says, 'Sure.' Craiger says, 'Can we do it again?'

"This is my life, what happened when the games were on."

The pizza was long gone by the time the other home teams won Game 3 and took a 2–1 lead in their Campbell series. The Red Wings scored four third-period goals to beat the Blues. Cliff Ronning scored twice—including a goal at 3:12 of overtime—as the Canucks beat the Kings 2–1. And Joe Murphy scored with 14 seconds left to lift the Oilers over the Flames.

Tuesday, April 9, 1991

Too little, too late.

NHL supervising official Wally Harris said Roenick's game-winning goal in Game 3 shouldn't have counted.

Without a win in Game 4, for which about 2,500 tickets remained available, the North Stars would need to win three straight to advance—including two at Chicago Stadium. While they won Game 1 there, and did so last season, those were their only victories in their last eighteen visits.

The players gathered for a meeting before a morning workout. Gainey surprised them, emphasizing what they were doing well instead of reaming them out for allowing six goals.

"All of us were understandably dreading practice," Bobby Smith recalled thirty years later. "We blew a 5–2 lead, and it was like, 'All right. Minnesota gave them a little scare, but the superior Blackhawks are back.' Gainey came in, and I thought, 'Holy smokes, get ready for it.' And he said, 'You guys were great. The best ten forwards on the ice were Jeremy Roenick and our top nine.' We're all thinking, 'Wow.'

"He started telling us how well we had played in the series up to that point and how good a team we were. None of us could believe it. At that exact moment our team changed. Things were never the same after that day."

Even still, it's probably a very good thing Gainey never found out about the Domino's delivery.

"There were a lot of things in Game 3 that went against the North Stars, even though I felt they played a better game than the score indicated," Gainey told me for this book. "We were over-penalized, and it was one of those things that happened often where you play well and you lose. You need to focus on the play well. Then there are other nights when you play shitty and you win, and you have to focus on the play-shitty. Sports don't always give you a fair result."

The Blackhawks dressed for practice and boarded a bus for the Eden Prairie Community Center, a tit-for-tat response after the North Stars had to practice in suburban Chicago before Game 2.

On Tuesday night, all four Wales Conference series were tied 2–2. Hartford scored four first-period goals and held off Boston, 4–3. Buffalo chased Patrick Roy and then his replacement, Andre "Red Light" Racicot, in a 6–4 win. Washington topped the Rangers, 3–2. And, while Lemieux scored, New Jersey beat Pittsburgh, 4–1.

Late that night, the Twins opened their 1991 season behind Jack Morris with a 7–2 loss at Oakland.

Wednesday, April 10, 1991: North Stars 3, Blackhawks 1, at Met Center

Casey settled for a pregame meal of spaghetti off the buffet at the Decathlon Club. It would become his ritual throughout the playoffs. As for other idiosyncrasies, he could only think of one: "I come in the east door to our dressing room every day—but only because that's the only door open. If they opened the door at the west end, I wouldn't have to walk as far."

As usual, Broten and Bellows rode to the rink together. Normally they don't talk that much about hockey, but on this afternoon, the magnitude of the game hung heavy.

The intensity of this series and importance of Game 4 became evident in pregame warmups as the teams got into a shouting match and a major scrum developed near the red line. No punches were thrown, but there were plenty of illegal blows once the puck dropped. McRae took a slashing penalty six seconds after the opening faceoff, and the teams combined for 139 penalty minutes.

The North Stars took advantage, scoring twice on the power play during a three-goal second period to delight 14,343 fans and those opting for pay-per-view on a clear, crisp evening with the temperature outside sinking almost to freezing.

Shortly after Broten made it 1–0, McRae fought Thomas, and the Blackhawks got an extra penalty. The North Stars didn't score, but they got two after Presley took a five-minute major for slashing Modano in the face at 9:53. Craig beat Belfour from the left circle at 11:30, and Tinordi did so from the right with one second left in Presley's penalty. Without even waiting for a wave from Keenan, Belfour skated to the bench, and Hasek came in to stop all 13 shots he faced the rest of the way.

Casey had 16 saves, allowing only a goal by Larmer with less than five minutes to go.

"We played a lot smarter," Wilkinson said. "We knew there would be a lot of pushing and shoving, but we wanted to keep a level head and let them take the dumb penalties… To legally hit another person is one of the best rushes you can get. I like punishing players I play against. I like to get hit, too. The best part of this game is the physical part."

In addition to Presley, Grimson got a game misconduct when he broke away from linesman Mark Vines. Grimson lost his jersey, equipment from the waist up, and quite possibly his mind. He shoved referee Dan Marouelli during an altercation involving all skaters on the ice late in the second period.

Keenan wondered how Minnesota had a 10–4 edge in power-play chances and was on the man advantage almost twenty-seven minutes more than Chicago through four games.

"I guess we could learn a lesson," Keenan said. "If we'd cry and whine about the officiating in the papers, it might serve us well. It served Minnesota well. We didn't complain when we served a penalty in overtime of Game 1. There's no question (officials) read the paper every day."

The North Stars sure hoped the Blackhawks picked up tomorrow's editions.

"They can't afford to lose the next game and are under a lot of pressure," Bellows said. "They know they have to come back to our rink, and they know how well we play here."

Since January 15, Minnesota was 13–2–2 at Met Center.

"We have three games left, with the home-ice advantage in two," Chelios said. "We need a big effort in the next game."

In attendance were former North Stars owners Gordon Ritz and Wheelock Whitney, who had been classmates with President George Bush at Yale.

Also on hand was Blackhawks owner Bill Wirtz, who said he didn't believe the deal with San Jose would affect the North Stars.

Blackhawks goalie Ed Belfour (30) stops a shot by Bobby Smith (18) at the right of the net as Chris Chelios (7) races to the crease during Game 4 on April 10, 1991, at Met Center. Smith said Bob Gainey's positive approach after losing two of the first three games was the key to putting the North Stars on a path to success in the playoffs. (St. Paul Pioneer Press/Buzz Magnuson)

"This franchise will be even better next year," Wirtz said. "A lot of people say this is not a good club. I wish I had this club."

And Green invited all the Timberwolves to the game. Tony Campbell, Gerald Glass, Scott Brooks, Tod Murphy, Bob Thornton, and Dan Godfread accepted.

Elsewhere, Detroit tipped St. Louis 4–3 to take a 3–1 lead in the other Norris Division semifinal. Edmonton beat Calgary 5–2 to take a 3–1 lead in one Smythe Division semifinal. In the other, Los Angeles drubbed Vancouver 6–1 to tie the series.

Thursday, April 11, 1991

Gainey no more than got off the North Stars' flight to Chicago when he was jumped by a Chicago TV crew seeking answers to what might happen in Game 5.

"The world wouldn't turn inside out if we lose," Gainey said. "But it is a very important game for us and our team and our franchise. We have the chance to do what this franchise hasn't done in six years—advance past the first round. We have a lot of players who have poured their heart and soul into this team without seeing results. They're not going to stop now."

The Blackhawks canceled practice and held mandatory team meetings. Perhaps the tide was turning.

"Chicago was a team that pressed hard in the offensive zone, so we needed to beat their press," Gainey recalled thirty years later. "They would gang attack you in front of their net after you had a scoring chance—whether you scored or not. So, we needed to be prepared for that, not back off and try to make the referees a little more aware of these tactics. By then, we had a much more open relationship between the coaches and players. We had a lot of smart players who could put a lot into those game plans that helped us as coaches."

The importance of Game 5 was on display later in the Wales Conference. In the Patrick Division, New Jersey downed Pittsburgh 4–2, and Washington won at New York 5–4 on Dino Ciccarelli's overtime goal. In the Adams, Boston broke through for six third-period goals to blast Hartford 6–1, and Montreal needed Russ Courtnall's overtime goal to beat Buffalo 4–3. Each of the losers were one game from elimination.

Friday, April 12, 1991: North Stars 6, Blackhawks 0, at Chicago Stadium

Propp scored two power-play goals and became the NHL's all-time leading playoff scorer at left wing, fittingly passing former Chicago star Bobby Hull.

The North Stars embarrassed the Blackhawks, setting a team postseason record for power-play goals in a game and tying marks for power-play goals in a period and largest margin of victory. Bellows also equaled a team record with four assists.

It was Minnesota's first shutout at Chicago since 1977, and the Blackhawks' worst shutout in the Stadium since a 7–0 loss to Detroit in 1966—before the North Stars existed.

Casey made 25 saves, with just four coming in the second period—after which it was 5–0.

Propp made it 1–0 late in the first after Murray went off for high-sticking. The North Stars added three more power-play goals in the first 7:16 of the second—thanks to Dave Manson high-sticking and cross-checking Craig, and Chelios slashing Tinordi.

Tinordi made it 2–0 on a shot from the slot, Gagner scored 5-on-3, and Smith tucked home a rebound to end Belfour's night early again.

Broten beat Hasek on a rebound late in the second period. By late in the third, after the organist played "Send in the Clowns" and fans littered the ice with garbage, the frustration became too much for Chelios. He earned a gross misconduct for attacking Bellows at center ice and gouging his eyes. Propp intercepted a pass from Hasek and scored on the ensuing power play, but Bellows suffered from blurred vision afterward. Chelios got an automatic $100 fine and the North Stars would send video from the KMSP-TV feed to the league in hopes the penalty would be escalated.

"A lot of their wounds were self-inflicted," said Gainey, shortly before the North Stars chartered home.

In Friday's other Norris Division semifinal, the Blues ripped the Red Wings 6–1 behind Adam Oates' hat trick and two assists. But Detroit still led the series 3–2. In the Smythe Division, Luc Robitaille scored two power-play goals as the Kings clobbered the Canucks 7–4, and Carey Wilson scored twice to lead the Flames over the Oilers, 5–3. Los Angeles and Edmonton took 3–2 series leads.

And, on the other side of Lake Michigan, Kalamazoo opened the IHL playoffs with a 4–3 win at Muskegon.

Saturday, April 13, 1991

Bellows had a scratched right cornea, similar to the injury keeping Paul Coffey out of action for Pittsburgh. That meant Broten would have to drive to the rink, but Bellows said after practice he expected to play in Game 6—the last tickets for which were sold. That made Sunday night the first advance sellout of the season. Green has decided not to sell standing-room tickets, though seventeen seats remain in the Founders Suite for $100 each.

Bellows, Broten, and Giles were the only players remaining from the 1985 North Stars—the last team to advance beyond the first round.

"We know people have heard a lot of promises before, but we hope to do our talking on the ice in Game 6," Gagner said. "If we win, then we can start thinking about what it means to the franchise."

Later Saturday night, the Capitals finished their upset of the Rangers 4–2, the Canadiens ousted Buffalo 5–1, and Boston bounced Hartford 3–1. The only series to go to Game 7 would be Penguins-Devils. Kevin Stevens scored twice for Pittsburgh, which won 4–3 after a potential tying goal was waved off with less than two minutes to go at New Jersey.

Sunday, April 14, 1991: North Stars 3, Blackhawks 1, at Met Center

On a cool, wet evening in Bloomington, the North Stars sent their first shock wave through the 1991 NHL playoffs.

A sellout crowd of 15,274 went increasingly berserk after Wilkinson and Bellows spotted Casey a two-goal first-period lead. Bellows added another early in the third as the North Stars tied an NHL postseason record with 15 power-play goals in the series. At that point, the people in the stands, the players on the bench, and certainly all of us working behind the scenes could smell victory. Keith Brown managed to spoil Casey's shutout attempt, but he stopped 26 shots. The crowd stood en masse for the final minute and—suddenly—was watching the first team in twenty years to knock the league's regular-season champion out of the playoffs in the opening round.

Out of mutual respect, Modano hugged Roenick in the postgame handshake line as Governor Arne Carlson applauded in the stands. Three Bloomington police officers stood on the Chicago bench as the Blackhawks filed out of the din toward the dressing room.

"We wanted to win this in front of the 7,000 fans who have come to see us through all of the bad times," said Bellows, who passed to Wilkinson for a 45-foot slap shot to make it 1–0 at 11:49. Barely a minute later, Bellows scored on a rebound. Later, Gagner set up Bellows, who shrugged off Chelios to score an especially satisfying goal with Thomas in the box for slashing.

"This was the most nervous I've felt in a long time," Gagner said. "It's been so tough here for so long. We wanted so badly to give the fans something to feel good about, and we wanted to do it here, in front of them. It really took me like the whole first period to feel like I had my legs under me. That's how nervous I was."

If Casey was uptight, it didn't show. He set a Stanley Cup playoff record with a scoreless streak of 120:09 in Games 4, 5 and 6. He stopped 67 of 69 shots in those games for a .971 save percentage.

"That's Jon," Resch said, laughing, thirty years later. "That year, he had the ability to find it in him to come up not just big but huge. He changed the momentum and changed the belief in our team. Some goalies, like Patrick Roy, they frustrate you, and they're so technical and they do everything right, and they don't give you anything, and you're like, 'It doesn't look like he's doing anything but standing there.' With Jon, when he was playing in those playoffs, you would chuckle. You were like, 'How did he make that save?'"

The Blackhawks were so convinced they needed help to beat Casey, they appealed for a two-man advantage after Gaetan Duchesne took an interference penalty midway through the third period. When Chicago assistant coach E. J. McGuire called down to tell the bench to ask for a measurement of the height of Casey's paddle, the message was misinterpreted to be a question about the width of the shaft. Whatever referee Don Koharski scrutinized, Casey's stick was legal. McGuire kicked the wall of the press box and screamed in anger as the Blackhawks' consequential delay of game penalty nullified their power play.

"This was a special night after the season we've had," Gainey said afterward, cautioning in his next breath. "All we did was win one series. I don't know if you can build a skyscraper out of it, but it's a start."

The delirium following the win pushed the North Stars over the 2,000 threshold in new season-ticket sales. Their regular-season winning percentage of .425 merely preceded the fifth-greatest upset in NHL history—and the second-greatest in 40 years. Since 1951, the only bigger surprise was Los Angeles (.394) over Edmonton (.694) in '82.

"I'll never forget the Chicago series," Electric Stars dancer Jennifer Shea said in an interview for this book. "When we beat them, the place erupted. The stairs were covered in beer. It was a party. I had a guy pick me up by the shins, and he was jumping up and down on the stairs. I thought, 'My God, I'm going to be paralyzed for the rest of my life if he drops me.' It all ended up fine. It was just this crazy celebration. We felt like we won the Stanley Cup that night."

In the pandemonium outside the west end, where the dancers exited from the same door as the players, even the Electric Stars were signing autographs—including one on a man's belly. The excitement spilled over to Joe Senser's, where the restaurateur and former Vikings tight end roped off an area for the North Stars to celebrate. Whenever a player came through the front door, the DJ played Gary Glitter's "Rock and Roll Part 2," and the crowd rose in a standing ovation.

By then the late Campbell Conference games were just finishing up on TVs around the bar. Theo Fleury scored in overtime (and proceeded to breakdance all over the ice) to lift Calgary 2–1 and force Game 7 against Edmonton, and Los Angeles eliminated Vancouver, 4–1. The one that mattered most, however, was St. Louis' 3–0 win behind 23 saves from Vincent Riendeau to force Game 7 against Detroit. The North Stars had nearly forty-eight hours to savor the fact that they would draw the winner.

Bob Gainey maintained a stern outlook even after the North Stars upset the Blackhawks in the first round of the playoffs. (Vintage Minnesota Hockey/Mike Thill)

CHAPTER 11

Norris Divison Finals: Do You Believe in Us Now?

Monday, April 15, 1991

Striking while his team was hot, Norm Green unveiled a plan to wrap a $30 million shopping mall, Arena of the Stars, around Met Center. At a news conference in the media lounge, where two weeks earlier Lou Nanne had announced his resignation, Green boasted that thirty to fifty shops and restaurants would ultimately be linked to the Mall of America, still a year from opening.

"From our viewpoint, we can't lose," Green said. "We're able to be almost parasitical."

His appetite must've been growing. For the North Stars to break even, Green said he needed a season-ticket base of 12,000. In his first season he had 3,500, although more than 2,000 were added by the late sales push and the improbable first-round playoff series victory.

"It's the impossible dream," said Green, who raised ticket prices $3 to a range of $14 to $34 for the second round. "To win a victory over Chicago, with all the talent they had, and the No. 1 team in the league; my dream was to put on a show, work hard and build for the future. I never dreamed we'd win."

While Green tried to work a power play on the press, the players and coaches got the day off—except for Curt Giles, who skated on his own, and Bob Gainey, who wore a suit and tie for a promotional ad shoot. He stood behind the bench, a couple of stand-ins dressed as anonymous North Stars in front of him. Behind the glass, fan extras cheered. The idea was to mock Gainey's unflappable demeanor in a TV commercial and print ads for Sunday's newspapers. They became so popular, we put out a poster.

"He was always calm behind the bench," Shawn Chambers told me for this book. "Compared to what it was like with Pierre (Page) the year before, it was quite a change. You could ask Bob about a play, and he could tell you exactly what happened. It was like he had a photographic memory. I'm like, 'He's not running the D. How can he tell me what I did the whole game?' It was kind of uncanny."

As excitement around the team built, Gainey continually bore the expression of someone waiting for the tires on his car to be rotated. Beating Chicago was monumental to Green and everyone else. But for Gainey, who'd played in the Stanley Cup Finals in 1976, '77, '78, '79, '86, and '89, this was just the first step in trying to get back.

"You don't get there by being happy that you won a game in the first series," Gainey told me in 2021. "You have to keep all these outside things where they belong—which is outside—and stay with your program. An owner who sells out the building one night and is feeling incredible, like, 'We've got it now; we know exactly what we should do,' you have to give them their time, but you also have to bring the people who are producing it back to reality."

Perhaps because the season was still going after some thought it would be over, the tension around the front office was heightened. That became clear when I made another mistake. Following the news conference, I was talking with Joanie Preston and said something to the effect that it was sure going to be interesting to see how all of this played out in the future. The implication was unspoken that I pretty well knew my future was in newspapers and not PR. She asked if I wanted to be done now. I gulped and got back to work.

Later Monday night, Frank Pietrangelo made 27 saves, Mario Lemieux scored a power-play goal (before leaving with back spasms), and Paul Coffey returned wearing a half shield as Pittsburgh beat New Jersey 4–0 in Game 7 of their Patrick Division semifinal.

Tuesday, April 16, 1991

Our office got a lot busier. Steve Aschburner joined John Gilbert, Rachel Blount, and columnists Dan Barreiro and Patrick Reusse on playoff coverage for the *Star Tribune*. All those writers needed people to talk to after practice, as did reporters from the *Pioneer Press* and most local TV and talk-radio stations.

Green, whose office was adorned with a good-luck bouquet from the Timberwolves, watched from the maroon theater seats with Rupert and Charles as the North Stars skated at Met Center. Jim Johnson didn't participate.

While media members were by no means the only ones jumping on the bandwagon, some people weren't surprised by what's happening.

"We had finished with 70 points in 1989 and 76 last year," Sharks GM Jack Ferreira told Reusse. "We felt like we were a team on the way up. That is a pretty good hockey club. Once they started concentrating on hockey and not the off-ice stuff, they were OK."

Derian Hatcher and Cal McGowan, whose Canadian junior teams had been eliminated from the playoffs, were recalled.[46] McGowan, the No. 3 scorer in the WHL, and Hatcher, who totaled 63 points in 64 games in the OHL, arrived Tuesday night—about when the coaches and players gathered to watch the satellite feed from St. Louis as the Blues overcame a 3–1 deficit in games to oust the Red Wings. Brett Hull, who had 10 of his 86 regular-season goals against Minnesota, scored on a breakaway in the third period to finish the 3–2 victory.

Andy Murray immediately went to work on another three-ring notebook.

"We had good knowledge of those (first two) teams because we played them so often," Gainey recalled in 2021. "The books that Andy put together were done in an academic way from a coach's point of view. I think it clarified things for our team and allowed us to approach our competitors with a full understanding of who they were as individuals and who they were as a team."

Murray's exposé had the Blues' logo inside the slashed circle this time. He was still putting it together when Esa Tikkanen completed a hat trick in overtime as the Oilers upset the Flames, 5–4. Edmonton would face old friend Wayne Gretzky and Los Angeles in the Smythe Division final.

Back in the Norris, the North Stars and Blues were set to play Game 1 of the division final at 7:35 p.m. Thursday at St. Louis. From there, they'd play every other day, with Minnesota hosting Games 3, 4, and—if necessary—6, until a winner was determined.

Green wanted to charge $12.95 per home game on pay-per-view during the second round, but cable operators, who share the proceeds 50–50, held the line at $9.95 again. The fee likely would increase if the North Stars make it to the Campbell Conference final.

Wednesday, April 17, 1991

The North Stars placed Johnson on the injured list before they took an afternoon charter to St. Louis. Johnson flew to Los Angeles to get treatment for his hip. It's a trip he'd make three times in less than three weeks.

46 Hatcher, McGowan and anyone called up from Kalamazoo during the playoffs would get $100 for every game they remained with the team.

Hatcher wasn't expected to step into the lineup, but he'd have a hard time taking Johnson's spot anyhow. Hatcher's size 13 1/2 skates have been lost in the mail from North Bay, Ontario, and you can't exactly find a pair like that at a sporting goods store. He watched practice from the stands.

Doug McLeod wasn't on the charter because he was broadcasting a Gophers baseball doubleheader at Iowa. He'd continue to St. Louis on Thursday, fly to California on Friday to work the Twins' game against the Angels, fly back to St. Louis for Game 2 on Saturday, and then return to California for Sunday's Twins game before coming home for Game 3 on Monday.

On Wednesday evening, Washington scored three times in the third period to steal Game 1 of the Patrick Division final, 4–2 at Pittsburgh. Larry Murphy and Lemieux had power-play goals for the Penguins, but Coffey suffered a broken jaw when he was hit by a shot from Dmitri Kristich, and Peter Taglianetti injured his foot. Elsewhere, Cam Neely scored two goals as Boston beat Montreal 2–1 in the opener of the Adams Division final.

Those were over by the time the Twins (2–7) lost 4–3 in 11 innings at Seattle and fell into sole possession of last place in the American League West.

Thursday, April 18, 1991: North Stars 2, Blues 1, at St. Louis Arena

Dave Gagner scores a lot. Shane Churla, not so much.

The unlikely duo netted first-period goals, and that was enough to open another series with a road victory.

Gagner scored on a power play 1:46 into the game—four seconds after Glen Featherstone tripped Neal Broten. Gagner won the ensuing draw and tipped in Mark Tinordi's shot from the point.

The deciding goal needed a little stardust considering Churla had never scored in 22 career playoff appearances—to go with just six goals in 162 regular-season games. St. Louis' Dan Quinn, a trade deadline pickup from Vancouver, checked Basil McRae but also wiped out two Blues teammates, leaving Churla free for an odd-man rush that he converted 11 seconds before intermission.

"Basil made a great saucer pass to me," Churla said. "I think Ray Charles could have put that one in."

It was McRae's second career playoff assist. His first came with Quebec in 1987.

"My middle name is Wayne," he joked, comparing himself to the Great One.

Rich Sutter cut the lead to one early in the third period, but Stew Gavin and Gaetan Duchesne nearly suffocated Hull—allowing him one shot in the game.

"That's the tightest I've been checked all season," Hull said. "With the way they're playing me, I'm not going to get that many shots. That means some of the other guys are going to have to score some goals if I'm taken away."

Jon Casey made 31 saves and withstood a two-man disadvantage in the final 26 seconds after Bobby Smith was called for high-sticking Paul Cavallini. Smith contended, and video appeared to show, the puck hit Smith's stick and deflected into Cavallini's face and that the stick never made contact. Regardless, the North Stars have allowed three goals in four games.

"No one knows who we are," Tinordi said. "We're a real no-name defense."

As the KMSP telecast outdrew "The Cosby Show," "The Simpsons," "Twin Peaks," and the entire night's lineups on ABC, CBS, and Fox, veteran *Pioneer Press* reporter Mike Augustin was in St. Louis with Gary Olson. Augie cornered Chico Resch to talk about Casey.

"He is just moving laterally so beautifully," Resch said. "Plus, he's standing up, not going down prematurely, and he's moving the puck to the right people."

Resch, who had 41 playoff appearances in his career, knew about performing under pressure. The most nervous he'd ever been was when he spoke before 20,000 people at a Billy Graham crusade.

Later, Luc Robitaille scored a power-play goal late in the third period and the game-winner 2:13 into overtime to lead the host Kings to a 4–3 victory in their opener against the Oilers. Les Jackson was at the Forum to scout that series in case the North Stars advanced.

Friday, April 19, 1991

The North Stars were overshadowed in the Adams Mark Hotel by Secretary of Defense Dick Cheney and the Philadelphia Phillies, in town to play the St. Louis Cardinals in the latter's home opener. Secret Service and autograph hounds were everywhere, but they weren't too concerned with hockey players.

At St. Louis Arena, Hatcher's skates finally arrived, and he participated in an afternoon practice. Johnson also returned and skated, but he'd be headed back to L.A. in the next week.

Green promoted Pat Forciea to vice president of communications and operations—essentially succeeding Nanne.

Ex-North Stars coach Page told *Star Tribune* columnist Sid Hartman his former team could go to the Stanley Cup Finals.

"There are better teams left in the playoffs, but the North Stars believe in themselves," Page said. "So anything can happen. It's not always the best team that wins the Cup. It's the one that's playing best at the right time."

Later, Stephane Richer scored 27 seconds into overtime as Montreal pulled even with Boston, 4–3. Soon after, Kevin Stevens scored 9:10 into overtime as Pittsburgh did the same with Washington, 7–6. The victory was costly for the Penguins, however. Ulf Samuelsson injured his hand, leaving Pittsburgh extremely short-handed on defense.

Saturday, April 20, 1991: Blues 5, North Stars 2, at St. Louis Arena

Gavin scored 26 seconds after the opening faceoff, Brian Bellows added another goal midway through the first period, and the North Stars had a 2–1 lead more than six minutes into the second. But Rod Brind'Amour was credited with the goal that tied it after Marc Bureau accidentally kicked the puck into his own net. And St. Louis capped a three-goal third with an empty-netter. Jeff Brown and Adam Oates, making up for Minnesota's stalking of Hull, each had a goal and an assist.

But not all was well with the Blues, even in victory. Their power play had converted just 3 of 44 chances in the playoffs and went 0-for-8 against the North Stars before Bureau's gift. After it, St. Louis went scoreless on three more chances. Hull, who had 45 power-play points during the regular season, was starting to get snippy.

"No comment," he said. "I'm not talking about the power play anymore. I have no idea what to do about it."

Darin Kimble, Mike Modano's linemate with the Prince Albert Raiders, picked a fight with Churla at 19:55 of the third period. Casey finished with 23 saves.

There were plenty of angry scowls when the North Stars boarded their charter to MSP. There were only tired scowls when they finally arrived at about 2 a.m. If they'd tuned in all-night sports talk radio (KFAN-AM 1130) on their way home from the airport, they'd have heard the Oilers beat the Kings in double-overtime on a goal by Petr Klima to square their Smythe Division final. And the Twins lost at California, 2–1, and now have the worst record in baseball (2–9).

There was no mention of Kalamazoo beating Muskegon 5–4 to win their first-round IHL playoff series.

Sunday, April 21, 1991

Elaine Waddell thought she was going to enjoy a day of golf as the St. Louis series moved to Minnesota. She left her Drew Avenue duplex near Lake Calhoun with her boyfriend and future second husband, Alexandria native Nate Digre, a graphic designer. They headed to Rich Acres in Rosemount. As he was about to hit a drive from one of the tee boxes, she was hit in the face by an errant shot from a nearby fairway. Although shaken, she wouldn't allow anyone to call an ambulance and instead was driven to Fairview Southdale, where doctors found she had broken bones above and below one eye socket. She was evaluated by an ophthalmologist, but the only thing to prescribe was rest.

That's what she was doing Sunday night when Lemieux had a goal and an assist and Tom Barrasso returned from a shoulder injury to make 26 saves to lead the Penguins over the Capitals, 3–1, in Game 3 of the Patrick Division final. Paul Coffey, who'd undergone surgery to put a metal plate in his jaw, played with a full-face shield, but an elbow from Dale Hunter aggravated the injury.

In Game 3 of the Adams Division final, former North Star Ken Hodge scored at 18:39 of the third period to help the Bruins past the Canadiens, 3–2.

And the Timberwolves closed their second NBA season with an 89–87 win at Washington to finish 29–53, good for 20th of 27 teams but more than a dozen games out of the playoff picture. Within twenty-four hours, they would fire coach Bill Musselman.

Monday, April 22, 1991: North Stars 5, Blues 1, at Met Center

Under sunny skies and with sixty-degree temperatures, many in the crowd of 14,341 lined up for the opening of the parking lot at 5:30 p.m. Attendance was nearly 1,000 short of a sellout but it was the last time in the playoffs when you could walk up and buy a ticket. Anyone who wasn't in their seats for the start missed the crucial action.

Giles and Gavin scored less than two minutes apart, Bellows and Neil Wilkinson added power-play goals in a span of less than three minutes, and this one was over before the game was 11 minutes

Gaetan Duchesne (10) smothers Brett Hull (16) in the corner as Chris Dahlquist (4) tries to clear the puck despite Gino Cavallini (17) hanging all over him in Game 3 of the Norris Division final against St. Louis on April 22, 1991, at Met Center. (St. Cloud Times/Chuck Kimmerle)

Jon Casey (30) keeps his eyes on the puck despite interference from Blues winger Rich Sutter, who has a hard time getting over the stick of Chris Dahlquist (4). Mark Tinordi (24) closes on the crease as Paul Cavallini (14) looks for a rebound. (St. Cloud Times/Chuck Kimmerle)

old. Vincent Riendeau, who was supposed to give the Blues a chance to win the Stanley Cup according to the St. Louis media, allowed four goals on eight shots and spent the rest of the night watching rookie third-stringer Pat Jablonski. The Blues' other goalie, Curtis Joseph, was out with a knee injury.

Brian Propp added a power-play goal early in the third period, and Casey made 29 saves – losing his shutout with 6:02 remaining. Hull, who took seven stitches in his right nostril after he was hit with the puck in the second period, set up Dave Thomlinson when it was 5–0. But Hull registered just three shots. Through three playoff games against the North Stars, he had no goals. He never went three games without a goal during the entire regular season.

"I'm in front of their net with either Gavin or Duchesne and a defenseman with me," pouted Hull, who seemed to sense that he might be headed to his offseason home in Duluth before he knew it. "Someone else has got to be open."

He wasn't the only one who needed repairs. Late Monday, Gretzky was hit by an errant shot in Edmonton and needed more than two-dozen stitches to close a gash near his left ear. It hurt even worse after Tikkanen scored in double-overtime to give the Oilers a 4–3 win and a 2–1 Smythe Division final lead over the Kings.

Tuesday, April 23, 1991

The Blues had a players-only meeting before practicing for nearly two hours at Met Center, trying to iron the kinks out of their power play and turn the series around. Hull said Game 4 would be "the biggest game in some guys' careers."

Later, Stevens scored his third consecutive game-winning goal, and Barrasso made 38 saves as Pittsburgh beat Washington, 3–1. Coffey did not play and would miss the rest of the Patrick Division final, which the Penguins led 3–1. And Montreal beat Boston 6–2 behind four points from Shayne Corson to square their Adams Division final at two games apiece.

Wednesday, April 24, 1991: North Stars 8, Blues 4, at Met Center

Modano and Brian Glynn (*Brian Glynn*?) each scored two goals and assisted on another, eleven different skaters had points, and scoreboard operator John Maher nearly wore out his recording of Rock & Roll Part 2.

A sellout crowd of 15,326, the biggest to date at Met Center during the playoffs, turned out either because of or in spite of the best weather yet (sunny and pushing seventy degrees). Mona Grudt of Norway, the reigning Miss Universe, and freshly fired Timberwolves coach Musselman were among the attending celebrities. And Broten's cousin, Shawn Broten, carried the US flag during the national anthem. He'd served with the Marines in the Gulf War.

The North Stars launched their own offensive soon after Ron Hoggarth dropped the puck at center ice to start the game. Bellows scored on his first shift, and Modano followed with goals less than six minutes apart to make it 3–0 before the game was nine minutes old.

Brian Glynn (6) gets congratulations from his teammates during Game 4 of the Norris Division finals against St. Louis on April 24, 1991, at Met Center. Glynn and Mike Modano (9) each scored two goals in an 8-4 victory over the Blues, giving Minnesota a commanding 3-1 lead in the series. Shawn Chambers (26), Mike Craig (20), Bobby Smith, and Dave Gagner join in the jubilation. (St. Paul Pioneer Press/Jean Pieri)

Oates scored on a rebound during a power play following a Smith tripping penalty, and the Blues clomped up the stairs at the first intermission to find their dressing room door locked. The furious players cooled their heels in the hallway for a couple of minutes before they were let in.

After Glynn's first goal, which came on a power play and during a delayed penalty, Hull made it 4–2 midway through the game—after a holding penalty on Duchesne. But then the North Stars put up a barrage of four more goals in an eight-minute span.

Propp scored on the power play, chasing Riendeau for the second time in as many games, and Gagner followed at even strength twenty-five seconds later, beating Jablonski with a slap shot from the top of the left circle. Then Bellows and Glynn each got their second goals on the man advantage, the latter on a shot from the point. Given that Churla—who was decidedly *not* a special-teams regular—started the sequence, everything was breaking the North Stars' way. Their sizzling 4-for-8 mark on the power play set an NHL record with four such goals in the second period. Just before intermission, the video screens on the scoreboard read: Lightning in their skates. Thunder in the stands.

This time, the Blues were able to get right into their dressing room. If not for the fact that they had four minutes carrying over from a five-minute power play (Tinordi high-sticked Jeff Brown), they might've kept walking to the bus.

Oates and Hull each scored early in the third before the penalty expired. But they would get no closer—even though Churla took a charging penalty and spearing double-minor with less than nine minutes to go. While Gainey seethed about that, the penalty killers brushed off the six-minute disadvantage, and Casey finished with 32 saves.

St. Louis had been an NHL-worst 4-for-57 (7.0 percent) on the power play through ten playoff games. The Blues went 4-for-12 in Game 4.

"The power play is easy when it's 8–2," Hull said sourly. "When it's 1–0 or 2–2 is when it's tough.... There was not a thing that was positive tonight. This is supposed to be the playoffs, but we've made it a joke."

Blues coach Brian Sutter wasn't laughing.

"We got down 3–1 after the first period because everything they had shot at the net went in," he fumed. "I've got no answers. If I had the answers, it wouldn't be happening this way."

Someone then asked whether the North Stars were better than the Red Wings, and without a printable word, Sutter bolted his postgame press conference.

More than 30 years after the series, Gainey can still recall with vivid detail the mechanics of shutting down the Blues.

"It was a very different era," Gainey told me for this book. "We did a lot of changing on the fly so you could get the forwards or defensive pairings you wanted. The pair that was on the ice would look for the first opportunity to come to the bench for the pair you wanted out there. Today, there might be some of that in the NHL with defensemen, but the forwards have gotten away from it. In today's game, the best forwards go against the best forwards.

"I felt we needed to have something different to present to St. Louis because our (regular-season) record against them (1–5–2) hadn't been good. They were a very strong team. We had, I thought, some advantages, but we needed to be able to nullify Hull and Oates. There really hadn't been in my own career a time when a player had been followed or shadowed. But I knew that it had happened previously. Teams used to do that to Bobby Hull or Gordie Howe. One player would play against them the whole game. We talked it through and came up with a plan. We had two great two-way players in Stew Gavin and Gaetan Duchesne, who could both match up and skate with Brett Hull. That threw a real wrench into the whole setup of the game in our favor. We were a step or two ahead of St. Louis and, by the time they figured out some of the mechanics of how to get around it, the series was half-over."

Gainey said matching Hull didn't matter to his defensemen.

"We didn't have a specific D-pair against him because Brett played a funny game," Gainey added. "He drifted away from the action until it became time for him to put the puck in the net. In the normal course of players' natural reaction, it's easy to forget about him because you're concentrated on other things. So, we pulled one player out of the normal format and had him think like Brett Hull. At that time in Brett's career, we'd seen where he could get a little pouty, and his body language would be off. Everybody on both benches and in the whole arena knew how Brett was feeling.... I think between the two of them, (Gavin and Duchesne) out-chanced Brett Hull 3-to-1. We got more scoring chances out of it, and Brett kept looking for different ways to avoid this method of coverage, but it got too late."

Elsewhere, Kalamazoo beat Fort Wayne 5–1 in their Turner Cup semifinal opener. And later, Grant Fuhr stopped 26 shots to lead Edmonton to a 4–2 win over Los Angeles and a 3–1 series lead. Gretzky had two assists despite a pregame xylocaine shot that he said made the left side of his face numb.

Thursday, April 25, 1991

When it hit doorsteps, the *Star Tribune* had a 1A centerpiece photo on the North Stars for the first time during the postseason.

The team's share from Monday's pay-per-view proceeds totaled about $70,000, meaning more than 14,000 households all over the Twin Cities ordered Game 3. On Wednesday night, more than 20,000 people ordered Game 4, and that produced another $100,000 for Green, who certainly looked like royalty as he and Kelly waved from the owner's suite during games. Combined with gross ticket sales of about $1.5 million total for the five playoff games thus far, the North Stars were cutting nicely into whatever losses Green may have incurred during the season.

"I never got this emotionally drained building shopping malls," he told *USA Today*. "Three months ago, Bob Clarke and I had many heart-to-heart talks, and I remember telling him: I don't know if we can make it here."

And now they're featured in the nation's most widely circulated newspaper, which also quoted Gainey on Casey: "He's not a textbook goaltender. You aren't going to map out his moves and sell them to youth hockey. He plays on the edge."

His teammates were right there with him.

"We're scared before each game," Gagner told the Associated Press. "There's not a lot of talk in the room. A lot of guys realize what's at stake."

Most of the North Stars didn't practice. Ulf Dahlen, Perry Berezan, Doug Smail, Rob Zettler, Hatcher, McGowan, McRae, and Brian Hayward skated before the team flew to St. Louis.

Meanwhile, Marines from Minnesota based in Saudi Arabia inquired about getting videotapes from Game 6 against Chicago and Games 3 and 4 against St. Louis. We gladly obliged and the tapes went out in the daily mail.

Thursday night, Barrasso made 33 saves and Pittsburgh advanced to its first Wales Conference final with a 4–1 win over Washington. Lemieux was pointless until he had an assist on an empty-net goal. Barrasso, who suffered a right shoulder injury in the first round, stopped 97 of 100 shots in winning Games 3, 4, and 5 in the Patrick Division final. Coffey (jaw), Taglianetti (foot), and Samuelsson (hand) all missed the game. In the Adams Division, Neely scored twice in eleven seconds and finished with his second hat trick of the playoffs as Boston beat Montreal 4–1, pushing the Canadiens to the brink.

Friday, April 26, 1991: Blues 4, North Stars 2, at St. Louis Arena

With my 22nd birthday coming in five days, I drove home to Garrison and later watched the KMSP-TV broadcast while visiting my paternal grandmother in Brainerd.

In St. Louis, a pair of columnists, the *Star Tribune*'s Dan Barreiro and the *Pioneer Press*'s Tom Powers, made a road trip for the first time in the playoffs. And, before the game, Green gave Joanie Preston a pair of gold star earrings in lieu of his patented lapel pin.

The night went downhill from there. Brind'Amour scored 1:46 into the game, and it stayed 1–0 midway through. But Craig's elbowing penalty led to Paul Cavallini's power-play goal, Quinn scored late in the second period, and, after McRae was called for unsportsmanlike conduct, Thomlinson made it 4–0 on the power play midway through the third. By then, the sellout crowd of 18,520—the largest the North Stars would face during the playoffs—was having a raucous time.

Gainey pulled Casey a few moments later to get him looking forward to Game 6. Then Oates got a double-minor for slashing, and Propp wrecked Riendeau's hope for a shutout at 14:04. Another slashing penalty on Quinn gave Modano an opening to score with just more than two minutes left.

But with Hayward off for a sixth attacker, the North Stars couldn't get anything more than a batch of penalties with fourteen seconds to go. McRae and Churla each got misconducts and stomped to the dressing room. St. Louis' Scott Stevens and Ron Wilson got misconducts, too, but their exit looked more like the departure of victorious Roman gladiators.

Giles and Modano each were minus-2. Casey made 25 saves, Hayward had two, and Riendeau finished with 24.

In Kalamazoo, the K-Wings lost to Fort Wayne 5–1, evening their Turner Cup semifinal at 1–1. Later in Los Angeles, as the North Stars were in flight to Minneapolis, Robitaille finished a hat trick and a 5–2 victory for the Kings to pull within 3–2 as the series shifted back to Edmonton.

A small group of fans greeted the North Stars in the wee hours of the morning on arrival of their charter at the Humphrey terminal.

Saturday, April 27, 1991

Dan Keczmer was recalled from Kalamazoo and joined the team for an afternoon practice. If you're not a player, there was almost no way to get into Met Center on Sunday night. Game 6 was sold out, though Green consented to add some $50 standing-room tickets to help meet demand.

"It's sweet," Bellows said. "You go to the same grocery store you've been going to for seven years and, all of a sudden, people are saying, 'Great game. Great game. Way to work.'… When you needed the pat on the back was when the team was getting twenty wins a season. That's when it would've been nice. But at least (the fans) are coming back, I guess."

Bellows, while an amazing talent, had been something of an enigma during his time in Minnesota:

- "Brian is Brian," Page said. "He's very demanding on other players."
- "If something isn't going right, he speaks his mind to the other players, and I think sometimes that gets misconstrued," Gagner said. "He almost gets condescending if we're not playing well, but I don't see anything wrong with that. He can back up his words. He's turned up his game ever since January, and we've counted on him for a lot of offense in the playoffs."
- "I enjoy it when Brian and I play on the same line together," Smith said. "You know when you go to the rink that Brian is going to give his best. That's not to say we don't butt heads once in awhile, but in a good way."

- "There was a time when Brian did whatever he wanted and didn't seem to care about too many people," Broten said. "I think he's grown up a lot. He's a guy now that you call if you're in trouble, because you know he'd be the first guy there to help you. A few years ago, he'd have probably told you off or something. Who knows what he'd have done? He's a good guy now. I don't know what else to say about him."
- "I tried to come in without any preconceived notions about any players," Gainey said. "I knew him as a driving power forward who could shoot and scored 55 goals last year. Since then, it's been a matter of trying to—whether he likes it or not—get him into the places that are best for the team. He told me what he thought he could do and I said, 'Show me.' And, for awhile, he didn't. For the last half of the season, he has."
- "One of the things that has been a pleasure is to see a player like Bellows working on his game at both ends of the rink," Clarke added.

Bellows has developed a tough public exterior. Whether it developed in response to being blamed for the North Stars' performance through their lean years, or if it was because of his own self-confidence or ego, many of his responses are blunt and colorless—at least to the media.

Pepsi took out a full-page ad in Saturday's newspapers saluting the North Stars and offering a year's supply of product for each pair of 1991–92 season tickets sold.

Former North Stars goalie and scout Gump Worsley, finally retired and living in Montreal, wasn't saluting. He left the franchise in the late years of the Gunds' ownership and doesn't think highly of the market.

"They've got a bunch of flat-footed front runners up there," Worsley said of Minnesota fans, talking on the phone to *Pioneer Press* columnist Charley Walters. "It only took them six months to realize they had a hockey team. And tell them I said it."

Bill Goldsworthy, despite working for the Sharks, was more diplomatic.

"As a player, you always want to bring a Stanley Cup to your city," he said. "As an ex-player, you still hope Minnesota will get that Cup."

Saturday night, on Hockey Night in Canada, the Canadiens got an overtime goal from Shayne Corson to beat the Bruins 3–2 and force Game 7 in the Adams Division final on Monday night in Boston.

And Kalamazoo beat Fort Wayne, 5–3.

Sunday, April 28, 1991: Stars 3, Blues 2, at Met Center

On a late afternoon (seventy-six degrees and clear) with little entertainment competition, the parking lot bulged with pregame tailgaters. They couldn't have cared less that the Twins finally escaped the basement of the AL West with a weekend Dome sweep of the Seattle Mariners.

Ryan Haney, a high school junior from Albertville, drove in and out of the rows of vehicles in his 1977 Chevy Chevette. Originally orange, it was now painted green and had a flashing yellow light, a flag on the roof, and various North Stars autographs on the hood. On the other side of Met Center, Todd Harris—originally from St. Paul—drove to the game from Missouri in a truck with a gas grill, table, and chairs. Kites flew overhead. People played catch with softballs, baseballs, footballs, and Frisbees. There was even a pair of pin jugglers.

Timberwolves owner Marv Wolfenson was inside, and Senator Dave Durenburger sat near Green in the owner's box. More than 31,000 households ordered the game on pay-per-view.

They all got an earful of Chuck Berry's "Johnny B. Goode," which became a major rock-and-roll hit when it was released in 1958 but was perhaps never played (repeatedly) to such an enthusiastic audience as it was that evening in Bloomington.

Casey, for whom the song was appropriated by the North Stars, made 18 saves and didn't allow anything until the final three minutes. By then, he had a two-goal lead, and St. Louis was forced to pull Riendeau for a sixth attacker. Brett Hull scored at 17:18 of the third period to provide some drama, but Smith scored his second goal of the game past Hull's outstretched leg into an empty net, clinching celebration for a sellout crowd of 15,274.

At one point, the fans chanted Green's name until he stood and turned over a placard that read: "If you're happy, please buy season tickets—Norm."

Through two periods, it was a tense scoreless tie. Murray overheard Sutter holler at his team, "We're going to win this thing," even after—or perhaps because—the North Stars outshot the Blues 18–2 in the second period.

Chris Dahlquist, pointless in two career playoff games prior to this spring, finally beat Riendeau with a slap shot from the right circle nineteen seconds into the third. Smith scored three and a half minutes later. That turned out to be the game-winner because Garth Butcher made it a one-goal game again with seventeen seconds left. But there was no keeping the North Stars from the Campbell Conference final.

"We worked hard all season, but it felt like it was one step forward, two steps back," Smith said after the North Stars mobbed Casey and waved themselves dizzy at the adoring crowd. "We had to doubt ourselves at some point."

Perhaps recognizing the magnitude of the accomplishment, Bellows asked for and received Hull's silver aluminum Easton stick for a souvenir as they passed in the handshake line. Hull's offensive output in the series (six points) was matched by Gavin.

In descending order, the three stars who took a postgame pirouette were Broten, Casey, and Dahlquist (!). At the top of the runway from the rink, an NHL official handed out Norris Division Champion hats and T-shirts to each of the North Stars as they whooped past.

Green, looking a little worse for wear, donned one of the tees over his designer dress shirt and hugged Broten.

"The cliches are all used up," Green said.

In the dressing room, the players alternated congratulations with teammates and from friends and family while answering questions from a growing media wave. Eventually, most got dressed, only to hang around and watch Game 6 of the Smythe Division final. Craig MacTavish scored 16:57 into overtime to give the defending Stanley Cup champion Oilers a series-clinching 4–3 win over Gretzky and the Kings. Finally, the North Stars knew: Their next game would be Thursday at Edmonton.

They weren't quite ready to stop the celebration, however. McRae and Churla still wore their championship T-shirts nearly an hour later.

"We said before the game it might not be easy," Gagner said. "We didn't care how we did it. If we all ended up with broken legs, if we could just win the game, we'd be happy."

Neal Broten (7) dangles around Blues captain Scott Stevens during Game 6 of the Norris Division finals on April 28, 1991, at Met Center. Broten set up a goal by Chris Dahlquist 19 seconds into the third period to break a scoreless tie. (St. Cloud Times/Chuck Kimmerle)

In perhaps the ultimate showdown, Jon Casey (30) stares down Brett Hull (16) as Shawn Chambers (26) tries to back up his goalie. After scoring eight goals on 34 shots in the first round against Detroit, Hull was repeatedly frustrated by the North Stars. In their six-game series, Hull scored just three times on 24 shots – and two of the goals came on the power play in Game 4, when he finished minus-3. (St. Cloud Times/Chuck Kimmerle)

When it was over and the teams were going through the traditional handshake line before the TV cameras, Brett Hull (16) could only congratulate Gaetan Duchesne (10) on the way the North Stars stifled him. Both photos this page: April 28, 1991. (St. Cloud Times/Chuck Kimmerle)

As the sellout crowd went berserk, the North Stars celebrated their Game 6 victory over St. Louis at Met Center. Somewhere in the the mass of players was Jon Casey, who saved 18 of 20 shots and won his eighth decision of the postseason, giving Minnesota a berth in the Campbell Conference finals.

Brian Propp (16) grimaces as he's blasted to the ice by New York Rangers defenseman David Shaw (27). Behind them, Brian Bellows (23) waits for an opportunity against goalie John Vanbiesbrouck on October 8, 1990, at Madison Square Garden. (Associated Press/Ron Frehm)

Mark Tinordi (24) checks Boston's Cam Neely (8) in front of goalie Brian Hayward and the Minnesota net, and Doug Smail (14) tries to beat Ray Bourque to a loose puck during a game December 22, 1990. Hayward was pulled early in the second period, trailing 4-0, but Jon Casey gave up two more goals and the North Stars lost for the fifth time in six games. (Associated Press/Winslow Townson)

April 6, 1991: Mark Tinordi (24) checks Chicago's Warren Rychel (42) in front of Jon Casey (30) during Game 2 of the Norris Division semifinals at Chicago Stadium. Also shown is Neal Broten (7) trying to impede Jeremy Roenick (27) from getting to a rebound. (Associated Press/Mark Elias)

April 12, 1991: Brian Propp (16), the hero of Game 1 in overtime, deflects a shot behind Blackhawks goalie Ed Belfour (30) during the first period of Game 5 at Chicago. Propp scored the first of the North Stars' four consecutive power-play goals (including five in the game) to earn a 6-0 win and a 3-2 series advantage. Also shown are Blackhawks defenseman Chris Chelios (7) and right wing Steve Larmer (28). Behind them is Brian Bellows (23), who had the initial assist on Minnesota's first four goals. (Associated Press/Fred Jewell)

April 14, 1991: Brian Bellows celebrates a first-period goal by Neil Wilkinson (5) that gave the North Stars a 1-0 lead over Chicago in Game 6 at Met Center. Bellows scored barely a minute later to make it 2-0 and added a third-period power-play goal as Minnesota ousted the Blackhawks for the second-biggest NHL playoff upset in the previous forty years. (St. Paul Pioneer Press/Joe Oden)

North Stars owner Norm Green often watched practice during the playoffs with his Cavalier King Charles Spaniels (brown-haired, four-year-old Charles, and black-haired, three-year-old Rupert). (Minneapolis Star Tribune/Mike Zerby)

Jon Casey (30) controls a shot during Game 1 of the Norris Division finals on April 18, 1991, at St. Louis Arena. Blues left winger Dave Lowry (10) lurks, looking for a rebound, but Neal Broten (7) has him well in check. Casey was almost perfect, stopping 31 of 32 shots as the North Stars stole home-ice advantage in the opener for the second consecutive series. (Associated Press/Leon Algee)

Shane Churla (27), who scored the winning goal in Game 1, gets back to more familiar duties, slamming into Blues captain Scott Stevens (2) during the first period of Game 2 on April 20, 1991, at St. Louis Arena. Churla later exacted what little satisfaction the North Stars got in a 5-2 loss, fighting Darren Kimble with five seconds left and setting the tone for Game 3 back at Met Center. (Associated Press/Andre Hoekstra)

Gaetan Duchesne (10) and Brett Hull (16) look like contestants at a marathon dance contest as a shot rings off the left post behind Jon Casey against the Blues at Met Center. (Both photos this page: Vintage Minnesota Hockey/Mike Thill)

After knocking off the Chicago Blackhawks in the Norris Division semifinals, the North Stars repeated their celebration in front of the fans at Met Center after ousting the St. Louis Blues in Game 6, April 28, 1991.

6

The scoreboard said it all at the end of Game 4 of the Campbell Conference finals at Met Center. All photos this page: May 8, 1991. (Vintage Minnesota Hockey/Mike Thill)

Jon Casey was a study in coolness throughout most of the postseason for the North Stars. Without him, they may not have made the playoffs in the first place.

Tempers flared with 1 minute and 19 seconds left in Game 4. As referee Dan Marouelli tried to keep track of the infractions, Jon Casey (30) wandered near where Stew Gavin (12) and Joe Murphy (8) were about to square off. Edmonton's Grant Fuhr soon crashed the party and both goalies were penalized for leaving their crease.

Long before the North Stars were halfway through their postseason run, every seat at Met Center was filled and the crowds let Norm Green know how happy they were with his change of fortunes.

Stew Gavin (12) stickhandles out of the corner, leaving in his wake Neal Broten (7) and three Oilers—Norm MacIver (36), Esa Tikkanen (10) and Anatoli Semenov (19).

May 10, 1991: Moments after Jon Casey withstood the last of 21 shots, his teammates celebrate a 3-2 win in Game 5 at Northlands Coliseum in Edmonton. As fans of the defending-champion Oilers finally realized their run was over, it dawned on the North Stars that they were going to the Stanley Cup Final. (St. Paul Pioneer Press/Joe Oden)

With their spirits perhaps at an all-time high, the North Stars playfully pepper goalie Jon Casey with shots at the end of practice on May 18, 1991, at Met Center in Bloomington, Minnesota. Also shown (from left) are head coach Bob Gainey, Stew Gavin, Neal Broten, Brian Propp, Larry DePalma, Gaetan Duchesne, Doug Smail, Mark Tinordi, and Mike Modano. About 24 hours later, the Met would be home to Game 3 of the Stanley Cup Final. (St. Paul Pioneer Press/Joe Oden)

Brian Propp (16) fights through a hook by former North Star Gordie Roberts (28) and an elbow from Penguins goalie Tom Barrasso (35) during Game 3 of the Stanley Cup Final at Met Center. Barrasso made 30 saves but gave up goals to Dave Gagner and Bobby Smith 33 seconds apart in the second period. All photos this page: May 19, 1991. (St. Cloud Times/Mike Knaak)

North Stars left wing Gaetan Duchesne (10) works the puck behind the Penguins' net as former teammate Peter Taglianetti (32) tries to cut him off. Duchesne scored on a rebound early in the third period to restore Minnesota's two-goal lead 38 seconds after Pittsburgh scored its only goal of the game.

Mike Modano (9) looks to make a pass as he cuts between Peter Taglianetti (32) and Mark Recchi (8) in the Penguins' zone. Modano found Dave Gagner for the North Stars' first goal early in the second period. Taglianetti, who was traded from Minnesota to Pittsburgh in December, was the only player in the game to finish minus-3. Recchi, who led the Penguins in scoring with 113 points during the regular season, did not have a shot on goal in the entire game.

May 19, 1991: All eyes are on the puck as Dave Gagner (15) tries to get to a rebound in front of Tom Barrasso (35). Mike Modano (9) jockeys for position behind Paul Stanton (22) as Ulf Samuelsson (5) makes sure he knows where he is in relation to the net. (St. Cloud Times/Mike Knaak)

May 21, 1991: Brian Bellows (23) led the North Stars in scoring during the playoffs, but by this point in Game 4 it looked like he was playing one against four. He suffered a knee injury in Game 2 that didn't keep him from leaping over Penguins winger Phil Bourque (29), but Joe Mullen (7), Jim Paek (2) and Tom Barrasso (35) remained between Bellows and the net. He managed five shots in the game and assisted on a goal by Dave Gagner. But that would be Bellows' last point in the series and Mullen later set up Bourque for an empty-net goal to seal it. (St. Cloud Times/Mike Knaak)

Neal Broten (7) goes to his backhand for a shot against Penguins goalie Tom Barrasso (35) during Game 4 of the Stanley Cup Final on May 21, 1991, at Met Center. Unfortunately for the North Stars, Pittsburgh scored three goals in the first three minutes and never trailed in a 5-3 victory. Broten was one of five Minnesota skaters to go minus-3, and Barrasso finished with 35 saves. (St. Cloud Times/Mike Knaak)

This moment was approximately when the North Stars' magic last appeared and began to sputter in Game 4. Dave Gagner (15) is exuberant and the Met Center crowd goes bananas after his goal at 18:22 of the first period. Jim Johnson, Brian Bellows, Ulf Dahlen and Brian Glynn share in the excitement. After dominating play late in the first period and much of the second, it looked like Minnesota might make a comeback. But Bryan Trottier scored the decisive goal midway through the game and the Penguins held on despite two more goals from the North Stars—who squandered an extended power play late in a one-goal game. (St. Cloud Times/Mike Knaak)

The puck has just dropped for Game 5 of the Stanley Cup Final on May 23, 1991, and the North Stars are on the attack at Civic Arena in Pittsburgh. Less than six minutes later, Mario Lemieux scored a power-play goal, the Penguins erupted for four consecutive goals in a span of about eight minutes, and the North Stars were on their heels for the rest of the series after a miraculous postseason run. (Associated Press/Chaz Palla)

Mario Lemieux (66) shuffles backward after scoring a short-handed goal on North Stars goalie Jon Casey (30) at 12:19 of the first period during Game 6 of the Stanley Cup Final, May 25, 1991, at Met Center. Lemieux outraced Brian Bellows to the net to make it 2-0. Even before the play, the Penguins had already all the offense they would need to win the series, 4-2. (Associated Press/Larry Salzman)

12

In the first period of Game 6, former teammates Larry Murphy (55) and Brian Bellows (23) clashed at the crease. But, try as they might, the North Stars just ran out of magic against the Penguins. Despite a two-games-to-one lead in the series, Minnesota was outscored 19-7 in the last three games. Tom Barrasso (35) registered a 39-save shutout and Maro Lemieux skated off with the Conn Smythe Trophy and, more important, the Stanley Cup. (Associated Press/Ann Heisenfelt)

Jon Casey (30) watches Marc Bureau (11) clear the puck away from the North Stars' goal. Shane Churla (27) waits for a breakout pass as Brian Glynn (6) takes out Bob Errey (12), and Ron Francis (9) and Mark Recchi (8) get caught behind the play. The way the Penguins defended, however, it was all over after they scored just two minutes into the game. (St. Cloud Times/Chuck Kimmerle)

Brian Bellows (left) and Ulf Dahlen chat in the North Stars' dressing room at Met Center following a team meeting on May 27, 1991. About 36 hours earlier, they'd suffered an 8-0 loss to the Pittsburgh Penguins in the decisive Game 6 of the Stanley Cup Final. Bellows, who had signed a three-year $2.1 million contract extension before the 1990-91 season began, knew he would return. But Dahlen wouldn't know for sure for another three days that he would stay in Minnesota and not go to the San Jose Sharks in the teams' dispersal draft. Of the players who had just appeared in the playoffs, the Sharks bit on Shane Churla, Brian Hayward, Neil Wilkinson, and Rob Zettler—although the North Stars quickly reacquired Churla. (St. Paul Pioneer Press/Neale Van Ness)

Mike Modano salutes the fans after his last NHL game in Minnesota, on April 10, 2010. The Dallas Stars beat the Minnesota Wild 4-3 in a shootout at the Xcel Energy Center. Modano was selected as the No. 1 star of the game and made his curtain call wearing a vintage North Stars jersey. (Associated Press/Ann Heisenfelt)

North Stars left wing Stew Gavin (12) tries to wrestle past Pittsburgh's Ron Francis (9) as Tom Barrasso (35) holds the puck in Game 3 of the Stanley Cup Finals. Gavin later assisted on a goal by Gaetan Duchesne that made the final score 3-1. (St. Cloud Times/Mike Knaak)

Norm Green (right) and his wife, Kelly, attend the inaugural celebration of the Dallas Stars Hall of Fame on October 30, 2022, at Gilley's Dallas event facility. Green, eighty-eight, lived in Calgary during much of the COVID-19 pandemic, but still spends time in Texas. He said he has not been back to Minnesota since 1992 and has no plans to return. (Dallas Morning News/Ben Torres)

MET CENTER . . . Home of the MINNESOTA NORTH STARS

CHAPTER 12

Campbell Conference Final: Daring to Do the Impossible

Monday, April 29, 1991

It was a rainy day all over the Twin Cities. If your newspaper wasn't soaked, you could have read a lead story on the North Stars for first time during the playoffs on the cover of the *Star Tribune*.

The team hadn't been this far in seven years and last won a game in the conference final just before vying for the Stanley Cup in 1981.

"This is more rewarding," said Bobby Smith, whose dressing room stall separated those of Neal Broten and Curt Giles—the only players who truly could compare the experiences—by about twenty feet. "To do what we've done has taken a tremendous effort from the players and from everyone, from the owner's suite to the coaches' room."

For all the first-round exits and years without a playoff berth, it was intoxicating to those who didn't know better.

"This is—what do you call it?—a fairy tale," said Gaetan Duchesne, who played in four of five postseasons with Washington but never made it past the second round. "To beat the first and second overall teams in the league, this is unbelievable. And our goal has not stopped there."

Smith said the playoff run was different from all his others. Usually, he was anxious until the first game, and then that feeling went away. This time, however, he'd had trouble sleeping, wasn't that interested in eating, and lost weight.

"It's not a bad thing unless you had to live with me," he said. "But I don't think it's a bad thing if you had to play on a line with me."

Brian Bellows and Stew Gavin generally had that pleasure. Bellows led the team with eight goals and 10 assists through 12 playoff games. Smith had four goals and six assists, and Gavin had two goals, six assists, and a team-best plus-6 rating.

"I'm in an ideal situation," Smith said. "I've got the team's best defensive player on my right side and the team's best goal-scorer on my left."

The North Stars didn't practice. We sent out a press release announcing that Games 1 and 2 at Edmonton could be seen on the video boards at Met Center for a $1 donation to the Special Olympics. The parking lot would open at 7 p.m., the arena at 7:30 p.m., and Game 1 would start at 8:35 p.m. Thursday. The Game 2 faceoff would be moved up one hour to 7:05 p.m. on Saturday. Games 3 and 4 would be at 7:05 p.m. May 6 and 8 at the Met. Games 5, 6 and 7, if necessary, would be at 8:35 p.m. May 10 in Edmonton, 7:05 p.m. May 12 at the Met Center, and 8:35 p.m. May 14 in Edmonton.

The pay-per-view telecasts increased to $12.95 per game, up $3 from the first two rounds. The price would stay the same for the Stanley Cup Final if the North Stars advanced.

Later, Oilers GM Glen Sather pronounced the North Stars "Odds-on favorites in this series." Asked about the quote, Broten countered: "Yeah, right."

Bobby Clarke laughed.

"The great thing about Sather is he'll not only BS you, but he'll expect you to believe it," Clarke said.

Clarke didn't deny that something special was happening, however.

"The chemistry is here," he said. "You get this far, it's not just on talent."

But you can probably put Sather's prediction with another mess he was trying to clean up. During Sunday night's game against Los Angeles, toilets on the upper levels of Northlands Coliseum clogged, leading to sewage being pumped into the Edmonton dressing room. Sather, appropriately, ordered the carpet replaced.

"It's not like this is the first time it happened," he said. "It's been happening for fourteen years. One time the power went out, and the meat in the freezers over our dressing room thawed, and blood was dripping through the ceiling."

Mike Modano recently moved from St. Paul's Lowertown to Uptown in Minneapolis. Reed Larson, Modano's road roommate in the 1989 playoffs, connected him with the owner of a duplex. Larson lived downstairs, and Modano moved into the upstairs portion of the home.

Tonight, Modano sank into the Porsche, which has a black interior and white mag wheels. His father found it through a listing in the Robb Report from a previous owner in Atlanta. Mike backed out of his driveway and was soon cruising I-94 en route to Highland Park, where he and Bellows appeared on a one-hour radio show hosted by Larry Fitzgerald on WMIN-AM (1010) at Champps on West 7th Street. Among the mounted TVs, you could follow Game 7 of the Adams Division final. Andy Moog made 35 saves and Dave Christian and Cam Neely scored to lead Boston to a 2–1 win over Montreal.

Elsewhere, Chicagoland Processing Corporation minted 5,000 commemorative silver coins celebrating the North Stars' Norris Division title. They sold for $30 apiece. Four years ago, the company produced similar coins following the Twins' world championship.

Tuesday, April 30, 1991

Before the players came in from an hour-and-a-half practice at Met Center, Andy Murray beat them to the dressing room and listed uniform numbers all over the whiteboard. Each of the North Stars was linked to numbers from the Edmonton Oilers they were to study. Murray broke the players into groups to analyze Edmonton's strengths and weaknesses. He then disappeared into the coaches' rooms to go over videotape with Bob Gainey and Doug Jarvis and meet with Les Jackson.

The North Stars' lines remained intact: Brian Propp-Dave Gagner-Modano, Bellows-Smith-Gavin, Ulf Dahlen-Broten-Duchesne, and Basil McRae-Marc Bureau-Shane Churla.

They already had far exceeded expectations for Norm Green, who seemed happier than if someone had just loaned him $10 million at a rate below prime.

"If you had asked me if we could turn this around in one year, I'd have said, 'Not in a million years,'" Green said. "I'm a pretty optimistic guy but, at the beginning of the year when we were talking about predictions, we said we wanted to build the best franchise in the National Hockey League but that it might take five years, or, if we were lucky, three. If I would have said the goal was to do it in one year—or in the three months since the all-star break, really—that would have been a little silly to say that. That would be like winning the lottery."

It was raining when we left for home. Later, Kalamazoo lost at Fort Wayne, 6–2. Their Turner Cup semifinal was tied 2–2.

Wednesday, May 1, 1991

Following a practice of not quite two hours at Met Center, the North Stars flew to Edmonton. After traveling separate on his private jet during the first two rounds, Green joined most of the players on a larger charter. Dan Keczmer was headed east, back to Kalamazoo since Jim Johnson was close to returning. Johnson flew to Los Angeles and would continue rehabilitation sessions multiple times each day before rejoining the team for Game 3.

Before departure, Murray distributed another forty-page pre-series binder. This time, the cover had the Oilers' logo inside the red circle and slash.

"We have to follow our gameplan and not be intimidated," said Giles, referring to the fact that Edmonton had won five of the last seven Stanley Cups.

The Oilers were trying to add to that after recovering from a slow start to the regular season. They won just five of their first twenty games but finished at .500 (37–37–6). Their record likely would be better had captain Mark Messier not missed twenty-seven games with knee and thumb injuries. He was back and ready to lead another run to the Stanley Cup Final.

Sather said what the North Stars had done was a "miracle." Gainey wasn't taking the bait.

"The fact that we're still playing is reward enough," Gainey countered. "All those teams that finished April 5 are tired of being away from the rink. We're still here, and we're enjoying it."

Ad sales at KMSP-TV became so overwhelming the station had to create a North Stars pregame show. Before Game 1, it will last an hour. Before Game 2 and subsequent road games in the series, it will be a half-hour.

Wednesday night, the team was able to watch on CBC as Boston opened the Wales Conference final with a 6–3 win over Pittsburgh. Neely scored twice as the Bruins overcame an early 2–1 deficit. Bob Sweeney hounded Mario Lemieux, holding him to one secondary power-play assist.

"If I shut him down, I'm doing my job," Sweeney told reporters.

In Kalamazoo, the Wings lost to Fort Wayne 4–3 in overtime and faced elimination from the Turner Cup semifinals on the road Friday.

Thursday, May 2, 1991: Stars 3, Oilers 1, at Northlands Coliseum

In the afternoon, the North Stars crossed the street from their hotel, the Hilton, to have lunch at a place called Smitty's. Speaking to Mark Tinordi, the manager said Minnesota had no chance against the Oilers. Eight hours later, he probably regretted that statement.

For the third series in a row, the North Stars won Game 1 on the road, but they also prevailed for the first time since the playoff opener at Chicago after giving up the first goal. Chris Dahlquist, the hero of Game 6 against St. Louis, took an interference penalty 48 seconds after the opening faceoff, and Steve Smith made it 1–0 on a slap shot at 2:15—the first shot Jon Casey saw. But Broten tied it with a shot over Grant Fuhr's right shoulder late in the first period, Gagner redirected Broten's shot on the power play at 8:05 of the second, and Duchesne added breathing room with his first point of the postseason—a goal off a pass from Dahlen at 16:21 of the third.

Casey made 27 saves, and it all amounted to Minnesota's first victory since its only one *ever* at Edmonton, back on October 24, 1980.[47] The North Stars had gone 0–12–4 during the regular season and 0–2 in the playoffs there since.

"You can't let yourself be satisfied," Gagner said. "You don't get this chance all the time. I mean, St. Louis isn't going to be any worse next year. Chicago isn't going to be any worse. They're going to be two

47 Fred Barrett played in that game. He'd made his NHL debut four months after Mike Modano was born.

angry teams. Detroit will get better. Toronto will get better. You never know what's going to happen in the future. We've got a good opportunity right now. We have to run with it.

"(Edmonton) is a pretty confident team by nature," he added. "I mean, they have a lot of guys who think they're unbeatable. We have to respect the situation we're in and hope they're overconfident."

The crowd of 17,802 fans at Northlands Coliseum, 411 short of a sellout, also might have been looking past Minnesota.

"The building was like church," Ralph Strangis remembered for this book. "They were there to watch another—*yawn*—Stanley Cup victory. This (the North Stars) was just a team we've got to play now and who do we get in the finals? I'm serious. The building was quiet. There was no atmosphere. Just think about that. This is a conference final. At Met Center, people had their hair on fire."

Almost literally. Back in Bloomington, nearly 4,500 showed up to watch on the video boards and skate on the ice. It didn't go well. Perhaps 100 of those fans acted like hooligans, removing decorative North Stars stickers from seats and walls, attempting to steal flags, and getting out of control in the parking lot. Fights broke out and an usher was bitten, according to Pat Forciea, who fielded a mayday call in Edmonton. Bloomington police sent thirteen squad cars to the Met between 10:10 p.m. and 11:20 p.m. Juveniles were arrested for disorderly conduct, fifth-degree assault, theft, and underage consumption. Bloomington Police Sergeant Cliff Bluml said there were as many complaints as at a typical North Stars game and that the team made no advance request for security. In any case, similar access for Game 2 was canceled.

Friday, May 3, 1991

Because Whitney Houston and her entourage took over Northlands Coliseum for a concert, the North Stars—except for Bellows (bruised leg)—practiced at Mayfield Twin Arenas.

Edmonton coach John Muckler blamed his team's Game 1 performance on "emotionally and physically draining" series in the first and second rounds.

"When we had a couple days off, the last thing anyone wanted to think about was hockey, and then we had to come back for the conference finals," Muckler said. "We don't see Minnesota or any Norris Division teams very often, so there's no hate. It's difficult to get up."

Nonetheless, he expected his players would outskate the North Stars.

"Speed kills," he said. "If it's a speed game, only one team can do it: The Oilers. We have to inject speed because they don't want it."

That dovetailed with what Gagner said about overconfidence after Game 1, and it made it a little easier for Gainey to fire up his team.

"I'm not sure they'll out-speed us that much," Gainey said. "We have a lot of speed in our forward skaters, and I'm not sure our defense is going to look like the front door of Eaton's."[48]

Meanwhile, the latest issue of *Sports Illustrated* hit newsstands. It led with the North Stars' miraculous story, although Bjorn Borg was on the cover. (Let's not get too carried away.) A two-page photo spread featured Gavin dumping Brett Hull on his derriere in front of Casey. On the subsequent four pages, writer Austin Murphy tried to explain why McRae and Churla, et al, aren't too thrilled at being called "Cinderfellas."

Back in the Twin Cities, all three possible home games against the Oilers were sold out. Ticket prices ranged from $17 to $38. For the finals, that would increase to $21 to $41.

48 Eaton's, founded in 1869, was Canada's largest department store chain. Competition from Sears and Walmart put Eaton's on a decline that—like many other organizations—would result in bankruptcy by 1999.

In Boston, the Bruins took a two-game series lead when they beat the Penguins 5–4 on Vladimir Ruzicka's goal 8:14 into overtime. Lemieux scored two goals and assisted on another to help Pittsburgh take a 4–3 lead late in the game. But Gordie Roberts took a high-sticking penalty, and Boston tied it on the power play with 3:11 left in regulation.

CBC got major pushback when it preempted the first ninety minutes of the game to accommodate the series finale of "Dallas." Apparently, no one north of the 49th parallel cared about the fate of J. R. Ewing and family.

The Wales Conference final would move to Pittsburgh on Sunday.

"We're confident we can beat this team," said Penguins winger Kevin Stevens, either whistling in the dark or incredibly confident. "And we will beat this team."

Also Friday night, Fort Wayne beat Kalamazoo 3–2 to eliminate the Wings in the Turner Cup semifinals, 4–2.

Saturday, May 4, 1991: Oilers 7, North Stars 2, at Northlands Coliseum

Despite a first-period trivia question about the "Minnisota" North Stars on the Northlands Coliseum scoreboard, Edmonton was serious about Game 2.

Gagner scored a power-play goal 1:55 after the opening faceoff, but then Petr Klima blew Minnesota away with a hat trick in a span of 5:13—the fastest in Oilers history.

Klima, who gave the Oilers all they needed to win, said before the series he'd had a dream that he would score on Tom Barrasso in this year's playoffs. For that to come true, Edmonton would have to reach the Stanley Cup Final against Pittsburgh.

The way Klima commanded the puck early, he looked clairvoyant. He scored from a sharp angle on Casey, beat Shawn Chambers on a rush to lift a shot under the crossbar with Giles off for cross-checking, and then faked out Casey again.

Tinordi's roughing penalty led to another goal late in the first period, and Brian Hayward went in to start the second. Midway through the game, Broten's forecheck created a turnover and Gavin scored the North Stars' first short-handed goal of the playoffs, cutting the deficit to two. But Edmonton struck twice late in the second period and again early in the third with goals from Glenn Anderson on either side of one by Anatoli Semenov. After that, the North Stars only had some fight left. McRae, who battled Kelly Buchberger in the first period, got a rare odd fighting penalty (no Edmonton player was given one) with three minutes left as part of a roughing exchange between Churla and Adam Graves.

Hayward made 18 saves on 21 shots after Casey stopped 7 of 11. Dahlquist and Bellows each were a team-worst minus-3.

"This has happened to us before," Gagner said. "It's not fatal."

Back in Minnesota, Herb Brooks told the *Pioneer Press* it will be Minnesota and Pittsburgh in the final. "Pittsburgh might have the most talent in the league," he said.

Sunday, May 5, 1991

A crowd of perhaps 100 fans greeted the North Stars' return after their charter landed at about 2 a.m. at the Humphrey terminal.

About six hours later, Forciea was roused from a deep sleep when his phone rang. It was Green, telling Forciea to create auxiliary press space in the northeast corner of the arena in case the team makes it to the Stanley Cup Finals.

The North Stars had a team meeting in the afternoon, followed by an optional practice. Johnson was one of only a few who skated.

"It's as good as it's going to get, and I'm ready," Johnson said of his hip.

Bellows was still steaming about Game 2, which he blamed on the officiating.

"We got the first goal, they got one back; the tempo was pretty close between both teams and then (Bill) McCreary just took the game over," Bellows said. "It's like a natural hat trick… he did it to us in Chicago, in St. Louis and now Edmonton, all in the second game. It's just something between Bill and our team. Surely, he can't be bad three times in a row. But he managed it."

Bellows might've taken one too many hits to the head. Paul Stewart refereed Game 2 against Chicago, and if Minnesota had a beef with any official against the Blackhawks, it was probably Denis Morel, who let Jeremy Roenick's controversial goal decide Game 3. McCreary, who didn't work any of the games against Chicago, called Game 2 at St. Louis and Game 2 in Edmonton, which the North Stars lost, 5–2 and 7–2, respectively—perhaps leaving lingering resentment in the minds of Bellows (and others). They were upset McCreary didn't call a penalty on Glenn Anderson, who scored the fifth goal immediately after he appeared to interfere with Basil McRae—who said Anderson gave him "the old slew-foot."[49]

"The game was taken away by the referee," Bellows persisted.

"It went from 4–2 with us getting a power play to them going ahead 5–2," McRae added.

Worse, Gainey told Smith to ask McCreary about the play on the ensuing faceoff.

"I asked him, 'What about Tinordi getting taken down?'" Smith said. "He said, 'It wasn't Tinordi, it was McRae.' So I guess he *must* have seen it."

Cal McGowan, a 20-year-old who benefitted from a couple weeks' exposure to the Stanley Cup playoffs, was sent back to Kamloops. And the North Stars recalled Larry DePalma, Keczmer and Jarmo Myllys now that Kalamazoo had finished its season.

On Sunday night, the Penguins got back into their series against the Bruins with a 4–1 win in Pittsburgh. Lemieux, despite shadowing from Sweeney and Dave Poulin, scored on a breakaway and assisted on another goal. And Samuelsson caught Neely with an open-ice hip check that put him out of the game with a bone bruise.

Monday, May 6, 1991: North Stars 7, Oilers 3, at Met Center

Right on cue Monday morning, construction workers knocked a wall out of the press dining room and an adjacent storage area under the deluxe suites. By seating overflow media there instead of the stands, 59 more seats will go on sale along with 100 standing-room tickets at $17 and $15, respectively. That amounted to $2,503 per game. The temporary remodeling was done by the time the players filed in for Game 3.

Outside, it was breezy with temperatures about forty-five degrees. But that didn't dampen the enthusiasm. A small army of autograph seekers was at the west end ramp by 3 p.m., waiting for the players to park in a reserved area nearby before running the gauntlet into the building. By 6 p.m., the parking lot was bonkers with the beginnings of a sellout crowd of 15,378. Souvenir sales grossed more than $17,000 (almost twice the playoff average), season-ticket sales passed 6,000, and approximately 30,000 homes ordered the $12.95 pay-per-view.

"These fans are really high," said former NHL winger Ace Bailey, an Edmonton scout who watched from the press box.

49 Slew footing is the act of a player using his leg or foot to knock or kick an opponent's feet from under him or pushes an opponent's upper body backward with an arm or elbow, and at the same time with a forward motion of his leg, knocks or kicks the opponent's feet from under him, causing him to fall. When called, it is a form of tripping.

Kelly Buchberger scores Edmonton's first goal, beating Jon Casey (30) inside the right post and cutting the North Stars' lead to 2-1 at 11:09 of the first period in Game 3 of the Campbell Conference finals, May 6, 1991. Dave Gagner (15) and Curt Giles (2) can only look on in disappointment. (St. Paul Pioneer Press/Jean Pieri)

Either these people are really pumped up or everybody has a fever," added Bailey, who helped Boston win the Cup in 1972. "This is a dull building. Even when the crowds used to be good, I've never seen the fans this excited. Six weeks ago I was here, and there was no feeling in the place at all."

The roof nearly came off after Modano streaked between Steve Smith and Jeff Buekeboom to burn Fuhr with a backhand four minutes into the game. The noise became maniacal when Propp scored his team-record seventh power-play goal of the playoffs at 9:52. After Buchberger broke through for Edmonton, Tinordi restored a two-goal lead late in the first period when his shot popped out of Fuhr's glove and into the net.

Muckler sent in Bill Ranford, last year's Conn Smythe trophy winner, to start the second. A holding penalty on Giles and a bench minor for too many men (served by Modano) led to a 5-on-3 Oilers goal, but Bobby Smith embarrassed Buekeboom and Ranford on a breakaway midway through to make it 4–2.

"The last time that move worked might have been when I was playing with the 67s," Smith said.[50]

Edmonton just couldn't catch up. After Craig Simpson scored for a second time, Bellows leaped over a defenseman to get to a loose puck and score on the power play. Bellows then scored again on a breakaway early in the third. Churla's goal with 1:15 left led to a thunderous ovation that continued long after the three stars were announced.

"When the North Stars scored a goal in the '91 playoffs at Met Center," Ralph Strangis told me

50 The Ottawa 67s became a team in the Ontario Hockey League in 1967, and Smith played for them from 1975-78.

Mike Modano (9) beats Oilers goalie Grant Fuhr (31) with a backhand just four minutes into Game 3. (St. Paul Pioneer Press/Buzz Magnuson)

Brian Bellows (23) moves the puck out of the corner just before Mark Messier (11) can break up the play in Game 3. Bellows broke open a one-goal game when he scored on a power play late in the second period and added an even-strength goal early in the third. He finished with a team-best three points. (St. Cloud Times/Chuck Kimmerle)

thirty years later, "it was like a collective orgasm."

Casey stopped 26 shots in his fifteenth playoff start and posted his tenth win—both franchise single-season records.

"Jon deserves a ton of credit," Hayward said in an interview for this book. "He was a guy who was able to turn the page mentally very quickly. I went in for him quite a few times during those playoffs, which was unusual. But he came back and won. It was always impressive to me. He was someone who could get kicked and dust himself off and get back after it."

Bellows (two goals and an assist) and Gagner (three assists) led the offense, while Broten centered Gavin and Duchesne on a line that shut down Edmonton's trio of Ken Linseman, Tikkanen, and Klima. They had one point, Klima's secondary assist on a power-play goal.

Messier had two second-period assists but took a slash on his left hand, the one with the broken thumb from February. He was one of several Oilers who ducked out the back door of the training room after the game to avoid the media. Later, I ran into Messier wandering the concourse after the building had emptied. Fans remained outside, and he asked me for directions on how to exit the arena without running into them.

The North Stars enjoyed the moment. Modano wore a Los Angeles Lakers cap while casually answering postgame questions, and the loading dock where the players exited looked like a mosh pit. Yet Bellows voiced what some must have been thinking.

"There's always doubt," he said. "People are wondering, 'When is it going to fall apart? When is it just going to come apart at the seams?' But our guys are always rallying, coming to the forefront for one another. Tonight was proof, yes, but only for tonight."

Tuesday, May 7, 1991

Floral arrangements crowded our executive offices. A man from Thunder Bay, Ontario, bought six season tickets. Visitors crowded the box office entrance and asked for tours of the building, which wasn't even a thing.

This was Met Center?

About 350 sixth-graders from Scott Highlands Middle School in Apple Valley decorated the concourse with hand-drawn posters of encouragement, then watched the morning skate.

The Oilers held a team meeting. Muckler said he made a bet (giving 5:1 odds) with an Edmonton reporter back in March that the North Stars would beat Chicago in the first round.

"Everybody in the media wants to make a Cinderella team out of Minnesota," Muckler said. "But anybody in the business doesn't say that. They definitely deserve to be here."

The North Stars also had a team meeting, absent Gagner because Jo-Anne went into labor. Their daughter, Jessica, was born at Fairview Ridges Hospital in Burnsville.

An *Edmonton Journal* column, written by John Short and reprinted in the *Star Tribune*, caused a stir. He wrote: "The rebirth of the North Stars is good for hockey, I guess, and for the economy of a region whose residents are best known for sleeping and wishing they lived anywhere else. But these jerks don't deserve a good team."

Short took issue with chants of "Oilers suck!" among others. The column provided a not very veiled counterpunch to those Dan Barreiro wrote after Games 1 and 2 calling Oilers fans dull.

Later Tuesday, Lemieux had a goal and an assist as the Penguins squared the Wales Conference final with a 4–1 win over the Bruins. Barrasso made 29 saves.

Wednesday, May 8, 1991: North Stars 5, Oilers 1, at Met Center

Temperatures barely reached fifty degrees before the gates opened, but another sellout crowd of 15,274 arrived to drink in the delirium of another home playoff game. Game 4 also drew more than 35,000 buys and was the most watched pay-per-view event to that point in Minnesota history.

Craig MacTavish became the first visiting player to score the opening goal of a game in this year's playoffs at Met Center. It held up until late in the first period when everyone looked on in wonder as Bureau scored his first NHL goal, and Modano added the game-winner eighteen seconds later. Bureau, who said he was shooting for Fuhr's stick side, had deadly aim. But he didn't even get to properly listen to his name announced before Modano shoved in a rebound.

Shortly after, the North Stars lost Bobby Smith to a cross-checking major and game misconduct when he knocked Martin Gelinas unconscious. The penalty was brewing after Johnson, in the lineup for the first time since Game 6 against Chicago, bulldozed Graves out of the crease near Casey. Gelinas, who'd lost his helmet on an earlier check by Johnson, clocked him from behind, and Smith got caught sticking up for his teammate.

Jim Johnson punches Martin Gelinas as linesman Wayne Bonney tries to separate them in the first period of Game 4 of the Campbell Conference finals at Met Center. Bobby Smith (18) had just taken a major for cross-checking and a game misconduct for trying to protect Johnson, who'd been waylaid from behind by Gelinas. (St. Paul Pioneer Press/Buzz Magnuson)

Smith raced up the steps to the dressing room and watched on TV as the North Stars not only survived the penalty, but didn't allow a shot for more than four minutes. Then Gagner made it 3–1 on a power play early in the second period. Neil Wilkinson sent a wrister through a screen less than four minutes later (the "Sieve!" chants raining down on Fuhr), and the game turned into a rout late in the second after Bellows' shot hit Broten and bounced into the net just as a 5-on-3 expired.

The third period turned ugly when Anderson caught Johnson in the face with a high stick. Anderson was ejected and Johnson was cut for eight stitches. Joe Murphy, who missed Game 3 with a sprained knee, took a double-minor for roughing and, by the time those penalties expired, only five minutes remained. At that point, there was no way Edmonton was going to come back on Casey, who finished with 20 saves.

"When they're down, they're a dirty hockey team," Johnson said. "They're trying to injure people out there. They stick you, stick you, stick you and try to hurt you. I want to win as bad as anybody, but I'm not out to end anybody's career."

With 1:19 left, the teams got into an all-out rumble—although technically there were no fights. Four Oilers got roughing minors, four North Stars totaled five roughing minors, Casey and Fuhr were penalized for leaving their crease to mill around those pushing and shoving, and Buchberger got a 10-minute misconduct.

"I've got a lot of welts and bruises," Broten said. "That was the dirtiest game of the playoffs so far. Maybe the next one will be even dirtier."

Gainey said videotape showed Anderson kicking Duchesne in the chest before high-sticking Johnson.

"It was a game with a lot of hate, a lot of hate that the referee (Dan Marouelli) let run over," Gainey said. "I don't think he had control… what happened tonight was dangerous."

Duchesne displayed a six-inch scrape from where Anderson's skate nearly sliced him open. Asked, however, whether Minnesota would send the videotape to the league office—seeking additional punishment for Anderson or others, Gainey sighed and gave a classic facetious-Gainey response: "No. It costs $8 apiece to send them in, and you never get them back."

Dave Gagner (15) and Brian Propp (16) celebrate a 5-on-3 power-play goal that finished the scoring in Game 4. Gagner won a face-off to the right of goalie Grant Fuhr (31). Propp moved the puck to Mike Modano at the right point. Modano passed to Neal Broten for a one-timer from the left circle at 19:33 of the second period. (St. Paul Pioneer Press/Buzz Magnuson)

The budget shouldn't have been much of a concern anymore. Tickets to all potential home games of the Stanley Cup Final, should the North Stars get there, were sold prior to Game 4.

"This game was unbelievably important," Broten told a growing mob of reporters. "We're one step away from making it to the finals. We played physical. We matched them hit for hit. If we wanted to win, we knew we had to keep sticking our noses in there."

The local media has been thoroughly mobilized. The *Star Tribune* had Rachel Blount, John Gilbert, and Jim Souhan covering the game with Patrick Reusse writing a column. (Barreiro had the day off.) By the finals, Jon Roe, Steve Aschburner, Dennis Brackin, Jerry Zgoda, Curt Brown, Jay Weiner, Roman Augustoviz, Randy Furst, Doug Grow, Howard Sinker, and even Judd Zulgad (my college classmate and a former North Stars intern) would join the mix in some capacity. The *Pioneer Press* used Gary Olson, Tom Powers, Bob Sansevere, Jim Wells, Mike Augustin, and Ray Richardson, adapted Timberwolves beat writer Mary Schmitt to hockey, and pulled Jim Caple away from the Twins.

As for the visiting media, fans chanted "John Short sucks!"

"This is like the girl with the glass slipper," Al Shaver said, concluding his broadcast. He looked like he'd been through a mild whirlwind. A Winnipeg radio station had begun picking up the KSTP radio feed.

In what the North Stars called the dirtiest game of the playoffs, Neil Wilkinson (5) wallops Martin Gelinas (20) while Adam Graves (12) gets the upper hand on Brian Bellows (23) during the second period. The game really got out of hand in the third, however, when the teams combined for 53 minutes in penalties. (St. Paul Pioneer Press/Buzz Magnuson)

The defensive pairings usually were Johnson with Wilkinson, Brian Glynn with Chambers, and Tinordi with Dahlquist. Johnson, who had missed the past nine games because of his injured hip, and Dahlquist, who spent some time in the minors during the 1989-90 season, were the only ones with at least 200 career games. The other four averaged less than 23 years and eight months in age but nonetheless had played every night in a 13-game stretch back to Game 4 against Chicago. In that stretch, the North Stars had allowed an average of 2.38 goals per game.

"Our defense is so young we don't know what we've accomplished," Tinordi said. "We're too stupid to know what we're doing. We just keep playing. Some of the older guys know what's going on, but we're just six guys doing their jobs and having fun."

With one exception in the postseason, when Johnson dressed that meant Giles was scratched. For such a veteran, it stung to be asked about it after the game.

"It was great to see the team play so well," said Giles, who made $220,000 this season but has worked a real job for the past few summers—selling building materials for Fridley-based API Supply Co.—perhaps sensing his playing days are numbered. "On the other hand, I didn't enjoy watching. You want them to do well, but you're hoping they miss you… I don't want to be a spare wheel."

That could be in conflict with strategy, however, if the North Stars advance to the Stanley Cup Final. He might have to subordinate himself to a championship.

"That's the ultimate goal," Giles said of winning the Cup. "I got goosebumps watching the Twins win the World Series."

It wasn't widely known, but earlier in the day Green fired Eric Kruse, director of operations at Met Center, apparently because he objected to the emergency demolition in the press dining room.

"Most of the people who are still working there are working in fear," Kruse said soon after. "Fear of not knowing what Norm is going to do next."

But it seemed like everyone else was rooting for the North Stars now. Bloomington resident George Konik's lawn sported a 15-foot by 15-foot North Stars logo carved in the grass. Konik[51] was one of the original Pittsburgh Penguins in 1967–68.

Thursday, May 9, 1991

With the weather sunny and temperatures in the seventies, everything looked bright. Even for Chambers, who underwent an MRI on his injured knee before joining the North Stars on their afternoon charter. They all heard a serenade of good-luck wishes from other Humphrey terminal travelers as they passed through the gate en route to Edmonton.

Pay-per-view ranged from 15,000 buys for the first two home games against Chicago to more than 31,000 for Game 6 against St. Louis to more than 35,000 for Game 4 against the Oilers. The strategy of selling the broadcast of playoff home games would generate more than $1 million in profits by the end of the postseason.

The North Stars also sold 125 season tickets on Thursday, the largest one-day total in team history. Season tickets had nearly doubled from the 3,331 that started the season. Some of that, according to Reusse, was undoubtedly because of the efforts of Strangis to use his post as radio color man to push the sales. That was not necessarily a compliment. Reusse's latest column referred to Strangis as the "third pooch in Norm Green's trio of Rupert, Charles and Ralph."

In any case, it was helping the bottom line. Forciea once estimated the team's losses would be $7 million, but a trip to the Stanley Cup Final could reduce that to $1 million—or perhaps break-even.

Later, Stevens scored twice and had three assists to lead Pittsburgh to a 7–2 win over Boston. Lemieux had a goal and three assists. The Penguins led the Wales Conference final 3–2 entering Saturday's Game 6 at the Igloo.

Friday, May 10, 1991: North Stars 3, Oilers 2, at Northlands Coliseum

Bobby Smith and Anderson each had an audience with NHL executive vice president Brian O'Neill the morning before Game 5.

"I've never even had a major penalty for high-sticking," Smith said. "I wasn't even suspended from high school and never had to sit on the wall during gym class."

No suspensions were announced.

Edmonton had a team meeting following the morning skate. Hours later, the Oilers tried to enforce their own justice. Dave Brown bumped Smith to the ice during pregame warmups, leading to a scrum.

---

51 Konik's major-league hockey career consisted of 52 games with Pittsburgh in 1967-68 and 54 games with the Minnesota Fighting Saints in 1972-73. A defenseman, he played in college at Denver University and settled in the Twin Cities after playing for the Minnesota Rangers of the Central Professional Hockey League in 1965-66. He scored a goal against St. Louis' Glenn Hall on Jan. 31, 1968, on the first penalty shot in Penguins history. He was seventy-nine when he died in 2016.

"I'll take the blame," Smith said. "I crossed on the wrong side of the red line and my skates hooked Brown's."

Brown then took a 10-minute misconduct twenty-six seconds into the game.

After Messier was called for cross-checking, Tinordi scored on a power-play rebound 2:06 into the first period. Twelve minutes later, Bureau converted a 3-on-2 rush for his second goal in as many games, and the North Stars enjoyed a 2–0 lead. But Tikkanen scored midway through the game, and Messier evened it early in the third period.

That only set the stage for Smith, more than ten years removed from being the North Stars' first teen phenom, to write the next chapter in this miraculous journey. Forty seconds after Messier scored, before Edmonton got to reframe the game as tied, Dahlquist head-manned the puck in his own zone to Gavin, who skated into the Edmonton end and dished to Smith, who deked Grant Fuhr and put a shot into the left side of the net.

Casey was unbeatable in the final fifteen minutes, finishing with 19 saves overall. Back in the Twin Cities, many of the players' wives and girlfriends jumped for joy watching the scene on Channel 9 at Beth Smith's house—rum punch spilled all over the carpet in celebration. On one wall hung a large framed photo of her husband scoring the goal against Calgary that put Minnesota into the 1981 finals. Now, history was repeating, and the North Stars were going to get a second chance at the Stanley Cup.

"This is a more complete team than we had in '81," her husband said afterward, his thinning hair drenched with perspiration. "We knew that, no matter how well we played, we weren't going to beat the Islanders. They were a great club. This time, there isn't a team we think should beat us."

After they pounded Casey on the back, the North Stars trooped off the ice. Oilers dressing room attendant Joey Moss delivered the Campbell Conference bowl, crafted in 1878 by a British silversmith, and set it next to a Gatorade bucket. The trophy, which had belonged to Edmonton until a few minutes earlier, was somewhat overlooked by the players in the media scramble and daze of what they'd accomplished.

"We've got eight reporters covering our team," said Bellows, sounding like the host of a beer bash. "There are reporters I don't even know. We're used to seeing two reporters write 'Stars Win' or 'Stars Lose,' see Page 10C.'... If anyone had predicted we would win this series in five games, I'd have said 'You've got to be kidding.'"

Perry Berezan, Mike Craig, DePalma, Giles, Derian Hatcher, Keczmer, Doug Smail, Rob Zettler, and Myllys all were scratched. But they were smiling, every one.

"I felt like a little kid, and I wasn't even in the lineup," Smail told me for this book. "I might have been happier than anybody, and I didn't even play a shift."

Green watched the game from a seat next to Chico Resch, whose shins ached from spontaneous kicks of excitement from the team's owner.

Later Friday night, Green ditched his tie and pulled on a Campbell Conference Champions T-shirt.

"I always thought it was more like someday the North Stars would win," Green said. "Never in my wildest dreams did I think that it would come this fast, that it would be this good."

"There has never been anything like this," Clarke added. "Never anything close."

In Minnesota, this scene was replicated in some fashion all over the state:

"You think they went crazy when the Twins won the World Series?" asked Rose Maxwell, who watched at the Little Wagon Bar in Minneapolis. "It's going to be even crazier. I can't even describe what it's going to be like. It's going to be wild.

"We're going to win the Stanley Cup," she added. "You betcha.... If you're a fan, you're a fan. You can't be a frontrunner. You've got to be with them until the very end. You can't give up. You've got to stick with them through thick and thin. I just wish I'd gone to Vegas and placed a bet."

As the final seconds ticked away on the TV, she chanted: "Na-na-na-na, hey-hey-hey, gooooodbye!"

At the Metrodome, some of the 16,012 fans abandoned the Twins during a 5–2 win over Detroit to watch the North Stars.

"I think they're going to go all the way," said Gregg Klohn, who headed across the street to Hubert's.

Within minutes of the final horn, drivers honked in the streets—just before Minnesota's midnight fishing opener drew excited anglers onto lakes all over the state.

Since expanding from six to 12 franchises, only three times had a team made the Stanley Cup Final with a losing record:

- 1967–68 St. Louis Blues (27–31–16, .473)
- 1981–82 Vancouver Canucks (30–33–17, .481)
- 1990–91 Minnesota North Stars (27–39–14, .425)

The Blues and Canucks were both swept.

But the North Stars couldn't have cared less about history as they rode their bus back to the Hilton. Some headed out for last call at a saloon a couple blocks away, though Tinordi was content to entertain his family and friends in the lobby. Green ordered a buffet for the entire travel party that would last well into the night, then went to the hotel bar with members of the media. Eventually, they all adjourned to the banquet room, shaking their heads in amazement. Gainey and Clarke, for whom the return to the Stanley Cup Final has special meaning, rehashed the game until they finally went to bed.

It was 4:30 a.m.

CHAPTER 13

Stanley Cup Finals: The Glass Slipper Shatters

Saturday, May 11, 1991

Dawn had barely broken when Doug Jarvis exited the Hilton for a brisk walk. He was too excited to sleep and wanted to stretch his legs before the North Stars boarded their charter. A few hours later, the plane winged home with green and gold crepe paper decorating the aisle between the passengers, and the replay of Friday night's game flickering on small TV screens set into the back of each seat. If the players couldn't believe they'd punched their ticket to the Stanley Cup Final, they had just enough time to watch it again through eyes wonderfully tired—but not so much they didn't respond with a back-slapping ovation when they saw Bobby Smith's goal all over again.

It was sunny and almost eighty when they arrived at the Humphrey terminal. More than 1,000 fans greeted the travelers—all wearing suits and ties—as they came through the jetway at about 3 p.m. With a big smile, Smith waved like a politician. Jon Casey, a pair of wire-rimmed glasses making him look like a college professor, signed autographs—including one on an electric guitar.

The proverbial bandwagon was overflowing.

"We back that thing up every morning," Pat Forciea said. "We're more than happy to let everybody on. We've had longtime fans say, 'Where were these people when the team needed them?' But I haven't heard anybody say it was more fun when there were 5,200 people."

As the players waded through screaming teens, baby strollers, young men with homemade Stanley Cup replicas, and assorted fans of all ages and sizes, Mark Tinordi sympathized with the latecomers: "What should we do, say, 'Stay home if you're only here because we're winning'? If I was paying money to come here the last two or three years, I'd have stayed home, too."

Shane Churla added to the carnival atmosphere as he lugged the rug from an 800-pound grizzly he'd shot with a rifle last summer in Canada. His father and his best friend had delivered it to him in Edmonton before Game 5. Watching him stuff it into his sporty black subcompact was good comedy, and later at the Met, he briefly spread it out in the dressing room before taking it home.

"We deserve to let our emotions run wild for a couple of days," said Stew Gavin, his playoff beard filling in dark brown and shaggy. "We worked hard. We've been underdogs. We've been low-key and tried to focus on what we had to do. Now it's just the time to celebrate what we've accomplished."

Casey and Basil McRae signed autographs until, finally, there were no more extended hands. Before driving home, Casey unveiled a wry goalie's sense of humor.

"We appreciate all the fans that are here, but we really respect the five or six who stayed with us all year," Casey said. "We'll have more than five or six next year. We'll have eight or ten, at least."

Pioneer Press columnist Bob Sansevere flew to Pittsburgh for Game 6 of the Wales Conference final, and Gary Olson called Gordon Gund for his reaction to the North Stars' amazing turnaround.

"I'm very excited for the guys we got to know and like very much," Gund said. "I'm happy they're doing so well. We always believed in that team.… I hope they win the Stanley Cup. There are people in Minnesota we think a lot of, and it's great to see this happen for them."

Shawn Chambers went right from the airport to the hospital for arthroscopic surgery to remove a loose piece of cartilage from his left knee. He'd reinjured it in Game 4 and woke up unable to walk Friday morning. The cartilage stuck in the joint, and the only way he could get to breakfast was to hobble down the hall. Miraculously, after stimulus treatment from Dave Suprenant and a pregame nap, Chambers felt fine and managed to play all through Game 5.

Saturday night in Pittsburgh, as the North Stars again gathered in Bloomington to scout their next opponent, the Penguins overcame a two-goal deficit to beat Boston 5–3 and advance to the Stanley Cup Final for the first time in franchise history. Former North Star Gordie Roberts scored one goal and set up Mark Recchi for the game-winner at 15:40 of the third period. Mario Lemieux, who had two assists, added an empty-net goal and subsequently skated around with the Wales Conference championship trophy.

"People were saying we weren't even going to make the playoffs; we're playing for the Stanley Cup!" Pittsburgh coach Bob Johnson hooted. "This team had many psychological barriers to overcome, but they overcame them all."

Games 1 and 2 of the Stanley Cup Final will be Wednesday and Friday, in Pittsburgh. Games 3 and 4 will be May 19 and 21 at Met Center. If the series goes that long, Games 5 and 7 will be May 23 and 28 in Pittsburgh, with Game 6 on May 25 at the Met. The games in Pittsburgh will start at 6:35 p.m. Central time, with the games at Met Center starting at 7:05 p.m.

"Even when we were down 2–0 (in the series), we knew we could beat Boston, even if a lot of people didn't," Kevin Stevens said in the jubilant Penguins dressing room at Civic Arena. "You could see it in everybody's eyes. You could see it in Mario's eyes… We're not going to think about Minnesota—at least not for a couple more hours."

Sunday, May 12, 1991

Mother's Day was like something from a Hallmark card: sunny and eighty-five degrees by late afternoon. Presumably, Jim Johnson spoke to his mom. But we know he called his former Pittsburgh defense partner, Paul Coffey, because Johnson told us so. He said Coffey is the Penguins' biggest leader—even bigger than Lemieux—because of the three Stanley Cups he won in Edmonton.

"One of the things he mentioned to me was that we had just beaten the No. 1 and No. 2 teams, and he thought we beat No. 3, too," Johnson said. "They're definitely aware of what we've done to get here, as we are aware of them."

Other than treatment with Surprenant, it was an off day for the players—many of whom desperately needed the sleep. The relative quiet left Bob Gainey time to reflect on the previous seven months.

"In October, it was too far out of reality to think we could go to the Stanley Cup Final," said Gainey, who'd stood behind the bench for just 17 playoff games in his young career as head coach. "Our goals were set as we moved along. Some of them, as we look back now, were very small. But we started to make things happen, one small bit at a time. Every marathon begins with one step."

For years, he was often asked which of the Stanley Cups he won was best. Gainey's answer was always the same: "The next one."

Monday, May 13, 1991

If you called Brian Bellows at home, you'd have heard this message on his answering machine: "We're not in, and we're out of tickets."

He wasn't the only one.

"Everyone I know in Minnesota is calling me, wanting me to get them tickets," said Bob Johnson, who previously coached at Warroad and Minneapolis Roosevelt high schools, at Colorado College and the University of Wisconsin, and with the Calgary Flames before Pittsburgh. "Where were those people all year? If they wanted to see the North Stars, there were tickets available all year, and nobody bought them."

Joanie Preston found dozens of messages from local and national reporters on her voicemail when she arrived at the office. With each round, the needs and attention of the media grew from onerous to almost impossible. Fortunately, the metro newspapers already had reporters in Pittsburgh where they had access to Penguins like Roberts. A defenseman who played for the North Stars with Bellows, Neal Broten, Dave Gagner, McRae, Curt Giles, Chambers, Smith, and Casey, Roberts still lived in the Twin Cities during the offseason and operated a wine store, The Connoisseur, in the IDS Crystal Court.

"What a difference Mario (Lemieux) makes," said Roberts, who played sixty-one regular-season games for the Penguins after his October trade from St. Louis. "He has made this franchise. When he came here, they were averaging 5,000 fans. Now they're selling out like the North Stars."

Roberts remembers, though, just several months earlier when the North Stars didn't draw—and he thought tartakes and the Electric Stars an embarrassment.

"I thought I was in some lounge in Las Vegas, with the music and the lights and the dancers and the cash giveaway," Roberts said of Pittsburgh's November 13 and December 1 visits to Met Center. "It was sad. I played in Minnesota for eight years. I couldn't believe the North Stars had reached a point where they were doing stuff like that."

Roberts said he didn't think Minnesota would be able to shadow Lemieux like they did Brett Hull. Mark Recchi, Stevens, Ron Francis, and Jaromir Jagr were four other forwards with at least 85 points or 25 goals. Recchi led all postseason players with 23 assists. Stevens's 13 playoff goals were more than anyone but Cam Neely.

"We have so much depth, they'll have more problems checking us," Roberts said.

Of course, the North Stars had Casey, who led all playoff goalies in goals-against average (2.63) and wins (12). His save percentage (.904) was second only to his Pittsburgh counterpart, Tom Barrasso (.914). Then again, Casey was the lightest player on either team—listed at 155 pounds—and that probably didn't reflect what was left on him after playing 788 of a possible 840 minutes in 14 games during the past 33 days. Where's the line between playing hot and getting fatigued?

It was sunny with temperatures in the eighties again when the North Stars reported for practice. Just before Smith exited I-494 at 24th Avenue, another driver recognized him and signaled thumbs up. Perhaps it was an omen. Indeed, the NHL announced it would not suspend Smith for his hit on Martin Gelinas during Game 4 of the Edmonton series.

Moments later, astoundingly, Chambers was skating less than forty-eight hours after arthroscopic surgery. If he couldn't go, Giles would be the next man in. Chambers' left knee would require draining before every game of the finals—a process not for the squeamish called arthrocentesis.

"I used to watch, until (Shane) Churla and some of the other guys were in the (training) room, and they're like, 'Oh, my God. That's a big syringe. I can't believe you're doing that,'" Chambers recalled for this book, sounding like he was reading from the script of a horror film. "Then I was like, 'OK. That's enough, Churls. Get out of here.'"

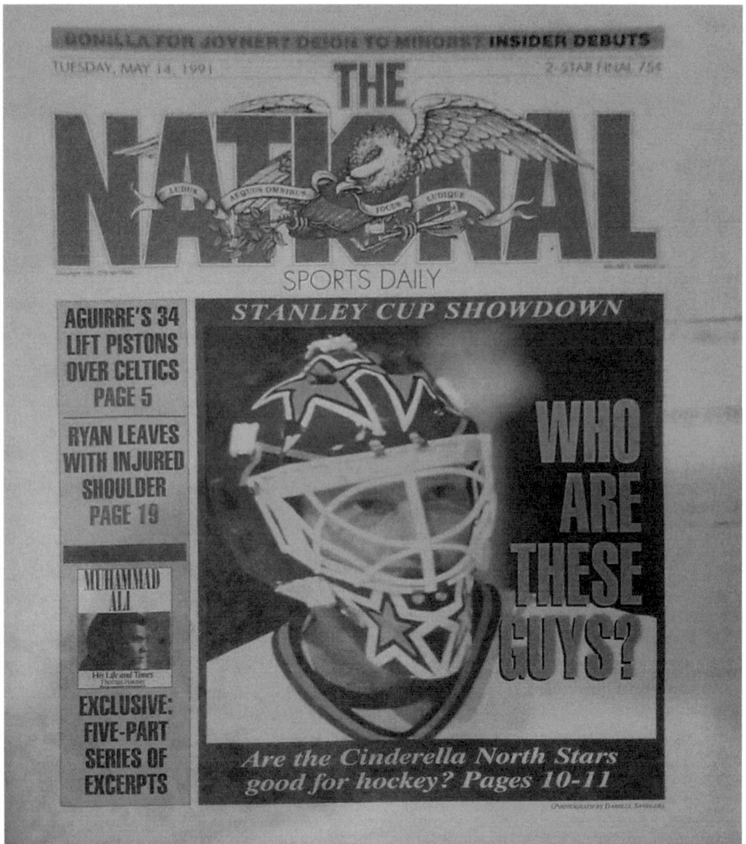

The cover of The National Sports Daily newspaper asked the question everyone in the hockey world wanted to know on May 14, 1991. Jon Casey was the masked man who had sparked the North Stars to the Stanley Cup Final.

The irony of the finals matchup between the Penguins and North Stars is that it might never have come to pass if not for one of the greatest collapses in NHL history.

In 1975, Pittsburgh had a 3-0 quarterfinal lead over the New York Islanders. But the Penguins lost 3–1 in Game 4 at Nassau Coliseum, 4–2 in Game 5 at the Igloo, and 4–1 in Game 6 back on Long Island. There was one goal in Game 7 back in Pittsburgh. The Islanders scored it, Chico Resch got the win, and the Penguins joined the 1942 Detroit Red Wings as the only NHL teams ever to blow a 3–0 series lead.[52]

As if that wasn't enough, two months later the IRS padlocked the doors of Civic Arena and the Pens went bankrupt. Coach Marc Boileau actually applied for unemployment. Former North Stars GM Wren Blair put together a partnership that allowed the team to survive. Otherwise, the NHL would've left Pittsburgh fifteen years ago.[53]

Tuesday, May 14, 1991

Fans lined up to buy souvenirs outside Pro Central in Bloomington even before the store opened Tuesday morning. The North Stars were off to Pittsburgh by then. As they waited for their charter to leave, a US Marine just back from Saudi Arabia—32-year-old Gary Jensen of St. Paul—gave his dog tag and a lucky coin he'd carried in battle to Smith.

KSTP-TV (Channel 5) sent eleven people to cover Games 1 and 2, including sports anchor Joe Schmit, co-anchor Randy Meyer, reporter Steve Hartman, sports reporter Robb Leer, two news producers, and five photographers.

WCCO-TV (Channel 4) sent eight, including sports anchor Mark Rosen, sports reporter Scott Reynolds, and news reporter Amy Marsalis—and they were planning a 30-minute special after Game 3. KARE-TV (Channel 11) had six people along for the ride, including sports reporters Jeff Passolt and Randy Shaver. For KMSP-TV (Channel 9), it was merely the regular road crew of Doug McLeod and Lou Nanne, though they'd be cut into an hour-long preview show from Benchwarmer Bob's (owned by former Vikings defensive lineman Bob Lurtsema) in Brooklyn Park.

52 The Red Wings met the Maple Leafs in the Stanley Cup Final, winning twice in Toronto and taking Game 3 in Detroit. But the Leafs won Game 4 4-3, romped 9-3 in Game 5 and earned a 3-0 shutout in Game 6. With Game 7 in Toronto, the Red Wings took a one-goal lead into the third period before losing 3-1.

53 Blair and his partners eventually sold to Eddie DeBartolo, Sr., in 1977. DeBartolo, perhaps best known for buying the San Francisco 49ers and giving them to his son, Eddie Jr., ironically threatened to move the Penguins in 1984 if $15 million in improvements weren't made to Civic Arena. Maybe that's where George and Gordon Gund got the idea.

The day grew hot. It was eighty-eight degrees by late afternoon, and Patrick Reusse made it even warmer with his column in the *Star Tribune*. Pay-per-view was the subject, and he became the first person to publicly refer to Norm Green as "Norm Greed."

But perhaps the day's best commentary came from an ABC announcer whose most famous call was from a hockey game but who had nothing to do with the finals.

"The NHL regular season has always been a charade, and no one should ever take it seriously," said Al Michaels, who broadcast the 1980 US Olympic victory over the Soviet Union. "Why do they play so many games to eliminate so few teams? We know why. Money. But the fans have let them get away with it, and they'll keep doing it as long as they keep getting away with it."

Nonetheless ...

"I think it's terrific, and I love when things like this happen," said Michaels, who knew a miracle when he saw one. "The Twins did the same thing in '87.... Maybe that shouldn't have been and maybe the North Stars shouldn't have been, but if sports were so predictable that all the teams that were supposed to win won all the time, would anyone be interested?"

The NHL wouldn't argue.

"The North Stars have captured the imaginations of the sports fans of North America," league president John Ziegler said. "Everyone is calling this that miracle in Minnesota."

"If you sat down and wrote this script before the season, people would have led you out with your hands tied behind you," NHL marketing VP Steve Ryan added.

But the sudden attention hadn't changed life for the North Stars.

"Dave Gagner told me he has been recognized twice in the Twin Cities," Smith said. "The assistant stick boy in Montreal can't get through the grocery store without being recognized."

Bobby Clarke sounded like he was ready to give a two-hand slash to anyone who suggested his team didn't belong in the finals.

"I don't give a damn what anybody thinks," Clarke said. "I think it's great. I think this is what the playoffs are all about. I think we struggled for a long time, stuck together, and came out of it when a lot of other teams would've been torn apart."

There were two concerns paramount to Gainey as the team settled into the William Penn Hotel. First, the North Stars went 0-for-11 against the Penguins on the man advantage during the regular season. Yes, Minnesota's power-play had already tied the NHL record for goals in a playoff year (32-for-119, 26.9 percent), but could that continue against Pittsburgh?

And then there was the little issue of the 6-foot-4-inch, 200-pound game-changer named Lemieux. Yes, Pittsburgh's first overall pick in the 1984 draft had back surgery last July, and he didn't participate in morning skates and sometimes took days off between games. But using his seven years of regular-season performance as a yardstick, there was an eighty percent chance Lemieux would score a goal in *every* game he plays. His postseason experience was a small sample but bore the same result. He had 12 goals and seven assists in 11 playoff games prior to this year, in which he led all scorers with 11 goals and 21 assists in 18 games.

In other words, if Lemieux dressed, the North Stars probably already trailed at least 1–0.

"They have a lot of other good forwards, but Lemieux can beat you by himself," said Les Jackson, who scouted Pittsburgh against Boston and would travel with the North Stars during the finals.

Andy Murray, for the fourth consecutive series, distributed the game plan. The three-ring binders had the Penguins' logo inside a circle and a slash, and the pages detailed every usable tactic Chris Dahlquist and Jim Johnson could conjure. For example, if the North Stars ever found Coffey in a scrum, they should chop his skates—right on the top of the laces. Coffey prefers to wear skates two sizes too small, Dahlquist and Johnson know, and his feet are tender as a result. Overall, the strategy is to force Pittsburgh's defense to carry the play, stay tight through the neutral zone, and not let their more talented forwards enter the Minnesota zone with possession.

Of course, Bob Johnson devised his own secret plan to beat Minnesota. Only he knew its details, but its focus was to stop Broten—the one player Johnson really fears.

"This is going to be an interesting series," Gagner said. "We don't know what to expect. We may be here next year; we may never be here again. We're going to make the most of it while we can."

Wednesday, May 15, 1991: North Stars 5, Penguins 4, at Civic Arena

The *Star Tribune* featured six pages dedicated to the North Stars and the Stanley Cup Final, not including Page 5A—a full-page Dayton's ad showed a hockey net with its goal mouth filled by bricks and mortar. Its text boasted to anyone from Pittsburgh that certain areas of Minnesota would be off-limits to visitors when the series shifts to the Met.

Nick's Sports World, with seven locations around the Twin Cities, advertised the "largest collection of Stanley Cup merchandise," including jackets, pucks, and mini sticks. By 10 a.m., a cottage industry of souvenir stands had sprung up in business and hotel parking lots all over the metro. All hawked T-shirts, caps, key chains, mugs, tankards, shot glasses, jerseys, sweatshirts, sweatpants, shorts, and infant clothing featuring the North Stars logo.

At the morning skate, Green proudly displayed a signed blank check he received from fellow mogul Harvey McKay, who'd sent it and an accompanying poem to Green requesting ten season tickets for 1991–92 to go with the six McKay already owns.

By late afternoon, it was eighty-seven degrees in Pittsburgh and little more than ten degrees cooler in Minneapolis. A sellout crowd of 16,164 packed into the Igloo. Mike Lange and Paul Steigerwald, handling the play-by-play and color, respectively, on the Penguins' TV/radio simulcast, sweated not far from McLeod and Nanne—staring at the ice as though they couldn't believe it.

Dave Smith, Mark Baribeau, and Lance Vogt ferried sticks and equipment across the ice to the bench. The Igloo was the only arena in the league with no other way to get there. Once play started, the only way off was to appeal a linesman during a stoppage.

Just after the Penguins took the ice for warmups, Tinordi followed Casey and Brian Propp through the doors in one corner of the North Stars' zone. Superstition dictated they had to pass in that order—and that Tinordi start getting his gear on exactly twenty-five minutes before they went out, and always the left side first. Just before leaving the dressing room, Churla used his stick to whack Stew Gavin, once on each shoulder, once on the helmet, and once on his backside. McRae and Churla, in order, followed Gavin onto the ice. Other than Gagner, who went out of his way *not* to be superstitious, everyone had some common routine.

Twenty minutes later, having worked up a light lather, they disappeared beneath the stands, where they fidgeted and wiggled their anticipation away waiting for the signal to return. The scratches (Perry Berezan, Mike Craig, Larry DePalma, Giles, Derian Hatcher, Dan Keczmer, Doug Smail, Rob Zettler and Jarmo Myllys) nearly made a small, well-dressed team of their own with no place to go.

Then it was time. The Penguins skated onto the ice, and the North Stars converged from an opposite corner. Each team was introduced, the loudest cheers reserved for last: "Number 66, Mario Lemieux!"

Barely had the din quieted before B. E. Taylor, a minor pop-rock singer from Aliquippa, Pennsylvania, launched into the longest and perhaps worst anthem in pro sports history. It ranged through a near-impossible range of octaves and took 2 minutes and 28 seconds—twice as long as those for subsequent games in the series. His performance left the fans and even players temporarily stunned.

"That was ridiculous," said Bryan Trottier, who had heard more than a few renditions in sixteen years in the NHL.

"It was funny," Churla said. "This was the moment I'd always been waiting for, and this guy just about puts me to sleep. I thought it was great, though, because I knew it had to be bringing that crowd down. What more could we want?"

Ulf Samuelsson brought everyone back to reality 3:45 into the game, making it 1–0 Penguins. Francis beat Marc Bureau on a faceoff, and Samuelsson shot through a screen and past Casey. But the North Stars responded with goals by Broten and Ulf Dahlen 3:17 apart before the midpoint of the first period.

Each team scored a short-handed goal early in the second. Pittsburgh's came from Lemieux, who would go on to score 49 during his career in the regular season and another seven in the playoffs. He blocked a shot by Chambers and took a head-man pass from Francis to beat Casey on a breakaway. Minnesota's came from Bureau—his third career goal in as many games and the only postseason shortie he would ever score. He stole the puck from Larry Murphy and beat Barrasso with a forty-foot slap shot.

"It was a scrambly game," Murphy said. "Not the type of game we want to play. I'm not surprised at how well Minnesota is playing."

Jim Johnson took a slashing penalty that led to Scott Young's first goal of the playoffs on a shot from the high slot at 7:43, but Broten scored again late in the second to retake the lead, and Smith got the game-winner, roofing a backhand early in the third. Joey Mullen, three months removed from neck surgery and looking like a football player with a padded collar sticking out of his sweater, made the final ten minutes more dramatic. He poked in a loose puck after Casey got caught out of the crease. But Casey kicked out everything else and the North Stars and Penguins started the finals just as they'd both started every series so far—with a road win for Minnesota and a home loss for Pittsburgh.

"Tonight, we didn't have the discipline of those past three openers," cautioned Broten, whose brothers, Aaron and Paul, watched on TV in the living room of their parents' home in Roseau.

Neal proved Bob Johnson's fears of his scoring prowess were not unfounded. Broten's first goal deflected off Roberts and eluded Barrasso. The second came on a third-chance rebound.

"I don't know if getting two goals is a reward or not," said Broten, who scored twice in a game for the first time since the playoff opener. "A reward is a win.... Most years, I can't tell you how many goals I've scored. This season, I knew. It's not hard to count to thirteen."

Jim Johnson somehow managed to finish with a plus-3 rating, the only player in the game to do so. It was especially satisfying since two of his former teammates, Roberts and Recchi, were minus-3.

"I think we all feel lucky to win the game because we didn't play our best," said Casey, who made 34 saves—10 more than Barrasso.

"Four goals should be enough to win against Minnesota," Barrasso countered in a bitter assessment of his performance.

The North Stars managed to kill seven of eight penalties, including two two-man disadvantages that totaled 1:21. Broten and Gavin usually started the PKs up front, with Bureau and Gaetan Duchesne coming off the bench. But the power play went 0-for-5. It was perhaps the only thing you could characterize as cold.

"That is as hot of an arena as I've ever played in," said Gagner, who was hit with a puck and needed seven stitches to close a gash to his jaw. "I think it had an effect."

But the Penguins refused to lose their cool because of the Game 1 loss.

"We're not panicking," said Lemieux, who led all skaters with seven shots. "We've done this before."

Back at the William Penn, Green opened a bottle of Courvoisier and asked Forciea, Elaine Waddell, Preston, and Ralph Strangis if they wanted a celebratory drink. Strangis, who had grown a playoff beard in solidarity with Duchesne, Gavin and Propp, politely declined. When pressed, Strangis revealed it was the fifth anniversary for his sobriety. He retired to his room and was watching TV when there came a knock on the door. A room service attendant entered bearing a piece of chocolate cake with a candle and a glass of milk. A note read "Your personal accomplishments far outweigh anything we'll do on the ice. Happy birthday. A secret admirer."

"It was from Norm," Strangis told me for this book. "That's not something people associate with him. I love Norm. He was mercurial and eccentric and tough and all those things. But Norman was really good to me."

Thursday, May 16, 1991

The Penguins couldn't see it yet, but in today's *Star Tribune* Reusse became the first Minnesota columnist to suggest a Stanley Cup parade in the Twin Cities. In the *Pioneer Press*, Nick Coleman wrote, "It's over. It's in the bag. The North Stars are going to win the Cup."

Eager to dive into his new role as an investment broker, Nanne returned to Minneapolis for the day off between Games 1 and 2 and found Minnesota had gone gaga. Game 1 drew the largest audience in KMSP-TV history. More than half of the one million TV sets in the Twin Cities were tuned to the game, although it was a smaller audience than watched the 1987 World Series on ABC.

McLeod rose almost at dawn and drove a rental car to Columbus, Ohio, so he could call Gophers baseball in the Big Ten tournament. By nightfall he would be back in Pittsburgh, having spent six hours behind the wheel. He'd repeat the tour on Saturday.

Meanwhile, the NHL announced a suspension of Edmonton forward Glenn Anderson for kicking Duchesne in Game 4 of the Campbell Conference final.

In Pittsburgh, Gainey canceled practice but the team held meetings. Frank Sinatra, playing at the Igloo, required the North Stars to temporarily remove their equipment from their dressing room in advance of a concert Thursday night. Perhaps it would shuffle their tendency to lose Game 2.

"When we look at those second games, we have to just shake our heads and kick ourselves in the pants," Broten said. "Chicago just blew us out in the second game. St. Louis blew us out. Edmonton blew us out. We've played poorly in the second game. We've been sitting back too much instead of creating our own chances."

The North Stars had been adamant about being respected for their accomplishments in these playoffs. But in almost the same breath, they seemed just as surprised as everyone else.

"If somebody had told us we'd be in the finals, I would not have believed it," Broten said.

When asked to recall his previous trip, in 1981—weeks after he'd left the University of Minnesota—Broten said, "It was so long ago, I can't remember half the guys who played for us."

He remembers the Islanders, however.

"Bryan Trottier would've had to break his leg and Mike Bossy break his arm for us to have a chance," Broten said. "It was fun, though. I was on a pretty good streak."

That included a run to the state high school tournament in 1978, an NCAA championship in 1979, the gold medal with the US Olympic team in 1980, and another appearance in the NCAA title game in 1981 before losing in the Stanley Cup Final less than two months later.

"Neal was so low-key," Smith said. "He had a wonderful view of hockey and of life. A lot of players will tell you, 'I don't even know who scored the goals tonight.' Neal is the only one I've ever played with who says that and is telling the truth. He is the same now as he was ten years ago."

What's different was that the '81 North Stars trailed in the finals three games to none before their lone victory. The '91 North Stars held a one-game lead.

"If we can win three more games, this will be a team that the people of Minnesota will be talking about for decades," Smith said.

Friday, May 17, 1991: Penguins 4, North Stars 1, at Civic Arena

It was a little more comfortable in Pittsburgh, with a Game 2 outdoor temperature of about seventy degrees. After missing Game 1, Coffey fired up another sellout crowd of 16,164 when he skated out for warmups wearing a full face shield to protect the metal plate in his jaw.

Nancy Wilson (of Heart) ripped through the national anthem in barely a minute. The North Stars lasted fourteen more before they cracked.

Bob Errey scored at 14:26, the second short-handed goal Minnesota allowed in as many games after giving up none in the first three rounds. Then, after Chambers took an interference call and forced his teammates to try to kill off back-to-back penalties, the theme from "Jaws" emanated from the loudspeakers. Fans waved 9x11-inch cards that showed shark fins. The scoreboard read "The Shark Attack is Back" and "Fins Up." On cue, Stevens scored on the power play for his first of two goals in the game.

A Pittsburgh bench minor for too many men at the end of the first period led to Mike Modano's power-play rebound goal in the opening minute of the second. But Lemieux—who set up Stevens' first goal—scored on a highlight-film breakaway that would be seen for generations to come. And Stevens added another goal less than a minute and a half later.

The only fireworks after that came during a fight between Tinordi and Troy Loney, once teammates in the WHL, at the horn for the second intermission. In the third period, Trottier got a 10-minute misconduct for punching Neil Wilkinson, and Roberts drew a major for spearing Brian Glynn. Roberts said the reason he lost his temper was because Modano had called him "Gramps." Roberts later got even by calling Modano a "pretty boy," and the major only allowed Barrasso to earn a couple more saves. He finished with 39.

"It's hard to say why this is happening to us," Tinordi said of a fourth straight Game 2 defeat.

Here's one clue: the North Stars' power-play units went 1-for-9. Add in Errey's short-handed goal and they were essentially worthless.

"The power play seemed to be the turning point of our game," Gainey said.

It didn't help that Bellows, who led the North Stars in goals and assists, injured his right knee in the first period on a hit by Samuelsson.

"I was not too happy," said Bellows, who tried to get up and take after Samuelsson to retaliate but couldn't initially put weight on his leg. "The puck was thirty feet away from me so you're not looking to get hit… not by most guys."

It was the first major blow in a game much more physical than the opener. Catastrophically, Gainey had scratched Churla and McRae in favor of Berezan and Smail, neither of whom had played since March 28. McRae watched the game from the coaches' room. Churla joined him for awhile but couldn't sit still long. They didn't know until after the morning skate that they wouldn't play. For as intimidating as Bump and Thump could be, however, they knew it would only be counterproductive to complain.

"That's a decision I made today for various reasons," Gainey said. "Some I can tell you and some I can't. ... I don't think that was a factor. We've had trouble in the second game of every series, and we came in standing pretty pat.… This gave us a chance to get new blood in there and try to get a little more speed in the lineup."

Berezan and Smail were fast, but they'd have needed rocket boosters to catch Lemieux on the third goal. After Berezan had a chance on a rebound in the Pittsburgh end, play went the other way, and Lemieux bore down on Chambers and Wilkinson. Lemieux offered the puck to Chambers, less than a week removed from his third knee surgery in eight months, and faked to the outside. As Chambers turned out, Lemieux cut in, zipped toward Casey, deked, lost his balance and wound up in the net with the goalie and the puck. The play would be seen for decades as part of a montage on the intro to Hockey Night in Canada.

"What can I say?" Chambers said. "It was ugly. Maybe if I had seen it happen to somebody else, I could say it was beautiful.... I'm sure there are other guys who can make that play, but I'm not just sure who they are."

Lemieux had been held off the scoresheet just once in the playoffs—April 11 against New Jersey.

"He was the difference in the game," Gagner said. "That was a huge goal for them. It's a different game when you're down by two."

While Lemieux played like a superhero, movie star and Pittsburgh native Michael Keaton posed for pictures with the Pens in their dressing room after the game. The North Stars, frustrated, chartered home into the dark night.

Saturday, May 18, 1991

It was cool in the Twin Cities the day before Game 3, with a high of fifty-three degrees. At the Hotel Sofitel, the Stanley Cup and other trophies were on display.

"When you get your name on it, that's about as close to heaven as you can get," Clarke said. Players and staff of winning teams get possession of the trophy for a day each, as well as a thirteen-inch version worth $1,000 to keep.

If that was in the stars for Minnesota, the power play—1 for 14 so far—had to wake up. All of the players involved in both units held a closed-door meeting at the back of the weight room before practice.

"I don't know if concerned is the right word," Gainey said. "I don't think something is wrong with the power play.... There are always small adjustments to make. It's a question of whether you make those adjustments."

Bellows sat out practice. Surprenant said Bellows had a bruise and would play Sunday night. Jim Johnson didn't skate, either.

The media spotlight was about to shine brighter than ever on Met Center and Green. Tony Danza would watch Games 3 and 4 from the owner's box, and "MacGyver" star Richard Dean Anderson would join him for the latter. But Green shunned talk of the celebrities and politicians that had visited during the playoffs.

"It sounds elitist," explained Green, a self-appraised man of the people—who happened to own a Rolls Royce and a private jet.

This week, he would try to convince the Metropolitan Sports Facilities Commission to make changes to the Met Center lease that would, among other things, allow him to build retail space around it and link to the Mall of America.

"If they want me to guarantee that the North Stars will play here for twenty-five years, I'll do that," Green said. "The North Stars aren't going anyplace."

Despite the team's on-ice success, some politicians weren't too keen on the idea because it would only offer competition to the brand-new publicly subsidized Target Center—where they'd prefer to have Green, too. But, thanks to playoff fever, he had them in a tough spot.

"If the season had ended with the regular season, I think he would've taken a close look and decided to move downtown," said Walt Dziedzic, a Minneapolis City Council member. "But the way things are going now, it's like it's a poker game and when it was his turn to draw, he drew aces."

Another politician found a more sympathetic target: the pay-per-view telecasts. Gerry Sikorski, the US representative from the Sixth Congressional district, wanted to draft legislation to require free broadcasts for hometown fans when a championship is on the line.

"This is the first time in American history it's happened," said Sikorski, a lawyer from Stillwater. "I want to make it the last."

San Jose GM Jack Ferreira was staying at a hotel across the street and would attend Game 3 as the guest of a season-ticket holder.

"I don't want to have to park at the Met Center and have to give Norm Green five dollars for parking," Ferreira said.

Sunday, May 19, 1991: North Stars 3, Penguins 1, at Met Center

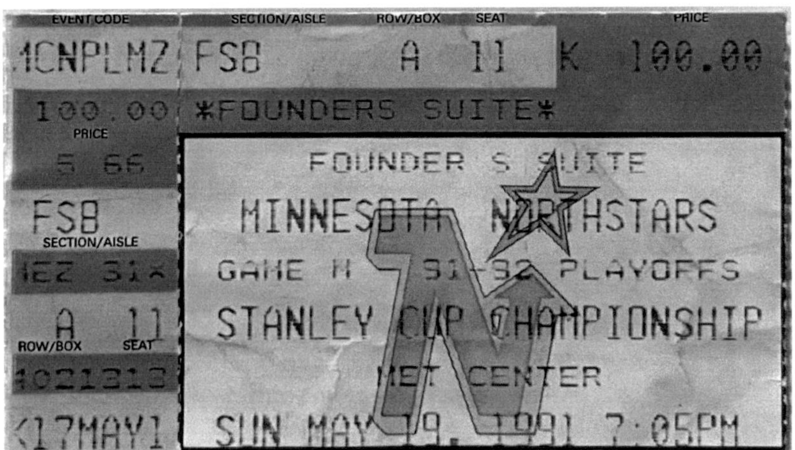

A ticket stub from a seat in the Founders Suite at Met Center for Game 3 of the 1991 Stanley Cup Final.

Lemieux woke up in his room at the St. Paul Radisson and knew something was wrong. His bed, too soft for his liking, triggered some back pain. Nonetheless, he pushed through, went to breakfast and, as usual, skipped the morning skate.

It was a mild afternoon—about sixty-two degrees at game time—but nice enough for Nanne to play golf with Ziegler at Interlachen Country Club in Edina. They chuckled about Nanne's failed attempt seven years earlier as North Stars GM to ship all 12 of his picks to Pittsburgh for the No. 1 overall draft selection, which was going to be Lemieux.

Around the time Nanne and Ziegler repaired to Met Center, there were three arrests for ticket scalping and one for selling illegal merchandise in the parking lot—which was otherwise well-behaved considering the throng on hand.

Inside, at about 6:45 p.m., came the announcement of the starters and scratches. Perhaps never in hockey history did the reading of the players who were *not* going to play have a bigger impact on a game and its atmosphere. Lemieux, the leading scorer in the playoffs and arguably the most intimidating offensive talent in the world, had experienced back spasms tying his skates before the warmup. He skated with the other Pittsburgh players but, after climbing the steps to the dressing room, he sat down and the spasms returned. For Lemieux, who missed fifty games during the regular season following back surgery, it was clear he could not play.

The sellout crowd of 15,378 was stunned, as though unsure whether to cheer, disbelieving what they heard.

In the North Stars' dressing room, Gainey took his copy of the game sheet—with circles around the starters—and asked Chambers to read them to the team.

"You won't have to worry about him tonight," Gainey said, pointing at Lemieux's crossed-out 66.

With Lemieux not playing, that meant Jiri Hrdina—a Czech who largely had been added as a mentor for Jagr—would suit up. Hrdina was pointless in 11 of 14 playoff games.

"It was like Christmas morning, practically," Gavin said.

There was an excruciating wait for the gift of the first goal to arrive. It didn't come until 7:21 of the second period. With his two-week-old daughter in the stands for her first game, Gagner took a pass from Modano, got behind Peter Taglianetti, and tucked a shot under Barrasso from the left side of the crease. The uproar had yet to subside before Smith scored thirty-three seconds later on the next shot, a wrister from the right circle that snuck under the crossbar.

During a delayed penalty 1:23 into the third, after Glynn hauled down Jagr, Phil Bourque cut the Penguins' deficit in half. But Duchesne got it back on a rebound thirty-eight seconds later.

Fueled by the home crowd, knowing McRae and Churla were in uniform again, and with a growing sense of confidence as the final minutes ticked away, Bureau ripped the helmet and half-shield off Coffey's head and, with 1:13 left, frustration boiled over. Stevens took a spearing major. Bellows and Randy Gilhen were given 10-minute misconducts at 19:53, and Smith tangled with Errey at the final horn. It was a continuation of the combativeness for which the NHL fined each team $25,000 in response to the Tinordi-Loney fight at end of second period in Game 2.

But this game was over. Casey made 29 saves, and the team that was sixteen games under .500 in mid-January had a 2-games-to-1 lead in pursuit of sport's greatest trophy. The North Stars were closer to the Stanley Cup than ever.

"It didn't happen like we wanted it to," Gagner said of the Game 3 victory. "We were tentative. We had trouble putting the puck in the net in the first period. We felt we had to win at home. I was pressing a little bit."

The goalie coaches for each team, separated by about 100 feet of press box, had hung on every moment. Resch said the first period was the most important 20 minutes in Casey's career—even though he only faced seven shots. Resch's counterpart with Pittsburgh was Gilles Meloche, who watched Barrasso make 30 saves and take a slashing penalty out of frustration in the final minute. Ten years earlier, Resch and Meloche were on opposing sides in the '81 Final.[54]

Smith, the only North Star to score in this game and in their only previous home victory in the finals, was cautiously optimistic.

"We have a huge game Tuesday," he said. "But we've got to like being in position where we have a home game to win to take a 3–1 lead."

In the euphoria, four fans were ejected—about the same as for games in the Edmonton series but many fewer than the approximate twenty-five per night against Chicago.

More than 41,000 households watched the pay-per-view. And the team sold $36,000 worth of merchandise during the game, more than doubling the previous record from Game 3 of the conference final.

Afterward, no one wanted to think about how the power play went 0-for-5, making it 1-for-19 in the series. Duchesne entertained his father, Rosaire, and his father-in-law and brother-in-law in the noisy dressing room. They were among relatives who drove from Quebec City in a van all weekend to see Gaetan's biggest games. Gaetan, whose nickname was "The Duke," wore a black hat with the word "Dukes," a gift from Danza. Later, Duchesne went home to Chanhassen, where fans had crowded his lawn with signs of congratulations, including one on his garage.

"It sure is a big change from the beginning of the year," he said.

And about twelve miles away in St. Paul, in Lemieux's room at the Radisson, Penguins team physician Charles Burke oversaw the installation of two slats under the mattress before his very important patient went to sleep.

54 Resch, whose career in the finals consisted of three saves on five shots in the third period of the New York Islanders' 8-3 loss to Philadelphia in 1980, didn't appear in any of the five games of the '81 finals. Meloche went 0-2 in his only finals appearances, losing Games 1 and 3 and allowing 12 goals on 51 shots for a save percentage of .765. Nineteen-year-old rookie Don Beaupre lost Game 2 6-3, won Game 4 4-2 and lost Game 5 5-1. He allowed 13 goals on 106 shots (.877).

Monday, May 20, 1991

Some of the Penguins found Charley Walters' column in the *St. Paul Pioneer Press* this morning. It detailed plans for a Stanley Cup parade in Minneapolis, St. Paul, and Bloomington.

Lemieux looked healthy as ever as he worked out on a stair climber at the St. Paul Athletic Club, where some of his teammates played basketball. How they felt about Game 3 or Game 4 remained a mystery because Pittsburgh GM Craig Patrick ordered them not to speak to the media. No Penguins attended the off-day press conferences because they were upset about a plan calling for them to bus to Met Center, dress, and then bus to Bloomington Ice Garden for practice. The Met was booked with an ice show. They took the day off instead.

The North Stars were more talkative. Bellows entertained a *Star Tribune* reporter in the sun on his Eden Prairie deck and waved to a neighbor who honked his horn and shouted congratulations and good luck.

"I think it's great," Bellows said of the way Minnesotans have caught Stanley Cup fever. "Too many years have gone by here where people didn't even want to be seen in a North Stars hat."

On Tuesday, he'd ride to the game with Broten as usual. The anticipation and magnitude wouldn't be anything they'd experienced before, however.

"If we can pull this off, we're going to enjoy it more than most players," Bellows said. "You have to remember that we've driven to the game and known there's only going to be 4,000 people watching us. We've walked through the community, and nobody's noticed us or even cared. This would make it all worth it. You win the Stanley Cup, and you'll be remembered in this town for a long time."

Another reporter spent part of the afternoon with Gavin, talking about what it was like to fly (he had a pilot's license), scuba dive, and ride his Harley-Davidson softail custom. He'd convinced Wilkinson and Zettler to buy them, too.

"We're hoping there's going to be a little North Stars posse riding around," Gavin said. "We want to take a few trips, just to some places that might be an hour from here but that you can take three or four hours to get there.... When I get that withdrawal this summer from not seeing the guys, that's what I'll do."

Not to be forgotten, however, was the urgency of maintaining the home-ice advantage they stole by winning Game 1.

"We have to win," Jim Johnson said of Game 4. "If you lose the momentum in a series like this, you never know when you're going to get it back."

Everywhere you looked, however, there was a state of delirium. A *Pioneer Press* columnist asked Dahlquist, McRae, Broten, and Modano about a potential visit to the White House. With wins in Games 4 and 5, Cinderella could hoist the Stanley Cup on Thursday in Pittsburgh. And there was a group of wives and girlfriends desperate to be there. The idea was too presumptuous for most coaches and players, who hadn't had travel companions of that sort since September. Still, some players seem caught in a crossfire of wanting to share the moment with those closest to them and yet maintain the tight bond and focus that brought them this far.

"There was less communication in the finals, particularly for the families, and I know that created some pressure," Gavin recalled thirty years later. "The spouses and girlfriends are now talking to the players: 'I want to go down to Pittsburgh. What if we win it in Game 5?' And, 'How am I going to get there? And where are my tickets?' Everyone was getting a little ahead of themselves. It got a little out of hand behind the scenes. It was a very small thing, but it made an impact."

Speaking of impact, Lemieux's back couldn't have bothered him too much. Late Monday night he was spotted visiting Solid Gold, a strip club in Minneapolis.

Brian Glynn (6) and Ulf Dahlen (22) clog the front of the net as Penguins defenseman Jim Paek tries to clear the way for goalie Tom Barrasso during the first period of Game 4. (St. Paul Pioneer Press/Chris Polydoroff)

Tuesday, May 21, 1991: Penguins 5, North Stars 3, at Met Center

This morning's *St. Paul Pioneer Press* includes Tom Powers' story about the possibility of a trip to 1600 Pennsylvania Avenue in Washington DC—something that had only occurred for a hockey team once before, in 1983 after the Islanders won their fourth straight Cup and Ronald Reagan could ignore them no longer.[55] Unfortunately, free copies of the paper were scattered around the banquet room at the Radisson, where the Penguins were eating bacon and eggs, pancakes, fruit, and oatmeal.

Casey arrived for the morning skate with his three children in tow. Usually, players didn't bring family—especially kids—to the rink on game days. It was evident to some of the North Stars that there had been a disagreement between their goalie and his wife, Brenda. Churla, Dahlen, Gagner, Jim Johnson, and Smith all said as much in interviews for this book.

Johnson said he asked Casey what was going on.

"And he goes, 'My wife and I got in a fight. I don't know if she left me, but I had nowhere to take the kids,'" Johnson said. "We're not in this situation without Jon Casey, I can tell you that right now. He played amazing. He was on fire. He was as good a player for us as anybody on our roster up to that point. But something changed in his focus."

Churla concurred.

---

55 From 1984 to 1990, a Canadian team won the Cup every year: Edmonton in 1984, 1985, 1987, 1988 and 1990; Montreal in 1986; and Calgary in 1989. It was the longest run of Canadian domination of the trophy since Toronto and Montreal each won it four times between 1962 and 1968.

"I've got to give (Casey) full credit for those first three rounds," Churla said. "It's hard to say it but, looking back, I think (the incident with his wife) played a part in what happened. Because you have to be so dialed in to what you're doing, with no distractions. His game, somehow, something changed."

Gagner could see it, too.

"It was really distracting and taxing on Jon, and it was the worst time, obviously, for that to happen," Gagner said. "Depending on who you talk to on our team, there was a lot of disappointment in what happened there. It started with the talk about travelling with the team. I think the majority of our players, and Jon was probably included in this, thought, 'We can't change anything now. Let's just win this thing and worry about celebrating later.' There could be some disagreement there, but it's clear that's when it unraveled."

Before Game 5 of the 1986 finals, the Montreal wives were flown to Calgary, but their husbands didn't see them until after it was over. Smith and Gainey, who played in that game, acknowledged there were disruptions five years later with the North Stars.

"I don't recall specifics, but at that point we'd been in this kind of bubble for six or seven weeks," Gainey told me in 2021. "Competition is heavy. The games are very competitive. There's a strain that comes on everyone, and you're trying to hold it all together as best you can. There are always seams and cracks that happen. You try to minimize them and overcome them. But, after all, people are human and they do things. Shit happens. You do the best you can.

"We're getting a lot of attention from outside the rink, and now that you're down to the last two teams, you've got media there from all NHL cities. The demands from the league are up about what you can do, when you can practice. It started out as a frolic, and it ends up being very organized from a different level. So, it was understandable to me that there were potential cracks in keeping everybody on a knife blade and a tight rope."

Compared to the Canadiens, the North Stars didn't have the culture to withstand such distraction.

"It was just so foreign," Smith said. "The talk in the Montreal dressing room had been that the wives can't help you, but they can hurt you."

Other North Stars, however, refused to believe even decades later that anything off the ice had an impact.

"I believe Jon was professional enough and strong enough that would not have affected him when he put his gear on," Wilkinson told me.

Whatever happened, Casey joined the others in the afternoon at the Decathlon Club for the pregame nap and meal. At about that same time, a meeting of NHL general managers was going on at the Hotel Sofitel and the San Jose Sharks posted their final payment of $22 million to become certified league members. Ferreira's first official act as GM of the league's twenty-second team was to attend Game 4.

It was warm and humid leading up to game time, with a temperature of seventy-six degrees. Gainey kept his lineup intact, but it didn't take long for the North Stars' confidence to thaw.

With Lemieux dressed, Pittsburgh scored three even-strength goals in the first 2:58. It was the fastest 3–0 lead in Stanley Cup Final history.[56]

After the North Stars thought an errant pass should've been icing, Stevens curled out of the right corner, evaded Bureau's sliding sweep check, and banked a ten-foot shot off Casey and into the net at fifty-eight seconds. A minute and a half later, Stevens shot from the right circle, and Francis shoved in the rebound. And thirty seconds after that, Lemieux—on his first shift since late in Game 2 at Pittsburgh—one-timed a pass from Recchi between Casey and the left post.

56 Ironically, the previous mark for fastest three goals in the finals came via the Islanders, who did it in 10:03 against the North Stars in Game 5 of the 1981 finals.

1991 North Stars Stanley Cup Finals program

"If you were writing a scenario for how not to start a game, that would be it," Gainey said.

"It cost us the game," Smith added.

The sellout crowd of 15,378 was in shock. After Game 3, when Pittsburgh's broadcast booth was under siege, Lemieux said the Minnesota crowd was louder than Chicago's—the loudest in the league. Now, the security guards posted near the Penguins' announcers stood silent and unchallenged.

The North Stars had won eight in a row at Met Center since the first home date in the playoffs, Game 3 against Chicago, the controversial 6–5 loss that hinged on Jeremy Roenick's late goal on April 8.

They got back into this one after Gagner scored at 18:22 of the first period. The Penguins restored a three-goal margin midway through the game following a faceoff in the North Stars' zone, when the defense lost track of Trottier. But three minutes later, Propp batted a pass out of midair and behind Barrasso on a power play. And Modano scored on a 5-on-3 slap shot late in the second to make it 4–3. A roughing call on Larry Murphy and Bob Errey's hooking penalty gave Modano all the space he needed for Minnesota's NHL-record thirty-fifth power-play goal of the spring. But it also would be the last.

The North Stars outshot Pittsburgh 14–13 in the first period and 17–5 in the second. Despite all the pleading the home crowd could muster in the third, however, the Penguins slowed play and crucially kept Minnesota without a shot during an extended power play late in the game that might've meant the difference between winning and losing the Cup.

Two games after they clashed for a $50,000 fight, Loney high-sticked Tinordi, cutting him in the face for a five-minute major with 6:57 remaining. The North Stars had a man advantage for 3:49, when Casey took an interference penalty for tripping Bourque with 3:08 left.

"I wasn't surprised he called an interference penalty on me," Casey told reporters, speaking of referee Andy vanHellemond. "I knew he was going to get me because I was screaming at him when they didn't call the penalty on Loney right away. He got even and it hurt us."

The North Stars were 2-for-7 on the power play, improving to 3-for-26 in the series, but couldn't manage the tying goal when the opportunity arose.

"We were completely disorganized," said Gagner, who had a goal and two assists. "The guy carrying the puck had no support. We had one guy carrying the puck and four guys on the other side of the ice. And we just couldn't get any whistles to get it organized. It was just kind of a mess.

"Maybe we ran out of gas at the end. That kind of play hasn't been characteristic of our power play—but maybe it has been in the last three or four games."

They never tested Barrasso the rest of the way, and Bourque scored from sixty feet into an empty net with fifteen seconds left.

Barrasso finished with 35 saves. Casey had 19.

Coming into Game 4, the North Stars had trailed at home a total of 18:12 out of 540 minutes in the playoffs, and they'd never been behind by more than a goal. Since the final 13:45 of Game 3 against Chicago, their only deficit was for 4:27 of the first period in the 5–1 win over Edmonton in Game 4 of the conference final.

"I don't know what happened," said Gavin, a team-worst minus-3 along with Broten, Chambers, Duchesne, and Glynn. "Everyone was so charged up. Everyone wanted to win so bad. Maybe we went out there too hard without thinking. At the beginning, we just wanted to skate, to get to the puck. But when it goes past you, it goes to someone else. There were just a lot of miscues out there. We wanted to do so well at home, but it backfired."

Perhaps former North Stars coach Pierre Page described it best:

"It was a great game with a great crowd pushing on the North Stars," he said. "Sometimes, with all that going on, you underestimate how hungry a team can be at this time of year. Everything was going Minnesota's way, but the Penguins stood up and said, 'No fucking way.'"

Suddenly, the magic was gone.

"When you get that close, I think the pressure starts getting on you," Modano said during one of our conversations for this book. "We were like, 'You have to take care of these home games.' It felt like if you let one of those slip, you're going to have to pull another one off in Pittsburgh, and that was a tall order. There was a lot of pressure on Game 4. Mario wasn't supposed to be 100 percent with his back issues. We had heard he could barely move. 'He can't lace his skates.' You know, this whole thing. But it didn't look like it was bothering him at that point."

Wednesday, May 22, 1991

It was hazy and eighty-four degrees in the Twin Cities when the NHL announced its expansion draft, originally scheduled for June 17, would be expedited to May 30.[57] The dispersal draft between the North Stars and San Jose Sharks also would be held that day. The change was made so all teams could meet a June 1 deadline for contract offers as set forth in the basic agreement with the NHL Players Association, which had rejected a request to alter the terms.

In Pittsburgh, where the Penguins flew soon after Tuesday night's game, people on the interstate highways saw travel message boards flashing: "You're on the road to the Stanley Cup," and "Let's go Pens!"

The North Stars canceled practice and took a late-morning charter to Pittsburgh. Since it was now impossible to win the Cup in Game 5, their wives and girlfriends stayed behind.

The Penguins had an optional practice with most choosing to participate. Lemieux settled for an off-day stretching routine.

Gainey met the media and had a hard time answering at least one question.

"I remember I was asked by the journalists, 'What do you think you'll do to stop Mario?'" Gainey recalled in an interview for this book. "My response was, 'I'm not really sure there's an answer to that.' He had matured to be this incredible player who understands how much work you have to put in to win. His only downside was that he had a sore back. They had a great team, and we did press them and push them. But (by Game 4) he'd scored an even-strength goal, a short-handed goal and a power-play goal. When you have those great players, there can be no answer when they want to produce."

Back in Minneapolis, where a North Stars' commemorative team photo filled the back page of

57 At this point, many of the North Stars realized that, instead of a decision on their future coming almost a month down the road, they might have to change teams and move across the continent just eight days hence—accelerating a potential distraction just before some of the most important games of their lives.

the *Star Tribune* sports section, customer receipts at Lund's grocery stores read "Go North Stars!" But Lund's employees, supposedly as a safety precaution, wouldn't be allowed to watch or listen to Game 5 at work—unlike in 1987 when Twins World Series broadcasts replaced the stores' Muzak.

The TCF building flashed "Go Stars" and the IDS building featured a North Stars logo several stories high. Just a few blocks away, Green's chauffeur parked his Rolls Royce during a meeting of the Metropolitan Sports Facilities Commission. The members debated Green's plan to buy Met Center or at least modify it with a $30 million retail plaza that would connect with the Mall of America. No decision was made. Green and his driver returned to find the Rolls' battery dead and a parking ticket on the windshield.

Thursday, May 23, 1991: Penguins 6, North Stars 4, at Civic Arena

The North Stars canceled their morning skate, unlike the Penguins, and informed the media that Game 6 on Saturday at Met Center would remain on pay-per-view. There had been discussions about moving the game to free TV, but Green wanted $460,000 ($300,000 in cash and $160,000 in season-ticket orders) to make it available. That was too rich for Norwest Banks, which was interested in sponsoring the game if TCF Savings, the exclusive rights holder for North Stars programming, was agreeable. Back in the Twin Cities, TCF and KMSP-TV officials were not amused to find they were being blamed for the failure to reach an agreement.

"Somebody with the North Stars doesn't know the difference between politics and business," said Bob Evans, president and chief operating officer of TCF. "We're made to look like shit, and we're the ones paying the bills and bringing the away games and the home games on cable to the people."

KMSP general manager Stu Swartz said he was "incensed" and, like Evans, focused return fire in thinly veiled comments at Forciea.

"It seems to me the North Stars are handling this like a political campaign instead of a business situation," Swartz said.

As a result, the North Stars would be the first major sports franchise (MLB, NFL, NBA, or NHL) to ask hometown fans to pay to watch a telecast of what might be a championship-deciding game.

It was sunny and warm in Pittsburgh, with a game-time temperature of about eighty degrees. Another sellout crowd of 16,164 packed the Igloo, making it feel even warmer for the same North Stars lineup. And, after the Penguins chased Casey with four goals in the first 13:41, it was clear whatever potion that got Minnesota to this point wasn't working anymore.

Hayward stopped 16 of 18 shots the rest of the way, including one from Lemieux on a breakaway, and Gagner scored twice to help make it a one-goal deficit with more than twelve minutes to go. But a couple quick penalties left the North Stars on the defensive and it got out of reach after Murphy shot, Loney crashed the net, and the puck bounced off Broten and past Hayward with 1:39 to play.

"I don't have an explanation," Gainey said. "We certainly wanted to do better than we did at the start of Game 4. But Pittsburgh got on a roll. They scored two power-play goals, and we weren't able to contain them after that."

Glynn was called for cross-checking Lemieux (Gainey called it a "push") behind the net 3:38 into the game. Two seconds before Glynn was to get out of the penalty box, Murphy's shot hit the end boards and caromed to Lemieux at the side of the net. He pulled it around the post to make it 1–0.

After Tinordi was called for hooking at 9:54, it took fourteen seconds for Stevens to score his playoff-best 17th goal. Murphy's errant pass could've gone for icing, but Stevens got to the puck first and one-timed a shot past Casey.

On their next two shifts, Lemieux set up Recchi, who'd been held to just one assist in the first four games. The first goal was a backhander inside the right post, the second a third-chance rebound following shots by Murphy and Lemieux.

"I don't know what's going on," Gagner said. "We are not reacting well enough in the first period. We're just digging ourselves too deep a hole."

Broten (on a thirty-foot slap shot) and Gagner (from between the circles) started the climb back with short-handed goals late in the first period and early in the second. But Francis scored on a slap shot from the left circle to restore a three-goal margin.

Dahlen and Gagner converted rebounds early in the third, and referee Kerry Fraser gave Minnesota a power play when Taglianetti took a cross-checking penalty at 8:40. But Gagner negated the last fifty-one seconds of that with a tripping call, and the North Stars went 0-for-4 on the man advantage, slumping to 3-for-30 in the series. Stevens and Trottier were among a few Penguins who tried to twist that knife deeper, leaning over the boards on their bench to question Bellows' manhood. He hadn't scored since Game 3 against Edmonton and, hampered by Samuelsson's check last Friday, already had the only points (two assists) he'd get in the finals.

Finally, Frank Pietrangelo—who replaced Barrasso (slight groin pull) during the first intermission—played just well enough to keep the North Stars at bay. The Penguins were outshot 18–7 in the first period and 31–25 in the game. Casey, who stopped nine of 13 shots, avoided the media afterward.

"It's a hard thing to get a handle on," said McRae, who joined Churla as the only North Stars who weren't on ice for a goal against—largely because their playing time was greatly reduced after it was 4–0. "The first twenty minutes has always been our better period. We know we may have gotten a little ahead of ourselves. We weren't skating and a couple of bounces went their way. We're going to have to think a lot about what has happened in the first period, but we will regroup."

Gavin said he thought the team had put the horrific start from Game 4 out of mind, that it was "buried." Now the North Stars had two terrible starts to forget before Game 6 on Saturday at Met Center.

"I don't know what the problem is," Gavin said. "Maybe we're all just trying to do too much instead of working together as a unit the way we have been through the playoffs."

Gagner, Tinordi, Gavin, Jim Johnson, and Propp were the only North Stars to finish plus-1.

"They picked us apart," Johnson said. "They made the right dumps at the right time, and they got a lot of speed going through the neutral zone. When you give them a big lead like that, they can gamble a little more. And we weren't making smart dumps or putting pressure on them. They play good hockey when they get the lead."

Gordie Roberts was the only player to finish plus-3.

"It's tough for me because I played with a lot of those guys, and now I've had to play like I hate 'em," Roberts said. "You have to give the North Stars credit. We can't sit back in a defensive shell no matter how many goals we get. If we can get up 8–0, we better get up 8–0… we know what their crowd enthusiasm is going to be."

But now, for the first time in these playoffs, the North Stars faced elimination.

"We're not far from the Cup," Tinordi said just before he climbed on the bus to Pittsburgh International Airport and the charter home. "We were far from the Cup at the start of the season. We were far from it at Christmas. We're closer to it than we've ever been. We're still on a roll at home, but we have to come out with more fire in our eyes. We're not going to just let it slip away."

It was after 2 a.m. when the North Stars touched down in Minnesota. In the parking lot outside the Humphrey Terminal, Berezan opened the wood-paneled driver's door of his Jeep Wagoneer and got in. Casey climbed into the passenger seat.

"You don't have interesting conversations with Jon," Berezan said in an interview for this book.

"There's not a lot of depth. But I remember I drove him home and he was *tired*.

"The way he played was unorthodox. You couldn't figure him out, even when he played in college, when he would charge at guys on a breakaway. He'd see their head go down, and he'd charge at them. When he used his instinct and it was on, things like that worked, and he was right more than he was wrong. There were times, even that year, when he'd go out of his way to be unorthodox, and he was off. That year in the playoffs, though, he was amazing until (Game 4). If you look at the ones after that, I bet there are a lot where you'd go, 'Ooh. Jeez.' Because by then he was guessing."

Mike Modano (left), Perry Berezan and Doug Smail, among others, catch a breath during practice on May 24, 1991, at Met Center. About 24 hours later, the North Stars would face a do-or-die situation against the Pittsburgh Penguins in Game 6 of the Stanley Cup Final. (St. Paul Pioneer Press/Eric Miller)

Friday, May 24, 1991

It was a delightful spring day with temperatures in the low seventies by the time the North Stars practiced for half an hour at Met Center. While the outlook was serious, it didn't seem grim. For example, a columnist marveled at how many shots Dahlquist blocked during Game 5 but also lamented that he looked like he took a couple off the face. Immediately, Wilkinson piped up.

"I wouldn't mind a Dahlquist nose," he said. "What I hope never to have is a Dahlquist goatee."

Dahlquist, who'd let his trademark mustache grow scraggly down each side of his mouth, went home to a furnished condo in West Bloomington. His attention had been diverted on recent off days by checking on a new home he was building in Eden Prairie. He was a week away from closing on it.

The last time the North Stars risked elimination was in Game 7 last spring at Chicago. They lost 5–2. But two nights before that, they could've been eliminated on home ice and they won, 5–3.

"We can't get down about being down," McRae said. "It's not a nice situation to be in, but we've been in a lot bigger holes than this before, and we've gotten out. It could be a lot worse. We could be sitting around a TV watching some other team trying to come back."

The last time the North Stars won back-to-back elimination games to win a series was the 1980 quarterfinals against Montreal. Then, McRae was playing with the London Knights, and Modano was nine years old.

Gainey was non-committal about who would start Game 6 in the net. In reality, he had no choice. It would be Casey. Hayward lobbied Gainey for a chance, warning that Casey was spent mentally and physically. But Hayward was almost assuredly going to be a member of the San Jose Sharks in a week, and there was no way Gainey could afford to lose with anything less than his best. And that was Casey.

"I don't think he's tired in the sense of being physically run down, but it's more difficult to stay fresh or perky when the red light keeps going on behind you," Gainey told reporters.

Hayward professed his focus on trying to win the next two games, but he didn't deny he was looking forward to a new beginning, too.

"I got a chance to play in only seven home games here," Hayward said. "At San Jose, I know I will get an opportunity to play."

He wasn't the only one with bruised emotions.

"Right now, we're not feeling very good about ourselves as a team, but we're used to being in that situation," Gagner said. "We know how to handle it. We know how to fight back from deficits, and we've done it before. Now we have to do it again."

Most of the regular season was an exercise in overcoming adversity. Did they have the willpower to do it some more?

"You learn how to prepare for a game and forget all the things that are going on around you," Gagner said. "There were so many things we had to block out earlier in the year: the lack of fan support, whether the team was going to move, not feeling good about ourselves. That's what we have to do now, block out all the distractions. We only have a few days left in the season, and we have to put everything we have into them."

As a result, for the first time, the team spent the night *before* a game at the Decathlon Club. Gainey thought it would be a worthwhile change because there were so many family and friends around for the finals. Propp even shaved his beard.

Game 6 would be Minnesota's 113th game of the season, which started just after Labor Day and included ten exhibitions (four on the trip to the Soviet Union), eighty regular-season games, and twenty-three in the playoffs.

"I don't know how any of us will duplicate what we've seen or experienced," Clarke said. "This has been a really special season.... I don't ever see it being duplicated."

I was extremely conflicted when I left Met Center that night. I knew my future was in sports journalism and it was important to maintain my part-time position at the *Pioneer Press*. As a result, I had no choice but to work at the paper on Saturday because our staff was reduced to a skeleton crew by the needs of Game 6 and the wedding of one of our copy editors—which took out most of our desk. I regretted I wouldn't be on hand for the last home game of my internship, but there was nothing I could do.

Dan Stuchal would go it alone. He'd recently accepted the offer to become a full-time PR assistant. "Full-time" should be a breeze compared to what we've been doing.

Later, in St. Paul, the Penguins were prepared with a special bed and lumber, if necessary, for Lemieux at the Radisson. They could see a difference in their captain since he missed Game 3.

"Mario is pretty excited about this," Stevens said. "He's playing hard both defensively and offensively, and it's obvious that his emotional level is pretty high."

Saturday, May 25, 1991: Penguins 8, North Stars 0, at Met Center

Prices were slashed in half this morning on all items at four remaining wildcat souvenir stands scattered around the Twin Cities—including one at the Thunderbird Hotel just across from Met Center. The vendors were eager to make sure they weren't stuck with leftover merchandise, especially in Minnesota if the series ended. Sales were expected to end at 8 p.m., by which time Game 6 would be well under way.

Barrasso donned a girdle beneath his equipment and felt good after taking some shots in practice. The North Stars also had their usual morning skate. George Brett, just coming off a knee injury with the Kansas City Royals (in town to play the Twins), was perhaps the most notable of onlookers and hung out in the dressing room with Giles, who showed him his own knee brace. After some final instructions, the players headed back to the Decathlon Club for their usual afternoon nap and pregame meal.

The parking lot opened a few minutes early, just after 5 p.m., greeting the usual sellout crowd of 15,378 and anyone else who wandered in. But the atmosphere wasn't quite as festive. While the game-time temperature was sixty-nine degrees, dreary weather arrived, and the lack of a breeze brought the first mosquitoes of spring.

Inside, George Gund had returned to see history. And one of Green's guests again was Richard Dean Anderson, wearing a North Stars pin in his lapel. His MacGyver character would've come in handy before the night was over. In the press box, the game notes included Forciea's reference to miracle comebacks, including those of the 1987 Twins (who won Games 6 and 7 of the World Series), Greg LeMond overcoming a fifty-second deficit to win the '89 Tour de France, and Governor Arne Carlson's win in the race for Governor. There was no mention of Paul Wellstone's upset in the US Senate.

There also was no possible way to prepare for what took place during the next three hours on the ice below.

Nine seconds after the opening faceoff, Broten was a little too aggressive in a race to the crease and bumped Barrasso. Referee Don Koharski waved Broten off for interference and, nine seconds before his penalty was to expire, Samuelsson struck for a power-play goal. Taglianetti passed D-to-D, and Samuelsson's wrister from the left point sailed through a screen and past Casey. It was the first shot he faced.

The score remained 1–0 until midway through the first period. The North Stars got a glorious chance to tie it after Stevens and Roberts took penalties in quick succession. A two-man advantage was supposed to last 1:26 but, after eighteen seconds, Lemieux stole a pass from Broten and Modano had to interfere with Lemieux to prevent a breakaway. One minute later, Lemieux took a long feed from Murphy, beat Bellows, and tucked a short-handed backhand behind Casey. Then, with Pittsburgh back at full strength and three seconds before Modano was to exit the box, Joe Mullen made it 3–0 by converting Stevens' one-handed shovel pass. Any momentum Minnesota might've generated was gone for good.

The power play failed on two chances late in the first period, the crowd begging for a shot—any reason to cheer. Gainey pulled Casey at the first intermission, and by early in the second period, the North Stars were playing with anxiety and desperation. Tinordi and Churla got in a scrap with Samuelsson and Recchi at 8:03. McRae earned a 10-minute misconduct, giving him a ringside seat to watch it grow worse. Errey redirected a pass behind Hayward at 13:15 and Francis followed with a breakaway shot between Hayward's pads at 14:28.

Moments later, Jim Johnson (who'd hacked Francis from behind but not enough to prevent his goal) got away without a penalty for a ramming Recchi headfirst into the boards. It infuriated the Penguins, who made it 6–0 when Mullen added his second goal of the game on another breakaway at 18:44. The outcome no longer in doubt, some fans began to leave. Perhaps it was because they had only recently hopped the bandwagon. Or maybe it was because they were diehards and couldn't stand to see such carnage after a storybook run.

The third period only got worse. Jim Paek, a rookie defenseman who played three regular-season games, scored his first NHL goal on a breakaway with Lemieux at 1:29. Gainey sent Casey back in, and with 8:52 remaining, public address announcer Dick Stanford (of his own volition and without prior approval from Green) read the words that appeared on the video boards: "Thanks for making us feel like Stars again." The crowd responded with a standing ovation that, briefly and fortunately for Stanford, was Green's highlight of the season, or so he said. Barely had it died away when Murphy, who'd played for the North Stars on this very ice in December, capped the scoring on a twenty-foot backhand with McRae off for slashing.

Barrasso finished with a 39-save shutout and made good on his vow not to talk about his 4-year-old daughter, Ashley, and her battle with leukemia until the season ended.[58] Casey finished with 13 saves on 17 shots. Hayward stopped 7 of 11. At one point, someone in the crowd pleaded for Kari Takko.

The remaining fans gave another ovation during the final minute. And then it was over.

Many of the North Stars gathered in a cluster in the west end of the rink, waiting for the Penguins to finish their spontaneous celebration. The familiar pose of many was one hand atop their stick, forming a chin rest with their glove. Glynn and Duchesne were bent over, resting their sticks on their knees. Churla stood out front.

Bob Johnson, who grew up thirty blocks north of Met Center, was one of the last to exit the Pittsburgh bench. He shook hands with Gainey, who turned and shoved his fists in his pockets and headed up the stairs to the North Stars' dressing room. Johnson quickly donned a hat confirming him as a Stanley Cup champion, the second American-born coach to do so—following Bill Stewart of the 1938 Chicago Black Hawks, the only team with a regular-season record worse than the North Stars to ever play for a major league sports title in North America.

Johnson waved to his wife, Martha, whom he'd courted since high school. They'd shared untold peaks and valleys. Their son Mark, Broten's US Olympic teammate, played eleven NHL seasons—including ten games with the '81–82 North Stars. Meanwhile, their 28-year-old daughter, Diane, had lived for more than two decades in the State Home for the Mentally Retarded in Union Grove, Wisconsin.

After the teams traded traditional handshakes, the North Stars vacated the ice to the victors.

Lemieux—who had a goal and three assists—was announced winner of the Conn Smythe Trophy

58 Ashley Barrasso was diagnosed with neuroblastoma in 1989, when she was two years old. Her parents started a cancer research fund in her name in October 1990. She recovered and lived a normal life until the cancer returned in 2000. She beat it again, although both battles left her with health complications for years to come. In late 2001, she was one of the torch bearers as the Olympic flame passed through Pennsylvania leading up to the 2002 Winter Games in Salt Lake City, taking a handoff from Lemieux, who in the mid-1990s had his own battle with Hodgkin lymphoma and became a cancer survivor. Barrasso later graduated from Springfield (Massachusetts) College and worked as a child life specialist at Children's Hospital of Pittsburgh. She eventually moved to North Carolina and married Jon Miles, an assistant coach with the Carolina Junior Hurricanes, in 2021.

May 25, 1991: Mario Lemieux (center) holds the Stanley Cup over his head at Met Center with a little help from Bob Errey (12). NHL President John Ziegler (right) presented the trophy. (Vintage Minnesota Hockey/Mike Thill)

as playoff MVP. The brown wood box with the large maple leaf on it wasn't what he was after, though. Moments later, he held the 98-year-old, 35-inch-tall, 32-pound Stanley Cup overhead without any hint of back pain. Shouts of the Pittsburgh players could be heard above golf-clap applause from the fans who'd stayed and moved close to the glass. Soon Lemieux, whose 41-point playoff total ranked third all-time behind 47- and 43-point efforts from Wayne Gretzky, carried his prize up to the visitors' dressing room.

"Winning the Cup is a greater feeling than I expected," Lemieux said in the steamy revelry that followed. "You want to keep it forever. There are guys playing ten, fifteen years in the league without a chance to win this.... This means everything. After the back problems and the surgery and infection, I never thought I could come back so strong. This is the ultimate dream."

Bob Johnson felt the same way.

"This is a great thrill, to reach the top of the mountain," he said. "It was a long road up there. ... To stand at center ice with the Stanley Cup is a dream come true. The hockey gods were good to us."

That means the hockey gods were, uh, something else to Minnesota. The North Stars' record-setting power play went 0-for-3 and finished the finals 3-for-33 (9.1 percent) while *allowing* three short-handed goals.

"There are no excuses," Broten said. "They played good, and we played disorganized. It's been a long two months and to lose like this is not fun."

His depression was obvious after a reporter asked him to compare this experience to the loss to the Islanders in 1981.

"We were young and didn't know a lot of the things we know now," Broten said. "This is definitely tougher to take."

The eight-goal margin was the most lopsided shutout of all-time in a Cup-clinching game and the worst playoff loss in North Stars history.

"We fought back the last two games so hard we just didn't have anything left," Gagner said. "We just ran out of gas. We just weren't on top of our game anymore. You can't blame us as much as give credit to them. They had the better team. But our standards have been raised. If this had happened a few years ago, we might have been pretty happy about it, but everyone is not happy about this.

"I think we expected to win once we got here. We just didn't play our game… we were taking penalties, not really concentrating, yelling at officials, just not focusing like we had before. I think over the last four to five games, we fell into a trap we said we wouldn't."

Jim Johnson and Dahlquist could only lament the joy their former teammates were experiencing. Murphy and Taglianetti were on top of the world, as was Roberts, who had played 555 regular-season games for Minnesota and another sixty-one in the playoffs.

"I couldn't believe the feeling of carrying the Cup out there," Murphy said. "It was like carrying every past winner of the Stanley Cup with you."

Half an hour after the North Stars left the ice, Duchesne had removed none of his uniform beyond his helmet and gloves. His tear-stained, reddened eyes looked out from under the Dukes cap, staring into nothing.

"We weren't even in the game," said Smith, who was minus-3—as were Glynn and Dahlen, the latter chagrined to have his father and future father-in-law in attendance. Bellows was a team-worst minus-4.

Less than 100 feet down the hall and well within earshot, champagne flowed for the joyous Penguins. Barrasso hugged his wife, Megan, then sat calmly and sipped a beer, saying, "This is the culmination of everything I've waited for."

"This series really ended at breakfast before Game 4," Stevens crowed to the Minnesota media while standing next to his wife, Suzanne, not far from where Jagr hugged his mother and posed for pictures as others donned championship T-shirts. "You guys were planning parades."

Later, to a more general audience, Stevens expanded: "I think they were getting a little ahead of themselves. Mario was ready, and when he's ready, everyone is ready. He had that thing in his eye all day, that we will do whatever it takes to win."

No shadow was going to stop him. While Gavin had pressed Gainey to let him try to cover Lemieux during the finals, Gainey said it was a different proposition than they had faced before.

"Stewart Gavin and Gaetan Duchesne did a terrific job on Brett Hull in the series against St. Louis, but Mario was a different case," Gainey said. "Hull had never experienced that kind of coverage before, and Mario has. Mario also has other tools. He's so big and has such a long reach, it's hard for anybody to stop him one-on-one. If you leave Mario on the ice in a one-on-one situation long enough, Mario wins."

Gavin, Duchesne, McRae, and Propp were the only North Stars to finish the game with an even plus-minus rating.

"We talked about it this morning, how we felt that if we took control of our game and played the way we played in the previous series, we'd have a chance at it," Gavin said, "if we could play smart and stay away from penalties and play tight defensively. But right off the hop, they get a goal, then another one, and it was like we kept digging ourselves in a hole. And then everything just collapsed.... We worked so hard at it. In some ways, it would have been easier to lose in the first round. It was the dream for everyone to win the Stanley Cup. You get so close and fall off at the end; it really hurts."

Anna, Steve, and Laura Gainey embraced their father after it was over. Colleen remained with Cathy, neither quite yet prepared for the emotion of the moment.

"I don't want to talk about the score or the game," Bob Gainey said. "I think the game was over in the first period."

He cut short his postgame comments, saying, "Whenever you're on the edge of a championship and you don't win, the pain is deep.... This is a night for the champions. They deserve it."

But he said the North Stars took a crucial step.

"The thing that was missing, and it was important, was to be respected," Gainey said. "We put ourselves in front of the community and in front of the league as an organization that wants to participate and to be competitive... I think it would be impossible to be anything but proud of our team."

Postgame, Green invited players, wives and girlfriends, and families to the Founders Suite, where a few stayed until late into the night dissecting what happened. Some were simply shell-shocked.

"The bubble burst badly," Green said. "That's all I can think about. There were no fans, and we filled the building. There were no wins, and we almost won the Stanley Cup. Tomorrow we will be proud, but tonight we are depressed."

Not even an $18,000 losing share for each of twenty-five players could change that.

Watching, in street clothes and unable to help, were Giles, Berezan, Craig, DePalma, Hatcher, Keczmer, Smail, Zettler, and Myllys. Only Berezan and Smail (both in Game 2) had appeared in the finals. Giles was scratched in eight straight after Game 3 against Edmonton. Craig never played after Game 5 at St. Louis. Ultimately, the others were interested observers.

"When it's all said and done, nobody cares who finished fourth, third or second," said Giles, especially bitter considering he played every game of the '81 playoffs. "There's only one team at the top of the heap, and that's the only one anyone cares a rip about."

Even before the players left in a drizzling rain, a public celebration was set for Tuesday night at Met Center. Tickets and parking would be free. Al Shaver and Doug McLeod would share emcee duties, and the proceedings would be shown on KMSP-TV.

As for the pay-per-view of Game 6, maybe some fans had a premonition. About 35,000 households bought the game, fewer than for Games 3 or 4. Or maybe the Saturday of a long holiday weekend had something to do with it.

In any case, thirty years later, everyone who participated in interviews for this book still replays that night in their minds:

- Mike Modano: "I was just looking at the clock like, 'Jeez, let's just get this over with. This is not how we envisioned this finishing.' Even the score; it was one thing if you lost, but to keep it somewhat respectable, we were far from it—worse than the previous couple games. Heads were down. We couldn't do a thing right, and everything they shot at the net seemed to go in. You get behind in those games like 3–0, 4–0, we couldn't flip the switch where we could go reel off five goals in a period. In Game 6, that meant we had to press it even more. For us to try to open the game up and score, that was the kiss of death. That just opened more holes in our game.

  "The last couple games, we just looked like a deer in the headlights. We just got skated to death, their speed finally got to us. I think we were, in a sense, unprepared for the type of skill and talent that they had. Once they started grinding us down and playing a little bit better defense, boy, then their offense just took off. I think they were just focusing. They just blew us out of the building. Barrasso started playing unbelievable. Casey started struggling. The tide turned really fast. And, once Mario smelled blood, that was it. We just ran out of answers at that point. Those last three games, it was just like he was just toying with us. He was on a mission and, once he started feeling better, it was over.

"But when I go back to Minnesota, there's not one person that doesn't bring up that whole thing. I mean, that whole run, people still talk about it, where they were, what they were doing, how old they were, this and that. It was unforeseeable. It was a Cinderella story. Not only who we beat, but what position those teams were in the league, how we did it, with the type of team we had, what we went through the regular season, how we got there. It was just weird. And it has legs. This thing just gets constantly talked about anywhere when you talk about crazy things happening in the playoffs. The hockey world understands the odds of that happening, and people in Minnesota claim it was some of the best two or three months they ever had."

- Stew Gavin: "You didn't know what to do going out for the third period. You didn't know if you wanted to fight someone or cry. It just was so embarrassing, and it couldn't get over fast enough. Hearing them celebrate in our building was one of the worst experiences of my life. It was wonderful to get (to the finals), and that was one of the most wonderful experiences of my hockey life. So it was a high and a low."
- Basil McRae: "I've been in worse games. They just didn't mean as much."
- Brian Bellows: "You have momentum, and wherever it ends, it ends. It's hard to get going again. We ran out of energy. People will say Casey had a tough time the last three games. Yeah, we all did. We all gave up opportunities we shouldn't have. We all started taking more penalties than we should have. You kind of get there together, and you leave together."
- Dave Gagner: "It was on the big stage, and for that to happen, it left a bitter taste in a lot of people's mouths. It was probably the most exposure we'd ever had in our careers. It was bad timing. People say you lose 3–2 or 8–0, you lost. But it probably would've been better to lose 3–2. I think we all knew we lost it because we got distracted. Our whole game plan went away."
- Bobby Smith: "It was a nightmare. I wish we could've called it off early."
- Brian Propp: "I still wanted to win, even if we were down and behind by a lot. I think that Gainey started to roll four lines and just kind of gave up. I would rather have just played two lines to try and get back in it. When I played for Mike Keenan, if he wanted to, he'd play two lines in a situation like that. I was disappointed. But we fell so fast, and then Casey, he had a couple of shots that he could have had, and maybe the pressure got to us. I was more disappointed with Game 6 than any other game in my career—and that includes Game 7 of the finals in 1987. In '87, it was completely different because we were down 3 to 1, we were beat up and Tim Kerr was out, and Dave Poulin had broken ribs, and we had other guys injured. We fought from behind. It was different because Edmonton was so strong. We were more evenly matched with Pittsburgh. To me, what happened in Minnesota was worse."
- Ulf Dahlen: "I remember seeing the Cup come onto the ice as we were walking off to head up the stairs to the dressing room. And I remember how tired we were and how much we invested in the playoffs and how many good memories it is because we won so many series. But at the end, I just remember those stairs and how tough it was going up them. That's the

toughest loss I've been involved in."

- Shane Churla: "At that time of year, people don't understand how many people are banged up. It's a war of attrition. I was getting my wrist shot up every game. You don't know how long it took just to get ready to play. At the end of the day, they just see the wins and losses. There's a lot of things people aren't aware of."
- Mark Tinordi: "It was like you were just numb. The magic was gone. No one knew where it went… It was like somebody just sucked the energy out of the team. It happened that fast. It's like they got the second goal, and, boom, it was gone. And we were just a regular team again."
- Shawn Chambers: "There was a point in that game when I looked around and I said, 'I'm done.' I'd never done that before, but my knee was rocking, and it was 7–0, and I'm like, 'There's no point in me going back out there.' The bench was so down. It was like one of those nightmares where you don't get your skates on in time or can't get to the rink. It was embarrassing. It was like we didn't put up a fight, and it wasn't because we weren't trying. It just went south that fast. You want to play the game of 'How could this have not happened?' But there was no way around it. That was how it was going to be."
- Neil Wilkinson: "Everybody had sacrificed, and then that happens. It's like laying a big fart in a room. You're so disappointed in the outcome you almost want to crawl out of the rink. You're proud of your teammates and your team for what you've done to that point, and you go through all that mantra in your head. But that bad taste in your mouth sticks for years and years and years."
- Jim Johnson: "That was the most embarrassing game I ever played in. And it came against a lot of guys that I knew and had a lot of respect for. But at that time, I had no friends on that team, and I played that way. Unfortunately, I probably don't have many friends among that group today for the way I hit Mark Recchi. The game was out of control, and I felt they were running the score up. I wasn't going to be a part of that. I was going to finish my check on him and right when I got there, he turned. I got him from behind. I was committed. And I was hitting to end all the bullshit. It was a bad hit. I admit it. He could have stayed facing me and taken the blow, but he didn't. And then, all hell broke loose. I feel bad that he got hurt. That was not the intention. My statement was that, when I'm on the ice, you're not going to run up the score on me."
- Chris Dahlquist: "It's one of those things where you grin and bear it. Get through it. (The Penguins) were loose and free and giggling and that bugs you. If this was Game 50 of the regular season, we'd have been clearing the bench. But at that point, the air was out of our balloon. You know you're going to lose. You just try to play through it. But the bruises started to hurt a little more when you realize it's coming to an end."
- Brian Glynn: "I didn't come to this conclusion right after, but thirty years later, I can say we got beat by a good team, and I can live with that. It is embarrassing what happened in Game 6, but there shouldn't be anything to be embarrassed about because the reality is you were a team with sixty-eight frickin' points that got there. Whether they beat you 8–0 or 1–0 doesn't really matter to me, but during the pandemic everyone got so starved for hockey that they kept playing all this old stuff (on television), and so we get to relive that. People would text me all the time and say, 'Hey, you're on TV.' And I'm like 'Great. No thanks. I know how it ends. I don't need to be reminded.'"
- Brian Hayward: "Game 6, I'll always regret. I remember every one of those goals. The first

was a two-foot slam dunk on a wraparound. The next two were breakaways. And the next one, I was guessing, and frickin' Jim Paek scored on me. I remember Andy Murray looking at me and saying, 'Look, this isn't your fault.' It was devastating… There's no question that it's embarrassing. You regret not being able to do something, and it was a tough way for a group of guys who had definitely overachieved and got to a Stanley Cup Finals and got through a bizarre season with everything off the ice—to have it finish that way was a shame. All of the accomplishments and good things get tarnished by that."

- Bob Gainey: "When you put those games (4–5–6) together, Pittsburgh won all of them, and they had the lead (and were never tied again after 58 seconds, 5:36, and 2:00, respectively). That's the best recipe you can have.… I think, at the end, you just have to ask yourself, 'Did we perform as well as we could? And did the team that won deserve to win?' If you can answer those correctly, then you're fine with any other minutiae that may have come into play. We would have liked to have been champions, but we could understand the team that won played better than we did. But then there was the other side. It looked like we had regained the attention of the fans in the Twin Cities. And if you compare where we were in May 1991 to where we were in November 1990, six months earlier, we were in a much better position to be a viable franchise. That was part and parcel of what we were trying to do. The North Stars had a long history there, and my memory was that, as a '67 expansion team, they always should be there in Minnesota, and maybe we'd been able to break through and help that happen."
- Doug Jarvis: "Game 4 was critical because if you go up 3–1, that's hard for a team to come back from. And if it's 2–2, the other team takes home ice back going into a game in their building. The momentum changes to them. Unfortunately, that's what happened. I reflect more on Game 4 than I do the 8–0 (Game 6)."
- Andy Murray: "I would disagree with the term 'embarrassing.' If any of the players have that attitude, they're being too hard on themselves. I never want my players to talk that way after a game. I can understand it because it's kind of common. But to me, it's only embarrassing if you're not trying. Whether we were mentally and/or physically just gone at that time, there wasn't any player or coach who wanted it to go that way. After what we'd accomplished, we just didn't have it. To me, we lost that series in some of the other games."
- Lou Nanne: "Once you can see that you're going to lose, I just tried to remind the people (on the TV broadcast) what a fantastic playoff run they had, the talent on the team and how exciting it was. ... I might have even said it, but I know I was thinking of it, that if I'm going to lose the game, I'd rather get blown out than lose by a goal because all I can think about if I lose by a goal is how many times we had a chance to change the outcome. But in that game, you know there's nothing you could have done."
- Pat Forciea: "I spent the second period trying to thank everybody I could see for everything they had done and same with the third period because, by the end of the first period, you pretty much knew it was over, right? People were pretty doggone gracious."
- Les Jackson: "The guys should be proud of what they did. There were a lot of other teams that would've liked to have been where we were."
- Mike Craig: "For sure, 100 percent, I thought it was going to happen that we were going to win the Cup. We've got some rhythm. Our goalie is hot. The power play is clicking. Guys were just grinding it out. We were so close, and it's what I've been dreaming about ever since I started playing. I try every year to make sure I witness that final game when they raise

the Stanley Cup. I was doing that when the Islanders were on their run. I remember Bob Nystrom scoring and winning the Cup (in 1980, when Craig was eight), and I was like, 'Oh, man. What a feeling.' You don't realize until later in life that it's not something you get to go to every year. We were so close, and I never got back. Never even got close to being back."

- Doug Smail: "The light at the end of the tunnel was gone. You could feel it. You want to participate and go, 'C'mon! C'mon!' But it became inevitable. You're trying to think of something to say to the guys to rally them, but they don't need that. It has to come from inside them. I played with Randy Gilhen and Peter Taglianetti in Winnipeg. I knew them both and was legitimately happy for them. But watching it was a disheartening thing. It's hard to describe. It doesn't matter if you are in lineup or not. You've got guys that have come that far and through so much from November through the playoffs. You're heartbroken for everybody. I spent some time in our locker room with the guys. There's nothing you can say. Everyone's dejected. There's no high-fives, knuckles, elbows, anything. You said how it was a great effort and a, 'Great run, guys,' and all that kind of stuff. There was a point when I walked down hall toward Pittsburgh, and I asked someone to tell Taglianetti and Gilhen I just wanted to say hello. They came out from their celebration, and I congratulated them and made sure I honored their effort and work. They were thankful, but then they looked at me and started laughing. My nickname (in Winnipeg) was Butchie. They were like, 'Sorry, Butchie. Gotta go, bud.'"
- Rob Zettler: "I remember feeling this ultra-disappointment. You're on such a high, such a ride for so long and to have it end like that, it was just like the old Charlie Brown cartoons, you know? 'Waa, waa' (he imitates Peanuts' school teacher noise). You started to expect to win. We were going, 'We got this! We can do this!' But Pittsburgh was a VERY good team. There's no shame in losing to them."
- Dave Smith: "I've been involved in a lot of games over my career and nothing stands out as bad as that Game 6. It was a nightmare.... It was like we got steamrolled by a freight train. I apologized to the Pittsburgh trainers later (for not shaking hands). I went off the bench, up the stairs and sat in my office with my head in my hands. I didn't talk to anybody. After guys left, I tidied up the room, locked up and headed home."
- Mark Baribeau: "I was looking at Smitty behind the bench after it was 3–0, and it was like, 'What are we going to do?' It was like we knew we were going to have to watch this for awhile.... That was *my* team, and I was crushed when we lost, not so much for myself but for some of those guys that I really thought highly of. But I remember talking to Gainey in Norm's suite afterward, and he told me: 'We're going to win it for real one day.'"
- Al Shaver: "After the game, I stopped at the Lincoln Del and had a sandwich and a Manhattan to drown my sorrows."
- Doug McLeod: "Through the first three rounds, you had this feeling, 'Boy, anything can happen.' I don't remember that anybody had that feeling going into Game 6. It wasn't like, 'Oh, no, we're going to get nailed.' But you could feel it coming from the Penguins. They were rolling.... My job has always been to make it feel (a comeback is) possible. But the way the North Stars had been playing catch-up the last couple games, you knew once they got down by a lot, they weren't going to catch up."
- Ralph Strangis: "Robb Leer was going to be set up in the North Stars dressing room after the game, regardless. I got the Pittsburgh dressing room, regardless. With a couple minutes left, I ran downstairs. I barely remember it. I couldn't hear the producer, and the producer couldn't

hear me, and guys are spraying champagne everywhere. After about fifteen minutes, I just put the mic down and walked away. This is sports. You don't always get a Hollywood ending. Sometimes a really good story has a really hard ending."

- Joanie Preston: "It felt like, 'Is this really happening? This is not how it's supposed to be.' It's kind of like we became the team from the beginning of the year again, right? It was like the stardust that carried us on this magical ride was gone."
- Dan Stuchal: "It was really hard, crushing. I still remember after the first intermission, and we're already down 3–0, and we hadn't even really threatened, I was standing over the copy machine, cranking out the first period stats to run up and down press row. You could see it in the eyes of the people we worked with. You knew it was over. You just didn't want it to get worse. And it did. It was such a gut punch. There was so much to be proud of over the previous three months. It just seemed like such a lousy way for it to end."

Sunday, May 26, 1991

For anyone who didn't catch the most regrettable performance in North Stars history live Saturday night, Midwest Sports Channel showed reruns of Game 6 at 10 a.m. and 9 p.m.

Why just undergo one root canal when you can experience it two or three times?

Amid all the postmortem coverage of the game and the rest of the news, Page 2A of the *Star Tribune* was a tribute from Dayton's that read: "Thanks North Stars, we had a blast."

The Cup run engendered goodwill. Now the challenge was to keep it.

"The fans are on a high for about two years," Twins GM Andy MacPhail said of the fallout from a World Championship run. "I would say the North Stars have earned a two-year honeymoon."

Green already was making plans for 1991–92, knowing that season tickets would grow to more than 7,000, based on more than 3,600 sold since February. He said the team lost $1.2 million this season after taking into account the playoffs, which generated about $4.5 million. Expenses didn't prevent him from handing out 650 North Stars pins during the playoffs and filling the Met Center urinals with almost 21,000 pounds of ice. By this afternoon, that was all down the drain—and the floor of the arena was bare. The dressing room was padlocked, the administrative offices dark.

"I'm more relaxed now than I've been since June," said Green, who received almost 1,700 letters in support of the team this spring. "Everything is now in place. Our team is accepted, and the fans that had turned their backs on us have come back. For the first time, I don't feel like we're in a panic situation."

Despite the recovery, former owner George Gund fired a parting shot on his way back to San Jose.

"We didn't want to leave here," he said. "The big problem is that there are now four arenas (Met Center, St. Paul Civic Center, Target Center, and Williams Arena) in the Twin Cities, and there isn't any way all are going to be profitable. We know this is a good hockey town, and it was tough to leave. But we couldn't compete with the Target Center unless the Met Center was fixed up."

The state of the arena may have been in question, but the players said they had a much better foundation now.

"We started from nowhere," Bobby Smith said. "When we went to Russia last fall, I felt like a new player with a new team and new management. Today, there is a special feeling among the players. We came together through those two months (of playoffs) and began to take pride in how the team was doing, not how we ourselves were doing or how a line was doing. When we go back on the ice next season, we will carry this with us."

But they'd also retain the bitter taste of defeat, knowing the Stanley Cup was within reach—only to see the Penguins take it away.

"If they had beaten us when we played our best, it would've been easier to swallow," Jim Johnson said. "But I don't feel like we played our best, and that's what's frustrating. We didn't play the way we played to get there. You can't downplay what we did, but you don't know how many chances you have to win the Cup. You have to reach out and grab it when it's there."

Monday, May 27, 1991

Memorial Day dawned sunny with temperatures in the low eighties, and the North Stars had a brief meeting at Met Center. Gainey advised the players to not let the trip to the finals alter their preparation for next season.

"I would feel we have to show improvement," Gainey said. "We have to continue to create high, realistic expectations for ourselves. When this season began, I don't think there were any expectations—good or bad. I just felt there was a feeling of indifference to this team. Even if the expectations are unrealistic, too high, that's better than to have no expectations at all."

Exposed to closer scrutiny than in the immediate hours after Game 6, a few statistics pointed to some reasons (not the only ones, but significant, nonetheless) why the dream of winning the Stanley Cup came up short:

- Casey made 41 saves on 53 shots in Games 4–6 for a save percentage of .774.
- Of course, it really didn't matter who was in net. Hayward saved 23 of 29 in Games 5–6 for a save percentage of .793.
- Between Games 4–6, Glynn and Smith each were minus-6. Smith and Brian Bellows each were minus-5 in Games 5–6. And Bellows, the team playoff scoring leader with a team-best 19 assists and 29 points, had one shot on goal in Game 6.

It wasn't a holiday for Clarke, who acquired 25-year-old goalie Darcy Wakaluk from Buffalo for future considerations. The acquisition meant Clarke expected to lose Hayward to San Jose in Thursday's dispersal draft.

Monday night, the players gathered to have their own private party. It was consolation for the celebration they wanted but weren't going to get. They rented a bus to tour some night spots in downtown Minneapolis. When those closed, they went back to the Met and opened the bar in the Founders Suite. Smith and Gavin sat in Green's box and drank some beer. Others called out to each other from various parts of the empty arena.

They didn't want the camaraderie to end.

Tuesday, May 28, 1991

As the city of Pittsburgh was in a bright mood and preparing for 80,000 people to attend its championship celebration, a late morning downpour brought nearly two inches of rain to the Twin Cities. Clarke met with Jackson to zero in on their choices for the expansion draft.

By late afternoon, there was a break in the weather as people began arriving at Met Center for the "Magic of the North Stars." While 12,000 tickets had been distributed and a larger crowd expected, about 7,000 people filled chairs on the floor and many of the sections in the lower bowl, before which the glass had been removed. No alcohol was served, and the most popular accessories were glow sticks that sold for $1. The production cost about $20,000. The KMSP-TV broadcast drew a 5.0 rating; about a fifth of the audience that watched Game 1 at Pittsburgh.

The show started with a parade of youth hockey players with flags, and Jim Bowers sang the national anthem. Wearing a tuxedo with a green bow tie, Al Shaver delivered perhaps the line of the night—unwittingly describing his appearance and foreshadowing the future: "Take a good look. You're never going to see this again."

The Electric Stars danced and the "Spirit of the North Stars," an actor in a gray wig, introduced a six-minute highlight video that appeared on the screens overhead. Seventeen-year-old magician Matthew Samp performed in a sparkling gold coat.

Finally, after more than a half hour of anticipation, the players were introduced and stepped through a giant star at the west end of the arena. They appeared in numerical order, escorted to positions along the stage by the Electric Stars: Brian Hayward; Curt Giles (carrying the Campbell trophy); Rob Zettler; Chris Dahlquist; Neil Wilkinson; Brian Glynn; Neal Broten; Jim Johnson; Mike Modano (who got the loudest cheers, mostly from teenage girls); Gaetan Duchesne; Marc Bureau; Stew Gavin (wearing shorts and still sporting his shaggy beard); Doug Smail; Dave Gagner; Brian Propp; Basil McRae; Bobby Smith; Mike Craig; Perry Berezan; Ulf Dahlen; Brian Bellows; Mark Tinordi; Shawn Chambers; Shane Churla; and Jon Casey. Staff members Chico Resch, Doug Jarvis, Andy Murray, Bob Gainey, and Norm Green followed.

Gainey, Giles, Gavin, McRae, and Green made brief comments. Governor Arne Carlson, wearing an "N" pin in his lapel, appeared on video and said: "None of us are going to rest until the Stanley Cup comes to Minnesota."

As the crowd filed out, Forciea said what was on the minds of most—whether their hearts were in it or not: "I'm sure every player and fan prefers to end the season this way, rather than letting it end Saturday night."

At about 10 p.m., more thunderstorms hit the Twin Cities and downed phone lines and trees. Three TV stations (Channels 4, 9, and 11) were knocked off the air at about the same time many people would've tuned in to see any coverage on the late evening news.

Assistant trainer Dave Smith holds the Campbell Conference championship bowl in the dressing room at Met Center. The North Stars wanted the Stanley Cup, but this was as close as they came. (Photo courtesy of Dave Smith)

Wednesday, May 29, 1991

The NHL reserve lists for Thursday's expansion draft were released and padded by some players who hadn't formally retired. For example, although he hadn't played since 1989, Gainey was available from Montreal. The Canadiens also chose not to protect Jayson More—the player they got for Hayward. Los Angeles left Ilkka Sinisalo exposed. And Pittsburgh didn't protect Gilhen, Randy Hillier, Hrdina, and Trottier less than twenty-four hours after they participated in the Penguins' Stanley Cup parade.

What would happen in the dispersal draft with San Jose remained a mystery, although Clarke offered one clue.

"Mike Craig is not going anywhere," Clarke said, indicating the price to keep him would be a second-round pick in 1991 and a first-rounder in 1992.

Not that Craig paid much attention to the drama with the Sharks.

"In all honesty, I didn't waste one minute thinking about it," Craig told me in an interview

As if losing the Cup wasn't enough, Minneapolis-based General Mills had to honor the Penguins for winning it.

for this book. "I wasn't frazzled by what was going on. It was all he-said she-said. You don't know what's going to happen. I was nineteen. I was living for today. I wasn't thinking about tomorrow or next week."

Thursday, May 30, 1991

Minneapolis-based General Mills announced this morning that the Penguins would be featured on boxes of Wheaties. Fortunately, they'd only target the Pittsburgh area.

The dispersal draft between the North Stars and San Jose Sharks was held at 9 a.m. via conference call. The NHL expansion draft followed at 3 p.m. Each lasted about a half-hour.

Clarke told the truth. The North Stars gave up a second-round pick in 1991 [which became Sandis Ozolinsh] and a first-rounder in '92 [Andrei Nazarov] to keep Craig, Derian Hatcher, Enrico Ciccone, Doug Barrault, and Jeff Levy.[59]

From the North Stars, San Jose took Churla, Hayward, Wilkinson, Zettler, Scott Cashman (a goalie from Boston University), Ed Courtenay (a right wing from Kalamazoo); Kevin Evans, Link Gaetz, Murray Garbutt (a center from Kamloops of the WHL), Rob Gaudreau (a right wing from Providence), Dan Keczmer, Dean Kolstad, Peter Lappin (a right wing from Kalamazoo), Pat MacLeod, Mike McHugh, Jarmo Myllys, Larry Olimb (a defenseman from the University of Minnesota), Tom Pederson (also a defenseman from the University of Minnesota), J.F. Quintin (a center from Kalamazoo), Bryan Schoen (a goalie from Denver University), John Weisbrod (a center from Harvard), Doug Zmolek (a defenseman from the University of Minnesota), Arturs Irbe (a goalie from Dynamo Riga), and Shaun Kane (a defenseman from Providence).

"We're relieved, and I'm sure the players are relieved, too," Clarke said. "We didn't want to lose anyone, but we knew we were going to, and we learned to accept that."

"It's like a huge mountain has been lifted off our club," added Green, who immediately phoned Churla personally and told him to "hang tough" with the expectation they would re-acquire him somehow.

"We've still got a long way to go," Sharks GM Jack Ferreira said. "We're not kidding anybody."

That didn't stop Sharks scout Chuck Grillo from raving about the prospects San Jose picked up—

59 Hatcher, a defenseman, would play a total of 110 regular season games for the North Stars during their final two seasons. Ciccone, a defenseman, appeared in 42. Barrault, a right wing, played four NHL games, including two with the '92–93 North Stars. The career of Levy, a goalie, topped out with Kalamazoo in '92–93 and '93–94.

especially Gaetz.[60]

"He's one of the meanest kids in hockey," Grillo said. "Heck, he may be one of the meanest kids alive."

When Wilkinson got the call from San Jose, he put on his most professional air and said he was proud and honored to be a Shark and would be happy to fly to California in a few days to do some publicity. Inside, he was nauseated.

But Ulf Dahlen finally had some closure, knowing he'd remain in Minnesota next season. He'd leave Saturday for Sweden, his wedding barely three weeks away.

"It's scary when you don't know where you'll be playing," he said. "A few months ago, I thought I would be going for sure. Then, a couple of weeks ago, I heard I might not be going. It was all over my head, so I had to decide I didn't care which way it came out. But I'm happy I'll be back."

Eleven minutes after the expansion draft began, a small tornado touched down in Bloomington, about six miles west of Met Center, and another funnel cloud was sighted about twenty blocks away. Sirens signaled a tornado warning that stayed in effect until 3:45 p.m.

By then, selected from the safety of Clarke's windowless office, Minnesota had four new defensemen: Rob Ramage (from Toronto), Dave Babych (Hartford), Allen Pederson (Boston), and Charlie Huddy (Edmonton), and six new forwards: Kelly Kisio (New York Rangers), Gilhen (Pittsburgh), Rob Murray (Washington—subsequently traded to Winnipeg for a seventh-round draft choice in 1991), Tyler Larter (Winnipeg), Jim Thomson (Los Angeles), and Guy LeFleur (Quebec).

LeFleur was chosen because the North Stars had to take a player from Quebec and Clarke didn't want any of the Nordiques available—including Aaron Broten.[61]

The Stars also acquired goalie Steve Guenette from Calgary for a seventh-round draft choice.[62]

When it was all over, Wilkinson and Modano went out to celebrate and commiserate.

"Whether it was chasing girls or driving cars or whatever, we hung out a lot," Wilkinson told me for this book.

They'd been road roommates most of the season.

"Let's just say that we enjoyed ourselves without ever missing curfew and without ever getting in trouble," he said, sounding like a cat with feathers in its mouth. "Basil and Stewie would often invite us to dinner, and then Mike and I would go find something to do. But I remember a lot of that playoffs just staying in because I was young in my recovery, and I didn't want to put myself in a risky situation. Mike wasn't a big drinker, so we pretty much kept each other out of trouble. The great thing is that I was the ugly kid from Canada, and Mike was the US first-round superstar. So we did not have to do a whole lot of chasing."

60 Of the players who hadn't appeared for the North Stars in 1990–91, Zmolek was by far the most significant of the skaters lost to San Jose. He totaled 905 career PIM in 467 games. Irbe went on to win 218 NHL games and had a Cup-losing effort with the Carolina Hurricanes in 2002. Cashman played three career AHL games. Courtenay's NHL career consisted of forty-four games for the Sharks. And Gaetz played forty-eight games (and totaled 326 PIM) in '91–92 with San Jose. Garbutt played twenty-five games with Kansas City of the IHL in 1991–92. Gaudreau totaled 51 goals in 231 career games with San Jose and Ottawa. Lappin appeared in one game with the Sharks on December 17, 1991. Olimb's career peaked with seventy-five games for the '94–95 Minnesota Moose. Pederson played a total of 240 career games with San Jose and Toronto. Quintin played twenty-two games with the Sharks. Schoen, a Minnetonka High School graduate, made it to the IHL for two games. Weisbrod played sixteen games for the '92–93 Kansas City Blades. And Kane totaled thirty-eight career IHL games and 147 in the AHL.

61 LeFleur, destined for retirement, was sent back to Quebec one day later for Alan Haworth, who was playing in Switzerland and had already played his last NHL game in 1988. Kisio was traded to San Jose on June 3 to bring back Churla, who never left his home in Burnsville. Ramage, who'd won the Cup with the '89 Flames, played thirty-four games for the '91–92 North Stars. He went to Tampa Bay in the next expansion draft and later joined Bellows with Montreal when the Canadiens won the Cup in '93. Babych was traded to Vancouver on June 22 for Tom Kurvers, who was instantly sent to New York for the Islanders' Craig Ludwig. Pederson played twenty-nine games with the '91–92 North Stars and was traded to Hartford. Huddy, Gilhen and Thomson were part of a June 22 trade for Los Angeles' Todd Elik. And Larter played three games for Kalamazoo in '91–92.

62 Guenette went 7–9–3 for Kalamazoo in 1991–92 before retiring.

With all the developments of the week, Green never addressed the plan to update Met Center with a $30 million shopping mall and other improvements. But North Stars counsel Jim Erickson indicated that it was dead. That meant Green was increasingly likely to look for another place for the North Stars to play. The question was: How far would he go to find one?

North Stars team awards from 1990–91:

- Masterton (most valuable player): Dave Gagner
- Memorial Cup (most proficient defenseman): Mark Tinordi
- Rookie of the Year: Mike Craig
- Most Improved: Tinordi
- Star of the Game: Gagner
- Community Service: Curt Giles

North Stars playoff records set in 1991:

- Team Wins: 14
- Home wins: 8
- Road wins: 6
- Power-play goals: 35 (*-still an NHL record in 2022; since '91, only one team, the 2006 Carolina Hurricanes with 31, has come within 10 goals of the total)
- Most games: 23
- Latest ending date: May 25
- Longest shutout sequence: 120:49, Casey vs. Chicago
- Most power-play goals in a series: 15 vs. Chicago (*-still an NHL record in 2022, tied with the New York Islanders in the 1980 Cup final. The most since '91 has been 12, by Colorado in 1997 and Philadelphia in 2012)
- Most power-play goals by both teams in a series: 21 vs. St. Louis (*-still an NHL record in 2022, matched five times, though only once since '91—by Philadelphia/Pittsburgh in 2012)
- Most goals against and worst shutout in a Cup clinching game: 8
- Most power-play goals in a game: 5, vs. Chicago on April 12; Most power-play goals both teams in a game: 8 vs. St. Louis, April 24 (*-still an NHL record in 2022; only Pittsburgh/Philadelphia, with 7 on April 18, 2012, totaled more than 6 since '91)
- Most power-play goals against in a game: 4 vs. St. Louis on April 24
- Most short-handed goals in a game: 2 vs. Pittsburgh on May 23
- Most PIM in a game: 77 vs. Chicago, April 6; Most PIM both teams in a game: 146 vs. Chicago, April 6
- Greatest playoff margin of victory: 6–0 vs. Chicago on April 12 (also achieved against St. Louis in 1984)
- Most goals in a period: 5 vs. Chicago on April 8

Individual

- Assists: Brian Bellows 19

- Points: 29 (Bellows tied Steve Payne, 1981)
- PIM: Basil McRae 94
- Power-play goals: Brian Propp 8
- Game-winning goals: Bobby Smith 5 (*-tied an NHL record set by Mike Bossy and Jari Kurri and matched by Mario Lemieux in '92; since eclipsed three times, the most being 7 by Brad Richards of the Tampa Bay Lightning in 2004)
- Wins: Jon Casey 14
- Games: Casey 23
- Goals by a defenseman: Mark Tinordi 5 (tied Brad Maxwell 1983 and Craig Hartsburg 1985)
- Point streak: Neal Broten 8 games (tied Dennis Maruk and Tony McKegney, who each had 8 in 1985)
- Assists in a game: Bellows 4 vs. Chicago on April 12 (tied three others)
- Points in a period: Dave Gagner 4 vs. Chicago on April 8

"The most beautiful vision I've seen in sports is Mike Modano winding up behind the net. He had those lengthy long strides that allowed him to blow by everybody. His jersey would be billowing behind him. I watched that in awe."

-Jeremy Roenick

"I don't know if Mike had his jersey specially cut, but it always looked like he had a cape on."

-Former NHL forward Bill Guerin,
Modano's US teammate in
international play
and eventual Minnesota Wild GM

CHAPTER 14

Penthouse to Poof! in Less Than Two Years

Nothing lasts forever.

On August 8, 1991, Neal Broten kissed his wife, Sally, hugged their daughters, and boarded a Northwest Airlines jet bound for Germany where he'd signed to play for a team in Berlin. He turned down a four-year, $2.6 million offer to stay in Minnesota. He wanted $2.9 million, matching what Michel Goulet got from Chicago. Instead, Broten will get $50,000 for eight games with SC Preussen, after which he can decide if he wants to stay and earn a tax-free salary of $400,000 for the season.

But after more than a month and a half of handwringing overseas, and just before a deadline by which he could either return to Minnesota or join the US Olympic team, Broten decided to come home. On October 3, he re-signed with the North Stars for $3.4 million—four years at $350,000 per and 10 years at $200,000 annually after that in exchange for making public appearances for the franchise. Bobby Clarke also promised he would not trade Broten to a team in Canada.

Meanwhile, Mike Modano agreed to a two-year, $1.2 million contract, a raise from the $265,000 he would have been paid for 1991–92. These were examples of how Norm Green's cost of running the team was rapidly increasing.

The North Stars opened the '91–92 season on October 5 against Chicago at Met Center. Dave Gagner scored a minute and forty seconds into the game, Brian Bellows added two goals, and Ulf Dahlen got the game-winner on the power play in a 4–2 victory. Seven minutes into the third period, just before Bellows' second goal finished the scoring, public address announcer Dick Stanford read notice of Curt Giles' retirement.[63] Broten was scratched but got a standing ovation when he returned to the lineup five days later.

The North Stars won their first three games, all at home, but fell under .500 at the end of October with an 8–1 loss at Pittsburgh. Minnesotans didn't really notice in the wake of another World Series title for the Twins, who went worst-to-first and beat the Atlanta Braves in an epic seven games, winning all four games at the Metrodome.

The Penguins also experienced seismic changes. Badger Bob Johnson underwent surgery for a brain tumor in August, and Scotty Bowman went behind the bench. On November 26, Johnson, who once lived in a Calgary condo next to Green, died from brain cancer. Johnson's death came almost exactly six months after Mario Lemieux raised the Stanley Cup at Met Center.

In an effort to ease travel on the players, Green leased a DC-9 for road trips but canceled the arrangement when the plane broke down before a December trip to the West Coast. The North Stars went back to commercial flights and flirted with .500 as late as January 22, when they were 20–20–4. But then they began to sink—going 12–22–2 the rest of the way. On February 15, they retired Bill Goldsworthy's number 8. He had become an assistant coach at Kalamazoo, but even his Midas touch couldn't send much young talent to Minnesota now that so many prospects were gone to San Jose. The North Stars finished with 70 points, a two-point improvement on 1990–91, fourth again in the Norris Division.

63 Giles later recanted, won a silver medal with Team Canada in the '92 Olympics and signed with the St. Louis Blues.

The playoffs were delayed by a ten-day players strike. NHL president John Ziegler was replaced by Gil Stein, and, when play resumed, Minnesota matched up with Detroit.

This time, the North Stars not only won the opener on the road—they swept two at Joe Louis Arena and came within an overtime goal in Game 3 of earning a sweep. But the Red Wings rallied with shutouts in Games 5 and 6, the latter scoreless through more than sixteen minutes of overtime. I was one of 13,177 people in the stands and just as curious as anyone when play stopped following a Detroit rush. Sergei Fedorov had fired a shot over Jon Casey's right shoulder but the puck ricocheted back so fast the goal judge didn't turn on his light. Did it hit the crossbar? I had a sinking feeling as referee Rob Schick skated over to the scorer's table to confer with replay officials upstairs. That feeling was justified a minute later. I'll never forget Red Wings captain Steve Yzerman skating halfway to his bench with no reaction until he finally couldn't contain himself. His upraised arms were the first signal Minnesota had lost.

It didn't go over well. A fan behind the North Stars' bench threw a whiskey bottle toward the ice and hit Modano. Others quickly hurled soda cups and plastic beer bottles. A seat bottom flew out of the west end stands.

We didn't know it yet, but that would be the last home playoff game in North Stars history. Two days later in Detroit, they trailed 3–0 before Bellows finally scored a power-play goal early in the third period. It ended Minnesota's scoreless streak at 2:08:36 en route to a 5–2 loss, a goal in the final minute by Mike Craig making it look closer than it was.

The Red Wings were swept by the Blackhawks, who advanced to the Stanley Cup Final against the Penguins, now owned by Howard Baldwin (you can't make this up). Pittsburgh swept the series, winning Game 4 on June 1 at Chicago Stadium, and Lemieux kept the Conn Smythe Trophy as well as the Cup.

A week later, Bobby Clarke returned to the Philadelphia Flyers, and Bob Gainey became the North Stars' GM as well as coach.

By the fall of '92, Modano had signed a four-year extension that made him the highest-paid North Star at $2 million per year. In turn, Green claimed losses of $11 million since he bought the team and publicly mused for the first time about moving—to the Target Center in Minneapolis, to the Civic Center in St. Paul, or even Anaheim, California. Never mind that regular-season attendance at Met Center almost doubled to 13,447 per game in 1991–92 and would reach 13,910 in '92–93—10th-best in team's 26-year history. Green needed to place blame somewhere—anywhere—if he was going to leverage what he wanted or actually move the team.

"I don't think I would have come here if I knew how little coverage the newspaper would give us," he said. "The effort would've been better spent in another place. The *Star Tribune* is the biggest business reason why NHL hockey has not had much greater success here. The philosophy of the *Star Tribune* is not to cover hockey ... it's a huge problem to us."

He didn't even mention the *Pioneer Press*.

Bill Lester, executive director of the Metropolitan Sports Facilities Commission, touted the North Stars' lease as one of the best in the NHL. Under its terms, Green paid 2 percent of adjusted gross revenue (including parking and concessions) as rent. In '91–92, that amounted to $250,000. The lease required him to pay for upkeep and improvements, but he controlled building dates and advertising. Yet Green was angry about the money he'd spent on the arena since taking over the team, about $3 million, and that the Commission wouldn't give him the land on which the arena sat in exchange for his financing a $30 million mall around the exterior.

"It absolutely escapes me," Green said. "I don't understand the motivation of the sports commission. I thought they would hold our hand and help us be successful. They've been more of an obstruction."

Lester said the MSFC needed to safeguard the interest of taxpayers.

"He wanted to take over a public asset for nothing," Lester said of Green. "Our position was that we would've sold him the land at market value. When he decided to withdraw because there were land costs involved, it was his personal decision. We are a public steward. Handing over large amounts of money to a private businessman doesn't seem like a good business arrangement on behalf of the public.

"We feel the NHL is an asset to the community, and we should work to keep it. The question we still ask is what does he need specifically to make hockey successful here? There's a constant vacillation. This idea is hot today. Another one is hot tomorrow. That makes it difficult as a public representative to fix on a plan."

With the expiration of the 3-for-2 deal, season-ticket sales shrank from approximately 8,600 in 1991–92 to 5,300 in '92–93.

Another landmark game came with the Penguins in town. On November 10, 1992, just before the North Stars lost to Pittsburgh 4–1, Minnesota center Dan Quinn was arrested on suspicion of sexually assaulting a woman the night before at the Bloomington Marriott, where the Penguins were staying. Quinn and Lemieux, his friend and former Pittsburgh teammate, had spent the night together with two women, one of whom was nineteen and made the complaint. Quinn, twenty-seven, had joined the North Stars in a September tryout and signed a one-year contract the day before the season began. He posted $30,000 bail and was released from Hennepin County jail before the game, but not surprisingly was scratched from the lineup. The embarrassment for the North Stars was complete and at their own hands when an ad they placed in the newspapers on the day of the game touted the sole regular-season visit by Lemieux as "Mario's One-Night Stand." (Elaine Waddell, who was among several employees laid off at the end of the '91–92 season, had nothing to do with the regrettable choice of words.) Charges against Quinn were later dropped, but the North Stars released him for what the team called a violation of curfew.

Then, on Sunday, November 22, the *Pioneer Press* reported allegations of sexual harassment against Green by a former employee, 30-year-old Kari Dziedzic, who had resigned in August. Green reportedly asked for kisses from his secretaries on National Bosses' Day and ordered some to wear more lipstick or dress provocatively. Green said the accusations resulted in lost sleep for him and his wife, Kelly, and there later was speculation in the media that she threatened to leave him if he didn't move the team to avoid increasing public ridicule. Dziedzic, from Edina, happened to be the daughter of Minneapolis City Council member Walt Dziedzic and sister of Gophers forward Joe Dziedzic.[64] Kari had once worked for Senator Paul Wellstone and became Green's executive assistant in September 1991.

On December 8, 1992, with the North Stars 16–9–3 (first place in the Norris Division and tied for the fifth-best record in the league), the NHL granted Green the right to move for the '93–94 season if he wished. He asked for the authorization to be confidential, but the news leaked. On December 13, Sid Hartman reported a rumor that the North Stars would move to Dallas, and Green made quiet visits there in January and February. Dallas, twice the size of Minneapolis-St. Paul, offered the prospect of better TV revenue, and Green later said it could support higher ticket prices than those in Minnesota that he claimed were $5.33 cheaper than the league mean. He set a January 15 deadline for proposals from locations wishing to lure the North Stars, then backed that off to February 15 so he could get input from a couple of consulting firms conducting market surveys. In the days leading up to the deadline, the North Stars were ten games over .500. That wasn't translating to season-ticket sales, however.

"I didn't believe the surveys (former owners George and Gordon Gund) had done about this market," Green told the *Star Tribune*'s Patrick Reusse. "I thought my confidence and enthusiasm would make up for any shortcomings. I was wrong. The Gunds were right."

64 Joe Dziedzic went on to play 126 of his 128 NHL games for the Penguins.

The North Stars lost both ends of a February 13–14 home-and-home series with Toronto. On February 16, Green was in Dallas for more talks about moving to Reunion Arena. The next day, after he was shown around by Hall of Fame quarterback Roger Staubach and had met with Cowboys owner Jerry Jones, Green said only that the North Stars would play at Met Center in 1993–94 if the team remained in Minnesota. That meant those courting him to Target Center or the St. Paul Civic Center could stand down. On February 18, Green went further:

"Maybe the media did not do a good enough job of making fans recognize the NHL is a phenomenal thing to have in the community," he said. "Maybe they should have talked about, 'Will you buy season tickets to save this team?'"

Green said the franchise was on pace to gross $14 million for the '92–93 season but that was offset by an $11 million payroll, up from $6 million in 1990–91. He called late January and February "the worst few weeks of my entire life," and said that he was "disappointed and hurt" by his treatment in Minnesota. He estimated his losses during three years at $16 million—ironically, the same total the Gunds tossed around in 1990.

"Everyone has to ask themselves if they have season tickets," Green said, sounding like a broken record. "There are no excuses. We have a great coach and the kids are working hard. But there are only 2,000 clients who have season tickets. That's not enough."

Green briefed Gainey on the Dallas situation and then did the same with the team. And, for the first time, players acknowledged the possibility of a move was crowding their thoughts.

"A week ago, I would have said I didn't see a disruption," Stew Gavin said. "We went through this three years ago, and we said, 'Here we go again.' But there's been so much talk about it, you start thinking about it. It does sidetrack you. When the reality of the situation hits you, that's when you start thinking about it."

Gainey agreed.

"What's happened in the last two to three weeks is that, as it's become more a civic issue than a sports issue, it's been harder for the players not to have to deal with it," Gainey said. "There is nowhere in the community the player can go and not hear about it and be asked about it."

Not even when they go on the road.

"It has been more of a distraction," Gagner said before a March 3 game in Toronto. "But I don't think anyone will admit it's so much of a distraction it's affecting our play."

Gainey ultimately ordered the players not to talk about a potential move, and the NHL insisted on a March 15 deadline for Green—who conducted negotiations in Dallas while staying at a hotel under an assumed name—to decide where the team would play in 1993–94.

Downtown Minneapolis interests revived late in the season, but any move of the North Stars to Target Center hinged on a public takeover of the building from Timberwolves owners Harvey Ratner and Marv Wolfenson. That was politically unpalatable in an election year, and it was difficult to see enough support rallying to meet Green's target of 10,000 season tickets at the Met, either. For example, Richard D'Amico, a partner in a company that owned several high-end restaurants in Minneapolis (Bocce, D'Amico Cucina, and the Azur) said the Met was too far away. And that wasn't all.

"Walking through the parking lot was like tailgating for a Twisted Sister concert," D'Amico said. "It's just not a very good corporate setting."

Even Pat Forciea, increasingly Green's stand-in responding to reporters, acknowledged as much.

"Corporations are looking for stability, and we have not been able to give them the kind of stability they need," Forciea said. "Ours is a franchise that has been struggling financially for over a decade, and for four years we've had this cloud over our heads where we would be playing.

"Some markets will consistently support mediocre teams. Minnesota will only consistently support a winner."

The North Stars' competition already included the two-time champion Twins (10,000 season tickets), resurgent Vikings (45,000), shiny new Timberwolves (12,000), and the Gophers football and men's basketball teams—never mind men's hockey. Additional major events like the '91 US Open, Super Bowl XXVI, and the NCAA men's basketball Final Four in '92 diluted support from big companies. There wasn't enough demand to go around. Six of Met Center's twenty suites were empty for '92–93.

"The corporations were tapped out," said Forciea, who'd had enough and also told Green he wouldn't be going with the franchise if it left Minnesota.

Ogden Management Corporation, the concessions company operating at the Target Center, offered $55 million to buy the North Stars. But by early March, Green said he wouldn't sell for less than $60 million—approximately twice what he'd paid in 1990.

On March 6, the first "Norm Green Sucks!" chants were reported during a home game against Montreal. On March 7, they intensified during a 7–1 loss to Detroit. The next day, Green was at Met Center for a monologue with the team—2–8–1 in 11 games since peaking at 29–19–8 in early February.

"He gave us all a blast for nonperformance," Gainey said. "As the president of the team, he made it clear to me and to the players that we're not fulfilling what we agreed to do. In my opinion, he hit the nail right on the head. We haven't been doing our jobs the way we should. He just told us to do what we're supposed to do. He's a businessman, and it's his job to understand the business of hockey. Our job is to play hockey and perform, not to try to understand what he's doing."

Two days later, it was over. At 8:42 p.m. on March 10, 1993, the saga finally ended when Green presented Dallas City Council members with Stars jerseys and an announcement was made that the team would move south. Perhaps fittingly, the North Stars were in Saskatoon to play a neutral-site game the following day.

On March 21, they lost to Detroit, 6–2, and the next night, St. Louis beat Vancouver 3–1. The combination gave the Blues, temporarily, sole possession of the Norris' fourth and final playoff spot. On March 23, Green suffered another setback when his attorney, Linda Holstein, said she would no longer represent him in any sexual harassment allegations. Two days later, Dzeidzic filed suit, seeking more than $50,000 and alleging various transgressions. Among them:

- Green told a female employee that, if she married his son, he would give her a mall.
- Green said he wanted the Met Center receptionist to have blond hair, a pretty face, and large breasts.
- Green shook the shoulder of a female employee (later revealed to be Waddell) to determine if she was wearing a bra and then made it clear bras were not required work attire.

Responding to the suit, Green said only that he was "misunderstood or misinterpreted." He'd stopped going to home games in November, choosing to watch on TV from his home in Palm Springs, California. On April 3, he ventured two hours west to the Forum in Inglewood to see his team play the Los Angeles Kings. The North Stars finished a 3–0 win and Modano had his final Minnesota point. And, as Green sat in the press box, a fan managed to get close enough to dowse him with a full cup of beer.

On April 10, the North Stars reeled in their banners and honored Bill Masterton, Goldsworthy, Broten, and Al Shaver before beating St. Louis 4–3 to move back into fourth place. It would be Minnesota's last victory at Met Center, incidentally with Giles and Basil McRae in the visiting lineup. But the next night, the Blues beat the North Stars 5–1 in St. Louis to take the playoff spot right back.

Gainey had wanted any pomp and circumstance over before the final regular-season home game against Chicago. It shaped up to be incredibly important if the North Stars were to make the postseason. But on April 13, they lost to the arch-rival Blackhawks, 3–2 before a standing-room sellout crowd of 15,445.

So, it all came down to April 15, the last night of the regular season. The Blues, playing host to the expansion Tampa Bay Lightning, had a one-point lead as the North Stars went to Detroit. Minnesota led 2–0, but St. Louis jumped out to a four-goal lead, and the Red Wings rallied. Dino Ciccarelli, acquired from Washington the previous summer, put Detroit ahead for good early in the third period. Sheldon Kennedy scored the game-winner on a breakaway, and Steve Yzerman, who could've been Minnesota property instead of Brian Lawton, beat Casey for the final goal against the North Stars. The last thirteen minutes were unremarkable except for Ulf Dahlen's goal with forty-nine seconds left. At 9:10 p.m. in the Twin Cities, the 5–3 loss was over before a KMSP-TV audience. As Doug McLeod called the final moments on radio, Shaver worked the telecast with his son, Wally, doing the color commentary. Al got the last word, as was fitting. Told by Green to avoid any melodrama, Al thanked all the players who had worn the North Star and said simply: "Goodnight, and goodbye."

Moments later, the Blues held on for a 6–5 win that no longer mattered. The North Stars had already backed out of the playoffs, and out of Minnesota.

"You say that none of the outside stuff should distract you, and it shouldn't, but it had to have some effect," Bobby Smith said. "Everyone was talking about it, and if you weren't talking about it, someone was asking you about it. It was the only subject of conversation."

Before the formal Dallas announcement, the North Stars were five games over .500. After it, they went 4–11–1. They'd won that game in Saskatoon, then went 0-8–1 in the next nine.

"Those last few games at the Met Center were pretty emotional," Modano said. "Seeing those little boys and girls in their North Stars gear—knowing they won't have a team the next year—that hurt."

On the morning of April 17, the players cleaned out their lockers and left Met Center for the last time. Gainey not only had to come to grips with moving to Texas, it was the first time in sixteen years as a player and another three as head coach that he hadn't made the postseason.

According to Financial World magazine, the North Stars were worth $42 million, less than the $57 million NHL average and a fraction of the Timberwolves ($65 million), Twins ($95 million), and Vikings ($123 million). But, even by that conservative yardstick, Green's $31 million investment just three years earlier had already grown by 28 percent.

"The move is something that shouldn't have happened, something that should have been avoided," Gainey told *Sports Illustrated*. "You have a place with a grass-roots interest and suddenly ... I was thinking about historical precedents. Hockey started in western Canada, you know. All the little towns had teams. Then there was a team in New York, in the big cities in the US. The players from the little towns went to New York, and suddenly there were no teams in western Canada. Same thing in France. I played over there. Hockey started in the Alps. Then a guy in Paris started a team, and all the players went, and there was no hockey in the Alps. It all winds up where the money is."

By the summer of 1993, that was Dallas. Green, seeming to increase the number with every interview, now estimated his losses with the North Stars at $24 million.

"When he came here, he said, 'Only an idiot could lose money on hockey in Minnesota,'" said Julie Hammond, president of the North Stars booster club. "Well, I guess he proved that point."

"Norm Sucks!" merchandise became a cottage industry.

"I never expected all this emotion, to be vilified the way I have been," Green told *SI* from Palm Springs. "I suppose I should have. My wife and I had bought a nice house on a lake in Minnesota, just beautiful, and I planned to spend summers there, no matter what happened. I said that to Frank Gifford, who is a friend. He said it wouldn't be possible. He said, 'Have you ever heard of Walter O'Malley?'"[65]

65 O'Malley, who at fifty-five years old moved the Dodgers to Los Angeles in 1958, was vilified in Brooklyn and never returned there during the rest of his life. In 1979, he was diagnosed with cancer and sought treatment at the Mayo Clinic. He died Aug. 9, 1979, at Methodist Hospital in Rochester.

What Green did was legal, if immoral in many eyes.

"It's a damn crime," said Brian Burke, an Edina native and GM of the Hartford Whalers.

On December 9, 1993, the Stars returned to Minnesota for a neutral-site game against the Ottawa Senators, winning 6–1 before 14,058 fans at Target Center. Modano, who had a solitary second assist in the North Stars' final nine games as they failed to make the playoffs the previous spring, scored twice.

"The more you come back, the harder it is to go away again," he said. "It's always tough to say goodbye. I know I wanted to do as well as I could. There are a lot of memories here that we wanted to revive, and I was excited to see my old friends and familiar faces from the Met. I hope they get a team back here as quickly as they can so we can come back and see them again soon."

In February 1994, Dziedzic reportedly received a $1.75 million settlement from Green. In depositions before a trial that never happened, Stanley Hubbard of Hubbard Broadcasting said he saw documents that showed the North Stars were profitable in their last years at Met Center. Forciea testified that Green asked him to provide pessimistic numbers when considering a move in 1993 and ultimately said the sexual harassment scandal was the real reason he took the team to Texas. Rachel Blount testified she received unwanted kisses and comments about her clothing from Green. And the former Joanie Preston, who'd become director of communications and media relations about the same time she married Dave St. Peter in 1991, swore to a telephone conversation in which Green said if Dziedzic had worked for Forciea, he (Forciea) "would be the one with the sexual discrimination case and the North Stars would still be in Minnesota."

On December 13, 1994, barely a year after the Stars briefly returned to Minnesota, the Met Center was demolished by dynamite. Early in 1995, Green won a $700,000 judgment against the Mall of America in a dispute over parking land. Ironically, Ron Rosenbaum, who served as Dziedzic's lawyer in the sexual harassment suit, represented Green against MOA. (Rosenbaum said he did so with Dziedzic's blessing.)

The Stars sold ninety-five percent of their tickets in their first two years at Reunion Arena. The 1993–94 season was the most successful in franchise history to that point, with forty-two wins and ninety-seven points. The Stars also built the two-sheet Dr. Pepper StarCenter in Valley Ranch, which housed the StarStuff pro shop and team administrative offices.

Green sold his commercial real estate company and built a new home in Dallas, but on December 13, 1995, exactly a year after the implosion of the Met, he sold the Stars to Dallas investor Tom Hicks. By 1998, the team was paying $17.5 million over three years to Brett Hull and $43.5 million over six years to Modano. It paid off on June 19, 1999, at Buffalo, when Hull scored off an assist from Modano in triple-overtime of Game 6 to win the Stanley Cup.[66]

In 2000, the Minnesota Wild brought the NHL back to Minnesota at the Xcel Energy Center in St. Paul. The building cost more than $130 million. It boasts sixty-six suites and 2,600 club seats. Naming rights alone brought in $80 million through 2025. But the new team has never been to the Stanley Cup Finals.

"There was always a business side," Modano told me as we wound down interviews for this book. "Even though we went to the finals in '91, we always heard rumors. We're like, 'How can this be?' There's no way in hell that you would take a team out of Minnesota where hockey's pretty much a religion, like it is in Canada. Maybe making a run like we did bought us a couple years. But what that (1990–91) team did will always show you, 'Hey, anything could happen.' You put it together, you make the playoffs, and weird things happen. But they've never been any weirder than they were that year in Minnesota."

66 Hicks owned the Stars until 2010, when he defaulted on $525 million in loans backed by the franchise. The team was sold at auction in 2011 to current owner Tom Gagliardi, a businessman from Vancouver, for $240 million.

"I think I'll take a moment, celebrate my age
The ending of an era, and the turning of a page
Now it's time to focus in on where I go from here
Lord, have mercy on my next thirty years"

-Tim McGraw, "My Next Thirty Years," 1999

CHAPTER 15

What Happened Ever After

The 1990–91 Minnesota North Stars, in ascending order of when they played their final NHL game:

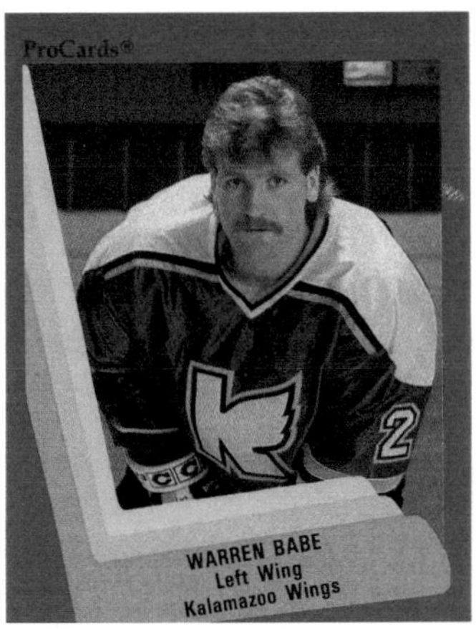

Warren Babe (December 8, 1990, Philadelphia at Minnesota)

Babe (9–7–68, Medicine Hat, Alberta) suffered a career-ending concussion at Kalamazoo later in the 1990–91 season—for which he earned a total of $32,100. In twenty-three career NHL games, all with Minnesota and including two in the playoffs, he had two goals and five assists.

After he retired from hockey, Babe worked as a powerline technician for the City of Lethbridge, Alberta, and later became an area foreman for FortisAlberta. He also participated in Natural Physique and Athletics Association (NPAA) and World National Bodybuilding Federation (WNBF) events. In 2015, he finished first in the Masters Male Bodybuilding competition at the Natural Nationals Championships in Calgary.

Steve Gotaas (January 2, 1991, Minnesota at Detroit)

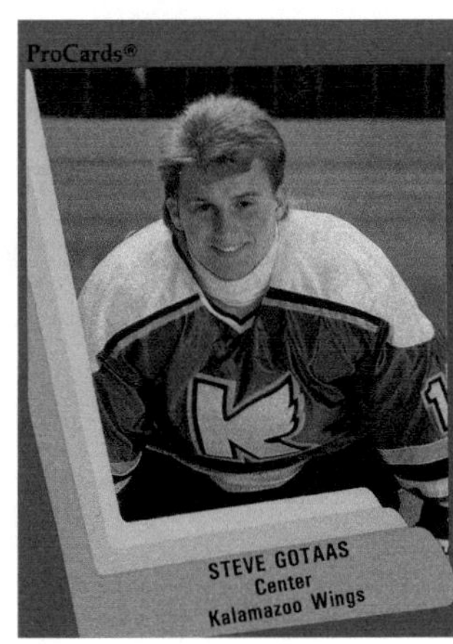

Gotaas (5–10–67, Camrose, Alberta) played the 1990–91 season on a two-way contract worth $130,000 in the NHL and $30,000 in the minor leagues. He earned an extra $1,266 for his one game with the North Stars. He played with Kalamazoo in '91–92, spent '92–93 in Europe, and retired after playing with Las Vegas of the IHL in '93–94. Thirty-six of his forty-nine career regular-season NHL games were with Pittsburgh in 1987–88, and he finished with six goals and nine assists.

He now lives in the Edmonton area and works in business development for Pioneer Truck Lines, part of the Pioneer Group of Companies, which provide pipeline supply materials. His son, Cam, was a forward and captain for MacEwen (Alberta) University, completing his career in 2019–20.

Mitch Messier (January 3, 1991, Toronto at Minnesota)

Messier (8–21–65, Regina, Saskatchewan) played in the IHL with Kalamazoo (1991–92), Milwaukee ('92–93), and sandwiched two seasons in Fort Wayne around one in Austria. His rights were traded to Utah, but he was injured in a truck crash on August 23, 1996, two days after his thirty-first birthday, in Canmore,

Alberta. He suffered head and neck injuries, and two people involved in the crash were killed, including former NHLer Jeff Batters. Messier's brother, Joby, who played for the New York Rangers, also was in the vehicle. They had spent that summer working together at a hockey school in Banff. Batters died on impact after he was thrown from the pickup truck, which then rolled over and crushed him. The Messier brothers, both injured, were taken to a hospital in Calgary. Mitch broke seventy bones all over his body, including four in his neck and seven in his back. Both his lungs were punctured, and his aorta was torn. He was airlifted to a hospital in Calgary and somehow survived. He even attempted to resume his career only to learn, after he began skating, that he still had a neck fracture and could've easily become a quadriplegic with one hit. He continued to experience severe back pain and coped with it via painkillers decades after the accident. His voice remains raspy because of a paralyzed vocal cord repaired with a silicon implant. Five screws and a titanium plate hold his spine together.

He had two assists in twenty career NHL games—all with Minnesota.

Messier eventually went into the real-estate business. He worked as a real estate agent in the Canmore/Banff area of Alberta until 2013 and coached minor hockey. He has continued to run the Messier Banff Hockey School. Mitch and his wife, Lisa, have three sons, including two (Jordan and Marcus) who were born in Kalamazoo and Fort Wayne, respectively. During stick hockey games, they put many a hole in the walls of the family home before going on to play in the WHL. Their youngest son, Ryan, also played hockey.

"I've got my three boys," Mitch told the *Calgary Herald* in 2012. "The most enjoyable thing in the world is watching them play."

When he's not scouting hockey games in Europe, Kari Takko enjoys spending time with his grandson, Kasper, who is growing up a Stars fan. (Photo courtesy of Kari Takko)

Kari Takko (February 8, 1991, Edmonton at Washington)

In the spring of 1991, Takko (6–23–62, Uusikaupunki, Finland) followed NHL scores in European newspapers and scant highlights on TV before returning to Minnesota to help his family pack up their house. He was in the stands at Met Center for Game 4 of the Stanley Cup Final against Pittsburgh.

He played professionally in Finland and in Sweden until 2000. He was 37–71–14 in 142 regular-season NHL appearances (all but eleven with the North Stars), with a 3.90 goals-against average and an .879 save percentage. In four playoff appearances, he went 0–1, 3.86, .873.

After Takko retired, Les Jackson recruited him to be a scout for Dallas. Takko eventually became director of European scouting for the Stars and continues to cross paths with Jarmo Myllys and Ulf Dahlen.

Takko's son, Karri, went on to a brief pro career in Finland as a defenseman, and it's Karri I owe for connecting me with his father. Kari and his wife, Kirsi, celebrated their fortieth anniversary in 2021 and their three children have given them four grandchildren. They maintain an apartment in Pori, Finland, but in 2016 moved to a cottage in the nearby forest.

Mike McHugh (October 17, 1991, Minnesota at San Jose)

Mike McHugh has found plenty of success in business with HydroWorx International, a company that makes aquatic therapy equipment. He discovered the benefits when he was injured in the AHL.

McHugh (8–16–65, Bowdoin, Maine) had a two-way contract in 1990–91 that paid him $125,000 in the NHL and $30,000 in the minor leagues. He earned $37,600 for the season. During the subsequent summer, he took karate lessons in Kalamazoo and spent several weeks in Brainerd at Minnesota Hockey Camps—which basically became training camp for the San Jose Sharks.

He played eight games and scored one goal for the Sharks in 1991–92. His goal, October 5 in a 5–2 loss against Vancouver, was his only NHL point in twenty games, twelve of which came for Minnesota. Coincidentally, his final game was against the North Stars—when he was minus-3 in an 8–2 loss. He was traded to Hartford the next day but was sent to the minors.

"They'd just told me to get a place in San Jose and all our stuff was in a moving van halfway across the country," McHugh remembered. "I get a call from Jack Ferreira. I'm like, 'Hey, Jack. What's up?' He's like, 'Uh, we just traded you to Hartford.' My wife was full of hormones (pregnant during the '91 finals with their first child). It was great. We turned the moving vans around, and I flew out to the east coast."

He never made it back up, but that's not to say McHugh wasn't successful. He finished the last of seven consecutive seasons in the AHL in '97–98, always one step away from the parent club. His final five seasons were with the Hershey Bears—first an affiliate of the Philadelphia Flyers and later the Colorado Avalanche, and he was named MVP of the '97 Calder Cup playoffs as he led the Bears to a championship.

"There was always hope," McHugh told me in 2021. "A couple of years in a row, I had made the AHL all-star team. Whether it was (Bobby) Clarke coming down from Philadelphia or (Colorado president) Pierre Lacroix showing up at our games or (Avs director of player personnel) Michel Goulet, you never knew who was going to be watching. It wasn't until my last year that I thought it probably wouldn't matter how I played, I wasn't going up again. And at that point, between the nicks and physical toll, I'd had enough."

McHugh suffered a knee injury in Hershey and rehabilitated in a unique therapy pool that featured a moveable floor, integrated underwater treadmill, resistance jets, and video analysis. He was sold on the idea of using the pool to loosen up pregame and recover postgame. When he retired, McHugh became one of the original investors in HydroWorx International, a company based in Middletown, Pennsylvania, that provides aquatic therapy equipment to clients worldwide. McHugh became director of sales development in 2019.

Mike and his wife, Cindy, are still married and have two daughters.

Ilkka Sinisalo (November 26, 1991, Toronto at Los Angeles)

Sinisalo (7–10–58, Valkeakoski, Finland) died of prostate cancer on April 5, 2017. He was fifty-eight and had battled it for more than three years. He's survived by his wife, Carina, whom he married when they were in high school. Their sons, Tomas and Niklas, were born in Philadelphia and turned thirty-six and thirty-four, respectively, in 2022.

One of the first Finnish NHLers, Sinisalo played a total of eleven years with Philadelphia, Minnesota and Los Angeles. He finished with 204 goals (the first of which came on a penalty shot) and 222 assists in 582 career regular season games, and 21 goals and 11 assists in 68 playoff games. He then returned to Europe, where he played from 1992–96.

"I think his motivation to go home was basically me," said Tomas Sinisalo, who went on to his own playing and coaching career and was in his fifth season as a Helsinki-based European scout for the New Jersey Devils in 2022-23. "I was going to start school. I would've gone to preschool for one more year, but the Finnish school system allowed me to hop into first grade because I'd already gone to first grade in the States. It was a chance for our family to settle down and my brother could get ready for school, too. My parents wanted to raise us in Finland."

Tomas has vague Minnesota memories of a big house in the suburbs, where deer would frequent the back yard. When he got home from Montessori school, he would don his skates and wait for his father to come home from practice and take him to the outdoor rink.

After Ilkka stopped playing, he served as GM of the Espoo Blues, a team in the Finnish Elite League for which Tomas eventually played as a forward. Ilkka also was a scout for the Sharks and Flyers until the time of his death.

"He enjoyed that part of hockey," Tomas said. "Going to games and seeing younger players and evaluating them. He loved his life and what he was doing. He was a very loyal and hard-working guy. He always had a great sense of humor. It was dry. I think he was really funny. He was my idol. I looked up to him.

"Ever since I was a kid, I would talk players with my dad. I enjoyed picking his brain and hearing what he had to say in general. He would take me on scouting trips, too. We'd take the ferry over to Sweden and then drive through Sweden and play golf and stay in hotels and watch hockey. I had a blast. When I would play video games, I never really enjoyed playing the game as much as I did building teams and figuring that stuff out. So (scouting) is sort of a dream job to me."

Tomas, who had a brief junior career with Green Bay of the United States Hockey League, played for Finland at the 2006 World Junior Championships. He bounced among eight teams at all levels of hockey in Europe but eventually earned an invitation to Philadelphia's training camp in 2009. He later signed to play in Denmark—an experience especially sweet because his father got to see his best two pro seasons before he died.

"He was always brutally honest," Tomas said with a chuckle. "He was a driving force for me. I was going to prove him wrong. In hindsight, it made me mentally strong because I never got that bothered when a coach told me I sucked as to when my dad told me I was awful. But he was proud of me, and that's how I look at my career. I have no doubts or regrets."

Jarmo Myllys in 2021.

Niklas lives In New Jersey and works as a carpenter. Carina splits her time between trips to America and visiting her grandchildren in Finland. Tomas is married and has a 10-year-old son and 5-year-old daughter.

Jarmo Myllys (March 26, 1992, San Jose at New York Islanders)

Myllys (5–29–65, Savonlinna, Finland) played twenty-seven games for the 1991–92 Sharks, going 3–18–1. He returned home after the season and chose to play in Europe even though his rights were purchased by Toronto, leaving behind a career NHL record of 4–27–1 with a 5.23 GAA and an .859 save percentage in 39 appearances—twelve of which came with the North Stars.

"Jarmo didn't speak much English at the rink, but if you got to the bar with him, he could speak perfect," said McHugh, his teammate in Kalamazoo and San Jose. "After a few beers, his English would get better. When we got to San Jose, the first time we played Minnesota, Jarmo was in net. The game didn't go well. We were never in it. I was back-checking, trying to work my ass off to prevent a goal. And I had two in the same game go off me and in, and that was like, impossible. One went off my skate and went in, and I was diving to stop a cross-crease pass, and the puck hit my stick and went in. So, in between periods, Jarmo said, 'Hey, you!' That's how he talked to everyone. No names. I looked at him, and he said 'You, no more backcheck.' The rest of whatever he said muttered off."

Myllys played in 188 games for the Finnish national team and picked up a gold medal in the 1995 IIHF World Championship—his country's first title. At the 1994 Winter Games in Lillehammer, Myllys was 5–0–0 with two shutouts and a 0.60 GAA as the Finns took bronze. He played in the Swedish Elite League from 1994–2001, and also helped Finland earn bronze at the '98 Winter Olympics in Nagano.

Myllys retired in 2005, was named to the Finnish Hockey Hall of Fame in 2008, and later served as a goaltending coach in Finland and for the Austrian national team. He got into a financial dispute with a Finnish team he coached that laid him off during the pandemic. The team later went bankrupt, and he's still involved in a suit to try to collect partial salary.

Myllys, who is quite famous in his homeland, is married, coaching in Kajaani, Finland, and lives in Savonlinna during the offseason.

Don Barber (April 16, 1992, Winnipeg at San Jose)

Barber (12–2–64, Victoria, British Columbia) scored six points in twenty-one games from 1990–92 with Winnipeg before the Jets let him go. He played two games with Quebec, which traded him to San Jose for the final twelve of his NHL career. He retired after nine games with Kansas City of the IHL in 1992–93.

After scoring 39 points in 49 games from 1988–90 at Kalamazoo, and 47 points in 67 games with the North Stars during the same time frame, Barber seemed to lose his touch. He had just two goals and eight assists in his final 48 NHL games. He totaled 115 regular-season games in his career and had 25 goals and 32 assists. In 11 playoff games for the North Stars in 1989 and '90, he had four goals and four assists.

During the 1990–91 season, Barber was single and made an estimated $75,200 on a two-way contract calling for $150,000 in the NHL and $30,000 in the minors. He later married and, with his wife, Stacy, had a son, Riley, who was drafted as a right wing by Washington in 2012 and played three games for the Capitals in 2016–17. He went pointless in those as well as nine games for the Montreal Canadiens in 2019–20 and four more for Detroit in '21–22, after which he signed as a free agent with Dallas Stars.

Don and Stacy, a former figure skater from Pennsylvania, live in Michigan, where she went into business as a power skating instructor.

Kevin Evans (October 13, 1992, San Jose at Chicago)

Five days after he was sent to Kalamazoo toward the end of November, the 1990–91 season ended for Evans (7–10–65, Peterborough, Ontario). He suffered a knee injury but came back to play five games for the '91–92 Sharks, totaling one assist in nine career NHL games. He spent most of his time in the IHL with Kansas City in '91–92 and then returned to Kalamazoo in '92–93. He played until 2000, winding up with stints in the Western Professional Hockey League (Tupelo T-Rex) and the Central Hockey League (Memphis RiverKings).

Evans was the career leader in penalty minutes in all of professional hockey (4,419, not including 472 during the playoffs in his 14-year career) until surpassed by Dennis Bonvie in 2007. Bonvie, who retired a year later, totaled 4,804 PIM (plus another 319 in the postseason) and played a total of 92 NHL games with six different teams. Evans, however, still holds the single-season pro mark of 648 PIM, recorded in 73 games of the '86–87 season with Kalamazoo (when he also had 19 goals and 50 points).

"He could get hit in the head with a two-by-four and just smile and say, 'Is that all you got?'" said Pat MacLeod, Evans' teammate in Kalamazoo and Kansas City. "Tough as nails. He didn't win every fight. But he would fight *anybody*—he'd fight Link (Gaetz)—and give everybody a good fight. He had stamina. I've never seen so many fights that lasted a minute and half or longer. He'd just wear 'em down. He was fighting with a broken hand when we won the Turner Cup in 1992. He'd been told not to. His hand was all purple and blue and swollen. But that was Kevin."

Two of Evans' brothers, Doug and Paul, also played in the NHL. Kevin and Doug both work in sales for Jack McGee, a Chevrolet-Cadillac dealership in Peterborough.

On March 1, 2019, Kevin appeared at a game in Kalamazoo (now in the East Coast Hockey League) as the first 1,000 fans through the doors got a Kevin Evans Bobble-Fist Doll.

"Best experience of my life was to step on the ice at the Met and even walk into the dressing room and get greeted with all the approvals," Evans told me in an email exchange for this book. "When I got sent down it took two games and I was off to year-ending knee surgery, so I first-hand got to watch the Wings and the North Stars from the couch—only hoping that I could have been there. Next year, going to San Jose was also one of the best moments but the comfort level did drop as my knee did not respond the best and I never felt the same again. Age also was not on my side after that and, after retiring and coming home, I've had many knee surgeries since. But I will always cherish the people I played with along with the coaches and the many years I got to play and coach the game I loved. Playing the way I did was easy as I grew up with five older brothers and it was just fun, and to get paid made it even so much more."

Brian Hayward (December 29, 1992, San Jose at Vancouver)

Hayward (6–25–60, Georgetown, Ontario) earned the first victory in Sharks history, but other joys thereafter were few and far between.

"That was the most difficult experience of my life, to get to San Jose and see this team is going to get hammered every night," Hayward told me. "I realized as a player they weren't trying to win. Their objective was *not* to be good and *not* to be competitive. It was horrible, and then I got hurt, and it got worse. I'd never missed the playoffs in my career, and we'd come off an experience where we almost

won the Cup. To go backward like that, I was like, 'Oh, my God.' But the Sharks are a whole other story."

Hayward suffered a degenerative back injury (two herniated disks) early in the 1991–92 season. After he played every second of an 8–2 loss to the North Stars on October 17, 1991, he didn't play again until December. He appeared in four more games—only one of them complete—but the back injury sidelined him for the rest of the season.

"I was literally unable to get off the floor for a month," Hayward said. "Then I'd get into physical therapy for three weeks and try to play again. Two weeks later, I'd be back on the floor. That went on for two years. It's so dumb. Rather than just say, 'I'm taking a season off,' I was wearing a girdle from under my armpits to mid-thigh. It was like a corset. It was tied up with straps, and I couldn't turn or rotate my body. And I was trying to play in the National Hockey League, on a bad team. It was a nightmare. I look back now and think, 'Boy, what an idiot.'"

Hayward made eighteen appearances in the first three months of the '92–93 season but went 2–16–1 and lost his last nine decisions. He filled in as a color commentator on San Jose telecasts the rest of the year and retired with a career record of 143–156–37. In 357 regular-season appearances (26 with the North Stars), he had a 3.72 GAA and an .874 save percentage. In 37 playoff games (the last six of which came in the '91 playoffs), he went 11–18, 3.50, .871.

His television experience provided a springboard into work (which continues today) as a color analyst for the Anaheim Ducks. He also is a partner in FanServ, a company that customizes digital sports advertising content.

He and his wife, Angela, live in Anaheim Hills, California. Their daughter, Courtney, also lives in southern California, where she is director of original content and strategy for Prime Video and Amazon Studios.

Perry Berezan (February 10, 1993, San Jose at Calgary)

Berezan (12–5–64, Edmonton) was summoned to Bobby Clarke's office in September 1991.

"I thought, 'Uh, oh,'" Berezan told me thirty years later. "During that summer, I knew I would be an extra. I knew when the playoffs were going on that I was in trouble—that Marc Bureau just took my spot. Then Neal Broten held out. I ended up filling Neal's spot until they signed him. (Clarke) said, basically, 'We don't want you anymore. We tried to trade you. Nobody wants you. We put you on waivers. If nobody picks you up, we'll buy you out of your contract.' He said the buyout would be two-thirds of what your contract called for. I was one of the lower-paid guys. I was thinking, 'Really? Are you going to do this to me?' I said, 'No. It's 100 percent.' He lost it on me. 'You want 100 percent, you'll earn it! I'll send you to every God-forsaken, minor-league team in this fucking country!' I just said, 'Call my agent,' and walked out."

Berezan got in touch with Jack Ferreira, who wanted to stick it to Clarke. Ferreira waited until Berezan cleared waivers and the North Stars had to honor his contract. As a free agent, Berezan then signed with San Jose and double-dipped.

Berezan played a total of ninety-four games in the next two seasons with the Sharks. During the summer of 1992, he suffered an ankle injury playing basketball with Hayward. Berezan hobbled through training camp, compounded by the stress of learning his wife, Marie, was suffering from multiple sclerosis. She'd just given birth to their oldest daughter.

"I'd go on a road trip, and my wife would cry," Berezan said.

Then, on February 10, 1993, he collided knee-to-knee with Ronnie Stern at Calgary. Berezan suffered a torn medial collateral ligament. As he lay on the stretcher in the visitors' dressing room in the Saddledome, where he'd started his NHL career not quite eight years earlier, he knew he was done. He'd totaled 61 goals and 75 assists in 378 regular-season games—132 with Minnesota. In 31 career playoff games, 11 for the North Stars, he had four goals and seven assists.

Twelve years after first leaving the University of North Dakota, Berezan returned and finished his degree and became a financial planner and investment advisor. He partnered with his best friend, former Sioux teammate and NHLer Gord Sherven, to form the Berezan Sherven Group at National Financial Bank in Calgary.

Perry and Marie remain married, and he said she has lived a relatively normal life since the years immediately after her MS diagnosis. They have three children, daughters now twenty-eight and twenty-two, and a son who's twenty-six.

Perry misses the atmosphere and competition of the NHL, but not the injuries, being away from his family, or "getting fired" and "having a coach telling me I'm no good."

"I look back now at all the games I sat out, and I know it was a blessing, because my hips and my knees and my shoulders are all good," said Berezan, who also has appeared on radio, TV and at alumni events for the Flames. "I don't have the wear and tear on my body as if I had played a long career. I'm happy with what I've got now.

"Players will cling to their career as long as they can," he added. "You can't pull it away from them. When you go on to that second career, you've almost got to go at it with that same intensity that you had in hockey. I think the average is that guys switch career paths about five times after they retire from the game. We don't know anything else. You never get the same type of fulfillment. Guys say, 'Oh, I don't like this. I don't like this.' But you stick with it. There were ugly parts to being an athlete, but you stuck with it. That's what I've done, and so have a lot of other guys. I've been able to build a nice (second) career for myself. This defines me more than, 'Perry is the former hockey player.'"

He tries to coach his clients to think of success beyond the rink.

"When you're a fifty-goal scorer in the NHL and an asshole, people will remember you are a fifty-goal scorer," Berezan said. "But when you retire, you're just an asshole. So remember how you treat other people when you're playing, because you'll get that back."

Doug Smail (March 2, 1993, Ottawa at San Jose)

Smail (9-2–57, Moose Jaw, Saskatchewan) was allowed to become a free agent and signed with Quebec for 1991–92 and Ottawa for '92–93, teams that lost a combined 118 games. He played thirteen seasons in the NHL, totaling 210 goals and 249 assists in 845 regular-season games, the vast majority with Winnipeg.

He also scored 28 shorthanded goals and had at least one each year for twelve consecutive seasons. He had nine goals and two assists in 42 career playoff games, all but the last of which (Game 2 in the '91 finals) were with the Jets.

Smail spent a portion of '92–93 in the minors for the first time, at San Diego of the IHL. From '93 to '96, he played in the UK before retiring. He later moved to Denver and has coached youth

hockey for the past 19 years. He adopted a daughter, Anna, and eventually divorced his first wife in 2001. (Lisa Smail ironically became an executive assistant in the Dallas Stars' hockey operations department.) Doug remarried in 2005 but, tragically, his son, Cody, died by suicide in 2011. He was twenty-one.

"It's sad, but it's real, and I don't run from it," Doug told me a decade later. "I've talked with a couple guys I played with whose sons took their own lives. (Former North Star) Kevin Maxwell is a scout in Philly, and I played with him at North Dakota. His son took his own life. It's almost epidemic in this day and age. I walk the halls in the arena here in Colorado with kids that I've coached from ages 15–18. Some of them were considering that. You talk with them and spend time and do what you can. It's more common than people understand."

Cody played youth hockey, but his real love was downhill skiing. Doug said Cody coming down a mountain looked like Mike Modano skating down the ice. Cody also dreamed of being a pilot or a broadcaster.

"But he just couldn't latch on," Doug said. "All the time, we were talking from the heart. But he just made some poor choices, and he was in a place that he never thought he could get out of."

If losing his son wasn't enough, Anna Smail died of an opioid overdose in 2016.

Doug's second wife, Wanda, had two daughters when they got married. He said they treat him like their own father, and he now counts six grandchildren.

His seven months with the North Stars are only acknowledged by a framed photo in his home office.

"Every inch of the walls is covered with my career, college through the NHL," Doug said. "No one comes in here, but I look up and see the North Star uniform and it brings back memories. And they're not memories of pain, but of thankfulness. It's not for my ego. I'll finish some work or writing or a conference call or whatever, and I take a breath and sit back. I see those images, and I'm so thankful I got a chance to be part of that, however small my role, I choose to look back on it with positive feelings.

"Bobby Smith called me 'Rocket' all year long. That was because Rocket Ismail was at Notre Dame at the time and my name was Smail. So, rather than, 'It's Smail,' he started calling me 'Rocket.' I remember the Christmas party, skating around the rink with our families at Met Center. Bobby said 'Hey, Rocket. This is great, isn't it?' It's little things like that you remember after all these years."

Dean Kolstad (March 11, 1993, San Jose at St. Louis)

Kolstad (6–16–68, Edmonton, Alberta) played 10 games for the Sharks in 1992–93, completing his NHL career with one goal and seven assists in forty games—thirty with Minnesota.

"The only reason I got those ten games (in San Jose) is because George Kingston was the coach, and his mom lived next door to my grandma," Kolstad remembered. "I'll never forget, he called me up, and I was in Kansas City, and at this time there was a lot going on. They took my assistant captain ('A') away, and (Blades coach) Kevin Constantine was going to be the (Sharks) coach that next year. I went from playing racquetball with Kevin and having a good old time when we were winning the Turner Cup to the second half of the next year having trouble getting into games. Dean Lombardi was in Europe, and they needed a defenseman in San Jose. They called Kansas City, and Kevin said, 'Well, I'll send you this guy or that guy.' George said, 'No, I want Dean.' And Kevin said, 'I can't do that.' George said, 'Yeah, you can.' When I went up there, I saw Lombardi in the hallway off the ice, and it was like he saw a ghost. He was

Dean Kolstad (center) towers over his golf group in 2022. (Michigan PGA)

like, 'What are you doing here?!' By the end of the year, I wasn't even playing."

Kolstad signed with the New York Rangers for '93–94 but played at Binghamton of the AHL—again on the outside looking in as the Rangers won the Cup. He then played in Minnesota (with the IHL Moose, '94–95) and Portland (AHL, '95–96). He retired after two seasons as player, assistant coach, assistant GM, and "assistant everything else" in the Western Professional Hockey League with the Central Texas Stampede. Each team was allowed five NHLers. One of Kolstad's teammates was Daniel Berthiaume.

"I had 73 points in 66 games, and I thought for sure by Christmas I would get called up and be in the IHL," Kolstad said. "It didn't happen, and that lost its luster."

In 2018, Kolstad became director of golf at Gull Lake View Golf Club and Resort in Augusta, Michigan, where he's been a pro for more than twenty-nine years. He also is president of the Michigan PGA and was its pro of the year in 2021. He also works for Athletic Mentors, a sports consulting and coaching business based in Richland, Michigan.

He and his wife, Amelia, live in Hickory Corners, Michigan. Their 27-year-old son, Dean, went to Notre Dame (Ohio) College and Madonna University in Michigan to play basketball. Their 29-year-old daughter, MacKenzie, played volleyball at Aquinas College in Ohio.

Dean Sr. coached a Bantam AA hockey team in 2019–20 at Kalamazoo and also coaches a high school team. He plays in NHL alumni charity games with other players who live in the Detroit area.

"I'm still playing with Larry Murphy," Kolstad told me. "People ask, 'How can Murph be in the Hall of Fame if he had to play with you?!'

"I could look at my career as a disappointment. Knowing what needed to be done at the time and if I had played a little differently, if I had fought more, I probably could've played a long time. But I didn't want to do that. If you look at my career, from juniors to the end, I averaged about thirty points a year. But I think it might have been Chuck (Grillo) who told me, 'I've got a bunch of guys who are 5-foot-8 who can score thirty points.' If I had played more like Mark Tinordi, I would've been fine. But it wasn't in my makeup. In juniors, I had more points, but he had more penalty minutes, and he became a tremendous NHL player because that allowed him more room to maneuver around."

Stew Gavin (April 3, 1993, Minnesota at Los Angeles)

Gavin (3–15–60, Ottawa, Ontario) continued to play for the North Stars until a knee injury, suffered April 3, 1993, at Los Angeles, forced him to retire. As the franchise transitioned to Dallas, he went into scouting for the Stars but came back for a brief stint in the IHL with Kansas City and Minnesota in 1994–95. He played 768 regular-season NHL games in his career (289 with the North Stars), totaling 130 goals and 155 assists. He was more dangerous offensively in 66 playoff games (40 with Minnesota), totaling 14 goals and 20 assists.

In addition to their son, Max, Stew and his wife, Phyllis, became parents to a daughter, Taylor, in 1993. They relocated to Toronto after Stew stopped playing, and he and Phyllis later divorced.

Stew became a senior vice president with Corporate Planning Associates in Toronto, and in 2003 founded Gavin Hockey Wealth Specialists, which continues today and has more than $500 million in client assets. It serves NHL players with a focus on educating them and protecting their finances, with special emphasis on tax planning.

"Coming out of hockey, everyone feels alone," Gavin said. "No one's taking care of you. No one's handing you your meal money. For a lot of guys, that was their identity."

Gavin maintains his private pilot license, owns a Cessna 172 amphibious float plane and enjoys golf and relaxing on his tree farm in the Ottawa Valley.

He continues to play recreational hockey two to three times a week. In some ways, he's still chasing an elusive goal.

Stew Gavin in 2022.

"I had dreams into my fifties of going back to that ('91) series to play, to win the Cup," Gavin told me in 2021. "It stuck with me for years and years. I can always relate to the losing team and how bad they've felt. I could never relate to the winning team until I had a couple of clients win the Cup, and that's only been in the last few years. But I saw how happy they were and the emotion of their win, and that kind of cured me I guess."

He's tormented by second thoughts, however.

Should he have shadowed Lemieux? Could they have avoided any of the overconfidence or friction that may have developed prior to Game 4?

"In the finals, everyone was eager to act out the street hockey scene from when we were kids and scoring the goal that won the Stanley Cup," Gavin told me. "Did guys step outside of their lane a little to try and do more and it cost us? I even question the little things, like should I have cut my hair? The little engine that could finally ran out of steam.

"Confidence is so precious, and it takes so much to get it, but you can lose it in a shift. We won as a team, and we lost as a team. Hey, I've spent a lot of time thinking about it. Frankly, if I could've checked Lemieux, and we could've won the Cup, it would be a whole different story you're writing. But that didn't happen. It's only part of my dreams."

Bobby Smith 🏆 (Won 1986 Stanley Cup; April 15, 1993, Minnesota at Detroit)

Smith (2–12–58, North Sydney, Nova Scotia) remained with the North Stars through their final game before announcing his retirement five days later.

In 1,077 regular-season NHL games, 572 with Minnesota, he scored 357 goals and assisted on 679 more for 1,036 points—but was also minus-9. He totaled 64 goals and 96 assists in 184 playoff games (77 with Minnesota) and appeared in the Stanley Cup Final four times, including his winning 1986 appearance with the Canadiens.

"I remember we checked into a hotel two nights before the series (with the Flames) started even though we had home-ice advantage, and the coach (Jean Perron) went around the room and asked guys to say a few words," Smith said. "We had quite a few guys who had won a Cup before, and at the end I said, 'I'd like to say something: I'm the only guy in here who's been to the finals who didn't win. We've got to play this like this is our last chance, because there's a really good chance it is going to be our last chance.'"

It wasn't. Montreal returned three years later, though that time the Flames prevailed.

Bobby Smith (left) sold the Halifax Mooseheads to Michigan buisnessman Sam Simon in 2023. (Photo courtesy Halifax Mooseheads)

The Canadiens' desperation to win didn't exist in Minnesota, Smith told me, until Bob Gainey brought it.

"We'd been to the finals (in '81) and the semifinals (in '80), and I got to Montreal, and I was shocked how serious they took hockey," Smith said. "We weren't a bunch of bums in Minnesota, but an example would be, generally an hour before warmups, you turn off the music. In Minnesota, it would be, 'Oh, come on! One more song. What's the difference?' In Montreal, forty-five minutes before the game you'd hear, 'Turn that crap off! Start thinking about the Boston Bruins!' It was driven by the fans and the history of the organization, but it felt like going from the American League to the NHL. Bob (Gainey) wanted to bring that to Minnesota."

Smith laid the credit for the first-round upset, if not the entire 1991 playoff run, on Gainey. His address to the players encouraging rather than berating them between Games 3 and 4 against Chicago, Smith said, was the single greatest piece of coaching he'd witnessed in his NHL career.

"I played fifteen years, way over 1,000 games if you count playoffs, and there are probably two coaching speeches I can remember that made a difference," Smith said. "That was one of them… and we outscored them 12–2 in the next three games, and it was over. I've heard thousands of speeches, pregame and between periods, but that one was a remarkable move, and you could feel the air rush into the dressing room.

"It was the one time where I could honestly say that a coaching decision won us a game."

Smith repeated a 46-point season in '91–92, but in '92–93 had career-lows in games (45), goals (5) and assists (7). From his second tenure in Minnesota, he prefers to remember the '91 playoffs.

"It was the best hockey I played in my return to the North Stars, and that was the last time I felt like a really good player," Smith said. "I remember walking down the steps (from the dressing room for a game) in February '93 and worrying about getting a stick in the eye. I said, 'You ARE finished. You should go back up and take your equipment off now.'

"People ask what you miss about the game and, invariably, people say, 'I miss being with the guys.' What I miss was being a good player. Being able to influence the game and be the difference between winning and losing. I think I was that in the '91 playoffs. When it came time for me to retire, it was an easy decision. It was time."

In retirement, he enrolled at the University of Minnesota and earned bachelor's and master's degrees from the Carlson School of Management in three years.

He became GM of the Phoenix Coyotes from 1996 to 2000 and bought the Halifax Mooseheads of the QMJHL in 2003. His son, Dan, later played for the team, and Bobby sold his interest in 2023.

Bobby and his wife, Beth, have been married thirty-nine years. They live in Phoenix, though Bobby also spends 60 to 70 days a year in Halifax. Their children are Ryan, thirty-six, a lawyer and graduate of med school at Mayo Clinic in Scottsdale; Meg, thirty-four, a mother of three who lives in San Diego; and Dan, thirty-two, who works for Grasslands Environmental in Nashville. The Smiths have five grandchildren.

Curt Giles (May 15, 1993, St. Louis at Toronto)

"Pengy" Giles (11–30–58, The Pas, Manitoba) signed with St. Louis on February 29, 1992, and played sixty-one games for the Blues before retiring in '93. He totaled 43 goals and 199 assists in 895 career regular-season NHL games, 760 with the North Stars—for whom he was plus-31. In 103 playoff games (all but 11 with Minnesota), he had six goals and 16 assists.

He later said not playing in the '91 finals was "the toughest thing I've ever been through." Perhaps that's why he didn't respond to repeated attempts to contact him for this book.

After retiring as a player, Giles coached youth hockey for six years before becoming head coach at Edina High School in 1999. His teams won state titles in 2010, 2013, 2014, and 2019. He continues to work in sales for Road Machinery & Supplies Co. He and his wife, Mary Pat, whom he met during freshman orientation at UMD, celebrated their fortieth wedding anniversary in 2019, at which time they had two grandchildren.

Brian Propp (April 14, 1994, Hartford at Boston)

Propp (2–15–59, Neudorf, Saskatchewan) re-signed with the North Stars for 1991–92 and stayed through '92–93, during which time he married his first wife (Kris) and was loaned to a team in Switzerland from November through March—returning after the North Stars announced their move to Dallas. He signed as a free agent with Hartford and finished his NHL career there in '93–94. Propp played fifteen seasons, totaling 1,016 regular-season games (147 with the North Stars), collecting 425 goals and assisting on 578 others for 1,003 points. Like Smith, Propp never played in the minors.

His career totals might have been much greater if not for the hit from Chris Chelios in 1989.

"In today's world, that would have been at least a 25-game suspension, and he got nothing… I missed only one game," Propp said. "We had baseline testing, then, too, so I must have passed, which is pretty amazing.

"You can see it on You Tube—it was nasty and on purpose, and I don't think he had a lot of remorse for it, at least he never said so. I know the type of person he is. It took me a couple years afterwards to really get over it. My reactions weren't slowed, but I would go into the corner flinching, thinking what might happen getting hit from behind again."

Prior to Chelios' hit, Propp had scored 26 goals or more in each of his ten NHL seasons. After his scare, he would never exceed 26 goals again. While he matched that with the 1990–91 North Stars, he never scored more than 16 in any of the rest of his five remaining seasons.

Chelios showed no remorse.

"Brian Propp is a jerk," Chelios told the *Pioneer Press* in 1993. "If he wants to meet me on West Madison (in Chicago), I'll be there. Anytime. And tell him not to bring his face shield."

The taunt never seemed to bother Propp, who chuckled thirty years after his overtime winner in Game 1 at Chicago presaged ousting the Blackhawks.

"Chelios still hates me because of that goal and that series," Propp told me with a laugh.

The unfortunate tag Propp will forever bear, however, is that he was on five Cup-losing teams (1980, '85, and '87 with Philadelphia; '90 with Boston; and '91 with Minnesota).

Brian Propp married the former Eileen McCay on May 14, 2021, in Stone Harbor, New Jersey. (Photo courtesy of Brian Propp)

"Hard to find someone who played in five finals and didn't win," said Propp, though actually there were four others: Regis Kelly (Toronto in 1935, '36, '38, '39, and '40), Norm Ullman (Detroit in 1956, '61, '63, '64, and '66), Gerry Melnyk (Detroit in 1956 and '61, Chicago in '62 and '65, and St. Louis in '68), and Bruce MacGregor (Detroit in '61, '63, '64, and '66, and New York in '72).

Melnyk was Philadelphia's western region scout in 1979 when he championed Propp in a draft that included Hall of Famers Mike Gartner, Ray Bourque, Michel Goulet, and Kevin Lowe in a star-studded first round from which no player went on to appear in fewer than 238 NHL games.

Propp's last playoff appearance came in the 1–0 double-overtime loss to Detroit in the North Stars' last postseason home game. It was the 160th of his career, one shy of Brad Park's record for most playoff games without winning the Cup.

Dave Gagner said Propp was the best left winger he ever played with, and indeed, Propp retired as the NHL's all-time leading playoff scorer at that position. He totaled 64 goals and 84 assists for 148 points—through 2022 more than Alex Ovechkin and every Hall of Fame left wing. That list includes Propp's contemporaries: Dave Andreychuk, Bill Barber, Clark Gillies, Goulet, Mark Howe, Bobby Hull (although he totals 209 if you include his WHA numbers), Luc Robitaille, Brendan Shanahan, Steve Shutt, and… Bob Gainey. All except Goulet and Howe won the Cup. (Goulet played in the finals in '92, and Howe did so in '85 and '87 when he was Propp's teammate, and in '95 when he was with Detroit for a sweep by New Jersey.)

"It's disappointing because the Stanley Cup is your ultimate goal," Propp said. "But all you can do is give it your best. People forget about how hard it is to get to a final, but in Philly, they don't forget how hard we played those three years to get there with a lot of injuries. Even when you do win and get all these awards, that's in the past. You think your kids are going to keep all your trophies when you are gone? They are going to wind up in an estate sale. You live on your laurels, you never will succeed in the next area of your life. I have always looked to the future."

Propp managed a New Jersey ice arena from 1995 to '99 and served as Flyers radio color analyst from 1999 to 2008. As a resident of Cinnaminson Township in New Jersey, he unsuccessfully ran as a Republican in 2007 for a seat in the state's General Assembly. From 2009 to '14, he served as VP of strategic account management for The Judge Group.

In the fall of 2015, just after he became Director of Strategic Relationships for Wolf Commercial Real Estate in Marlton, New Jersey, Propp suffered a massive stroke. While he'd never lost a tooth during his playing career, he lost two of them in the middle of the night, September 3, 2015, when he crashed and hit the floor of a vacation home in Annapolis, Maryland.

Propp had been diagnosed with atrial fibrillation in the left side of his heart in 2000. In 2009, he underwent a cardiac ablation and was placed on blood thinners.

"I got to where I didn't want to take the blood thinners anymore," Propp said. "I was in good shape. I was skating in the morning a couple of days a week with a group of guys, and I felt good. When I had the stroke, I wasn't feeling that well the week before that, but then we went on a trip with my family. The first day was OK, and then I had a bad headache, and I stayed in. That night it just hit. I don't remember that much. I couldn't speak. I couldn't move. Thankfully, my family was there."

Propp believes a blood clot developed in his heart and eventually led to his stroke, which left him with limited use of the right side of his body. He suffered some loss of movement and needed intense speech, occupational, and physical rehabilitation. He was in Philadelphia's Magee Rehabilitation Hospital for more than a month and continued outpatient therapy long after his release.

"The only thing I could say was 'and' and 'Bernie Parent[67],'" Propp told me. "I had to relearn with my brain how to talk. It was really tough. It took me a long time, a year and a half. But I've come a long way."

He still struggles to pronounce some names (Tinordi comes out "Tornado," for example), and there is the occasional glitch in conversation where his mind and voice may not be in synch (his brother, Ron, moved from Calgary to Philadelphia to assist him), but Brian hasn't lost his sense of humor.

"All the hockey players that I know, they don't talk so well anymore, either," he said.

Nonetheless, Propp has recovered, learned to sign his name left-handed, returned to work and considers himself lucky not to have any facial paralysis and steady use of both legs. He got divorced but subsequently married the former Eileen McCay. He often talks publicly about his stroke and recovery and has become a spokesman for Bancroft NeuroRehab in New Jersey.

"My right fingers don't work that well—they're pretty straight," Propp said. "I still skate, but I can't shoot the puck like I could. I golf right-handed, but I can only hit the ball about 220 yards now. It used to be a little longer than that. But I have fun, and it all works well."

His daughter, Paige, is twenty-six and works for Comcast in Philadelphia. His son, Jackson, is twenty-three and was a member of the rowing crew at Rutgers until his graduation in 2021. Whenever Brian visits his relatives in Saskatchewan, he changes planes in Minneapolis. That has led to him keep in contact with other former North Stars. One night after a missed connection, he stayed at Brian Bellows' house. Propp, who also played in one of Mike Modano's celebrity golf tournaments, singled out Gagner, Broten, and Mark Baribeau among others with whom he still communicates.

Propp, who continues to serve as a Flyers goodwill ambassador at Wells Fargo Arena in Philadelphia, also has cultivated a relationship with a small factory in the Dominican Republic to import fine rolled tobacco under his own brand ("Guffaw" cigars). That leads to the obvious denouement: No one can ever tell him he was always close but no cigar.

Larry DePalma (April 21, 1994, Pittsburgh at Washington)

DePalma (10–27–65, Trenton, Michigan) signed as a free agent with San Jose on August 30, 1991. He played twenty games for the Sharks in '92–93 and wound up his NHL career with seven games for the '93–94 Penguins. He totaled 21 goals and 20 assists in 148 regular-season games (121 with the North Stars). He was pointless in three playoff games—two in 1989 with Minnesota and one with Pittsburgh in 1994.

"I screwed up my career; no one else is to blame," DePalma told the *Pioneer Press* in 1995, when he played for the Minnesota Moose. "No one ever sat me down and told me they wanted me to be a

67 Parent was in goal as the Flyers won Stanley Cups in 1974 and '75, and was one of the greatest goaltenders of all-time. His playing career ended in 1979 following an eye injury and the franchise immediately retired his uniform number (1). He was Philadelphia's goalie coach during the early years of Propp's career and Parent—like Propp—has long been employed by the Flyers as an Ambassador of Hockey.

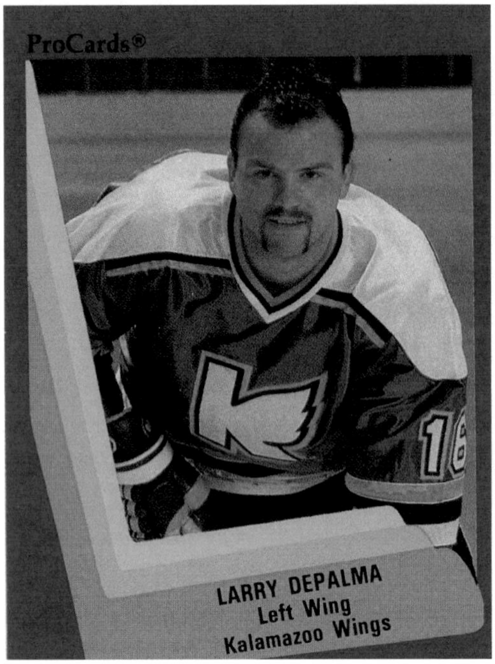

third- or fourth-line player, to just play tough. Of course, it wouldn't have mattered if they had; I never would have accepted that role. I thought I was better than that. I could never understand how some guys could come out of juniors with 50 goals and be seen as goal scorers. I scored 61 goals my last year (in Saskatoon of the Western Hockey League), and everyone looked at me as a grinder."

From 1994 to '97, he played with four teams (Cleveland, San Diego, Minnesota, and Milwaukee) in the IHL. DePalma, who gained distinction with the Moose for his claim to having seen a UFO, suffered at least eight significant concussions (and many lesser ones), which were then treated with addictive pain medications that left him dependent after he retired. He was sentenced to a year in jail on an attempted extortion conviction in 2008, and later described bouts with depression and even suicide attempts. He said several times he put a gun in his mouth, but that cannabis saved his life, allowing him to control rage and counteract depression. He spoke about it publicly during a 2016 campaign, also featuring former Detroit forward Darren McCarty—whom DePalma once fought—backing a ballot question to make cannabis legal in Michigan.

"It was bad," DePalma said in a YouTube video (since taken down) and also reported by Rick Thompson, editor of *Michigan Medical Marijuana Magazine*—which lasted two years in publication. "I couldn't talk, my speech was slurred, people thought I was drunk or high or something. It got so bad to where I couldn't even walk, my equilibrium was off. I couldn't stand on one leg for more than three seconds; I couldn't look up, because I would fall right backwards ... concussions ruin people's lives."

He and his wife, Jacquie, had two daughters, Hunter and Lauren, after their son, Larry, but later divorced. I reached Larry Jr. through Facebook Messenger in January 2021 and finally communicated with his dad a month later. Larry Sr. said he recently had elbow surgery, the latest and one of the worst of approximately twenty surgeries he'd undergone. In mid-March 2021, he told me via email that much of what was reported about substance abuse when he was arrested in 2008 was not true. We were set to talk by phone when I contracted COVID-19 in March 2021 and was down for a couple weeks.

Unfortunately, after many messages, DePalma texted to say he was sorry, but he had to feel like talking to tell his story or he wouldn't do it. He said he would let me know when he felt up to it. Late in 2021, he was engaged, buying a new house in Michigan and dealing with COVID himself. I'm sure this is a tiny fraction of his story, and Larry, if you read this, I'd love to update a new edition with your voice.

Gaetan Duchesne (May 3, 1995, Florida at Pittsburgh)

Duchesne (7–11–62, Quebec City, Quebec) died of a heart attack while training at a gym in his hometown on April 16, 2007. He was forty-four and had played in a Washington Capitals alumni game eight days earlier—when his former teammates marveled at his physical condition, so strong that he broke his own stick on a breakaway.

Duchesne played for the North Stars until they left Minnesota. His son, Jeremy, then six, burst into tears at news the team would move to Dallas. He told his parents to go without him, but Gaetan got him to stop crying and reconsider by showing pictures from Texas.

They moved, but not to Dallas. On June 20, 1993, the rechristened Dallas Stars traded Gaetan to San Jose for a sixth-round draft pick. Six days later, Dallas' selection turned out to be Petri Varis, whom they traded to San Jose for Dean Evason, who later became the Minnesota Wild's sixth head coach in 2020. Varis played one NHL game with the Chicago Blackhawks.

Gaetan played with the Sharks in 1993–94, his second consecutive year appearing in the maximum 84 regular-season games. He played 46 of a possible 48 during the lockout-shortened '94–95 season, which included a trade to Florida. He then moved home and played 69 games over the '96–97 and '97–98 seasons with the IHL's Quebec Rafales before retiring as a player.

In 1,028 career regular-season NHL games (297 with the North Stars), he totaled 179 goals and 254 assists. Incredibly, he was plus-108. In 84 career playoff games (37 with Minnesota), he added 14 goals and 13 assists. In retirement, he coached in the QMJHL, where one of his brothers was an official, and later ran an architectural supply business in Quebec City.

Gaetan is survived by two sisters, eight brothers and his wife, Gina. They met when he was playing junior hockey and, in addition to Jeremy, had a younger daughter, Chloe.

A goalie, Jeremy played in the QMJHL beginning in 2003 with Victoriaville, about an hour and a half southwest of Quebec City. Gaetan saw Jeremy play there often until he was moved to Bobby Smith's Halifax Mooseheads and, in 2005, was drafted by the Philadelphia Flyers. Father or son was sure to call the other before or after every game.

"He never pushed me to play," Jeremy told me. "As long as I had fun, he wanted me to continue. What he helped me most was with the mental aspect—controlling pressure."

When his father died, Jeremy was with the Val d'Or Foreurs, deep in the QMJHL playoffs. He went home several days for the funeral, then returned to help Val d'Or win a semifinal series in a seventh game. However, the Foreurs lost four straight in the finals to Lewiston (Maine) and fell short of the chance to play in the Memorial Cup.

"It was a very emotional time being that it was my last year (of junior eligibility) and trying to get a contract," said Jeremy, who played 18 of the 20 postseason games that spring. "It was tough. My father was in great shape. From what we learned, he'd just recently been tested for cholesterol for insurance, and while that test was fine, he had a blocked artery. One of the ones to his heart was blocked to 98 percent. Why? You don't know ... when there's no direct explanation, it makes it more mysterious, and you search more for a reason. You have to accept sometimes that you won't get it and you've got to move on."

Jeremy signed with the Flyers soon after and bounced between the AHL and the ECHL for almost four years. In 2009, he and Tomas Sinisalo went to training camp together. At the end of March 2010, Jeremy was in Wilkes-Barre, Pennsylvania, when an injury with Philadelphia created his chance to play in the NHL. He traveled all night to join the Flyers, on the road for the regular-season finale, April 1, 2010, at Nassau Veterans Memorial Coliseum against the New York Islanders.

"I barely slept and got there for the morning skate, but I didn't expect to play," said Jeremy, who'd been called up other times that season only to dress as a back-up. "Nassau Coliseum was so old, and I remember sitting down and thinking, 'My dad sat in this same dressing room.'"

Brian Boucher, who went on to a long career as a broadcaster, started in goal for Philadelphia. But 2:30 into the third period, trailing 5–1, coach Peter Laviolette sent Jeremy into the game. He allowed one goal on four shots the rest of the way as a Flyers' rally came up just short, 6–4.

It turned out to be Jeremy's only NHL appearance, although he remained with Philadelphia as a third goalie during the playoffs—when he went on a ride similar to what his dad experienced in 1991. The Flyers qualified seventh in the Eastern Conference. After a first-round upset, they trailed Boston 3–0 but became the first team since the 1975 Islanders to overcome such a deficit. They beat Montreal and advanced to the Stanley Cup Final, where they lost in six games to Chicago.

"I felt it a few times in my career where the fans and the town behind you create this whole other energy," Jeremy said, recalling what he could from the spring of '91. "That year, the support in Minnesota made it almost feel like everyone was one big family. I remember wearing a North Stars shirt at daycare and going around with my dad. He was always getting stopped, and he didn't mind. He'd stop and talk to anybody. I found it quite annoying because I was ready to leave, and then we'd have to stay and talk some more, but that's part of who he was and why people liked him."

Jeremy lives in Quebec City, where he works as a craft brewer for Archibald Microbrasserie. He has two sons, twelve and ten, who weren't fortunate enough to meet their grandfather.

"He was known for his personality, and I think Minnesota was his favorite (place) in which he played," Jeremy said. "He wore his emotions on his sleeve, but they didn't affect him in the same way, good and bad. The good ones, he would express and cherish and have. But the bad ones wouldn't bring him down as much as the highs would bring him high. He taught me the same things I used in my career. I remember him saying (1991) was his most cherished season. I don't think it took him too long to get over (losing to Pittsburgh), but there was always a sense of 'what if?' Of course, that was his only chance. I don't think he looked back on it as a disappointment as much as a missed opportunity."

Peter Taglianetti 🏆🏆 (Won 1991 and 1992 Stanley Cups; May 22, 1995, New Jersey at Pittsburgh)

Taglianetti (8–15–63, Framingham, Massachusetts) also won the Stanley Cup with the Penguins in 1992—although he had back surgery that spring and didn't appear in the postseason. Left unprotected in the '92 expansion draft, he was selected by Tampa Bay but traded back to Pittsburgh the following season. He played parts of two more years with the Pens, spent '95–96 with Providence of the AHL, and retired. He totaled 451 regular-season NHL games, scoring 18 times and collecting 74 assists. In 53 career playoff games, he had two goals and eight assists.

Taglianetti told me his time with the North Stars didn't get off to a great start.

"I didn't know anybody but the player rep, Stew Gavin, and there was no one from the east, either," Taglianetti said. "You've got Bob Gainey and Doug Jarvis and Andy Murray, and all three might be the greatest guys in the world, but they wouldn't smile and wouldn't laugh. If you made a joke, they'd stare at you like, 'Why the fuck would you tell jokes in the locker room?' In Winnipeg, it was loud and boisterous. We made fun of each other. In Minnesota, it was very stoic. If somebody made a mistake in practice or fell down, you couldn't laugh. It made for some real tense moments, especially since you weren't winning. It was hard to go into that locker room every day.

"I don't think they liked me. I still joked around. I laughed and I did things. In practice every day, we were on the ice for two frickin' hours. It's like, 'This is not training camp. What are we doing?' They probably didn't think I was taking it seriously. But I was."

Taglianetti worked in radio and TV for the Penguins, owned an office products supply business, and worked thirteen years as foreman for a paving company. He divorced his first wife, Allison, in 2003 and later married an orthopedic surgeon, Dr. Vonda Wright. They've gone on to raise a blended family of six children and moved to Alpharetta, Georgia. In 2021, Peter became manager of the southeast division for Crews Control, a company that provides traffic control for construction projects. His oldest son, Patrick, now thirty-five, once served as an Igloo arena worker when his father was broadcasting. Twins Andrew and Jon, now thirty-three, played football at the University of Pittsburgh and also worked for the Penguins and won Cups of their own. Jon has been a longtime member of the equipment staff and in 2021 became head equipment manager. Andrew became the Pens' manager of amateur hockey development before taking a job in the technology sector. Peter and Allison also had another set of twins now twenty-eight—a son, Louis, a football captain at Bucknell, and a daughter, Corey.

Peter still attends Penguins reunions and said he stays in touch with former teammates like Mario Lemieux, Mark Recchi, Troy Loney, and Randy Hillier.

"I'll never forget that ('90–91) season," Peter said. "It changed all of our lives."

Pat MacLeod (November 22, 1995, Vancouver at Dallas)

MacLeod (6-15-69, Melfort, Saskatchewan) was 21 in 1990–91—just six weeks younger than me—during his brief tenure with the North Stars. Taken by San Jose in the dispersal draft, he scored twice in the Sharks' first NHL game and stayed with them through '92–93. The rest of his career came in the minors, except for two games for the Dallas Stars in November 1995. He totaled five goals and 13 assists and was minus-50 in 53 NHL games.

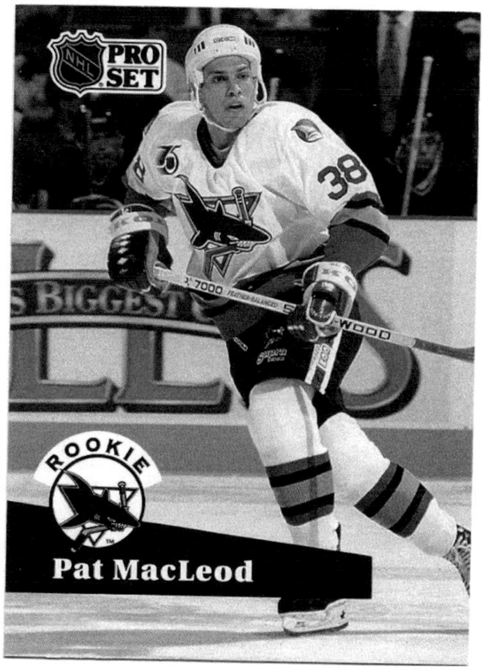

"I always say I should've paid a little more attention to the fact I was a defenseman," MacLeod laughed. "Maybe I'd have spent a little more time in the NHL."

He played briefly in Sweden in '96–97, and then played four seasons with Cincinnati (IHL), interrupted only by three games with Florida of the ECHL in the 1999–2000 season.

"In a lot of ways, playing in the NHL is easier than playing in the minor leagues," MacLeod said. "The reason is, it's more professional right from the get-go with everything: the attitude of the players, the feel of the locker room, and you only have to worry about you. You do your job, and the other guy's going to do his job. When I'm on the ice as a defenseman, my partner isn't going to miss his guy. He's going to be there to back me up. He's going to be there when I go pick up the puck in the corner, and I know he's going to be on the other side of the net waiting for my outlet pass. In the minors, you pick up the puck, and you might be getting run through the boards because the winger forgot to pick up his coverage, or you go for the outlet pass and he's not there. In the NHL you're expected to be more professional, on and off the ice. It's walk out, look good."

He often did, until his second-to-last pro game in Cincinnati, when he suffered a knee injury and tore his MCL, ACL, and meniscus. At 30, MacLeod retired as a player. He became operations manager, first for an overhead door company and then for one specializing in insulation. He worked as a supervisor in plant operations and shipping for Kellogg's before relocating to Phoenix. He now works as operations manager for Cosentino, a Spain-based company that provides granite for countertops and other surfaces.

He and his wife, Kenley, have been married for seven years but together more than ten. He has two sets of twins from a previous relationship: 29-year-old daughters and a son and daughter who are twenty-seven. He's also a stepfather to Kenley's 18-year-old daughter and 15-year-old son.

MacLeod taught hockey at camps in the Cincinnati area for many years. About three years ago at a shooting camp, his slap shot was still clocked at more than 97 miles per hour.

"Did I play as long as I wanted in the NHL? No," MacLeod said. "But I got there. I think the work ethic that it took to get there—and that may have come from my parents—is ingrained. To me, knowing how hard you have to work just to get there, I've tried to instill that in my kids. If you're going to do something, do it right. I say to them, 'Look, your first job might be bagger at the grocery store, and that's not your career. I understand that. But do the best you can because it will always reflect on you.'"

Chris Dahlquist (April 13, 1996, Ottawa at New Jersey)

Dahlquist (12–14–62, Fridley, Minnesota) remained with the North Stars in 1991–92, then was claimed off waivers by Calgary before the '92–93 season.

"I was really glad I wasn't here for that," Dahlquist said of the turmoil the led to the move to Dallas. "I remember them coming up to Calgary (on April 1, 1993), and it was just a shell of a team. I felt bad for them because at that point, they were just not even trying."

He played two years with the Flames, who had the best record in the Pacific Division during his tenure. But they were bounced in the first round by the eventual Cup contestants, Los Angeles and Vancouver. Dahlquist then signed with Ottawa and endured a season when the Senators posted the worst record in the league. Despite being one of their captains, he was demoted to Cincinnati of the IHL to start 1995–96.

Chris Dahliquist in 2022.

"(The Senators) went on a long losing streak (nine in a row and 13 of 14), they fired everybody, and (later) Jacques Martin took over," Dahlquist said. "He wanted to bring me back up. We never lost in Cincinnati. I didn't want to go, but they said I couldn't stay."

In 1996, he signed with Las Vegas of the IHL. His career ended there with a shoulder injury.

Dahlquist played 532 career regular-season NHL games (116 with Minnesota), with 19 goals and 71 assists. In 39 playoff games (30 with the North Stars), he had four goals and seven assists.

He and his wife, Jeanie, have two children. Their son, Chad, now twenty-seven, won a state hockey title with Eden Prairie High School and went on to play club hockey at North Dakota. Their daughter, Charly, twenty-four, played two years at North Dakota, transferred to Ohio State after UND cut its program, and eventually played in the Frozen Four.

Before he stopped playing, Chris sold two businesses that he started. One was Dahlquist Properties (he bought single-family homes, fixed them up and rented them out). The other was Dahlquist Purification (a company that provided water and air cleaners). He began a career as a financial advisor during the NHL lockout that shortened the '94–95 season—when he was Ottawa's representative on the players' negotiating team. He has been with Prudential since 1998 and works in St. Louis Park. A framed team photo of the '91 North Stars adorns his office wall. He also serves on the board of the Minnesota chapter of the NHL Alumni Association, which provides various benefits to members—including tickets to Minnesota Wild games. He and Jeanie still live in the house they built in 1991, near where Highway 169 crosses the Minnesota River.

He said the December 11, 1990, trade of him and Jim Johnson for Peter Taglianetti and Larry Murphy was crucial for both teams.

"I always say the Pens never would have won two Cups in a row if they hadn't got rid of me," Dahlquist said with a chuckle. "I was the key to that deal. You have to hang your hat on something."

Basil McRae (November 30, 1996, Chicago at Los Angeles)

McRae (1–5–61, Beaverton, Ontario) played for the North Stars in 1991–92. He had a cameo appearance with Mike Modano in "The Mighty Ducks," but also suffered a severed tendon when Shane Churla sliced McRae's left foot with his skate blade on February 29 in a loss to Hartford. Eight weeks later, rehabilitating alone on the Met Center ice, McRae broke his left leg.

Claimed by Tampa Bay in the expansion draft, he broke his left leg again (in practice this time) on October 10, 1992. He underwent surgery for a third time and played just fourteen games for the Lighting, who dealt him to St. Louis on January 28, 1993. His stay there was much more positive. He had a song written about him ("The Blues and Basil McRae," by Consolation Champ) and a beer named in his honor (Sweet Basil McRae IPA by Sawdust City Brewing). In the fall of '96, he signed as a free agent with Chicago and played eight games with the Blackhawks before retiring. He totaled 576 career regular-season NHL games (323 with the North Stars), with 53 goals, 83 assists and 2,457 penalty minutes. That ranks 25th on the NHL's all-time PIM list and fifth in penalty minutes per game (4.27) among players with at least 2,000 in their career. He moves up to 18th if you add the postseason. In 78 playoff games (34 with Minnesota), McRae totaled eight goals, four assists, and 349 PIM.

Basil McRae in 2022.

He went on to become part-owner of the London Knights and was GM in 2016 when they won the Memorial Cup. He worked as a scout for Columbus and St. Louis before becoming assistant GM for the Blue Jackets in 2019. He also operates a company in London, Ontario, that markets insurance to pro athletes.

McRae enjoys long distance running and biking and has competed in more than a dozen marathons—including qualifying for and completing the Boston Marathon twice. Preparing for one of those crystallized his place in

Minnesota sports lore, at least in his own mind. While staying in a Minneapolis hotel one winter, he Googled running clubs to find one with which he could get in a workout.

"I called them, and they were like, 'Oh, yeah, we go for a long run on Saturday,'" McRae told me in 2021. "So, I was up at 7:30 in the morning and met down there, and it was a big running group. Anyone new from out of town, they introduced you. They were like, 'We have someone here from Columbus; Basil McRae.' And everyone gave a little clap. Nobody said anything, and I remembered it was twenty-five years since I'd been in Minnesota playing. My ego was a little bruised. I thought someone would recognize me. So, we did this long run, twenty miles all around the lakes, and by the time I got back, a lot of younger people running had called their parents. And their parents came down and took a picture with me. I was like, 'Oh, OK. I'm just with the wrong generation here.'"

Basil and his wife, Jill, have been married for more than thirty-eight years, together for more than forty-three, and split their time between Columbus, a vacation home near Fort Myers, Florida, and a cabin near Haliburton, Ontario. They have two granddaughters from their oldest daughter, Alexandra. Their son, Phil, went on to a brief NHL career with the Blues. He played 15 games in 2010–11, totaling one goal, two assists, and two penalty minutes. He continues to live in St. Louis, where he works for Total Package Hockey, which provides an academic and training alternative for high school students in more than a dozen cities across the US. Their youngest daughter, Abbey, was born in St. Louis and played at St. Lawrence.

During an interview for this book, Basil glanced at his phone to find a text from Churla.

"That was thirty years ago but we still call each other partners in crime, and he'll be a friend for life," McRae said. "He's a good person, and he makes me laugh. I've been watching 'Yellowstone' (the TV show), and now he wants me to come to Montana. I told him to find me a good trail run, but the grizzly bears kind of scare the crap out of me. But I told my wife, 'If I'm with Shane, there's not a better guy I could be with when it gets dangerous.' Back in the day, there were some scary times going into certain buildings, and we'd kind of look at each other and say, 'OK. Who do you want tonight?' If I was ever in a foxhole, there's no one I wanted to be with other than Shane Churla."

McRae routinely talks to Dave Gagner and Stew Gavin, remains in contact with Modano, Neal Broten, and Bobby Smith, and sees Brian Bellows, it seems, whenever his son, Kieffer, plays the Blue Jackets.

"There's a bond there," McRae said. "That ('91 playoff run) was thirty years ago. You don't appreciate it until years later. I've never won the Stanley Cup. When it's being rolled out on the ice and you're asked to leave, that's a pretty hollow feeling. We had a great team; great guys. And we lived in a great neighborhood. People were so excited and supportive ... it was like time stood still. The playoffs were so fun, and it just did a complete 180. I think we're all still proud of what we did. But you only get so many chances to win the Stanley Cup, and I never got (another) one. A lot of us didn't. But I wouldn't trade those two months for anything. That was the highlight of my career."

Jon Casey (April 10, 1997, Toronto at St. Louis)

Casey (3–29–62, Grand Rapids, Minnesota) remained with the North Stars until they left Minnesota. Traded to Boston for Andy Moog on June 25, 1993, he played one season for the Bruins before signing with St. Louis as a free agent. He went 7–5–4 as a backup to Curtis Joseph in 1994–95, then spent most of '95–96 in Peoria of the IHL. Back in St. Louis for the playoffs, Casey stepped in for an injured Grant Fuhr and helped a team with Wayne Gretzky, Brett Hull, Al MacInnis, and Chris Pronger take a 3–2 lead over Detroit in the Western Conference semifinals. But they lost Game 6, and Casey never really recovered from a Game 7, double-overtime goal by Steve Yzerman, a shot under the crossbar that was a classic in NHL history. Casey went 3–8 for the Blues the following year and wound up his career with Kansas City of the IHL in '97–98.

"He was definitely unorthodox, especially compared to today's goalies," Bob Gainey said with a chuckle during an interview for this book. "He had his own style. He was athletic and spontaneous. He liked to be involved outside the crease area. In the first part of the ('90–'91) season, we played him mostly because we had to. When Brian (Hayward) came in, I think we put them into a little bit of competition to see who was going to be our player, and (Jon) won the competition. He played brilliantly through the playoffs, and maybe we wore him down at the end."

In 425 career regular-season NHL games (325 with the North Stars), Casey was 170–157–55 with a 3.21 GAA and an .888 save percentage. In 66 playoff games (41 for Minnesota), he went 32–31, 3.08, .895.

"Jon was a very competitive person," Dave Gagner said. "As players, we didn't like to practice against goalies who didn't like to practice. You didn't want to shoot against a goalie who was just going through the motions. You want them to try because you're trying to get better. Jon certainly was doing that. He was as competitive as they come. It was almost like listening to a play-by-play announcer the way he'd talk to us and try to get in our heads. We had a lot of characters on that team, and he was one."

Shawn Chambers remembers the cat-and-mouse game the players played with Casey during practice. As one of the coaches diagrammed a drill or made a point, inevitably somebody would find a loose puck and shoot it into Casey's net. It would drive him bananas.

"Jon never wanted a puck in his net," Chambers told me. "I can't remember another goalie acting that way up to then. Even in practice, he'd dive to keep the puck out of his net. Even when guys kind of half-heartedly threw it on there, he wasn't going to let that happen. I respect him a ton for his mentality, which was, 'Nothing is going in my net.' We were always trying to get under his skin that way."

Casey likely never played better than in 1991. After he was pulled on January 15 and benched for four games, he returned to go 12–1–3 with a .907 save percentage in 16 games through the night the team clinched a playoff spot.

In the postseason, discounting the final three games against Pittsburgh, Casey was 14–4 with a .915 save percentage. He allowed three or fewer goals in 11 of 17 games against Chicago, St. Louis, and Edmonton. Those 11 were all wins.

"He was unpredictable," Chambers said of Casey's unconventional style. "I always gave him a hard time about that goal (Mario Lemieux scored in Game 2). I'm like, 'Just stay in the net. You stop that, and I'm never on TV then.' Was he tired? Probably. He'd played a ton of hockey for us. But he wasn't the reason we lost the Cup. He was the reason why we had a chance at it in the first place."

Neil Wilkinson said Casey stood "as tall as a red oak tree" in the '91 playoffs.

"He never looked like a goalie, but he got the job done so well," Wilkinson told me. "I have the utmost respect for Case'. . . He was a player I learned from that your energy goes into your team and your teammates. When you're away from them, people want to suck that energy out of you. He had time and energy for anybody on the team and his close circle. But outside of that, he remembered that people didn't believe in him, that people always questioned him. He never gave those people the time of day."

Never one who enjoyed the spotlight, Casey shunned reporters. When he left Minnesota in 1993, he said, "I won't trust anybody (in the media) again." He blamed columnists who "don't understand hockey, don't like hockey, and are negative about every sport."

"I had one reporter tell me, 'I'm not like those other people,'" Casey said. "He even came into my home. And when I was making $140,000, I could do no wrong. But when I started making $600,000, I was 'terrible.'"

After retiring as a player in 1998, Casey completed his college degree. He lives in De Soto, Missouri, southwest of St. Louis, where he and the former Brenda Olason celebrated their thirty-sixth anniversary in 2021.

I tried repeatedly through phone calls and letters to appeal to Jon, even enlisting former teammates and coaches to intervene. Unfortunately, nothing brought a response. If he ever decides to add his perspective, doubtless a second edition will be necessary.

"For a guy who didn't want to speak off the ice, the rink was his stage," Gagner said. "He was clever and witty but very quiet. With his glasses on, he looked like a guy you'd see in the library."

Neal Broten 🏆 (Won 1995 Stanley Cup; April 29, 1997, Edmonton at Dallas)

Broten (11–29–59, Roseau, Minnesota) moved with the franchise and scored the first goal in Dallas Stars history.

"I played all my youth hockey in northern Minnesota and with the University of Minnesota for two years and then with the North Stars for thirteen," said Broten, who was even based in his home state with the 1980 Olympic team. "For the first time in 1993, I left Minnesota and played somewhere else. It was kind of surreal. I knew where Texas was, but I had only been there once before. It didn't really hit me until the moving van pulled up in my driveway and they started moving the furniture down to Dallas.

"Once we got down there, the people were really awesome and treated us great. It was kind of refreshing and something different. It re-energized my career. I would have rather stayed in Minnesota and played there, but you've got to do what you've got to do."

He was traded to New Jersey on February 27, 1995, under the perception that his playing days were winding down. Instead, despite being the oldest player on the Devils, Broten finished second in team scoring with 19 points in 20 playoff games. He scored four game-winning goals, including in Games 3 and 4 of the finals, the last of which made him the first American-born player to clinch the Cup. New Jersey captain Ken Daneyko later said that, without Broten, the Devils don't win.

"I would have rather won a Stanley Cup in Minnesota," Broten said. "I had more connection with that organization. Not to say that winning in New Jersey wasn't awesome; it was. But it would have meant more to me if it was in Minnesota."

He became the first player to win an NCAA championship, an Olympic gold medal, and the Stanley Cup. Ed Belfour joined him on that very short list in 2002. Unlike Belfour, Broten accomplished the first two of the three—and had a crack at the third—in a span of barely two years and before he was 22.

"I felt like, 'This is pretty smooth sailing,'" Broten said of his career through 1981. "You just feel how fortunate you are to be involved with the University of Minnesota, which was a great team, and then the Olympic team, which was a Cinderella upset story, then with the North Stars and making it all the way to the final. It's hard to get to that final again. It's a tough road."

In '96–97, Broten was traded to Los Angeles, released, and returned to Dallas for the final twenty games of his career. In 1,099 regular-season NHL appearances (876 with the North Stars), he scored 289 goals and had 634 assists. In 135 playoff games (104 for Minnesota), he added 35 goals and 63 assists.

In 1997, he entertained a reporter at his 75-acre farm near River Falls, Wisconsin, wearing a Vikings hat, work boots, a flannel shirt, and holey blue jeans. Broten was cleaning horse stalls—and not necessarily disliking it.

"There's not much pressure in this job," he said, "unless you get kicked."

At the time, his daughters, Brooke and Larissa, were fourteen and twelve, respectively.

The Stars retired his No. 7 on February 7, 1998, just a few weeks after he'd been on hand to unveil the Wild logo in St. Paul. "It doesn't seem appropriate for my number to be hanging in Dallas, but I'm not going to say no," he said.

He was inducted into the US Hockey Hall of Fame in 2000.

Broten was named a grass-roots advisor prior to the Wild's inaugural season in 2000–01, helping build awareness in the Twin Cities and around the state. It was on one of his visits to St. Cloud that I talked with him in-depth about the '90–91 season.

"We didn't think we had a chance going into the playoffs, but once we started winning, then we started thinking about it," Broten said. "Those playoffs were one of the highlights of my career. Beating those teams—Chicago, St. Louis and Edmonton—was exhilarating. But losing to Pittsburgh was one of the toughest experiences of my life.... We thought we had a chance to win the Cup, and then, to get beaten 8–0 in the sixth game of the finals, it was humiliating."

Broten remained with the Wild, making appearances on the team's behalf through the 2002–03 season. But...

"I got kind of bored with that," he said. "That's not what I enjoy doing. (Wild GM Doug Risebrough) said, 'If you're interested, you could be a scout for us.' Scout? That's on the road five days a week. I played over 1,000 games and went to the rink twice a day for seventeen years, except for the summer. I needed a break. I just kind of had my fill with hockey. I just like to sit back and maybe go to a few games every now and then. I just hang back."

The modern NHL became a different world to him.

"I don't really know anyone who is playing anymore," Broten said. "I don't follow it very closely. I couldn't tell you who is in first place or who is in last place."

Lou Nanne said that's easy to understand—if you understand Broten.

"What he loved about the game was playing the game," said Nanne, who served as Broten's agent in his final season. "He didn't get involved in other parts of the game, like management, coaching, or any of that stuff. He just loved playing the game. He had a tremendous amount of fun playing the game. It was a joy for him. It didn't matter if he was playing in an outdoor rink or the Stanley Cup playoffs. He felt the same way about it. That's his attitude."

For a while, Broten's mornings typically started around 7 a.m., tending to the forty-four horses of the Sally Broten Horse Company. But they began selling those horses a decade ago (making more off the receipts than he ever took home in an NHL season), and he increasingly spent much of his time removing snow during the winter and working the grounds during the summer.

"I kind of just do what I want to do," Broten told NHL.com in 2014. "Summers are a lot of mowing and keeping the place looking halfway decent; golf two or three days a week. That's about it. There is no schedule. I do what I want to do. It's a nice situation. I could get a job and go to work and have to put on a suit or whatever. Go to Minneapolis and go to work and give the government half of what I make. I have enough money to be happy and do what I want to do. We don't live an extravagant lifestyle. Some days I do nothing. Other days, I babysit (my grandchildren) until 5 o'clock and come home and have dinner and relax."

Perhaps all wasn't idyllic, however. In 2019, he was arrested a third time for drunken driving, following previous convictions in 1995 and 2003. All were in western Wisconsin. He and Sally also divorced. He now has two grandsons a 20-minute drive away with one of their daughters.

Neal proved to be enigmatic to many of his former teammates, and—like Casey—couldn't be roused by phone and text messages or other attempts to convince him to participate in the preparation of this book beyond our long ago interview. Regardless, it's virtually impossible to overestimate his importance to hockey in Minnesota—or underestimate his desire to get credit for it.

"I was struggling to make the team and had a two-goal game one night," recalled Dave Gagner, who roomed with Broten for five seasons. "The other team had pulled their goalie. Neal was out there, but he came off the ice after only about ten seconds because I was up. At the time, he was getting criticized in the papers because he wasn't producing. But he was the kind of guy who wanted to help me. He was so unselfish. Even when people were picking on him for a lack of production, it was more important to Neal that he be regarded by his teammates as a good team guy."

Even if he didn't say much.

"Neal was pretty quiet," Mike Modano said. "We were both quiet guys, but Neal had a real inviting kind of attitude and personality where you could come to him and talk about anything. He was very supportive of me. And he was a great guy to watch. Bob Gainey would tell me, 'Just watch Neal and see how he plays.'"

Broten forever will be the North Stars' leader in scoring, assists, games played, seasons, shorthanded goals, playoff games, and playoff assists.

"I'm still always so happy when I see someone wearing an old North Stars jersey or I see a sweatshirt with that old logo on the front," he once said. "I'll always consider myself a Minnesota North Star."

Shane Churla (May 25, 1997, New York Rangers at Philadelphia)

Shane Churla in 2022.

Churla (6–24–65, Fernie, British Columbia) stayed with the Stars until February 17, 1996, when he was traded to Los Angeles. Less than a month later, the Kings sent him to the New York Rangers. By then he'd injured just about everything possible in his left knee. Doctors even tried using ligaments from a cadaver to extend his career. But Churla developed a staph infection, and the ligaments had to be removed. The only alternative in 1997 would have been a knee replacement.

"At that point, a prosthetic knee only had a life expectancy of about six to seven years," said Churla, who suffered his original injury against St. Louis in the '91 playoffs. "At my age, I was going to go way by that. They said it would be best to let technology catch up and go as long as you can."

He told me the only recurring physical issues he has today are with his neck from, "all those years of guys trying to steal my head."

In 488 career NHL regular-season games (246 for the North Stars), Churla had 26 goals and 45 assists—and 2,301 penalty minutes. His average of 4.72 PIM per game ranks No. 1 all-time among players with at least 2,000 and is likely to never be topped. Chris Nilan (4.42), Kelly Chase (4.40), Dave Schultz (4.29), and Basil McRae (4.27) round out the top five.

Churla, who had five goals, seven assists, and 282 PIM in 78 playoff games (29 for Minnesota), always will believe he was capable of much more than dropping his gloves. In 1992–93, he had a career-best 21 points and got time on Gainey's second power-play unit. But at that point, McRae was gone, Churla was the sheriff, and he didn't have a deputy.

"We weren't very good," Churla said of the North Stars' last season in Minnesota. "Let me make that point. That's why I got on the second power play. But (Gainey) was going to allow that transition, and he told me, 'I don't want you to fight as much anymore. I want you on the second power play. We're going to do this.' That's everything that I wanted. But at that point in time, he didn't bring anybody else in and so every time something went sideways, everybody's looking down the bench at me. I was in a tough spot. I still think about that quite a bit."

Along with Modano, Churla was one of the Stars' most popular players in the early years in Dallas, when they introduced hockey to the American South. While Modano was unequivocally their best player, it was Churla—a second cousin to former Super Bowl XXVI MVP Mark Rypien—who routinely was announced last during pregame player introductions. In a market where football is religion, fans craved Churla's smash-mouth style and treated him like a rock star.

"I wouldn't say it was embarrassing, but I didn't feel right around my teammates with that," said Churla, who nonetheless said Dallas was probably the best stop of his career.

After he retired, Churla spent a few years as a brown bear hunting guide in Alaska, then became a scout for Arizona in 2000, Dallas in 2005, and moved into a similar role with Montreal in 2013. He often attended more than 200 games per year. And just because he wasn't lacing up skates anymore didn't mean he couldn't still be pugnacious. On April 20, 2011, he was arrested for a misdemeanor in a road rage incident near Eau Claire, Wisconsin. But nothing overshadowed his devotion to the game, and on November 23, 2020, he was named director of amateur scouting for the Florida Panthers.

Shane and his first wife, Stephanie, had two daughters (Morgan and Lierin) but later divorced. He's remarried, and when not in Florida or scouting around the world, lives with his second wife, Melissa, on Flathead Lake near Kalispell, Montana.

"I know what era I played in and what my role was, but it's always funny to me when I talk to some of these young lads and they go, 'Man! That was a tough series we just played in,'" Churla said. "You just kind of snicker to yourself and go, 'You have no idea.' If a team was up 3–0 (in the 1990s), it would usually turn into a four-hour game. Now, you can watch an 8–0 game and nobody gets mad. Now that I'm on the building side, I kind of have to park that stuff. But you still want highly competitive people. That's always a gene I look for in anybody that we draft."

Would he scout Shane Churla?

"I always played my best hockey in the playoffs, when fighting wasn't as prevalent," said Churla, who had 5 goals, 7 assists, and 260 PIM in 78 playoff appearances (29 for Minnesota and all but 26 with the Stars' organization). "One thing I could do is I could skate and pressure and get there and put bodies on people. Unfortunately, guys don't like to get hit. So, they take exception to it, and next thing you know, you're in a dust-up. Today's game is fast; a lot faster than it was when I was playing. But I know I could play because of that ability to skate. And you have to remember, at that time (thirty years ago), every time you went in to forecheck somebody, you had that guy's D-partner waterskiing off your back. They could do anything they wanted then, and in this game (today), they can't. But you still have Tom Wilsons running around, and when you get in the playoffs, the games get hard, so you need toughness."

One of the toughest to ever play, Churla has a soft spot for the '91 North Stars, how close they came, and how painful it was to fall short.

"I'll walk with those guys for the rest of my life off that team," he told me. "That's something we'll always have. When I watch the Stanley Cup Finals today, I put myself in the shoes of the loser, because I know how he's feeling. I think I know how excited I would be to win, because I know how bad it felt to lose it. They never talk about those guys. They always just remember who won. To this day, it still bothers me. I'm still in the same business, trying to do the same thing more than thirty years later: trying to win the Stanley Cup."

Brian Glynn (October 8, 1997, Pittsburgh at Hartford)

Glynn (11–23–67, Iserlohn, Germany) signed a three-year, one-way contract in September 1991, guaranteeing him an NHL salary for the first time in his career. Fortunately, he and his wife, Cindy, were renting an apartment in Bloomington. He went minus-16 through the first 37 games and was traded to Edmonton on January 21, 1992. He went plus-11 with the Oilers the remainder of that season but was minus-13 in '92–93. In training camp the following September, he was traded to Ottawa for future considerations. The Senators placed him on waivers in February 1994, and he was claimed by Vancouver.

Glynn had a second brush with the Cup and came even closer with the Canucks in the '94 finals, losing to the New York Rangers in seven games after trailing 3–1 in the series. He played in seventeen playoff games that year, including all seven against New York.

"While you're going through those first three rounds, everything's good," Glynn told me. "The Rangers were up 3–1 and people started talking about the parade routes and that fired us up. We got it back to 3–3, and there was the same thing (that happened in Minnesota): Are we going to fly the wives in? All of a sudden, guys are thinking about things they wouldn't have in the first few series. Instead of, 'How do we get this job done?' it's like, 'I need tickets' or, 'I've got this family member coming in,' and you kind of lose focus. So I've been on two teams that went through that."

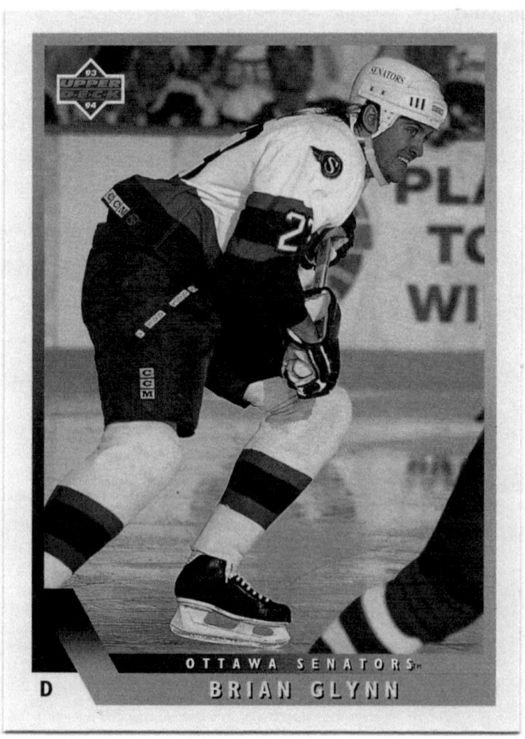

In January 1995, Glynn was claimed on waivers again, this time by Hartford. After a full season with the Whalers, he played in the season opener on October 8, 1996, and the following day was a throw-in on a trade that moved Brendan Shanahan to Detroit for Keith Primeau and Paul Coffey. Glynn was sent to San Antonio of the IHL and never joined the Red Wings. He played in 1997–98 in Germany, where he'd been born when his father was serving in the Canadian armed forces. By then, he and Cindy had two daughters. The oldest was starting kindergarten, and he decided he'd had enough hockey at age thirty. He retired after 431 career NHL games (103 with the North Stars), in which he had 25 goals and 79 assists. In 57 career playoff games (23 of them on the'91 run), he added another six goals and 10 assists.

They settled in Cindy's hometown of Prince Albert, Saskatchewan, a city of about 35,000 that is nonetheless the third-largest city in the province. He was an insurance broker for five years, then an assistant coach with Swift Current of the WHL for one season. He said he "was a terrible insurance salesman and not a very good hockey coach."

At thirty-seven, he submitted an application to join the Prince Albert Police Service.

"I thought I was way too old and they'd never hire me," Glynn said in 2021. "That was in 2005, and I've been here ever since."

After attending police school in Regina, with most other candidates in their early 20s, Glynn became an officer and spent fifteen years on patrol. He saw situations that make the crease in front of a net in the Stanley Cup playoffs look tame. He's negotiated with people at risk for suicide or who have barricaded themselves from authorities. In 2019, he was promoted to sergeant overseeing six officers who handle traffic enforcement and others who do foot patrol and community relations. His duties are mostly in an office now, and he doesn't work nights.

"It's a nice change because, after fifteen years of working the street, there are a lot of things you see and do that are awful and terrible," Glynn said. "I'm not going to hide from it. It took its toll on me. I ended up going to the hospital because I thought something was going on. It turns out I just had a panic attack. There's been some anxiety and mental health stuff, but I took some time to work through it and things are good. I'm in the right spot at the right time. Some people are great investigators and others cut out for something else. But I think where I excel most is being a street cop. I love being on the street. I'm in a break period right now and embracing that and enjoying that. But before I'm done, I'll go back to the street. That's where I belong."

His daughters, born in 1993 and 1995, both excelled as volleyball players. The oldest, Tori, played at the University of Regina and now teaches high school in Prince Albert. His younger daughter, Lauren, played at St. Johns River College in Palatka, Florida, and later returned home and applied with the police service to be a dispatcher. After three years, she began training in 2021 to follow in her father's footsteps and become a constable.

"Hockey seems like it was another lifetime," Glynn told me. "Police work is the closest thing I've ever done to being an athlete on a team. My twelve-year pro career was great training for me to become a police officer. In our city, we have about 100 sworn members and forty-eight of them work in the patrol section. You have four platoons of twelve, and you have a staff sergeant, who is kind of like your head coach, and a sergeant who is like an assistant coach. The rest of you are brothers and sisters, and at the end of the day, you work as a team and your teammates are the most important things to you as police officers. Yes, we carry guns and we play for keeps and do what we do, but it's so similar. I loved being a hockey player and all the things that came with it, but I love being a policeman more."

Jim Johnson (November 11, 1997, Tampa Bay at Phoenix)

Johnson (8–9–62, New Hope, Minnesota) stayed with the Stars into their first season in Dallas.

"It was disappointing," Johnson told me. "I thought Minnesota should have hockey way over Dallas. But that's my job. I'm going to go down there and play."

Jim and his wife, Jody, had a house in Bloomington by then and put it up for sale in August 1993, when they went to look at homes in Dallas. As the real estate agent drove them around, the sun baked Texas in 110-degree heat.

"I sweat pushing a pencil," Johnson said. "By the time we get to the second house, I've got a towel, and I handed $20 to the agent and said, 'Keep the car running. Keep the air on.' By the second day, I was like, 'Jody, we can't live here in the summer. I can't train in this fucking humidity. Why are we selling our house?'"

Jim Johnson in 2022.

They took it off the market and rented in Dallas.

"I think (the Stars) looked at it like I wasn't committed," he said.

On March 21, 1994, Johnson was traded to Washington for Alan May. (The same Alan May who incensed Johnson on January 17, 1991, the night the North Stars started their climb from rock bottom.) In 1996, Phoenix GM Bobby Smith convinced Johnson to sign with the Coyotes. But he retired in 1998 following issues with concussions. He had more than a half-dozen during his career, including two that knocked him out. The cumulative effects made each more difficult. At the beginning of the '97–98 season, he was checked and hit the back of his head on a stanchion near the bench. Three weeks later, he got knocked out again and began suffering serious symptoms.

"For the first time in my professional career, my wife had to wake me up to go to the morning skate," Johnson said. "I was tired. It's like I was out of shape or something. Jody was like, 'Jimmy, you're one of the best conditioned guys for the Coyotes at thirty-six. You're not out of shape.' I knew something was wrong. I'd walk to the mailbox and get back, and I'd have to lay down and sleep. I kept sleeping. And she'd wake me up. She'd wake me up for the game."

On November 11, 1997, in a home game against Tampa Bay, Johnson scored a goal against Darren Puppa.

"I couldn't even see the net," Johnson said. "It was blurry. I knew something was wrong when I got back to the bench, and I couldn't read the board advertising. I called the trainer over, but I finished that game, which is amazing in hindsight."

That was his 829th and last career regular-season game. Johnson, who played in 194 with the North Stars, had 29 goals, 166 assists, and totaled 1,197 penalty minutes. In 51 playoff games (21 for Minnesota), he added one goal, 11 assists, and another 132 PIM.

He wrestled with post-concussion syndrome for another two and a half years. He couldn't get on a ladder. He often slept sixteen hours a day. After the first few months, he went to the Mayo Clinic, where he was diagnosed by Drs. Ronald Petersen and David Dodick, two of the foremost head trauma experts in the world. Petersen once treated Muhammad Ali. After a week of tests and driving back and forth from Bloomington, they told him his brain was functioning at thirty percent capacity.

"They were 99.9 percent sure I would recover, but if I went back and played and got hurt again, they were dealing with people who were functioning like a twelve-year-old for the rest of their life," Johnson said. "They asked 'Could you do that?' I said, 'Nope.' I realized at that time that my career was over. I called my wife on the way home and told her."

Dodick remains Johnson's attending physician. He still visits the Mayo Clinic once a year, but feels fully recovered.

The Coyotes honored Johnson's contract, which ran through 1999. In return, he was a consultant, did some broadcasting, and helped with coaching and player development. He was an assistant to Bobby Francis when the latter won the Jack Adams Award (coach of the year) in 2002. Two years later, after the staff was fired following an ownership change that brought in Wayne Gretzky, the Johnsons decided to stay in Phoenix to raise their family. In addition to their son, Derik, they had a daughter, Mia, just before the move to Dallas.

Jim coached with the US National Team Development Program, but found that took him away from home as many as 200 days per year.

"I was coaching the (2002 US) World Junior team in the Czech Republic and Derik said, 'Dad, I wish you'd just coach me,'" Jim said. "I broke down and said, 'That's it.'"

He coached youth hockey in Arizona and co-founded flexxCOACH, a web-based program that provides practice plans and education. He coached the VOSHA (Valley of the Sun Hockey Association) Mustangs to a USA Hockey Amateur National Championship in 2005 and established a Phoenix elite program sponsored by P. F. Chang's.

"I started getting calls to come back to the NHL, and I kept turning them down," said Jim, whose son had moved away to play junior hockey in 2008. "Finally, I said, 'Jody, I better jump at this because eventually they're not going to call anymore.'"

He was an assistant with Tampa Bay from 2008–10. After a year in Switzerland, he went to Washington in '11–12 and moved to San Jose the following season. In 2015, he followed former Sharks head coach Todd McLellan to Edmonton, serving there until 2018. After a year off, he became associate head coach at San Antonio of the AHL. When the team moved and became an affiliate of the Vegas Golden Knights and COVID shut down other AHL opportunities for '20–21, Blues GM Doug Armstrong brought Johnson to St. Louis to work with their young defensemen. In 2022, he became director of player development for the Anaheim Ducks.

Derik played defense (naturally) at Minnesota-Duluth (naturally) and went on to a three-year pro career that topped out in the AHL. He became a minor-league video coach for Edmonton and Los Angeles and, in 2022, became a skills coach for the Kings.

Jim and Jody have spent their offseasons at a home on Gull Lake near Brainerd since 1993. They also keep a condo in Scottsdale, Arizona. They celebrated their thirty-fifth wedding anniversary in 2021.

"You build memories off teams that have success," said Jim, who said the most fun of his thirteen-year playing career came during the '91 playoffs. "That group of people was special.... We didn't have the ultimate success, but one way or another, just about everybody from that team has gone on to success, and I'm still chasing that dream—even today."

Mark Tinordi (February 22, 1999, Toronto at Washington)

Tinordi (5–9–66, Red Deer, Alberta) suffered nerve damage to his left leg (foot palsy) when he was struck by a dump-in from Al MacInnis on October 15, 1991. Tinordi returned six weeks later and captained the Stars before and after they moved to Texas. He played one season in Dallas but suffered a broken femur on February 23, 1994, at Los Angeles when he lost his balance and crashed into the end boards during a race with John Druce to touch the puck for icing. Tinordi recovered during the '94–95 lockout and was traded to Washington a week after play resumed. He lost a shot at the Cup with the Capitals in '98 (swept by Detroit) and was picked in the '99 expansion draft by the Atlanta Thrashers but chose to retire.

In 663 career regular-season NHL games (314 with the North Stars), he totaled 52 goals, 148 assists, and 1,514 penalty minutes. In 70 playoff games (42 with Minnesota), he added another seven goals, 11 assists, and 165 PIM.

Tinordi and his first wife, Lorene, divorced soon after he stopped playing. They had four children (Matt, Jarred, Ellie, and Jake). Matt and Jarred had been born in Burnsville, the latter a year before they moved to Dallas. Mark coached them through youth hockey and with the Washington Junior Nationals of the Atlantic Junior Hockey League, for whom he also served as director of the team's college development program.

"It was fun, but it's really hard here," said Mark, who settled in Millersville, Maryland, about thirty miles east of Washington, DC. "These kids here, you can't believe they do what they do to play hockey. The odds of success in Maryland are tough. Very few kids play Division I, let alone make the NHL. We had to drive an hour to practice, each way, several times a week. That's a lot when kids are going to school. We played teams in Philadelphia, which was an hour and forty-five minutes away. Most of the others were in New Jersey and New York. We'd go to showcases in Boston. One year, I think we went there seven times. It's a lot of travel and a lot of weekends gone, so it was a full-time commitment."

Matt played at RPI, where he was a captain as a senior, and went on to a brief career in the ECHL.

Jarred joined the US National Team Development Program, played for London of the OHL, and was a first-round draft pick of the Montreal Canadiens in 2010. He's had a spotty NHL career with six teams, ultimately landing in Chicago in 2022, where Blackhawks fans now cheer *for* a Tinordi.

While Mark occasionally would run across former teammates when he was coaching or following his sons on their paths to the pros, he's fallen out of touch with most.

"No one retires here," he said of the suburban DC area. "Peter Bondra (a former Caps forward) is about the only one. A lot of guys stayed in Dallas or went to Florida or they're from Toronto. In those places, if you're a former hockey player, you're out at charity golf events or doing things where you hear stuff about your former teammates. For me, once hockey was over, it's like, '*Poof*.' That was the end of that.... Now all my friends have nothing to do with hockey."

Mark married his second wife, Jessica, in 2010. Two years later, he transitioned from coaching into the hospitality industry. He was one of several investors who turned a former biker hangout in nearby Severna Park into a sports bar.

"It's your typical bar or restaurant story, I think," he said. "We were getting in as silent partners and weren't going to have anything to do with it, and the main guy got off the rails, and we ended up having to buy him out to keep it moving. So, me and another guy have owned it for about eight years. I go in every day. Jessica runs it, but we do the daily stuff. It's a lot of work."

Severna Park Taphouse played host to the Stanley Cup for a day in 2018. After the Caps finally won it for the first time in franchise history, Zach Leonsis, son of Washington owner Ted Leonsis, brought it to Tinordi's establishment for a day-long party.

"It was fun," Mark said. "We got some pictures of the staff with the Cup."

But not as fun as it would've been twenty-seven years earlier if the North Stars had just gotten a few more breaks as Tinordi went from journeyman to star.

"He was known as a very reliable and tough defensive guy that nobody wanted to play against because he was so mean," Gagner said of Tinordi. "Nobody knew Mark's hockey sense was off the charts. All of a sudden, after we traded Larry Murphy to Pittsburgh, Mark was given an opportunity to play on the power play and add some offensive flair to his game. He was so calm at the point with the puck, and nobody even knew that existed. It was unbelievable how he emerged. Mark just became a force in all areas of the ice. The maturation process must've happened in about a week. He shocked a lot of guys that year."

Neil Wilkinson (March 27, 1999, Buffalo at Pittsburgh)

Wilkinson (8–15–67, Selkirk, Manitoba) played in San Jose from 1991 to '93. Traded to Chicago, his one season with the Blackhawks culminated in the final game at Chicago Stadium. He signed with Winnipeg and essentially played in his hometown until Christmas 1995.

"On the morning of December 26, we flew to Chicago," Wilkinson recalled for this book. "We get in the hotel, and I get a phone call from (Jets GM) John Paddock. 'We've made a deal. We just acquired Norm MacIver for you.' I'm like, 'Fuck, John, I do not want to go to Ottawa.' He said, 'Neil, Norm was playing for Pittsburgh.' I said, 'What time is my flight?'"

While eager to join the Penguins, abdominal injuries plagued Wilkinson in Pittsburgh and ultimately forced his retirement in 1999.

"My last three years in Pittsburgh, I had five sports hernia surgeries," he said. "Given the choice of hockey or (being able to have) kids, I decided to walk away from hockey."

In 460 career regular-season NHL games (86 with the North Stars), he totaled 16 goals, 67 assists, and 830 penalty minutes. In 53 playoff games (29 for Minnesota), he had three goals, six assists, and just 41 PIM. He was minus-93 for his career—an incredible minus-50 rating with the Sharks in '92–93 accounting for most of that. San Jose was 11–71–2 that season, its .143 winning percentage second-worst in NHL history to the 1974–75 Washington Capitals (8–67–5, .131).

Neil and his wife, Kristin, moved to Durango, Colorado, and had their first child (a daughter, Muriel, named for both of their mothers).

"I always said I wasn't getting married until after my career," he said. "The reason was I wanted to be around to raise my kids. I watched guys for years miss things in their kids' lives."

But in 2002, he was offered chance to play with the Tulsa Oilers of the Central Hockey League—with the caveat that he would get into coaching.

"I wanted to have fun again playing hockey because the last three years in Pittsburgh were not fun," he said. "I wanted to leave the game on a good note. I loved it going in and didn't want to hate it going out."

In 2003–04, he played for the Jacksonville (Florida) Barracudas of the WHA2 and had a stint with the Fresno Falcons of the ECHL with the possibility of becoming their head coach. In the end, he decided family time was more valuable.

The Wilkinsons went back to Colorado and had a son (Cayden Maxx, who goes by Maxx). For eight years there, Neil was a stay-at-home dad. He would take his daughter, barely old enough to speak, riding in the wilderness on an ATV. She would huddle inside his hunting jacket while clutching the handlebars. When they saw deer, she would call them "jumpy jumps."

"Those memories are invaluable to me," Neil said. "It feels like it was a few days ago, and it was really seventeen years ago when she was two. That's what's important to me now. Not the kind of car I drive."

After Kristin's father developed cancer, they moved to Sherwood, Oregon, to be near her parents. As the kids got older and Neil had more freedom, he took a job mowing at a golf course—at least in part so he could play for free.

"I was working one day and they brought in a tree crew, and they were removing a tree," he said. "A guy climbed up and started cutting stuff and I said, 'You know what? I want to do that.'"

So, he went to work for a tree service. He started on a crew but is now in management—although occasionally he still gets behind a chainsaw.

"I like being outdoors, and I like being active," Wilkinson said. "I can't sit around. Being here in the northwest, you're always guaranteed a job if you're in the tree industry."

In 2009, he started coaching with Sherwood Ice Arena's Learn to Play Hockey Program. In 2011, he was inducted into the Manitoba Hockey Hall of Fame. He began coaching Maxx when he turned ten.

"We have a great relationship," Neil said. "He calls me dad off the ice. He calls me coach when we're on it. And I'm sure he's called me a few other things under his breath."

At sixteen, Maxx attended Elite Hockey Academy in Connecticut. In 2022, he joined the AAA midget Colorado Rampage as a defenseman. Muriel is now at Wellesley College, outside Boston. That puts Neil a long distance from his children, but they're not really kids anymore, and besides, their bonds are unbreakable.

"Mine was a family path more than a professional path," Neil said. "Other guys make different choices and they're happy with that, but I have many blessings in my life and my family is the biggest one. Other than five or six hunting days each year, I spent every day with my kids as they were growing up. I look at where I've come from to where I am now; I wouldn't change a thing."

Throughout his playing career, he continued to attend Alcoholics Anonymous meetings and was open about discussing his past in the hope his story might help someone else.

"I'm doing great, but I'm still nervous," Wilkinson said of his sobriety. "Back in 1991, I didn't know any better. I didn't know what was important. Now I have everything to lose. I know one is too many, and a thousand is never enough. I never put myself in those situations. I still work the program, and I reach out to people I know and respect when I'm struggling. Because I do struggle. Everybody does. But I've got a good group around who know how to handle me."

It's up to him to deal with any disappointment from the '91 finals.

"It's one of those things where the stars didn't align," Wilkinson told me. "As the playoffs went on, it's like being a tight-rope walker—'Don't look down. Don't look down. Oh, shit! Look how far it is down.' The comeback in Game 5 (of the finals) was a snapshot of our season. We were always down, whether it was in the standings or people's minds. The only thing we could control at that point was what we did on the ice in the next shift. We chipped away. Had we gotten a bounce, maybe the series swings back to us."

More than thirty years later, he still has the Harley-Davidson that Stew Gavin convinced him to buy with his playoff bonus.

"That bike, to me, symbolizes my Stanley Cup," Wilkinson said.

Dave Gagner (April 14, 1999, Calgary at Vancouver)

Gagner (12–11–64, Chatham, Ontario) played for the Stars until 1996, when he got into a contract dispute, played one pro game in Italy as a holdout, and was traded to Toronto. Five months later, he was dealt to Calgary. He signed with Florida in 1997 and in '99 was sent to Vancouver in the trade that brought Pavel Bure to the Panthers.

Retiring after 946 career regular-season NHL games (440 with the North Stars), Gagner totaled 318 goals, 401 assists, and 1,018 penalty minutes (and was minus-65). In 57 playoff games (37 for Minnesota), he added 22 goals, 26 assists, and 64 PIM.

In 2000, Gagner founded Custom Ice Inc., a company that builds permanent and portable skating rinks. It continues to this day. He coached the London Knights, finishing his business degree at Western University along the way. In 2008, he became director of player development for the Canucks, a position he held until 2013, when he became an NHLPA certified agent and director of player development for the (Bobby) Orr Hockey Group. He eventually was named executive vice president at Wasserman Hockey. His duties include advising on finance, contract work, player development, and recruiting for the agency, which counts among its clients Connor McDavid, Auston Matthews, Roman Josi, Jordan Kyrou, and Nick Suzuki.

Dave Gagner in 2022.

Dave and his wife, Jo-Anne, high school sweethearts who have three grandsons and a granddaughter, have been married for thirty-five years and live in Oakville, Ontario.

Their son, Sam, was a first-round pick like his dad and has gone on to a long NHL career that began in 2007 in Edmonton, with stops in Arizona, Philadelphia, Columbus, Vancouver, and Detroit along the way. In 2022 Sam signed with Winnipeg. Their oldest daughter, Jessica, played at Dartmouth. They also have a younger daughter, Renee, born in Dallas, who is an actress based in New York City. It's at least a little ironic that her career is flourishing in the city where Dave's languished in the mid-1980s.

"I felt it was so much easier lifestyle-wise to play in Minnesota because when I was with the Rangers, it was stressful just getting to the rink," he told me. "We lived in Westchester, and I had to drive an hour through traffic, and people were very aggressive on the roads. Coming from a small town in Canada, I felt exhausted by the time I got to practice."

Their home in Apple Valley was footsteps away from Basil and Jill McRae's house, and it was a simple commute to Met Center.

"Literally ten minutes and no traffic," Gagner said. "You'd walk in and walk out, no autograph people. It was like playing junior hockey again. You could just be focused, and all your energy could go toward that instead of just coping with things. We're all different. Some guys wanted the New York thing. They drew adrenalin from it. But it took adrenalin away from me."

He said the '91 playoffs were the most fun he ever had.

"Game 4 against Chicago was the turning point," Gagner recalled for this book. "Our line (with Mike Modano and Brian Propp) didn't have a very good game, and we found a way to win. It really showed how our team had become a unit because everybody was contributing. Everybody. And our power play was unconscious. Of course, we had about 150 opportunities because I was a small guy. Mike wasn't a fight-back kind of guy at the time, and Brian is very competitive but not a fighter. Everybody was going after us hard."

If the North Stars hadn't scored two power-play goals that night, the book you're reading might not exist. But as much as he cherishes 1991, his final weeks in Minnesota are a bitter memory.

"The last two months in Minnesota were a disaster," Gagner said. "We were well within a playoff spot but, after the announcement was made, we just threw in the towel. I guess guys were a little too distracted. Players worry about getting traded, sent down, and what's happening at home—all the things that distract you from being a successful athlete. With a whole team, you can multiply that by twenty. You worry about schools for your kids and whether your wife is going to enjoy the new city. Back then, players weren't used to that type of distraction. Nowadays, there's so much talk about ownership changes and collective bargaining and such, guys are just immune to it."

Our interview came during the height of the COVID pandemic in North America, when Sam was diagnosed with it and consequently inactive for the Red Wings. Dave lamented the restrictions that closed the Canadian border and kept people from socializing. Fortunately, his phone provided a link to McRae, Stew Gavin, and other former teammates.

"I'm not really an extrovert," Gagner said. "I grew up on a farm, so I'm kind of used to social distancing. But my wife is very much a people person, and she found it really tough. It's different for everyone, but I don't think it's good for anyone. You've got to stay busy and do positive things."

Brian Bellows 🏆 (Won 1993 Stanley Cup; April 18, 1999, Washington at Buffalo)

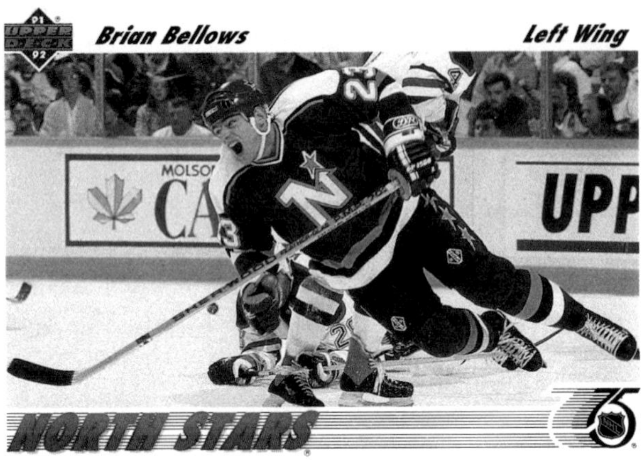

Nicknamed "B. B." or "BeeBee," Bellows (9-1–64, St. Catherines, Ontario) played with the North Stars in 1991–92. On August 31, 1992, he was traded to Montreal for Russ Courtnall. Bob Gainey had decided Bellows "directed his career in the way he thought was best for him."

"The record over the period Brian was here wasn't very good," Gainey told the Associated Press in 1993. "He has to be held accountable."

Bellows struggled to fit into a system he described as a neutral-zone trap, designed to create offense from defense—which was never his strong suit. Initially disappointed to be jettisoned by the franchise, the move turned out to be a good one as the '93 Canadiens won the Cup.

"I think it was Bob Gainey doing me a helluva favor," Bellows said at the time. "He knows how good of an organization this is. I think in his own way he was showing me some respect.

"Well, here I am," Bellows added, standing under a photo of Gainey in the uproar of the victorious Forum dressing room. "After all the bull, it was nice to go somewhere with a clean slate. There was so much bull in Minnesota. The trade rumors. You get blamed for this, you get blamed for that. Different players. Different coaches. Different owners. Then you had to worry about what Norm was going to do. So much bull… Minnesota didn't make the playoffs this year, and I didn't get blamed for it."

Eventually, Bellows said the trade to Montreal made him a more complete player and allowed him to finally understand Gainey.

"He was trying to achieve something with us (in '91) that he had achieved in Montreal," Bellows told me in an interview for this book. "You listen, but I didn't really get it until I was in Montreal in those other shoes. Then you understand the ways they want you to play, and the type of player they want you to be. I was surrounded by a lot of similar-type guys. We had good, quality, talented people—similar to what we had with the North Stars when we went to the finals. There, you had the experience of the team but also the expectations of the city. When you have a Monday night game in Minnesota and a Monday night game in Montreal, there's a huge difference. You get a higher preparation level."

Bellows married Tracy Sullivan on July 25, 1993, a month after winning the Cup. During the summer of '95, he was traded to Tampa Bay for Marc Bureau. Early in the '96–97 season, Bellows was dealt to the Mighty Ducks of Anaheim for a sixth-round pick. He played a portion of '97–98 in Germany but signed with Washington and made it to the finals again with the Capitals (and Mark Tinordi) in '98. Bellows retired in '99 after 1,188 career regular-season NHL games (753 for Minnesota). He posted 1,022 points—722 for the North Stars. He also was a career minus-128, and minus-87 with Minnesota.

For more than twenty years, Bellows has worked as an institutional equity trader for Piper Sandler, which had been Piper Jaffray until 2020. It's similar to what Lou Nanne still does.

"I don't know if I want to be working at 80," Bellows laughed between interruptions by other traders in his Minneapolis office, creating a din that sounded a little like the New York Stock Exchange. "But we both got in fields that are similar to pro sports. Every day you have to prepare, and you have to compete. We both like to talk a lot, too. I'm sure that helps. It's interesting. A lot of the guys who retire now, they don't have to work. How do you transfer for skills and preparation and your discipline on to your kids if they don't see you working? It's a hard thing."

Brian and Tracy live in Edina. Their son, Kieffer, was a first-round pick of the New York Islanders in 2016 and made his NHL debut in February 2020, just before COVID shut down the NHL. In October 2022, he was claimed off waivers by the Philadelphia Flyers. Brian and Tracy also have two daughters, Brianna and Lydia, who played hockey and lacrosse for Edina High School. Brianna lives in New York City, where she works in marketing for United Health Group. Lydia graduated with a degree in advertising and public relations from the University of Nebraska in 2022.

With the passing of time, Bellows has come to grips with how he was often the hero or the goat, depending on whether the North Stars won.

"It was part of the territory," he told me. "I think not having a centerman for the longest time was probably one of the biggest things. I know I picked up when I started playing with Dave Gagner, but we could've had (Steve) Yzerman. That would've made a huge difference. When you're in one place and you've had five or six coaches and three or four GMs, it was like it was always a rebuild."

During the '91 finals, Bellows was on the receiving end of brutal verbal abuse by Kevin Stevens and Bryan Trottier. Video of the rants can still be found on YouTube. It added insult to injury after Bellows suffered a sprained knee on the hit by Ulf Samuelsson.

"That really hurt us," Dave Gagner said. "(Bellows) was really a catalyst for us offensively—so strong on the puck. He was a bear in the corner. He'd have three guys on him, throw them all off and come out with the puck. When he was determined to do something, he could do it. He wasn't really able to compete at his level in the finals because of the injury."

Bellows said the Samuelsson collision resulted in a bone compression injury beneath his right knee.

"I could barely move for the rest of the series," Bellows said. "You try to remember the people across from you are probably in just as bad shape. But it does affect you. It's the Stanley Cup Finals. You live for that and want to perform then."

But he also said the North Stars needed even more than he would've been able to deliver at full strength.

"We needed (Mario) Lemieux's back to go out again," Bellows said. "It was disappointing not to finish it off, but we made a good run. We didn't have a Lemieux or a (Wayne) Gretzky. We were a bunch of guys who had to work hard to succeed, who got along really well, and pulled together to get on a roll."

Shawn Chambers 🏆🏆 (Won 1995 and 1999 Stanley Cups; October 8, 1999, Dallas at Anaheim)

Chambers (10-11-66, Sterling Heights, Michigan) was traded to Washington on June 21, 1991, three weeks after his wedding to the former Lisa Miller. He played two games for the Capitals, and his left knee was a wreck. Whenever he skated, it blew up like a basketball.

Chambers underwent his fourth operation in eighteen months and was selected by Tampa Bay in the '92 expansion draft. Operation number five, which removed floating bone chips, came at the Mayo Clinic in the fall of '92, just before the Lightning followed him to Minnesota for an early-season game.

Shawn Chambers in 2022.

He was given an extensive rehabilitation assignment, and as a result, found a reason to laugh (if not cry) at the release of NHLPA 93, the first hockey video game to feature real player names. It came out in time for Christmas and included the first-year rosters of the Lightning and Ottawa Senators. As video game blogger Jon Bois later pointed out, the player rankings for both expansion teams were not kind. Ottawa's best forward was Sylvain Turgeon with a 62 rating overall, on a 0–99 point scale—an average of composite scores in various skills. Top defenseman Brad Shaw was a 44, and goalie Peter Sidorkiewicz was a 40. The lowest-rated Senators were defensemen Kent Paynter, Darren Rumble and Dominic Lavoie, all of whom were 2s.

Tampa Bay fared a bit better, with top forward Anatoli Semenov a 77, top defenseman Joe Reekie a 60, and goalie Wendell Young a 58. But not Chambers. He was given a 0 in speed, a 0 in agility, a 0 in offensive awareness, a 0 in defensive awareness, a 0 in shot power, a 0 in shot accuracy, a 0 in stickhandling, a 0 in passing accuracy, a 13 in endurance, a 13 in checking, a 66 in aggressiveness and a 0 in fighting. All told, this gave him an overall rating of 1. When Bois wrote about it in 2012, Chambers remained the lowest-rated player in video-game history.

"Oh, yeah. I know, I've got the worst video rating of any sport," Chambers laughed during our interview for this book. "I think the first I ever knew about it was that one of my friends bought it and they were like, 'What the hell?' I'm in the NHL—I should have *some* ability."

After playing just three games in 1993–94, Chambers suffered again from swelling—this time in his right knee—prompting another operation. When it looked like he was going to return, he was involved in a car accident. A swerving motorist forced him off the road and into a tree. Chambers suffered bruised ribs, a bruised shoulder, and a cut over his eye, but he returned less than six weeks later and was only scratched once the rest of the season.

After 145 games over three seasons with the Lightning, on March 14, 1995, he was traded to New Jersey and reunited with Neal Broten. The Devils went 12–7–4 the rest of the way in a 48-game regular season and Chambers played in all 20 postseason games to become the only player ever taken in the NHL's supplemental draft process (which existed from 1986–94) to win the Stanley Cup.

"Other than having kids, that's your ultimate goal and dream—to win the Stanley Cup," Chambers told me. "Ninety-five was super weird… I got traded with Danton Cole, and both our wives were eight months pregnant at the time. We're playing in Philly, and I got a call that my wife was in labor. I went to Tampa, where we were going to play in a few days, so I was there for my baby (birth of his second son, Connor). But my family was in Tampa, and I was in Jersey living in a hotel with Broten. My kid was born March 31st, and we won the Cup June 24th. I think I saw him twice in that time.

"I scored two goals in the fourth game (of the finals), and no one ever wants to show highlights of that. But I was in a car at eight the next morning driving to Detroit because my mom was watching our kids. It was awesome, something I've dreamed about since I was 7 years old playing street hockey, but all I could think about was, 'I've got to get home.' I'd only known those guys for two and a half months. I felt like I was a big part of that hockey team but at the same time, your life moves on."

From 1995 to '97, Chambers played 137 games with New Jersey—his highest two-season total since his first two full seasons with the North Stars. He then signed with Dallas and, in 1999, he and Mike Modano became the only former members of the '91 North Stars to achieve their ultimate goal of winning the Stanley Cup with the franchise. Even then there were echoes of '91. After a collision with Chris Pronger, Chambers had problems with his right knee and had to have it drained during the playoffs. But he played in every game of the finals against Buffalo, including the triple-overtime victory in Game 6.

Chambers played four games the following fall before he went down with yet another knee injury that required yet another operation. It shelved him for the remainder of the season, which was also the last year of his contract. He planned to see two knee specialists during the summer of 2000 but, expecting both to suggest he undergo surgery—for the fourteenth time in nine years—Chambers instead retired.

"I would've played if it was up to me," he said. "I was thirty-two. I was willing to get cortisone shots, whatever it took. But my body couldn't take it anymore."

In 625 career regular-season NHL games (198 for the North Stars), he had 50 goals and 185 assists. In 94 playoff games (33 for Minnesota), he added another seven goals and 26 assists.

Shawn and Lisa have three children: Cody, Connor, and Courtney, who in 2021 were twenty-eight, twenty-five, and twenty-two, respectively. During his playing days, the family had a cabin on Daggett Lake in Crosslake, Minnesota. In retirement, they lived in Ideal Township before moving to a home on Gull Lake, north of Brainerd in 2016.

Shawn coached both of his sons from mites through Pequot Lakes High School. Then he coached a Tier III junior team in Minnesota, and from 2016 to '18, joined the staff of the Prince George Cougars of the WHL. Their head coach was former North Stars teammate Richard Matvichuk.

"I enjoyed it except for the bus rides," Chambers said. "Matty always wanted to leave after the game and ride all night, and we didn't have a sleeper. I'm like, 'I'm too old for this.' I did it for two years, though, and really had fun."

Connor played junior hockey in the US and Canada before going on to Division III Wisconsin-Stout. He graduated in 2020 and even played three games in the Southern Professional Hockey League. Shawn became a grandfather on August 20, 2019, with the birth of Cody's son, Jack Shawn Chambers. Grandpa already got him Rollerblades for Christmas in 2020.

Shawn's place in hockey history is secure, even if more people are probably familiar with his presence for Mario Lemieux's highlight-reel goal in Game 2 of the '91 finals than anything else.

"I think that will be forever remembered," Chambers chuckled. "It was pretty ugly. I don't think I'll ever be forgotten.… That play, it wasn't that bad until they started showing the back angle, and you could see the name on my jersey. Any normal fan isn't going to know who that is, but then they'd show me from the back and ran it in slow motion. My name is as clear as day. To this day, I still have buddies and friends who say, 'Yeah, I saw you on TV last night.'

"But it's all good, the Mario goal and all that stuff. I'm in good company. (Lemieux) was the best player I ever played against. (Wayne) Gretzky is Gretzky, but Mario is Mario. One-on-one, he's the greatest. Gretzky had eyes for everybody. But when it was just you against him, Mario was the greatest. He was so big and so fast that you'd see him coming, and he was around you before you knew it. And his reach was so long; he was a game-changer."

Shawn can only wonder what his career might have become if his left knee would have fully recovered from those early surgeries, including the one before the Pittsburgh series in '91.

"In hindsight, I should either have never played or never had the surgery, one of the two," Chambers said. "If I knew it would be such a setback, I wouldn't have come back so quickly. But nobody told me not to, and it *was* the Stanley Cup Finals."

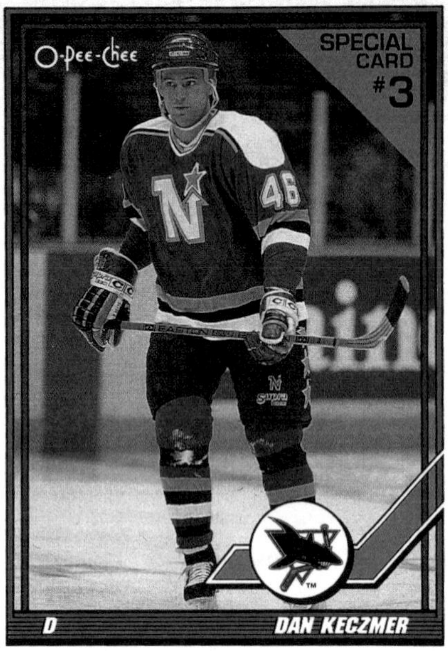

Dan Keczmer (December 2, 1999, Nashville at St. Louis)

Keczmer (5–25–68, Mount Clemens, Michigan), turned twenty-three the day of Game 6 of the '91 finals and went to San Jose in the dispersal draft five days later. But on October 2, 1991, he was moved to Hartford in *another* trade for future Wild coach Dean Evason—this one preceding Gaetan Duchesne's exchange by more than a year. Keczmer was dealt to Calgary in '93 and New Jersey in '96. But he only played in the minors for the Devils. Then Dallas signed him as a free agent. Bob Gainey liked Keczmer enough to convert him from defense to left wing in 1998. It prolonged his NHL career, but he was placed on waivers on March 12, 1999, just before the Stars won the Cup. Nashville picked him up, and he played forty games over two seasons with the Predators. He was traded to St. Louis in 2000 but retired after twenty-five games in the AHL.

In 235 career regular-season NHL games (9 with the North Stars), Keczmer had eight goals and 38 assists. He had one assist in 12 playoff games (none with Minnesota).

Keczmer settled in Brentwood, Tennessee, and in 2012 became vice president of sales and marketing for Carlin O'Brian Batson, a food broker and manufacturer representative. As recent as 2016, he also coached high school hockey at Ravenwood High School in Brentwood.

Marc Bureau (March 23, 2000, Calgary at Buffalo)

Bureau (5–19–66, Trois-Rivieres, Quebec) went home after the 1991 playoffs and trained hard for '91–92.

"Nobody told me I was going to stay the next year," he told me in an interview for this book. "I came to camp in great shape, expecting to make the team."

With Neal Broten holding out, Bureau was used on the point on the power play during the preseason. But after Broten signed, Bureau got much less ice time. He scored one goal and had one assist through 15 games, prompting a demotion to Kalamazoo.

"They said, 'Go get your confidence back,'" Bureau recalled. "I had 10 points in seven games and they brought me back. But it's like what happened to Perry Berezan. Even if I didn't know him from before, Perry was a great guy. They put me in his spot, and he didn't bitch me… That year after, they did the same to me. They brought Todd Elik in, and they put him in my position. We went to the playoffs against Detroit and lost. I didn't have much ice time there, and my season was kind of so-so."

In '91–92, Bureau had 10 points in 46 regular-season games and was shut out while playing in five of the seven postseason games against the Red Wings.

Bureau was left exposed in the '92 expansion draft, and former Calgary coach Terry Crisp wanted him in Tampa Bay. After three seasons with the Lightning, he was traded to Montreal for Brian Bellows. After three seasons with the Canadiens, Bobby Clarke signed Bureau to play in Philadelphia. He was traded back to Calgary at the deadline in 2000. The next fall, at Saint John of the AHL, he suffered a career-ending back injury in practice.

In 567 career regular-season NHL games (55 for the North Stars), he had 55 goals and 83 assists. In 50 playoff games (28 for Minnesota), he added five goals and seven assists.

"I'd played baseball before I went to major junior," Bureau told me in 2021. "I was a catcher, and I had back problems then. My L5 and L4 vertebrae were cracked. I'd been born that way. At fifteen, the doctors warned me to stop playing hockey. No way. But at thirty-five, I was sore and not able to get out of bed. I went to Calgary, and they looked at it. They basically told me to go home and go to a chiropractor. Now, I have no troubles, and I'm feeling OK."

Marc Bureau (left) looks like he could still take a few faceoffs. He retired as a player after he and his wife, Louise (center), had a son, Alex (right), who went on to be a goalie in the Quebec Major Junior Hockey League. (Photo courtesy of Marc Bureau)

Another reason Marc had for hanging up his skates was that he and his wife, Louise, had a son, Alex, on February 1, 1996. By 2001, Alex was ready to start school.

"I remember Jeremy Duchesne was (almost) 7 when he knew he was going to be moving to San Jose," Bureau said. "My wife and I were there, and he said to his mom and dad, 'Go ahead. I'm not going.' All of his friends were in Minnesota. It's hard on the kids to go to another school and in a different language."

In retirement, Marc appeared on a French-language television sports program in Quebec. It was called "110%," a Québécois sports, Habs-centric show where talking heads debated every weeknight. Other primary debaters were former coaches like Jean Perron and Michel Bergeron, ex-players like Dave Morissette and PJ Stock, or journalists and Québécois celebrities. The show ran until 2009.

By then, Marc had coached Alex through the Atom and Peewee levels of Canadian youth hockey.

"Then I let him go," Marc said. "My dream was always to have a coffee and sit in the stands and watch him play."

Alex ultimately became a goalie and played three seasons in the QMJHL. He's since gone on to become a history teacher.

Marc maintains a connection to hockey as a coaching consultant specializing in faceoff technique.

"Bob (Gainey) was always using me in those key faceoff situations, and I always take pride in my percentage," Bureau said. "I never had a season below 51 percent."

While faceoffs didn't become an official NHL statistic until 1997, Bureau won 53.4 percent of his draws from 1997–2001—ranking him among the top twenty-five during that era among players with at least 200 games. One of the pupils he later tutored in the QMJHL was Patrice Bergeron. Through 2022, Bergeron had the highest faceoff winning percentage (57.5) of any center with at least 700 career NHL games. In interviews with the *Boston Globe* and New England Sports Network, Bergeron credited Bureau for helping him hone his skill.

Marc and Louise are still married and have lived in Trois-Rivieres since he retired, but he says he'll never forget his time in Minnesota. Two nights before I talked with him, Game 2 of the '91 finals—complete with Lemieux's breakaway goal against Bureau's line—was re-aired in Quebec.

"I had to check him and play against him in short-handed situations," Bureau said of Lemieux. "I'd played against him in junior when he was playing in Laval."

In 1983–84, Bureau had 22 points in 56 games for the Chicoutimi Sagueneens, and Lemieux had 282 points in 70 games for the Laval Voisins.

"You've got two great players in Mario Lemieux and Wayne Gretzky," Bureau said. "I know (Lemieux) is a French guy, but he was the toughest. You can see all the highlights where he has a guy over his back. Wayne was a smart player and he could see to pass the puck, but Mario never had the same team around him Gretzky had in Edmonton.

"I remember I went to hit him one time when he had back problems," Bureau added of Lemieux. "I lined him up and it was like, 'Pow!' Running into a blank wall. I saw him a few years ago when he was with Marc Bergevin (who was GM of the Canadiens), and Mario called me over and said, 'Hey, Marc. How is your shoulder?' He had the size and the moves. For me, he's the best player there was."

And there's no shame in losing to the best.

"When we won against Edmonton and they brought the Clarence Campbell trophy in the room, I remember you'd look at Bob, and you couldn't see whether he was happy or not," Bureau said. "But he took his jacket off, and he had sweat underneath his armpits, and the pressure kind of (Bureau makes a long exhaling sound) in the room. It was kind of our Stanley Cup."

Frantisek Musil (January 5, 2001, Edmonton at Chicago)

Musil (12–17–64, Pardubice, Czech Republic) played for Calgary until he was traded to Ottawa in 1995. The Senators sent him to Edmonton in '98. He suffered a spinal cord injury when he fell head-first into the boards during an Oilers practice on October 2, 1999. He missed the entire season but came back in 2000–01 before suffering another injury. He attempted a brief comeback in his native country in '01–02 and then retired.

In 797 career regular-season games, Musil totaled 34 goals, 106 assists, and 1,241 penalty minutes. He had two goals, four assists, and 47 PIM in 42 playoff games (9 for Minnesota). None of them ever came after the first round.

After his playing career, Musil became a scout for Edmonton and an assistant with the Czech national team. His son, David, made it to the NHL briefly with the Oilers, collecting two assists in four games during the spring of 2015. Another son, Adam, was drafted by St. Louis that same year and played a couple of seasons in the AHL. Both have since migrated to play in the Czech Republic. Frantisek's daughter, Dana, played volleyball at the University of Buffalo.

As of 2022, Frantisek was a scout for the Buffalo Sabres covering Eastern Europe.

Larry Murphy (Won 1991, 1992, 1997 and 1998 Stanley Cups; April 23, 2001, Detroit at Los Angeles)

Murphy (3–8–61, Scarborough, Ontario) helped Pittsburgh win the Cup in 1992 and played for the Penguins through '95. Traded to Toronto, he played two seasons before the Maple Leafs gave him to Detroit for "future considerations," and his career was rejuvenated.

"I tell you, it was exciting beating a team I played for," Murphy said of the '91 final. "I don't remember how much we were up in the second period (of Game 6), but I was never so excited in my life. I couldn't even sit still that second intermission. We were comfortably in the lead. How nervous and excited. I felt like a little kid. I couldn't even sit still."

Murphy, who had more than $18 million in career earnings, retired as a player in 2001, becoming a broadcaster with the Red Wings and NHL Network. He was inducted into the Hockey Hall of Fame in 2004, the fifth-highest scoring defenseman in NHL history. In 1,615 regular-season NHL games, the most

by a defenseman when he retired, he totaled 287 goals and 929 assists and was a career plus-199. In 215 playoff games (12 for Minnesota), he added 37 goals and 115 assists.

Murphy has lived in Birmingham, Michigan, for more than twenty years. He enjoys auto racing and has run in the 24 Hours of LeMans. He and his first wife, Nancy, divorced. In 2014, he married his second wife, Jaimee. In the summer of 2022, Murphy was a head coach in the 3ICE hockey league, whose commissioner is Craig Patrick.

"Other than Thomas Steen, Larry Murphy is the most underrated NHL player of all time," Peter Taglianetti told me. "People have no idea how good he was. Day in and day out, he was solid. He wasn't a physical guy, but he was a big dude, and he always made the right plays. He was great on the power play. He never left the blue line too early… he really solidified our offense."

Mike Craig (March 23, 2002, San Jose at Los Angeles)

Craig (6–6–71, London, Ontario) scored 15 goals in each of the final two seasons in Minnesota and remained with the Stars through 1993–94. Then he married the former Krissie Anfinson, who is from Spicer, Minnesota, and signed a four-year, $2.3-million contract with Toronto. But he totaled just 20 goals and went minus-49 in 172 regular-season games over three seasons before the Maple Leafs let him go. He signed with San Jose, which six years earlier would have chosen him in the Sharks-North Stars dispersal draft if not for Bobby Clarke's desire to keep him. Craig played just three games with the Sharks and 300 in the minors between 1997 and 2002.

At that point, the NHL was through with him. In 423 career regular-season games (176 for the North Stars), he scored 71 goals, had 97 assists, and was minus-98. In 26 playoff games (14 for Minnesota), he had two goals and two assists.

But Craig wasn't through with hockey. He played one season in Switzerland and followed that with ten more in Austria. He won Austrian League championships in 2005 with the Vienna Capitals and 2009 with Klagenfurt Athletic Club.

"The body still said, 'Go' and, more than that, my kids did," Craig told me in an interview for this book. "They were still kind of young and they liked watching me play. We went for a year to try it, and fast forward, I was there for eleven years. We met a lot of great people along the way.… In Europe, when you have success on the ice, scoring goals and winning championships, you build a resume and it compounds. How they live is awesome, too. You'd go to the grocery store every day, and no one has a huge double-door fridge that stockpiles for weeks on end. You go and get what you need for that day, and everything's fresh. You walk everywhere or bike everywhere. My son was born in Vienna, and my daughter got to see Rome and Paris."

Mike was the last former North Star still playing pro hockey when his career finally ended in 2013 in Italy. He played more games in Europe than he did in the NHL. After he retired, he returned to Canada and joined the coaching staff of the WHL's Lethbridge Hurricanes for four seasons. Eventually, he became the Calgary Flames' Midwest amateur scout and today watches a lot of US college games, looking for free agents.

Mike and Krissie have two children. Their daughter, Kenzie, graduated from St. Cloud State University in 2020. Their son, Colton, played high school hockey for Northern Lakes (a co-op of school districts serving Aitkin, Crosby-Ironton, Pequot Lakes, and Pine River-Backus in Minnesota) and in 2022–23 was playing for the Minnesota Squatch of the US Premier Hockey League. Mike and Krissie have lived near Pequot Lakes for almost twenty-five years, but they also spend time in Eden Prairie, where he coaches skill development among high school players. For the past six years, he has coached each fall in the Upper Midwest High School Elite League and, for the past five, has overseen the summer and fall captains' practices in Edina, getting prospective Hornets ready to play for Curt Giles.

"I'm on the ice every morning Monday through Friday somewhere," Craig said.

And while those Austrian trophies weren't the Stanley Cup, he doesn't spend much time wondering how life might be different if the North Stars won in '91.

"Honestly, I don't look back a whole lot," he said. "There's not a whole lot of time to worry about yesterday's news. I'm all about moving forward."

Rob Zettler 🏆 (April 13, 2002, New Jersey at Washington; Won 2021 Stanley Cup as an assistant coach with Tampa Bay)

Zettler (3–8–68, Sept-Iles, Quebec) played in San Jose from 1991 to '94, when he was traded to Philadelphia. The following year, he was dealt to Toronto. The Maple Leafs left him unprotected in the '98 expansion draft, and he was selected by Nashville. In '99, he signed with Washington, where he played until his retirement as a player in 2002.

In 569 career regular-season NHL games (80 for the North Stars), he had five goals, 65 assists, and 920 penalty minutes and was minus-121—including, like Neil Wilkinson, a minus-50 rating in his second season with the Sharks. (Doug Zmolek matched them for worst plus-minus on the team.) Zettler also was pointless with four PIM in 14 playoff games, none with Minnesota.

"In hindsight, it was a great thing for me to go to San Jose," Zettler told me for this book. "If I would have stayed in Minnesota, I'm sure it would have worked out. I'm sure I would have played, but at the end of the day, this was like a whole new adventure for me. I had no wife, no kids. I found out I was going, and I was thrilled. It was a new opportunity, a new experience and a chance for me. ... I'd known Jack Ferreira, and he talked to me and said, 'You're going to be a big part of this.' It didn't feel like there was a question of whether or not I was going to be there. It was just, 'Let's get you out here, get yourself settled, get a place to live, and let's go. You're going to play.' That was pretty cool. Unfortunately, we didn't win a whole lot of games, but it was an opportunity, and that's what I was looking for: to be a regular in the NHL. Selfishly, I kind of got over the Stanley Cup loss pretty quick."

Zettler has since worked in radio for Washington and San Jose and been an NHL assistant for several teams. From 2013 to '16, he was head coach of the Syracuse Crunch of the AHL, then an assistant with the Sharks for two seasons. He left to take a position with Oates Sports Group, an organization founded by Adam Oates, which offers services in player assessment, skill development, and group training/seminars.

Zettler's wife, Shannon, is from the San Jose area, where they have settled, and he coached his son, Robert, now fifteen, in youth hockey. They also have two daughters (Emma, twenty-three, and Laney, twenty-one) in college. Rob and Shannon met when he was with the Sharks, and she was just out of UCLA and working at Nordstrom in Hillsdale, California. Their first date was for a Sharks game in which he was playing.

On December 7, 2020, Rob became an assistant coach with the Tampa Bay Lightning. Exactly seven months later, he was behind the bench, running the defensive corps for head coach Jon Cooper, during the Bolts' 1–0 victory over Montreal in Tampa, Florida. In the celebration that followed, Zettler finally got the chance to lift the Stanley Cup.

More than thirty years on, he's still at a loss to explain the 1990–91 North Stars.

"I don't really have an answer as to how that team did what it did," Zettler said. "I feel like we had some high-end players in Neal Broten and Mike Modano. At the same time, I thought we learned how to play defense. We really tightened up and weren't giving up as many chances as the season went on. That's probably what helped us the most.... We weren't a team full of stars, but we had enough depth, and we were real competitive."

Zettler said he looks forward to this book because he and so many teammates have gotten out of touch.

"I lived with Neil for two years in San Jose," Zettler said. "I talk to him once in a while. We exchange Christmas cards or a phone call once a year, that's about it. Perry Berezan I see when we go to Calgary and some of the other guys in press boxes or in passing when they're scouts. But it was the kind of team where when you see somebody, time kind of melts away."

Ulf Dahlen (May 5, 2003, Dallas at Anaheim)

Dahlen (1–21–67, Ostersund, Sweden) and the former Maria Forslund were married on June 21, 1991. They returned to Minnesota, and he stayed with the Stars until March 19, 1994, when he was traded to San Jose for Doug Zmolek. Dahlen played for the Sharks until January 25, 1997, when he was dealt to Chicago.

Ulf and Maria's first child, a daughter, Johanna, was born in 1995 in San Jose. When Ulf reported to camp with the Blackhawks in the fall of '97, Maria was pregnant again. But Bob Murray had replaced Bob Pulford as GM, and it was clear a youth movement was under way.

"We were waiting to get traded, but it never happened," Ulf told me in an interview for this book. "The season started and (the Blackhawks) said to just wait. But I had a lot of contract left and ended up being bought out on a Monday. On Tuesday we flew back to Sweden because Wednesday or Thursday was going to be the last day Maria could fly."

Four days later, in Ostersund, the Dahlens had a son, Jonathan. Ulf, admittedly sick of the North American pro game at the time, played the next two seasons with HV71 Jonkoping in the Swedish Elite League. Ironically, one of his first games brought him right back to Minneapolis for an exhibition against the Minnesota Gophers. Dahlen and Kari Takko both played for the Swedes in a 10–2 win, with Dahlen scoring two goals and adding two assists and Takko stopping 24 of 26 shots. The team visited the Mall of America, and Dahlen said it was "weird" not seeing the Met Center.

In 1999, he returned to the States and signed with Washington. After three increasingly productive seasons with the Capitals, he signed with Dallas for 2002–03. He posted 37 points in 63 games, but an ankle injury led to him needing painkillers and yards of tape in order to play. He took a year off and considered a comeback but was still unable to train to his standard. Instead, he retired.

In 966 career regular-season NHL games (241 with the North Stars), he had 301 goals and 354 assists. In 85 playoff games (29 for Minnesota), he added 15 goals and 25 assists.

Dahlen became an assistant with the Swedish National Team for a year, then went into scouting with the Stars—for whom Doug Armstrong had climbed from director of team services to GM. In 2006, Dahlen filled a vacancy on the Dallas coaching staff when Guy Carbonneau went to Montreal. Dahlen coached from 2006–08 as an assistant under Dave Tippett.

"I thought coaching would be more fun, and it was," Dahlen said. "I worked on the power play but, eventually, it was clear I was going to have to move more."

The Dahlens had had enough of that, so they returned to Sweden and Ulf coached six seasons in the Swedish Elite League.

In 2014, he quit coaching and he and Maria moved back to Ostersund to live full-time.

"When you move around for thirty years, you accumulate a lot of stuff on the side that you say, 'I'll deal with that later,'" Dahlen told me. "So, 'later' has been the last few years here. We're starting to get organized.... Sooner or later, you kind of get fed up with moving around. We bought some land, and I like to hunt and fish a lot because what we have here is similar to Minnesota weather."

In 2016, Jonathan became a second-round pick of the Ottawa Senators. Soon after, Johanna became a sports journalist and broadcaster on radio and TV in Sweden. Ulf and I spoke in March 2021, shortly after I'd had my own bout with COVID-19, but I was quite certain I heard him right: His daughter had become a *sportswriter*!

"There have been times when we're watching Jonathan play on TV but without the volume because we're listening to Johanna broadcast the game on the radio," Dahlen said. "It's kind of fun. They play mostly Wednesdays and Fridays. Jonathan skates (with his feet) at a quarter to three, too, and he calls after the games. And Johanna wants feedback, as well. I enjoy it."

Jonathan, whose rights were traded to Vancouver in 2017, played three full seasons with Timra IK of the Swedish Elite League. Then he played in the AHL in 2018–19, first for the Canucks' affiliate in Utica, New York, and later for the San Jose Barracuda, after he was traded to the Sharks. He returned to Sweden, had the best two years of his career with Timra IK, and finally played in the NHL with San Jose in 2021–22. With his debut on October 16, 2021, he and Ulf became the first father-son duo ever to play for the Sharks. Jonathan totaled 22 points in 61 games for San Jose and was the team's rookie of the year. Nonetheless, he didn't receive a qualifying offer in 2022 and returned to play in Sweden.

While seeing his son make it to the NHL was one of Ulf's proudest moments as a parent, he said reaching the finals in 1991 was the highlight of his career.

"It really, really makes me respect players who've won the Cup, because I know how tough it is," he told me. "We got so close to doing it, and it was a Cinderella story. You know how long the road is, a couple of months battling, and you win series and it builds. I won the world championship and there you're together for three weeks. It's a great thing to win, but this is a team (the North Stars) that was together for a whole season, and then you're in the playoffs for two months. It was my greatest memory as a hockey player—even though we didn't win."

Mike Modano ♆ (Won 1999 Stanley Cup; May 10, 2011, San Jose at Detroit)

Modano (6–7–70, Livonia, Michigan) was the only player from the 1990–91 North Stars who continuously remained with the franchise until the Stars finally raised the Stanley Cup on June 19, 1999. Modano played in Dallas until 2010 and retired after a forgettable 40-game stint with Detroit in 2010–11. He was inducted into the Hall of Fame in 2014.

Mike Modano joined the Minnesota Wild as a senior advisor in 2019. He consults with Wild management and makes occasional appearances on behalf of the team. (Photo courtesy Minnesota Wild)

His 561 goals and 1,374 points (in 1,499 career regular-season games; 317 for Minnesota) are the most in NHL history by an American-born player and ranked twenty-sixth among all players through 2022. His 146 playoff points (in 176 games; 39 with the North Stars) also is a record for a US native.

He netted seven career hat tricks, though only one came with Minnesota (March 17, 1990, in a 6–2 win at Pittsburgh), and curiously went scoreless on five career penalty shots.

Modano played in every game of his rookie season, and only accomplished that feat once more in his career (2007–08). He won gold at the 1996 World Cup and silver at the 2002 Olympics. But his entire career path might've changed had the North Stars won the Cup in '91.

"It was pretty electric," he told me in a series of interviews for this book. "You get to that point at an early age, you couldn't wait to do it next year, but it didn't happen for another eleven years. You took it for granted, and you didn't realize how hard it is to make it to the finals."

That makes what happened all the more special, especially in light of the way it started with the smallest crowd he'd played in front of since juniors on opening night.

"It was shocking," Modano said. "I think being so young, you really didn't understand the magnitude of what was happening. I was just twenty years old, playing and having fun and getting acclimated to the league. I didn't really understand what the details were behind the scenes. ... We just had a horrible start to the season, just an abysmal start to October (2–8–3), even November (4–7–3).

"It's hard to say when the bottom came because I scored three goals in my first nineteen games. So, you're almost looking at a quarter of the season. But then I got on a clip where I was almost scoring every two games the rest of the way. It's frustrating to wonder what could have happened if I'd played well in the one-third of the games that I went cold on. I just recall the start being more difficult than the middle. And by that point, we all got going. ... We had little bits and pieces, little runs here and there, and it kept our interest. I think it was just a total confidence thing. Something magical at the Met Center started happening, too. We started getting fans, and the place was starting to get full."

Looking back, he finds it humorous that the team traveled on commercial flights throughout the regular season.

"You'd have to go through security, wait at the gate to get on the plane, and board," Modano told me. "We were on there with everybody else travelling. We would always try to get the windows and aisles. They booked those for us. But it was frowned upon if you checked your bag, so we were all trying get our travel bags on the overhead on a seven-, eight-day trip. It was tough. We'd have to stay over every night after the game and get the first flight out of town, which was, you know, crack of dawn, 8 or 8:30. So, you play a game. You get done at 10:30. You're sitting around trying to get something to eat, trying to find somewhere that's open. Then, you get maybe five hours of sleep, and you got to get back on a commercial flight back home. And then we often had practice. We'd drive right to the rink when we landed. The players nowadays would have a heart attack if they had to fly commercial."

Although he was the same age as many of the Americans in uniform in the Middle East in 1991, Modano insulated himself from the news.

"I would take a look at our game notes, and I would take a look at the standings, but I didn't get too caught up in what was going on in the world," he said. "You just knew that the Gulf War was on, and at that point, I think there was a lot of pride in the country."

And the North Stars' pride grew as they won in February and March.

"We were dominant at home," he said. "We barely ever lost there. I think we all felt there was just the challenge of trying to make something of the season and feeling like, if you had a good playoffs, you'd feel better. Great players and consistent players are made in the playoffs. So, for me, that was motivation. By the end of the regular season, I could keep my legs. I wasn't exerting a lot of energy (playing) on the wing defensively. Once the puck turned over, I could get going. Our power play was clicking at a rate like no other. We really frustrated teams if they took penalties. We'd score, and that would piss them off even more. So, they would take some more runs at us. Then they'd be in the box again. Before they got a grasp of it, the series was over."

Between Game 2 of the Norris Division semifinals against Chicago and Game 4 of the finals against Pittsburgh, only Brian Bellows (27 points) and Dave Gagner (24) had more points than Modano (20).

"Mike was so easy going," Brian Propp said of Modano as a 20-year-old. "He was a pleasure to play with because he didn't get bothered by anything. He was happy-going, and after a time, he learned how to win. I think us going to the finals at a young age like that made a big difference for him to understand what it takes to get there. We had a good mix of veterans, and we had some younger guys and good coaching. But for him to play as well as he did in the playoffs was huge, especially when you're at the start of your career."

That's perhaps one reason Modano averaged more than a point per game for the first time in 1991–92.

"At that age, I was just thinking to myself that I couldn't wait for the next year to do this all over again," Modano said. "I took it *so* much for granted. Because we went to the final, I was like, 'Let's have a fun summer. We've got a good team. We'll be back.' Lo and behold, it took another nine years to do that. It was naïve on my part. When you're young and you have success, you think that's capable every year. Then you get older, and you really have a whole different respect for winning and going to the finals and that whole deal.

"Ninety-one was just one of those runs you don't see. The parity (now) isn't like it was back in the day. You had these high-level teams and then you had your bottom ten. They were struggling to get by. Nowadays, it's like, anybody who gets in the playoffs, you feel like you're only about a half a dozen points between eighth place and first place in a conference. It's hard to gauge and compare but, getting in at 68 points and making the run that we did, I would safely say I don't think you're ever going to see that again. Nothing has ever really been explained yet that's done justice to those North Stars."

Modano's two best seasons, statistically, were his final one in Minnesota and his first in Dallas. He had 93 points in each.

"We knew a move was inevitable, but taking the North Stars out of Minnesota was really hard for a lot of us," Modano said. "It was one of those things that you just never could imagine. People to this day are still devastated about it.

"I was petrified to think of going someplace that hadn't seen ice before, and I wasn't looking forward to the thought of having to educate people to the game of hockey. But, hey. I was single, and I knew Dallas had great golf courses. So, it was easier on me than the married guys."

In 1993–94, he scored 50 goals for the only time in his career. His first four seasons in Dallas, the Stars won one playoff series and missed the postseason entirely in 1996. Changes were in order. Gainey relinquished head coaching duties to Ken Hitchcock but remained GM. Under Hitchcock, Modano's ice time jumped from 15–18 minutes a game to more than 25. And the Stars finally began traveling exclusively by charter. Perhaps not surprisingly, they won the Central Division title in '97 and reached the Western Conference final in '98.

It all came together in 1999, when Dallas' lineup included six Hall of Famers (Modano, Brett Hull, Joe Nieuwendyk, Sergei Zubov, Guy Carbonneau, and Ed Belfour). The Stars raced through the season to 114 points and the best record in the NHL. They swept Edmonton, ousted St. Louis in six games (thanks to Modano's first career playoff overtime goal in the decisive game), and needed seven to top Colorado.

Perry Berezan said Modano never would've got there if Gainey hadn't persuaded him to be coachable.

"Mike was this amazing talent, and Bob was the right guy to get him to grow up without breaking him," Perry Berezan said. "He was so gifted. You had to play him. But he also had to learn what it took to be one of the best players in the league. In '99, I was doing radio work for the Flames, and Mike and Brett Hull were walking into the building before the game. I'm like, 'Hey, guys. How's it going?' They were kind of down and like, 'Fine. We're playing for (Ken) Hitchcock.' I said, 'How's Hitchie?' Brett looked at Mike and says, 'You want me to tell him or are you going to tell him?' Mike said, 'You tell him.' Brett said: 'Dump it in, dump it out. Blah. Blah. Blah. We hate it.'

"But that was the year they won the Cup. What does that mean? Those two needed to conform to win. They needed to buy in, and they did. You have to sacrifice something to get the ultimate prize for your team. I'm sure Mike learned a lot from Bob Gainey, and it was painful early in his career. But if he'd had a coach that pampered him, he might've become one of those wasted talents."

Modano led the Stars with 81 points during the 1998–99 regular season—23 more than the next-best player. But he suffered a broken left wrist in the second game of the finals against Buffalo when he was slammed into the boards by the Sabres' Jay McKee. Incredibly, Modano continued to play in every game and assisted on Dallas' last five goals of the series. When the Cup was finally won, Modano—who led his team with 23 playoff points—flung the brace from his wrist into the crowd and collapsed on the ice in a pool of tears.

"I remember hugging him, and you could feel his emotion," said Craig Button, a longtime member of the front office who was Dallas' director of player personnel at the time. "You could feel the release—it was like, 'I won, and now no one can ever say I didn't win.'"

The Stars, who had an affinity for metal bands like Metallica, partied like it was 1999. The Stanley Cup became worse for wear during a celebration at the home of Pantera drummer Vinnie Paul, whose band recorded the "Dallas Stars Fight Song." The Cup was thrown off a balcony and bounced into the swimming pool, shades of what happened when Mario Lemieux celebrated with it in '91.

"Yeah, that's pretty accurate," Modano said. "It had a couple of good dents on it. It got put through the wringer that two or three weeks it was in town. It wasn't a good group of guys to leave that Cup with."

Modano's 1999–2000 season was marred by a broken engagement to his longtime girlfriend, Kerri Nelson. They'd been planning to build their dream home in Dallas. Then, Anaheim's Ruslan Salei added injury to insult when his check from behind into the boards gave Modano a concussion, strained neck ligaments, and a broken nose. He narrowly avoided a career-ending injury, and although he came back a few games later and had an 81-point season, it proved painful in multiple ways. It ended with a six-game loss to New Jersey in the final, although the series wouldn't have gone that long if not for his triple-overtime winner for the only goal in Game 5.

In 2003, the town of Westland, Michigan, where Modano lived during his minor hockey career and his parents still reside, renamed their rink Mike Modano Ice Arena. The parking lot is a cut-off throw away from the baseball diamond where he played Little League. While some of the trophies from his youth remain at his parents' home, the arena is where you can see a collection of his jerseys behind glass in the lobby, along with the puck from his first NHL goal, on October 5, 1989, at Pittsburgh.

"I've always had some humbling parents and family and friends that never once let you forget where you came from," said Modano, who nonetheless had a six-bedroom, seven-bath, 11,435-square-foot home in the Highland Park area of Dallas—which he sold in 2004 for roughly $8 million. "They taught you to treat people how you wanted to be treated. And I think that's always been a big thing: remembering people that were a part of your life growing up and helped get you there and pushed you and supported you."

Modano was the Stars' captain from 2003 to '06, serving as alternate from 1995 to 2003 and again from 2006 to 2010. On November 7, 2007, Modano's shorthanded breakaway goal broke Phil Housley's career scoring record for Americans, and he got a congratulatory call from President George W. Bush, who was aboard Air Force One. Mike Modano Night was held two weeks later at American Airlines Center in Dallas, and Housley, Hull, Joe Mullen, and owner Tom Hicks helped decorate a pregame program. Modano then scored the game-tying goal and the shootout winner in a 3–2 victory over the Ducks.

He played out the rest of his contract, concluding with a game April 10, 2010, at Minnesota where he was named the game's No. 1 star and skated out for the curtain call wearing a North Stars jersey—to a standing ovation.

Not quite ready to quit, but with his tenure in Dallas at an end, Modano cast for offers and considered joining the Wild. In the end, he signed with the Red Wings but suffered a freak injury when a skate blade severed a tendon in his wrist. He had 15 points in 40 games and was a healthy scratch for a late-season game against Dallas and for Detroit's playoff opener. He played in just two of 11 postseason games before the Wings were eliminated.

Modano signed a one-day contract with Dallas on September 23, 2011, in order to retire as a Star. He was the last remaining NHL player from the 1980s and the final North Star in the NHL. Although Modano split from his longtime agent Howard Gourwitz in 1998, and was burned by an unscrupulous money manager who cost him millions in 2004, he earned more than $77 million in contract revenue alone during his career.

Despite his success, Modano never won a major NHL award. He finished fourth in balloting for the Selke Trophy in 1997 (behind Michael Peca, Peter Forsberg, and Jere Lehtinen) and third in 2001 (edged out by John Madden and Joe Sakic). Modano was fifth in the Lady Byng voting in 2000 (Pavol Demitra, Nicklas Lidstrom, Teemu Selanne, and Pavel Bure claimed the top four spots) and third in 2003 (behind Alexander Mogilny and Lidstrom). The highest Modano ever finished in the Hart Trophy voting was seventh (1997 and 2003). He appeared in seven all-star games and was named to the league's second all-star team in 2000.

Off the ice, he started the Mike Modano Foundation and had his own clothing line (Inspired by Mike) in the 1990s. He appeared in magazine photo shoots for *Cosmopolitan*, *Mademoiselle* and *Marie Claire*. He's had his own beer with a company called Rabbit Hole Brewing and helped market a product from Mineral Wells, Texas, called Crazy Water. Hull and Modano also ran a Dallas establishment, Hully & Mo's Restaurant and Tap Room, from 2008 to 2012.

After a Hall of Fame career as a bachelor, when pictures of his golden retrievers decorated almost every room in his palatial Dallas home, he married singer/songwriter Willa Ford on August 25, 2007. (She'd performed on "Dancing with the Stars," appeared in *Maxim*, and once portrayed Anna Nicole

Mike Modano and his wife, Allison Micheletti, have enough kids to start their own hockey team. The family includes (from left) daughter Reese, Mike, son Luca, Allison holding daughter Quinn, and twins Kate and Jack. (Photo courtesy of Mike Modano)

Smith in a movie.) They'd been together for five years before they took the plunge. Hull and Daryl Sydor served as Modano's co-best men. However, five years later, Modano and Ford divorced, and she later married former NFL player Ryan Nece.

On September 1, 2013, Modano married Allison Micheletti, a pro golfer and daughter of former Gophers and NHL defenseman Joe Micheletti—who'd been the North Stars color commentator during the 1991–92 season. They met on a Florida golf course and later honeymooned on the Caribbean island of St. Bart's.

Modano, also an avid golfer, has collected autographed pictures of Byron Nelson, Arnold Palmer, Ben Hogan, and Tiger Woods.

Modano wore No. 9 throughout his career, an homage to Ted Williams (his father's favorite baseball player) and Gordie Howe. The only time he wore anything else was his season in Detroit, when he wore No. 90 because Howe's No. 9 already was in the rafters. The Stars retired Modano's number on March 8, 2014, before a game against the Wild in Dallas.

Neal Broten was on hand, as well as family members of the late Bill Masterton and Bill Goldsworthy. Dan Stuchal, my onetime fellow intern who was the Stars' VP of Business Development at the time, helped plan the event. Norm Green was one of the tributaries, and Stars president Jim Lites feted the most important player in Dallas Stars history. That was the last time Modano saw Green until the Stars inaugurated their first Hall of Fame class in 2022.

Modano later became executive adviser and alternate governor for the Stars for two seasons before joining the Wild in a similar capacity on May 24, 2019. He and Allison have five children. The oldest, twins Jack and Kate, were born in 2014. A daughter, Reese, came two years later, followed by a son, Luca, in 2018 and a daughter, Quinn, in the summer of 2020.

"The timing worked out well for me," Modano said. "I like that I get to be around them every day. I like to get to watch them grow. I'll just go in there and watch them sleep sometimes; it's an incredible experience."

While he expects to relocate with his family to Minnesota in 2023, they own a modern farmhouse-style estate in Phoenix's Tierra De Paz community. The Arcadia-area mansion was built in 2019 and features a formal dining area, white oak wood flooring, and a separate guest house. The 6,712-square-foot home has four bedrooms and five and a half bathrooms. They also have a vacation property in Park City, Utah.

But Mike's legacy goes far beyond his life off the ice. Lou Nanne, who ought to know, said Modano was the fastest skater and had the best slap shot of anyone in North Stars history—forever frozen in memory as a youngster.

"The first time he practiced with us, he'd come in from Prince Albert and had a broken wrist," Stew Gavin, Modano's road roommate, recalled for this book. "He could *still* shoot the puck harder than anyone else on our team—*with a broken wrist*. Churls (Churla) went and got the same stick Mike was using because he figured if it worked for Mike, maybe it would make him shoot like that. There was a commercial about that time (featuring Michael Jordan) with the saying, 'Be like Mike.' We started to be like Mike and do the things he was doing. His curve was really different, and a bunch of us began emulating him. The talent and skill was oozing out of him. He just had to get his feet wet and mature and learn to play at both ends of the rink.

"Some players questioned his compete level when he was young because the game was so tough, and he'd shy away from the physical part," Gavin added. "Basil (McRae) and Churls would protect him, but to his credit, he battled and evolved and grew into the player he needed to be. He was such a great kid. He was this good-looking guy with blond hair and tall, and after the game, we'd be out somewhere, and he wasn't even old enough to drink. Obviously, he was interested in girls, but if someone said hi to him, it was like he had marbles in his mouth. He couldn't speak. We'd laugh because he didn't have to say anything to strike up a relationship with a woman. She'd leave, and he was like, 'She really likes me!' And in reality, he couldn't get two words out. He eventually got a lot more confident in that area, too."

His teammates took Modano in like a little brother. A *very talented* little brother.

"He never whined, or if he did say something negative, it was always funny," Gagner said. "So, he could even pick you up with negativity. He was just a kid, but he was good at everything. You go golfing with him, he'd hit the ball a mile. Everything he did, he was the best at it, and he did it naturally. You could tell he was going to be a star. He just galloped down the ice… he was very confident in himself. He knew what he could do, but he wasn't boastful about it. I always said that if my son could grow up to be like that, I'd be pretty happy."

Ralph Strangis, who saw more of Modano's career than anyone else, says he's honestly not much different today than he was in 1991.

"He's always been a kid, and today he's a kid," Strangis told me. "I've always liked that about him, because I am, too. Just the other night, we texted a juvenile exchange that we used to do with Gaetan (Duchesne), and it was hilarious because we're both like that. But I think the thing Mo doesn't get credit for is how tough he was. He was never hurt. He didn't miss a lot of games. For a guy who had a bull's eye on his back, in an era where that meant something and you were getting welts and bruises and bruises on top of bruises, he always smiled.

"I think the public made him nervous and uncomfortable. He couldn't have a private life. I was with him over those years, and we're not talking about Tiger Woods, but (Modano) would come out, and he wouldn't sign a lot of times. He'd have a snack in the afternoon or a coffee and he'd walk out, and there would be 100 guys there trying to get their cards signed—usually dealers. He'd just head right to the bus, and everybody would go, 'Mo, what the fuck?' I'm like, 'Are you shitting me? Give the guy a break.'"

Whether it was as a 20-year-old center or a 50-year-old adviser to the front office, Modano is pretty happy to have bonded with Minnesota.

"My five years when I played there was the best five years I've had in my life," Modano said. "You always have a fun part in your heart for where it started and for the people who were there at the beginning. It still strongly resonates with me."

Coaches, Front Office, Support Staff and Media

Bob Gainey ♆♆♆♆♆♆ (Won 1976, 1977, 1978, 1979, and 1986 Stanley Cups as a player with Montreal; Won 1999 Stanley Cup as Dallas' general manager)

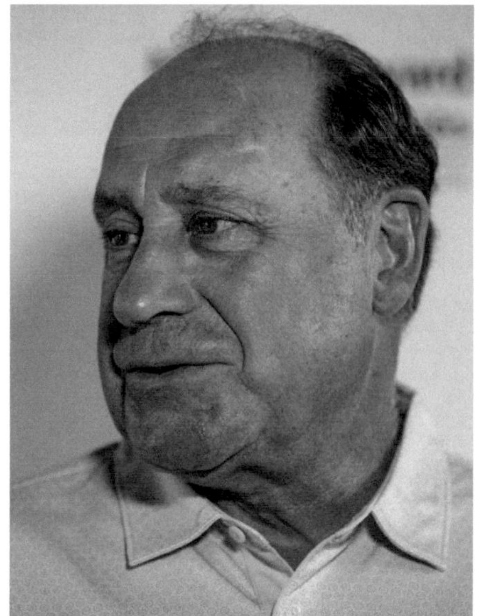
Bob Gainey in 2021.

Gainey (12–13–53, Peterborough, Ontario), who was inducted to the Hall of Fame in 1992, continued as GM and coached the North Stars through tumultuous times, including Norm Green's move out of Minnesota and the first three seasons in Dallas.

"I think in '91–92 we felt like we had to absorb a lot of changes because of the agreement in place with San Jose," Gainey recalled for this book. "There was disruption there that really made it impossible. There were draft picks and players leaving, and we were a middle-of-the-road team that got into the playoffs. From the community side, I felt the euphoria had dissipated, and we were back to who we were in January of 1991. We had our fan base, but it wasn't large. The performance in the spring of '91 didn't translate into lots of season tickets and participation by ('92–93). We worked hard (in '91–92) from a hockey and business point of view. The following year was a different kind of turmoil. It was almost entirely business related, and there were several players who were there throughout very trying times—Dave Gagner, Mark Tinordi, Neal Broten—and you can't keep applying that amount of stress on people without having it show up in some kind of way that's recognizable. You can't go through repeated stress of not being good enough on player personnel or not good enough in our revenues. It wears you down. You can try to separate those emotions from what happens on the ice, but you can't do it all. You ultimately drop your arms a little bit, and then you're not as good as you should be."

It wasn't enough to keep them in Minnesota, but they improved their point totals each year from 1991 through '94, peaking during the first season in Dallas with 97.

"I could not see any way that the North Stars were going to survive in Minnesota," Gainey told me. "Player salaries were escalating, and the players' union had changed dramatically by the early '90s. We were starting to have labor stoppages, and the escalation in costs was dramatic between 1990 and 1995. There did not seem to be any break possible between the different groups who controlled arenas. There were too many obstacles.

"And, realistically, the North Stars had been on life support a number of times in the past fifteen years. Sometimes you just have to burn it down. Rebuilding a house with a bad foundation is not a good plan. Norm took the brunt of it. He took a lot of heat and a lot of anger, but I don't think he had any choice but to make the move he made. Happily, some of those things resolved, and a team showed up in St. Paul where there was a greater love for the sport and a real commitment. They now have a vibrant and strong franchise there, which the state of Minnesota deserves."

In 1994–95, Dallas slumped to fifth place in the Central Division during a lockout-shortened schedule. On June 22, 1995, not long after they'd been eliminated in the first round of the playoffs, Cathy Gainey succumbed in her battle with cancer.

That began a tumultuous period for Bob. After a last-place division finish in 1995–96, he stepped down as head coach but retained his GM duties. (His record behind the Stars' bench was 165–190–60 during the regular season and 23–21 in the playoffs.) He began to feel the weight of the loss of his wife and the demands of his high-profile job. While his oldest daughter, Anna, went to McGill University in Montreal and his son, Steve, began a junior career with Kamloops of the WHL, their younger siblings, Laura and Colleen, were just thirteen and ten when their mother died. Colleen underwent treatment for depression, and Laura descended into destructive behavior, eventually entering a rehabilitation program for drug use.

The Stars won the Stanley Cup in '99, and Bob's father, George, died in 2000. In 2001, Bob announced his decision to step down as GM after the 2001–02 season. The Stars had returned to the final in 2000 but subsequently lost in the second round and were en route to their first season out of the playoffs in six years. He said his reasons were similar to why he gave up coaching: "Most of these trains end up off the rails. I'd rather get off at a station."

By then, Steve Gainey was in the NHL. He played 33 games, including 13 for the Stars between 2000 and 2004. Anna Gainey became active in the Liberal Party of Canada, a prelude to becoming an advisor to Canadian Prime Minister Justin Trudeau and her own election as party president in 2014.

Laura Gainey followed a different compass. Despite growing up in Montreal, Minnesota, and Texas, she eventually found her passion in sailing tall ships on the open oceans. In 2006, she joined the crew of the 55-meter, 300-ton *Picton Castle* for the last three months of a world voyage. She was on board for another tour, 500 miles off Cape Cod, on December 8, 2006, when she was on deck in the dark of night during rough seas and was swept overboard. Her body was never found.

The news was shattering for Bob, who had become Canadiens GM in 2003. As a public figure, his nation shared in his grief. But just as his father was a humble man who never talked about himself or the war he fought, Bob wouldn't court publicity for his on-ice accomplishments or off-ice heartbreak.

"My father," Anna Gainey said years later, "is a very private man."

Bob Gainey, in the opinion of legendary *Montreal Gazette* sportswriter Red Fisher, "played through more pain, I think, than any athlete I have ever known."

"I don't think you can really get to know him," Dave Gagner said of Gainey. "He doesn't have a lot of highs and lows. The best way I can describe him is he's a hockey man to the highest level. He approaches life with a quiet calm… He played in a very intense media center, where it could be brutal. He learned to keep his private life private."

On February 23, 2008, the Canadiens retired Gainey's No. 23. Decked out in full equipment, he took a last lap around the ice at the Bell Centre. It was there that he stepped down as Habs GM on February 8, 2010, having coached the team briefly in 2006 and 2009—including a 29–21–7 record in the regular season and two wins in ten playoff games. He stayed on as a consultant until 2012, when he moved on to similar capacities in Dallas and, in 2014, St. Louis.

"Then I broke my work-related ties," said Gainey, who splits his time between an urban home in Montreal, a country house north of Peterborough, and a vacation spot along the Atlantic Coast of Florida. "I was ready for that. I still follow the NHL. I don't watch that many games on TV, but every morning I check the scores and who's going up and who's going down."

Bob's mother, Anne, a member of her church parish for more than seventy years, died in 2016 at the age of ninety-six. In 2018, he was named as a senior advisor to the Peterborough Petes. Today, he continues to be involved with the Gainey Foundation, which honors the memories of Cathy and Laura. Anna lives in Montreal and has three children. Colleen, who he affectionately calls his "leftover hippie," lives in the mountains of British Columbia and has a son. Steve lives in Kamloops, British Columbia, and has three children.

"Bob is the most interesting man I know," Ralph Strangis told me. "He's not an eat-drink-sleep hockey guy. In fact, he's famous for *not* watching hockey with the coaches in the bar on the road. He'd frequently call me and say, 'Hey, ah, I don't want to watch hockey with those guys. You want to go down to this little piano bar I found about a short walk from here?' The short walk turns out to be about four miles. But that's Bob, right? And then about an hour into it he'd say, 'All right, well, maybe you want to go back. I'm going to hang out for awhile.' That's Bob, too. I was like, 'OK, I'll see you tomorrow.'"

In 2020, Gainey auctioned off sixty-six pieces of memorabilia, including Stanley Cup rings he said he never wore in public, raising more than $300,000 for charity. In 2021, his 1999 Stanley Cup ring was offered for sale at a price of $23,000.

The one he came close to but can't show you from 1991 remains a priceless memory.

"You find opportunity in chaos, and the North Stars were definitely in chaos when I got there," Gainey said. "There was nothing we could do about all the past errors. The best response was to give (fans) something people will want to see. If your team is competitive, can win some games, people will respond."

He said he "wasn't very sharp" at his job when Cathy was diagnosed and that midway through the '90–91 season, "there were times you had to look seriously at the team and the franchise and wonder how long you go on."

"That one year, though it held a lot of turmoil, it turned into an incredible journey," Gainey told me. "That was a great streak of seeing a group of players join together and access all their tools. To be so functional and competitive, to be a part of that was a great experience. I would've loved to have been a Stanley Cup–winning coach, but I've bumped into some of the players along the way, and we have these kinds of brief revisits, and it's always very positive and enjoyable.... To see that enthusiasm at Met Center and in the community was great fuel for our team. And it was great medicine for that group after the long and dreary days early in the year. It was a reminder that in sports, you're never over until it's over."

Doug Jarvis 🏆🏆🏆🏆🏆🏆 (Won 1976, 1977, 1978, and 1979 Stanley Cups as a player with Montreal; Won 1999 and 2011 Stanley Cups as assistant coach with Dallas and Boston, respectively)

Jarvis (3–24–55, Brantford, Ontario) remained with the Stars for fourteen seasons—longer than any NHL assistant has stayed with one team. He helped win the Cup for Dallas in 1999 and departed with Bob Gainey in 2002. Jarvis coached Montreal's AHL team at Hamilton from 2003 to '05. Then the two reunited again with the Canadiens—Jarvis becoming an assistant coach while Gainey was GM. When new head coach Jacques Martin brought in a different staff in 2009, Jarvis was dismissed but was hired as an assistant in Boston and helped the Bruins win the Cup in 2011. After six years in Boston, he took a similar job for two seasons in Vancouver and has been a senior advisor for the Canucks since 2018.

Doug Jarvis in 2016.

Doug and his wife, Linda, live in rural Ontario, near the Rideau Canal about forty miles north of Kingston—where they originally bought a cottage in the early 1980s. They've since torn it down and built a four-season home. Their children both attended Wake Forest and now live in North Carolina. Their daughter, Laura, thirty-eight, is a family practice/sports medicine doctor. Their son, Landry, thirty-five, went on to a fellowship at Duke and became an orthopedic surgeon. Doug and Linda eagerly waited for the US/Canada COVID border freeze to thaw in 2021 so they could see their five grandchildren—with a sixth on the way.

Doug traveled routinely to evaluate Vancouver's AHL affiliate in Utica, New York, until it relocated in 2021 to Abbotsford, British Columbia. One of the vehicles he still drives today is a black 1991 GMC Sonoma that he bought in Apple Valley with his North Stars Stanley Cup playoffs bonus.

"I'm eager to read the book," Doug told me during our interview. "I was with the Canadiens when Ken Dryden wrote 'The Game' about his team in Montreal, and I know how those moments in time can be captured in written form.

"You have great memories of finals when you're successful, but those ones that you weren't—and I've had three of those experiences—they're still alive in your memory," Jarvis added. "You think back on them and wish certain games had gone different."

Andy Murray

Murray (3–3–51, Gladstone, Manitoba) coached with the North Stars through 1991–92, after which he returned to a previous stop in Lugano, Switzerland. Later, he coached in Germany before returning to the NHL as an assistant with the Winnipeg Jets until 1995. He then coached the Canadian national team and was an associate to head coach Marc Crawford at the 1998 Olympics in Nagano, Japan. The Canadians lost to the Czech Republic in a semifinal shootout, a crushing defeat that ranks with the North Stars' loss in Game 6 against Pittsburgh as the most haunting of Murray's career. After Canada lost the bronze medal to Finland, Murray was a candidate to become head coach in Anaheim but instead landed quite a few rungs lower in 1998–99 at Shattuck-St. Mary's, a prep school in Faribault, Minnesota, near where his family has a lake home.

Perhaps even more unlikely than his original rise to becoming an NHL assistant, Murray was named head coach of the Los Angeles Kings on June 14, 1999, five days before the Stars won the Stanley Cup. In seven years, his teams never posted a losing record or finished lower than third in the Pacific Division, but they ran into Detroit or Colorado in the playoffs and then missed the postseason in 2003 and 2004. After the lockout, the Kings were 37–28–5 on March 21, 2006, when he was fired. He'd won more games (215) and coached more (480) than anyone in franchise history.

Gainey hired Murray as a consultant with the Canadiens, but on December 11, 2006, he was hired as head coach of the St. Louis Blues. In four seasons, his teams went 118–102–40 but made the playoffs just once and were swept in 2009. He was fired on January 2, 2010. His overall NHL head coaching record was 333–278–58.

Andy Murray in 2022.

Murray, who coached Canada to three gold medals at the IIHF World Championships, took over as head coach at Western Michigan in Kalamazoo in 2011. He was coming off a 10–12–3 season and had a 167–156–43 record with the Broncos when he resigned on August 3, 2021.

"I am in great health and full of energy, so this is not a retirement," said Murray, who had three years remaining on his third five-year contract. "I still have a number of things on my bucket list and now is the time to pursue those."

Andy and Ruth continue to live near Faribault. Their older son, Brady, played at North Dakota and was drafted in the fifth round by Los Angeles in 2003. He had a four-game stint with the Kings to start the 2007–08 season, but concussion issues later forced him to retire to a financial services career in Minneapolis.

Their younger son, Jordy, played at Wisconsin, and their daughter, Sarah, played at Minnesota-Duluth, where she won two NCAA championships. All three siblings played pro hockey in Switzerland, and Sarah went on to coach the unified Korean women's team at the 2018 Winter Olympics in South Korea. In 2019, she became head coach of the women's team at St. Mary's University in Winona. In 2022, Jordy joined the coaching staff at Michigan Tech.

Other than Brady, who according to his mother was crying and inconsolable during Game 6 of the '91 Stanley Cup Finals, they can't remember the North Stars. But their father will never forget how that team almost pulled off the unbelievable.

"The way we were playing was not a finesse game—it was a demanding kind of game," Murray told me. "But they just stayed after it, grinding it out. I attribute a lot of that to Bob Gainey, Bob Clarke, and Doug Jarvis. That's what their careers were all about. We became a real lunch-bucket crew. And, later on, I always told my players: the greatest talent in the game of hockey is not skating. It's not passing. It's not shooting. It's not checking. It's the ability to work. Some players, some people, just outwork other people."

Chico Resch 🏆 (Won 1980 Stanley Cup as a player with New York Islanders)

Resch (7–10–48, Moose Jaw, Saskatchewan) parted ways with the North Stars before the 1991–92 season, when he became general manager of the Tri-City Americans of the WHL.

"I was there the whole ('91) playoffs, and I can't imagine how much money Norm Green took in," Resch recalled for this book. "And Bobby Clarke and I played against each other and had some battles, verbal and otherwise. There was some slashing, and he wasn't my best friend. But he'd talked me into coming back with the Flyers and working with (Ron Hextall), and he talked me into coming back (in Minnesota). I thought, 'OK, that's six weeks that I'm down in Minneapolis. I'm sure he's going to give me something (for a bonus).'"

During the summer, Resch checked with Doug Jarvis to confirm the coaches had received playoff money.

"The players and coaches got (almost) $19,000," Resch said. "I was waiting and waiting, and nothing came. I didn't know what it would be. Even if he'd given me half—$10,000—I would've been really happy. I think if he'd given me $5,000, I'd have been happy. If he'd given me $1,000, maybe I would've been happy. I don't know. But we're in July and nothing's coming."

Resch called Clarke. After mentioning that he knew the coaches had received their bonuses, Resch asked whether anything was forthcoming for him.

Chico Resch in 2022.

"He says, 'No, Chico, I don't think you deserved to get any bonus,'" Resch said. "I was like, 'Really, Clarkie? Do you know what I did? I want you to call Bob Gainey and ask him how much of an impact I had.' He said, 'OK, I'll do that.' So, I called Bob and said, 'Clarkie's going to call you. I don't want you to embellish.' I refreshed all that I had done and how well Jon had played. I said, 'I'm not trying to put you in between. I know you're caught in the middle. I just want you to be truthful.' 'Oh, yeah (Gainey said). Sure, Chico. You had a big impact. Da-da-da-da-da.' So, I waited a week or so, and I called Clarkie. I said, 'Well, Bob, did you talk to Bob Gainey?' 'Yup. I did.' I said, 'Well, what do you think?' He says, 'Nah. I still don't think you deserve anything.'

"I've got to tell you, I was really hurt," Resch added. "It's not going to change my life, but I thought maybe

Clarkie had feelings from when we played. I don't know what it was. I said, 'OK, Clarkie. But I'm not coming back, obviously. And don't ever ask me to work for you again.' He just said, 'Sorry you feel that way, Chico.' It just bothered me that a fellow player and someone I helped build the team would react that way. We made Norm Green a ton of money. I'm not bragging, but I don't think I had more of an impact on games other than when I played. But they couldn't take $10,000 of the millions that they made. I've never asked (Clarke), but I'd just like to ask if he had a budget, and I would've put him over? Or why?"

From 1992 to '96, Resch scouted and served as goalie coach with the Ottawa Senators. In November of 1995, Ottawa head coach Rick Bowness was fired and replaced by Dave Allison, who was coaching their AHL team. Resch joined Allison's staff as a bench coach, but after a 27-game record of 2–22–3, Allison was fired in favor of Jacques Martin.

Resch went on to a long career in TV and most recently, radio (beginning in 2017–18) for the New Jersey Devils. In the thousands of games he's witnessed, he has yet to see anything approaching the North Stars' story from the 1990–91 season.

"It's the reason why people play," Resch said. "It's the intangible story, almost indescribable in pro sports, of a team coming together. You know it. The room knows it. But there's more to it than that. Dick Irvin was a great player (in the 1920s) and went on to be a great coach (winning Cups in 1944 and '46 with Montreal). He would say, 'Well, the Unseen Hand was on our side.' Meaning, you shot the puck wide, it hit a shin pad, ricocheted off another guy and went in the net. That's not a designed play. It's the unseen hand of how things transpire that are beyond description other than, 'We just got lucky.'"

The North Stars' luck ran out in Game 4 of the finals. Resch said it was because of a cold power play and Mario Lemieux's return. Asked whether any discord between Jon and Brenda Casey played a role in the collapse, Resch said suggesting as much is ludicrous.

"When (Lemieux) skated out for Game 4, he was going to be the game-changer," Resch said. "He was going to be decisive in what happened. If he hadn't come back, our confidence level probably would've stayed high. But there was a psychological, confidence switch there. You heard he couldn't tie his skates, and then he came out and played like he did, you start subconsciously thinking 'The guy is superhuman.' The rest is just a great story. Brenda's not going to affect Jon. We knew Game 4 was huge. Were we as uptight as we were the first round? No. Who knows why he had his kids with him that day? Maybe it was just trying to give them the experience like players do today when their kids are on the field after the Super Bowl. People try to point to that, but this is hard to write: our power play was good, but we weren't out-skilling teams or out-surprising them with strategy that nobody else had seen or done. No. The puck was going in for us. You could throw a puck across on a one-timer, dot to dot, five times. Maybe on three of those, the puck finds a hole, not by skill, but it just went in. It will hit something, or it will come off the blade a little different. But then they stopped, and the Unseen Hand somehow healed Mario's back."

Later that spring, Casey gave Resch the gift of the goalie pads he'd worn during the playoffs—signing them to his goaltending coach. Resch still keeps them among other souvenirs from that season, which he still sometimes can't believe.

"It came out of nowhere and mushroomed into a mountain," Resch said. "You knew it wasn't a group that was going to last a long time. It was kind of like a vortex, how all these humans rose together and played their best hockey. I think we knew that couldn't be duplicated. It was a special moment, something athletes dream of. It's just not the story that we who were involved wanted."

In November of 2015, he held the Stanley Cup in Brainerd—living a tradition where winners get control of the trophy for a day, which wasn't a thing when he won it in 1980. One of the places he took it was his church in Baxter. Today, Chico and his wife, Diane, rent a place in New Jersey during the season and spend the rest of their time at their home on Little Trout Lake in rural Emily, Minnesota. Their daughter, Holly, lives in Kentucky and they have one granddaughter.

Chico remains one of the supporters and coaches for Hockey Ministries International, teaching hockey and ethic skills to boys and girls at Christian Hockey Camps. During the Covid shutdown, he began participating in a Zoom chapel for ex-NHLers to talk about their faith. Mark Johnson, Bob Johnson's son, was a guest on the call the day after our interview. Paul Henderson, Al Secord, and Bobby Smith also have been speakers.

"In this crazy world, you better have a foundation more than sports, politics, money, or power," Resch said. "That stuff, as we're seeing, will all pass away. It won't be there. That's why I think you see athletes become Christians. They've done, in some cases, everything they dreamt of in a worldly sense, and it wasn't enough. It wasn't satisfying or fulfilling."

Norm Green 🏆 (Won 1989 Stanley Cup as owner of Calgary)

Green (6–12–34, Winnipeg, Manitoba) moved to Dallas in the summer of 1993 and enjoyed a robust first season in Texas as the Stars had the third-best record in the Western Conference. Then they fell six games under .500 in the lockout-shortened 1994–95 season, after which financial pressures—stemming at least in part from his business ventures outside of hockey—began to mount. In November 1995, the *Dallas Morning News* reported Green was $60 million in debt, including $10 million owed to Howard Baldwin and Morris Belzberg and another $6 million to the NHL. The following month, Green agreed to sell the franchise to Tom Hicks for $84 million. The sale closed early in 1996.

"He's really a great guy, one of those guys that I enjoyed playing for, and he took care of the players," Mike Modano said of Green. "He was a real players' type owner."

Out of hockey, Green and his wife, Kelly, continued to keep a home in the Dallas area and maintained others in Palm Springs, California, and Calgary. He generally resisted the public eye but continued to follow the Stars so closely that Hicks awarded him a Stanley Cup ring in 1999. Green says he wears it every day, except when he plays golf.

In 2003, Green got back into hockey as part-owner of the Central Hockey League's Austin (Texas) Ice Bats. In 2007, he told NHL.com that he understands now why people in Minnesota continue to harbor such ill will against him.

"I don't blame them because the North Stars, even though they weren't being supported, were part of their culture," Green said. "We didn't plan this—we had to do this because there was not support—but in retrospect, they needed to have a little shot in the arm. And what happened? Amazingly, when we left, the government (in Minnesota) did a great thing. They built a great building, they got a new team, and now there's a waiting list for season tickets. Quite incredible. We couldn't fill our 16,000-seat building with 7,000 people. But it was a good process in the final analysis."

Not that he would know first-hand.

"I haven't been back since '92, and I'm not going back," Green laughed. "Well, I may one day. I may go sit in a box with (former North Star GM) Lou Nanne and put a mustache on."

Green continues to remain a Stars suite holder and season-ticket holder. He occasionally drops by the team's practice facility. Contacted by WCCO-TV in 2016, he declined an interview when the Wild played the Stars in the playoffs for the first time. "Too many folks still hold (bad) feelings toward me," Green wrote in an email, "and I do not want to give them any more fuel."

Norm and Kelly remain married and spent most of their time during the recent pandemic in Calgary. I was unable to communicate with him but several sources in this book are still in contact. I encouraged those people to at least let him know of the project, with little expectation he would participate.

"He's an old guy, and this is very much in his rear-view mirror," Strangis told me. "I don't think he's doing much. I don't think he wants to do much. And I get the sense that he had a very public, busy, complicated life. He's just tired and wants to play golf, and Kelly will let him and that's that. It's my sense he doesn't want to talk about any of this."

(Norm, if you ever do, I'd be happy to add your perspective—which might be worth another book entirely.)

Bob Clarke 🏆🏆(Won 1974 and 1975 Stanley Cups as a player with Philadelphia)

Bobby Clarke in 2017.

Clarke (8–13–49, Flin Flon, Manitoba) remained the North Stars' GM in 1991–92, after which he returned to Philadelphia to serve as senior vice president and as a mentor for Eric Lindros, whom the Flyers acquired in a trade with Quebec. Clarke become GM in Florida in '93–94 but reprised his role as GM in Philadelphia in '94–95. Under Clarke, the Flyers made one other finals appearance—swept by Detroit in 1997.

For the next six seasons, Philadelphia made the playoffs every year but only once advanced to the conference final, losing to New Jersey in 2000. That was after coach Roger Neilson took a medical leave to undergo cancer treatment and was replaced by Craig Ramsay. Some in the media thought the way Clarke replaced Neilson was disrespectful.

"The Neilson situation—Roger got cancer—that wasn't our fault," Clarke said at the time. "We didn't tell him to go get cancer. It's too bad that he did. We feel sorry for him, but then he went goofy on us."

Clarke also had some legendary battles with Lindros, whom he traded to the New York Rangers in 2001. Afterward, Clarke said, "I don't give a crap whether he ever plays again or if I ever see him again. All he ever did was cause aggravation to our team."

By 2003, Clarke's reputation with the Philadelphia media, if not the fans, had cratered.

"I don't have anything to prove to you people; I've won in this league," Clarke told reporters after a second-round loss to Ottawa. "If the writers judged themselves the way they judge me, they would all be fired. The papers are losing readers, they're losing advertisers, losing money, everything. But you never judge yourselves. You judge me. You say that I should be fired. Maybe it should be you guys that are fired."

The Flyers lost to Tampa Bay in the 2004 conference final but—after the 2005 lockout—were eliminated in the first round in 2006. Early the following season, Clarke resigned to become a senior vice president again. When Lindros retired a year later, Clarke remained ever enigmatic and was one of Lindros' most ardent supporters for the Hall of Fame.

As recent as 2011, Clarke and his wife, Sandy, lived in Haddonfield, New Jersey; however, they eventually sold their home and began spending more time in Florida.

On January 14, 2017, Clarke played in Philadelphia's 50th-anniversary alumni game, which he announced would be his last ever.

Hockey would remain prominent for all his children. His oldest daughter, Jody, worked in hockey operations for the Flyers and is divorced from former Philadelphia forward Peter White, who scored the first goal in the history of the Xcel Energy Center. Clarke's youngest daughter, Jakki, went on to write a book about the team's former greats. His oldest son, Wade, played at Division III Hobart College from 1991 to 1994 and has been a Philadelphia scout since 2007, and his youngest son, Luke, became a network engineer who nonetheless assists the Flyers' trainers at home games.

And they've combined to give Bobby enough grandchildren to form his own hockey team.

Les Jackson in 2022.

Les Jackson

Jackson (12–21–52, Manning, Alberta) followed the Stars to Texas and was assistant GM from 1993 to '98, when he left to take the same role with the Atlanta Thrashers, who would play their first season in 1999–2000. His timing was bad as Dallas won the Cup immediately after he left. After the Thrashers debuted with the worst record in the league, Jackson rejoined the Stars in 2000 as director of hockey operations and later assistant GM again. From 2007 to '09, Jackson and Brett Hull were co-GMs. They were replaced by Joe Nieuwendyk in 2009, when Jackson became director of scouting and player development. He served in that role until 2013, when he again became assistant GM. In 2016, he became a senior advisor to the GM, a position he held until his contract was not renewed in 2020, ending a 33-year tenure—the longest of any employee in franchise history.

Since the 2020–21 season, Jackson has been a pro scout with the Florida Panthers.

Before they left Minnesota, Les and Melanie had three boys (Brock, Drake, and Reid). They later divorced. Their older sons live in Saskatchewan, where they work as an electrician and for a gas company, respectively. Their youngest, Reid, played in the WHL before his career was cut short by concussions. He later became an amateur scout for the Calgary Flames.

Les has since remarried and lives in Coppell, Texas.

Doug Armstrong in 2022.

Doug Armstrong 🏆 🏆 (Won 1999 Stanley Cup as assistant general manager with Dallas; won 2019 Stanley Cup as GM with St. Louis)

Armstrong (9–24–64, Sarnia, Ontario) became assistant GM to Bob Gainey during the North Stars' last season in Minnesota and served in that role until 2002, when he succeeded Gainey as the GM in Dallas. Armstrong held the position until 2007, when he was fired. Within six months he became director of player personnel for the St. Louis Blues. He was promoted to GM in 2010, named NHL GM of the Year in 2013—when he added the title of president of hockey operations—and helped forge the team that won the Stanley Cup in 2019.

Armstrong and his wife, Kelly, had a son, Blake, and a daughter, Kayla, and now live in Creve Coeur, Missouri.

Dave Surprenant in 2022.

Dave Surprenant 🏆 (Won 1999 Stanley Cup as trainer with Dallas)

Surprenant married the former Julie Wesselman in 1992 and remained head trainer for the Stars until 2008. He then became an outreach coordinator at the Institute for Orthopedic Sports Rehabilitation at the Carrell Clinic Center and served as an independent consultant based in The Colony, Texas. In 2013, he was inducted to the trainers' area of the Hockey Hall of Fame. He and Julie live in Lewisville, Texas, with their sons, AJ and Bryan, both of whom have special needs.

Dave Smith spends much of his time tying flies for fly fishing these days. He lives in Carrollton, Texas, but travels all over the US for his passion. (Photo courtesy of Dave Smith)

Dave Smith 🏆 (Won 1999 Stanley Cup as equipment manager with Dallas)

Smith, who stayed to the end with the North Stars, was blind-sided by the move to Texas, which came just a few weeks after he'd bought a new snowblower. He worked with the Stars until the lockout in 2004, after which GM Doug Armstrong told Smith his contract wasn't going to be renewed.

"We had an assistant GM at that time who was a bean counter," Smith said. "He gave me a booklet that showed the salary, playoff bonuses, health/dental insurance, tickets, and per diem I got. It was like he was structuring a picture to get rid of me, financially. I was disappointed (Armstrong) didn't stand up for me."

Smith worked nineteen seasons with the Stars organization and thirty-nine years in hockey. He then went to work for his son, Kevin, as manager of a rink in Richardson, Texas. Dave drove the Zamboni, managed the work crew, and oversaw recreational leagues until he retired in 2008. That same year, at sixty-four, he was inducted into the equipment managers section of the Hockey Hall of Fame.

He turned seventy-seven in 2021, and lived with his wife, Maxine, in the same Dallas area home they owned since 1993, until her death in 2022. He has three grandchildren and has become an avid fly-fisherman.

Mark Baribeau in 2022.

Mark Baribeau

Baribeau served as equipment manager for the North Stars until the move to Dallas in 1993. He might've gone with the team if not for some entrepreneurship that riled Norm Green.

In the early 1990s, Baribeau increasingly worked side hustles in addition to his duties as equipment manager. He got into buying and selling sports trading cards, brokering some purchases in the height of a boom in the hobby with help from players as investors. He also produced and sold a "9" cap in partnership with Mike Modano, a poster of Modano and Russ Courtnall together, and several T-shirts. One last attempt at that proved his undoing.

Once it became clear in the spring of '93 that the team was moving, Baribeau created a T-shirt with facsimile autographs of all the players on the back and "Thank You, Minnesota" on the front. It was available in the parking lot before the final home game, April 13 against Chicago. The next day, the T-shirt was prominent in a picture on the cover of the *Star Tribune*.

"Norm went ballistic and wanted to know who did that T-shirt," Baribeau told me in 2021. "I'd gotten into doing some of the team services stuff that season, and I was coming in the next day to arrange meal money for the trip to Detroit. (Bob) Gainey came in, and I knew something was wrong. He says, 'Hey, can you come into my office.' He said, 'I'm going to have a new job for you in Dallas, so you can just go home and I'll call you later.' I got a sick feeling in the pit of my stomach. I didn't go to Detroit and some of the guys were like, 'Where's Babby?'"

Baribeau says he has a letter signed by Pat Forciea authorizing him to sell the T-shirts outside Met Center.

"Somehow, I got ratted out," Baribeau said. "Later on, I found out there was talk about cards and the (other) T-shirts we'd done. Basically, Bob was told from Norm that, 'Whoever did this, I want them out of here.' That's not the way you want your tenure to end, and it shook me to the core… it was a heartbreaker. I played things back in my head, and I think there was a misconception of what I was doing."

He also believes he may have been a victim of his relationship with some of the players, including Modano.

"I tried to keep my boundaries, but when Mike came in (in '89), I felt it was important that I did the most I could to help somebody in the transition he faced," Baribeau said. "So, I felt a kinship to him. He's a really nice guy; a good-looking stud of an athlete. He liked to laugh, and I don't know if he knew what he was getting into. Did I go out and hang with him? Not really. Maybe some on the road. We would get something to eat when it was our responsibility to get something to eat. During that last season, Ralph Strangis would join us. I remember one night we were having a bite to eat and three Pepsis in St. Louis. I was with Mike and Ralph, and the brass comes walking by.

"By the end, with guys like Gainey, I had been there a long time, and I'm sure they were trying to figure out what guys they could trust. In the locker room, I was kind of a sounding board even though I was fairly young. I tried to be a good, all-around teammate from that standpoint. If guys were complaining or bitching, I would never go talk to anybody about it.… I feel like I was the fall guy. Easy to get rid of."

Baribeau had a year remaining on his contract and eventually reached a settlement that bridged until he landed in pro team sales for CCM and Easton. He has worked in marketing for CCM since 2003.

Now fifty-seven, he and his wife, Julie, live in Hudson, Wisconsin. They have three children.

"In hindsight, the best thing that ever happened to me was getting canned," Baribeau told me. "I regret to this day that I wasn't around when they won (in '99)… just like players, when they don't get to leave on their own terms, it's disheartening and discouraging."

Less than two months after Dallas won the Cup in 1999, Baribeau started the Met Center Classic golf tournament for former arena employees. It's been an annual event for the past twenty-two years, and they never tire of revisiting '90–91.

"It was a miracle year," Baribeau said. "We had 5,000 people for opening night. I was embarrassed for the guys. And, somehow, we got to the end of the year where the building is jammed and the parking lot is jammed. The whole thing seems like a frickin' dream. But what a dream it was… you couldn't make it up. The only thing that would've made it more silly is if we'd won."

Lance Vogt

Vogt continued with the team as an equipment manager before and after the move to Dallas. He became an equipment assistant with the Minnesota Wild in 2000 and continues to work primarily with visiting teams at the Xcel Energy Center.

Lance Vogt in 2022.

Lou Nanne

Nanne (6-2–41, Sault Ste. Marie, Ontario) retired from hockey at fifty to enter the world of finance, starting at Piper Capital Management and then moving to the institutional sales department for Voyageur Asset Management. When RBC Global Asset Management purchased the firm in 2000, he stayed on as RBC's senior managing director for institutional sales.

Lou and Francine Nanne have been married more than sixty years. He's still working and calling the Minnesota State High School hockey tournament on TV in his 80s. (Photo courtesy of Lou Nanne)

"I'm still working," said Nanne, who turned eighty just after we spoke in 2021. "I still love what I'm doing. I don't call it work, and I do what I want, when I want to do it. And it's just dealing with people, and you know, I can't stop doing that."

Lou and his wife, Francine, were high school sweethearts. They eventually settled in Edina and had four children: sons Michael, Marc, and Marty, and a daughter, Michelle. Michael became a dentist, which was his father's failed pursuit. Michelle married former Minnesota Strikers pro soccer goalie Tino Lettieri. Marc became a real estate broker. And Marty played at the University of Minnesota, was a Chicago Blackhawks draftee, and finished the first of two seasons with Indianapolis of the IHL in 1989–90. Michael died of brain cancer at age forty-eight in 2013. They also have eleven grandchildren. One grandson, Louis, was a draft pick of the Minnesota Wild, and another, Tyler, was a New York Rangers draftee and played in the AHL and ECHL. One of their granddaughters, Erin, worked in community relations for the Wild. They have four great-grandchildren, all living within a fifteen-minute drive of their home. They also have a family cabin on Balsam Lake in Wisconsin, northeast of Taylors Falls.

Lou opened Lou Nanne's Steakhouse in Edina in 2016. It has since been renamed Tavern23 as a tribute to his jersey number. He knows he's been fortunate compared to some other former players.

"People don't just ride off into the sunset and be successful," Nanne told me. "That's what I try to tell college kids and young kids about going to school because, as I say, you might have forty years to work after you're done. Not everyone's going to make the pros, and if you do make the NHL, it doesn't mean you're going to make a lot of money. You might make a lot for a short time. But that's not a lot over a long period of time. I've talked to a lot of former players that have had tough times in their lives. There aren't many guys left from when I played on our team. There's (Bobby) Rousseau, Cesare (Maniago) and Tommy Reid and Ray Cullen, maybe one or two others, and that's it. It's just a microcosm of life. That's what happens. And hockey is actually much better than basketball or football. If you look at the guys who really made big money, five to seven years after they are done playing, many of them are bankrupt. But fortunately, the percentages are much more favorable on the hockey side."

For all his experiences, Nanne never witnessed anything like that run to the finals in '91.

"It was amazing," he said. "I just couldn't believe what I was seeing, but they were playing so well. It's not like they were fluke wins. They were good enough to win. They had good talent. We had a good team by that time. And the atmosphere was unlike anything I've ever seen. The excitement and electricity going through the building, through the Twin Cities, I mean, through the state, was unreal. When you look back at opening night compared to that, all of a sudden it's just unbelievable what you're seeing. You keep asking yourself, 'Is this really gonna happen? Is this really gonna happen?!'"

Pat Forciea

Forciea described his time with the North Stars as a "walk through the valley of death." He said the last year the team was in Minnesota was "the worst year of my professional life," and that's saying something.

After the Stars moved to Dallas, he went to work in marketing for the University of Minnesota athletic department and later worked on the Twins' efforts to get a new ballpark. As those efforts were frustrated, he invested in a couple of Tier I junior teams in the United States Hockey League—first in Cedar Rapids, Iowa, and later in Omaha, Nebraska. While trying to buy a third team, he forged several signatures (including that of Minnesota Wild owner Robert Naegele Jr.) on bank documents to get financing. Forciea was caught, and in 2004, pleaded guilty to two counts of fraud and embezzlement. He was sentenced to six years in federal prison and ordered to pay $5 million in restitution, mostly to Minnesota banks from which he fraudulently received loans. Ironically, when Forciea lost control of the USHL's Omaha Lancers and was in deep legal trouble, Mario Lemieux emerged as a candidate to be one of the new owners.

Pat Forciea in 2022.

While serving his sentence, Forciea said he was diagnosed as having bipolar disorder. He was treated at a facility in Rochester and then served the remainder of his sentence at a prison in Colorado.

"That was awful," Forciea told me in an interview for this book. "I tried to serve my sentence with as much dignity as I could. But you think you understand what the bottom is, and then you find out there's a couple more fuckin' levels to that than you thought. But I'm the luckiest guy you could ever meet in terms of the support I got in my time in prison."

He worked ten hours a day, six days a week in the penitentiary bakery. Being busy helped pass the time. So did a realization people hadn't given up on him. Although he and his wife, Cathy, divorced, Pat highlighted her support, that of their daughter and son, and of former business partners—including Naegele—as being compassionate throughout his ordeal.

"A lot of guys in prison don't have any support at all, right?" Forciea said. "They kept me on my feet and gave me a second chance."

After his release, Forciea became part owner of Hell's Kitchen, a downtown Minneapolis restaurant, from 2010 to 2017. He cultivated a consulting business in which he advises clients on communications and branding. He has worked with the Nova Group, which owns restaurants in the Twin Cities and Rochester, and his clients include Tavern 4&5 in Eden Prairie, Hazelwood in Bloomington and Minnetonka, and Pier 500 in Hudson, Wisconsin.

In 2021, Forciea publicly revealed he has battled Parkinson's disease since 2017. He struggles with handwriting, his voice has become quieter, and he has minor balance issues that have partly been addressed by spinal fusion back surgery in 2020 and a left hip replacement in 2021. Part of his treatment program for staving off any effects of the disease includes boxing workouts (footwork drills and punching a heavy bag) twice a week. He also hosts a podcast on Parkinson's with former KARE-TV news and sports anchor Tim McNiff.

At sixty-two, Forciea said he's "fortunate and blessed" to feel as good as he does. His daughter, Grace, was a track athlete at St. Thomas, worked in politics for Governor Mark Dayton and Senators Tina Smith and Amy Klobuchar, and is now VP of public policy with the Minneapolis Regional Chamber. His son, Jack, works as a scouting coordinator for Minnesota United FC—otherwise known as the Minnesota Loons soccer team.

Elaine Sullivan (Waddell)

Elaine Waddell moved to California at the prospect of connections with Jim Goddard and Frank Jirik, former Met Center executives who went to San Jose to work for George and Gordon Gund. Goddard, who had been VP of Met Center, went on to a similar role at the SAP Center, future home of the Sharks. Jirik, who'd been in charge of marketing for Met Center, became VP of building operations in San Jose and offered a role

Elaine Sullivan in 2022.

to Waddell. From 1994 to 1999, she was VP of sales and marketing for the Sharks. From 1999 to 2001, she was VP of consumer services for the NBA's Houston Rockets and WNBA's Houston Comets. Then she moved back to San Jose and co-founded SullivanWorks, a marketing and communications agency, with her second husband, Nate Digre. They were married for more than twenty years and remain business partners although they divorced in 2013.

Waddell turned seventy-one in 2021 and said the 1990–91 North Stars remain a hazy memory—regardless of the fact that she lost most of the sight in one eye from the golf injury that spring.

"I never had surgery, though I'm getting a cataract now, so I suppose that could change," she told me in an interview for this book. "Even now when I go to an eye doctor, they'll say, 'Wow, what happened to your eye?' I've got blotches in there. I can still see 20/20 out of the other eye. I've never worn distance glasses. I wear reading glasses now for work. But that season is really a blur to me… I'm traveling with the team (to Russia and in the playoffs), and then all of a sudden I get hit in the eye with a golf ball, and then we're in the finals. It was crazy."

Joanie Preston

The former and once again Joanie Preston did not go with the team to Dallas. One of her last tasks was to package front-office materials and ship them to Texas. She said she intentionally held out some artifacts significant to Minnesota and later sent them to the US Hockey Hall of Fame in Eveleth.

She worked briefly in public relations for Aveda, then for a small PR agency. As her husband, Dave St. Peter, worked his way up through the Minnesota Twins front office, they started a family. They adopted their oldest son, Jack, and she later gave birth to twins Eric and Ben. In a little more than a decade, Dave climbed from Twins pro shop manager to team president in 2002. Joanie started her own communications company and wrote a couple of books for teen readers about NHL teams. They divorced nearly a decade ago, but they remain amicable and focused on the welfare of their sons, who were twenty-four and twenty-three, respectively, in 2021.

Joanie Preston worked in the Minnesota Wild press box for awhile but now spends most of her time as an administrator and management specialist with School Technology Associates in Chaska or at home in Eden Prairie. (Photo courtesy of Joanie Preston)

Joanie jumped back into the job market as communications project coordinator for Westwood Community Church in Excelsior and now works as an administrator and management specialist with School Technology Associates in Chaska. She lives in Eden Prairie and recently worked several seasons with the Wild press box crew for home games at the Xcel Energy Center.

"Life is a ride, and sometimes you just shake your head," Joanie told me. "Hopefully, you can take it and enjoy it and learn from it."

Dan Stuchal 🏆 (Won 1999 Stanley Cup as director of team services with Dallas)

Stuchal moved to Dallas with the team and became an assistant to the hockey department and in charge of team video in 1993–94. But it almost didn't work out that way. Since Joanie St. Peter had decided

Dan Stuchal has risen from a PR intern with the Minnesota North Stars to chief communications officer with the Dallas Stars—though it hasn't exactly been a straight path. (Photo courtesy of Dan Stuchal)

she wasn't moving with the team, Dan flew down with Norm Green for the initial reveal that the team was coming to Texas.

"I was with Norm for two days," Stuchal recalled. "The morning after the announcement, I was staying in one hotel and he was in another. I called him, feeling pretty cocky. I said, 'Norm, congratulations on everything that just happened yesterday. It was great to be part of. I just want to let you know I would really like to be your media relations director in Dallas.' I don't think it took him two seconds to say, 'Absolutely not. I want somebody who knows this market. I want somebody with way more experience than you.' *Click*.

"I remember sitting on my bed going, 'Oh, no.' I was on a plane that afternoon back to Minnesota and started dusting off my resume."

But two days later, Doug Armstrong—by then assistant GM—called Dan and asked him to come to his office.

"He said, 'Bob Gainey and I have been talking and we need some help in the hockey department down in Dallas, and we'd like you to join us. Are you willing to come?'" Dan said. "I said 'Am I willing to come?! Just tell me where to sign!' I got very fortunate."

In 1995–96, Stuchal became director of team services. He was in charge of travel and all administrative duties for the coaching staff. It was a role he maintained through the Stars' Stanley Cup victory.

Stuchal, who was married and divorced during his tenure in Dallas, left the team after the 2000 finals to become assistant GM in Calgary. Longtime Stars scout Craig Button had been hired as Flames GM at the draft that year and invited Dan to come along. They served in those positions for three seasons, during which time Stuchal remarried. His second wife, Shauna, worked for a travel agency with offices in the Saddledome. He met her on one of the many occasions of booking a flight.

On April 11, 2003, Calgary fired Button. Stuchal, whose contract had expired, was suddenly without a visa in Canada.

"What now? I couldn't even legally work there," Stuchal said. "I didn't have a professional network outside of hockey and the paperwork to stay because I'd gotten married was a nightmare."

Ralph Strangis, by then entrenched on TV and radio with the Stars, brokered Stuchal's return to Texas as a consultant for Big Brothers Big Sisters Lone Star. He "fell in love with the mission" and was soon hired full-time. He served until 2013, rising to vice president of sales and marketing. Offered a chance to return to the Stars, he was VP of brand development and broadcasting, responsible for Mike Modano's jersey retirement in 2014, and remains the last Minnesota connection for the franchise.

"We have internal discussions all the time about what is important from a Dallas or franchise perspective," Stuchal said. "The retired numbers are a good example. People down here don't really know anything about Bill Masterton or Bill Goldsworthy, but I've always thought we need to respect that history. But it's like the Brooklyn Dodgers moving to Los Angeles, or how much do the Twins observe their Washington Senators heritage?"

Stuchal became senior VP of marketing in 2019, overseeing game production, digital content for social media and the web, graphic design, and advertising, and in 2022 moved to chief communications officer. He and Shauna have two daughters, Talia and Sydney, who are sixteen and nine, respectively. They live in Coppell, Texas.

Dan maintains contact with Joanie, and has occasionally played golf with his boyhood idol, Neal Broten, when he gets back to Minnesota and Wisconsin in warmer months. Stuchal remains close friends with Les Jackson and Bob Gainey, calling the latter "the most powerful mentor in my life."

"He has reached the highest of highs and the lowest of lows in his unbelievable life," Stuchal said of Gainey. "The way he has navigated through it all is remarkable. It's one of the many reasons I look up to him so immensely. He's been a real guide for me throughout my professional journey. I just have so much respect for him. He's a man of few words, but when those words come out, they always mean something. There's no idle chit-chat."

That's one of the reasons I was so honored when Gainey gave me a couple of hours of uninterrupted time for this book. And it wouldn't have been complete without contrasting my own experience with Dan, who has done extremely well since we were once interns.

"You've gotten amazing access to a lot of people, and I think it goes to show they believe there's a story to be told there," he told me. "They want to contribute. There were so many good stories and so many good characters on that ('91) team. It just seemed wrong the way we exited. I knew that morning (of Game 6) that Pittsburgh could be skating around with the Cup that night, but to see it happen, it never leaves you… and I wasn't playing. I can't imagine what it feels like for the guys who never got a chance to win one."

Al Shaver

Shaver, who had two years left on his contract (to do only home games) when the team moved to Dallas, stayed in Minnesota and called Gophers hockey from 1993 to '96 before retiring. He was honored with the 1993 Foster Hewitt Memorial Award for outstanding contributions to radio and TV broadcasting and the game of hockey.

Al Shaver (Vintage Minnesota Hockey)

When the NHL returned to Minnesota with the debut of the Wild, the team named the press box in his honor. He later settled on Vancouver Island in Qualicum Beach, British Columbia. He and his wife, Shirley, had a condo, and he moved into a senior apartment after her death in 2019. They were married sixty-seven years and had five children (Wally, Jim, Judy, Gary, and Susan) all of whom had been born in Edmonton.

Their oldest son, Wally, has become the radio voice for the Gophers men's hockey team. Jason Shaver, one of their nine grandchildren, was a goalie at Augsburg in the early 1990s and has had several stops as a minor-league broadcaster, including with the Wild's AHL affiliate and, most recently, the Chicago Wolves.

Al also has eight great-grandchildren. He was ninety-three when I spoke with him in 2021, battling the effects of asthma and diabetes but still going strong.

"I sleep well at night," he told me. "I'm gone as soon as my head hits that pillow. My appetite is still good.… I've got no complaints. I've had a great life and loved every bit of it."

Ralph Strangis

Ralph Strangis banters with Mike Modano (left) on the night the Dallas Stars retired his number in 2014. (Photo courtesy of Ralph Strangis)

Strangis moved to Dallas as the only employee of the team outside hockey operations who worked for the franchise in Minnesota. He continued as color analyst until 1996, when he took over play-by-play.

"Norm trusted me," Strangis said in an interview for this book. "He knew I wanted to do business. This is a craft but also a business. My job is to bring eyeballs and listeners and to sell. I think Norm understood that. I remember I called him in the spring of '93 once the team was moving. He answered, and I said, 'Hi, Norm. How you doing?' 'Nice. Nice.' He always said 'Nice.' I said I was still young in my efforts at sobriety, and I had all my friends and family in Minnesota. But I wanted to stay with the Stars, and I told him, 'I'll go on your say-so.' He said, 'OK.' I got there Memorial Day weekend. I was the first guy from the organization to go down there. I went to every Rotary Club and church meeting in Texas. Then, in 1996–97, I got The Chair."

With former NHL goaltender Daryl "Razor" Reaugh as color analyst, Strangis became synonymous with the team until he left the Stars in April 2015. His run was only briefly interrupted in 2001 when he was injured in a car accident and suffered a broken vertebra.

"This is my team," Strangis said of the Stars. "I mean, I'm the only one to say, 'the Dallas Stars have won the Stanley Cup,' as their radio voice."

Strangis sent a letter to Al Shaver right after first speaking those words in 1999.

"I thought about him all day," Strangis said of that Saturday, June 19, the day of Game 6 in Buffalo. "He was with me, and so were all the things he had taught me."

Strangis became a seven-time Emmy winner and called more than 2,300 NHL games. He wrote speeches for Mike Modano's Hall of Fame induction and scripted the program for his number retirement ceremony.

In 2016, Strangis finished his degree (Applied Technology and Performance Improvement) from the University of North Texas. He moved to Palm Springs, California, and in 2017 published a novel (*Saving Lenny Franks*). Strangis has called some games for the Los Angeles Kings and worked the 2018 Olympics, several NHL outdoor games, and the Stanley Cup playoffs.

"Act 2" in his life has involved creation of 3rd Period Media, for which he is a consultant (the Minnesota Loons are a recent client). He produces films, podcasts, and stage plays for his own company, Senseless Productions, and is a corporate speaker.

"I'm really happy that I left (Dallas)," Strangis told me. "It was time, and I needed a rinse."

Since leaving the Stars, he has traveled the world. He's ridden his bike in France and Croatia, saw The Cure in Italy, and drives his Jeep to Joshua Tree National Park.

In 2020, he was diagnosed with bladder cancer. (It's the same cancer famed Dallas announcer

Norm Hitzges fought, while Dave Strader, the broadcaster who replaced Strangis with the Stars, developed a different form of cancer in 2017.)

He was scheduled to call the 2020 NHL conference finals until he learned of his diagnosis, but that hasn't kept him from getting involved in a local community college. He started to teach and also began working with a local theater group—even winning an award in "The Diary of Anne Frank," for playing the girl's father. Strangis, who got married and divorced in Dallas, has his own daughter, Savannah, who is twenty-five and pursuing a career in the production side of the film industry in Los Angeles.

Strangis called 2020 a "thorn bush." You didn't know how much he was referring to his health or the COVID-19 pandemic. But every day he strived to smell the roses, most notably when his daughter moved in with him. She was there if he needed her, and they got to watch their team, the Dallas Stars, play the Tampa Bay Lightning in the Stanley Cup Final. He turned sixty on February 27, 2021, and embarked on a list of sixty things—a bucket list, if you will—that he planned to experience during his sixtieth year. He's kept only a few mementos from his broadcasting career, including his credentials from the '91 finals, in a couple of scrapbooks at home. He rarely looks through them.

"I've lived a remarkable first two periods," Strangis told me. "I had some health stuff this year, but I feel great. I want to get to overtime, which is ninety, and then the shootout is 100. My dad lived until he was eighty-two and biked until he was eighty-one. If I can have that quality of life at that age, that's enough for me."

Doug McLeod

McLeod didn't know his job as the North Stars' TV voice was in jeopardy until he learned he was being replaced for 1991–92 by Dave Hodge, who had been the Hockey Night in Canada studio host from 1971 to 1987.

"Nothing had been said," McLeod recalled. "I mean, we had all these record ratings, which I don't take credit for at all—people weren't tuning in to see me, and things had gone very well. But my contract was up at both Channel 9 and Midwest Sports Channel. I couldn't get a response from anybody beyond, 'We're going to work it out. We'll work something out.' Ok. So, I went on vacation. I'll never forget. I was on the Isle of Skye in Scotland, and my folks had come up from Iowa to housesit and dog-sit. I called home one day, and Dad said, 'Hey, your name's in the paper.' Immediately, I think, 'Oh, fuck.' I'd called to tell him, among other things, that I'd just seen the most beautiful triple rainbow. I'd never seen a triple rainbow, and there was one on the Isle of Skye. I thought, 'Boy, that's gotta bring good luck.' Instead, Dad said, 'Yeah, looks like they're gonna get some Canadian guy in there.'"

Doug Mcleod in 2022.

McLeod continued a hodgepodge of other broadcasting duties, and he and his wife, Catherine, had a daughter, Caitlin. In 1992, Pat Forciea reached out to ask if McLeod would return for the '92–93 season, and he welcomed the opportunity.

After the Stars moved to Dallas, McLeod moved his family to Pittsburgh where, ironically, he became a TV voice for the Penguins from 1993 to '96. He had a role as a broadcaster in the film "Mystery Alaska," and later, had a similar position with the Phoenix Coyotes from 1996–2003. From 2012 to '19, he called Gophers hockey, something he'd done in the late 1970s and '80s. Doug turned sixty-eight in 2021. He and Catherine live in Mesa, Arizona.

Rachel Blount

Rachel Blount in 2022.

Blount remains a sports reporter for the *Star Tribune*, covering a variety of topics, including the Olympics, Wild, college sports, and horse racing. She has written extensively about Minnesota's Olympic athletes and won numerous state and national writing awards.

A Notre Dame alum with a graduate degree from the University of Missouri at Columbia, she lives in Minneapolis with her husband, Pat Borzi, who also is a sportswriter. Reached about participating in this book, she never went further than a promise to think about it. Unfortunately, she was diagnosed with gallbladder cancer in 2022 but has met the fight bravely and with beautifully written updates on her CaringBridge page. Rachel, perhaps winning this battle can be your Stanley Cup.

Gary Olson

Gary Olson retired from the St. Paul Pioneer Press in 2002, a year before his death.

Olson covered the North Stars through their departure to Texas and worked for the *St. Paul Pioneer Press* for thirty-two years. He placed third in the national AP sports reporting competition with his copyrighted story in 1995 on Bill Goldsworthy's battle with AIDS. Olson was a pallbearer and gave a eulogy, along with Al Shaver, at Goldsworthy's funeral in 1996.

Olson loved that his career allowed him to combine his passions for sports and dining as he traveled around North America, a pursuit for whom Shaver made the ideal companion.

"We both liked good food," Shaver told me. "We had lunch at Bookbinder's (in Philadelphia) and the bill was $100 without any drinks."

That was back when $100 went a long way.

Olson took an early retirement in 2002 because of complications from diabetes, but it was a cancerous tumor that paralyzed him from the waist down for the last five months of his life and ultimately led to his death August 1, 2003. He was fifty-six, survived by his wife, Deborah, whom he married in 1987, and daughters Michelle Olson and Kim Brackett.

Other Faces In The Crowd:

Dick Arneson, whose contract was not renewed in the spring of 1991 as the North Stars' VP of administration, died of cancer in 2002. He was sixty-two.

Steve Aschburner continued at the Star Tribune through 2007, after which he became a writer for NBA.com.

Mike Augustin, who was the sports editor at the St. Cloud Times before joining the Pioneer Press in 1969, died of cancer in 1997. He was fifty-seven.

Roman Augustoviz covered mostly high school sports, Gophers men's hockey, and the Minnesota Lynx before moving to the Star Tribune copy desk in 2012. He continues to produce occasional stories.

Ace Bailey was director of pro scouting for the Kings and was aboard United Airlines Flight 175 to Los Angeles on September 11, 2001. Shortly after take-off from Boston, terrorists took control of the plane and crashed it into the south tower of the World Trade Center in New York. Bailey was fifty-three.

Dan Barreiro remained a columnist at the Star Tribune until 2004, when he became a full-time sports radio personality with KFAN. In 2022, he was inducted into the Minnesota Broadcasting Hall of Fame.

Eddie Belfour, who rose to prominence as a goalie with the Blackhawks, would go on to play for the Dallas Stars, helping them win the Stanley Cup in 1999. One of the most distinct characters in the league during his career, he was arrested on March 8, 2000, in Dallas, after a bizarre series of drunken events. According to Sports Illustrated, an intoxicated Belfour—who was playing for Dallas at the time—checked into an upscale hotel with a woman. She became frightened by the loud and belligerent goalie and called hotel security. Security personnel escorted the woman to a cab. When one of the guards confronted Belfour, he slammed the 50-year-old man against a wall and put him in a headlock. When police arrived, they were forced to pepper spray him because he also kicked two officers in the chest. He was taken into custody and spent six hours in a holding cell before being released on bond. It was only the first of several arrests for Belfour, who was inducted into the Hall of Fame in 2011. He went on to launch a whiskey distillery and was arrested again in 2020 following an alcohol-induced incident in which he attempted to assault a Kentucky hotel employee.

Morris Belzberg died in 2020 at the age of ninety. He was part of the Penguins' ownership group, with Howard Baldwin when they won the Cup in 1992. Baldwin, who turned eighty in 2022, and his wife, Karen Mulvihill Baldwin, remain married and in 2020 produced their latest film, "Odd Man Rush," about an American who plays professional hockey in Sweden and develops a relationship with a local woman. Howard also wrote a book (*Slim and None: My Wild Ride from the WHA to the NHL and All the Way to Hollywood*) about his hockey and movie-making careers.

Wren Blair, the North Stars' first coach and general manager, died in 2013. He was eighty-seven. From 1979 to '85 he served as player personnel director for the Kings.

Jim Bowers sang the anthems for the North Stars through their final home game in 1993, when he was given a rocking ovation before and after his performance. Bowers, who sang at Herb Brooks' wedding and funeral, died in 2019 after a bout with cancer. He was eighty-four.

Dennis Brackin continued to be a writer and editor at the Star Tribune until he retired in 2016.

Herb Brooks, who coached the Penguins in 1999–2000, reprised his role with the US Olympic team in 2002 but settled for a silver medal. The following year, he was killed in a one-car rollover on I-35 south of Forest Lake, Minnesota, as he returned from Biwabik and a fundraiser for the US Hockey Hall of Fame. He was Pittsburgh's director of player personnel at the time of his death. He was sixty-six.

Curt Brown worked as a journalist for more than thirty years and has become an author of many books about Minnesota history. He continues to write a weekly historical feature for the Star Tribune.

President George H.W. Bush, who lost to Bill Clinton in the 1992 election, died in 2018. He was ninety-four.

Walter Bush, the original North Stars president, died of a heart attack in 2016. He was eighty-six.

Craig Button scouted for the North Stars from 1988 to '92, when he became director of scouting. He followed the team to Dallas and was director of player personnel from 1998 to 2000. After a three-year stint as GM of the Calgary Flames, he became a scout for Toronto and later a broadcaster with the NHL Network and TSN.

Jim Caple covered the Twins for more than a decade before leaving the Pioneer Press to write for ESPN.com. He has written a couple of books on baseball and in 2021 was living in the Seattle area and writing for SportsPressNW.com. He later joined The Athletic, a sports journalism website.

Arne Carlson served as Minnesota's governor until 1999. He has remained involved in politics in retirement and turned eighty-eight in 2022.

Nick Coleman continued as a columnist at the Pioneer Press until 2003, when he returned to the

Star Tribune—where he'd worked as a reporter from 1973 to '86. He left the Star Tribune in 2009. He died after a massive stroke in 2018. He was sixty-seven.

Clark Donatelli, who played twenty-five games for the 1989–90 North Stars, played the 1990–91 IHL season with the San Diego Gulls, then signed with the Boston Bruins and played ten games for them in 1991–92. He retired after five more minor-league seasons and later coached in the ECHL with the Wheeling Nailers (2011 to '15) and the AHL with the Wilkes-Barre/Scranton Penguins (2015 to '19). In 2021, he was indicted on sexual assault charges stemming from a 2018 incident in which he was accused by the wife of his former assistant coach. According to a lawsuit filed against him, Donatelli apologized to the couple and said he would inform Pittsburgh Penguins assistant GM Bill Guerin of the incident. A subsequent investigation was launched into conduct by Guerin and the NHL team as to whether they allowed Donatelli to continue to coach despite knowledge of the assault. In 2019, Guerin became GM of the Minnesota Wild.

Kari Dzeidzic became a spokesperson for the Hennepin County attorney's office, a political activist, and has been a Minnesota state senator since 2011. She turned sixty in 2022, when she became Minnesota's Senate Majority Leader. Walt Dzeidzic served the Minneapolis city council until 1998. He died in 2018. He was eighty-five.

Jack Ferreira, who turned seventy-seven in 2021, served as GM of the Mighty Ducks of Anaheim from 1993 to '98. He later became director of player personnel for the Atlanta Thrashers, a special assistant to the general manager of the Los Angeles Kings, and from 2018 to '21 served the Wild as a senior advisor.

Larry Fitzgerald has been a sports editor and columnist for the Minnesota Spokesman-Recorder for more than thirty-five years. He was a radio broadcaster, including a stint at KFAN, and continues to appear on Twin Cities radio and TV. He has two sons, Marcus and Larry Jr., the latter of whom went on to a standout NFL career.

Theo Fleury scored 1,000 NHL points despite being 5-foot-6. But drug and alcohol addictions led to the end of his NHL career in 2003. He later revealed he had been sexually abused by his former junior coach Graham James, who served two terms in prison—one for abusing Sheldon Kennedy and later, again, for abusing Fleury. Since retiring, Fleury has become a best-selling author, sex-abuse victim advocate, speaker, and businessman.

Randy Furst continues to write for the Star Tribune in a career that has spanned more than forty-five years. In 2019, he underwent open-heart surgery at seventy-three.

Link Gaetz truly earned his nickname, "the Missing Link." His NHL career ended when he was thrown from the passenger seat of a friend's car on April 2, 1992, hours after a brief players strike went into effect. The driver was later charged with driving under the influence for losing control on a Bay Area freeway ramp at eighty miles per hour. Gaetz suffered back and facial injuries and was semi-comatose for eight days. When he regained consciousness, he suffered from some left-side paralysis. However, he regained movement through several months of rehabilitation, only to be arrested for driving under the influence himself. His career then spiraled through twenty-one different teams in fourteen different leagues between 1993 and 2007. In none of those stops did he play more than thirty-five games in a season—reduced to sideshow status in small arenas where fans often wanted to see more fights than hockey. In 2011, the San Jose Mercury News found him living in Surrey and working for a recycling company. His most recent appearance in a North American newspaper came in 2014, when Mounties in British Columbia issued a warrant for his arrest because he failed to appear for a charge of causing a disturbance in 2012 at a fast-food restaurant in Cache Creek.

John Gilbert left the Star Tribune after thirty-one years and moved to Duluth, where he continues to write for an alternative weekly and has a daily radio show.

Gary Glitter, the English glam rock star whose anthem punctuated North Stars goals at Met Center, has spent much of the past 20-plus years in jail. Glitter, whose real name is Paul Gadd, was sent to prison after downloading child pornography in 1999. He was later convicted of child sexual abuse in 2006 and attempted rape in 2015.

Bill Goldsworthy continued to scout for the San Jose Sharks, but he was diagnosed with AIDS in November 1994. He told the Pioneer Press in 1995 that his health problems stemmed from drinking and promiscuity, and he died March 29, 1996. He was fifty-one. His son, Sean, whom I got to know when he was a graduate assistant with the St. John's University hockey team in the mid-1990s, went on to coach at St. Olaf and is now the head coach at Minnetonka High School, which won the Class AA state tournament in 2023.

Wayne Gretzky played with the Kings until 1996, followed by a brief stint with the Blues and three years with the Rangers. He retired in 1999 and remains the NHL's all-time leader in goals, assists, and points. He later was a part-owner and coach of the Coyotes. From 2016 to 2021, when he turned sixty, he had an ownership stake in the Oilers. While he won four Cups in Edmonton, his only appearance in the finals after his trade to L.A. in 1988 came in 1993, when the Kings lost in five games to the Canadiens. He recently joined TNT as a studio analyst for its coverage of NHL games.

Chuck Grillo was the Sharks' director of player personnel and later GM from 1992 to '96. He later scouted with the Penguins from 2001 to '11. In 2020, he and his family divested their interest in Minnesota Hockey Camps.

Doug Grow left the Star Tribune in 2007 but continues to write about politics and public affairs for MinnPost, a nonprofit online newspaper covering Minnesota.

George Gund died of cancer in 2013. He was seventy-five. In February 2002, the Gunds sold the Sharks to a consortium, named San Jose Sports and Entertainment Enterprises. While George retained his share, Gordon Gund sold his outright. He turned eighty-three in 2022 and remains CEO of the Gund Investment Corporation.

Sid Hartman continued to write a column in the Star Tribune until his death in 2020. He was 100.

Brett Hull played for the Blues until 1998, after which he signed free-agent contracts with the Stars and later, the Red Wings, with whom he won the Cup in 2002. He retired after five games with the Coyotes in 2005. Hull, who turned fifty-eight in 2022, has been an executive vice president with St. Louis since 2013.

Frank Jirik, who spent forty years in the sports and entertainment industry with the North Stars, Twins, Met Center, the San Jose Sharks, the Minnesota Wild, and the Excel Energy Center, died following a battle with lymphoma in 2009. He was sixty-nine.

Brenda Knight worked for the Sharks for thirteen years and married Joe Will, a former North Stars intern who went west with Jack Ferreira. Will, who is four years older than I, became the Sharks' scouting director, then director of hockey operations, and ultimately assistant GM.

Eric Kruse landed at the University of Minnesota after he was fired in 1991. Kruse served as a facilities manager and director of facilities operations and was an associate vice-president and later VP of university services. In 2001, he started his own business, Pegasus Group, which represents owners in strategic facilities planning and capital project delivery.

Peter Lappin played most of the 1991–92 season at Kansas City of the IHL, then retired. His son, Nick, appeared in sixty games with the New Jersey Devils from 2016 to 2019.

Robb Leer worked as an investigative reporter for KSTP-TV until 2003, after which he created his own company, Leer Communications & Consultants.

Mario Lemieux never played a full season in his entire career, which nonetheless was showered with decorations. He is the only person to win the Stanley Cup as a player (1991 and '92) and owner (2009, '16, and '17). He missed the 1994–95 season as he battled Hodgkins Lymphoma, which caused him to temporarily retire in 1997, when the Hall of Fame waived its normal three-year waiting period and inducted him immediately. But he returned in 2000 and played until 2006, after which he was diagnosed with atrial fibrillation and retired for good.

Bill Lester remained executive director of the Metropolitan Sports Facilities Commission until 2012. He turned seventy-seven in 2022.

Eric Lindros finished his career with Dallas in 2006–07, at which point multiple concussions and problems associated with them forced his retirement. He played eight seasons with the Flyers, three with the Rangers, and one with the Maple Leafs and was inducted to the Hall of Fame in 2016. He never won the Stanley Cup.

Dean Lombardi was GM of the Sharks from 1996 to 2003 and held the same position with the Kings from 2006 to '17. His teams won the Stanley Cup in 2012 and 2014.

Bill Mack went on to sculpt the statues of Twins greats that adorn Target Field, as well as likenesses of Kareem-Abdul Jabbar, Peggy Fleming, and Arthur Ashe.

John Maher worked for the North Stars until the move to Dallas, and in 2002 joined the Minnesota Wild. He became VP of brand, broadcast, and production in 2017 and a senior brand advisor in 2020.

Sergei Makarov posted declining point totals in his second, third, and fourth NHL seasons, making his choice as the Calder Trophy recipient in 1989 seem even more of a travesty. He had 57 points in 1992–93, his last season with Calgary, played two diminishing years in San Jose, and was out of the NHL at thirty-six, except for a four-game stint with the Dallas Stars in November 1996.

Mark Messier was traded to the Rangers on the eve of the 1991–92 season. He helped them end a 44-year championship drought in 1994 and became the only man to captain two different teams to the Stanley Cup. He later played three seasons for the Canucks before returning to New York. When he retired in 2004, he was the last remaining player from the WHA and the last NHLer from the 1970s. He is now a studio analyst for NHL games on ESPN and ABC.

Alexander Mogilny scored 473 goals in 990 career NHL games. Late in the 1999–2000 season, he was traded from Vancouver to New Jersey in time to help the Devils beat the Stars in the Stanley Cup Final.

Jayson More played 287 games for the San Jose Sharks from 1991 to '96, then played 113 games with four different NHL teams over three seasons until he suffered a career-ending injury with the Nashville Predators. He later became a senior partner with Players Capital Group, a private investment and marketing partnership of former professional athletes.

John Muckler continued to coach in the NHL with the Sabres and Rangers until he was fired in 2000. He was GM for the Senators from 2002 to 2007 and also served as an advisor for the Coyotes. He contracted COVID-19 in late 2020 and died January 4, 2021, in Buffalo. He was eighty-six.

Joe Murphy, who won NCAA and AHL championships before getting his name on the Stanley Cup with the 1990 Oilers, had a 15-year NHL career, including stints with the Blackhawks, Blues, Sharks, Bruins and Capitals. His last stops, in Boston and Washington, resulted in suspensions—first for screaming profanities at Bruins coach Pat Burns and second after an altercation at a New York nightclub. He retired in 2001 and later struggled with post-concussion issues. Despite earning more than $15 million in his career, he was living on the streets in Costa Rica when he was deported to Canada in 2017. In 2018, he was homeless, using drugs and alcohol, and living on the streets of Kenora, Ontario. Although he completed a mental health services program in 2019, he has either relapsed or refused more help. In 2020, he surfaced—homeless—in Regina, Saskatchewan, a circumstance that has regrettably continued.

Dr. George Nagobads, who served as the team doctor for the 1980 US Olympic hockey team, was inducted into the US Hockey Hall of Fame in 2010 and continued to live in Edina until his death on March 31, 2023. He was 101.

Jeff Passolt, a one-time hockey player at St. Cloud State, left Channel 11 in 1993 to go to a station in Denver but returned to KMSP-TV as a news anchor in 1996. He was inducted to the Minnesota Broadcasting Hall of Fame in 2018 and retired a year later.

Tom Powers retired in 2015 but continued to write a column in the Pioneer Press until 2017, when he went on a Twitter rant about "liberal pussies," called Hillary Clinton "the devil incarnate" and told Democrats "go fuck yourself."

Bob Probert played for the Red Wings until 1994 and then the Blackhawks from 1995 to 2002. He retired in 2003, at which time he re-entered rehab. He died of a heart attack in 2010. He was forty-five. In 2017, his family scattered his ashes in the penalty box at the final game in Joe Louis Arena.

Jean-Francois Quintin spent most of his time with Kansas City of the IHL from 1991 to '98. He then played five seasons in Europe before retiring in 2003.

Patrick Reusse, who wrote for the St. Cloud Times in the 1960s, continues to write columns for the Star Tribune and was inducted to the Minnesota Broadcasting Hall of Fame in 2019.

Ray Richardson left the Pioneer Press in 2013 but continued as an on-air personality for KMOJ-FM until 2019. He now works for the Urban League Twin Cities but also covered some of the protests in the wake of George Floyd's killing by a Minneapolis police officer in 2020. Richardson oversaw the CDL truck-driving training program at the YWCA in St. Paul and got to know Floyd in the process.

Gordon Ritz, the North Stars' first governor, died of cancer at his Wayzata home in 2001. He was seventy-four.

Jon Roe retired in 1999 after working thirty-two years at the Star Tribune.

Jeremy Roenick played with the Blackhawks, Coyotes, Flyers, Kings, and Sharks until he retired as a player in 2009. He was the third American-born player, after Joe Mullen and Mike Modano, to score 500 goals. Roenick then became a broadcaster for NBC until 2020, when he was fired for making suggestive sexual comments about colleague Kathryn Tappen.

Mark Rosen worked for WCCO-TV for fifty years until he retired in 2019. He turned seventy in 2022 and continues to make regular appearances on KFAN.

Ron Rosenbaum, who represented Kari Dzeidzic and Norm Green in separate cases, died of cancer in 2016. He was sixty-eight.

Steve Ruane later served as Xcel Energy Center's security projects coordinator. He died of natural causes in 2019 at his Bloomington home. He was sixty-four.

Art Savage was president and CEO of the Sharks until 1997. He died of lung cancer in 2009. He was fifty-eight.

Dr. John Schaefer continues to practice as an emergency medicine physician at Fairview Southdale Hospital.

Mary Schmitt Boyer covered the Timberwolves for the Pioneer Press until 1995, when she moved to the Cleveland Plain Dealer, where she continues to cover sports.

Randy Shaver, no relation to Al, was inducted into the Minnesota Broadcasting Hall of Fame in 2020, when he was sixty-one. He continues his career at KARE-TV, now in his thirty-ninth year, and has prevailed in a couple bouts with cancer.

Gerry Sikorski lost his seat in the House of Representatives in 1992, after a scandal in which he was found to have hundreds of overdrafts on the House Bank. Needless to say, his efforts to stop pay-per-view never amounted to anything. He turned seventy-four in 2022 but continues to work as a Washington lobbyist.

Dr. William Simonet served as a team physician with the North Stars from 1987 to '93 and continues to practice as an orthopedic surgeon with Twin Cities Orthopedics.

Howard Sinker remains at the Star Tribune, where he is a digital sports editor. He also teaches media and cultural studies at Macalester.

Glen Sonmor, who coached more than 600 NHL and WHA games—the vast majority with the North Stars—died of pneumonia at a Brantford, Ontario, nursing home in 2015. He was eighty-six.

Jim Souhan continues to write for the Star Tribune, where he's worked for more than thirty years.

Kevin Stevens, a key factor in the 1991 Stanley Cup Final, was named to three All-Star teams during his career and won two Cups, but he was arrested on January 23, 2000, after being discovered with a prostitute and crack cocaine in a Collinsville, Illinois, motel room. According to the New York Times, Stevens, a

Ranger at the time, was celebrating a 4–1 win over St. Louis that night. At the time, he was married with two children and a third on the way. Stevens went through rehabilitation and behavioral health counseling but continued to struggle with an addiction to prescription drugs, a condition that dated to when he suffered a massive facial injury during a game in 1993. In 2017, he pleaded guilty to federal drug charges but also was rehired by the Penguins as a special assignment scout. He had scouted for Pittsburgh from 2005 to 2012.

Stu Swartz remained as GM at KMSP-TV until 2001. He later launched his own sports media consulting company.

B. E. Taylor died in 2016 from a brain tumor, less than two months after the Penguins won their fourth Stanley Cup. He was sixty-five.

Mario Thyer played the entire 1990–91 season and most of '91–92 in Kalamazoo before he was traded to the New York Rangers. They sent him back to Minnesota for future considerations during the summer of 1992, but the rest of his career consisted of a full season with Cincinnati of the IHL in '92–93, and three games in the AHL and a brief tenure in Germany the following year.

Charley Walters, who turned seventy-five in 2022, continues to write a weekly sports column for the Pioneer Press, where he went to work after a short major league career as a pitcher with the 1969 Twins.

Jay Weiner worked twenty-six years at the Star Tribune before leaving in 2007. He specialized in off-the-field sports issues, mostly the public financing of sports facilities, and covered every Winter and Summer Olympic Games between 1984 and 2010. He later covered politics for MinnPost, was a speech writer for University of Minnesota president Eric Kaler, and was manager of communications for the Minneapolis Federal Reserve. He has written several books, including *Stadium Games: 50 Years of Big-League Greed and Bush-League Boondoggles.* He turned sixty-eight in 2022, continues to be a mentor for me, and was crucial to the progress of this book.

Jim Wells was a sportswriter for the Pioneer Press for more than thirty-five years, retiring in 2006. He was inducted into the Minnesota halls of fame for boxing and horse racing. He died in 2019 following complications from angioplasty. He was seventy-three.

Paul Wellstone defeated Rudy Boschwitz in a rematch to retain his Senate seat in 1996. Eleven days before the 2002 elections, Wellstone was killed in a plane crash near Eveleth with his wife and daughter. He was fifty-eight. While the DFL nominated Walter Mondale to run in Wellstone's place, Republican Norm Coleman, who'd been instrumental in creating an environment to build the Xcel Energy Center as mayor of St. Paul, won the election.

Wheelock Whitney, an original North Stars investor, died at his home in Independence, Minnesota, in 2016. He was eighty-nine.

Marv Wolfenson, the former original owner of the Timberwolves (along with Harvey Ratner), died in La Jolla California, in 2013. He was eighty-seven. Ratner died of cancer in 2006. He was seventy-nine.

Doug Woog coached the Gophers hockey team through 1999, then went on to a long career as a color commentator for college hockey games on Fox Sports North. He died in 2019 after battling Parkinson's. He was seventy-five.

Steve Yzerman led the Red Wings to Stanley Cup titles in 1997, 1998, and 2002. He played with Detroit until his retirement in 2006. He later became GM of the Lightning and returned to the Red Wings in the same capacity in 2019.

Jerry Zgoda continues to write for the Star Tribune, where he has worked for more than thirty-seven years.

John Ziegler, who succeeded Clarence Campbell as NHL president and was succeeded by Gil Stein, presided over the league until 1992. He returned to his career as an attorney, served as a governor of the Chicago Blackhawks, retired to Florida, and died in 2018. He was eighty-four.

Judd Zulgad wrote for the Star Tribune, and covered the Vikings as recently as 2011, before joining Hubbard Broadcasting as a radio and podcast host and writer for its SKOR North platform.

"A guy tells me one time—he was a writer this guy—I'm trying to learn about writing a screenplay and he says 'Remember, anybody can write a good first act.' He tells me this like 20 years ago and it's been bangin' around in my head ever since.

"What he doesn't tell me—this guy—and it's something I only find out by working on writing books and movies and plays in my spare time over the years—he doesn't tell me how hard it is to know when to end Act 1. And how to start Act 2. Turns out art's like life that way. Messy. No straight lines. No right or wrong answer. Just yours.

"My timeline isn't your timeline—I know that. You wish I'd be here forever. I would if I were you. I always wanted Ray Scott to do the Vikings and Al Shaver to call the Stars games forever. See how it works—Al has the chair—then another guy has the chair—then I have the chair—then another guy has the chair. It ain't our chair to begin with...

"Act 1? I got no complaints. None at all. The opposite for sure. What a ride... Not easy this Act 2 business. Nope—not hardly easy at all. But you look in the mirror and check the clock and make a call. Ships in port are safe but that's not what ships are built for. And so on... Act 2. Scary—exciting—exhilarating—complicated. But here I go..."

-Ralph Strangis, in an open letter to Stars fans, on his decision to leave as a broadcaster in 2015

EPILOGUE

Kevin Allenspach (5-1-1969; St. Louis Park, Minnesota)

Kevin Allenspach in 2023.

In the summer of 1991, I knew what I needed to do; what I wanted to do.

I needed to graduate, and I wanted to be a sportswriter.

With two quarters of college left, I took a promotion at the *Minnesota Daily* to cover Gophers football. It was, by far, the choice beat at the paper—and I had a blast, though it was like writing about one comical car crash after another.

The '91 Gophers went 2–9 overall, 1–7 in the Big Ten (back when the Ten stood for something). For many years, I debated with Patrick Reusse whether it was the worst team in school history. He preferred the '83 Gophers, who went 1–10 and lost at home to top-ranked Nebraska, 84–13.

The '91 squad won its season opener against San Jose State, 26–20, which came during the lull between summer school and the start of fall classes—so the *Daily* wasn't even publishing. The same was true the following week, when we didn't travel to Colorado, and the Gophers were rolled, 58–0.

But the rest of the way, while Minnesota got caught up in the Twins' second World Championship in four years, I was at Gophers practice every day—trying to keep up with Curt Brown, who always seemed one step ahead in the *Star Tribune*, and Charley Hallman (God bless him), who got my foot in the door at the *Pioneer Press*. I had a few small scoops and felt like a big shot when former Vikings receiver Paul Flatley interviewed *me* at halftime of the homecoming game on WCCO-AM. The Gophers won a thriller that day, 6–3 over Purdue.

The rest of the season I can only liken to what it must've been like to cover the 1962 New York Mets. The Gophers didn't kick an extra point until week 6. The next Saturday, Michigan barely broke a sweat in maintaining possession of the Little Brown Jug, 52–6. The historic Halloween blizzard cost me a trip to beautiful Bloomington, Indiana, and the other trophies (Paul Bunyan's Axe and Floyd of Rosedale) remained with Wisconsin and Iowa, respectively. The offense averaged 8 points per game in conference play, and the defense allowed 302 points during the season (27.5 per game).

I learned a ton. I found how valuable it was to always be around, to develop rapport with everyone from the fourth-string punter and the equipment staff right up to the head coach. That season, it was John Gutekunst. As rumors swirled that he would be fired, I'll never forget how he cut short his last weekly media luncheon and offered me a ride from Williams Arena, where they were held, back to the Bierman Athletic Building in his big, white Cadillac. He dallied, long enough to tell me what was really happening. I could never understand why he showed such deference to a lowly student reporter. The best answer I got was from his administrative assistant. She said, "He likes you."

Without sacrificing objectivity and journalistic integrity, I tried to grow similar relationships wherever I've gone since. Sometimes it didn't work as well. Like during the subsequent winter when I covered the Gophers men's basketball team. Clem Haskins built a wall around his players, creating an adversarial relationship with the media that only heightened scrutiny and criticism for a team that went 16–16. (Six years later, some of those chickens came home to roost. The *Pioneer Press* scooped everyone with a Pulitzer Prize–winning expose that proved academic fraud for more than twenty players since 1993.)

I graduated in the spring of '92, after I'd lucked into some major events for the *Daily*. Super Bowl XXVI was at the Metrodome on January 26, 1992, and I got to cover the game from a press seat high in what would have been the upper-deck right-field stands for a baseball game. Then the NCAA men's basketball Final Four was at the Dome a couple months later. Since it was a college event, they respected the *Daily* much more. My press seat was right behind one of the benches. I could've reached my hand forward and touched the back of Michigan forward Chris Webber while he shook with sobs under a towel as Duke won the national championship on April 6.

I continued working at the *Pioneer Press* and later moved to Woodbury. I filled my spare time playing amateur baseball and hockey, and my job search was voluminous. I sent out hundreds of resumes and clips to newspapers all over the country. My "part-time" job (which averaged about thirty-eight hours per week) allowed me to be selective, however. I wasn't going to move to Missouri or New Mexico or Pennsylvania unless it was a good situation. Secretly, perhaps not even admitting it to myself, I didn't want to go that far from Minnesota. I liked the Twin Cities, where most of my friends lived. One of my first interviews was in Marshall. It was a daily newspaper, with a college in town, but that's about all that could be said for a position where the starting pay was going to be less than $16,000 per year.

I said no thanks and kept looking. During the North Stars' final season, I worked for New York hockey columnist Stan Fischler as his Minnesota correspondent. Before long, I also was writing for *Minnesota Hockey Magazine*, *Full Court Press*, *Minnesota Basketball News*, and *Collegiate Basketball News*, among other freelance opportunities—even in radio.

Working at the *Pioneer Press* was like hanging out with my favorite uncles every night. We had games on the TV and access to news from all over the country—the world. It's hard to explain to anyone who has only known the Internet Age. But at that time, there were two primary repositories of the latest, most complete and best sports information in Minnesota: the sports departments at the *Pioneer Press* and the *Star Tribune*.

Our reporters would call in from every press box in the American League, the NFL, the NHL, and the NBA. Our newspaper provided coverage of those and an incredible smorgasbord of college sports (big-time and small school), as well as high school sports throughout the metro area and even the entire state. Preps were where I was most valuable at the time. I'd cover some games, write a feature on the athlete of the week, cover the new fad of independent professional baseball in the summer, and be available in emergencies.

Occasionally, that presented when an out-of-town newspaper needed a reporter in a pinch. It happened on January 8, 1994, when a snowstorm prevented the *Boston Globe* basketball writer from following the Celtics to Minneapolis for a game against the Timberwolves. The *Globe* appealed to me and, the following day, I had multiple bylines—including on the front of the sports section of one of the biggest dailies in the nation.

Inevitably, I would be at some event in one of my expanding freelance roles, and my colleagues at the *Pioneer Press* would ask for my help in getting quotes or to write a sidebar.

On February 27, 1994, I was at Williams Arena to see the Gophers destroy Indiana, 106–56. At the time, it was Bobby Knight's worst loss and only the largest margin of defeat for the vaunted Hoosiers (then ranked No. 12) since 1905. The desk at the *Pioneer Press* quickly asked me to write something on the volatile visiting coach.

He didn't disappoint.

"Fucking back off so the rest of the people can see," Knight hollered at a camera encroaching on his postgame press conference. "They should find an island for you TV people. Then they could put the newspaper writers in a cave under the island."

Knight had benched three of his starters to open the second half. Steeling myself, I asked him what he wanted to accomplish when the game got out of hand.

"You wouldn't understand if I explained it to you anyway," he said, figuratively handing me my head on a platter. But that's one of the risks I had to run to get a story.

I always enjoyed playing sports, especially baseball and hockey. In April 1995, my Minneapolis-based amateur hockey team advanced to play in a Hockey North America tournament in Toronto. I took advantage of the trip to visit the Hockey Hall of Fame and take in a game at Maple Leaf Gardens. (Author photo)

By then I'd moved to an apartment in North St. Paul. I was getting antsy, and finally, in February of 1995, the path of my life was forever altered. Dave DeLand, sports editor at the *St. Cloud Times*, hired me full-time, and I moved to another apartment in St. Cloud. Part of my new position involved covering recreation and outdoor sports (like hunting and fishing). While I'd fished a little as a kid with my dad and occasionally shot some birds or squirrels with my .22, I had no interest in anything that didn't include a ball, a stick, or a puck. But I was working, writing a regular column, and I immersed myself in coverage of local high schools and any way I could think of linking Central Minnesota with major college and professional athletics. We routinely covered Vikings home games and, occasionally, the Twins and Timberwolves. When a trip to cover the St. John's University hockey team in the NCAA Tournament took me to Vermont via Montreal, I wrangled a reason to cover a Canadiens game at the Bell Centre.

I kept looking for the next job on the ladder and perhaps came closest when I interviewed to be a back-up Packers writer and beat reporter covering the University of Wisconsin-Green Bay basketball team for the *Green Bay Press-Gazette*. I remember the prediction of my college mentor, *Star Tribune* sportswriter Jay Weiner, who heard of my desire to climb to New York. He responded: "You'll probably move around a few times, and at some point, you'll get married and settle down." (He also thought if I got to New York, I might find it wasn't quite what I expected or hoped.)

After I finished second for the Green Bay job, narrowly missing the chance to cover Brett Favre, Weiner's prediction came true before I went anywhere else. I met the former Danell Tatro, who worked in IT for the Times, and we married in 1997. We briefly lived in her tiny house, and then bought our first home together. By then, I got the opportunity for which I'd been waiting. Our assistant sports editor, Mike Killeen, moved on from covering the St. Cloud State hockey program in 1998. I took over, and the next twelve years were (unknown to me at the time) some of the halcyon days of my life.

I covered the Huskies, who had the unique appeal of playing in a sterile concrete building (the National Hockey Center) but before spirited crowds of as many as 7,000 people per game in the Western Collegiate Hockey Association. It was like covering one of the Davids in a league with several Goliaths. The 10-team conference provided some of the best Division I college hockey in the country, routinely before its biggest crowds. The University of Minnesota and the University of Wisconsin, both Big Ten schools, had a different level of media exposure. And Denver University was another example of a school located in a major metropolitan area, with all four major pro sports, that competed on the same footing as a relatively small city like St. Cloud (population 68,000).

I covered my share of Wild games in the 2000s. During the 2004-05 lockout, the team invited the media to participate in a one-day fantasy camp. I lived to tell about it, as you can see from this photo after it was over with Wild coaches Mike Ramsey, Bob Mason, Jacques Lemaire and Mario Tremblay.

I traveled regularly to Minneapolis, Duluth, and Mankato in Minnesota; Denver and Colorado Springs in Colorado; Madison, Wisconsin; Grand Forks, North Dakota; Houghton, Michigan; and even once to Anchorage, Alaska. There were trips to nonconference series and NCAA Tournaments all over the country.

By then, St. Cloud also had what could sort-of pass for minor-league baseball. It had a team (the River Bats[68]) in the Northwoods League. Using some of the best college undergrads in the country, they played more than seventy games a summer, traveled on buses all over the Midwest and played before crowds of as many as a couple thousand people. We seldom went on the road, but my calendar was full of hockey from September through April (and offseason news during the summer) and baseball from May to August. What wasn't to like?

Until 2000, there was no NHL team in Minnesota, so the college game took top billing in the State of Hockey. I couldn't have created a better job description in St. Cloud and, after the Wild arrived I even became a semi-regular at some games throughout the 2000s. I got to know well players who would eventually make it to the NHL, NFL, NBA, and Major League Baseball. None of them are household names, but it was rewarding to chronicle their days of ascension.

Of course, I was rarely satisfied, always striving to provide "better" coverage. I didn't realize those were the dying days of a media we now hardly recognize. With the rapid expansion of the web, soon there were more platforms available, continually eroding the need for newspapers.

There's nothing inherently wrong with that. It's just the way it is. It's one of the things that became clear to me in writing this book. Thirty years is a long time. Hopefully, we all live longer than that—maybe a couple of times around. But the world is often a much different place in the span of three decades. In 1961, most people didn't have color television. By 1991, the VCR had revolutionized how we watched TV. And in 2021, you were behind the times if you weren't streaming video on your 65-inch, 4K flat screen.

That's just one example. Look anywhere else and you find others: automobiles, the way we listen to music, advances in medicine, and the advent of smartphones. And that's just off the top of my head.

The athletes and others I detailed in the previous pages all experienced this same shelf life. A pro hockey player's career might last a few years. Anything more than ten is exceptional. What do you do with the rest of your life?

A sportswriter's timetable is only a little different. Sure, Sid Hartman worked until he was 100. And I know some who have worked forty or even fifty years in sports media. But for me, the time came to move on in 2010. I could see the future: earlier deadlines, smaller news hole, reduced road trips, and more responsibilities with fewer resources. I'd always danced with anxiety and depression, and I

68 The Bats later changed their name to Rox—reflecting what had been a minor-league team in St. Cloud from 1947-71. The original Rox were affiliated with the New York Giants, the Chicago Cubs and later the Minnesota Twins.

reached a breaking point. I dreaded that someone on the street would strike up a conversation about why our coverage wasn't as good anymore. If I couldn't meet my personal standard, I wanted out.

By the end of the SCSU season that year, the program finally won an NCAA Tournament game (after a record seven consecutive losses in other attempts) and came within one win of the Frozen Four. I was so stressed that I felt as though I was constantly attached to an electric cord. When the Huskies lost their last game, for a couple days, I felt like that cord had been pulled from its socket. But that feeling—as though I was being fried by some invisible current—soon returned. I've never felt worse. I couldn't eat. I couldn't sleep. I couldn't stay upright because all I wanted to do was sleep to escape.

What tipped my decision, I believe, was that my son, William, and daughter, Anna, (then ages six and four) were just getting to be school-aged. We'd moved to a lovely home on the northwest edge of St. Cloud. Watching William begin to experience some of the things I had from my earliest memories triggered a need to be around him more. That didn't jive with working nights and weekends, covering games or working on the sports copy desk.

It's the hardest thing I've ever gone through. I swapped roles with a former sportswriter who'd become our community news editor (think of all the submissions you might find in a small-town weekly, about some kid becoming an Eagle Scout or a big donation from the VFW). It felt alien and uncomfortable. Later, I worked as a night news editor a few days a week and then became our business reporter. As the *Times*, then owned by Gannett (publisher of *USA Today*), spiraled downward like most newspapers, we began to experience more and more layoffs. My wife had been one of the first in 2008, though she landed on her feet in another job in the computer sector. After a trickle of middle managers, by 2014 it was a wave at all levels of the company. At one point, we had to re-apply for our jobs and some people left or were laid off. I became part of a three-person investigative team with two fellow U of M graduates and reporters for whom I have the highest respect.

But it only delayed the inevitable. I was never comfortable away from sports. Roger Kahn once said that, if you're going to write, write about what you know. But eventually, there was no one to pay the bills for a sports department as we knew it.

Then in late 2015, my father died after a short battle with lung cancer. Like his father, he didn't make it to seventy-nine. My mother had been partially paralyzed in a car accident two years earlier, and suddenly it was on me to place her in senior care and divest the family homestead near Garrison.

By the time I accomplished that, I knew I needed to try something else to save my own health. I left the *Times* of my own volition in mid-2016. That summer was a delightful time of coaching my son's baseball team of 11-year-olds to an extremely unlikely state title, spending time on my boat and watching my daughter dance.

By the fall, I took a job as a grant writer with CentraCare Health—the largest employer in Central Minnesota. It probably wasn't the best fit, but at least I worked for a growing organization, had some pride in my position, and made a good salary while working business hours. Like Neil Wilkinson, I didn't want to miss my kids growing up. And like him, I don't regret the way it played out.

After a little more than three years at CentraCare, a declining economy brought another reorganization. That spelled layoff for me and another writer from our department just a couple months before COVID-19 became a reality.

Trying to make something positive from a bad situation, I used my time while unemployed during the pandemic to fulfill a 30-year-old desire to tell this story. This book is my gift to myself, though I certainly hope others find value in it. I don't know what the future holds. I may get to a point, like Wilkinson or Brian Glynn, where I do something entirely different. (I don't imagine I'll make a living trimming trees or become a police officer. But, hey, you never know.) If so, that's OK. I'm fifty-three, and I've done many of the things I've wanted to do. For much of my life, I got paid to write sports. I covered them all, at the highest levels—even though I never got to the *New York Times* or *Newsday*. Officially or as a fan, I've been to the Super Bowl and the World Series, the Stanley Cup Final, all-star games in Major League Baseball, the NHL, and NBA, and the Final Four and Frozen Four. I talked with Joe DiMaggio and Wayne Gretzky and dozens of other Hall of Famers in all sports. I've been to Comiskey Park and Tiger Stadium, Fenway and Wrigley, the original Yankee Stadium, Lambeau and Soldier fields, Chicago Stadium and Maple Leaf Gardens, and dozens of other stadiums, arenas and ballparks still in use or faded into the scrapbooks of history.

I was fortunate to receive many writing awards at state and national levels. I'm proud of the work I did, and in review, I believe it stands up well through time. But it's all yesterday's news—fun to look back on, but as Brian Propp said, nothing on which to stake your reputation.

My dad was so proud of the things I'd done and the stories I'd written. I remember soft-pedaling when he boasted about me to other people in my presence. I understand now as I look at my own kids. I have no doubt they will be my greatest contribution to this world.

William is eighteen, bright and sensitive, and he has succeeded athletically so far beyond his dad that it's silly. He's a captain of his high school football team and has played varsity hockey and baseball. One of my greatest joys is watching him play.

Anna is sixteen, with a near-perfect grade-point average, and she has been on her varsity high school dance team since she was in seventh grade. What's more, I can see she is fast becoming a beautiful young woman, and I can't wait to see how far she'll go.

As for me, my life is far from over, I hope. I still have a lot I want to do. There are many lakes to visit, games to watch, and the works of other writers to read. Like Ralph Strangis, completing this book is a major step in figuring out what's next. For all the words I've written (I calculated more than six million in my tenure at the *Times* alone), I've never devoted more of myself to one project than this one. It was more than a year in the making, and it feels rewarding in more ways than I can express to finish the final page.

Maybe there will be other books. Perhaps not. But at least there will always be this one. Like Mike Modano's Stanley Cup, you won't be able to take it away from me.

I hope something has seeped between the lines if you've read all this. I spent a lot of my life striving to be the best I could be. I don't regret that at all. But I also spent a lot of time comparing myself to others. In high school, it was to those more popular—like a classmate who ultimately pitched in the majors. In college, it was to peers who went on to earn much more than I ever would or fellow journalists who wrote stories I wish I could say were mine. Heck, look where Dan Stuchal is now. But I believe the 1990–91 North Stars offer a lesson and admonition: Celebrate your highs and persevere your lows. Let the lens of history put them in perspective. And, even if you didn't achieve something you wanted, honor yourself for having run the race.

I'm sure there is a lot more for me to discover, but now I can own with satisfaction what I've done to this point in my life. I never played professional baseball. The peak of my sports writing career probably came in some college hockey arena more than a decade ago. I am not wealthy and am curious where I will go from here. But I'm not afraid anymore.

As a youngster, I was scared of being left on my own. In high school, I fretted that others couldn't see my gifts—that I wasn't worth a rightful place alongside talented or privileged peers. By the time I was in college, I worried about when I would find love and whether it would be possible with the future I wanted to pursue. In my 30s, I fought to balance building a career with having a family. And, by my 40s, I discovered that was what was most important to me, after all.

And you know what? Life went on.

It didn't fade to black when I was no longer a sportswriter or a journalist or even any kind of writer. There are other things. I'm just now beginning to discover them. And it's OK to move on, just as I hope it is or was OK for everyone I wrote about in these pages.

I obviously never won the Stanley Cup. I had my photo taken with it three times. The first was in 1995 at the Hockey Hall of Fame in Toronto. I was there with my amateur hockey team, playing in a tournament, and I got to see not only the Cup but a playoff game between the Maple Leafs and Blackhawks. Then, in the lead-up to when the NHL all-star game was in St. Paul in 2004, the Cup made a visit to St. Cloud State. It was inside a protective Plexiglas case on the back of a snowmobile at the National Hockey Center.

The last time I saw the Stanley Cup, I broke with tradition and actually touched it. You're not supposed to lay a finger on it unless you win it. Knowing my future only held experience as a writer, I figured nothing was holding me back in 2006 when Bret Hedican and Matt Cullen brought the trophy to their alma mater, St. Cloud State University. (Author photo)

Finally, in 2006, after SCSU alums Bret Hedican and Matt Cullen won it with the Carolina Hurricanes, they brought it to campus. During the hoopla, I managed to sneak a photo of myself in the Huskies' dressing room, my right hand cradling the trophy.

Will there be another opportunity? Who knows?

We can't all be Modano. We shouldn't—and I don't—begrudge him one bit for the wonderful things that have happened in his life. Of all the sports figures in my lifetime, I personally rate him and Derek Jeter, who won five World Series and shined as the Yankees shortstop for twenty years, as the two individuals with the most storybook, fantastic, Cinderella-like existences I can imagine. It's great that *somebody* got to experience what they did, otherwise what would the rest of us have to dream about?

For myself, I've done—and will continue to do—the best I can. I'm grateful for the life God has allowed me to live. Just like those '90–91 North Stars, there's been plenty of what you might call good and bad. And, while it hasn't always turned out the way I wanted—or thirty years ago the way *we* wanted—it's enough to say I was there and a part of it all.

Kevin Allenspach
St. Cloud, Minnesota
December 2022

The tumult and the shouting dies;
The Captains and the Kings depart:
Still stands Thine ancient sacrifice,
An humble and a contrite heart.

~Rudyard Kipling, 1897

(Al Shaver recited this portion of the poem from memory during our conversation for this book. ~Kevin Allenspach)

APPENDIX I

No Comparison: The '90-91 North Stars & Other Rags-to-Riches Stories

Perspective on the 1990–91 North Stars

Through 2022, only one playoff upset in NHL history ranks greater based on regular-season points than Minnesota (68) dumping Chicago (106) and St. Louis (105) in 1991. That was in 1982 when Los Angeles (63) beat Edmonton (111) in a five-game division semifinal.

The last team to win the Cup after a sub-.500 regular season was the Toronto Maple Leafs in 1949. They were 22–25–13 (.475). The only other loser to win the Cup was Chicago in 1938: 14–25–9 (.385).

Teams with losing records to make it to the finals and lose:

- 1937 New York Rangers (19–20–9, .490); lost to Detroit 3–2 (6–3 in playoffs)
- 1939 Toronto Maple Leafs (19–20–9, finished 3rd of 7, .490); lost to Boston 4–1 (5–5 in playoffs)
- 1942 Detroit Red Wings (19–25–4, finished 5th of 7, .438); lost to Toronto 4–3 (7–6 in playoffs)
- 1944 Chicago Black Hawks (22–23–5, .490); lost to Montreal 4–0 (4–5 in playoffs)
- 1950 New York Rangers (28–31–11, .479); lost to Detroit 4–3, including Game 7 in 2OT (7–5 in playoffs)
- 1951 Montreal Canadiens (25–30–15, finished 3rd, .464); lost to Toronto 4–1 (5–6 in playoffs)
- 1958 Boston Bruins (27–28–15, .493); lost to Montreal 4–2 (6–6 in playoffs)
- 1959 Toronto Maple Leafs (27–32–11, .464); lost to Montreal 4–1 (5–7 in playoffs)
- 1961 Detroit Red Wings (25–29–16, .471); lost to Chicago, 4–2 (6–5 in playoffs)
- 1968 St. Louis Blues (27–31–16, .473), beat Stars 4–3 in semifinals; lost to Montreal, 4–0 (8–10 in playoffs)
- 1982 Vancouver Canucks (30–33–17, .481); lost to New York Islanders 4–0 (11–6 in playoffs)
- 1991 Minnesota North Stars (27-39-14, .425); lost 4-2 to Pittsburgh (14-9 in playoffs)

The two most massive upsets of the Original Six era came in 1951 and '61. In '51, the Montreal Canadiens (.464 winning percentage) totaled 65 points and yet shocked Detroit (101 points) before falling to Toronto in the finals. Ten years later, the Red Wings (.471; 66 points) knocked off Toronto (90 points) before bowing to Chicago.

The biggest playoff upset of the first expansion era prior to 1980 was when the St. Louis Blues (.429) totaled 67 points in 1972 and ousted the North Stars (86 points) in seven games before bowing to Boston in the semifinals.

The league played 80-game schedules from 1974–75 through '91–92. During that stretch, seventeen teams made the postseason with fewer than 68 points. Three won first-round series when they were best-of-five ('82 Los Angeles Kings with Larry Murphy; '85 North Stars with Brian Bellows, Neal Broten, and Curt Giles; and '86 Toronto Maple Leafs). Only the 1989 Chicago Blackhawks, with 66 points, won first- and second-round series before losing in the conference final.

Beginning in 1992, further expansion increasingly made it more difficult to get to the playoffs.

There were 84 regular-season games in 1992–93 and '93–94. San Jose (.488, 82 points in '94, including Ulf Dahlen, Gaetan Duchesne, and Rob Zettler) was the worst team to make the postseason in that window. The Sharks shocked Detroit before falling to Toronto.

A lockout shortened the '94–95 season to 48 games, none against opposing conference teams, when the Sharks and Stars both made the playoffs with .438 winning percentages and 42 points. Dallas (featuring Broten, Shane Churla, Dave Gagner and Mike Modano) was dumped in the first round. San Jose (with Dahlen and Duchesne) upset Calgary before falling to Detroit in the conference semifinals.

The only other lockout-shortened season was 2012–13, likewise cut to 48 games, when the New York Islanders (.531, 55 points) punched the last ticket to the playoffs and lost in the first round.

Since 1995–96, a full regular season has been 82 games. Ottawa and Montreal (each .470 and 77 points in '97, Ottawa featuring Frantisek Musil and Montreal featuring Marc Bureau; both lost first round) had the worst regular-season record for a playoff team through 1998–99, after which additional points first became available via overtime losses. Removing those points, the lowest winning percentage to make the playoffs between 1999 and 2004 was .493 (Buffalo, 2000, lost first round; New York Islanders, 2003, lost first round). Shootouts first became possible after the 2004–05 season was canceled by labor conflict, further clouding comparison. However, based on the same logic of removing points not gained by an overtime tie, the lowest winning percentage to make the postseason between 2006 and 2019 was .476 (Minnesota, 2016, lost first round; and Colorado, 2019, beat Calgary before losing in second round).

Since 1991, the team with the lowest winning percentage to reach the finals was Vancouver (.506 and with Brian Glynn) in 1994. The Canucks, who were 41–40–3 en route to 85 points, lost to the Rangers in seven games. The 2010 Philadelphia Flyers had a .518 winning percentage (not including overtime losses), totaled 88 points, and lost to the Chicago Blackhawks in six.

Some people falsely identify the 2019 St. Louis Blues, who were in last place in the NHL in January and went on to win the Cup, as succeeding in a similar situation to the '91 North Stars. However, the '19 Blues were never more than four games under .500 (as late as December 9, 2018), and were 15–18–4 on New Year's Day. From that point, they went 30–10–5 to finish the regular season 45–28–9 (.604). So, while their turnaround was amazing (and inspired a rebirth for their chosen victory song "Gloria," by Laura Branigan), they tied for the tenth-*best* record in a 31-team league. Nonetheless, GM Doug Armstrong, who was manager of team services for the '91 North Stars, deserves a lot of credit for making the moves necessary for St. Louis to post such a strong second half. The Blues then beat Winnipeg (4–2), Dallas (4–3), San Jose (4–2), and Boston (4–3) to raise the Cup.

The 2019–20 season was marred by the Covid-19 pandemic, and the playoffs were expanded to include twelve teams from each conference. Montreal had the worst winning percentage (.384) and beat Pittsburgh 3–1 in the qualifying round. The Canadiens lost to the Flyers in the subsequent first round. Chicago (.486) also made the playoffs that season, winning a qualifying round matchup before losing to Vegas in the first round.

The worst team ever to make the NHL playoffs was the 1988 Toronto Maple Leafs (.325). Ironically, they squeezed past the North Stars by one point and were eliminated in the first round by Detroit. The 1986 Leafs (.356) were the worst team ever to advance, knocking off Chicago before losing in the second round.

The worst WHA team to make the postseason was the 1976 Edmonton Oilers (.364). The worst team to win a playoff series was the '76 New England Whalers (.456), who swept Cleveland 3–0 in the preliminary round and ousted Indianapolis 4–3 in the quarterfinals before bowing to Houston 4–3 in the semifinals. The team with the worst winning percentage ever to appear in an Avco Cup final was the 1974 Chicago Cougars (.519), who upset New England and Toronto before losing to Houston.

National Basketball Association

No team has ever won an NBA championship with a losing record. NBA teams to make the finals with a losing record: (3)

- 1957 St. Louis Hawks (34–38, .472); lost to Boston 4–3 (8–4 in playoffs)
- 1959 Minneapolis Lakers (33–39, .458); lost to Boston 4–0 (6–7 in playoffs)
- 1981 Houston Rockets (40–42, .488); lost to Boston 4–2 (12–9 in playoffs)

National Football League

Only two teams in NFL history have won a postseason game after a losing regular season. NFL teams to make the playoffs with a losing record: (4)

- 1982 Cleveland Browns (4–5, .444); lost wild-card game at Los Angeles Raiders, 27–10[69]
- 2010 Seattle Seahawks (7–9, .438); won home wild-card game over New Orleans, 41–36; lost divisional playoff at Chicago, 35–24
- 2014 Carolina Panthers (7–8–1, .469); won home wild-card game over Arizona, 27–16; lost divisional playoff at Seattle, 31–17
- 2020 Washington (7–9, .438); lost home wild-card game vs. Tampa Bay, 31–23

Major League Baseball

The only Major League Baseball teams to make the playoffs with a losing regular-season record (3) came in either the strike-shortened 1981 season or in 2020, ravaged by COVID:

- 1981 Kansas City Royals (50–53 overall, .485; won 2nd half after going 20–30 in 1st half); lost divisional playoff to Oakland, 3–0[70]
- 2020 Houston Astros and 2020 Milwaukee Brewers (29–31, .483); Houston won wild card series at Minnesota 2–0 and Milwaukee lost wild card series at Los Angeles 2–0; Houston then beat Oakland in divisional playoff 3–1 before losing to Tampa in ALCS 4–3

Dallas Stars in the Stanley Cup Final

In 2020, the Dallas Stars went 37–24–8, 15–8 in postseason, and lost to Tampa Bay 4–2 in the finals.

In 2000, they were 43–23–10–6 and lost to New Jersey 4–2 in the finals.

They won the Cup in 1999, after a 51–19–12 season that culminated with a triple-overtime win in Game 6 at Buffalo.

69 The 1982 NFL season was marred by a 57-day players strike that reduced a 16-game regular season to just nine.

70 The 1981 MLB season became the first where games were lost because of a players strike. Play was halted from June 12 to Aug. 9, resulting in the cancelation of 713 games—38 percent of the entire schedule.

APPENDIX II

The '90-91 North Stars,
The Complete Game-by-Game Record

Stats for each skater represent: goals-assists-points plus/minus penalty minutes (shots)
Shading = home games.

Date/Opponent	Result	Record	Attend./TV	Babe	Barber	Bellows	Berezan	Broten	Bureau
Oct. 4 vs. STL	3-2 L	0-1-0	5,730/KMSP	minors	0-0-0 E 0 (1)	1-0-1 +1 0 (2)	0-0-0 -1 0 (2)	0-2-2 +1 0 (3)	CAL
Oct. 6 vs. NYI	4-2 W	1-1-0	5,970	minors	DNP	0-0-0 -1 0 (5)	0-1-0 +1 0 (3)	0-1-1 -1 0 (2)	CAL
Oct. 8 at NYR	6-3 L	1-2-0	15,286	minors	DNP	1-1-2 -1 0 (3)	DNP	0-1-1 E 0 (1)	CAL
Oct. 9 at NJD	5-2 L	1-3-0	8,448/KMSP	minors	0-0-0 E 0 (0)	0-0-0 -1 0 (3)	0-0-0 -1 0 (1)	0-1-1 E 2 (3)	CAL
Oct. 11 vs. BOS	3-3 T	1-3-1	5,280	minors	DNP	0-2-2 E 0 (6)	0-0-0 -1 0 (0)	0-0-0 -1 0 (0)	CAL
Oct. 13 vs. CHI	4-1 L	1-4-1	9,129/MSC	minors	DNP	0-1-1 -1 0 (2)	0-0-0 E 2 (0)	0-1-1 E 0 (2)	CAL
Oct. 17 at LAK	5-2 L	1-5-1	12,281/KMSP	minors	DNP	1-0-1 E 2 (6)	DNP	0-1-1 -1 0 (3)	CAL
Oct. 20 at STL	2-2 T	1-5-2	17,177/MSC	minors	0-0-0 E 2 (0)	0-0-0 E 0 (5)	DNP	0-0-0 E 0 (3)	CAL
Oct. 21 at CHI	7-1 L	1-6-2	17,782KMSP	minors	0-0-0 E 0 (1)	0-0-0 -1 0 (3)	DNP	0-0-0 -1 0 (1)	CAL
Oct. 24 vs. HAR	3-0 W	2-6-2	4,646	minors	DNP	0-1-1 E 0 (0)	0-1-1 +1 0 (1)	0-1-1 E 0 (2)	CAL
Oct. 26 at DET	8-6 L	2-7-2	19,875/MSC	minors	DNP	1-2-3 E 0 (3)	0-0-0 -1 2 (0)	1-2-3 E 2 (3)	CAL
Oct. 27 vs. DET	2-2 T	2-7-3	6,164	minors	0-0-0 -1 0 (4)	0-1-1 +1 0 (3)	DNP	0-0-0 E 4 (0)	CAL
Oct. 30 at TOR	5-4 L	2-8-3	15,524/KMSP	minors	0-0-0 -1 2 (3)	1-0-1 E 0 (3)	DNP	2-1-3 +1 2 (5)	CAL
Nov. 1 at PHI	6-3 L	2-9-3	17,151/KMSP	minors	0-0-0 -1 0 (1)	1-0-1 -3 0 (2)	DNP	0-2-2 +1 0 (4)	CAL
Nov. 3 at QUE	2-0 W	3-9-3	13,795/MSC	minors	DNP	0-0-0 E 0 (2)	DNP	0-2-2 +2 0 (3)	CAL
Nov. 4 at MON	2-2 T	3-9-4	16,210/MSC	minors	DNP	0-0-0 E 0 (2)	0-0-0 -2 0 (0)	0-0-0 -2 0 (2)	CAL
Nov. 8 vs. QUE	3-2 W	4-9-4	5,286	minors	DNP (traded)	0-0-0 E 2 (2)	DNP	0-0-0 +1 0 (3)	CAL
Nov. 10 vs. HAR	3-2 L, OT	4-10-4	8,624	minors	WPG	0-0-0 -1 5 (2)	DNP	0-0-0 E 2 (4)	CAL
Nov. 13 vs. PIT	4-1 L	4-11-4	5,429/MSC	minors	WPG	1-0-1 E 0 (9)	0-0-0 E 0 (0)	0-1-1 E 4 (2)	CAL
Nov. 15 vs. NYR	4-2 L	4-12-4	6,677	minors	WPG	0-1-1 -1 0 (8)	DNP	1-0-1 -1 0 (2)	CAL
Nov. 17 vs. STL	3-2 L	4-13-4	7,926/KMSP	minors	WPG	0-0-0 -1 0 (3)	minors	0-0-0 E 0 (6)	CAL
Nov. 19 at NYR	2-2 T	4-13-5	15,260	minors	WPG	0-1-1 E 0 (2)	0-0-0 E 2 (1)	0-0-0 E 0 (5)	CAL
Nov. 21 at DET	4-3 L	4-14-5	19,584/KMSP	minors	WPG	0-0-0 -2 0 (2)	0-1-1 +1 0 (1)	0-0-0 E 0 (1)	CAL
Nov. 23 vs. VAN	6-4 W	5-14-5	7,889	minors	WPG	3-1-4 +2 0 (5)	DNP	0-1-1 E 0 (2)	CAL
Nov. 24 vs. NJD	5-3 L	5-15-5	8,138/MSC	minors	WPG	0-1-1 E 0 (3)	DNP	0-2-2 +1 0 (4)	CAL
Nov. 27 at VAN	1-1 T	5-15-6	12,292/KMSP	minors	WPG	0-0-0 E 0 (2)	0-0-0 -1 0 (1)	0-1-1 E 0 (2)	CAL
Nov. 30 at WPG	4-2 W	6-15-6	12,394/KMSP	minors	WPG	0-1-1 +1 0 (6)	0-0-0 +1 0 (0)	0-1-1 +1 0 (0)	CAL
Dec. 1 vs. PIT	6-3 W	7-15-6	7,225	minors	WPG	0-0-0 -1 0 (5)	2-0-2 +1 0 (5)	1-2-3 +2 0 (6)	CAL
Dec. 5 at TOR	3-2 W	8-15-6	16,115/KMSP	minors	WPG	0-1-1 +1 0 (4)	0-0-0 E 2 (0)	0-0-0 E 0 (3)	CAL
Dec. 6 vs. TOR	2-1 L, OT	8-16-6	6,345	minors	WPG	0-0-0 -1 0 (3)	0-0-0 +1 0 (3)	0-0-0 +1 2 (3)	CAL
Dec. 8 vs. PHI	7-0 W	9-16-6	6,711/MSC	0-1-1 +1 0 (0)	WPG	0-0-0 E 0 (2)	DNP	0-2-2 E 0 (4)	CAL
Dec. 11 vs. CAL	7-4 L	9-17-6	6,658	DNP	WPG	0-0-0 -1 0 (6)	DNP	1-3-4 E 0 (5)	CAL
Dec. 13 at STL	4-2 L	9-18-6	16,472/KMSP	minors	WPG	0-0-0 -1 2 (4)	0-0-0 -1 0 (1)	1-0-1 +1 0 (3)	CAL
Dec. 15 vs. CHI	5-1 W	10-18-6	9,438	minors	WPG	0-1-1 E 0 (4)	1-0-1 E 4 (4)	0-2-2 +2 0 (3)	CAL
Dec. 16 at CHI	5-2 L	10-19-6	18,059/MSC	minors	WPG	0-0-0 -1 0 (3)	0-0-0 E 0 (1)	0-0-0 E 2 (3)	CAL
Dec. 20 at PIT	4-3 L	10-20-6	15,140/KMSP	minors	WPG	0-1-1 +1 0 (4)	0-0-0 -1 0 (0)	2-0-2 +2 0 (6)	CAL
Dec. 22 at BOS	6-2 L	10-21-6	14,448/KMSP	minors	WPG	1-0-1 E 0 (6)	0-0-0 -1 0 (1)	0-0-0 -1 0 (2)	CAL
Dec. 23 at HAR	5-2 W	11-21-6	11,525/MSC	minors	WPG	0-1-1 E 2 (7)	0-0-0 E 0 (0)	1-1-2 -1 0 (4)	CAL
Dec. 26 vs. WPG	6-4 L	11-22-6	7,948	minors	WPG	1-1-2 -1 0 (3)	1-0-1 E 0 (4)	1-0-1 -1 2 (3)	CAL
Dec. 29 vs. BOS	4-4 T	11-22-7	11,639	minors	WPG	0-2-2 +2 0 (3)	0-0-0 E 0 (1)	0-1-1 E 0 (4)	CAL
Dec. 31 vs. LAK	4-2 L	11-23-7	12,015/MSC	minors	WPG	0-1-1 E 0 (3)	0-0-0 -1 0 (1)	0-0-0 -1 0 (4)	CAL
Jan. 2 at DET	6-2 L	11-24-7	19,507/KMSP	minors	WPG	0-2-2 E 0 (3)	0-0-0 -1 0 (2)	0-0-0 -3 0 (1)	CAL
Jan. 3 vs. TOR	3-3 T	11-24-8	6,253	minors	WPG	0-0-0 -1 0 (4)	DNP	0-1-1 +1 0 (0)	CAL
Jan. 5 vs. VAN	6-5 L	11-25-8	9,445	minors	WPG	0-2-2 E 2 (5)	DNP	0-1-1 E 0 (0)	CAL
Jan. 8 at NYI	3-0 W	12-25-8	10,260/KMSP	minors	WPG	0-0-0 E 0 (3)	1-0-1 +1 0 (2)	0-1-1 +1 0 (1)	CAL
Jan. 12 vs. BUF	5-3 L	12-26-8	7,045	minors	WPG	0-0-0 E 0 (3)	DNP	0-0-0 -2 0 (1)	CAL
Jan. 13 at CHI	5-3 L	12-27-8	17,577/KMSP	minors	WPG	2-1-3 -1 2 (6)	DNP	0-1-1 -1 0 (0)	CAL
Jan. 15 vs. MON	5-1 L	12-28-8	5,375	minors	WPG	0-0-0 -1 0 (3)	0-0-0 E 0 (1)	0-0-0 E 2 (1)	CAL
Jan. 17 vs. WAS	5-2 W	13-28-8	6,301	minors	WPG	1-1-2 +1 0 (6)	DNP	0-1-1 E 0 (0)	CAL
Jan. 21 at WPG	2-0 L	13-29-8	11,061/MSC	minors	WPG	0-0-0 -1 0 (2)	0-0-0 E 0 (2)	0-0-0 -1 0 (0)	CAL
Jan. 22 vs. STL	7-3 W	14-29-8	5,901/MSC	minors	WPG	2-0-2 +1 0 (8)	0-2-2 +2 0 (1)	0-1-1 -2 2 (4)	CAL
Jan. 25 at WAS	2-2 T	14-29-9	16,859/KMSP	minors	WPG	0-0-0 E 0 (1)	0-0-0 E 0 (0)	0-1-1 -1 0 (2)	CAL
Jan. 26 at NJD	3-1 W	15-29-9	14,842	minors	WPG	0-0-0 +1 0 (5)	0-0-0 +1 0 (1)	0-0-0 -1 0 (3)	CAL
Jan. 28 at TOR	4-0 L	15-30-9	15,993/KMSP	minors	WPG	0-0-0 -1 0 (4)	0-0-0 E 0 (1)	0-0-0 -1 0 (4)	CAL
Jan. 30 vs. DET	5-2 W	16-30-9	5,965	minors	WPG	2-0-2 E 0 (5)	INJ (shoulder)	1-0-1 +2 0 (1)	CAL
Feb. 2 at QUE	6-4 W	17-30-9	14,306	minors	WPG	1-2-3 +1 0 (4)	INJ (shoulder)	0-0-0 E 0 (1)	CAL
Feb. 4 at MON	5-3 L	17-31-9	16,164/KMSP	minors	WPG	0-0-0 -1 0 (4)	1-0-1 E 0 (3)	0-1-1 E 0 (1)	CAL
Feb. 7 vs. TOR	4-2 W	18-31-9	7,084/MSC	minors	WPG	2-0-2 E 4 (3)	0-0-0 -1 0 (2)	0-2-2 E 0 (0)	CAL
Feb. 9 vs. DET	6-5 W	19-31-9	11,836	minors	WPG	0-0-0 -1 2 (1)	1-0-1 E 0 (2)	0-0-0 -1 0 (2)	CAL
Feb. 12 at NYI	5-4 L	19-32-9	10,191/KMSP	minors	WPG	0-0-0 -2 0 (3)	1-0-1 E 0 (2)	0-0-0 -3 0 (1)	CAL
Feb. 13 at BUF	6-6 T	19-32-10	15,017	minors	WPG	2-1-3 -1 4 (5)	0-0-0 +1 2 (3)	0-2-2 -2 0 (3)	CAL
Feb. 16 at DET	3-0 W	20-32-10	19,875	minors	WPG	1-0-1 E 0 (1)	0-1-1 +1 0 (1)	0-1-1 E 0 (1)	CAL
Feb. 20 vs. EDM	5-1 W	21-32-10	6,195/KMSP	minors	WPG	1-1-2 +2 0 (6)	0-0-0 E 0 (3)	0-2-2 +1 0 (2)	CAL
Feb. 23 vs. CHI	3-3 T	21-32-11	14,832/MSC	minors	WPG	1-1-2 -1 2 (4)	0-0-0 E 0 (3)	0-0-0 -1 0 (3)	CAL
Feb. 26 vs. PHI	2-2 T	21-32-12	8,866	minors	WPG	0-0-0 E 0 (4)	0-0-0 -2 0 (1)	1-0-1 +1 0 (5)	CAL
March 1 at EDM	1-1 T	21-32-13	16,516/KMSP	minors	WPG	0-0-0 E 0 (1)	0-0-0 E 6 (2)	0-0-0 E 0 (0)	CAL
March 2 at CAL	5-1 L	21-33-13	19,844/MSC	minors	WPG	0-0-0 -1 0 (0)	0-0-0 -2 0 (2)	0-0-0 -1 0 (4)	CAL
March 6 vs. EDM	5-1 W	22-33-13	6,888	minors	WPG	1-1-2 E 0 (3)	1-0-1 +1 0 (3)	0-0-0 E 0 (2)	DNP
March 9 vs. DET	6-2 W	23-33-13	11,607	minors	WPG	0-3-3 +1 0 (3)	0-0-0 E 2 (0)	0-2-2 +3 0 (4)	DNP
March 10 vs. CAL	7-3 W	24-33-13	7,082/MSC	minors	WPG	1-0-1 +1 0 (2)	1-0-1 +2 0 (1)	0-2-2 +1 0 (4)	0-2-2 E 0 (0)
March 12 vs. BUF	5-2 W	25-33-13	8,546	minors	WPG	0-1-1 +1 0 (3)	1-0-1 +1 2 (2)	0-0-0 +1 0 (1)	0-1-1 E 0 (4)
March 14 at STL	2-2 T	25-33-14	17,908	minors	WPG	0-0-0 +1 0 (4)	0-0-0 -1 4 (0)	0-2-2 +1 0 (2)	DNP
March 16 at TOR	4-3 L, OT	25-34-14	16,382/MSC	minors	WPG	0-0-0 E 2 (2)	0-0-0 E 0 (1)	0-0-0 E 0 (0)	DNP
March 17 vs. TOR	4-3 W	26-34-14	7,234	minors	WPG	1-0-1 E 0 (5)	DNP	0-0-0 -1 0 (6)	0-2-2 +1 0 (0)
March 22 at WAS	3-1 L	26-35-14	15,655/MSC	minors	WPG	0-0-0 -1 0 (3)	0-0-0 E 0 (0)	0-0-0 -1 0 (3)	0-0-0 E 0 (1)
March 24 at CHI	5-4 L	26-36-14	18,472/KMSP	minors	WPG	2-1-3 +2 4 (7)	DNP	0-2-2 +2 0 (1)	0-0-0 -3 2 (0)
March 25 vs. STL	5-4 L	26-37-14	10,070	minors	WPG	1-0-1 -1 2 (6)	DNP	0-1-1 +1 0 (1)	0-0-0 -2 0 (0)
March 28 at LAK	6-5 L	26-38-14	16,005/KMSP	minors	WPG	0-2-2 -1 2 (3)	0-0-0 E 2 (1)	DNP	0-1-1 +1 0 (1)
March 30 vs. CHI	2-1 W	27-38-14	15,213/MSC	minors	WPG	1-0-1 E 4 (5)	0-0-0 E 0 (1)	DNP	0-0-0 E 2 (1)
March 31 at STL	2-1 L	27-39-14	17,344/KMSP	minors	WPG	1-0-1 E 0 (5)	DNP	0-0-0 -1 0 (4)	0-0-0 E 0 (1)
80 GP	256 GF	19-15-6 (home)	316,605 (home)	1 GP	7 GP	80 GP	52 GP	79 GP	9 GP
	266 GA	8-24-8 (road)	624,536 (road)	0-1-1 +1 0 (0)	0-0-0 -3 4 (10)	35-40-75 -13 43 (296)	11-6-17 -2 30 (73)	13-56-69 -3 26 (191)	0-6-6 -3 4 (8)

Stats for each skater represent: goals-assists-points plus/minus penalty minutes (shots)
Shading = home games.

Date/Opponent	Chambers	Churla	Craig	Dahlen	Dahlquist	DePalma	Duchesne	Evans	Gagner
Oct. 4 vs. STL	INJ (knee)	DNP	0-0-0 +1 0 (3)	INJ (hand)	PIT	minors	DNP	minors	1-0-1 -2 0 (3)
Oct. 6 vs. NYI	INJ (knee)	1-0-1 +1 0 (1)	0-0-0 -1 0 (4)	INJ (hand)	PIT	minors	DNP	minors	1-1-2 +2 0 (2)
Oct. 8 at NYR	INJ (knee)	0-0-0 E 7 (1)	1-0-1 -1 0 (2)	0-0-0 -1 0 (1)	PIT	minors	DNP	minors	0-0-0 -1 E (3)
Oct. 9 at NJD	INJ (knee)	0-0-0 -1 8 (1)	0-0-0 -1 2 (0)	DNP	PIT	minors	0-0-0 E 2 (0)	minors	1-1-2 +1 0 (2)
Oct. 11 vs. BOS	INJ (knee)	0-0-0 E 0 (2)	0-0-0 E 4 (1)	1-0-1 E 0 (1)	PIT	minors	DNP	minors	DNP (father)
Oct. 13 vs. CHI	INJ (knee)	0-0-0 -1 10 (0)	0-0-0 E 0 (1)	0-0-0 -1 0 (0)	PIT	minors	0-0-0 -1 2 (3)	minors	DNP (father)
Oct. 17 at LAK	INJ (knee)	0-0-0 -1 2 (1)	1-0-1 -2 4 (2)	0-0-0 E 0 (2)	PIT	minors	DNP	minors	0-1-1 E 0 (3)
Oct. 20 at STL	INJ (knee)	0-0-0 E 4 (2)	1-0-1 +1 0 (2)	DNP	PIT	minors	0-1-1 +1 0 (3)	minors	1-1-2 +1 0 (1)
Oct. 21 at CHI	INJ (knee)	0-0-0 E 16 (1)	0-0-0 -2 0 (0)	DNP	PIT	minors	0-0-0 -1 0 (1)	minors	0-0-0 -1 0 (2)
Oct. 24 vs. HAR	INJ (knee)	0-0-0 E 2 (0)	0-0-0 E 4 (3)	DNP	PIT	minors	DNP	minors	2-0-2 +1 0 (3)
Oct. 26 at DET	INJ (knee)	0-0-0 -2 2 (1)	0-0-0 -2 0 (2)	DNP	PIT	minors	DNP	minors	1-0-1 -1 10 (4)
Oct. 27 vs. DET	0-0-0 -1 0 (3)	0-0-0 E 7 (0)	1-0-1 +1 0 (2)	0-1-1 +1 2 (1)	PIT	0-0-0 +1 0 (0)	0-0-0 E 0 (2)	minors	0-0-0 -1 0 (1)
Oct. 30 at TOR	0-0-0 E 0 (2)	0-1-1 E 4 (1)	0-0-0 -1 0 (1)	0-0-0 -1 0 (1)	PIT	1-0-1 E 2 (2)	DNP	minors	0-0-0 -1 0 (5)
Nov. 1 at PHI	0-0-0 -1 0 (1)	0-0-0 E 12 (0)	0-0-0 -3 0 (2)	DNP	PIT	DNP	0-0-0 E 0 (0)	minors	0-0-0 -3 2 (0)
Nov. 3 at QUE	DNP	0-0-0 E 0 (0)	0-0-0 E 2 (2)	DNP	PIT	1-0-1 +1 2 (1)	0-0-0 E 0 (1)	minors	0-0-0 E 0 (2)
Nov. 4 at MON	0-0-0 -1 0 (2)	0-0-0 E 14 (1)	DNP	0-0-0 E 0 (2)	PIT	0-0-0 E 0 (1)	INJ (head)	minors	1-0-1 +2 2 (4)
Nov. 8 vs. QUE	0-0-0 E 0 (2)	1-0-1 E 17 (1)	DNP	0-1-1 +1 0 (1)	PIT	0-0-0 E 4 (1)	1-0-1 +1 0 (3)	minors	1-0-1 +1 0 (2)
Nov. 10 vs. HAR	0-0-0 -1 2 (1)	0-0-0 E 27 (0)	0-0-0 E 0 (0)	DNP	PIT	1-0-1 -1 0 (3)	0-0-0 E 0 (1)	minors	0-1-1 E 2 (0)
Nov. 13 vs. PIT	0-0-0 -1 0 (1)	0-0-0 E 4 (3)	0-0-0 -2 0 (1)	DNP	PIT	0-0-0 -1 0 (3)	0-0-0 E 0 (2)	minors	INJ (knee)
Nov. 15 vs. NYR	0-1-1 -1 0 (3)	0-0-0 -1 12 (1)	0-0-0 -1 0 (0)	0-0-0 -1 0 (2)	PIT	0-0-0 -1 2 (3)	DNP	0-0-0 -1 9 (0)	INJ (knee)
Nov. 17 vs. STL	0-0-0 E 2 (0)	0-0-0 -1 0 (1)	0-0-0 E 0 (1)	0-0-0 E 0 (2)	PIT	DNP	0-0-0 E 0 (0)	0-0-0 E 0 (1)	INJ (knee)
Nov. 19 at NYR	0-0-0 E 7 (4)	INJ (ribs)	DNP	0-0-0 E 0 (4)	PIT	0-0-0 E 2 (3)	0-0-0 E 0 (2)	0-0-0 E 10 (0)	INJ (knee)
Nov. 21 at DET	0-0-0 +2 0 (2)	INJ (ribs)	DNP	0-0-0 -1 0 (4)	PIT	0-0-0 E 0 (1)	0-0-0 E 0 (2)	DNP	0-0-0 -1 2 (2)
Nov. 23 vs. VAN	0-0-0 +2 2 (1)	INJ (ribs)	0-0-0 E 0 (1)	1-1-2 +1 0 (2)	PIT	0-0-0 -1 0 (0)	0-0-0 -1 0 (1)	DNP	0-4-4 +2 0 (2)
Nov. 24 vs. NJD	0-0-0 E 0 (2)	INJ (ribs)	DNP	0-0-0 +1 0 (0)	PIT	0-0-0 -2 7 (0)	1-0-1 +1 0 (2)	0-0-0 -2 0 (1)	1-0-1 +1 2 (4)
Nov. 27 at VAN	0-0-0 E 0 (4)	INJ (ribs)	0-0-0 -1 2 (0)	0-0-0 E 0 (3)	PIT	DNP	0-0-0 E 0 (0)	minors	0-0-0 E 2 (2)
Nov. 30 at WPG	1-0-1 +3 0 (2)	0-0-0 E 0 (0)	DNP	0-0-0 +1 0 (1)	PIT	DNP	0-0-0 E 0 (0)	minors	1-0-1 +1 2 (3)
Dec. 1 vs. PIT	0-0-0 +3 7 (2)	0-0-0 +2 6 (0)	DNP	0-0-0 -1 0 (1)	PIT	DNP	0-0-0 +2 0 (1)	minors	0-0-0 E 0 (3)
Dec. 5 at TOR	0-0-0 E 0 (0)	0-0-0 E 2 (0)	DNP	0-1-1 +1 0 (0)	PIT	DNP	0-0-0 E 0 (1)	minors	1-0-1 +1 0 (1)
Dec. 6 vs. TOR	INJ (knee)	0-0-0 E 2 (3)	DNP	0-0-0 E 0 (0)	PIT	DNP	0-0-0 E 0 (1)	minors	0-0-0 E 0 (0)
Dec. 8 vs. PHI	INJ (knee)	0-0-0 +2 4 (2)	DNP	DNP	PIT	0-0-0 E 5 (0)	1-0-1 +2 0 (4)	minors	1-0-1 E 0 (6)
Dec. 11 vs. CAL	INJ (knee)	0-0-0 E 2 (3)	DNP	0-0-0 -1 0 (2)	DNP	0-0-0 -1 2 (0)	0-0-0 E 0 (1)	minors	2-0-2 -1 0 (4)
Dec. 13 at STL	INJ (knee)	INJ (shoulder)	Canada	0-1-1 -1 0 (3)	0-0-0 E 0 (1)	minors	0-0-0 -1 2 (2)	minors	0-0-0 -1 15 (4)
Dec. 15 vs. CHI	INJ (knee)	INJ (shoulder)	Canada	2-0-2 +2 2 (7)	0-0-0 +1 2 (0)	minors	0-0-0 +1 0 (3)	minors	0-0-0 E 0 (1)
Dec. 16 at CHI	INJ (knee)	INJ (shoulder)	Canada	0-0-0 -1 0 (2)	0-0-0 +1 0 (1)	minors	0-0-0 E 0 (0)	minors	1-0-1 -2 0 (3)
Dec. 20 at PIT	INJ (knee)	INJ (shoulder)	Canada	1-1-2 +1 0 (3)	0-0-0 -1 0 (0)	minors	0-0-0 E 0 (1)	minors	0-1-1 E 0 (2)
Dec. 22 at BOS	INJ (knee)	INJ (shoulder)	Canada	0-0-0 E 0 (2)	0-0-0 -2 0 (0)	minors	0-0-0 -1 0 (4)	minors	0-1-1 -1 0 (1)
Dec. 23 at HAR	INJ (knee)	INJ (shoulder)	Canada	0-1-1 +2 0 (0)	0-0-0 -1 0 (0)	minors	0-1-1 +1 2 (0)	minors	3-1-4 +1 0 (9)
Dec. 26 vs. WPG	INJ (knee)	INJ (shoulder)	Canada	0-0-0 -2 0 (3)	0-2-2 +2 0 (1)	minors	0-0-0 E 0 (2)	minors	1-0-1 E 2 (3)
Dec. 29 vs. BOS	INJ (knee)	0-0-0 E 17 (0)	Canada	2-1-3 +2 0 (3)	0-0-0 +2 4 (1)	minors	0-0-0 E 0 (2)	minors	1-0-1 +1 0 (5)
Dec. 31 vs. LAK	INJ (knee)	0-0-0 E 17 (1)	Canada	1-0-1 E 0 (3)	0-0-0 +1 2 (0)	minors	0-0-0 E 0 (1)	minors	1-0-1 -1 2 (4)
Jan. 2 at DET	INJ (knee)	SUSP	Canada	1-0-1 E 0 (3)	0-0-0 -1 0 (2)	minors	0-0-0 -1 0 (2)	minors	0-1-1 +1 0 (1)
Jan. 3 vs. TOR	INJ (knee)	0-0-0 E 0 (0)	Canada	0-0-0 E 0 (1)	INJ (wrist)	minors	1-0-1 +1 0 (3)	minors	1-0-1 E 0 (4)
Jan. 5 vs. VAN	INJ (knee)	0-0-0 E 2 (0)	DNP	1-0-1 +1 0 (5)	INJ (wrist)	minors	0-2-2 +1 2 (1)	minors	0-0-0 -1 2 (2)
Jan. 8 at NYI	INJ (knee)	DNP	0-1-1 +1 2 (1)	0-0-0 E 0 (2)	INJ (wrist)	minors	0-1-1 +1 0 (3)	minors	1-0-1 +1 0 (3)
Jan. 12 vs. BUF	INJ (knee)	0-1-1 +1 2 (0)	1-0-1 +2 0 (3)	0-0-0 -1 0 (5)	INJ (wrist)	minors	0-0-0 E 0 (0)	minors	1-1-2 +2 0 (1)
Jan. 13 at CHI	INJ (knee)	0-0-0 E 15 (0)	0-0-0 -1 2 (1)	0-0-0 E 0 (0)	INJ (wrist)	minors	0-0-0 E 0 (1)	minors	1-2-3 -2 4 (8)
Jan. 15 vs. MON	INJ (knee)	0-0-0 E 2 (0)	0-0-0 +1 0 (1)	DNP	0-0-0 E 0 (0)	minors	0-0-0 -1 0 (2)	minors	0-0-0 E 0 (1)
Jan. 17 vs. WAS	INJ (knee)	0-0-0 E 0 (1)	1-0-1 +1 2 (3)	1-0-1 +1 0 (2)	0-1-1 +2 0 (1)	minors	0-0-0 E 2 (0)	minors	1-0-1 +2 0 (2)
Jan. 21 at WPG	INJ (knee)	INJ (shoulder)	0-0-0 E 0 (3)	0-0-0 E 0 (1)	0-0-0 E 0 (2)	minors	0-0-0 E 0 (4)	minors	0-0-0 -1 0 (2)
Jan. 22 vs. STL	INJ (knee)	INJ (shoulder)	0-1-1 +2 0 (1)	0-1-1 +1 0 (4)	0-0-0 -1 0 (0)	minors	1-0-1 +2 0 (3)	minors	1-1-2 +3 0 (6)
Jan. 25 at WAS	INJ (knee)	INJ (shoulder)	0-0-0 E 0 (1)	1-0-1 +1 0 (1)	0-0-0 E 0 (1)	minors	0-0-0 E 0 (0)	minors	0-0-0 -1 0 (2)
Jan. 26 at NJD	INJ (knee)	INJ (shoulder)	0-1-1 E 0 (0)	0-0-0 E 0 (0)	0-0-0 +1 0 (1)	minors	1-0-1 +1 0 (1)	minors	0-0-0 +1 0 (4)
Jan. 28 at TOR	INJ (knee)	INJ (shoulder)	0-0-0 -2 0 (1)	0-0-0 -1 0 (1)	0-0-0 -1 0 (0)	minors	0-0-0 E 2 (0)	minors	0-0-0 -2 0 (4)
Jan. 30 vs. DET	INJ (knee)	INJ (shoulder)	0-0-0 E 0 (0)	0-1-1 +1 0 (3)	0-0-0 +2 0 (0)	minors	1-0-1 +1 0 (1)	minors	0-0-0 E 0 (6)
Feb. 2 at QUE	INJ (knee)	INJ (shoulder)	1-0-1 +2 2 (2)	0-0-0 +1 0 (0)	0-1-1 E 0 (0)	minors	0-0-0 E 0 (4)	minors	1-4-5 +1 2 (4)
Feb. 4 at MON	INJ (knee)	INJ (shoulder)	0-0-0 -1 0 (2)	0-0-0 -2 0 (2)	DNP	minors	0-0-0 -1 0 (2)	minors	1-0-1 -1 0 (3)
Feb. 7 vs. TOR	INJ (knee)	INJ (shoulder)	INJ (hand)	0-1-1 E 0 (1)	0-0-0 E 2 (1)	minors	0-0-0 +1 0 (1)	minors	1-0-1 +1 2 (5)
Feb. 9 vs. DET	INJ (knee)	INJ (shoulder)	INJ (hand)	1-0-1 E 0 (1)	1-0-1 -1 2 (5)	minors	0-0-0 +1 0 (2)	minors	1-2-3 +2 10 (7)
Feb. 12 at NYI	INJ (knee)	INJ (shoulder)	INJ (hand)	0-0-0 E 0 (2)	1-1-2 +1 2 (2)	minors	0-1-1 +1 0 (0)	minors	0-2-2 -1 0 (1)
Feb. 13 at BUF	INJ (knee)	INJ (shoulder)	INJ (hand)	0-0-0 -1 0 (0)	0-0-0 -1 2 (1)	minors	0-2-2 -1 0 (0)	minors	1-2-3 -1 0 (7)
Feb. 16 at DET	INJ (knee)	INJ (shoulder)	INJ (hand)	0-1-1 E 0 (2)	0-0-0 E 0 (1)	minors	0-0-0 E 0 (1)	minors	0-1-1 +1 4 (2)
Feb. 20 vs. EDM	INJ (knee)	INJ (shoulder)	INJ (hand)	1-0-1 +1 0 (5)	0-0-0 E 2 (0)	minors	0-0-0 E 0 (1)	minors	0-3-3 +3 2 (1)
Feb. 23 vs. CHI	INJ (knee)	INJ (shoulder)	INJ (hand)	0-1-1 +1 0 (3)	0-0-0 -2 2 (1)	minors	0-0-0 -1 0 (0)	minors	1-1-2 -1 0 (4)
Feb. 26 vs. PHI	INJ (knee)	INJ (shoulder)	INJ (hand)	0-0-0 E 0 (0)	0-0-0 E 4 (3)	minors	0-0-0 -2 0 (0)	minors	0-1-1 +1 0 (5)
March 1 at EDM	minors	INJ (shoulder)	INJ (hand)	0-0-0 E 0 (4)	0-0-0 -1 0 (0)	minors	0-0-0 E 0 (0)	minors	1-0-1 -1 15 (2)
March 2 at CAL	minors	INJ (shoulder)	INJ (hand)	1-0-1 -2 0 (4)	0-0-0 -1 0 (0)	minors	0-0-0 E 0 (4)	minors	SUSP
March 6 vs. EDM	0-1-1 +2 0 (4)	INJ (shoulder)	INJ (hand)	1-0-1 E 0 (4)	0-0-0 E 0 (1)	minors	0-1-1 +1 0 (3)	minors	0-3-3 +3 6 (2)
March 9 vs. DET	0-0-0 +2 2 (1)	INJ (shoulder)	INJ (hand)	3-2-5 +4 0 (3)	0-0-0 E 2 (0)	minors	0-0-0 E 0 (1)	minors	1-0-1 -1 0 (5)
March 10 vs. CAL	0-0-0 -2 0 (3)	INJ (shoulder)	INJ (hand)	0-1-1 +1 0 (1)	0-1-1 +2 0 (1)	minors	1-0-1 E 2 (4)	minors	0-1-1 -1 4 (2)
March 12 vs. BUF	0-1-1 +3 0 (2)	INJ (shoulder)	INJ (hand)	1-0-1 +1 0 (1)	0-0-0 +2 0 (2)	minors	1-0-1 E 0 (2)	minors	1-1-2 +2 0 (4)
March 14 at STL	0-0-0 E 0 (1)	INJ (shoulder)	INJ (hand)	0-0-0 E 0 (1)	0-0-0 -2 0 (0)	minors	0-0-0 -2 0 (0)	minors	1-0-1 +1 0 (4)
March 16 at TOR	0-0-0 -1 0 (0)	0-0-0 +1 0 (0)	INJ (hand)	1-0-1 E 0 (4)	0-0-0 E 0 (1)	minors	0-0-0 -1 0 (1)	minors	0-1-1 E 2 (3)
March 17 vs. TOR	DNP	0-0-0 +1 0 (1)	INJ (hand)	0-0-0 -1 0 (1)	0-0-0 -2 7 (1)	minors	0-0-0 E 2 (3)	minors	0-1-1 E 0 (5)
March 22 at WAS	0-0-0 E 0 (1)	DNP	0-0-0 E 0 (1)	0-0-0 -1 0 (1)	0-0-0 -2 0 (3)	minors	0-0-0 E 0 (0)	minors	0-0-0 -1 0 (2)
March 24 at CHI	0-0-0 -2 0 (2)	0-0-0 E 31 (0)	1-0-1 -1 2 (3)	0-0-0 E 0 (3)	0-0-0 -1 0 (0)	minors	DNP	minors	1-0-1 +1 0 (2)
March 25 vs. STL	0-0-0 -2 0 (2)	DNP	0-1-1 -1 2 (3)	DNP	0-0-0 E 0 (0)	minors	0-0-0 -1 0 (2)	minors	0-0-0 E 0 (0)
March 28 at LAK	0-0-0 -2 0 (5)	DNP	DNP	0-1-1 -1 0 (3)	INJ (knee)	minors	DNP	minors	1-1-2 -3 2 (3)
March 30 vs. CHI	0-0-0 E 0 (1)	0-0-0 E 16 (0)	0-0-0 E 2 (1)	0-1-1 E 0 (1)	0-0-0 +2 0 (1)	minors	0-0-0 E 0 (1)	minors	0-1-1 +1 0 (7)
March 31 at STL	0-0-0 E 2 (1)	0-0-0 E 18 (0)	0-0-0 E 0 (2)	0-0-0 +1 2 (2)	0-0-0 +1 0 (2)	minors	0-0-0 E 0 (1)	minors	0-0-0 +1 16 (1)
	29 GP	40 GP	39 GP	66 GP	42 GP	14 GP	68 GP	4 GP	73 GP
	1-3-4 +2 24 (55)	2-2-4 +1 286 (32)	8-4-12 -11 32 (59)	21-18-39 +7 6 (133)	2-6-8 -1 33 (37)	3-0-3 -5 26 (18)	9-9-18 +4 18 (100)	0-0-0 -3 19 (2)	40-42-82 +9 114 (223)

Stats for each skater represent: goals-assists-points plus/minus penalty minutes (shots)
Shading = home games.

Date/Opponent	Gavin	Giles	Glynn	Gotaas	Johnson	Keczmer	Kolstad	MacLeod	McHugh
Oct. 4 vs. STL	0-0-0 E 0 (1)	0-0-0 -1 2 (1)	CAL	minors	PIT	minors	minors	minors	minors
Oct. 6 vs. NYI	0-0-0 E 2 (4)	0-0-0 +1 0 (2)	CAL	minors	PIT	minors	minors	minors	minors
Oct. 8 at NYR	0-0-0 -1 0 (1)	0-0-0 -2 0 (1)	CAL	minors	PIT	minors	minors	minors	minors
Oct. 9 at NJD	0-0-0 -1 0 (5)	0-0-0 -1 0 (0)	CAL	minors	PIT	minors	minors	minors	minors
Oct. 11 vs. BOS	0-0-0 -1 0 (1)	DNP (flu)	CAL	minors	PIT	minors	0-0-0 E 2 (6)	minors	minors
Oct. 13 vs. CHI	0-0-0 E 0 (1)	0-0-0 -1 2 (1)	CAL	minors	PIT	minors	0-0-0 -1 9 (0)	minors	minors
Oct. 17 at LAK	0-0-0 E 0 (0)	0-0-0 E 0 (0)	CAL	minors	PIT	minors	0-0-0 -1 0 (2)	minors	minors
Oct. 20 at STL	0-0-0 +1 0 (3)	0-0-0 +2 0 (0)	CAL	minors	PIT	minors	0-0-0 E 2 (0)	minors	minors
Oct. 21 at CHI	0-0-0 +1 7 (2)	0-0-0 -1 0 (0)	CAL	minors	PIT	minors	0-0-0 E 2 (1)	minors	minors
Oct. 24 vs. HAR	1-0-1 +1 0 (1)	0-1-1 +1 0 (1)	CAL	minors	PIT	minors	DNP	minors	minors
Oct. 26 at DET	1-0-1 +2 0 (1)	0-0-0 E 0 (1)	CAL	minors	PIT	minors	minors	minors	minors
Oct. 27 vs. DET	0-0-0 E 2 (2)	0-1-1 +2 0 (0)	0-0-0 E 0 (2)	minors	PIT	minors	minors	minors	minors
Oct. 30 at TOR	0-1-1 +1 0 (1)	0-0-0 -2 0 (0)	0-0-0 +1 0 (2)	minors	PIT	minors	minors	minors	minors
Nov. 1 at PHI	1-0-1 +1 0 (4)	0-0-0 E 0 (2)	0-0-0 -1 0 (0)	minors	PIT	minors	minors	minors	minors
Nov. 3 at QUE	0-0-0 +1 0 (1)	0-1-1 +1 0 (0)	0-0-0 E 0 (0)	minors	PIT	minors	minors	minors	minors
Nov. 4 at MON	0-0-0 -2 0 (1)	0-0-0 E 0 (0)	0-0-0 E 0 (1)	minors	PIT	minors	minors	minors	minors
Nov. 8 vs. QUE	INJ (knee)	0-0-0 -1 0 (2)	0-1-1 +3 4 (3)	minors	PIT	minors	minors	minors	minors
Nov. 10 vs. HAR	INJ (knee)	0-0-0 E 2 (0)	1-1-2 E 0 (3)	minors	PIT	minors	minors	minors	minors
Nov. 13 vs. PIT	INJ (knee)	0-0-0 +1 0 (2)	0-0-0 -1 0 (3)	minors	PIT	minors	minors	minors	minors
Nov. 15 vs. NYR	INJ (knee)	0-0-0 -1 0 (1)	0-1-1 -2 0 (2)	minors	PIT	minors	minors	minors	minors
Nov. 17 vs. STL	INJ (knee)	0-0-0 -1 0 (2)	0-0-0 -1 0 (2)	minors	PIT	minors	minors	minors	minors
Nov. 19 at NYR	INJ (knee)	0-0-0 E 0 (0)	0-0-0 E 0 (3)	minors	PIT	minors	minors	minors	minors
Nov. 21 at DET	INJ (knee)	0-0-0 E 0 (1)	0-0-0 -3 2 (0)	minors	PIT	minors	minors	minors	minors
Nov. 23 vs. VAN	INJ (knee)	0-0-0 -2 2 (0)	0-0-0 E 0 (0)	minors	PIT	minors	minors	minors	minors
Nov. 24 vs. NJD	INJ (knee)	0-0-0 E 0 (0)	0-0-0 E 0 (2)	minors	PIT	minors	minors	minors	minors
Nov. 27 at VAN	INJ (knee)	0-0-0 E 2 (0)	0-0-0 E 2 (0)	minors	PIT	minors	minors	minors	minors
Nov. 30 at WPG	INJ (knee)	0-0-0 +1 2 (2)	0-0-0 -1 2 (3)	minors	PIT	minors	minors	minors	minors
Dec. 1 vs. PIT	INJ (knee)	0-0-0 E 0 (0)	0-1-1 E 2 (1)	minors	PIT	minors	minors	minors	minors
Dec. 5 at TOR	INJ (knee)	0-0-0 +2 0 (0)	0-0-0 +1 2 (0)	minors	PIT	minors	minors	minors	minors
Dec. 6 vs. TOR	INJ (knee)	0-0-0 +1 0 (0)	0-0-0 -1 0 (3)	minors	PIT	minors	minors	minors	minors
Dec. 8 vs. PHI	INJ (knee)	0-0-0 E 0 (1)	1-0-1 +1 0 (1)	minors	PIT	minors	minors	minors	minors
Dec. 11 vs. CAL	INJ (knee)	0-0-0 -1 0 (2)	0-0-0 +1 0 (0)	minors	0-0-0 -1 6 (0)	minors	minors	minors	minors
Dec. 13 at STL	INJ (knee)	0-0-0 -2 0 (2)	0-0-0 E 0 (2)	minors	0-0-0 E 0 (4)	minors	minors	0-1-1 +1 0 (1)	minors
Dec. 15 vs. CHI	INJ (knee)	0-1-1 +1 0 (0)	1-0-1 +1 2 (3)	minors	0-0-0 +1 6 (1)	minors	minors	DNP	minors
Dec. 16 at CHI	INJ (knee)	0-0-0 E 4 (0)	0-0-0 -2 4 (3)	minors	0-0-0 +1 2 (1)	minors	minors	minors	minors
Dec. 20 at PIT	0-0-0 +1 2 (2)	0-0-0 E 2 (0)	0-0-0 +1 0 (1)	minors	0-0-0 -1 2 (1)	minors	minors	minors	minors
Dec. 22 at BOS	0-0-0 -2 0 (1)	0-0-0 E 0 (0)	0-0-0 -1 5 (1)	minors	0-0-0 -3 2 (2)	minors	minors	minors	minors
Dec. 23 at HAR	INJ (ribs)	0-0-0 E 0 (0)	0-0-0 E 0 (1)	minors	0-0-0 +1 4 (2)	minors	minors	minors	minors
Dec. 26 vs. WPG	0-0-0 E 4 (2)	0-2-2 E 0 (4)	0-0-0 -1 0 (3)	minors	0-1-1 E 0 (0)	minors	minors	minors	minors
Dec. 29 vs. BOS	0-0-0 -1 2 (3)	0-0-0 E 0 (0)	0-0-0 -2 0 (1)	minors	0-1-1 E 4 (2)	minors	minors	minors	minors
Dec. 31 vs. LAK	0-0-0 -1 0 (1)	0-0-0 -2 2 (0)	0-1-1 E 0 (2)	minors	0-0-0 E 2 (2)	minors	minors	minors	minors
Jan. 2 at DET	0-0-0 -2 2 (4)	0-0-0 E 2 (0)	DNP	0-0-0 -1 2 (2)	0-0-0 -2 2 (1)	minors	minors	minors	minors
Jan. 3 vs. TOR	0-0-0 +1 2 (5)	0-1-1 +1 2 (2)	0-1-1 E 2 (3)	DNP	0-0-0 -1 2 (0)	minors	minors	minors	minors
Jan. 5 vs. VAN	1-1-2 +1 0 (3)	0-0-0 -1 0 (1)	0-0-0 E 2 (0)	minors	0-1-1 +3 0 (2)	minors	minors	minors	minors
Jan. 8 at NYI	0-1-1 +1 0 (0)	0-0-0 +2 2 (0)	0-0-0 E 2 (1)	minors	0-0-0 +1 2 (3)	minors	minors	minors	minors
Jan. 12 vs. BUF	0-0-0 -2 0 (0)	0-0-0 -1 0 (0)	0-1-1 E 4 (0)	minors	0-0-0 E 2 (1)	minors	minors	minors	minors
Jan. 13 at CHI	0-0-0 -1 0 (0)	0-0-0 -1 2 (0)	0-0-0 E 0 (1)	minors	0-0-0 -1 12 (0)	minors	minors	minors	minors
Jan. 15 vs. MON	INJ (knee)	0-0-0 E 2 (1)	0-0-0 -1 0 (1)	minors	INJ (neck)	DNP	minors	minors	minors
Jan. 17 vs. WAS	INJ (knee)	0-0-0 E 4 (0)	DNP	minors	0-1-1 +2 19 (0)	minors	minors	minors	minors
Jan. 21 at WPG	INJ (knee)	0-0-0 E 0 (0)	DNP	minors	0-0-0 -1 2 (1)	minors	minors	minors	minors
Jan. 22 vs. STL	INJ (knee)	1-0-1 +3 0 (1)	0-1-1 +2 0 (0)	minors	0-0-0 +2 2 (2)	DNP	minors	minors	minors
Jan. 25 at WAS	INJ (knee)	0-0-0 E 2 (1)	0-0-0 -1 0 (1)	minors	0-0-0 -1 0 (1)	DNP	minors	minors	minors
Jan. 26 at NJD	INJ (knee)	INJ (knee)	0-0-0 E 4 (1)	minors	0-0-0 E 0 (0)	0-0-0 E 4 (1)	minors	minors	minors
Jan. 28 at TOR	INJ (knee)	INJ (knee)	0-0-0 -2 0 (3)	minors	0-0-0 E 2 (2)	0-0-0 -1 0 (1)	minors	DNP	minors
Jan. 30 vs. DET	INJ (knee)	INJ (knee)	0-0-0 +1 0 (0)	minors	0-0-0 -1 0 (2)	0-1-1 +2 2 (0)	minors	minors	minors
Feb. 2 at QUE	INJ (knee)	0-0-0 +1 2 (1)	0-0-0 +1 0 (3)	minors	0-0-0 +2 7 (2)	DNP	minors	minors	minors
Feb. 4 at MON	INJ (knee)	0-0-0 -3 2 (0)	0-1-1 -3 2 (1)	minors	0-1-1 E 0 (2)	0-0-0 E 0 (0)	minors	minors	minors
Feb. 7 vs. TOR	INJ (knee)	0-0-0 E 0 (1)	0-0-0 E 0 (1)	minors	0-1-1 +1 0 (2)	DNP	minors	minors	minors
Feb. 9 vs. DET	INJ (knee)	0-1-1 +1 0 (0)	0-0-0 +1 4 (3)	minors	0-0-0 +1 0 (0)	DNP	minors	minors	minors
Feb. 12 at NYI	INJ (knee)	0-0-0 -1 0 (0)	1-0-1 -1 2 (4)	minors	0-0-0 -1 0 (1)	0-0-0 E 0 (0)	minors	minors	minors
Feb. 13 at BUF	INJ (knee)	1-0-1 +1 0 (3)	0-0-0 E 2 (6)	minors	0-0-0 -1 0 (1)	DNP	minors	minors	DNP
Feb. 16 at DET	0-0-0 E 0 (0)	0-0-0 +1 0 (0)	0-0-0 +1 2 (2)	minors	INJ (neck)	0-0-0 E 0 (1)	minors	minors	0-0-0 E 0 (0)
Feb. 20 vs. EDM	INJ (knee)	0-0-0 +1 0 (2)	0-0-0 +1 2 (1)	minors	0-0-0 +3 0 (1)	DNP	minors	minors	0-0-0 E 0 (0)
Feb. 23 vs. CHI	INJ (knee)	0-0-0 +1 0 (5)	1-0-1 E 2 (1)	minors	0-0-0 -1 0 (3)	DNP	minors	minors	0-0-0 E 0 (1)
Feb. 26 vs. PHI	INJ (knee)	DNP	0-0-0 E 0 (5)	minors	0-1-1 E 0 (2)	0-0-0 E 0 (1)	minors	minors	0-0-0 -2 0 (2)
March 1 at EDM	INJ (knee)	0-0-0 E 2 (0)	0-0-0 E 2 (1)	minors	DNP (flu)	0-0-0 E 0 (2)	minors	minors	0-0-0 E 0 (1)
March 2 at CAL	INJ (knee)	0-0-0 -1 0 (1)	0-0-0 -1 10 (2)	minors	DNP (flu)	0-0-0 -1 0 (0)	minors	minors	0-0-0 -1 0 (0)
March 6 vs. EDM	0-0-0 E 0 (0)	0-1-1 +1 0 (2)	0-0-0 +1 2 (2)	minors	DNP (flu)	minors	minors	minors	minors
March 9 vs. DET	0-1-1 +1 2 (0)	1-0-1 +2 2 (3)	1-1-2 +2 0 (5)	minors	0-0-0 +1 0 (3)	minors	minors	minors	minors
March 10 vs. CAL	0-0-0 E 7 (0)	1-1-2 +2 2 (1)	1-0-1 +1 0 (5)	minors	0-0-0 -1 14 (1)	minors	minors	minors	minors
March 12 vs. BUF	0-0-0 E 0 (1)	0-0-0 -1 2 (0)	0-0-0 -1 2 (1)	minors	0-1-1 +4 2 (2)	minors	minors	minors	minors
March 14 at STL	0-0-0 -2 0 (0)	0-0-0 E 0 (0)	0-0-0 E 4 (1)	minors	0-0-0 E 0 (1)	minors	minors	minors	minors
March 16 at TOR	DNP	0-0-0 +1 0 (0)	0-0-0 +1 2 (0)	minors	0-0-0 +1 4 (1)	minors	minors	minors	minors
March 17 vs. TOR	DNP	0-0-0 E 0 (0)	0-0-0 +1 4 (0)	minors	1-0-1 E 2 (2)	minors	minors	minors	minors
March 22 at WAS	0-0-0 E 0 (2)	INJ (knee)	0-0-0 E 0 (2)	minors	0-0-0 E 0 (2)	minors	minors	minors	minors
March 24 at CHI	0-0-0 E 0 (1)	INJ (knee)	0-1-1 +1 0 (1)	minors	0-0-0 +1 2 (0)	minors	minors	minors	minors
March 25 vs. STL	0-0-0 -1 2 (0)	0-0-0 -1 0 (0)	0-0-0 -1 0 (2)	minors	0-0-0 -2 0 (0)	minors	minors	minors	minors
March 28 at LAK	0-0-0 +1 0 (0)	DNP	1-0-1 E 0 (2)	minors	0-1-1 +1 0 (2)	minors	minors	minors	minors
March 30 vs. CHI	DNP	DNP	0-0-0 E 2 (1)	minors	0-0-0 -1 0 (3)	minors	minors	minors	minors
March 31 at STL	0-0-0 E 2 (2)	DNP	0-0-0 -1 0 (0)	minors	0-0-0 E 0 (0)	minors	minors	minors	minors
	38 GP	70 GP	66 GP	1 GP	44 GP	9 GP	5 GP	1 GP	6 GP
	4-4-8 -3 36 (56)	4-10-14 +3 48 (53)	8-11-19 -5 83 (111)	0-0-0 -1 2 (2)	1-9-10 +9 100 (61)	0-1-1 E 6 (6)	0-0-0 -2 15 (9)	0-1-1 +1 E (1)	0-0-0 -3 0 (4)

Stats for each skater represent: goals-assists-points plus/minus penalty minutes (shots)
Shading = home games.

Date/Opponent	McRae	Messier	Modano	Murphy	Musil	Propp	Sinisalo	Smail	Smith
Oct. 4 vs. STL	0-0-0 -1 4 (1)	minors	0-0-0 -2 0 (3)	0-1-1 E 0 (2)	0-0-0 -1 0 (0)	0-0-0 -1 0 (1)	0-0-0 -2 0 (1)	WPG	0-1-1 E 0 (0)
Oct. 6 vs. NYI	0-1-1 +1 0 (3)	minors	0-1-1 +2 0 (4)	1-0-1 +1 0 (2)	0-0-0 +1 4 (3)	1-1-2 +2 0 (2)	0-0-0 E 0 (4)	WPG	0-1-1 +1 2 (1)
Oct. 8 at NYR	0-0-0 E 15 (0)	minors	0-1-1 -2 2 (1)	0-0-0 -1 2 (4)	0-1-1 E 4 (1)	1-1-2 +1 0 (4)	0-0-0 -1 0 (3)	WPG	0-0-0 -1 2 (3)
Oct. 9 at NJD	DNP	minors	0-1-1 +1 4 (0)	0-0-0 E 0 (6)	0-0-0 E 2 (1)	0-1-1 +1 0 (4)	DNP	WPG	1-0-1 -1 0 (2)
Oct. 11 vs. BOS	0-0-0 E 5 (1)	minors	1-2-3 +1 0 (2)	0-0-0 +1 0 (6)	0-0-0 -1 E (0)	1-0-1 -1 2 (4)	0-0-0 -2 E (0)	WPG	0-0-0 -1 0 (4)
Oct. 13 vs. CHI	0-0-0 -1 12 (1)	minors	1-0-1 -1 0 (6)	0-0-0 -1 8 (0)	0-0-0 E 0 (0)	0-0-0 E 2 (1)	DNP	WPG	0-0-0 E 0 (0)
Oct. 17 at LAK	0-0-0 -1 0 (7)	minors	0-0-0 E 2 (3)	0-0-0 -1 22 (3)	DNP	0-1-1 -1 0 (4)	0-0-0 E 0 (4)	WPG	0-1-1 -1 0 (1)
Oct. 20 at STL	0-0-0 E 5 (0)	minors	0-0-0 E 7 (0)	0-0-0 E 0 (4)	0-0-0 E 11 (0)	0-1-1 +1 0 (2)	DNP	WPG	0-0-0 E 0 (2)
Oct. 21 at CHI	0-0-0 +1 5 (0)	minors	1-0-1 +1 0 (2)	0-0-0 -1 2 (7)	DNP	0-0-0 -2 0 (3)	DNP	WPG	0-1-1 -1 7 (0)
Oct. 24 vs. HAR	0-0-0 E 0 (2)	minors	0-0-0 E 0 (3)	0-0-0 E 0 (1)	0-1-1 +1 2 (0)	0-0-0 +1 0 (2)	0-1-1 +1 2 (0)	WPG	0-0-0 +1 2 (1)
Oct. 26 at DET	0-0-0 -2 0 (0)	minors	0-0-0 -1 0 (4)	1-3-4 -3 0 (4)	DNP (traded)	0-1-1 E 15 (1)	0-2-2 -1 2 (1)	WPG	1-1-2 -3 0 (2)
Oct. 27 vs. DET	INJ (abdomen)	minors	DNP	0-0-0 E 0 (4)	CAL	0-0-0 -1 0 (1)	INJ (groin)	WPG	1-0-1 +2 0 (3)
Oct. 30 at TOR	INJ (abdomen)	minors	0-1-1 E 0 (1)	0-1-1 E 0 (4)	CAL	0-0-0 E 0 (2)	INJ (groin)	DNP	0-0-0 -2 0 (4)
Nov. 1 at PHI	0-0-0 -1 2 (2)	minors	0-1-1 -2 0 (0)	0-1-1 -1 0 (3)	CAL	1-0-1 -2 0 (3)	INJ (groin)	DNP	0-0-0 E 0 (2)
Nov. 3 at QUE	0-0-0 E 2 (0)	minors	0-0-0 E 2 (3)	0-0-0 E 0 (4)	CAL	1-0-1 +2 0 (2)	INJ (groin)	DNP	0-0-0 E 0 (0)
Nov. 4 at MON	0-0-0 E 0 (1)	minors	0-0-0 +1 0 (1)	1-0-1 +1 0 (4)	CAL	0-0-0 +2 0 (1)	INJ (groin)	DNP	0-1-1 +1 0 (2)
Nov. 8 vs. QUE	0-0-0 E 10 (0)	minors	0-0-0 E 0 (2)	0-1-1 +3 0 (3)	CAL	0-0-0 +1 0 (1)	INJ (groin)	0-1-1 +1 4 (1)	0-1-1 E 0 (0)
Nov. 10 vs. HAR	0-0-0 E 11 (0)	minors	0-1-1 E 0 (2)	0-0-0 -1 0 (3)	CAL	0-1-1 E 0 (3)	INJ (groin)	0-0-0 E 0 (0)	0-0-0 -1 2 (1)
Nov. 13 vs. PIT	INJ (abdomen)	minors	0-0-0 -2 0 (3)	0-0-0 -2 0 (2)	CAL	0-0-0 -1 0 (1)	0-0-0 -2 0 (3)	0-1-1 +1 0 (2)	0-0-0 -1 0 (5)
Nov. 15 vs. NYR	INJ (abdomen)	minors	0-1-1 E 0 (4)	0-0-0 -1 0 (3)	CAL	0-0-0 E 0 (0)	0-0-0 E 0 (1)	1-0-1 -1 0 (2)	0-0-0 -1 0 (2)
Nov. 17 vs. STL	INJ (abdomen)	minors	1-0-1 E 0 (5)	0-0-0 E 0 (3)	CAL	1-1-2 E 0 (2)	0-1-1 E 2 (2)	0-0-0 E 2 (4)	0-1-1 -1 0 (0)
Nov. 19 at NYR	INJ (abdomen)	minors	0-1-1 +1 0 (4)	0-0-0 +1 0 (3)	CAL	1-1-2 +1 0 (7)	0-0-0 +1 0 (1)	0-0-0 E 2 (0)	1-0-1 E 2 (2)
Nov. 21 at DET	INJ (abdomen)	minors	1-1-2 E 0 (4)	0-0-0 -3 2 (2)	CAL	0-2-2 E 0 (0)	0-1-1 E 0 (1)	0-0-0 E 0 (0)	1-0-1 E 0 (3)
Nov. 23 vs. VAN	INJ (abdomen)	minors	0-0-0 E 2 (3)	0-2-2 +1 0 (2)	CAL	2-0-2 E 0 (2)	0-1-1 +1 0 (2)	0-0-0 E 0 (2)	0-0-0 -1 0 (1)
Nov. 24 vs. NJD	INJ (abdomen)	minors	0-0-0 -2 0 (4)	0-0-0 -1 0 (6)	CAL	0-0-0 -1 0 (1)	0-0-0 -1 0 (5)	1-1-2 +1 0 (2)	0-0-0 -2 0 (0)
Nov. 27 at VAN	INJ (abdomen)	minors	1-0-1 E 0 (2)	0-0-0 -1 0 (1)	CAL	0-1-1 -1 0 (2)	0-0-0 E 0 (1)	0-0-0 E 0 (0)	0-0-0 E 4 (0)
Nov. 30 at WPG	INJ (abdomen)	minors	0-1-1 +1 2 (2)	0-0-0 -1 0 (0)	CAL	0-0-0 +1 0 (0)	1-0-1 +1 4 (2)	1-0-1 +1 0 (3)	0-1-1 E 0 (3)
Dec. 1 vs. PIT	INJ (abdomen)	minors	0-0-0 -1 0 (3)	1-0-1 +2 2 (4)	CAL	0-2-2 +2 0 (3)	1-0-1 +1 2 (2)	0-1-1 +1 0 (1)	1-1-2 +2 0 (1)
Dec. 5 at TOR	INJ (abdomen)	minors	1-0-1 +1 2 (3)	0-0-0 +1 0 (3)	CAL	0-1-1 +2 0 (2)	0-1-1 +2 0 (1)	0-0-0 E 0 (4)	0-0-0 +1 0 (1)
Dec. 6 vs. TOR	INJ (abdomen)	minors	0-0-0 E 0 (0)	0-0-0 -2 0 (7)	CAL	0-0-0 -2 0 (3)	0-0-0 -1 0 (1)	1-0-1 +1 0 (1)	0-0-0 -2 0 (0)
Dec. 8 vs. PHI	INJ (abdomen)	minors	1-2-3 +2 0 (2)	0-2-2 +1 0 (3)	CAL	1-1-2 +2 0 (2)	0-0-0 +1 0 (1)	0-0-0 E 0 (2)	1-0-1 +2 2 (1)
Dec. 11 vs. CAL	INJ (abdomen)	minors	1-2-3 +2 0 (5)	DNP (traded)	CAL	0-1-1 E 0 (2)	0-0-0 E 0 (0)	0-2-2 E 0 (3)	0-0-0 E 0 (2)
Dec. 13 at STL	INJ (abdomen)	minors	0-0-0 -2 0 (4)	PIT	CAL	0-0-0 -2 0 (0)	1-0-1 -2 0 (3)	0-1-1 +1 0 (2)	0-0-0 -1 0 (0)
Dec. 15 vs. CHI	INJ (abdomen)	minors	0-0-0 E 2 (2)	PIT	CAL	0-1-1 E 0 (1)	0-1-1 +1 0 (4)	0-0-0 +1 0 (2)	1-0-1 +1 0 (3)
Dec. 16 at CHI	INJ (abdomen)	minors	0-1-1 E 0 (2)	PIT	CAL	1-0-1 E 0 (4)	0-1-1 +1 0 (2)	0-0-0 E 0 (1)	0-0-0 -1 2 (3)
Dec. 20 at PIT	INJ (abdomen)	minors	0-0-0 -1 0 (3)	PIT	CAL	0-0-0 -2 0 (1)	0-0-0 -1 0 (2)	0-0-0 E 0 (0)	0-0-0 +1 0 (4)
Dec. 22 at BOS	INJ (abdomen)	minors	1-0-1 +1 0 (6)	PIT	CAL	0-2-2 E 2 (0)	0-1-1 E 0 (2)	0-0-0 -2 2 (1)	0-0-0 -1 4 (1)
Dec. 23 at HAR	INJ (abdomen)	minors	1-0-1 +2 0 (4)	PIT	CAL	0-0-0 -1 4 (4)	0-0-0 E 2 (1)	0-0-0 -1 2 (3)	0-0-0 E 0 (4)
Dec. 26 vs. WPG	INJ (abdomen)	DNP	0-0-0 -1 0 (2)	PIT	CAL	0-0-0 -1 0 (2)	0-0-0 -1 0 (2)	0-1-1 E 0 (1)	INJ (foot)
Dec. 29 vs. BOS	INJ (abdomen)	minors	0-1-1 E 2 (0)	PIT	CAL	1-0-1 +1 0 (2)	0-0-0 +1 0 (1)	0-0-0 -1 0 (1)	INJ (foot)
Dec. 31 vs. LAK	INJ (abdomen)	minors	0-0-0 E 0 (6)	PIT	CAL	0-0-0 -1 0 (3)	INJ (thumb)	0-0-0 E 0 (1)	INJ (foot)
Jan. 2 at DET	INJ (abdomen)	0-0-0 -1 0 (0)	1-0-1 -1 2 (5)	PIT	CAL	0-1-1 -1 0 (2)	INJ (thumb)	0-0-0 E 2 (3)	INJ (foot)
Jan. 3 vs. TOR	INJ (abdomen)	0-0-0 -1 0 (0)	0-0-0 -1 0 (4)	PIT	CAL	0-1-1 -1 0 (2)	INJ (thumb)	0-0-0 +1 0 (0)	1-0-1 E 2 (3)
Jan. 5 vs. VAN	INJ (abdomen)	minors	2-1-3 +1 2 (2)	PIT	CAL	0-1-1 -1 0 (1)	0-0-0 E 0 (0)	0-0-0 E 0 (0)	1-0-1 +1 0 (2)
Jan. 8 at NYI	INJ (abdomen)	minors	0-0-0 E 0 (5)	PIT	CAL	0-1-1 +1 0 (2)	INJ (thumb)	1-0-1 +1 2 (4)	0-0-0 E 0 (0)
Jan. 12 vs. BUF	INJ (abdomen)	minors	0-0-0 E 0 (2)	PIT	CAL	0-1-1 +2 0 (1)	INJ (thumb)	0-0-0 -1 0 (2)	0-0-0 E 0 (2)
Jan. 13 at CHI	INJ (abdomen)	minors	0-0-0 -1 0 (6)	PIT	CAL	0-2-2 -2 0 (4)	INJ (thumb)	0-0-0 -1 0 (0)	0-0-0 -1 0 (4)
Jan. 15 vs. MON	INJ (abdomen)	minors	0-0-0 -1 6 (1)	PIT	CAL	0-0-0 E 0 (2)	1-0-1 E 0 (3)	0-0-0 E 0 (0)	0-0-0 -1 0 (1)
Jan. 17 vs. WAS	INJ (abdomen)	minors	0-1-1 +1 0 (0)	PIT	CAL	0-0-0 +2 4 (0)	0-0-0 E 0 (1)	1-0-1 +1 0 (2)	0-0-0 E 0 (2)
Jan. 21 at WPG	INJ (abdomen)	minors	0-0-0 -1 0 (1)	PIT	CAL	0-0-0 -1 0 (3)	0-0-0 -1 0 (1)	0-0-0 -1 4 (1)	0-0-0 -1 4 (1)
Jan. 22 vs. STL	INJ (abdomen)	minors	0-0-0 +1 0 (0)	PIT	CAL	1-2-3 +2 0 (1)	0-1-1 -1 2 (1)	0-1-1 -1 0 (5)	1-1-2 +2 0 (3)
Jan. 25 at WAS	INJ (abdomen)	minors	0-1-1 +1 0 (1)	PIT	CAL	1-0-1 -1 2 (4)	0-0-0 -1 2 (0)	0-0-0 -1 2 (3)	0-1-1 +1 2 (2)
Jan. 26 at NJD	INJ (abdomen)	minors	0-1-1 E 0 (0)	PIT	CAL	1-0-1 +1 0 (1)	0-0-0 -1 2 (0)	0-0-0 -1 0 (0)	1-0-1 +1 0 (2)
Jan. 28 at TOR	INJ (abdomen)	minors	0-0-0 -1 0 (4)	PIT	CAL	0-0-0 -1 0 (2)	0-0-0 -1 0 (1)	0-0-0 -1 0 (0)	0-0-0 -1 0 (3)
Jan. 30 vs. DET	0-0-0 E 19 (0)	minors	0-1-1 E 2 (1)	PIT	CAL	0-1-1 +1 0 (1)	1-0-1 +1 0 (2)	0-1-1 E 0 (4)	0-1-1 E 0 (2)
Feb. 2 at QUE	0-0-0 E 0 (1)	minors	1-0-1 +1 0 (2)	PIT	CAL	2-2-4 +1 2 (3)	0-0-0 E 0 (3)	0-0-0 E 0 (1)	0-0-0 E 0 (0)
Feb. 4 at MON	0-0-0 E 2 (2)	minors	0-0-0 -3 0 (2)	PIT	CAL	0-0-0 -1 0 (2)	DNP	0-0-0 E 0 (3)	1-1-2 +1 0 (1)
Feb. 7 vs. TOR	0-0-0 -1 2 (1)	minors	0-1-1 +2 2 (2)	PIT	CAL	0-1-1 +1 2 (1)	0-0-0 -1 0 (1)	0-0-0 +1 0 (2)	0-0-0 +1 2 (0)
Feb. 9 vs. DET	0-0-0 E 7 (1)	minors	1-1-2 +1 2 (3)	PIT	CAL	1-1-2 +1 2 (8)	0-0-0 E 0 (1)	0-1-1 E 0 (1)	0-1-1 E 0 (1)
Feb. 12 at NYI	0-0-0 -1 0 (1)	minors	1-0-1 E 0 (4)	PIT	CAL	0-2-2 -1 0 (2)	0-0-0 -2 2 (1)	INJ (knee)	0-1-1 +1 2 (4)
Feb. 13 at BUF	0-0-0 E 17 (0)	minors	0-1-1 -1 4 (2)	PIT	CAL	0-1-1 -1 2 (0)	0-1-1 E 2 (0)	1-0-1 -2 2 (1)	0-2-2 -1 2 (4)
Feb. 16 at DET	0-0-0 E 5 (1)	minors	0-1-1 E 0 (2)	PIT	CAL	1-0-1 +1 0 (4)	DNP	INJ (knee)	1-0-1 E 0 (2)
Feb. 20 vs. EDM	0-1-1 +1 2 (1)	minors	2-2-4 +3 0 (5)	PIT	CAL	1-0-1 +1 15 (1)	0-0-0 E 0 (0)	INJ (knee)	0-0-0 E 2 (1)
Feb. 23 vs. CHI	0-0-0 E 2 (0)	minors	0-1-1 -2 0 (1)	PIT	CAL	SUSP	0-0-0 E 0 (0)	0-0-0 -1 2 (2)	0-2-2 E 0 (0)
Feb. 26 vs. PHI	0-0-0 E 2 (1)	minors	1-0-1 +2 0 (4)	PIT	CAL	0-0-0 +2 0 (4)	DNP	0-0-0 E 0 (2)	0-0-0 E 0 (0)
March 1 at EDM	0-0-0 E 0 (0)	minors	0-0-0 -1 4 (1)	PIT	CAL	0-1-1 -1 0 (1)	DNP	0-0-0 E 0 (3)	0-0-0 E 0 (3)
March 2 at CAL	0-0-0 -1 17 (1)	minors	0-0-0 E 2 (5)	PIT	CAL	0-0-0 E 0 (0)	0-0-0 E 0 (0)	0-0-0 E 2 (0)	0-1-1 -1 0 (0)
March 6 vs. EDM	0-0-0 E 0 (4)	minors	1-0-1 +2 2 (3)	PIT	CAL	1-1-2 +2 0 (2)	DNP (traded)	0-0-0 E 0 (1)	0-0-0 E 2 (1)
March 9 vs. DET	0-0-0 E 0 (1)	minors	0-1-1 E 0 (9)	PIT	CAL	0-0-0 E 0 (1)	LAK	0-0-0 E 2 (2)	0-0-0 E 0 (0)
March 10 vs. CAL	0-0-0 +1 9 (1)	minors	1-0-1 E 0 (2)	PIT	CAL	0-1-1 -1 0 (2)	LAK	0-1-1 +1 4 (0)	DNP
March 12 vs. BUF	0-1-1 +1 2 (2)	minors	1-0-1 +2 0 (6)	PIT	CAL	0-2-2 +2 0 (0)	LAK	0-0-0 +1 0 (1)	DNP
March 14 at STL	0-0-0 -1 6 (0)	minors	1-0-1 +1 0 (2)	PIT	CAL	0-1-1 E 0 (5)	LAK	0-0-0 E 2 (2)	0-1-1 +1 2 (4)
March 16 at TOR	1-0-1 +1 2 (3)	minors	1-1-2 E 0 (5)	PIT	CAL	0-1-1 E 0 (2)	LAK	0-0-0 -1 0 (0)	0-2-2 E 0 (2)
March 17 vs. TOR	0-0-0 E 20 (0)	minors	1-1-2 E 0 (7)	PIT	CAL	1-1-2 E 0 (3)	LAK	0-1-1 +1 0 (2)	0-1-1 E 7 (1)
March 22 at WAS	0-0-0 E 2 (2)	minors	0-0-0 -1 2 (4)	PIT	CAL	1-0-1 -1 0 (4)	LAK	DNP	DNP
March 24 at CHI	0-0-0 -2 19 (0)	minors	0-1-1 +1 2 (5)	PIT	CAL	0-1-1 E 0 (3)	LAK	DNP	0-1-1 +1 0 (1)
March 25 vs. STL	0-0-0 -2 2 (2)	minors	0-1-1 E 0 (4)	PIT	CAL	1-0-1 +1 0 (4)	LAK	0-0-0 -1 0 (1)	1-2-3 -2 2 (2)
March 28 at LAK	0-0-0 E 0 (0)	minors	2-0-2 -2 0 (4)	PIT	CAL	1-1-2 E 0 (3)	LAK	0-0-0 E 2 (1)	0-2-2 -1 0 (0)
March 30 vs. CHI	0-0-0 E 16 (1)	minors	0-1-1 +1 0 (5)	PIT	CAL	1-0-1 +1 0 (3)	LAK	DNP	0-1-1 E 0 (2)
March 31 at STL	DNP	minors	0-0-0 E 2 (1)	PIT	CAL	0-0-0 -1 4 (2)	LAK	DNP	0-0-0 E 0 (1)
	40 GP	2 GP	79 GP	31 GP	8 GP	79 GP	46 GP	57 GP	73 GP
	1-3-4 -8 224 (44)	0-0-0 -2 0 (0)	28-36-64 +2 61 (232)	4-11-15 -8 38 (103)	0-2-2 E 23 (5)	26-47-73 +7 58 (171)	5-12-17 -10 24 (68)	7-13-20 -2 38 (89)	15-31-46 -9 60 (121)

Stats for each skater represent: goals-assists-points plus/minus penalty minutes (shots)
Shading = home games.

Date/Opponent	Taglianetti	Tinordi	Wilkinson	Zettler	Casey	Hayward	Myllys	Takko	Shots For	Shots Against
Oct. 4 vs. STL	0-0-0 E 0 (1)	SUSP	0-0-0 -1 5 (0)	0-0-0 -1 0 (1)	0-0-0	MON	DNP	DNP	26	38
Oct. 6 vs. NYI	0-0-0 E 0 (1)	SUSP	0-1-1 E 4 (3)	0-0-0 +1 0 (0)	0-0-0 2	MON	DNP	DNP	46	29
Oct. 8 at NYR	0-0-0 +1 0 (0)	SUSP	0-1-1 -1 2 (1)	0-0-0 E 0 (0)	DNP	MON	0-0-0	minors	30	40
Oct. 9 at NJD	0-0-0 E 0 (3)	SUSP	0-0-0 -1 2 (3)	0-0-0 E 0 (1)	0-0-0	MON	DNP	minors	35	29
Oct. 11 vs. BOS	0-0-0 -2 0 (0)	SUSP	0-1-1 -1 0 (4)	0-0-0 -1 0 (1)	0-0-0	MON	DNP	minors	39	35
Oct. 13 vs. CHI	DNP	SUSP	0-0-0 -1 4 (1)	0-0-0 E 0 (0)	0-0-0	MON	DNP	minors	19	31
Oct. 17 at LAK	0-0-0 -1 2 (1)	SUSP	0-0-0 -1 5 (1)	0-0-0 E 0 (0)	0-0-0	MON	DNP	minors	43	27
Oct. 20 at STL	0-0-0 +2 2 (0)	SUSP	DNP	0-0-0 E 4 (0)	0-0-0	MON	DNP	minors	27	25
Oct. 21 at CHI	0-0-0 -1 2 (0)	SUSP	0-0-0 E 0 (0)	0-0-0 E 4 (1)	0-0-0	MON	0-0-0 2	minors	25	32
Oct. 24 vs. HAR	0-0-0 +2 0 (2)	SUSP	0-0-0 E 0 (0)	0-0-0 E 0 (1)	0-0-0	MON	minors	DNP	23	33
Oct. 26 at DET	0-0-0 -1 0 (2)	0-0-0 -1 0 (0)	0-0-0 E 0 (1)	0-0-0 E 4 (1)	DNP	MON	minors	0-0-0	31	47
Oct. 27 vs. DET	0-0-0 +1 0 (1)	0-0-0 E 0 (0)	DNP	DNP	0-0-0 2	MON	minors	DNP	29	24
Oct. 30 at TOR	0-0-0 -1 0 (1)	0-0-0 E 9 (1)	DNP	DNP	DNP	DNP	minors	0-0-0	39	28
Nov. 1 at PHI	0-0-0 -3 0 (1)	0-0-0 -2 2 (1)	DNP	DNP	0-0-0	DNP	minors	DNP	28	24
Nov. 3 at QUE	DNP	0-0-0 +2 0 (0)	0-0-0 +1 4 (0)	0-0-0 E 0 (1)	0-0-0	DNP	minors	DNP	22	24
Nov. 4 at MON	DNP	0-0-0 E 0 (0)	DNP	0-0-0 E 0 (0)	0-0-0	DNP	minors	DNP	25	28
Nov. 8 vs. QUE	DNP	0-0-0 E 0 (0)	DNP	0-0-0 -1 2 (0)	0-0-0 2	DNP	minors	DNP	27	26
Nov. 10 vs. HAR	0-0-0 E 4 (1)	0-0-0 E 30 (0)	minors	DNP	0-0-0	minors	minors	DNP	24	26
Nov. 13 vs. PIT	DNP	0-0-0 -1 0 (1)	minors	0-0-0 +1 0 (0)	0-0-0	DNP	minors	DNP	43	23
Nov. 15 vs. NYR	DNP	0-0-0 -1 0 (1)	minors	0-0-0 E 0 (0)	DNP	0-0-0	minors	DNP	35	32
Nov. 17 vs. STL	DNP	0-0-0 +1 0 (1)	minors	0-0-0 -1 0 (1)	0-0-0	0-0-0	minors	DNP	36	23
Nov. 19 at NYR	DNP	0-1-1 +1 10 (1)	minors	0-0-0 E 0 (1)	DNP	0-0-0	minors	DNP	43	37
Nov. 21 at DET	DNP	0-0-0 +2 0 (1)	minors	1-0-1 E 2 (1)	DNP	0-0-0	minors	DNP (traded)	28	29
Nov. 23 vs. VAN	DNP	0-2-2 +3 0 (0)	minors	0-0-0 -2 4 (0)	0-0-0	DNP	minors	EDM	26	38
Nov. 24 vs. NJD	DNP	0-0-0 -1 0 (3)	minors	0-0-0 E 0 (3)	DNP	0-0-0	minors	EDM	42	22
Nov. 27 at VAN	DNP	0-0-0 E 14 (1)	minors	0-0-0 -1 0 (0)	0-0-0	DNP	minors	EDM	21	33
Nov. 30 at WPG	DNP	0-2-2 +3 0 (0)	minors	0-0-0 +1 0 (2)	0-0-0 2	DNP	minors	EDM	29	34
Dec. 1 vs. PIT	DNP	0-0-0 +1 0 (1)	minors	0-1-1 +2 2 (1)	0-0-0	DNP	minors	EDM	40	22
Dec. 5 at TOR	DNP	1-0-1 +1 0 (1)	minors	0-0-0 +1 0 (0)	DNP	0-0-0	minors	EDM	24	28
Dec. 6 vs. TOR	0-0-0 E 2 (0)	0-0-0 -1 0 (0)	minors	0-0-0 +1 0 (1)	0-0-0 2	DNP	minors	EDM	30	22
Dec. 8 vs. PHI	0-1-1 +3 2 (1)	1-1-2 +3 7 (4)	DNP	0-0-0 E 15 (1)	DNP	0-0-0	minors	EDM	37	22
Dec. 11 vs. CAL	DNP (traded)	0-0-0 E 0 (1)	DNP	0-0-0 E 2 (1)	0-0-0	DNP	minors	EDM	37	22
Dec. 13 at STL	PIT	DNP	0-0-0 -1 0 (0)	0-0-0 -3 0 (1)	DNP	0-0-0	minors	EDM	37	32
Dec. 15 vs. CHI	PIT	0-2-2 +2 2 (2)	0-0-0 +1 0 (0)	0-1-1 E 12 (1)	0-0-0 2	DNP	minors	EDM	41	22
Dec. 16 at CHI	PIT	0-0-0 -1 10 (2)	0-0-0 E 5 (0)	0-0-0 -1 5 (1)	0-0-0 2	DNP	minors	EDM	32	23
Dec. 20 at PIT	PIT	0-0-0 +1 2 (1)	DNP	0-0-0 -1 4 (1)	DNP	0-0-0	minors	EDM	32	37
Dec. 22 at BOS	PIT	0-0-0 -1 0 (3)	DNP	0-0-0 E 2 (0)	0-0-0	0-0-0	minors	EDM	33	35
Dec. 23 at HAR	PIT	0-1-1 E 2 (0)	0-0-0 E 5 (2)	0-2-2 +2 2 (0)	0-0-0	DNP	minors	EDM	41	26
Dec. 26 vs. WPG	PIT	0-0-0 -3 0 (2)	0-0-0 +1 0 (2)	0-0-0 -2 4 (1)	0-0-0	DNP	minors	EDM	40	28
Dec. 29 vs. BOS	PIT	0-0-0 -1 0 (3)	DNP	0-0-0 +2 7 (1)	0-0-0	DNP	minors	EDM	33	32
Dec. 31 vs. LAK	PIT	0-1-1 -1 0 (2)	0-0-0 E 10 (0)	0-0-0 -2 5 (1)	0-0-0	DNP	minors	EDM	35	23
Jan. 2 at DET	PIT	0-0-0 -1 0 (1)	0-0-0 -1 5 (0)	0-0-0 E 10 (0)	0-0-0	0-0-0	minors	EDM	32	24
Jan. 3 vs. TOR	PIT	0-1-1 -2 2 (1)	0-0-0 E 0 (1)	0-0-0 +1 0 (1)	0-0-0	DNP	minors	EDM	34	29
Jan. 5 vs. VAN	PIT	0-0-0 E 14 (2)	0-1-1 +2 2 (2)	0-0-0 -2 2 (1)	0-0-0	DNP	minors	EDM	29	30
Jan. 8 at NYI	PIT	0-0-0 +2 0 (0)	0-0-0 E 0 (0)	0-0-0 +1 2 (0)	DNP	0-0-0	minors	EDM	32	15
Jan. 12 vs. BUF	PIT	0-1-1 E 0 (3)	1-0-1 E 5 (2)	0-0-0 E 4 (0)	DNP	0-0-0	minors	EDM	26	27
Jan. 13 at CHI	PIT	0-0-0 -1 4 (0)	0-0-0 -1 0 (1)	0-0-0 -1 0 (0)	0-0-0	DNP	minors	EDM	32	26
Jan. 15 vs. MON	PIT	0-0-0 -1 7 (3)	0-0-0 E 5 (0)	0-0-0 E 0 (1)	0-0-0	0-0-0	minors	EDM	22	27
Jan. 17 vs. WAS	PIT	0-1-1 +2 12 (0)	0-1-1 +2 5 (0)	0-0-0 -2 19 (0)	DNP	0-0-0	minors	EDM	20	36
Jan. 21 at WPG	PIT	0-0-0 E 0 (3)	0-0-0 -2 0 (1)	0-0-0 E 2 (0)	DNP	0-0-0	minors	EDM	28	28
Jan. 22 vs. STL	PIT	0-1-1 +1 7 (0)	0-0-0 +1 0 (0)	INJ (hip)	DNP	0-0-0	minors	EDM	40	25
Jan. 25 at WAS	PIT	0-0-0 E 9 (2)	0-0-0 -1 2 (0)	INJ (hip)	DNP	0-0-0	minors	EDM	23	20
Jan. 26 at NJD	PIT	0-0-0 +1 0 (0)	0-0-0 E 2 (2)	INJ (hip)	0-0-0	DNP	minors	EDM	22	33
Jan. 28 at TOR	PIT	0-0-0 -3 6 (1)	0-0-0 -1 9 (0)	INJ (hip)	DNP	0-0-0	minors	EDM	32	27
Jan. 30 vs. DET	PIT	0-1-1 +2 0 (2)	0-0-0 -2 2 (1)	INJ (hip)	0-0-0	DNP	minors	EDM	31	34
Feb. 2 at QUE	PIT	0-0-0 -1 0 (2)	0-0-0 E 4 (0)	INJ (hip)	0-1-1	DNP	minors	EDM	33	21
Feb. 4 at MON	PIT	0-1-1 E 0 (0)	0-0-0 E 0 (1)	INJ (hip)	DNP	0-0-0 2	minors	EDM	31	34
Feb. 7 vs. TOR	PIT	0-0-0 -1 4 (3)	1-0-1 +2 0 (4)	INJ (hip)	0-0-0	DNP	minors	EDM	31	18
Feb. 9 vs. DET	PIT	0-1-1 E 2 (1)	0-1-1 E 0 (0)	INJ (hip)	0-0-0 2	DNP	minors	EDM	39	31
Feb. 12 at NYI	PIT	0-1-1 E 0 (2)	0-0-0 -1 0 (0)	INJ (hip)	DNP	0-0-0	minors	EDM	30	26
Feb. 13 at BUF	PIT	1-0-1 -2 4 (1)	0-0-0 -2 0 (3)	INJ (hip)	0-0-0	DNP	minors	EDM	40	40
Feb. 16 at DET	PIT	0-0-0 E 0 (0)	0-0-0 E 9 (0)	INJ (hip)	0-1-1	DNP	minors	EDM	21	18
Feb. 20 vs. EDM	PIT	0-0-0 E 0 (2)	0-0-0 +3 0 (2)	INJ (hip)	0-0-0 2	DNP	minors	EDM	34	17
Feb. 23 vs. CHI	PIT	0-0-0 -2 4 (2)	0-0-0 E 2 (3)	INJ (hip)	0-0-0	DNP	minors	EDM	36	39
Feb. 26 vs. PHI	PIT	0-0-0 E 0 (1)	0-1-1 E 0 (4)	INJ (hip)	0-0-0	DNP	minors	EDM	44	21
March 1 at EDM	PIT	0-1-1 -1 0 (1)	0-0-0 E 0 (0)	INJ (hip)	DNP	0-0-0	minors	retired	22	31
March 2 at CAL	PIT	0-0-0 -1 4 (0)	0-1-1 -1 2 (4)	INJ (hip)	0-0-0 2	DNP	minors	retired	27	31
March 6 vs. EDM	PIT	0-0-0 E 0 (2)	0-0-0 +2 5 (0)	INJ (hip)	0-0-0	DNP	minors	retired	39	24
March 9 vs. DET	PIT	0-1-1 E 0 (1)	INJ (thumb)	INJ (hip)	0-0-0	DNP	minors	retired	42	28
March 10 vs. CAL	PIT	1-2-3 +2 0 (5)	INJ (thumb)	INJ (hip)	DNP	0-0-0	minors	retired	35	29
March 12 vs. BUF	PIT	0-0-0 +1 4 (1)	INJ (thumb)	INJ (hip)	0-0-0	DNP	minors	retired	35	32
March 14 at STL	PIT	0-0-0 -1 2 (3)	INJ (thumb)	INJ (hip)	0-0-0 2	DNP	minors	retired	30	28
March 16 at TOR	PIT	0-1-1 E 0 (0)	INJ (thumb)	INJ (hip)	DNP	0-0-0	minors	retired	25	31
March 17 vs. TOR	PIT	0-0-0 -1 4 (0)	0-0-0 +1 0 (0)	INJ (hip)	0-0-0	DNP	minors	retired	37	27
March 22 at WAS	PIT	0-1-1 -2 0 (1)	0-0-0 E 2 (2)	INJ (hip)	0-0-0	DNP	minors	retired	34	26
March 24 at CHI	PIT	0-0-0 +1 4 (3)	0-1-1 E 2 (2)	INJ (hip)	DNP	0-0-0	minors	retired	34	26
March 25 vs. STL	PIT	1-2-3 E 4 (3)	DNP	INJ (hip)	0-0-0	DNP	minors	retired	32	32
March 28 at LAK	PIT	0-1-1 -1 0 (2)	0-0-0 E 0 (1)	0-0-0 -2 0 (1)	0-0-0	DNP	minors	retired	33	25
March 30 vs. CHI	PIT	0-0-0 +2 4 (3)	0-0-0 -1 4 (0)	DNP	0-0-0	DNP	minors	retired	37	28
March 31 at STL	PIT	0-0-0 +1 0 (2)	0-0-0 -1 4 (1)	DNP	DNP	0-0-0	minors	retired	28	31
	16 GP	69 GP	50 GP	47 GP	55 GP	26 GP	2 GP	2 GP		
	0-1-1 E 14 (15)	5-27-32 +1 189 (92)	2-9-11 -5 117 (55)	1-4-5 -10 119 (30)	0-2-2 22	0-0-0 2	0-0-0 2	0-0-0 0	2565	2266

Stats for each skater represent: goals-assists-points plus/minus penalty minutes (shots)
Shading = home games.

Date/Opponent	Goalie	PIM	Opp PIM	PPG/PPO	PK/PKO	PP	SH	ENG	GW
Oct. 4 vs. STL	Casey 35/38 L	11	13	1-4	3-3	Gagner			
Oct. 6 vs. NYI	Casey 27/29 W	14	16	1-6	4-5	Gagner			Murphy
Oct. 8 at NYR	Myllys 34/39 L	36	17	1-4	5-7	Bellows			
Oct. 9 at NJD	Casey 24/29 L	24	24	1-5	4-7	Smith			
Oct. 11 vs. BOS	Casey 32/35 T	13	19	2-5	2-2	Modano, Propp			
Oct. 13 vs. CHI	Casey 27/31 L	51	65	1-5	6-8	Modano			
Oct. 17 at LAK	Casey 22/26 L	41	21	1-6	4-6	Craig			
Oct. 20 at STL	Casey 23/25 T	37	31	0-4	5-7				
Oct. 21 at CHI	Casey 10/14; MYLLYS 15/18 L	47	53	0-6	4-8				
Oct. 24 vs. HAR	Casey 33/33 W	12	12	1-5	5-5	Gagner		Gavin	Gagner
Oct. 26 at DET	Takko 39/46 L	37	31	3-5	1-3	Bellows, Murphy, Smith			
Oct. 27 vs. DET	Casey 22/24 T	17	19	0-5	3-4				
Oct. 30 at TOR	Takko 23/28 L	19	23	0-6	4-4		Broten		
Nov. 1 at PHI	Casey 18/24 L	18	8	2-4	3-4	Bellows, Propp	Gavin		
Nov. 3 at QUE	Casey 24/24 W	12	8	0-3	5-5			Propp	DePalma
Nov. 4 at MON	Casey 26/28 T	18	19	0-3	3-3				
Nov. 8 vs. QUE	Casey 24/26 W	47	33	0-4	5-6				Gagner
Nov. 10 vs. HAR	Casey 23/26 L	89	77	2-9	8-10	DePalma, Glynn			
Nov. 13 vs. PIT	Casey 19/22 L	8	10	0-5	3-4				
Nov. 15 vs. NYR	Hayward 28/32 L	23	17	1-3	1-1	Broten			
Nov. 17 vs. STL	CASEY 17/20 L; Hayward 3/3	6	6	1-2	1-2	Propp			
Nov. 19 at NYR	Hayward 35/37 T	35	37	0-4	2-4	Smith			
Nov. 21 at DET	Hayward 25/29 L	8	8	0-3	3-3				
Nov. 23 vs. VAN	Casey 34/38 W	10	19	2-3	4-5	Bellows, Propp			Dahlen
Nov. 24 vs. NJD	Hayward 17/21 L	9	9	0-2	1-2		Smail		
Nov. 27 at VAN	Casey 32/33 T	26	29	1-5	5-5	Modano			
Nov. 30 at WPG	Casey 32/34 W	14	6	0-2	5-6				Sinisalo
Dec. 1 vs. PIT	Casey 19/22 W	21	21	0-4	3-4		Broten, Sinisalo		Murphy
Dec. 5 at TOR	Hayward 26/28 W	8	10	0-5	2-4				Tinordi
Dec. 6 vs. TOR	Casey 20/22 L	8	8	0-4	4-4				
Dec. 8 vs. PHI	Hayward 22/22 W	35	59	3-5	3-3	Gagner, Modano, Propp			Tinordi
Dec. 11 vs. CAL	Casey 17/22 L	12	16	2-7	3-5	Gagner (2)			
Dec. 13 at STL	Hayward 28/32 L	19	12	1-5	1-1	Sinisalo			
Dec. 15 vs. CHI	Casey 21/22 W	34	52	2-10	5-6	Berezan, Smith			Smith
Dec. 16 at CHI	Casey 18/22 L	36	34	1-5	3-6	Gagner			
Dec. 20 at PIT	Hayward 33/37 L	12	8	0-2	3-4				
Dec. 22 at BOS	Casey 21/23; HAYWARD 8/12 L	17	17	1-4	2-4	Bellows			
Dec. 23 at HAR	Casey 24/26 W	25	37	2-7	6-6	Gagner, Modano			Modano
Dec. 26 vs. WPG	Casey 22/28 L	12	10	0-2	3-3				
Dec. 29 vs. BOS	Casey 28/32 T	32	21	0-5	3-5				
Dec. 31 vs. LAK	Casey 19/23 L	40	27	1-4	4-5	Gagner			
Jan. 2 at DET	HAYWARD 18/24 L; Casey 0/0	27	33	1-7	2-4	Modano			
Jan. 3 vs. TOR	Casey 26/29 T	12	8	1-3	4-5	Gagner			
Jan. 5 vs. VAN	Casey 24/30 L	30	18	1-6	3-6	Modano			
Jan. 8 at NYI	Hayward 15/15 W	10	8	0-2	3-3		Berezan		Gagner
Jan. 12 vs. BUF	Hayward 22/26 L	17	17	0-6	5-6				
Jan. 13 at CHI	Casey 21/25 L	41	38	3-8	3-5	Bellows (2), Gagner			
Jan. 15 vs. MON	Hayward 11/14; CASEY 11/13 L	24	15	0-5	7-10				
Jan. 17 vs. WAS	Hayward 34/36 W	67	58	0-4	8-8		Smail		Craig
Jan. 21 at WPG	Hayward 26/27 L	12	10	0-3	4-4				
Jan. 22 vs. STL	Hayward 22/25 W	13	9	1-2	3-4	Bellows			Gagner
Jan. 25 at WAS	Hayward 18/20 T	21	31	1-9	4-4	Propp			
Jan. 26 at NJD	Casey 32/33 W	12	20	1-9	5-5	Smith		Duchesne	Propp
Jan. 28 at TOR	Hayward 23/27 L	19	23	0-7	5-5				
Jan. 30 vs. DET	Casey 32/34 W	25	37	1-4	3-3	Bellows			Bellows
Feb. 2 at QUE	Casey 17/21 W	19	15	2-4	4-6	Bellows, Gagner			Craig
Feb. 4 at MON	Hayward 29/33 L	8	8	1-2	2-2	Gagner			
Feb. 7 vs. TOR	Casey 16/18 W	22	20	1-4	5-5	Bellows			Gagner
Feb. 9 vs. DET	Casey 26/31 W	33	21	2-5	4-6	Dahlen, Gagner			Berezan
Feb. 12 at NYI	Hayward 21/26 L	8	10	1-5	4-4	Glynn	Berezan		
Feb. 13 at BUF	Casey 34/40 T	43	39	3-6	9-9	Bellows, Gagner, Tinordi			
Feb. 16 at DET	Casey 18/18 W	20	22	2-4	3-3	Bellows, Smith			Smith
Feb. 20 vs. EDM	Casey 16/17 W	27	23	1-4	5-6	Modano			Bellows
Feb. 23 vs. CHI	Casey 36/39 T	16	18	2-8	7-7	Bellows, Gagner			
Feb. 26 vs. PHI	Casey 19/21 T	6	12	0-4	4-4				
March 1 at EDM	Hayward 30/31 T	29	20	1-6	4-4	Gagner			
March 2 at CAL	Casey 26/31 L	39	17	1-5	4-6	Dahlen			
March 6 vs. EDM	Casey 23/24 W	17	23	1-3	5-5	Bellows			Bellows
March 9 vs. DET	Casey 26/28 W	12	30	2-8	3-4	Dahlen, Gagner			Dahlen
March 10 vs. CAL	Hayward 26/29 W	46	48	3-8	6-7	Bellows, Glynn, Modano	Berezan		Duchesne
March 12 vs. BUF	Casey 30/32 W	14	8	0-2	4-5			Berezan	Dahlen
March 14 at STL	Casey 26/28 T	22	26	1-4	4-4	Gagner			
March 16 at TOR	Hayward 27/31 L	12	10	1-3	2-4	Dahlen			
March 17 vs. TOR	Casey 24/27 W	46	50	1-5	3-3	Propp			Modano
March 22 at WAS	Casey 23/26 L	6	8	1-3	1-2	Propp			
March 24 at CHI	Hayward 21/26 L	68	64	0-8	4-5				
March 25 vs. STL	Casey 27/32 L	14	18	3-4	1-2	Bellows, Propp, Smith			
March 28 at LAK	Casey 19/24 L	10	12	1-3	3-3	Gagner			
March 30 vs. CHI	Casey 27/28 W	52	36	0-3	6-6				Bellows
March 31 at STL	Hayward 29/31 L	52	24	0-4	7-8	Bellows			
	Casey 21-20-11; Hayward 6-15-3								
	Casey 2.98, .891; Hayward 3.14, .886	1964	1869	76-382 (19.9)	303-378 (80.2)				
	Myllys 0-2-2, 6.12, .860; Takko 0-2-0, 6.06, .838								

Stats for each skater represent: goals-assists-points plus/minus penalty minutes (shots)
Shading = home games.

Date/Opponent	Result	Record	Attend./TV	Babe	Barber	Bellows	Berezan	Broten	Bureau
April 4 at CHI	4-3 W, OT	1-0	18,102/KMSP	minors	WPG	0-2-2 +1 0 (3)	DNP	2-1-3 +1 0 (3)	0-0-0 E 0 (1)
April 6 at CHI	5-2 L	1-1	18,190/KMSP	minors	WPG	1-0-1 -2 2 (5)	DNP	0-1-1 E 0 (3)	0-0-0 E 10 (0)
April 8 vs. CHI	6-5 L	1-2	12,753/PPV-MSC	minors	WPG	1-0-1 -2 0 (3)	DNP	0-1-1 E 0 (0)	0-0-0 E 0 (0)
April 10 vs. CHI	3-1 W	2-2	14,343/PPV-MSC	minors	WPG	0-1-1 E 0 (4)	DNP	1-0-1 +1 2 (4)	0-0-0 -1 0 (1)
April 12 at CHI	6-0 W	3-2	17,641/KMSP	minors	WPG	0-4-4 E 6 (4)	DNP	1-0-1 +1 0 (6)	0-0-0 E 2 (1)
April 14 vs. CHI	3-1 W	4-2	15,274/PPV-MSC	minors	WPG	2-1-3 +2 0 (4)	DNP	0-0-0 -1 0 (1)	0-0-0 E 0 (3)
April 18 at STL	2-1 W	5-2	16,911/KMSP	minors	WPG	0-0-0 E 0 (0)	DNP	0-0-0 +1 0 (2)	0-0-0 E 0 (0)
April 20 at STL	5-2 L	5-3	18,051/KMSP	minors	WPG	1-0-1 E 2 (7)	DNP	0-0-0 -1 2 (2)	0-0-0 -1 0 (0)
April 22 vs. STL	5-1 W	6-3	14,341/PPV-MSC	minors	WPG	1-1-2 +1 0 (3)	DNP	0-1-1 E 0 (2)	0-1-1 +1 0 (0)
April 24 vs. STL	8-4 W	7-3	15,326/PPV-MSC	minors	WPG	2-0-2 +1 0 (5)	DNP	0-2-2 E 0 (1)	0-0-0 E 0 (1)
April 26 at STL	4-2 L	7-4	18,520/KMSP	minors	WPG	0-0-0 E 0 (4)	DNP	0-2-2 -1 0 (4)	0-0-0 E 0 (1)
April 28 vs. STL	3-2 W	8-4	15,274/PPV-MSC	minors	WPG	0-1-1 E 0 (0)	DNP	0-1-1 +2 0 (1)	0-0-0 E 0 (1)
May 2 at EDM	3-1 W	9-4	17,082/KMSP	minors	WPG	0-1-1 E 0 (1)	DNP	1-1-2 +2 0 (4)	0-0-0 E 0 (1)
May 4 at EDM	7-2 L	9-5	17,503/KMSP	minors	WPG	0-1-1 -3 4 (4)	DNP	0-1-1 -1 0 (0)	0-0-0 -1 0 (0)
May 6 vs. EDM	7-3 W	10-5	15,378/PPV-MSC	minors	WPG	2-1-3 +1 0 (5)	DNP	0-1-1 +1 0 (0)	0-1-1 +1 0 (1)
May 8 vs. EDM	5-1 W	11-5	15,274/PPV-MSC	minors	WPG	0-3-3 +1 0 (1)	DNP	1-0-1 E 0 (6)	1-0-1 E 0 (1)
May 10 at EDM	3-2 W	12-5	17,503/KMSP	minors	WPG	0-1-1 E 0 (2)	DNP	0-0-0 -1 0 (2)	1-0-1 +1 0 (1)
May 15 at PIT	5-4 W	13-5	16,164/KMSP	minors	WPG	0-0-0 E 0 (2)	DNP	2-0-2 +2 0 (6)	1-0-1 -1 4 (1)
May 17 at PIT	4-1 L	13-6	16,164/KMSP	minors	WPG	0-0-0 -1 2 (1)	0-0-0 -1 0 (2)	0-0-0 -1 0 (2)	0-0-0 -1 4 (2)
May 19 vs. PIT	3-1 W	14-6	15,378/PPV-MSC	minors	WPG	0-1-1 +2 12 (3)	DNP	0-1-1 +1 0 (0)	0-0-0 E 0 (0)
May 21 vs. PIT	5-3 L	14-7	15,378/PPV-MSC	minors	WPG	0-1-1 E 2 (5)	DNP	0-0-0 -3 0 (3)	0-0-0 -1 0 (0)
May 23 at PIT	6-4 L	14-8	16,164/KMSP	minors	WPG	0-0-0 -1 0 (1)	DNP	1-0-1 E 0 (2)	0-0-0 E 0 (0)
May 25 vs. PIT	8-0 L	14-9 (.609)	15,378/PPV-MSC	minors	WPG	0-0-0 -4 0 (1)	DNP	0-0-0 -1 2 (1)	0-0-0 -1 0 (3)
23 GP	81 GF	8-3 (home)	164,097 (home)			23 GP	1 GP	23 GP	23 GP
	78 GA	6-6 (road)	207,995 (road)			10-19-29 -6 30 (68)	0-0-0 -1 0 (2)	9-13-22 +2 6 (55)	3-2-5 -4 10 (19)

Date/Opponent	Chambers	Churla	Craig	Dahlen	Dahlquist	DePalma	Duchesne	Evans	Gagner
April 4 at CHI	0-1-1 E 0 (2)	0-0-0 +1 2 (2)	0-0-0 E 4 (1)	0-0-0 -1 2 (2)	0-1-1 E 0 (0)	minors	0-0-0 E 0 (0)	minors	0-2-2 -1 2 (2)
April 6 at CHI	0-0-0 -1 0 (1)	0-0-0 E 17 (0)	0-0-0 E 2 (0)	0-0-0 -1 0 (3)	0-0-0 -1 2 (2)	minors	0-0-0 E 0 (0)	minors	0-0-0 -2 0 (2)
April 8 vs. CHI	0-0-0 -1 0 (3)	0-0-0 E 4 (0)	DNP	0-1-1 -3 0 (2)	0-1-1 E 0 (1)	minors	0-0-0 E 2 (1)	minors	2-2-4 +2 0 (8)
April 10 vs. CHI	0-0-0 E 0 (4)	0-0-0 -1 14 (0)	1-1-2 +1 4 (1)	DNP	0-0-0 -1 0 (2)	minors	0-0-0 +1 10 (0)	minors	0-0-0 E 0 (0)
April 12 at CHI	0-2-2 +1 2 (3)	0-0-0 E 0 (0)	0-0-0 +1 (3)	DNP	0-0-0 E 4 (1)	minors	0-0-0 +1 0 (1)	minors	1-0-1 E 0 (4)
April 14 vs. CHI	0-0-0 E 0 (6)	0-0-0 E 0 (2)	0-0-0 -1 2 (1)	DNP	0-0-0 E 0 (0)	minors	0-0-0 E 2 (3)	minors	0-1-1 E 0 (3)
April 18 at STL	0-0-0 E 0 (1)	1-0-1 +1 0 (3)	0-0-0 E 0 (5)	DNP	0-0-0 E 0 (1)	minors	0-0-0 E 0 (1)	minors	1-0-1 -1 4 (3)
April 20 at STL	0-0-0 -2 0 (1)	0-0-0 E 17 (1)	0-0-0 -2 2 (0)	DNP	0-0-0 +2 0 (1)	minors	0-0-0 -1 0 (0)	minors	0-0-0 -2 0 (1)
April 22 vs. STL	0-0-0 E 2 (2)	0-0-0 +1 4 (0)	0-0-0 E 0 (1)	DNP	0-0-0 E 2 (0)	minors	0-0-0 E 2 (1)	minors	0-1-1 -1 0 (4)
April 24 vs. STL	0-1-1 +3 0 (2)	0-1-1 E 10 (0)	0-0-0 E 4 (0)	DNP	0-1-1 +1 0 (0)	minors	0-0-0 E 2 (2)	minors	1-2-3 +3 0 (5)
April 26 at STL	0-0-0 E 2 (4)	0-0-0 E 10 (0)	0-0-0 -1 2 (0)	DNP	0-0-0 E 2 (0)	minors	0-0-0 -1 2 (0)	minors	0-1-1 E 2 (3)
April 28 vs. STL	0-0-0 E 0 (2)	0-0-0 E 0 (1)	DNP	0-0-0 E 0 (2)	1-0-1 +1 0 (2)	minors	0-0-0 E 2 (3)	minors	0-0-0 E 2 (2)
May 2 at EDM	0-0-0 E 0 (2)	0-0-0 E 0 (0)	DNP	0-2-2 +2 0 (2)	0-0-0 +1 2 (2)	minors	1-0-1 +2 0 (1)	minors	1-0-1 E 0 (2)
May 4 at EDM	0-0-0 E 2 (1)	0-0-0 -2 2 (1)	DNP	0-0-0 -1 0 (1)	0-0-0 -3 0 (0)	minors	0-0-0 E 2 (1)	minors	1-0-1 +1 0 (1)
May 6 vs. EDM	0-1-1 +1 0 (1)	1-0-1 +1 2 (2)	DNP	0-1-1 +2 0 (0)	0-0-0 +3 2 (1)	DNP	0-1-1 +1 0 (1)	minors	0-3-3 -1 0 (6)
May 8 vs. EDM	0-0-0 -1 0 (0)	0-0-0 -1 0 (0)	DNP	0-0-0 E 2 (2)	0-1-1 +1 2 (0)	DNP	0-0-0 E 4 (2)	minors	1-1-2 +2 0 (4)
May 10 at EDM	0-0-0 -1 2 (1)	0-0-0 E 4 (0)	DNP	0-0-0 -2 0 (0)	0-1-1 +2 0 (0)	DNP	0-1-1 E 0 (1)	minors	0-0-0 E 4 (3)
May 15 at PIT	0-1-1 E 2 (2)	0-0-0 E 0 (0)	DNP	1-1-2 +2 0 (3)	0-0-0 -1 0 (1)	DNP	0-0-0 -1 0 (3)	minors	0-0-0 E 0 (1)
May 17 at PIT	0-1-1 -1 2 (0)	DNP	DNP	0-0-0 E 0 (2)	0-0-0 -1 0 (2)	DNP	0-0-0 E 4 (3)	minors	0-0-0 -2 2 (6)
May 19 vs. PIT	0-0-0 -1 2 (1)	0-0-0 E 0 (0)	DNP	0-0-0 +1 0 (2)	0-1-1 +2 2 (2)	DNP	1-0-1 +1 2 (1)	minors	1-0-1 E 2 (6)
May 21 vs. PIT	0-0-0 -3 0 (2)	0-0-0 -1 0 (0)	DNP	0-1-1 +1 0 (2)	0-0-0 E 0 (0)	DNP	0-0-0 -3 0 (0)	minors	1-2-3 E 2 (5)
May 23 at PIT	0-0-0 E 0 (2)	0-0-0 E 2 (1)	DNP	1-0-1 -1 0 (2)	0-0-0 -1 2 (2)	DNP	0-1-1 E 0 (0)	minors	2-0-2 +1 6 (4)
May 25 vs. PIT	0-0-0 -1 0 (1)	0-0-0 -1 2 (1)	DNP	0-0-0 -3 0 (1)	0-0-0 -1 0 (1)	DNP	0-0-0 E 0 (1)	minors	0-0-0 -1 2 (3)
	23 GP	22 GP	10 GP	15 GP	23 GP		23 GP		23 GP
	0-7-7 -7 16 (44)	2-1-3 -2 90 (14)	1-1-2 -2 20 (12)	2-6-8 -4 4 (26)	1-6-7 +4 20 (21)		2-3-5 E 34 (26)		12-15-27 -4 28 (78)

Date/Opponent	Gavin	Giles	Glynn	Gotaas	Johnson	Keczmer	Kolstad	MacLeod	McHugh
April 4 at CHI	DNP	DNP	0-0-0 -1 0 (4)	minors	0-0-0 E 0 (2)	minors	minors	minors	minors
April 6 at CHI	DNP	0-0-0 -1 0 (0)	0-0-0 -1 0 (0)	minors	0-0-0 E 17 (1)	minors	minors	minors	minors
April 8 vs. CHI	0-0-0 E 0 (3)	DNP	0-2-2 -1 2 (5)	minors	0-0-0 +1 15 (0)	minors	minors	minors	minors
April 10 vs. CHI	0-0-0 E 6 (1)	DNP	0-0-0 E 2 (1)	minors	0-0-0 +1 0 (0)	minors	minors	minors	minors
April 12 at CHI	0-0-0 E 0 (2)	DNP	0-2-2 +1 2 (3)	minors	0-0-0 E 2 (1)	minors	minors	minors	minors
April 14 vs. CHI	0-2-2 +2 0 (0)	DNP	0-0-0 E 2 (2)	minors	0-0-0 +1 2 (1)	minors	minors	minors	minors
April 18 at STL	0-0-0 E 2 (2)	0-0-0 E 2 (2)	0-0-0 E 0 (1)	minors	INJ (hip)	minors	minors	minors	minors
April 20 at STL	1-1-2 +1 0 (3)	0-0-0 -1 2 (0)	0-0-0 -2 2 (1)	minors	INJ (hip)	minors	minors	minors	minors
April 22 vs. STL	1-0-1 +1 0 (2)	1-0-1 +1 4 (1)	0-1-1 E 0 (0)	minors	INJ (hip)	minors	minors	minors	minors
April 24 vs. STL	0-3-3 +3 2 (1)	0-0-0 E 0 (2)	2-1-3 +3 2 (3)	minors	INJ (hip)	minors	minors	minors	minors
April 26 at STL	0-0-0 E 0 (2)	0-0-0 -2 4 (0)	0-0-0 E 0 (0)	minors	INJ (hip)	minors	minors	minors	minors
April 28 vs. STL	0-0-0 -1 0 (3)	0-0-0 E 0 (1)	0-0-0 +1 2 (0)	minors	INJ (hip)	DNP	minors	minors	minors
May 2 at EDM	0-0-0 E 2 (0)	0-0-0 +1 0 (0)	0-0-0 E 0 (4)	minors	INJ (hip)	minors	minors	minors	minors
May 4 at EDM	1-0-1 E 0 (3)	0-0-0 -1 2 (1)	0-0-0 -1 0 (3)	minors	INJ (hip)	minors	minors	minors	minors
May 6 vs. EDM	0-0-0 +1 0 (1)	0-0-0 -1 2 (0)	0-0-0 +1 0 (1)	minors	INJ (hip)	DNP	minors	minors	minors
May 8 vs. EDM	0-0-0 E 4 (1)	DNP	0-0-0 -1 0 (0)	minors	0-0-0 +2 2 (0)	DNP	minors	minors	minors
May 10 at EDM	0-1-1 +1 0 (5)	DNP	0-0-0 -2 0 (3)	minors	0-0-0 E 4 (0)	DNP	minors	minors	minors
May 15 at PIT	0-1-1 +2 0 (2)	DNP	0-0-0 +1 0 (2)	minors	0-0-0 +3 2 (0)	DNP	minors	minors	minors
May 17 at PIT	0-0-0 E 0 (4)	DNP	0-0-0 E 2 (2)	minors	0-0-0 E 0 (1)	DNP	minors	minors	minors
May 19 vs. PIT	0-1-1 +1 0 (0)	DNP	0-0-0 E 0 (2)	minors	0-1-1 +1 4 (0)	DNP	minors	minors	minors
May 21 vs. PIT	0-0-0 -3 0 (2)	DNP	0-0-0 -3 0 (4)	minors	0-0-0 E 2 (4)	DNP	minors	minors	minors
May 23 at PIT	0-1-1 +1 0 (1)	DNP	0-0-0 E 4 (0)	minors	0-0-0 +1 0 (1)	DNP	minors	minors	minors
May 25 vs. PIT	0-0-0 E 2 (2)	DNP	0-0-0 -3 0 (2)	minors	0-0-0 -2 2 (1)	DNP	minors	minors	minors
	21 GP	10 GP	23 GP		14 GP				
	3-10-13 +9 18 (40)	1-0-1 -4 16 (7)	2-6-8 -8 20 (43)		0-1-1 +8 52 (12)				

Stats for each skater represent: goals-assists-points plus/minus penalty minutes (shots)
Shading = home games.

Date/Opponent	McRae	Messier	Modano	Murphy	Musil	Propp	Sinisalo	Smail	Smith
April 4 at CHI	0-0-0 +1 0 (0)	minors	0-0-0 -1 0 (3)	PIT	CAL	1-0-1 -1 2 (2)	LAK	DNP	0-0-0 -1 0 (3)
April 6 at CHI	1-0-1 E 7 (4)	minors	0-1-1 -2 0 (6)	PIT	CAL	0-0-0 -1 0 (0)	LAK	DNP	0-0-0 -2 2 (2)
April 8 vs. CHI	0-0-0 +2 0 (2)	minors	1-1-2 +2 0 (7)	PIT	CAL	0-2-2 +1 0 (3)	LAK	DNP	1-0-1 -3 0 (2)
April 10 vs. CHI	0-0-0 -1 9 (1)	minors	0-1-1 E 0 (3)	PIT	CAL	0-1-1 E 0 (2)	LAK	DNP	0-0-0 E 0 (4)
April 12 at CHI	0-0-0 E 0 (1)	minors	0-1-1 E 0 (1)	PIT	CAL	2-1-3 E 0 (5)	LAK	DNP	1-0-1 E 0 (4)
April 14 vs. CHI	0-0-0 -1 0 (0)	minors	0-0-0 E 0 (1)	PIT	CAL	0-1-1 E 0 (3)	LAK	DNP	0-1-1 +2 0 (3)
April 18 at STL	0-1-1 +1 0 (0)	minors	0-0-0 -1 0 (0)	PIT	CAL	0-0-0 -1 0 (0)	LAK	DNP	0-0-0 E 5 (4)
April 20 at STL	0-0-0 E 8 (1)	minors	0-0-0 -1 0 (2)	PIT	CAL	0-0-0 -1 0 (1)	LAK	DNP	0-1-1 +1 2 (1)
April 22 vs. STL	0-0-0 +1 4 (1)	minors	0-1-1 -1 4 (0)	PIT	CAL	1-1-2 -1 0 (5)	LAK	DNP	0-2-2 +1 8 (2)
April 24 vs. STL	0-0-0 E 4 (0)	minors	2-1-3 +3 2 (2)	PIT	CAL	1-2-3 +1 2 (1)	LAK	DNP	0-2-2 +1 2 (1)
April 26 at STL	0-0-0 E 14 (0)	minors	1-0-1 -2 0 (2)	PIT	CAL	1-0-1 E 6 (1)	LAK	DNP	0-0-0 -1 6 (3)
April 28 vs. STL	0-0-0 E 0 (0)	minors	0-2-2 +2 0 (3)	PIT	CAL	0-0-0 E 0 (3)	LAK	DNP	2-0-2 E 0 (6)
May 2 at EDM	0-0-0 E 0 (0)	minors	0-0-0 E 0 (1)	PIT	CAL	0-0-0 E 2 (5)	LAK	DNP	0-0-0 E 0 (3)
May 4 at EDM	0-0-0 -2 20 (0)	minors	0-0-0 E 2 (1)	PIT	CAL	0-1-1 -1 2 (2)	LAK	DNP	0-0-0 -1 0 (0)
May 6 vs. EDM	0-0-0 +1 0 (0)	minors	1-0-1 E 2 (2)	PIT	CAL	1-1-2 -1 4 (3)	LAK	DNP	1-0-1 +2 0 (3)
May 8 vs. EDM	0-0-0 E 0 (1)	minors	1-2-3 +2 0 (1)	PIT	CAL	0-1-1 +2 2 (0)	LAK	DNP	0-0-0 E 15 (0)
May 10 at EDM	0-0-0 E 0 (0)	minors	0-0-0 E 0 (3)	PIT	CAL	0-1-1 +1 4 (5)	LAK	DNP	1-0-1 E 0 (3)
May 15 at PIT	0-0-0 -1 2 (0)	minors	0-1-1 E 0 (2)	PIT	CAL	0-0-0 +1 2 (1)	LAK	DNP	1-1-2 +1 0 (2)
May 17 at PIT	DNP	minors	1-0-1 -1 2 (4)	PIT	CAL	0-0-0 -2 0 (1)	LAK	0-0-0 -1 0 (0)	0-0-0 E 2 (4)
May 19 vs. PIT	0-0-0 E 2 (1)	minors	0-1-1 E 0 (4)	PIT	CAL	0-0-0 -1 0 (4)	LAK	DNP	1-0-1 +1 4 (3)
May 21 vs. PIT	0-0-0 -1 4 (1)	minors	1-0-1 -1 2 (4)	PIT	CAL	1-1-2 -1 2 (1)	LAK	DNP	0-0-0 -1 0 (2)
May 23 at PIT	0-0-0 E 6 (1)	minors	0-0-0 -1 0 (3)	PIT	CAL	0-2-2 +1 0 (1)	LAK	DNP	0-1-1 -2 0 (2)
May 25 vs. PIT	0-0-0 E 12 (1)	minors	0-0-0 -1 2 (4)	PIT	CAL	0-0-0 E 0 (3)	LAK	DNP	0-0-0 -3 0 (3)
	22 GP		23 GP			23 GP		1 GP	23 GP
	1-1-2 -3 94 (15)		8-12-20 -3 16 (59)			8-15-23 -4 28 (52)		0-0-0 -1 0 (0)	8-8-16 -5 46 (60)

Date/Opponent	Taglianetti	Tinordi	Wilkinson	Zettler	Casey	Hayward	Myllys	Takko	Shots For	Shots Against
April 4 at CHI	PIT	1-1-2 -1 2 (3)	0-0-0 E 4 (1)	DNP	0-0-0	DNP	minors	retired	34	23
April 6 at CHI	PIT	0-0-0 -1 16 (1)	DNP	DNP	0-0-0 2	0-0-0	minors	retired	30	36
April 8 vs. CHI	PIT	0-0-0 E 4 (7)	0-0-0 -1 2 (0)	DNP	0-0-0	0-0-0	minors	retired	47	31
April 10 vs. CHI	PIT	1-0-1 -1 2 (3)	0-1-1 +1 0 (3)	DNP	0-0-0	DNP	minors	retired	34	17
April 12 at CHI	PIT	1-0-1 E 2 (2)	0-0-0 E 0 (1)	DNP	0-0-0	DNP	minors	retired	43	25
April 14 vs. CHI	PIT	0-0-0 E 2 (0)	1-0-1 +1 2 (1)	DNP	0-0-0	DNP	minors	retired	34	27
April 18 at STL	PIT	0-1-1 E 0 (2)	0-0-0 E 0 (0)	DNP	0-0-0	DNP	minors	retired	27	32
April 20 at STL	PIT	0-1-1 +1 0 (0)	0-0-0 -1 0 (0)	DNP	0-0-0 2	DNP	minors	retired	22	28
April 22 vs. STL	PIT	0-0-0 E 12 (1)	1-0-1 +1 0 (1)	DNP	0-0-0	DNP	minors	retired	26	30
April 24 vs. STL	PIT	0-0-0 +1 15 (2)	0-0-0 E 0 (3)	DNP	0-0-0	DNP	minors	retired	31	36
April 26 at STL	PIT	0-0-0 -1 2 (0)	0-1-1 -1 0 (2)	DNP	0-0-0	0-0-0	minors	retired	26	31
April 28 vs. STL	PIT	0-0-0 E 0 (1)	0-0-0 E 0 (1)	DNP	0-0-0	DNP	minors	retired	32	20
May 2 at EDM	PIT	0-0-0 +2 2 (3)	0-0-0 E 0 (1)	DNP	0-0-0	DNP	minors	retired	32	28
May 4 at EDM	PIT	0-0-0 -1 2 (1)	0-0-0 -2 0 (1)	DNP	0-0-0	0-0-0	minors	retired	21	32
May 6 vs. EDM	PIT	1-1-2 +1 0 (6)	0-0-0 +1 0 (3)	DNP	0-0-0	DNP	DNP	retired	36	29
May 8 vs. EDM	PIT	0-1-1 E+1 0 (3)	1-1-2 +2 0 (4)	DNP	0-0-0 2	DNP	DNP	retired	26	21
May 10 at EDM	PIT	1-0-1 +1 2 (3)	0-0-0 E 2 (1)	DNP	0-0-0 2	DNP	DNP	retired	33	21
May 15 at PIT	PIT	0-0-0 -1 2 (1)	0-0-0 +2 0 (0)	DNP	0-0-0 2	DNP	DNP	retired	29	38
May 17 at PIT	PIT	0-0-0 -2 5 (3)	0-0-0 -1 2 (1)	DNP	0-1-1	DNP	DNP	retired	40	31
May 19 vs. PIT	PIT	0-0-0 +1 0 (2)	0-0-0 +1 0 (2)	DNP	0-0-0	DNP	DNP	retired	33	30
May 21 vs. PIT	PIT	0-0-0 -1 0 (3)	0-0-0 E 0 (0)	DNP	0-0-0 2	DNP	DNP	retired	38	24
May 23 at PIT	PIT	0-1-1 +1 4 (1)	0-0-0 -1 0 (1)	DNP	0-0-0	0-0-0	DNP	retired	25	31
May 25 vs. PIT	PIT	0-0-0 -1 4 (6)	0-0-0 -1 0 (4)	DNP	0-0-0	0-0-0	DNP	retired	39	28
		23 GP	22 GP		23 GP	6 GP				
		5-6-11 -1 78 (54)	3-3-6 +1 12 (31)		0-1-1 12	0-0-0 0			738	649

Date/Opponent	Goalie	PIM	Opp PIM	PPG/PPO	PK/PKO	PP	SH	ENG	GW
April 4 at CHI	Casey 20/23 W	18	29	3-11	5-6	Broten, Propp, Tinordi			Propp
April 6 at CHI	CASEY 21/25 L; Hayward 10/10	77	69	1-5	2-4	Bellows			
April 8 vs. CHI	HAYWARD 11/13 L; Casey 14/18	31	22	3-9	4-7	Bellows, Gagner, Smith			
April 10 vs. CHI	Casey 16/17 W	49	90	2-10	4-4	Craig, Tinordi			Craig
April 12 at CHI	Casey 25/25 W	20	52	5-12	6-6	Gagner, Propp (2), Smith, Tinordi			Propp
April 14 vs. CHI	Casey 26/27 W	12	18	1-7	4-4	Bellows			Bellows
April 18 at STL	Casey 31/32 W	13	8	1-4	5-5	Gagner			Churla
April 20 at STL	Casey 23/27 L	39	29	0-6	5-6				
April 22 vs. STL	Casey 29/30 W	42	38	3-9	7-7	Bellows, Propp, Wilkinson			Gavin
April 24 vs. STL	Casey 32/36 W	45	38	4-8	7-11	Bellows, Glynn (2), Propp			Propp
April 26 at STL	CASEY 25/29 L; Hayward 2/2	52	52	2-8	6-8	Modano, Propp			
April 28 vs. STL	Casey 18/20 W	6	2	0-1	3-3			Smith	Smith
May 2 at EDM	Casey 27/28 W	8	12	1-5	2-3	Gagner			Gagner
May 4 at EDM	Hayward 18/21; CASEY 7/11 L	38	25	1-7	5-7	Gagner	Gavin		
May 6 vs. EDM	Casey 26/29 W	14	14	2-6	5-6	Bellows, Propp			Smith
May 8 vs. EDM	Casey 20/21 W	33	49	2-7	4-4	Broten, Gagner			Modano
May 10 at EDM	Casey 19/21 W	24	38	1-8	6-6	Tinordi			Smith
May 15 at PIT	Casey 34/38 W	16	10	0-5	7-8		Bureau		Smith
May 17 at PIT	Casey 27/31 L	29	54	1-9	7-8	Modano			
May 19 vs. PIT	Casey 29/30 W	30	47	0-5	4-4				Smith
May 21 vs. PIT	Casey 19/23 L	16	33	2-7	5-5	Modano, Propp			
May 23 at PIT	HAYWARD 16/18 L; Casey 9/13	24	18	0-4	5-7		Broten, Gagner		
May 25 vs. PIT	CASEY 13/17 L; Hayward 7/11	28	14	0-3	3-6				
	Casey 14-7; Hayward 0-2								
	Casey 3.04, .893; Hayward 3.86, .853	664	761	35-152 (23.0)	24-136 (82.4)				

AFTERWORD

By Patrick Reusse

Kevin Allenspach and I were going to be in the same building at the College of Saint Benedict in St. Joseph, Minnesota, on a night in December 2022. We talked beforehand and Kevin asked if there might be a few minutes to discuss a book he was finishing on the 1990–91 Minnesota North Stars, carrying the title *Mirage of Destiny*.

As fellow alums of the *St. Cloud Times*, me in the late '60s, Kevin a few decades later, this wasn't going to be a problem. My only issue was, "Why does Kevin feel as if that team is worth a book?"

I had the seventy minutes it takes to get from a first-tier Minneapolis suburb to Saint Ben's to contemplate this.

I thought about the Gund brothers deciding they wanted to move the North Stars to San Jose, and the NHL turning down the move because it wanted to split expansion money for a Bay Area franchise;

And I thought of those seven months from January 1990 to July 1990 looking for a new owner, with no Minnesota money people showing up as we went from Howard Baldwin to Slick Norm Green;

And an empty Met Center to start a season in which the North Stars would finish 16th among 21 teams in points;

And then a Game 3 win in an overflowing Met as the North Stars took a 2–1 lead over Pittsburgh in the Stanley Cup Final, and I had not yet made it to the Hasty truck stop on the drive when saying to myself:

"That's why Kevin is writing a book about the 1990–91 North Stars—because it was the goofiest, most otherworldly ride we've ever had with a Minnesota pro sports franchise since the Twins and the Vikings made this a big-league market in 1961."

That was true in 1991, and that remains true three decades later. You know what it was? It was a version of "Major League," the smash baseball comedy from 1989, come to real life on ice.

The only difference was the Cleveland ballclub had Harry Doyle on the mike and we had Al Shaver.

The *Star Tribune* was between NHL writers that spring and utility player Jon Roe, double-duty Jerry Zgoda, and I were charged with attempting to follow the ownership drama.

Baldwin became "Howie the Hairdo" in my *Star Tribune* columns, and he was prancing around in high style until one day telling team president Lou Nanne: "We're bringing in Norm Green from Calgary to take care of our money problems."

Louie's response was: "I didn't know we had money problems."

They did, and Norm finally became majority owner in July 1990, and Baldwin soon went away. Norm and I talked a few times during that drama, to the point that he must have decided that I was an ally.

This is based on one of the strangest early-morning calls at home received from a sports figure. Checking the records, the call had to be on January 16, 1991, since it was the previous night when the Montreal Canadiens defeated the North Stars 5–1, and there was an actual crowd of fewer than 5,000 at Met Center.

The loss dropped the North Stars to 12–28–2. And it was Norm Green on the phone.

Norm had tried to replicate the expansion Timberwolves' provocatively attired dance team with his "Electric Stars" cheerleaders. He also had people walking through the stands giving away cash.

Those efforts didn't work, which was disappointing... but fewer than 5,000 customers for the Canadiens was disaster for Green, a Canada native.

I don't think Norm could've been sadder that morning if one of his King Charles spaniels—Charles or Rupert—had been struck by a car on a walk in the Met Center parking lot.

Somehow, the North Stars crawled on their stomachs to hold off the lowly Toronto Maple Leafs—who had the second-worst record in the league—to squeeze into the playoffs. Then Bob Gainey's 68-point bunch beat NHL royalty in the Chicago Blackhawks (106 points) and the St. Louis Blues (105) in six games each, and then they took care of Edmonton in five games in the Campbell Conference finals.

By then, Met Center had been a madhouse for weeks. Green had built himself a highly visible booth in the southwest corner of the arena. Those getting invitations to sit among the fifteen or twenty elite became time travelers—sent back to Ancient Rome, sitting with Nero as he stood to wave to the masses.

"Norm! Norm! Norm!" you—*yes, you!*—would chant, and then Mr. Green, looking very distinguished with the silver hair and $3,000 suit, would stand again and give a slow wave of approval.

On it went as the snow left, as the leaves and then flowers started to appear... "Norm! Norm! Norm!" ...our savior of the North Stars, through the playoffs.

Then, the Stanley Cup Finals arrived and it was revealed that Green had decided to restrict the telecasts for home games to pay-per-view in the metro area. The legend became that only 35 percent of metro residents were equipped to have the games in their homes, even if they were willing to pay Norm's tariff.

I wrote a column in the Star Tribune rather critical of Green's TV strategy. I believe it was the first time "Norm Greed" was used, although that could've been on radio at the mighty 1500 AM ... I'm not sure.

Anyway, goalie Jon Casey and the North Stars defeated Pittsburgh 3–1 in that first home game. That gave them a 2–1 lead in the series—two wins from the Cup.

I was driving home late after writing an ode to those miracle Stars and turned on WCCO, where Dark Star (among my closest pals) was taking calls.

And his topic for the night was: "Does the Twin Cities need a negative sports columnist like Pat Reusse?"

I didn't take it personally. I realized the Darkman's motive: to support Norm for allowing him and an attractive young companion to occupy a couple of seats in the owner's booth on occasion during the playoff run.

As for Green, the North Stars lost the next three, the Cup still hasn't made it here, and a couple of years later—well, I was lamenting not having copyrighted "Norm Greed."

Which gets us back to the best thing Allenspach told me about this book in that first conversation: The first half is the gutter-to-almost-glory season of 1990–91; the second half is what has happened over the past three-plus decades to the principals in the drama.

The Boys of Summer in hockey form, Allenspach said.

I was hooked right then, since Roger Kahn's story then and after about the 1952 Brooklyn Dodgers remains my all-time favorite sports book a half-century after being published in 1972.

The 1990–91 North Stars. A fine drama, indeed.

Patrick Reusse
Golden Valley, Minnesota
February 2023

ACKNOWLEDGMENTS

This book was possible through the help of dozens of people—more to thank than I can possibly remember. Alan Warmka, my first college roommate and best friend, created the cover concept and was always a humble hockey fan, just like me. Aaron Sickman, a junior in high school when he was captivated by the '91 playoffs, is director of media relations with the Minnesota Wild and my conduit to the NHL for the past twenty-three years. Carly Napier, senior manager of licensing and special accounts for the NHL Alumni Association, connected me with several former players. Chris Garner, once an equipment manager for the St. Cloud State men's hockey team—who has taken that role to a new level with NCAA titles in 2011, 2018, and 2019 at Minnesota-Duluth, put me in touch with Derik Johnson and, ultimately, his father. John Peterson, a PR director with the Kalamazoo Wings, was pivotal in reaching Kevin Evans and Dean Kolstad. Thank you to Lelisa Rozendal of the Pacific Edge Hockey Association for helping me find Neil Wilkinson. Charles Saindon-Courtois, who works in communications for the Montreal Canadiens, was crucial to getting Bob Gainey to participate so beautifully. *Merci!* Vonda Wright took my appeal seriously and encouraged her husband, Peter Taglianetti, to give me one of the most colorful interviews in the book. Without Wally Shaver, I wouldn't have had the chance to speak once again with Al Shaver, one of the finest human beings I know. Scott MacIntosh of the Halifax Mooseheads found Jeremy Duchesne for me, and that was also an important addition to this book. If not for Mike Bialka, longtime sports editor at the Brainerd Dispatch, this book might not exist. He gave me my first job in journalism, and almost thirty-five years later he helped me find Chico Resch. Thank you to my college mentor, Jay Weiner, for his encouragement. He aptly said publishing a book is like "birthing a porcupine." Bob Showers, who predated me in the North Stars front office and later collaborated with Lou Nanne on the best pictorial celebrating the team, also pumped my tires when I needed it. Barb Regal helped me find images from the *Pioneer Press*, as did Matt Lutts with AP Images and John Wareham at the *Star Tribune*. Dave Schwarz and Mike Knaak, both first-class former photo editors at the *St. Cloud Times* and friends, helped me with research and listened over occasional lunches when I didn't know where this was going. Jason Soria, whose talent with a camera defies his young age, shot the author portraits. Thank you to: Terry Magnuson, once a receptionist in the front office at Met Center and now an assistant to Lou Nanne; my attorney, Tim Reuter of Kelm & Reuter, P.A., for important counsel; another college buddy, Patrick Donnelly, for making the manuscript sing; and Mike Killeen, who has a habit of vacating positions for me to succeed him—and still being a friend and reading the manuscript against his vast knowledge of hockey.

Finally, thank you to all the sources who participated and I am forever grateful to Curtis Weinrich and Liz Dwyer of North Star Press, and anyone who has read this far, for helping me realize a dream.

BIBLIOGRAPHY

Much of my career was as a beat writer covering a hockey team. As such, I had great interest in and respect for those who covered the Minnesota North Stars—primarily, but not exclusively, those from the *Minneapolis Star Tribune* and the *St. Paul Pioneer Press.* This project would not have been possible without reference to the published articles of Rachel Blount and Gary Olson and others from their organizations who were there every day in 1990–91. Most of the quotes from that season in this book, unless otherwise cited, came from the pages of those newspapers. I am indebted to those writers and reference them here because crediting every single quote would be redundant and detract from the overall tale.

When quotes from those newspapers were written by columnists, I tried to make that clear. I also have cited other newspapers from around North America if information did not come from an outlet in the Twin Cities or a wire service such as the Associated Press.

While those newspaper stories provided a framework from which to start, my own correspondence and interaction with approximately four dozen sources—more than sixty-five hours of one-on-one interviews—provides the perspective that I hope makes this work valuable. I indicated in the diary of the '90–91 season when quotes are from 2021 looking back. Much of the biographical information in the what-happened-ever-after section came from each person, although occasional quotes from more recent articles were used.

I have an extensive collection of North Stars memorabilia, including a complete run of media guides, many game programs, and magazines, and some of that provided depth and information as well. My video library includes hundreds of hockey games and films, including twenty-six telecasts from the team's 1990–91 regular season and every one of the '91 playoffs, the official Stanley Cup Final video, and season highlight films for both the North Stars and Pittsburgh Penguins.

The following are books that either contained valuable information about the North Stars which I used for this project or that I recommend to interested readers:

Before the Stars: Early Major League Hockey and the St. Paul Athletic Club Team by Roger Godin, 2005, Minnesota Historical Society Press.

The Bird by Wren Blair with Rob Brown and Jill Blair, 2002, Quarry Press.

The Blazing North Stars by Stan Fischler, 1972, Prentice-Hall.

Henry Boucha: Star of the North by Mary Halverson Schofield, 1999, Snowshoe Press.

Frozen in Time: A Minnesota North Stars History by Adam Raider, 2014, University of Nebraska Press.

The Goldy Shuffle by Richard Rainbolt and Ralph Turtinen, 1971, T.S. Denison and Company.

A History of Professional Hockey in Minnesota: From the North Stars to the Wild by George Rekela, 2014, The History Press.

Mario Lemieux Overtime 66 by Chrys Goyens and Frank Orr, 2001, Team Power Publishing.

Minnesota North Stars by Ross Rennie, 1990, Creative Education.

Minnesota North Stars History and Memories with Lou Nanne by Bob Showers, 2007, Beaver's Pond Press.

Nine: A Salute to Mike Modano 2014, Dallas Stars Hockey Club.

A Passion to Win by Lou Nanne, with Jim Bruton, 2010, Triumph Books.

Penguin Profiles: Pittsburgh's Boys of Winter by Jim O'Brien, 1994, James P. O'Brien Publishing.
Stadium Games by Jay Weiner, 2000, University of Minnesota Press.
They Call Me Gump by Lorne Worsley, with Tim Moriarity, 1975, Dodd, Mead and Company.
Naturally, many web sources provided invaluable information. Those most often used are noted here:
www.hockeydb.com
www.hockey-reference.com
www.hockeyzoneplus.com
www.mikemodano.com
www.newspapers.com
www.nhl.com
www.nhlmedia.com
www.vintagemnhockey.com

Finally, for more information or to contact the author, please visit www.kevinallenspach.com.